WINSTON CHURCHILL

HENRY PELLING

WINSTON
CHURCHILL

E. P. Dutton & Co., Inc., 201 Park Avenue South, NY 10003

ISBN: 0-525-23510-8

Apr. 10, 1975

Library of Congress Catalog Card Number: 73-21276

Printed in Great Britain

Contents

Illustrations

Between pages 356 and 357

Preface

IN the late 1960s, when I was preparing a book on *Britain and the Second World War* – published by Messrs Collins in 1970 – it occurred to me that there was no serious critical study of the life of Winston Churchill which in any way covered the entirety of his career. The official biography, now being most ably written by Mr Martin Gilbert, promises to be of very considerable length: the last volume to be published as I write this preface covers the years 1914–16. But the Public Record Office has now made available the great bulk of the official papers of Churchill's years in office up to the end of his first Premiership in 1945; and there is an abundance of material in the form of the memoirs, diaries and biographies of his colleagues, in addition to the documents published by the official biographer as companion volumes. In view of the extent of the evidence, I have not endeavoured to seek direct assistance from members of the Churchill family, or from surviving colleagues, of whom there are of course many. To some extent this has enabled me to write with more freedom than would otherwise be the case; but it would be difficult for a person of ordinary temperament to write the biography of so versatile a statesman without developing sympathy for his attitudes and feelings.

Miss E. D. Box typed almost the entire work for me and gave me valuable suggestions for its stylistic improvement. Both Mr James Wright of Macmillan and his wife Gilli also helped me to eliminate errors and to make the text crisper and clearer. Mr Peter Collenette helped me with the illustrations and my colleague Mr Mervyn King kindly assisted by reading the proofs.

My obligations to archivists, to librarians and their staffs are too numerous to list in detail: they will be obvious to the reader.

St John's College, Cambridge HENRY PELLING
February 1970

WINSTON CHURCHILL

1. *Birth and Parentage*

ON Monday May 25th 1874 the younger son of the seventh Duke of Marlborough brought his American bride to his ancestral home for the first time. Lord Randolph Spencer Churchill, who only four months earlier at the age of twenty-four had in effect been nominated by his father to represent in Parliament the family borough of Woodstock in Oxfordshire, had married Jennie Jerome in Paris in mid-April. Six weeks later the newly-weds drove through the narrow streets of the little town, which lay at the gates of the great palace of Blenheim. The townsfolk were expecting them, but had only received one day's notice, which was hardly sufficient to enable them to prepare as good a reception as they wished to offer. Furthermore, the day on which Lord and Lady Randolph arrived was one of thunder and torrential rain. But the greeting was none the less warm. Although the Blenheim brass band was fulfilling an engagement elsewhere, the town was bedecked with flags and bunting, and, as the local correspondent of the *Oxford Times* put it,

> On the arrival of the happy pair, the horses were detached from their travelling carriage and [the carriage] triumphantly drawn into the town, thence to the palace, by the populace, conspicuous among whom were the members of the Woodstock Lodge of Foresters in full regalia (of which lodge his Lordship is a member).[1]

But before the carriage was taken along the drive to the palace, there was a halt at the Bear Hotel, where the Mayor delivered an address of welcome, declaring that 'the Corporation and Inhabitants of Woodstock ... cannot be unmindful of anything which concerns the happiness of any member of the noble house of Churchill', and wishing the couple 'many years of unclouded happiness'.[2]

As the carriage passed through the triumphal arch which divides the town from the grounds of the palace, Jennie was enchanted by the expanse and beauty of the park, whose landscaping was the work of 'Capability' Brown, and by the prospect of the palace itself, Vanbrugh's monumental achievement.[3] Blenheim Palace had been designed more as a national memorial to Marlborough's victories than as a home for his descendants; and the discomforts of the building, combined with the formalities of old-fashioned English country society, were to be something of a trial for Lady Randolph, who was only twenty years of age and as vivacious as American girls can be. It was not that she was unused to life among the aristocracy: born in Brooklyn, the daughter of Leonard Jerome, a prominent New York businessman, she had been brought up in Paris, where her parents, who had developed a taste for the culture and amusements of European high society, had made a second home. Compared with Paris, life at Blenheim seemed provincial and old-fashioned. The seventh Duke, John Winston Spencer-Churchill, and his Duchess, Frances, daughter of the third Marquess of Londonderry, were very conscious of their dignity and rank, which was, to be sure, inferior only to that of royalty. Apart from members of the royal family, there were no more than twenty dukes of the United Kingdom peerage, and of these Marlborough was tenth in seniority. The Duke and Duchess conducted their home life in a patriarchal fashion, maintaining strict formality at mealtimes and personally cutting the joints for the entire family, including all the children, governesses and tutors.[4]

Fortunately for Jennie, Randolph now had to have a home of his own in London in order to attend Parliament. He had delivered his maiden speech only three days before he brought her to Blenheim; and although he had no reason to take his parliamentary duties seriously – for few of his constituents were likely to make an issue of his absence from the lobbies – it was not long before the young couple returned to London, where the pleasures of the season were a considerable attraction for the young bride. But both Parliament and London season lasted only until July; and as their permanent London home would not be ready until

December, Randolph and Jennie spent the late summer and autumn at Blenheim. There was now another reason why Jennie should find life a little dull: by the late autumn she was well on in pregnancy, and in early November could not attend the few gay occasions which Woodstock had to offer, in particular the Nobility Ball at the King's Arms, to which Lord Randolph went with his mother and one of his sisters as well as various cousins.[5] She was still prepared to go out with shooting parties, but on November 24th she had a fall, which shook her somewhat. This did not prevent Lord Randolph from going off to Oxford two days later to take his MA degree in person at the usual formal ceremony before the Vice-Chancellor of the University.[6] Perhaps as a result of sheer boredom, Jennie went out again on Saturday (28th) for what Lord Randolph later described as 'an imprudent and rough ride in a pony carriage'. This 'brought on the pains' that night, and the local doctor was summoned.[7] Attempts were made on Sunday to delay the delivery, but after eight hours' labour on Sunday evening a baby was born at 1.30 a.m. on Monday November 30th. *The Times* (of London) and the *Oxford Journal* briefly reported the event: 'On the 30th Nov., at Blenheim Palace, the Lady Randolph Churchill, prematurely, of a son.' The *Oxford Times* added the information that 'In the evening a merry peal on the church bells was rung in honour of the event'.

If the people of Woodstock were somewhat taken aback by the hasty arrival of Lord Randolph with his bride in May, they must have been even more surprised by the appearance of a first child after only seven and a half months of marriage. There seems to be no doubt that Winston was a premature baby. It was evidently the intention of his parents that he should be born in London, where the best medical advice would be readily available; and Lord Randolph's correspondence shows that he was unhappy at having to rely upon the services of a country doctor – who nevertheless proved very competent. Winston's arrival caused a household crisis: there was a shortage of baby linen at Blenheim, and some had to be borrowed from the wife of the Woodstock solicitor. Curiously, however, the correspondence of the family betrays no anxiety for the life of the child, which if almost two months premature must have been in grave danger for some weeks. Lord Randolph's comment on him was 'wonderfully pretty so everybody says dark eyes and hair & vy healthy considering its prematureness'.[8] As the weight at birth does not seem to have been recorded, or if recorded has not been revealed, it is perhaps idle to speculate whether the baby was in fact only two or three weeks premature, which would imply that his parents had seriously offended against the proprieties of the time. So we must suspend judgment on whether this was simply the first instance of Winston's impetuosity or whether it also involved yet another example of Lord Randolph's.

Winston Leonard Spencer Churchill was thus a direct descendant of the great John Churchill, first Duke of Marlborough, Captain-General of the Forces in Queen Anne's reign and the victor of the battles of Blenheim, Ramilles, Oudenarde and Malplaquet. So direct, indeed, was the line of descent that Winston was for a time the heir presumptive to the dukedom. This occurred in the 1890s, after the death of his father and before his cousin the ninth Duke had a son. The real family name, however, was Spencer, for John Churchill had had no son, and his titles descended by special remainder through his daughter Anne, who had married Charles Spencer, Earl of Sunderland. It was only in 1817 that the fourth Duke assumed by royal licence the surname of Churchill as well as that of Spencer. Lord Randolph preferred to drop the 'Spencer' for everyday use, for he had a dislike of what he called 'double-barrelled' names; but he could not always avoid the fact that it was part of his legal surname.

Even in the later nineteenth century a great deal of political power, as well as wealth and social eminence, still remained in the hands of the landed aristocracy, of which the dukes were the foremost and most illustrious leaders. Some of the dukes, to be sure, had run into debt owing to too lavish personal expenditure or the mismanagement of their estates: a good example was the second Duke of Buckingham, who was obliged to sell his great house at Stowe in order to pay his debts in 1847. But those who held their estates more or less intact were still able to live up to their traditional privileges and responsibilities – and these were great indeed. To act as the leader of local society, and, as often as not, as the Queen's Lord Lieutenant for the county; to control the patronage of many livings of the Church; to sustain a regiment of Yeomanry, by providing accommodation for their annual camp and manœuvres; to support almshouses and give aid to the deserving poor; to be able to nominate a son or a kinsman for election to Parliament, and to have him elected at a modest expense; all these things went with the possession of broad acres of cultivable land, and the income that could be derived therefrom. The growth of industry and the spread of towns threatened the great landed magnates with a new type of society which would not recognise their pre-eminence; but it could also still further increase their wealth, if they were fortunate enough to own land which was wanted for urban or industrial development.

Lord Randolph's father, the seventh Duke of Marlborough, was, as Benjamin Disraeli, the Conservative Prime Minister, told the Queen in 1876, 'not rich for a duke'.[9] This was probably partly due to the extravagance of his father and grandfather, and partly to the fact that the family estates remained overwhelmingly rural. The seventh Duke also had the heavy responsibility for providing dowries for six daughters as well as a settlement for his younger son. In 1875 he sold off his land in the adjoining county of Buckingham to the wealthy Jewish financier Ferdinand de Rothschild, and he also sent the 'Marlborough gems' to be auctioned at Christies. This left him with about 25,000 acres, almost entirely in Oxfordshire, and producing an annual income of about £35,000 – at a time when the pound was worth about seven times as much as it is worth now. In addition, he had a perpetual state pension of £4000 a year, originally granted in Queen Anne's reign. Nevertheless much of this income must have been committed to maintaining the various responsibilities of the estates and the Duke's position and dignity. The Duke did not like the idea of his younger son marrying an American girl; but he assumed that one compensation would be that her father would provide the bulk of the settlement for the young couple. Leonard Jerome did in fact undertake to provide them with an annual income of £2000, and to this the Duke added another £1000. The only difficulty was that Jerome seemed to think that Lord Randolph ought to be able to earn his own way if necessary, and that all his own contribution to the settlement ought to be vested in his daughter. Randolph would not accept this, as it was contrary to British ideas of a gentleman's position in society and of the correct relationship between the sexes. In the end Jerome rather reluctantly agreed, as he put it, to 'waive all my American prejudices', and to divide his own contribution equally between the couple.[10]

An unencumbered £3000 a year should have been ample to maintain Lord and Lady Randolph and their family in the utmost comfort and security. But both of them had been brought up to spend freely without counting the cost; and, incredible as it may seem, they failed to live within their very generous income. Jennie had grown accustomed to all the enjoyments of high society – dances, parties and balls – and she and Lord Randolph were soon in the smart and expensive circle of the Prince of Wales. Randolph did not enjoy dancing, but he expected his wife to give dinner parties to their friends, at which no expense was spared; and he was a devotee of the turf. All this left him with little time for his parliamentary duties, as it left Jennie with hardly any opportunity to look after her infant son. But in those days the Member of Parliament who rarely attended debates was by no means an untypical case; and the children of the upper classes were normally looked after by nurses or governesses, rather than personally ministered to by their mothers.

But the round of society pleasure on which the young couple were engaged was suddenly interrupted by the repercussions of a scandal affecting the Prince of Wales himself, and in which Lord Randolph himself was directly involved. In 1876 Randolph's elder brother, the heir to the dukedom who was known by the courtesy title of Marquess of Blandford, was contemplating an elopement with a Lady Aylesford, whose husband was a close friend of the Prince and was at the time accompanying the Prince on a visit to India. Lord Aylesford proposed to initiate divorce proceedings, whereupon Lord Randolph, in the hope of preventing the publicity that would ensue, wrote to the Prince urging him to use his influence to deflect Lord Aylesford from this course. Unfortunately Randolph did not merely request the Prince's assistance; he threatened that if he did not co-operate, he would publish the Prince's own correspondence with Lady Aylesford, which was distinctly compromising. The Prince, who had helped to persuade the Duke of Marlborough to agree to Randolph's wedding, and whose private secretary, Francis Knollys, had been Randolph's best man, was infuriated by this apparent perfidy and, as he saw it, attempted blackmail. The matter reached the ears of the Queen and was pondered upon both by the Prime Minister, Disraeli, and by the Leader of the Opposition, Lord Hartington; and in the end Randolph was forced to sign an apology to the Prince in terms laid down by the Lord Chancellor. But the Prince's wrath was still not appeased; and he let it be known that henceforth he would refuse to accept the hospitality of any host who received Lord and Lady Randolph.

This social boycott was acutely embarrassing, not only to the young Churchills but also to the entire family of the Duke and Duchess of Marlborough. Under the circumstances the Duke decided to accept an opportune invitation from Disraeli to serve a term as Lord Lieutenant of Ireland. This meant setting himself up in state at Dublin, at a cost which far exceeded the annual salary of £20,000 that he would receive. Because of the great expense of the post, Marlborough had turned it down when it was first offered to him in 1874; but now that it was again vacant and available to him, he accepted, and took Lord Randolph with him as an unpaid private secretary. With Jennie and the baby Winston, Randolph was installed in an official house in Phoenix Park near the Viceregal Lodge in Dublin. He did not give up his seat in Parliament, but his appearances in the House were naturally even less frequent than before.

Yet the effect of the scandal was to turn Randolph more and more towards a serious study of political problems. To begin with, he learnt a great deal about Ireland, whose affairs were constantly being debated at Westminster. In 1879 he helped to administer a relief fund launched by his mother as a result of the agricultural distress of that year. This brought him into direct touch with the social and administrative problems of the Irish countryside. When, shortly afterwards, Disraeli's government was defeated in the 1880 general election, the Duke's term as Viceroy came to an end and Randolph returned to Westminster with a new interest in politics and a new confidence in his own capacity.

In the course of the ensuing seven years Lord Randolph's political career was truly meteoric. His success was due to the skill that he displayed as a parliamentarian and to the power of his speeches on public platforms throughout the country. He was, like his father, a Conservative; and his party, humbled by defeat in the 1880 election, and after the elevation of Disraeli to the Lords and his subsequent retirement lacking any spokesman in the Commons of the quality of Gladstone, discovered in Randolph a debater who could effectively puncture the solemn pretensions of the great Liberal leader. His weapon was ridicule, and his speeches, which he prepared with great care and then committed to memory, were delivered with the skill of a trained actor. His distinctive appearance – a slight figure with bulbous eyes and an extra large moustache – was a gift to cartoonists and added to his celebrity. In the early stages of the 1880 Parliament he attacked his own front bench almost as much as the government, for he deplored the failure of Sir Stafford Northcote, the Conservative leader in the Commons, to produce any effective criticism of Liberal policy. With three colleagues, Sir Henry Drummond Wolff, J. E. Gorst and Arthur Balfour, he formed a 'ginger group' on the Conservative side, which became known as the 'Fourth Party'.

Lord Randolph soon became something of a national figure, and he was invited to address political meetings throughout the country. The social boycott imposed by the Prince of Wales was now relaxed as it was said that the Prince always worshipped success. But Randolph found himself being drawn into the adoption of policies which contradicted those natural to an aristocrat representing a rural nomination borough. When he visited Lancashire in the autumn of 1881, he was as he later said 'particularly enjoined by the leading gentlemen in those places not to say a word against the assimilation of the county and borough franchise'[11] – that is, not to oppose an extension of the vote to the working men in the counties. He found that within the Conservative Party 'many borough members & particularly Lancashire members' were in favour of this reform. This was because large numbers of Lancashire workingmen were in fact Conservatives: they thought that the Liberals were too friendly to the Irish, many of whom they knew and disliked as immigrants in their midst. There was no need, therefore, to fear that a wide enfranchisement would lead to the triumph of extreme Liberalism and the destruction of existing social institutions. So Lord Randolph gradually gave up his opposition to parliamentary reform and adopted a new policy, that of 'trusting the people'. He spoke warmly of the 'Tory democracy', and demanded that the programme of social reform which he associated with Disraeli's ministry should not be allowed to disappear under his successors.

Lord Randolph never produced any coherent social reform programme of his own, and it is easy to come to the conclusion, which he himself is said to have admitted, that 'Tory democracy' was 'principally opportunism'.[12] All the same, he had stumbled upon an important political truth, namely, that a large proportion of the working-class electorate, and also of those not yet admitted to the electorate, were willing to support the Conservative Party if they were encouraged to believe that they were not unwelcome in its ranks. When in 1883 a Corrupt Practices Act was passed which drastically limited expenditure at election time, Randolph and his friends founded a body called the Primrose League to provide voluntary assistance to candidates. The League took its name from what was supposed to be Disraeli's favourite flower; it had a hierarchy of medieval-sounding titles for its members, and a semi-secret masonic ritual; and for some time the new party leaders, Lord Salisbury and Sir Stafford Northcote, laughed it off as an absurdity. But in 1884 membership was opened to women, and after this it immediately became a great social success. It spread throughout the constituencies and in some areas, not least Lancashire, it had a strong working-class membership.

If Salisbury and Northcote laughed at the Primrose League, they were less amused by the way in which, in 1883, Lord Randolph deliberately set about using the National Union of Conservative Associations as a vehicle for an attack upon the party leadership and its policies. He appeared to be claiming that the National Union, which was normally regarded as merely the servant of the leaders, should help to determine party policy. At the Union's annual conference at Birmingham in October 1883 he declared: 'If you want to gain the confidence of the working classes, let them have a share and a large share – a real share and not a sham share – in your party councils and in your party government.'[13] In 1884 he became chairman of the National Union, and for some months there was a complex struggle between himself and his supporters, and the acknowledged leaders of the party. In the end, an agreement was reached between Lord Salisbury and Lord Randolph which brought the conflict to an end, on terms which suggested that Randolph had been keener on establishing his own personal position than on furthering the representative rights of the working classes. Salisbury undertook to take him into his group of frontbench colleagues and to give official recognition to the Primrose League; Randolph called off the campaign in the National Union and later in the year went off on a visit to India. When a Conservative government was formed in June 1885, Lord Salisbury became Prime Minister and Lord Randolph became Secretary of State for India.

Lord Randolph soon showed that he could work hard as a minister, and that he could take important decisions. He secured the appointment of the capable soldier General Sir Frederick Roberts as Commander-in-Chief in India, in the face of strong hostility from the Queen, who had taken a dislike to the General's wife; he arranged for a reinforcement of the strength of the Indian army, which he thought necessary in view of the possibility of a Russian invasion; and he authorised the annexation of Upper Burma, in order to put an end to a state of uncertainty and intrigue in that region where British and French traders were bidding against each other at the court of the native ruler. But Randolph's career at the India Office lasted only seven months, as a general election in November 1885 failed to give the Conservatives the overall majority in the Commons that they required, and the Liberals returned to office after Gladstone had won the support of the Irish Nationalists by promising to introduce a bill for Irish Home Rule.

By this time a new Parliamentary Reform Act had been passed, and Randolph had to find a new constituency, as the little parliamentary borough Woodstock had been abolished. He fought a brave battle in the Central Division of Birmingham, at that time a Liberal stronghold, but was defeated and forced to fall back on the safe Conservative seat of South Paddington, on his own doorstep in the West End of London. He was now for a few months on the Opposition front bench; but Gladstone's Irish Home Rule Bill was defeated by a combination of the Opposition and a substantial minority of the Liberal Prime Minister's own followers. A fresh general election followed in July 1886, and this resulted in a great victory for the Conservatives and their new allies, who were to hold office for most of the ensuing twenty years. Salisbury became Prime Minister once more, and this time he made Randolph Chancellor of the Exchequer and Leader of the House of Commons. With a clear Commons majority for the Conservatives for the first time since 1880, it looked as if Randolph was assured of a long tenure of his high office.

But this was not to be. Salisbury had found him a difficult colleague when he was at the India Office, and his behaviour as Chancellor was even more perverse. He interfered in foreign policy, publicly demanding closer ties with Germany and Austria; and he planned a Budget on Gladstonian lines, reducing taxation and cutting expenditure on the armed forces to a point which the rest of the Cabinet could not tolerate. Having grown to regard himself as indispensable to the Government, he impatiently tried to win his point by offering his resignation, and was astounded when Salisbury, realising that the issue was not one that would discredit himself or the Cabinet, calmly accepted the resignation and appointed an ex-Liberal frontbencher, G. J. Goschen, to assume Churchill's responsibilities. There was a great sensation: but the government survived, and Randolph went to the back benches, from which he was never to return. He had been Chancellor of the Exchequer for only five months.

Lord Randolph had evidently made a mistake in trying to force the hand of a Prime Minister with a large Commons majority. He later acknowledged the mistake himself, admitting that he 'forgot Goschen'. At first there seemed no reason why after a few months or even years on the back benches he should not be restored to high office. But for some time already his health had been poor, and by now he had contracted one of the most dreadful of diseases, in those days virtually incurable – syphilis. Some of the symptoms of this disease are clear enough when it is first contracted, but a period of dormancy of about eight to ten years thereafter is not uncommon. Although the nature of his misfortune was kept secret at the time, it has since been suggested that his lack of judgment in resigning so precipitately at the end of 1886 was a sign that his mind was already being affected. But his life had been marked by many hasty and even reckless actions, and if he usually suffered little as a result, it was perhaps because his opponents were taken by surprise. In Salisbury, however, he at last met his match. By the early 1890s, when the government had served most of its term and a new general election was imminent, it should have been possible for Churchill to recover his position. But worsening health, lack of interest in his own political future, and a tendency to veer still further away from distinctively Conservative attitudes all alienated him from his party. In 1891 he went on a long trip to South Africa, in search of better health and also with the intention, which he successfully realised, of making useful investments in the mining boom. By 1893 his condition was such that his old friends could hardly bear to listen to his speeches; as Rosebery put it, 'he died by inches in public'.[14] In 1894 he took Jennie on a tour round the world, to get away from politics and to try to overcome his debility. It was without avail; he returned to England at the end of the year in a state of almost complete collapse and died within a month. He was still less than forty-six years old.

All was not 'unclouded happiness', then, for the young couple who had been fêted at Woodstock in the spring of 1874. Jennie had a buoyant, extrovert character and was probably not much upset by the early quarrel with the Prince of Wales and her exile to Dublin, where at least there was some society and a great deal of racing and hunting. Her second and last child, John – usually known as 'Jack' – was born in 1880, shortly after the family had returned to London. For a time they lived in St James's Place, Mayfair, but later took a house in Connaught Place, near Marble Arch, which had a view across Hyde Park; this became the social centre of the 'Fourth Party'. Jennie was drawn into the excitement of Randolph's political activities, and it seems that she enjoyed it thoroughly. She often listened to debates from the Commons gallery, and she played a full part in the early days of the Primrose League as soon as women were allowed to join. In 1885 she took charge of her husband's candidature at a by-election at Woodstock, and soon found that electors of all classes were as susceptible to her charm as were the young aristocrats whom she met at society functions.

But Lord Randolph was not an easy man to live with at the best of times: he was often moody and irritable without apparent reason. As the 1880s wore on, his periods of political activity were increasingly interrupted by long holidays or journeys to France or Scotland in search of rest and recreation. For a time he and his wife appear to have become estranged, although there was never any question of formal separation. The nature of Randolph's illness, once it was diagnosed, was such that he could no longer claim his conjugal rights, and it is not surprising that Jennie began to seek the company of other men. The conventions of high society were not so strict as to make such behaviour seem exceptional or to arouse the hostility of others not directly affected. The Prince of Wales himself set the pattern of irregularity, and where he led others were naturally not afraid to follow. It was understood, of course, that these affairs had to be conducted with discretion. The occasional open scandal or legal case affecting the nobility or even the Court could lead to permanent social ostracism for those concerned. But society reporters were primly able to reveal, without mentioning names, that things went a lot deeper than this:

Go into any London ballroom and listen to the conversation. The name of lady after lady is coupled with that of a man in a manner which shows what the meaning of these relations is. Her frivolity is

28

spoken of not as a suspicion but as a fact, and is treated simply as amusing material for gossip.[15]

Jennie was so attractive and so ready to take part in social activities of all sorts that there was much gossip about her, and it is easy to exaggerate her liaisons. She was again very friendly with the Prince of Wales, but there is no evidence that she was ever his mistress. Her most serious romance was with the Austrian Count Charles Kinsky, four years her junior, who was an honorary attaché at the Austrian Embassy in London for a period in the 1880s, and who astonished the racing world by winning the Grand National on his own horse in 1883. The Count was handsome and dashing, and for many years and in spite of moves to diplomatic posts in other countries was remarkably faithful to Jennie. Naturally there could be no question of their getting married while Randolph was alive.

As for Lord Randolph, he sought some compensation in the affection of his mother, the Duchess Frances, who may never have been fully acquainted with the nature of his illness. When in the late 1880s he began to feel that his political career was largely over, he returned to his old interest in the turf, and entered a racing partnership with Lord Dunraven. The stable was at Newmarket, and for his own convenience Randolph took a small house outside the town. For some years he and Jennie could if they wished play Box and Cox in London, at Newmarket, at various house parties and at health resorts in Britain and on the Continent. But as the illness began to affect Randolph's mind Jennie recognised that it was her duty to stay with her husband and to look after him. Her decision to accompany him on his world tour in 1894 was an act of self-sacrifice which impressed her friends. One heavy blow that befell her before the tour ended was a telegram from Count Kinsky to say that he had just got engaged. Life must have seemed bleak for her in the aftermath of Randolph's funeral; at the age of forty-one, apart from her children she was more truly alone than she had ever been in her life before. But her elder son was now approaching manhood, and it is to an account of his early development and progress that we must turn.

2. *Schoolboy and Cadet*

HOWEVER small Winston had been at birth he was soon a chubby baby, and the 'dark eyes and hair' which his father noticed at his birth became blue eyes and ginger hair. His parents obtained a middle-aged nurse to look after him – Mrs Elizabeth Ann Everest, a kindly woman born in Chatham in Kent and evidently imbued with strong Low Church principles. She was to stay with the family until Winston was grown up, looking after the two children and later keeping house. Winston gave her the nickname of 'Woom', and responded warmly to the affection that she showed him. Some years after she had died, he was to reflect on the nature of a relationship of this kind, describing it as 'perhaps ... the only disinterested affection in the world' and 'one of the few proofs ... that the nature of man is superior to mere utilitarianism, and that his destinies are high'.[1] Mrs Everest was already looking after Winston in 1876 when the family moved to Ireland; in later life his earliest recollection was of the house in Phoenix Park, and of his nurse's fear of the Fenians, the Irish revolutionaries who were engaged on a campaign of violence against the union of Britain and Ireland. Winston found more to be afraid of in the advent of a 'governess', who already before he was five was temporarily engaged to teach him to read. He saw little of his parents: his father was busy in various political activities, and his picture of his mother was of her 'in a riding habit, fitting like a skin and often beautifully spotted with mud'.[2]

It is dangerous to generalise about environmental factors in the formation of character. Winston was, in his mother's words, 'a most difficult child to manage',[3] and some students of his life have argued that this was due to being neglected by his parents in early childhood.[4] But this type of upbringing was normal among upper-class families at the time. As a society journal of the time put it, it was customary for a young mother of social position 'to shirk the nursery, and to content herself with having "the Baby" or Miss Ethel brought down into the drawingroom once or twice a day to be played with and treated as if they were pet kittens'.[5] His brother Jack, who was over five years his junior, in spite of incitement from Winston was to be regarded as a well-behaved child. If Winston's character suffered exceptionally from parental neglect, it was not when he was still at home but when he was already at school.

For although it was quite in accord with the habitual procedure that he should be ruthlessly despatched to boarding school at the age of seven, it was his special misfortune to be sent in the first instance to a particularly bad school. This was St George's, Ascot, founded only four years earlier by a young High Church clergyman, the Rev. H. W. Sneyd-Kynnersley. Although the school specialised in preparing boys for Eton, and was well equipped even to the extent of having installed electric light – a novelty in those days – it was run on a very mechanical system of instruction in Latin grammar and other subjects. If the pupils showed any signs of recalcitrance, they were beaten unmercifully until they bled. The headmaster's reports show that Winston's best subjects were history and geography; but he was regarded as 'troublesome' and 'greedy at meals',[6] and he had his share of the flogging. In his letters home he bravely insisted that he was happy, but one vacation, it appears, Mrs Everest discovered the signs of ill-treatment on his body, and showed them to his mother.[7] As a result, after only two years at Ascot Winston was transferred to a less pretentious establishment run by two Misses Thomson in Brighton. This had the advantage of being not far from the home of the Churchill family doctor, Robson Roose; and here the methods of instruction were altogether less severe.

At Brighton Winston found life much happier, and he was soon making better progress than at Ascot. The more formal academic subjects were accompanied by instruction in riding, dancing and swimming. By the time he was eleven he was collecting postage stamps and gaining a vicarious prestige among his contemporaries from the eminence of his father, now at the height of his parliamentary career. Although he suffered a setback as a result of a severe attack of pneumonia, which brought both his parents rushing to his bedside, he was more or less at the top of the school by the time he was thirteen, and was grappling with such advanced subjects as Greek, ancient history and algebra. He had to face the entrance examination to Harrow, where his father now intended him to proceed. The examination in Winston's case at least was no more than a formality, for the young and new headmaster of Harrow, the Rev. J. E. C. Welldon, had no intention of rejecting the son of so distinguished a parent as Lord Randolph. But Winston was not to know this, and he took the examination very seriously. He blacked out completely in the Latin paper, and wrote nothing; and he was sick on the train on the way home to Brighton. Next day, however, he was told that he had been accepted.

Harrow ranked then, and probably still ranks, as socially the most distinguished of the public schools, with the sole exception of Eton; and the prominence of Etonians and Harrovians in various spheres of national life has frequently been remarked upon. As an Etonian, Lord Randolph would probably have preferred to send his son to his old school if medical advice had not suggested that Harrow-on-the-Hill was a healthier place for a boy with a 'weak chest', which Winston was presumed to have after his attack of pneumonia. Lord Randolph could console himself with the knowledge that among his contemporaries in the House of Commons there were no less than fifty-six Harrovians – and the great majority of them were members of his own party.[8] Clearly whatever career Winston was later to fashion for himself, he could expect to know personally quite a large proportion of those who would govern the country.

Harrow was not as free and easy a school as the establishment run by the Misses Thomson, but Winston was at once attracted by several features of it: 'such a nice place – beautiful view – beautiful situation – good swimming bath – a good Gymnasium – & a Carpentering shop & many other attractions,' he wrote to his mother.[9] Certainly Harrow-on-the-Hill was an attractive place – more so then than now. It was still in the country in those days, although it could easily be reached by the Metropolitan Railway. As a contemporary of Winston's was later to write, 'from the churchyard you had an uninterrupted view of English landscape as far as Windsor, which was visible on a clear day'.[10] And Winston found other things to enjoy at the school – for instance, drill and shooting in the Rifle Corps, and also the 'sham fights' or tactical excursions which the Corps undertook against other schools. He had long possessed a small army of toy soldiers – as many as a thousand by the time he was seven – and he had spent much of his spare time marshalling this army for battle and engaging in tactical manœuvres. Before he reached his fifteenth birthday his interest in soldiering, and his father's growing conviction that his son had no marked academic leanings, had led to a decision that he should aim for the Royal Military Academy at Sandhurst, with a view to becoming an officer in the army. He therefore joined the special Army Class at Harrow, so as to prepare for the entrance examination. The Army Class, we are told by one of his Harrow contemporaries, was regarded by the other members of the school as 'a sort of dunce's paradise'.[11]

At this time the most obvious professions for a young man of good birth were the Church, the Law and the Army. The Church and the Law obviously required ability in the classics, and it was here that Winston was lamentably unsuccessful. Although he had been subjected to instruction in Latin since the age of seven, he had learnt very little. This may seem puzzling in the light of his later achievements. It was true enough that he did show ability in some fields of study, and this his schoolmasters were always willing to concede. He was, however, utterly lacking in the self-discipline that is the mark of the academic mind. In a subject which he enjoyed, such as history, he secured excellent marks; and he won a prize open to the whole school for reciting Macaulay's *Lays of Ancient Rome* from memory. But in Latin, which he did not enjoy, he was hopeless; and in French and mathematics his performance was indifferent.

His general conduct also left much to be desired. According to the reports, he was 'not *wilfully* troublesome' but forgetful, careless and unpunctual.[12] His misbehaviour was not serious, and apparently the only occasion on which he was 'swished' – that is to say, caned – by the headmaster was after he had been caught breaking a few windows in an already derelict building near the school. (His father could not take him to task for this, as he had had trouble as an Oxford undergraduate after breaking some glass in the far from derelict Randolph Hotel.) Somehow or other, Winston could not make up his mind to fit into the pattern imposed by school discipline, by the curriculum and by the examination system. Richard Meinertzhagen, a fellow-Harrovian who was three years younger, later described him as 'a lonely boy, usually walking by himself, but the whole school knew him'.[13]

It is perhaps not surprising in view of his individualistic attitude that Winston did not enjoy team games. He got a good deal of pleasure out of swimming, and spent a lot of time in the summer terms at 'Ducker', the large open-air swimming-pool at the school. It was here, shortly after his arrival, that he had his famous encounter with an older boy named Leopold Amery, whom he had the temerity to push into the pool when he was standing on the bank. Amery was no larger than Winston, but he was stronger, and quickly got his revenge. Winston later apologised to Amery, pointing out that he thought he was no more than his own age because he was so small, and adding more felicitously, 'My father who is a great man is also small'.[14] Like Amery, Winston became keen on gymnastics; but his greatest success was in fencing, in which he won a Public Schools competition and was awarded a silver medal: according to the school magazine, 'his success was chiefly due to his quick and dashing action, which quite took his opponents by surprise'.[15] Winston's one close friend at Harrow was Jack Milbanke, who was two years older than himself and much more self-assured. He envied the way in which Milbanke could talk to Lord Randolph 'as if they were equals', on the occasions when his father visited the school.[16]

But Lord Randolph's visits to the school were infrequent, although when Winston was in his teens he was no longer in office. Jennie wrote to Winston affectionately, and expected regular letters home: but she also visited him very infrequently, and was often away when he was on vacation. Winston felt neglected, and even at the age of sixteen his letters are full of entreaty to his mother: 'Please do do do do do do come down to see me.... Please do come I have been so disappointed so many times about your coming'.[17] He would perhaps not have written in such terms to his father, who was less approachable. Jennie was still very young-looking and in the American fashion was inclined to treat her sons as equals: her letters show little sign of serious admonishment and no trace at all of bad temper. But Randolph was often irritable and usually unapproachable. One of Jennie's sisters thought it very painful to see him refusing to talk to his children when they saw him briefly at breakfast-time at their London home: he was too busy with his newspaper to do more than return their greeting, and 'the two pairs of round eyes, peeping around the screen, longed for a kind word'.[18] It is not surprising that both Winston and Jack continued to depend a good deal on the devotion of their old nurse, Mrs Everest, who looked after them when they were at home, and wrote to them at school, telling them to watch their health and warning them of the dangers of 'sitting in wet feet'. But Winston needed a father substitute. Perhaps Milbanke filled the part to some extent, and when Winston was at home there was often Count Kinsky, whose panache impressed him considerably.

Winston did not enjoy his schooldays. They were, he said in middle age, 'the only barren and unhappy period of my life ... a time of discomfort, restriction, and purposeless monotony'.[19] The vacations, on the other hand, were a great relief because they enabled him to do what he, and not his schoolmasters, wanted. One of his first seaside holidays was spent at Ventnor, where at the age of seven he was taken by Mrs Everest to stay for a time in the home of her sister and brother-in-law. The brother-in-law was a prison warder and this was probably the humblest British home in which Winston ever lived. When he was ten he spent a holiday at Cromer, and was able to bathe and to hunt on the rocks for sea anemones; but this holiday was rather spoiled for him by the presence of a governess whom he found 'very unkind, so strict and stiff, I can't enjoy myself at all'.[20] There was always Blenheim to be visited occasionally, and when Winston was in his teens there was for a time the house near Newmarket, Banstead Manor, where he and Jack could go out with the keeper hunting rabbits. At Banstead Winston developed a whole menagerie of pets – a guinea-pig, a cat, puppies, rabbits and chickens – but they had to be left to Mrs Everest's care during term-time. He and Jack built a log house for themselves, which they called 'the Den': it had a ditch round it which was filled with water, and a drawbridge. A young female cousin of theirs was taken to visit 'the Den' but found it a dangerous environment – 'War' was taking place: 'The fort was stormed. I was hurriedly removed from the scene of action as soon as stones began to fly with effect.'[21]

Winston's games could, however, be dangerous to himself. He had a serious accident on a holiday at the Bournemouth estate of his aunt, Lady Wimborne, when he was eighteen. He was trying to escape from his brother and a cousin, who were chasing him, when they suddenly closed in on him as he was crossing a bridge

35

over a deep gulley. Determined to avoid 'capture', Winston leapt off the bridge, hoping to break his fall by sliding down a tree. Unfortunately the tree gave him no hold and he fell almost thirty feet. He ruptured a kidney, was unconscious for three days and took more than three months to recover his full health.

The vacations were always a time of enjoyment, and it distressed Winston that the harsh necessity of preparing for the army entrance examination should intrude upon them. But it was essential for him, as his Latin was so bad, to get up a good knowledge of French, and much against his will it was arranged when he was seventeen that he should spend a month at Christmas living with a French family in Versailles. Rather to his surprise, he quite enjoyed the experience. His mother gave him a number of introductions to friends in Paris and he got on well with his hosts. His letters to his mother contained quite a lot of French idiom and he got into the habit of speaking French boldly if ungrammatically – a habit which stood him in good stead throughout his later life. In spite of this, Winston failed his first attempt at the Sandhurst entrance examination, and as he was now eighteen his father decided that he should leave Harrow and go to a 'crammer'. The tutor (recommended to Lord Randolph by the headmaster of Harrow) was Captain W. H. James, who provided instruction at a house in Kensington.

If the 'crammer' could not get Winston through the Sandhurst examination, nothing could. Captain James had a remarkable record of success with pupils who were generally thought to be unintelligent. His system was to work out, by a careful comparison of past examination papers, what questions were likely to be asked, and to coach his pupils methodically in answering these. Not surprisingly, he did not find Winston a very satisfactory student. He wrote to Lord Randolph that he was 'casual' and 'inattentive' and 'too much inclined up to the present to teach his instructors'.[22] He thought it presumptuous of Winston to suggest to him that he did not need any more instruction in history – though this was no more than the truth. Nevertheless Winston did his best to accommodate himself to Captain James's system, and when he next took the Sandhurst examination he just scraped in, not at the infantry level which his father had hoped he would obtain, but high enough to qualify for the less exacting standards of the cavalry.

Lord Randolph had arranged for a young Eton master to take Winston and Jack on a walking tour of Switzerland after the examination, and Winston obtained his result just as he was about to cross the Channel. He was naturally in high spirits on the tour, until he received a far from congratulatory letter from his father, which caught up with him at Milan. Lord Randolph was annoyed by the fact that his son had not done better, and in particular by the knowledge that to maintain him in the cavalry rather than in the infantry would be more expensive to the tune of £200 a year. There was a touch of petulance and lack of sympathy in the letter which suggests that his physical and mental decline was affecting his judgment: he told Winston that his performance was 'discreditable' and reflected 'beyond refutation your slovenly happy-go-lucky harum-scarum style of work'.

Winston was not unnaturally upset by this letter, but he had been enjoying his holiday, and he knew that his father would not prevent him from going to Sandhurst. So he replied humbly, acknowledging faults in his behaviour in the past, and promising that he would 'try to modify your opinion of me by my work and conduct at Sandhurst'.[23] As it turned out, however, when he got back to London he found that he had been transferred to the infantry after all. He was still less than nineteen when he began his first term at the Royal Military College.

The college, situated at Sandhurst, in Berkshire, just a few miles from the railway station at Camberley in Surrey, was the training college for cadets for commissions in the infantry and cavalry. At this time commissions in the army were almost entirely restricted to those of the upper classes whose parents could afford not only a good private education for their sons, including the fees of the college, which amounted to £150 a year, but also a generous allowance for the early stages of their careers as commissioned officers. There was consequently little likelihood of finding men of humble birth among the cadets. But this would have been true of the entrants to any other profession at the time; and there is no doubt that, after the reforms instituted by the Prince Consort, Sandhurst did provide a genuine professional education. Instruction began daily at 6.45 a.m. and continued with intervals for breakfast and lunch until about 4 p.m. The cadets engaged in drill, map-reading, tactics, studies of military administration and law, trench-digging, musketry, gymnastics, and riding. After 4 p.m. they were free to play games, to explore the countryside, or to relax in any way they liked. Dinner was a formal meal in 'mess'; and there was a strict 'lights-out' at 11 p.m.

This was of course a stricter discipline than Winston liked, though not quite as strict as that which he had experienced at school. In this case, however, it was at times tightened still further by his father's refusal to allow him to visit London more than one weekend in four while the term lasted. Lord Randolph thought that this would ensure that his son worked harder and obtained a better result on passing out; and indeed it may have had this effect. Fortunately Winston enjoyed many aspects of the training – especially the riding – and he often managed to improve the 'quality of life' for himself by giving generous tips to non-commissioned instructors and servants. When he was ill for a few days and had to go into the college sick-bay, he 'judiciously distributed a few half-crowns' and was 'consequently looked after *en prince*'.[24] Winston saw no reason for personal austerity if there was an opportunity of escaping from it.

Now that Winston was an infantry cadet, Lord Randolph began to take a more favourable view of him. He thought that his son had 'much smartened up', and that 'he holds himself quite upright and he has got steadier'.[25] He allowed Winston to accompany him on a weekend visit to Nathaniel Lord Rothschild's house at Tring in Buckinghamshire, and even discussed politics with him – which he had not done before. He also gave the young man a present of some of his best cigars and cigarettes, while exhorting him to be sparing in their use. But this close association of father and son was abruptly terminated by the rapid deterioration of Lord Randolph's health. When he and Jennie went off on their world tour, Winston managed to persuade Dr Roose to show him the medical reports on his father's condition. Whether or not he discovered the true character of his father's illness is not clear; but at least he learnt that the illness could only lead to further decline and early death. Naturally this was a severe shock to him: and his letters show an increased warmth towards his mother, who had undertaken the cruel task of accompanying a dying man on a world tour.

While his parents were abroad, Winston took part in an escapade which must rank, for all its anonymity as far as he was concerned, as the first occasion on which he made a speech in public with the intention of influencing an election. Winston occasionally visited the Empire Theatre in Leicester Square, which was popular for its variety performances. The theatre had a bar and promenade in full view of the stage, and this was to some extent a resort of ladies of ill repute and also naturally for gentlemen who sought their company. When the Empire's licence came up for renewal in 1894, a Mrs Ormiston Chant, who was a champion of various causes including that of 'purity', opposed its renewal, and secured a compromise whereby the management undertook to abolish the promenade and to stop the sale of drinks in the auditorium. The licensing authority was a committee of the London County Council, then dominated by the Progressive Party, which was largely Liberal in membership and consequently inclined to sympathise with advocates of moral improvement by legislation. But a large section of the press and public thought that it was impossible to make people behave themselves by law. Winston, from the depths of his personal inexperience, warmly embraced this point of view, and wrote to the *Westminster Gazette* and the *Daily Telegraph* to explain why he thought the 'prudes' were wrong. His letter to the *Telegraph* was not published; but that to the *Westminster Gazette*, which he signed only with his initials, argued quite sensibly that 'the only method of reforming human nature and of obtaining a higher standard of morality is by educating the mind of the individual and improving the social conditions under which he lives'.[26] He also decided to join a new society which he saw advertised under the name of the 'Entertainments Protection League', and attended its first meeting, but was dismayed to find that the League had been inaugurated by a single person, and that he himself was the only reader to respond to the advertisement.

It was with a sense of frustration, therefore, that Winston and a number of other cadets attended the Empire Theatre on the first Saturday night in November 1894 to discover that canvas screens had been erected in front of the bar to separate it from the auditorium. At the end of the performance a number of 'well-dressed men, some of them almost middle-aged',[27] but also including Winston and his party, set upon the canvas screens and demolished them. According to a newspaper account, 'The party was led by a young man in a light coat, covering evening dress. ... "Now boys", said the man in the light coat, "we have pulled them down, and what you have to do is to see that they are not put up again."' This young man is not mentioned in Winston's own account of the incident, described many years later in *My Early Life*; but he records that he himself 'made my maiden speech' on this occasion.[28] The newspaper account proceeds:

> Another young gentleman, amid the whirling of sticks and umbrellas, improved the occasion by a speech in which he said that the pulling down of the partitions was only a metaphorical illustration of what they intended to do with the County Council.[29]

Winston and his friends then made off. The Liberal papers deplored the 'hooliganism' and the Conservative papers suggested that it was only to be expected if silly regulations were made; but the LCC elections in 1895 failed to unseat the Progressive majority, and the reform initiated by Mrs Ormiston Chant remained in force.

When Lord and Lady Randolph returned to England in December 1894, Lord Randolph was already so ill that he could hardly conduct a conversation. In January he gradually weakened, and he subsided into a coma from which he died on January 24th. Winston and Jack were with Lady Randolph at his bedside when he died. A memorial service was held at Westminster Abbey, attended by the Prime Minister, Lord Rosebery, and by many leading politicians. The funeral was conducted simultaneously at Woodstock, in the church which had pealed out a 'merry peal' when Winston was born. The interment took place in the churchyard at Bladon, within sight of Blenheim, where many of the members of the Churchill family already lay. It was a cold but sunny day, and as an Oxford paper reported, 'The snow lay thick in the long avenue stretching through Blenheim Park from the Woodstock arch to Bladon. . . . Lady Randolph Churchill, supported by her sons, stood at the foot of the grave [and] . . . scattered lilies of the valley in the coffin'.[30]

This year of 1895 was a year of maturing for Winston. Of those who had guided his early years, it was not only his father who died in the course of the year. His mother's mother, Mrs Leonard Jerome, died in April, and in July he lost Mrs Everest, with whom he had kept in touch to the end. Mrs Everest had left the service of the Churchill family as a result of the economies forced upon Lady Randolph by her husband's illness; but she received an allowance from Lord Randolph until he died and perhaps from Lady Randolph afterwards. Winston visited her before she died, attended the funeral and paid for a headstone for her grave. He did not think that loyal service and affection, such as Mrs Everest had given, should lightly be forgotten.

Just before his father's death Winston had passed his final examination at Sandhurst, in which he was placed twentieth out of 130 cadets – a distinct improvement upon his position at the time of his entry to the college. His best marks were in riding, and he had developed a keen desire to join the cavalry after all. He decided that he would like to be posted to the 4th Hussars, whose mess he had visited and whose commanding officer, Colonel J. P. Brabazon, he had met and admired. Early in February he at once set about pulling the necessary strings: he got his mother to write to Colonel Brabazon, who thereupon wrote several letters on Winston's behalf and advised Lady Randolph herself to write to the Duke of Cambridge, the Commander-in-Chief of the Army. This was done; the Duke replied favourably, and when Winston was formally commissioned on 20th February he found himself posted to the 4th Hussars. There was, he reported to his mother, a 'very large Harrow element in the regiment'.[31] He found it agreeable to have this element of continuity, at any rate, in his new career.

3. Subaltern and War Correspondent

By deciding after all to join the cavalry, Winston had followed his own personal preference, but it placed a serious financial burden upon his mother. At this time an officer in the army needed a private income 'ranging from £150 a year, in the more economical infantry regiments, to £600 a year and upwards in the regiments of cavalry of the line'.[1] Jennie had of course benefited from her husband's will, but Lord Randolph's successful investments in South Africa, based upon £5000 loaned him by Lord Rothschild and rapidly built up in the Rand boom to about £70,000, were largely required to pay his enormous outstanding debts.[2] Jennie was left with about £2700 a year, which was mostly the income settled on her by her father; and now her own expensive tastes competed with the needs of her two sons, Winston and Jack – the latter being still at Harrow. Although Winston began to receive officer's pay of £120 a year, he found that the subalterns of his regiment reckoned to need an extra £500 a year to enable them to maintain their position. In addition, an officer on joining his regiment had certain initial expenses, including the cost of polo equipment, which Winston reckoned at over £650.[3] It would have been more had not his aunt by marriage, the Duchess Lily, second wife of the eighth Duke of Marlborough and like Jennie an American, helped out by giving him £200 to purchase a cavalry charger.

In the course of his education Winston had never had a

regular allowance from his parents, and his letters home from Harrow and Sandhurst were constantly burdened with requests for money and explanations of why he was hard up. Now he persuaded his mother to pay him a regular £125 a quarter. Unfortunately things began to go wrong at the outset owing to expenses additional to those which he had anticipated. There were mess and club subscriptions to be paid, and the cost of the transport and maintenance of the horses had to be met. Winston had never learnt to live economically, but it is clear that most of his obligations were unavoidable – given that he was to be a cavalry officer. A fellow-subaltern who was a close friend of his – in fact, the son of a peer – had to throw up his commission when through no fault of his own his private income fell to a mere £200 a year.[4]

Furthermore, if Winston was careless about financial matters, his mother was far worse. 'In money matters', it was said of her, 'she was without sense of proportion. The value of money meant nothing to her: what counted with her were the things she got for money, not the amount she had to pay for them.'[5] Three years after Lord Randolph's death she found that she had built up debts of her own amounting to about £14,000 – which was about a quarter of what was left of the family's accumulated wealth under her father's settlement, the seventh Duke's will and the sum left by Lord Randolph. The only way in which these obligations could be met, she was advised, was by raising a loan, which she, and in the event of her death her sons, would have to pay off at £700 a year. Thus the expectations of Winston and Jack of some £1800 a year each would be reduced accordingly. Winston was naturally very unhappy about this arrangement, though he consented to it for his mother's sake. He wrote very frankly to her:

I sympathise with all your extravagances – even more than you do with mine – it seems just as suicidal to me when you spend £200 on a ball dress as it does to you when I purchase a new polo pony for £100. And yet I feel that you ought to have the dress & I the polo pony. The pinch of the whole matter is we are damned poor.[6]

Poverty, the reader will hardly need to be reminded, is a relative matter. At this time Winston understood the capital remaining to the family to be of the order of at least £40,000 – and the value of money was many times what it is today. Soon, however, he discovered that his mother was getting into such

43

difficulties that she could no longer afford to pay his allowance of £500 a year. He therefore raised a loan of £3500 to pay his allowance and Jack's for three years, and to pay off some £400 of debt which he himself had accumulated with tailors and other tradesmen. This was a heavy charge for him to assume, as the value of his reversion on the Jerome settlement – the capital of which Jennie could not touch – was at this time worth much less than £3500, though it was certain gradually to grow.[7]

In February 1895, when Winston was commissioned, his regiment was stationed at Aldershot, which had already for forty years been a permanent military base. In his first six months as a newly joined subaltern he had to undergo the same rigorous riding exercises that were practised by the ordinary recruits – and he suffered accordingly, although unlike them he was able to ease the stiffness of his muscles with hot baths and massage. In some ways he lived comfortably, having breakfast in bed and playing bezique after dinner. But there was no escaping the daily routine of two hours' riding, one hour's 'stables' and ninety minutes' drill. The drill Winston heartily disliked, but in spite of his aches and pains he enjoyed the riding. He played polo regularly and was bold enough to take part in a steeplechase at the Aldershot races.

At this early stage of his military career he was already marked out by the army's most senior officers, who wanted to know what Lord Randolph's son was like. He was selected to escort the Duke of Cambridge – the aged royal duke who was Commander-in-Chief of the Army – when he paid an official visit to Aldershot, and on this occasion he also met the Prince of Wales and 'had a long talk with' Lord Roberts, now a field-marshal and ten years earlier Lord Randolph's appointee to the command in India.[8] A few weeks later he was invited to meet the Duke and Duchess of York – later King George V and Queen Mary – and the Duke of Connaught, their uncle. He 'had a great many invitations & could go to a ball every night should I wish to': but he did not do so, partly because he found his training so exhausting. But it was about this time that Mrs Everest died, and he found time to go to her funeral. He also visited his father's grave at Bladon: 'I was so struck by the sense of quietness & peace as well as by the old world air of the place – that my sadness was not unmixed with solace.'[9]

It is clear that Winston was thinking a good deal about his

father – perhaps surprisingly in view of their lack of intimacy while he was alive. But he felt drawn towards the ambition of emulating his father's brilliant career in politics. He watched the 1895 general election with close attention and imagined himself taking part in a similar contest of oratory in a few years' time. He wrote to his mother:

> It is a fine game to play – the game of politics and it is well worth waiting for a good hand – before really plunging. At any rate – four years of healthy and pleasant existence – combined with both responsibility & discipline – can do no harm to me – but rather good. The more I see of soldiering – the more I like it – but the more I feel convinced it is not my *métier*.[10]

Considering the expense of keeping him in the cavalry, his mother may well have been rather taken aback by this lack of military zeal. But Winston disliked the 'mental stagnation' which began to afflict him and which he realised to be 'quite in accordance with the spirit of the army'. He determined to resist it by reading systematically in economics and history. His mother urged him to get up some subject relevant to his profession, such as 'Supply of Army Horses'; but he replied this was a topic 'calculated to narrow and groove one's mind'.[11] He deplored the fact that his education, even at Harrow, had been so vocational in character; and he at once tackled Henry Fawcett's *Political Economy*, and planned to follow up with Gibbon's *Decline and Fall* and Lecky's *European Morals*.

One advantage of military life – if one wished to combine it with other pursuits – was that leave was very generous. In October 1895, eight months after being commissioned, Winston became entitled to two and a half months' freedom. With a fellow-subaltern, Reginald Barnes, he made a sudden decision to go to Cuba, where the Spanish army was fighting a guerrilla uprising. He broke the news gently to his mother, telling her that he proposed to visit 'America and the Indies';[12] but even this startled her not a little, since as usual she was expected to provide extra funds for travel and expenses. It was a great advantage to the project that Lord Randolph's old friend Sir Henry Drummond Wolff was now Ambassador at Madrid: the two young officers thereby obtained an introduction from the Spanish Minister of War to Marshal Martinez Campos, the officer in charge of operations in Cuba. Winston also personally visited Field Marshal

Lord Wolseley, who had just replaced the Duke of Cambridge as Commander-in-Chief of the British Army, in order to get formal permission to make the journey. Here again the Field Marshal's friendship with his father was the instrument which enabled him to secure a personal interview. Lord Wolseley gave his permission and passed Winston on to the intelligence department, which invited him to find out what he could about the capabilities of the new bullets which the Spanish army was using. Finally, as the two officers were to travel by way of New York, Jennie provided introductions to a number of her American relations and also to a leading Democratic politician whom she had met in Paris – Bourke Cockran, who was intermittently a Congressman for New York and always a skilful advocate of his party's cause.

Winston enjoyed his few days in New York. He and Barnes stayed in Cockran's comfortable Fifth Avenue apartment and did a good deal of sightseeing. But for Winston, the most exhilarating experience was simply to engage in conversation with Cockran, who was one of the ablest of contemporary American orators. In the tradition of the British aristocracy, Winston came to the conclusion that there was much 'vulgarity' in the United States: he wrote rather quaintly to his brother that 'their best papers write for a class of snotty housemaids and footmen'. But he was favourably impressed with many aspects of American life, and his general assessment was not unjust:

> Picture to yourself the American people as a great lusty youth – who treads on all your sensibilities perpetrates every possible horror of ill manners – whom neither age nor just tradition inspire with reverence – but who moves about his affairs with a good hearted freshness which may well be the envy of older nations of the earth.[13]

This was to be the basis of a special sympathy for the United States which he retained throughout his life – and which, of course, his American parentage and connections had helped him to develop.

The two officers did not reach Cuba until late in November. After meeting Marshal Campos, they joined a column of Spanish troops proceeding on a punitive expedition under General Juarez Valdez. They spent eight days on the march with the troops, moving through virgin forest, being harassed by the guerrillas, and finally witnessing an assault on an enemy position. The General was himself prominent in the final action – he was well within sight and range of the enemy – and he drew a good deal of fire upon himself and upon the two British officers who were at his side. Winston received his baptism of fire on November 30th – his twenty-first birthday. Fortunately, the guerrillas were very poor shots – or had very poor rifles. But there were also the dangers of being caught in an ambush, or of catching one or more of the many diseases that were prevalent in Cuba at the time.

Although Winston congratulated himself on his good fortune when it was all over, he admitted that 'there were moments ... when I realised how rash we had been in risking our lives – merely in search of adventure'.[14] He made a little pocket-money on the side by writing letters for the *Daily Graphic*, which had previously commissioned his father as a correspondent when he visited South Africa in 1891. He was only paid five guineas each for his letters – which he took the trouble to illustrate with sketches – whereas his father had been paid a hundred guineas a letter. But Winston had the additional consolation that both he and Reginald Barnes were awarded a Spanish decoration, the Order of the Red Cross, for their 'gallantry' in the campaign which they had witnessed.

After this exploit Winston's appetite for more travel and campaigning, and for more journalistic commissions, was very keen. He began to calculate on the political advantages of having had a wide range of military experience, with medals to indicate the fact. Journalism, he realised, would not only help to pay his way but would also bring him to public notice and perhaps even fame. He approached the *Daily Chronicle* with the suggestion that he should go as the newspaper's special correspondent to Crete, where the islanders were in revolt against Turkish rule. But the *Chronicle* was not prepared to pay the expenses of a special correspondent, and so this project collapsed. He then persuaded his mother to approach Lord Wolseley about the possibility of his getting leave to go to South Africa, where worsening relations with the Boer Republics after the Jameson Raid fiasco threatened to produce an armed conflict between Boer and Imperial forces. He also made a direct application to the Colonel of the 9th Lancers, a cavalry regiment which had been detailed for service in South Africa, in order to obtain a transfer. Winston's ambitions were made ruthlessly clear in a letter to his mother at this time:

A few months in South Africa would earn me the S.A. medal and in all probability the [British South Africa] Company's Star. Thence hotfoot to Egypt – to return with two more decorations in a year or two – and beat my sword into an iron despatch box.

He expected his mother's keen assistance in all his plans. 'I put it down here – definitely on paper – that you really ought to leave no stone unturned to help me at such a period.'[15]

For the time being, however, all his mother's best efforts and those of himself were of no avail. One reason was that there had been a minor scandal in the 4th Hussars. The father of one of his fellow-subalterns, who had proved an unpopular member of the officers' mess, accused Winston of homosexual practices, and he was obliged to bring a libel suit. The case was settled out of court, and Winston obtained £400 damages. But when the officer concerned left the regiment he brought further charges against his fellow-subalterns which in the opinion of the War Office at least required investigation. The Radical journal *Truth*, run by Henry Labouchere, MP, endeavoured to bring the whole episode into politics, perhaps as a means of attacking the social and financial exclusiveness of the officer class, which was certainly a matter for some remark in what was supposed to be a democratic country. These tactics did not prove successful, and the affair was allowed to die: but Winston was advised not to try to leave the 4th Hussars for the time being, in case it should seem that he was seeking to avoid enquiries into his conduct. In September 1896 the regiment was posted to India, and with it, willy-nilly, went Lieutenant Winston Churchill.

By October Winston and the 4th Hussars were established at Bangalore in southern India – a hill station with an equable climate. With Reginald Barnes and another subaltern, Winston occupied a bungalow with 'a large and beautiful garden'.[16] Indian servants were numerous and inexpensive: each subaltern had a 'butler', two 'dressing boys' or valets, and a syce or groom for each of his ponies. The three officers shared the services of two gardeners, three water-carriers, four washermen and a watchman. Winston had three rooms and plenty of space in which to spread out his books, photographs and other reminders of home. Owing to the heat of the afternoon sun, the regimental routine was to parade at 6 a.m., and after 'stables' from 9.45 to 10.45 a.m. there were no engagements until polo at 4.15 p.m. The afternoon could be spent in sleeping, writing or even in catching butterflies: there were many beautiful butterflies in the garden of the bungalow, and Winston was determined to form a collection. For the rest, he particularly enjoyed the polo, and had a prominent part in the success of his regiment at the Hyderabad Polo Tournament that autumn; an account of one of his successes appeared in the London magazine the *Field*: 'Captain Hoare made one of his familiar runs, Mr Barnes backing well. Then Mr Churchill got his chance, and in two grand strokes the ball went between the posts.'[17]

Winston was later to write of polo as one of the most valuable recreations for army officers, and as a significant social link between the army and the Indian princes, against whose teams they often played.[18] But on the whole he thought the life he was living in India was 'stupid dull & uninteresting'.[19] He had no letters of introduction to senior officers in India, as he had had in Cuba, and he felt that as a soldier he could learn little about the way the country was governed. He made little effort to make friends in the 'Anglo-Indian' – that is, the expatriate British – community at Bangalore, which he thought very dull; and, as for the Indians, apart from the occasional game of polo it was out of the question to mix socially even with the aristocracy.

Towards the end of the year, after only three months in India, Winston was agitating for a transfer to Egypt, where he had reason to believe that action was impending to assert Anglo-Egyptian control over the Sudan. He persuaded his mother to write on his behalf to General Kitchener, who was in charge there. 'I thirst for excitement of some sort or other', he wrote to her at this time.[20] Meanwhile he was busy with his programme of self-education, and soon found his way through Gibbon's *Decline and Fall*, Macaulay's *History of England* and *Essays*, Plato's *Republic* in translation, and Winwood Reade's *Martyrdom of Man* – a work whose criticism of Christianity he thought was 'the crystallisation of much that I have for some time reluctantly believed'.[21] He also arranged for his mother to send him a run of volumes of the *Annual Register* so that he could study the political history of recent times.

In the spring of 1897 Winston was due for a period of leave, and he spent it on a hasty visit home. In London he called at the Conservative Central Office and by consultations with the secretary he arranged to make his first political speech – at a Primrose League meeting at Bath. The occasion convinced him that speech-making was not beyond his powers. Previously he had had some doubts about the matter as he could not properly pronounce the letter 's' and thought that this defect might put off his audience. But the speech went down well: 'At the end they clapped loudly and for quite a long time. So I could do it after all! ... I began to be much pleased with myself and the world.'[22]

But before his leave was up Winston learnt that there was trouble on the North-west frontier of India, in the mountains not far from where the great empires of Asia – the Russian, the Chinese and the Indian – all converged. He realised that this might give him the possibility of action that he had sought, and so he at once set off back to India, despatching in advance a fusillade of telegrams to General Sir Bindon Blood, who was in charge of the so-called Malakand Field Force, now being formed for action in this area. He had met Sir Bindon at Deepdene, the home of Lord William Beresford and his wife Lily, the former Duchess of Marlborough now remarried. The General replied cordially, pointing out that although he could not himself appoint Winston to his command he was willing to receive him as a newspaper correspondent, and would probably be able to give him a fighting post as soon as there were any casualties. So Winston got extra leave from his regiment, and with the General's help obtained credentials as a correspondent from the *Calcutta Pioneer*. Later he also arranged to send letters to the *Daily Telegraph* in London.

The Malakand Field Force was engaged in making reprisals against the nomadic tribes of the frontier which had attacked various British outposts. Columns of troops would go forward to burn villages, and would then return to their bases, not without harassment from the enemy. Often the withdrawal to base was very dangerous as the tribesmen had obtained modern rifles and could wound at least a proportion of the soldiers. The wounded could not be allowed to fall into enemy hands; and usually each casualty had to be carried home by four of his able-bodied companions. This meant that each retiring column lost the firepower of five rifles for every casualty it suffered. The casualties among the officers were especially high, and so Winston was soon able to join the force. At first he acted as a liaison officer on the staff of the General. He galloped around visiting the various columns, at first by himself, but later, after nearly being caught by hostile tribesmen on horseback, in the company of two *sowars* or Indian cavalrymen. On September 16th he was with one of the retreating columns when it was in acute difficulties. As he wrote to his mother, it was 'an awful rout in which the wounded were left to be cut up horribly by these wild beasts'. Winston himself at first joined in the task of helping to carry the wounded, and later took part in the defence of the column, shooting at the enemy at a range of about forty yards, first with his revolver and later with a wounded man's rifle. 'I cannot be certain, but I think I hit 4 men.' Out of 1300 men in the column, 150 were killed or wounded.

Considering the dangers in this campaign, Winston sometimes took quite unnecessary risks in order to get a reputation for conspicuous gallantry. His motives were carefully calculated, as he revealed to his mother: 'I rode on my grey pony all along the skirmish line where everyone else was lying down in cover. Foolish perhaps but I play for high stakes and given an audience there is no act too daring or too noble. Without the gallery things are different.'[23]

Early in October Sir Bindon Blood appointed Winston to an Indian regiment which had run short of officers – the 31st Punjaub Infantry. The General approved of this young officer of his acquaintance and described him in a letter to Winston's old regimental commander, Colonel Brabazon, as 'working away equal to two ordinary subalterns'.[24] But Indian Army Command had never approved of Winston's self-transfer from Bangalore to the Frontier; and after a few days he was ordered to rejoin the 4th Hussars, and so his part in the campaign came to an end.

Somehow during the battles Winston had managed to write his letters for the *Daily Telegraph* and the *Pioneer*, describing the events he had personally witnessed, and giving such news as he could obtain of other actions by the force. His letters were vivid enough in their descriptions of the fighting, but they did not reveal its full dimensions. He was reluctant to admit that British and Indian troops had been thrown back in a 'rout', and that terrible atrocities had been inflicted on the wounded who fell into enemy hands. Nor did he like to say that when the enemy casualties were in British or Indian hands the troops 'do not hesitate to finish their wounded off'. He did not reveal to the British public that the troops were supplied with Dum-Dum expanding bullets, 'the shattering effects of which', he said, 'are appalling',[25] and which were later banned, albeit ineffectually, by the Hague Convention of 1899. He was after all a British officer who owed his presence on the battlefield to the courtesy of the general in charge. But it was significant that he noticed these things, repeated them to his family and friends, and reckoned them in his mind as thoroughly unpleasant.

From his own point of view, the campaign was a great success. He gained fresh confidence in his own courage: as he told his mother, 'I never found a better than myself as far as behaviour went'.[26] He returned to Bangalore with the knowledge that he had qualified for a medal and 'I think two clasps';[27] and he later heard to his great satisfaction that Sir Bindon Blood had given him a mention in despatches. He at once conceived the plan of transforming his newspaper correspondence into a book to be called *The Story of the Malakand Field Force*. One reason why he wished to do this was because his name had been omitted from the letters published in the *Daily Telegraph*. Since his purpose was in large part that of 'bringing my personality before the electorate',[28] he was much disappointed by the cloak of anonymity which had been thrust upon him by his mother, after consultations with her friends in London. Lady Randolph had been given to understand that a young officer might get into serious trouble for discussing in print the strategical and political questions which exercised his superiors.

The Story of the Malakand Field Force was published by Longman in the spring of 1898. Winston had been unable to correct the proofs, as he was anxious for the book to be published as soon as possible in order to anticipate a rival correspondent's account. He therefore asked his mother to have Moreton Frewen, her sister's husband, look through the proofs and correct the style and punctuation. This was a disastrous decision as Frewen had no idea of English style, and introduced far more errors than he removed. It was a tribute to the real merits of the book that in spite of this most reviewers recognised its quality. The *Athenaeum*, whose literary standards were perhaps exceptionally high, described it as 'in style a volume by Disraeli revised by a mad printer's reader'[29] – a comment which hit Winston hard.

But most reviewers thought that they recognised in it many of the qualities of Lord Randolph Churchill. *The Times* said that 'the power of direct expression, the unhesitating candour, and the sense of humour displayed by the young author will be noted as a striking instance of heredity'.[30] The *Spectator* thought that the author showed 'abundantly keen powers of soldierly observation' upon which he based 'much shrewd argument'.[31]

The *United Services Magazine*, a journal for officers of the forces, described it as 'a most excellent work' and recommended it to be read by every officer in the army:[32] and the editor promptly invited Winston to write a special article on frontier policy for the magazine. In this article, which Winston quickly composed and despatched, he summed up the conclusions of his book. The 'Forward Policy' on the frontier should perhaps never have been begun, he thought, because it made the task of subordinating those mountainous districts, suitable as they were to guerrilla warfare, one of constant difficulty and expense both in money and in men. But since the policy had been accepted in the past, it could not now be abandoned without serious consequences. The main thing was to economise on the expense, by moving cautiously rather than hastily, by limiting the total number of frontier forts, and by using subsidies, rather than major military expeditions, as the means of gradually extending British control into this wild borderland of Afghanistan.[33] On the whole, this was in fact what the government was now trying to do; but there were still some advocates of a more vigorous action, of whom the most important was Field Marshal Lord Roberts. It was into this conflict of ministers and generals that Lieutenant Winston Churchill thrust himself with as much confidence as he had shown on the hills of Malakand.

In the summer of 1898 Winston resumed work on a novel which he had begun to write the previous year. He had worked out the plot in advance, and only had to modify it slightly in the course of composition. It is a tale of civil war in a mythical state entitled 'Laurania' – obviously an imitation of the 'Ruritania' which appears in Anthony Hope's *Prisoner of Zenda*, published in 1894. The title of the novel is *Savrola*, which is the name of the hero, a young political leader who combines all the qualities which Winston most admired – courage, intelligence, wide reading, oratorical power and the outlook of the philosopher and rationalist as well as of the 'human man who appreciated all earthly pleasures'.[34] Savrola is the leader of an opposition party, based on popular support, which seeks to overthrow a military dictatorship. The dictator's wife, Lucile, secretly sympathises with Savrola, and there is a mutual attraction between them which develops when the dictator sends her to him to learn his plans. Winston does not describe his heroine beyond telling us that she is 'beautiful' and that her *salon* had been 'crowded with the most famous men from every country.... Suave and courtly ambassadors had thrown out delicate hints, and she had replied with unofficial answers'.[35] There is a hint of Lady Randolph about this character; but when it came to the love scene Winston was quite at a loss and had to ask for help from a brother officer at Bangalore – without much improvement of the dialogue or description.[36] Much of the book, however, is taken up with an account of the civil war itself, and here Winston is in his element. There is a vivid account of street fighting and of the final capture of the presidential palace. But the plot, which has become somewhat complicated by this time, is never properly disentangled except by a rather artificial summary in the last few pages.

Although the novel reads easily and is quite good light entertainment its interest now is almost entirely confined to the fact that it was written by a man who for other reasons has become famous. We notice, for instance, that Winston includes among his minor characters some figures who clearly come straight out of his own experience. One of them is an old nurse, Bettine, who looks after Savrola in the way in which Mrs Everest looked after Winston: 'She had nursed him from his birth up with a devotion and care which knew no break.'[37] Another is Lieutenant Tiro, a subaltern who might be Winston himself in his earliest military phase – anxious to see combat and to win medals, keen on polo, loyal to his cause. But most of all Savrola himself reflects Winston's own ideal self – not unmixed with recollections of his father:

He hoped for immortality, but he contemplated annihilation with composure. Meanwhile the business of living was an interesting problem. His speech – he had made many and knew that nothing good can be obtained without effort. These impromptu feats of oratory existed only in the minds of the listeners; the flowers of rhetoric were hothouse plants.[38]

The novel first appeared in serial form in *Macmillan's Magazine*, for which Winston was paid £100. Longman published it as a book in February 1900, and Winston, who evidently had some doubts about its merits, wrote in the preface: 'I now submit it with considerable trepidation to the judgment or clemency of the public.'[39] On the whole the reviews were reassuring, but they did not encourage him to repeat the experiment. According to the *Globe*, the book was 'only too obviously the work of an amateur';[40] and in the view of the *Athenaeum* it was 'not a remarkable contribution'.[41] But most reviewers thought, as the *Outlook* put it, that it was at least 'interesting, and will improve the "shining hour" of idleness'.[42] The *Academy* called it 'an agreeable, "rattling" book',[43] and the *Manchester Guardian* saw it as 'full of life and cheery vigour'.[44] *The Times* said that 'all that is good in *Savrola* is in the nature of war correspondence', and that 'it lacks the lightness of Mr Anthony Hope's style, and, of course, it is very far away from Stevenson'.[45] The *Saturday Review* said, 'His events are real, his people abstractions'.[46] The *Spectator* was perhaps the most generous, although still indicating faults:

> If he has not the elegance and urbanity of Mr Anthony Hope, he displays a genuine rhetorical gift of expression, his characters are boldly outlined and his incidents well-planned.... The strength of the novel does not lie in its character drawing, which is conventional, so much as in its political satire – the account of the Lauranian press is decidedly entertaining – its vigorous rhetoric, its effective if not always original epigrams.[47]

While he was still working on the novel in his spare time at Bangalore, Winston was urging his mother to try to get him a transfer to Egypt. 'It is a pushing age and we must shove with the best' he wrote. In the summer of 1898 he again became due for leave, and at once returned to England, depositing his 'native servant and campaigning kit' in Egypt so that he could join General Kitchener's army without inconvenience if the opportunity arose.[48] Kitchener, however, was proving somewhat obdurate, in spite of pressure brought to bear upon him by Lady Randolph and her friends and by Winston himself. Apparently the General had discovered that Winston was proposing to leave the army shortly, and he thought that military experience in the Sudan would be wasted upon him. He therefore at first refused to oblige, even when solicited by Sir Evelyn Wood, the Adjutant-General, who was a friend of Lady Jeune, one of Lady Randolph's society intimates. Winston, on his return to England, went one better, and got in touch with Lord Salisbury, the Prime Minister, who at once undertook to ask Lord Cromer to approach Kitchener. As Cromer was British agent and Consul-General in Egypt, and Kitchener depended on his close collaboration, this promised well; but Kitchener had already discovered that he needed an emergency replacement in the 21st Lancers, a cavalry regiment, and it seems that he had agreed that Winston should be appointed before he received Cromer's letter.

By early August Winston was moving up the Nile on a river boat to join his new regiment, having arranged to send letters to the *Morning Post*, his father's old ally, which had in any case promised to pay him rather more than he had previously been paid by the *Daily Telegraph*. He joined the 21st Lancers as the army was moving south, and the regiment made long marches through the desert – about thirty miles a day, in conditions of great heat. They lost five or six horses a day, and many of the soldiers suffered from heat exhaustion or sunstroke. Winston remained in good health but on one occasion lost his way after nightfall while trying to catch up the column: he spent a 'miserable night and day without food or water' in the desert.[49] Somehow he managed to thrive on the monotonous diet of bully-beef, biscuits and warm beer. Expecting a battle before Khartoum was taken, he wrote to his mother urging her to 'avail yourself of the consolations of philosophy and reflect on the utter insignificance of all human beings'. But he added a cautious rider to this lofty sentiment. Having discovered that the medical arrangements were less than adequate, he added 'If a severe wound, you would do well to come out and help me back.'[50]

Shortly afterwards the battle of Omdurman was fought as Kitchener's little army thrust its way forward towards Khartoum. Winston was on patrol early in the morning of September 2nd and was the first to see the Dervish mass of some 40,000 men preparing to attack. His cavalry troop was hotly engaged by the enemy but escaped without loss. Then as the enemy attack developed the cavalry were placed in reserve, and Kitchener's infantry and artillery broke up the Dervish charge. The enemy fell into confusion and most of them retreated, but they left, facing the Anglo-Egyptian army, what appeared to be a thin line of spearmen. The 21st Lancers galloped alongside this line with the object of turning its flank and attacking the fugitives; but it was suddenly discovered that the spearmen were in fact riflemen who produced a sharp fusillade at close range. The Lancers at once wheeled into a charge – the only alternative being a precipitate retreat – and soon overran the enemy line, only to find beyond it a packed mass of spearmen whom they had not previously noticed. Winston wrote to a friend:

Opposite me they were about 4 deep. . . . We passed through without any sort of shock. One man in my troop fell. He was cut to pieces. Five or six horses were wounded by back handers etc. But otherwise unscathed. Then we emerged into a region of scattered men and personal combats. The troop broke up and disappeared. I pulled into a trot and rode up to individuals firing my pistol in their faces and killing several – 3 for certain – 2 doubtful – one very doubtful.[51]

The Dervish mass gradually re-formed and Winston saw a couple of men aiming at him with rifles at only twenty yards range. So he galloped off to where the squadron was re-forming about 150 yards away. The regiment's casualties had not been light. 'Out of 310 . . . one officer and twenty men killed, 4 officers & 45 men wounded. . . . All this in 120 seconds!'[52]

Winston was impressed with the courage of his men who in spite of their losses were quite ready to make a fresh charge through the enemy ranks. He was, in the heat of the moment, all in favour of such a course himself. But to his disappointment the commander of the regiment wisely decided that dismounted fire would be equally effective and much less costly. In this way the enemy was routed and the Lancers were left in possession of the field, from which they could recover their dead. Rifle and artillery fire on the Anglo-Egyptian side was in general what decided the battle: about 10,000 of the enemy were killed, for a loss of only about 500 among those under Kitchener's command. Kitchener had not ordered the charge of the 21st Lancers, and he was probably disappointed by their heavy losses, but he recognised their gallantry, and on his recommendation no less than three Victoria Crosses as well as many other awards were made to those who took part in the charge. Winston's work was not specially remarked, perhaps because he was a newcomer to the regiment and was in any case not much in favour with the army commander.

After the destruction of the Dervish army Khartoum was at once occupied and all else was anti-climax. Winston noticed as he had expected that the wounded were quite inadequately cared for. He also saw that Kitchener did not discourage his troops from killing or ill-treating the Dervish wounded and permitted desecration of the Mahdi's tomb. It confirmed his impression of Kitchener, already expressed to his mother: 'He may be a general – but never a gentleman.'[53] This time he did not fail to mention these matters critically in his correspondence to the *Morning Post*. It was just as well that he was not permanently under Kitchener's command. In October he returned to England for leave before returning to the 4th Hussars in India.

Once again Winston determined to reorganise his correspondence into a book on the campaign. He envisaged the work on a larger scale than his study of the Malakand Field Force, and decided to include an account of Britain's earlier relations with the Sudan, culminating in the siege of Khartoum and the death of General Gordon in 1885. Fortunately his regimental duties at Bangalore were far from taxing, and although he spent some time playing polo, and helped his regiment to win the Inter-Regimental Polo Tournament – himself scoring three out of four goals for his team in the final – he still had a great deal of spare time for the book. By March 1899 when he left India for the last time he had written eighteen out of twenty-three chapters. He paused in Cairo on his way home in order to consult Lord Cromer on aspects of the narrative; Cromer proved most obliging and also gave him useful introductions to other officials, British and Egyptian, from whom he could obtain extra information. The work was quickly finished on his return to England, and by August he was receiving proofs. He asked Lord Salisbury to accept dedication of the work, and the Prime Minister cautiously agreed, after first discovering that there was nothing politically controversial in its pages. There were, however, some sharp remarks about Kitchener: 'The General who never spared himself, cared little for others'; 'Of all the departments of his army the one neglected was that concerned with the care of the sick and injured'; he allowed 'acts of barbarity' by his soldiers which were 'not always justified' by the behaviour of the enemy.[54]

The work was published in the autumn of 1899 under the title of *The River War*. It was 950 pages long, and was lavishly produced in two volumes at a price of 36s – ten times as much as

The Story of the Malakand Field Force. At first it probably attracted less attention than the publishers had expected, owing to the outbreak of the South African War shortly before it appeared. But it won high praise from reviewers for its descriptive qualities. The *United Services Magazine* – his friend as before – thought it 'without doubt the best and most comprehensive book yet written on the subject',[55] and the *Pall Mall Gazette* took the same view: '... to our mind a long way the first among the literature of the Soudan War'.[56] The *Outlook* went so far as to say that its author came 'very near doing for the Soudan what Kinglake did for the Crimea'.[57] The *Manchester Guardian*, as an organ of Liberal opinion, was especially impressed by 'the chivalrous attitude of Mr Churchill towards the enemy'.[58] But other reviewers thought that he was too critical of Kitchener. The *Field* thought that his remarks conveyed 'the impression of personal dislike';[59] *The Times* spoke of the author's 'bumptious self-assertion'[60] and the *Saturday Review* said in an unconsciously prophetic reminder of Walpole's comment on William Pitt the elder, 'He is perpetually finding fault in this "terrible cornet of horse" '.[61]

Winston had resigned his commission in the spring of 1899, and so in any case could not suffer the fate that befell William Pitt, of actually being dismissed from the army. He fought a parliamentary by-election at Oldham in June/July, which will be described later (pp. 70–3), but was narrowly defeated. The defeat was not a dishonourable one, and it looked as if his entry into Parliament would only be postponed by a few months. By September, however, it was clear that war with the Boer Republics was only a matter of weeks; and so he arranged to go to South Africa as correspondent of the *Morning Post* – for which he was to be paid £1000 for the first four months, and £200 a month thereafter, with expenses paid and also the copyright of his articles. He sailed for the Cape on October 14th. On board ship he met J. B. Atkins, the correspondent of the *Manchester Guardian*, with whom he soon made friends. Atkins later described him on the voyage as 'slim, slightly reddish-haired, pale, lively, frequently plunging along the deck "with neck out-thrust", as Browning fancied Napoleon; sometimes sitting in meditation, folding and unfolding his hands, not nervously but as though he were helping to untie mental knots'.[62]

On arrival at Capetown Winston immediately arranged to obtain a commission in a yeomanry regiment, as he thought it would be useful to have officer's rank. The Oxfordshire Yeomanry, his first choice, was full up, and so he secured a place in the Lancashire Hussars. It seems likely that his second choice was dictated by the fact that he had been a candidate for a Lancashire constituency, and probably would be so again.

Winston decided to go at once to the Natal front, where it looked as if there might be the most serious fighting. He took a small steamer along the coast to Durban – an uncomfortable journey through a storm, which made him very seasick – and joined up with the British troops at Estcourt, where they were held up by the Boers who were investing Ladysmith. Here he encountered an officer he had known in India, Captain Aylmer Haldane, who offered him a place on an armoured train which he was taking forward on reconnaissance. The train was armed with a 9-pounder muzzle-loading naval gun and carried two companies of soldiers as well as a crew of civilian railwaymen. It was, however, very vulnerable to ambush by the enemy; and when a party of Boers armed with artillery placed a stone on its line of retreat, it suffered an immediate disaster. The lookouts on the train failed to see the stone, and the impact caused the derailment of two of the armoured trucks, one of which remained partly on the line preventing the escape of the engine and other trucks.

In this predicament Haldane had his work cut out supervising the fire of his troops in defence of improvised positions on and around the wrecked train. Winston volunteered to take charge of operations to clear the line, so that the engine and other trucks could make their escape. Haldane later formally reported of Winston that 'while engaged in the work of saving the engine, for which he was mainly responsible, he was frequently exposed to the full fire of the enemy. I cannot speak too highly of his gallant conduct.'[63] What he had to do was to persuade the civilian engine-driver – who was wounded and about to abandon his duty – to move his locomotive to and fro, butting at the truck which was partly on the line, so as gradually to ease it away. This difficult task took altogether an hour and a half, amidst heavy enemy shellfire. In the end, only the engine and tender escaped along the line, but some fifty or sixty of the party, including many wounded, were on board. Meanwhile Haldane was preparing to undertake a fighting retreat on foot with the remaining force; but two of his soldiers suddenly raised the white flag, and the Boers emerged and invited the remainder to surrender. In the confusion Haldane and another officer, with about fifty soldiers, were all made prisoners of war. Winston had decided to leave the engine and rejoin Haldane, and he returned alone and unarmed along the railway track, only to be caught and forced to join the other prisoners.

Winston was for some time confident that as a newspaper correspondent he would soon be released from captivity. But he was taken to Pretoria with the other prisoners, and placed in an officers' prison camp in a school. He at once applied to the Boer authorities for his release; but they realised that he had played an important part in the escape of the railway engine and tender and about half the party which had been ambushed. The British South African papers were full of the heroism of 'Lieutenant Churchill', who had been warmly praised by members of the escaping party. So Winston was kept as a prisoner for some weeks, and it was only after much hesitation that it was finally decided that he should be released. Actually, he did not have a very strong case for release as when he had started the expedition he was armed with a Mauser pistol, and it was only in the effort of freeing the engine that he had put it aside.

But before Winston had time to be notified of his release he had escaped from captivity. The plan for an escape was originally made by Captain Haldane and a regimental sergeant-major called Brockie who was himself a South African and knew Afrikaans and Kaffir. It was decided to make a break over the wall of the school, while the closest sentry was momentarily inattentive. When Churchill asked to join the escape, Haldane and Brockie had serious doubts as they thought he was regarded by the Boers as a specially valuable prisoner, and so there would be a very keen hunt for him. Also, he did not appear to be very fit; his shoulder had not fully recovered from a fall in India and so he might have difficulty in climbing over the wall. In the end, however, it was only Winston who found a suitable opportunity for jumping over the wall while the sentry was not looking. Although he waited for well over an hour for the others to join him, they could not do so, nor could he climb back without danger of detection. So he set off by himself, with little real hope of being able to get away. He had some chocolate and about £75 in cash

– a remarkable sum for a prisoner to have in his possession – but he had no map or compass.

It was already dark. Winston was dressed in a civilian suit with a slouch hat, and was therefore able to walk straight out of the town through the suburbs without arousing suspicion. Soon after passing a railway station, he jumped on to a slow-moving freight train which was on its way eastwards – that is, towards the frontier of Portuguese Mozambique. He slept for a while, but woke in time to jump off the train before it was light. Next day he lay low – accompanied, somewhat to his concern, by a 'gigantic vulture'[64] – and planned to catch another train during the following night. But he soon discovered that no more trains were running at night, and so in desperation he had to make for what at first he took to be a Kaffir village. By good fortune it turned out to be the residence of a colliery manager called John Howard. Howard was a naturalised Transvaal citizen, but he was of English origin, and he undertook to look after Winston and to send him on his way after the hue and cry had died down.

The Boers did not discover that Winston had escaped until the morning after his departure. During the night his fellow-prisoners had placed a dummy in his bed, which next morning was solemnly offered a cup of tea by an orderly. When his absence was reported, a vigorous search was organised and a description of him was issued, with a reward of £25 for his apprehension, dead or alive. He was described as

25 years old, about 5 ft 8 in tall, average build, walks with a slight stoop, pale appearance, red brown hair, almost invisible small moustache, speaks through the nose, cannot pronounce the letter 'S', cannot speak Dutch, has last been seen in a brown suit of clothes.[65]

Meanwhile for three days Winston was actually living down the mine, in complete darkness except for the occasional light of a candle. He was visited and supplied with food by Howard and a few others of the colliery staff who were entrusted with the secret because they were of British origin. His sleep was disturbed by rats, but they were afraid of the light, and if he prevented them from eating his candles before they were lit, he could keep them at bay. But the strain of living underground soon began to tell on him, and after three days Howard decided that the worst of the hue and cry was over, and that Winston could be brought to the surface and installed in the back room of his office. Here he stayed another three days, after which Howard gave him some food and a revolver and put him on an eastbound train, on which after a weary journey of almost three more days he reached the Portuguese port of Lourenço Marques.

The rest of Winston's journey was an easy one. He made his way to the British Consulate in the town and had a hot bath and a good dinner. The weekly steamer for Durban by a fortunate chance was leaving the same evening, and so he was soon on his way back to British territory. The news of his escape preceded him, and when he reached Durban on December 23rd he was given a great ovation.

> Mr Winston Churchill ... was carried shoulder high from the steamer and conveyed to town from the docks in a jinricksha drawn by a band of enthusiastic admirers and followed by a large crowd cheering and waving Union Jacks. His arrival at the Commandant's office occasioned another outburst of patriotic fervour. Demands were made for a speech and Mr Churchill willingly complied. ... [66]

Meanwhile British arms had suffered a series of defeats in the field, and the home government and public opinion were just beginning to wake up to the magnitude of the task that lay ahead before victory could be achieved. Winston decided to hasten this awakening, and having obtained a healthy respect for the Boers as a result of the armoured train incident and what he had seen during his captivity he decided to put the matter bluntly to his *Morning Post* readers. Writing on the day of his arrival in Durban, he declared:

> The individual Boer, mounted and in a suitable country, is worth from three to five regular soldiers. The only way to deal with them is either to get men equal in character and intelligence as riflemen, or failing the individual, huge masses of troops. ... There is plenty of work here for a quarter of a million men. ... Are the gentlemen of England all fox-hunting? Why not an English Light Horse? ... [67]

These views aroused some criticism in London, even among the *Morning Post*'s own contributors. Spenser Wilkinson, the military historian, who was the paper's leading analyst of the progress of the war, thought that the case for sending a quarter of a million men was by no means proved[68] – though in the end Winston was justified by events. Others were offended by Winston's implication that man for man the Boers were better soldiers than the British. Some critics even sent him a wire: 'Best friends here hope you will not continue making further ass of yourself.'[69] But Winston believed in his own analysis of the situation and suited his action to his words by obtaining a commission for himself in the South Africa Light Horse, a regiment recruited in the Cape Colony. As the *Morning Post* was still paying him a salary, it was agreed that he should not draw army pay, but should have some freedom to carry on with his duties as a correspondent.

For the next two months the South Africa Light Horse was engaged in the fighting which, under the command of General Sir Redvers Buller, led to the relief of Ladysmith. Buller was by no means a competent commander, but Winston's despatches betrayed no disloyalty to him. For one thing Buller, unlike Kitchener in the Sudan, had made himself very accessible to Winston, and had indeed arranged for his commissioning. Also, Winston enjoyed his regiment's life of skirmishing with the enemy, in which no heavy casualties were incurred. 'We lived in great comfort in the open air, with cool nights and bright sunshine, with plenty of meat, chickens and beer.'[70] He had a lot to write about to the *Morning Post*, and as he had no way of spending money, his salary accumulated at home. He had obtained a commission in his regiment for his brother Jack, now aged nineteen, but after the brothers had been together for only a few weeks Jack was wounded in the leg. He was sent back to Durban where by a coincidence he was one of the first casualties to be treated on board the hospital ship *Maine*, which his mother Lady Randolph had accompanied from England. The *Maine* had been equipped out of funds raised from American sources, largely as a result of Lady Randolph's initiative. Meanwhile Buller was at last able to raise the siege of Ladysmith, and Winston was with the first troops to enter the town. 'At the head of a battered street of tin-roofed houses [we] met [General] Sir George White on horseback, faultlessly attired.... I dined with the Headquarters staff that night.... Jealously preserved bottles of champagne were uncorked.'[71]

Realising that it would take a long time to mount an assault on the Transvaal itself, Winston decided to join the army of Lord Roberts, which had been moving up from Cape Colony into the Orange Free State. He had no great difficulty in getting leave for this from the South Africa Light Horse, but it took him some time to secure permission to join Roberts. The General had disliked his criticism of Kitchener, who was now his Chief of Staff, in *The River War*; and he was also offended by a sharp attack made by Winston in his *Morning Post* correspondence on the type of sermon preached by army chaplains on the battlefield. When Winston finally received permission to join Roberts' headquarters, he found that the General would not speak to him and that he was subject to a mild form of censorship. But this did not hinder him unduly, and he was able to see many of the actions of Roberts' advancing troops, and particularly those of General Sir Ian Hamilton, who had befriended Winston on one of his trips home from India. Winston as usual got involved in the fighting – on one occasion to the extent of nearly being caught by the enemy while with a scouting party. Later dressed in civilian clothes, he bicycled through Johannesburg before the Boer troops had finally departed; and he was one of the first into Pretoria and had the satisfaction of raising the Union Jack at the prison camp where he had been held. It was now June 1900; the major enemy forces had been broken, and the main towns occupied. Winston felt free to return home.

A few days after his return to England, his mother married again. The bridegroom was George Cornwallis-West, a lieutenant in the Scots Guards, born in the same year as Winston and hence twenty years younger than his bride. Tall, handsome, and, if not rich, at any rate the heir to a fine inheritance – Ruthin Castle in North Wales – Cornwallis-West was more interested in sport than in anything else. His family hotly opposed the marriage, but Winston and his brother felt that their mother should be free to do as she wished. The ceremony took place at St Paul's, Knightsbridge, and was attended by the Churchill family in force, including the Duke of Marlborough, who gave away the bride, but by none of the Cornwallis-Wests except for the bridegroom. Jennie's finances now became entangled with those of her second husband, who could not obtain any large allowance from his indignant father. He soon found it necessary to leave the army, and Sir Ernest Cassel, an old friend of Lord Randolph, found a job for him in industry.

Winston, too, was thinking of marriage. Throughout his youth he had had few opportunities for meeting girls of his own age, for he was never at a mixed school – unknown in those days except in the state primary system – and at Sandhurst his closest contact with the opposite sex appears to have been a visit to the dressing room of an actress at the Gaiety Theatre in London, from whom he obtained a signed portrait. There is no evidence that he engaged in the sowing of wild oats: perhaps the terrible fate of his father inhibited him from doing so. In India, however, he met a girl whom he came to like very much – Pamela Plowden, the daughter of the British resident at Hyderabad. She was a few months older than Winston, and generally regarded as very attractive. Although she returned to England before Winston completed his service in India, they kept in touch by correspondence, and in November 1898 Winston was chiding her gently for saying that he was 'incapable of affection'.[72] When he fought the by-election at Oldham in 1899 he went so far as to invite her to join him in campaigning, but when she refused he agreed that 'it would perhaps have been a mistake'.[73] Pamela knew other eligible bachelors, but after she had visited him at Blenheim Winston was confident that 'if there be any possibility of marrying she would marry me'.[74] It seems clear that he felt he could not marry while he was still risking his life in battle and was acutely short of money. While he was in South Africa Pamela wrote to him regularly for some time, but Winston seems to have been lax in replying. It was an on-and-off affair; and Pamela had other, more ardent suitors than Winston. In 1902 she finally decided between them and married the Earl of Lytton, who was slightly younger than Winston, but undoubtedly more handsome.

Although he was still a bachelor, Winston had urgent need of a degree of financial independence so as to devote himself to a political career. He could no longer look to family sources for his upkeep, but he now knew that he could easily make money out of journalism and the writing of books. In 1900 he published two books containing his South African correspondence – *London to Ladysmith* and *Ian Hamilton's March*. The earlier of the two, *London to Ladysmith*, contained his account of the armoured train ambush and of his imprisonment and escape: it received warm praise in the press and sold some fifteen thousand copies within about four months. The *Globe* and the *United Services Magazine* both thought that the author was 'somewhat self-assertive',[75] but almost all the journals stressed his ability as a reporter. The *St James's Gazette* said that 'as an accurate reporter of events within the limits of his vision we consider him un-equalled amongst living war correspondents',[76] and the *Pall Mall Gazette* asked:

> What need is there to run through the combination of qualities which make him the most popular of living war correspondents – the grasp of war, happily wedded to a knowledge of the way to make it easily intelligible to the average civilian; the vividness which is not allowed to draw him into mere picture-drawing; the fearlessness in expressing his judgments on war and politics alike with a cocksureness that sometimes impresses, sometimes amuses, but always scores?[77]

All this success began to make Winston quite prosperous. The royalties of *The River War*, his salary as *Morning Post* correspondent in South Africa, and now the royalties of these two latest books brought him a total of about £4000. After fighting the general election of 1900, and narrowly winning a seat at Oldham, he undertook a lecture tour throughout Britain which in the course of November brought in another £4000. As he put it, 'All the largest halls were crowded with friendly audiences, to whom, aided by a magic lantern, I unfolded my adventures and escape, all set in the general framework of the war.'[78]

In December he went to America, hoping to repeat this success, but was disappointed to find himself hindered by 'a strong pro-Boer feeling'.[79] His own takings, after allowing for expenses, amounted to only about £50 for each lecture, which was half of what he had made in Britain. In New York, where the celebrated novelist Mark Twain presided at his lecture, he made £150; but this was the highest figure. He spent Christmas in Canada, staying with the Governor-General, Lord Minto, and then in January he lectured to rather larger audiences in the dominion – but as his agent had sub-contracted the lectures for a fixed sum, he benefited little. At any rate, when he returned home he was able to put together a total capital sum, from all his earnings, of about £10,000. This sum he handed over to Sir Ernest Cassel to invest on his behalf. It was enough to live on for several years, in the course of which it would be possible for him to devote himself more or less fulltime to his political career.

4. *Member of Parliament*

It seemed obvious from the start that Winston Churchill should choose the Conservative Party as the vehicle of his political ambitions. His father was still regarded as the man who, more than anyone else, had revived Conservatism in the country after the electoral defeat of 1880 and the retirement of Disraeli; and Winston took his politics 'almost unquestioningly' from him.[1] The Churchill family remained closely associated with the Primrose League, the Conservative Party's auxiliary organisation, of which Lord Randolph had been the original driving-force. Winston himself had been made a Knight of a local 'Habitation' or branch of the League, when he was only fifteen years old, and the first speech of his political career, as we have seen, was made at a meeting of the Bath Habitation of the League in 1897, when he was on leave from India. In the course of his speech on that occasion Winston made approving reference to the government's firm foreign policy and to its Workmen's Compensation Bill – which, of course, his father would have endorsed – and for the rest he had only to mention his father's name to arouse the enthusiasm of his audience.

But behind all this, the young Churchill had doubts about where to take his political stand. After all, although Lord Randolph had never left the Conservative Party, he had developed opinions, especially towards the end of his life, which did not fit in at all with the policy of Lord Salisbury's government.

Lord Randolph's closest friends were as often Liberals as Conservatives, although some of the Liberals became Liberal Unionists in 1886. At the age of twenty-one his son was much impressed by a speech of Randolph's old friend Lord Rosebery, who had been Liberal Prime Minister after Gladstone's retirement in 1894. Winston suggested to his mother that a fusion between Rosebery and Joseph Chamberlain, the Liberal and the ex-Liberal, would be the best thing for the country. It would create a new centre party which would exclude on the one hand the 'Fenians' – by which he meant the Irish Nationalists – and on the other hand the 'fossils' – the unprogressive elements of the Conservative Party. 'Lord Rosebery and Joe Chamberlain would be worthy leaders of the Tory Democracy,' he wrote.[2]

Reading Gibbon and Macaulay in India made Winston even more inclined to Liberalism – or at least to Whiggism. Early in 1897 he was annoyed by Salisbury's apparent unwillingness to help the Cretans in their revolt against Turkish rule, and wrote to his mother from India:

> I am a Liberal in all but name. My views excite the pious horror of the Mess. Were it not for Irish Home Rule – to which I will never consent – I would enter Parliament as a Liberal. As it is – Tory Democracy will have to be the standard under which I shall range myself.[3]

But this Tory Democracy, as he defined it, went beyond what most Conservatives of the day would accept, though it was very much on the lines of his father's attitude to politics. It meant universal suffrage, the payment of Members of Parliament, a progressive income tax, and a stern limitation on the size of the army. In spite of his military career, Winston agreed with his father that the army was quite large enough for a predominantly naval power. His opposition to the 'Forward Policy' on the Indian frontier, expressed in the *Story of the Malakand Field Force*, was in accordance with this view.

Churchill was not, however, a Little Englander, as many of the more extreme Liberals were. He believed in the maintenance and in the consolidation of the existing Empire, perhaps by some form of federation. Such a policy, in his view, required caution rather than assertiveness. He disliked jingoism or flag-wagging for its own sake: 'Patriotism', he declared, 'shades into cant; Imperialism sinks to jingoism.' A great war with Russia, for instance, he regarded as likely to do more harm to Britain than to her enemy.[4] When his mother was planning the publication of the *Anglo-Saxon Review*, a monthly journal which she edited for a time, and which had the motto 'Blood is thicker than water', he told her that the idea of an Anglo-American alliance was a 'wild impossibility' and that 'blood and thunder' would not do for a journal which was presumably intended to be read by educated people. 'Literature', he said, 'is essentially cosmopolitan.'[5] In October 1898, when on leave after his service in the Sudan, he delivered several speeches from Conservative platforms, and as the diplomatic conflict with France known as the Fashoda crisis was at its height he could not but stress the need for a determined attitude in the face of what he took to be French intervention in a British sphere of influence. But he went out of his way to praise the Liberal Unionists, and also that section of the Liberal Party known as the Liberal Imperialists, and led by Lord Rosebery, who supported Salisbury's foreign policy. He also argued that Empire and Social Reform went hand in hand as twin objects of policy: 'To keep our Empire we must have a free people, an educated and a well-fed people. That is why we are in favour of social reform. That is why we long for Old Age Pensions and the like.'[6] Clearly, he saw his place as being on the most advanced wing of the Conservative Party, if it was to be within the Conservative Party at all.

In February 1899 Churchill received a letter from Robert Ascroft, one of the two Conservative MPs for the double-member borough of Oldham in Lancashire, suggesting that he might care to contest a by-election there if his colleague, J. F. Oswald, who was in poor health, were to resign his seat.* The electors of Oldham, an overwhelmingly working-class town near Manchester, were predominantly engaged in cotton manufacture and in textile engineering. It was a marginal constituency, falling sometimes to the Liberals and sometimes to the Conservatives at general elections. It had become Conservative in 1895 because the cotton workers were very hostile to the fact that the Liberal ministry of 1892–5 had allowed the Indian government to place an import duty on

---

* At general elections (and at double by-elections) electors in double-member boroughs had two votes each, but could not give more than one vote to a single candidate. If one of the two seats fell vacant and there was a single by-election, the conditions of a single-member constituency would apply.

textiles, which seemed to them to be unfair discrimination against Lancashire. The Salisbury ministry had removed the duty, and the issue had largely dropped out of current politics; but a working-class constituency in Lancashire was obviously the most suitable possible challenge for an aspiring Tory Democrat, and so Churchill was eager to accept the invitation. It was agreed that he and his cousin, the Duke of Marlborough, who might be prepared to help finance the contest, should visit Oldham in mid-June 1899.

When the time came, however, Ascroft himself died suddenly and it was decided that Oswald should resign at once and that a double by-election should be held – naturally a most unusual event. Churchill was forthwith adopted as one of the two Conservative candidates, and as he was an outsider, and an aristocrat, it was thought that it would 'balance the ticket' in an impressive way if his colleague were to be a local trade-union leader, James Mawdsley. Most trade-union leaders were Liberals, and there were already a few of them in Parliament – the 'Lib-Labs' as they were called. But as we have seen, Conservatism was strong among the Lancashire working class, and it was not unreasonable that there should be at least one 'Tory-Lab' in Parliament, to show that the Liberals did not have a monopoly of the representation of working-class interests. Mawdsley was the secretary of the Amalgamated Association of Operative Cotton Spinners – an important union, many of whose members lived in Oldham – and he had for long been prominent in the counsels of the Trades Union Congress. Churchill was delighted by the choice, and thought for a time that it might guarantee their joint victory.

In his election address Churchill declared himself a Tory Democrat and said that he expected to be able to work closely with Mawdsley if they were both elected. Mawdsley for his part welcomed him as a colleague and spoke of what he called 'a compliment to the freedom of British institutions – the standing together on the same platform of a son of the old and world-famed British aristocracy and a spinner from the jinny-gate'.[7] It would certainly have made history if this remarkable pair of candidates had been elected. But the fact was that although there were several thousand textile trade unionists among the electors, they were no more willing to support a working-class spokesman and a trade-union leader at the poll than any other type of candidate. The issues of the by-election turned out to be such things as the Tithes Rent

Charge Bill which the Salisbury government had introduced, and which was disliked by Nonconformists and Low Churchmen because it sought to provide funds for Anglican clergy out of the rates. During the campaign, the Conservative MP for the neighbouring borough of Stockport actually crossed the floor of the House of Commons because of his hostility to this measure.

Churchill nevertheless enjoyed the contest. He found the air of Oldham 'invigorating', and it was easy to get away from the smoke of Oldham industry by visiting the neighbouring hills.[8] On his first day in the constituency he went up 'the high hill that rises towards Mossley' and looked down upon the town that he hoped to represent at Westminster:

> I saw the multitude of tall chimneys, the big square factories, the rows and rows of cottages filling up the valleys, and over all the black smoke from the factories. It came over me strongly then what a responsibility I was taking by asking you to return me to Parliament. I said to myself that if ever I had the honour to represent that great town I would rest neither night nor day, working in and watching over its interests, and the increase of its wealth should be my constant and ceaseless care.[9]

His meetings were well attended, not least by Liberals, who nevertheless gave him a courteous hearing. 'I shall never forget', he later wrote,

> the succession of great halls packed with excited people ... speech after speech – meeting after meeting – three even four in one night – intermittent flashes of Heat & Light & enthusiasm – with cold air and the rattle of a carriage in between.[10]

He vigorously rebutted a charge made by one of the Liberal candidates, Walter Runciman, that he had been 'swashbucklering' round the world:

> That is the sort of attitude the Radical Party takes towards the two fighting services; but a county like Lancashire, fond of manly games, will not take up that attitude. Why, a Lancashire regiment was up the Nile! Was that swashbucklering? Mr Runciman, of course, has not had the same experience as the Queen's Own Lancashire Fusiliers....[11]

But although Churchill declared himself to be in favour of the consolidation of the Empire, he went out of his way to indicate that he was not a 'jingo'. In Whiggish fashion he praised the 'continuity of English foreign policy', and declared that it was more important to control the waterways of the world than to conquer vast tracts of land. His list of waterways, to be sure, went far inland, for it included the Irrawaddy, presumably to show that he approved of his father's action in annexing Burma. And he again emphasised the importance of social reform, which in his view was essential to a sane Imperial policy:

> The strength of the British Empire does not depend so much on ships and guns as on the stamina and magnificence of our race.... To keep the Empire we must have an Imperial stock.... To keep our Empire we must have a free people and an educated people and a well-fed people. That is why we are in favour of social reform.[12]

For all the energy that he put into electioneering, Churchill began to feel that the tide was flowing against him. He had declared himself a Low Churchman, as indeed he safely could, having been brought up to be so by Mrs Everest. He was, he said, 'a member of the Church of England, with moderate views, and an affection for a good plain service'.[13] But the pressure of the Nonconformists and the opponents of Anglo-Catholicism were so strong that he felt obliged to go further, and to disavow his party's attitude on tithes. At the close of the campaign his mother joined him for the canvassing: but it was to no avail. The result of the polling was:

A. Emmott (Liberal)	12,976	Elected
W. Runciman (Liberal)	12,770	Elected
W. S. Churchill (Conservative)	11,477	
J. Mawdsley (Conservative)	11,449	

At the count Churchill showed no signs of disappointment, and went out of his way, in congratulating the victors, to say that 'he had been delighted by the kindness with which he had been received by his political opponents'.[14] It was a well-fought contest, and by no means a dishonourable defeat under circumstances in which the government was not as popular as it had been at the general election.

The Conservatives of Oldham had liked what they had seen of Churchill, and they were keen to keep him as one of their candidates. He visited the constituency again in October 1899, accompanied by his cousin the Duke, and they both spoke about the prospect of war in South Africa, which was then imminent. In the immediately ensuing weeks, Churchill's popularity in Oldham was naturally enhanced by his exploits in South Africa. A group of Liberals in the constituency wrote to him when he escaped from the Boers to express their admiration, and to say that they would vote for him 'irrespective of politics' at the next election.[15] He and the Duke of Marlborough visited Oldham again in August 1900, both of them having lately returned from South Africa, and the Duke promised £400 towards Churchill's election expenses and £100 a year for the upkeep of the party organisation.[16] Churchill addressed an audience which was warmly in favour of the war, but as usual he put in a note of warning about being too jingoistic: 'I come before you not as a representative of any policy of jingo annexation of territory but simply as a young man who desires to see this country powerful abroad and its people happy at home.'[17]

When the general election took place in September, at a most favourable moment for the Conservative government, Churchill again had the help of his mother in the campaigning, and he was able to persuade Joseph Chamberlain, the Colonial Secretary and the minister responsible for policy in South Africa, to speak at a meeting on his behalf in Oldham. Mawdsley had died since the by-election, and Churchill now had as colleague in the fight a more conventional type of Conservative candidate – a stockbroker named C. B. Crisp. Crisp, who was new to the constituency, was naturally not so popular as Churchill; and the strength of the parties was so closely balanced that this was an instance where the personal popularity of the candidate made a vital difference to the result. The Lancashire cotton district was less strongly Conservative in 1900 than it had been in 1895, although in the country as a whole the Conservatives held the ground that they had won at the earlier general election. The slight Liberal reaction in 'cotton' Lancashire was probably due in part to the same factors that had operated in the 1899 by-election – namely, the loss of interest in the Indian Cotton Duties question, and the residue of feeling on the Clerical Tithes and other Church questions, which tended to benefit the Liberals in a strongly Nonconformist and Low Church part of the country. So Oldham remained Liberal – albeit only marginally so. But Churchill had a personal vote of about 400, which just put him ahead of the less popular of the two Liberal candidates. The result was:

A. Emmott (Liberal)	12,947	Elected
W. S. Churchill (Conservative)	12,931	Elected
W. Runciman (Liberal)	12,709	
C. B. Crisp (Conservative)	12,522	

Churchill was generous in the moment of his triumph, as he had been courteous in defeat. He said:

> I regret personally that Mr Runciman, who is a very clever and able gentleman – there is no doubt that you had three candidates whose ability is above the average, the fourth is myself (laughter) – I am personally sorry that Mr Runciman is among the defeated; but we cannot be all victors (laughter and cheers).[18]

Runciman's career was interrupted only temporarily, for he returned to the Commons at a by-election at Dewsbury in 1902 and was to be a colleague of Churchill's in Cabinets of the future. But the Liberals, for their part, recognised the quality of the young Conservative who had snatched a victory at Oldham; their leading organ, the *Manchester Guardian*, described Churchill as 'a courageous, engaging, and remarkably able young man in whom the spirit of militarism is embodied more amiably than it deserves'.[19]

In those days the polling at a general election did not all take place on one day but was spread over a period of about three weeks. As Oldham had been one of the first constituencies to poll, the success of one of the Conservative candidates there in recapturing a seat lately lost had an invigorating effect on Conservative hopes elsewhere. Churchill was in great demand as a speaker in other constituencies which had not yet polled. The first invitation he accepted was one from Arthur Balfour, his father's own colleague and now the Leader of the House of Commons, who was defending his seat in a working-class constituency in Manchester. When Churchill joined Balfour he found him already addressing an audience, but as he later recorded, 'The whole meeting rose and shouted at my entry.... After this I never addressed any but the greatest meetings.'[20] Already, before making his maiden speech in the House of Commons he was much more of a draw in the country than many parliamentary veterans.

*　　*　　*

In November and December 1900, and in January 1901, the newly elected MP spent his time, as we have seen, not at Westminster but on a tour of the cities of Britain, the United States and Canada giving lectures on his South African experiences and raising enough money to enable him to concentrate on politics for several years without having to worry about earning his living. He took his seat in the Commons in February, and a few days later made his maiden speech. He rose from the seat which his father had occupied after his resignation – the corner seat above the gangway, immediately behind the front bench. Like his father, he had prepared his speech with the utmost care, and had learnt it off by heart. The speech was a defence of British policy in South Africa, but it had some very distinctive touches, including several signs of respect for the enemy – particularly in the remark, 'If I were a Boer I hope I should be fighting in the field', and in a call for generous terms of surrender. The speech ended with a reference to Lord Randolph: 'I cannot sit down without saying how very grateful I am for the kindness and patience with which the House has heard me and which have been extended to me, I well know, not on my own account, but because of a certain splendid memory which many honourable Members still preserve.'[21]

The speech was heard by a crowded House and there was also a good attendance in the gallery, for the young Churchill had loyal friends and relations and was nothing if not newsworthy. It was well received in newspapers of very varying views, though some commentators expressed doubt whether the new MP would ever be the equal of his father as a Parliamentarian. But Churchill was determined to master the art of debate, and he attended Parliament assiduously thereafter. He took up in particular the question of army reform, on which subject he had reason to feel himself specially equipped to speak. It was in line with his previously expressed general attitude that he believed that the army should not be permanently expanded above its pre-war establishment, but should be reformed on its existing peacetime strength. Consequently he objected strongly to a plan put forward by the Secretary for War, St John Brodrick, to enlarge the regular army from two army corps to three, with three more in reserve. In criticism of this plan he delivered a powerful speech in the House in May 1901, quoting his father's views as Chancellor of the Exchequer on the need for military economy and on the desirability of keeping out of Continental entanglements. His main practical argument was that one army corps was 'quite enough to fight savages', while three were 'not enough even to begin to fight Europeans'. The essential thing was to have a 'supreme Navy'.[22]

For some months after this Churchill concentrated his parliamentary activities on opposition to the army scheme; but he also allied himself with a group of Conservative back-bench 'rebels' which included Lord Hugh Cecil, a younger son of Lord Salisbury. Cartoonists likened the little group to Lord Randolph's 'Fourth Party', and it was true that one survivor of the rebels of those days, Sir John Gorst, did join in their attacks on the government, though another, Arthur Balfour, was the Commons leader of the government they were attacking. By early 1903 Churchill was pleased to find that he was only one of nineteen government supporters who were prepared to vote against the Address to the Crown on the issue of army reform. As Henry Lucy, the veteran parliamentary commentator, pointed out, it was an issue that 'would have tempted Lord Randolph Churchill to action', and there seems no doubt that Churchill was the man who organised this rebellion.[23]

Like his father, Churchill believed in politics at the dinner table, and was not averse to mixing socially with political opponents. He was a member of the 'Hooligans' or 'Hughligans' – a group of five younger Conservative MPs including Lord Hugh Cecil, who entertained to dinner one by one a succession of political leaders of both parties. Lord Rosebery was one of those that they invited, and Churchill soon struck up a special friendship with the distinguished Liberal ex-Prime Minister, formerly a close friend of his father, and a man whose political independence and originality he had long admired. Rosebery was one of the last British statesman in the Whig tradition – rich, generous, well read, capable of making brilliant speeches yet curiously unambitious; the advocate of a strong foreign policy and also (here was his bridge with the twentieth century) a man who had pondered over the problem of Britain's future in a world of increasingly powerful nation-states. In a striking speech at Chesterfield in December 1901 Rosebery called on the Liberal Party to start off afresh with a 'clean slate' and to concentrate on how to secure national and personal 'efficiency' by better education and housing and so on. Churchill's interest in social problems had lately been sharpened by reading – at the suggestion of another Liberal leader.

John Morley – a study of social conditions by Seebohm Rowntree entitled *Poverty*. He readily fell in with Rosebery's views, and Rosebery appears to have sounded him on the possibility of forming a 'Middle Party' of right-wing Liberals and left-wing Conservatives. Churchill consulted Lord Hugh Cecil, who was inclined to be very cautious about the overture: 'It is wise to play a waiting game & not to respond to the invitations until he has built himself a house to entertain you in. Now he has only a share – in a dilapidated umbrella!'[24]

Lord Hugh was really too much of a Tory to favour Rosebery's ideas to the extent that Churchill did. But the comment was true enough in any case. If other Liberal leaders who favoured a strong foreign policy and supported the government on the South African War – in particular, Sir Edward Grey, H. H. Asquith and R. B. Haldane – could be brought under the 'umbrella', then Rosebery could perhaps appeal more successfully to a section of government supporters to join him. The possible 'middle party' supporters on the government side were the Liberal Unionists – those who had split off from the Liberal Party in 1886 over Irish Home Rule, including Joseph Chamberlain and the Duke of Devonshire. If these elements came together, they would indeed form a substantial 'Middle Party' – though it is difficult to believe that they would have had much success in a general election. But even to bring together such a union of forces seemed to be beyond the realm of immediate possibility. Chamberlain and the Duke of Devonshire were both in the existing Cabinet, and even Rosebery's friends inside the Liberal Party were not inclined to think there was much future in the policy of the 'clean slate' – which was at once denounced by the official leader of the party, Sir Henry Campbell-Bannerman. Churchill, however, was impatient for a new development in national politics. He felt increasingly restless inside the Conservative Party. He told Rosebery in June 1902: 'I cannot make speeches in the country with any satisfaction now. I cannot work up the least enthusiasm on the Govts behalf: and yet popular audiences seem to gape for party clap trap.'[25]

In October there came some changes: Salisbury at last retired from the Premiership, which he had held for seven years, and Balfour took his place. Sir Michael Hicks Beach, who had been Lord Randolph's closest ally within the Conservative leadership, took the opportunity to retire from the Cabinet, and Churchill sensed that Beach might be somewhat at odds with his former colleagues. He at once wrote to Rosebery:

> I should like to bring you and Beach together. There lies the chance of a central coalition. 'Tory-Liberal' is a much better name than 'Tory Democrat' or 'Liberal Imperialist': & certainly neither paradoxical nor unprecedented. The one real difficulty I have to encounter is the suspicion that I am moved by mere ruthless ambition: & if some definite issue – such as Tariff – were to arise – that difficulty would disappear.[26]

But Rosebery was not in favour of immediate action, and showed signs of alarm lest Churchill should raise the standard too hastily: 'You must not compromise your career by premature action. Some day, perhaps not long hence, the psychological moment may come for a new departure, but it is not yet.'[27]

For Rosebery, in fact, the moment never came. A return to active politics had little attraction for him, as unlike Churchill he had little to gain from attaining high office once more. Churchill gradually became aware that the leader whom he most admired would not provide the leadership that he sought.

It was, in fact, Joseph Chamberlain who 'opened a new chapter in British politics'.[28] He did this by announcing, in May 1903, his own conversion to the belief that it was essential for Britain to introduce Tariff Reform, with a system of preferences to assist the countries of the Empire. Up to this time, Tariff Reform had been the creed of only a small minority of Conservatives; but Chamberlain was a Minister of the Crown, and indeed after Balfour the most prominent figure in the government. Although now in his late sixties, he remained as he had been for thirty years a dynamic force in British politics. He was not speaking for his colleagues in making his demand for Tariffs; and it was clear that he would either have to convert them at once, or resign his post as Colonial Secretary. The realignment of politics and perhaps the realignment of parties which Churchill longed for appeared to have begun.

It was quite open to Churchill to join the Tariff Reformers. He could cite the fact that his father, before he became Chancellor, had shown a good deal of sympathy with the so-called 'Fair Traders' of the 1880s, who wished to return to the system of Protection which had been abandoned in the 1840s. He had in fact been thinking the matter over since April 1902, when Chamberlain had dined with the 'Hooligans' and warned them that the issue was likely to return to practical politics.[29] He had consulted one of his father's old advisers at the Treasury, Sir Francis Mowatt, who was now Permanent Under-Secretary. Mowatt was a convinced Free Trader; he put his own point of view to Churchill and referred him to other Treasury officials for guidance on particular aspects of the question.[30] Churchill also had the interests of his constituency to think of. Oldham depended on the maximum freedom of trade, not only to get cotton as cheaply as possible but also to enable cotton manufactures to be sold as cheaply as possible in other countries. Whatever might happen to other industries, it was clear that Lancashire cotton had nothing to gain and a good deal to lose from the introduction of Tariff Reform. In October 1902, well before Chamberlain announced his conversion to Tariff Reform, Churchill told his Oldham constituents that he stood firmly by the principle of Free Trade:

> What Protection means is that all the people of this country would subscribe together, through the taxes, to make a payment towards keeping certain trades going.... Every trade in the country would agitate for protective assistance.... The lobbies in the House of Commons would be crowded with touts, and I foresee corruption all round.... Protection would not help the cotton trade in any way.... I can quite understand an agriculturalist being in favour of Protection, but I cannot understand a Lancashire man favouring a general system of Protection.[31]

When, seven months later, therefore, Chamberlain announced his conversion to Tariffs, Churchill was ready to play his part in scotching the heresy. Before the end of May he had written to Balfour to say that if he, the Prime Minister, did not repudiate Chamberlain, 'I must reconsider my position in politics'.[32] Balfour, who was not prepared to show his hand to a backbencher, returned a typically non-committal reply, and a few days later Churchill wrote to the Leader of the Opposition, Sir Henry Campbell-Bannerman, to suggest a co-ordination of parliamentary tactics between the Liberals and the Conservative Free Traders. In doing this he was acting on his own initiative, and Lord Hugh Cecil, who was equally keen on Free Trade, berated him severely for writing without consulting him. Lord Hugh was anxious to rally the 'trembling sheep' within the Conservative Party and felt that any attempt to forge an alliance with the Liberals before this had been done would simply push the waverers over to Chamberlain's side.[33] Churchill had to admit that Lord Hugh's policy was sound, but he clearly found it hard to curb his impatience.

In the course of the summer of 1903 the sharp disagreements on fiscal policy that arose inside the Cabinet itself led to the resignation of rival factions, and this in turn suggested to the public that the government was on the point of collapse. Chamberlain himself was the first to go, saying that he would carry on his campaign for the conversion of the party from the back benches. But Balfour endeavoured to avoid completely alienating the Tariff Reformers, and acknowledged that there might well be a case for reconsidering aspects of existing fiscal policy. This attitude, however, distressed the convinced Free Traders within the Cabinet, such as the Duke of Devonshire and C. T. Ritchie, and they also resigned. Churchill and his Free Trade allies now set up an organisation within the party which they called the Unionist Free Food League, of which the Duke of Devonshire became President and Sir Michael Hicks Beach and C. T. Ritchie – both former Chancellors of the Exchequer – became Vice-Presidents.

But the prospects of saving the party from becoming committed to Chamberlain's proposals seemed dim. There was a great deal of latent protectionist feeling in the Conservative ranks – not least at Oldham, where 'Fair Trade' had been very popular in the 1880s among the party activists. Churchill found that his own local party would not continue to support him if he continued to attack Tariff Reform, and on one occasion he arrived at a local club in his constituency to find that the committee refused to allow him to speak. Elsewhere throughout the country, and especially in Birmingham, Chamberlain's home town, Conservatives and Unionists rallied to the new gospel. In November 1903 Churchill and Lord Hugh Cecil bravely addressed a meeting in Birmingham, and rather to their surprise escaped unhurt; but a hostile crowd surrounded the hall where the meeting was held, and it was obvious that the audience, which was not unfriendly, largely consisted of Liberals. For a time Churchill toyed with the idea of fighting the next election in the Central division of Birmingham, which his father had fought in 1885: the prospects did not look very good there, but they seemed better than at Oldham, where his own party was repudiating him, and where the Liberals were far more likely to adopt a Labour candidate to run as

Emmott's colleague than to accept Churchill as an ally or as a convert.

There was still a chance that the Liberal Party might be prepared to come to some sort of electoral treaty with the Unionist Free Traders if they formed a substantial and relatively homogeneous political group – and indeed there were more than fifty MPs who had joined the Free Food League. The Conservative Party in 1886 had been similarly generous to the Liberal Unionists, and this had proved a wise policy in the long run from their own point of view. Churchill wrote to the Duke of Devonshire to suggest that the Liberal Unionist organisation might perhaps revert to the Liberal Party: his idea was that it would provide a suitable channel for both Liberal Unionist and Conservative Free Traders to regroup alongside the Liberal Party. 'The reconstitution of the Liberal Party in its old power and integrity', wrote Churchill, 'was greatly to be desired. I implore you not to leave that work uncompleted; and I venture with great respect to offer such faithful service as is in my power.'[34] But Churchill could not help the Duke in the conflict within the Liberal Unionist organisation; and here Chamberlain won a speedy victory and forced the Duke to leave its ranks.

Churchill was now coming to the conclusion that he personally had no future with the Conservatives. It was just at this time that he wrote an article for the *Monthly Review*, which was full of criticisms not only of the Conservative Party, but of the entire party system:

> The position which many moderate reasonable people occupy is one of great difficulty. They lie between the party organisations. They take a sincere pride and pleasure in the development and consolidation of the Empire, but they are not prepared to see Imperialism exploited as a mere electioneering dodge. They would not support a Government prepared to deal with delicate and momentous questions of Colonial and inter-Colonial administration on the narrow principles and extensive prejudices of Exeter Hall. But they recoil from that preaching which reduces all the noblest sentiments of the British race to planks in the platform of a party leader.[35]

Churchill's vision of the future was gloomy. He saw the Press being steadily taken over by the Tariff Reformers and the Conservative Party becoming the 'slave of great interests'. He concluded with a vision of the party led by Chamberlain: 'Over all, like a red robe flung about the shoulders of a sturdy beggar, an extravagant and aggressive militarism, and at the top, installed in splendour, a party leader, half German Chancellor, half American boss.'[36]

He was certainly correct in seeing no future for the 'moderate, reasonable' people in the centre. Balfour staved off the immediate danger of a general election, and by refusing to adopt an out-and-out protectionist policy himself he managed to retain the sympathies of many who might otherwise have defected. The Liberal leaders, for their part, were unwilling to come to an electoral agreement with the Unionist Free Traders unless the latter adopted Liberal policy on other questions as well. The reasons for the stiffness of the Liberal attitude were, first, that they were confident that public opinion was moving strongly to their side, and secondly that they had already made agreements for an electoral alliance with the nascent Labour Party, and this distinctly reduced the possibility of further alliances. Consequently the Unionist Free Food League gradually broke up. Churchill had an interview with the Liberal Chief Whip, Herbert Gladstone, to see if he could be accommodated without Liberal opposition at Oldham, or at Birmingham Central, or perhaps elsewhere.[37] At the same time, he decided to break his last links with the Conservative Party. He told the Oldham Conservatives that he was doing so, and offered to resign and fight a by-election in the constituency as a Free Trade candidate. This offer was refused by the officers of the Oldham Conservative Association, who realised that the seat could not be won by a Tariff Reformer; and so Churchill was allowed to continue as the junior member for Oldham as long as the Parliament survived.

In the winter of 1903–4 Churchill's links with the Conservative Party at Westminster were finally severed. In December he sent a letter of support to a Liberal candidate at a by-election at Ludlow; and as a consequence in January the Conservative whip was withdrawn from him. In March, when he rose to speak on Tariff Reform, a large body of government supporters, led by the Prime Minister himself, immediately deserted the Chamber. But he received encouragement from the Liberal benches, and perhaps especially from David Lloyd George, the brilliant Radical who was twelve years older than himself, but still relatively young in comparison with most members. At the end of May Churchill moved to a seat on the Opposition side of the House – and again he chose a seat which had been occupied by his father, this time below the gangway. He had now been invited to contest the North-Western division of Manchester as a Free Trade candidate with Liberal support, and had accepted. The constituency was the Manchester equivalent of the Central division of Birmingham: it contained the city centre, the civic buildings, the exchanges and the major shops. It would not be easy to win, as it had long returned a Conservative MP, who in 1900 had been unopposed. But it did contain many businessmen who though normally Conservative might support a Free Trade candidate who was not too Radical. For that reason the Liberals were prepared to give him a clear run.

Meanwhile on several issues, some of them newly arisen, Churchill was able to bring his views into line with those of the great body of the Liberal Party. With the end of the South African War there was an extension of mining operations in the Transvaal, and owing to the fact that there was a shortage of native labour, and since white labour was relatively expensive, the mining companies persuaded Lord Milner, the High Commissioner for South Africa, and through him the British government in London, to agree to the importation of indentured labour from China. Owing to the fear of hostility to the Chinese on the part of the existing population, both white and black, it was decreed that the Chinese labourers should come without families and should live in segregated compounds. Churchill joined the Liberals in opposing the proposal, which not only seemed inhumane but also caused strong ill-feeling among the existing inhabitants of South Africa and deep disappointment in Britain among workers who had been led to hope that the South African War would expand the opportunities for migration from the home country.

Churchill accepted the Liberal view that too much money and effort had been spent on foreign and imperial affairs. He called for retrenchment in both military and naval expenditure, arguing that this would 'produce a corresponding restraint in the foreign and colonial policy of Great Britain, and the restraint will be all in the interests of the workers at home and all in the interests of peace'.[38] There now seemed to be no trace of martial influence in his attitude to politics; and when his old friend J. B. Atkins of the *Manchester Guardian* invited him to take part in a symposium of essays on the proposal to establish a system of physical training for British youth his contribution recalled the message of Rowntree's *Poverty* and urged instead 'the provision of meals for children who are underfed'. This, he thought, if combined with opportunities for playing games, would be sufficient to produce healthy physique.[39]

On the question of trade-union rights also Churchill now accepted the Liberal standpoint. For some time he had been pressed by J. R. Clynes, the secretary of the Oldham Trades Council, and later a leader of the Labour Party, to support the trade unions' demand for legislation to restore the legal position of the unions to that which existed before the famous Taff Vale case of 1901. For some time Churchill had resisted, arguing that 'it would be most unwise to free commercial combinations from the restraints and protection of the law';[40] but Clynes, who was nothing if not persistent, kept writing to him, replying with care to every argument that he used; and in 1903 Churchill was one of seventeen nominal government supporters to vote in favour of a resolution put forward by David Shackleton, the Labour MP, calling for new legislation.

In 1904 when the issue came up again Churchill actually made a speech in support of the proposal, arguing that in the existing situation after an adverse judgment in the courts,

> ... trade union funds, accumulated shilling by shilling during many years, and inextricably mingled with moneys intended for friendly and provident purposes, might be swept away. That is a situation which has produced profound anxiety all over industrial Lancashire. ... It cannot, I think, be said that Labour bulks too largely in English politics at the present time.[41]

Churchill was in the habit of learning his speeches off by heart, but on this complicated and perhaps somewhat uncongenial subject he suffered from a lapse of memory and had to sit down in confusion without completing his speech. Some of his friends, fearing that he was going the way of his father, were very concerned. But it was a problem that could best be remedied by the simple expedient of holding in his hand full notes of what he wanted to say, in case his memory failed him; and this was what he was always careful to do thereafter.[42]

Churchill's change of view on the trade-union question might have won him some votes in Oldham, but it would not cut much ice in Manchester North-West, where the electors were predominantly middle class. On another question, however, he was able to commend himself to a section of his prospective constituency. The Manchester Jewish community was anxious to do what it could for those of the Jewish faith who were trying to escape from the pogroms in Russia, and its leaders asked Churchill if he would oppose the government's proposal to restrict alien immigration. The level of immigration into Britain was not high, taking the country as a whole, but many of the immigrants had crowded into East London and formed a substantial community there. Conservative MPs for East London constituencies had discovered in the elections of 1895 and 1900 that any proposal to ban further immigration was popular with their constituents; and it was clear that the passing of a measure for this purpose would strengthen the position of Conservative candidates in East London and perhaps elsewhere. But Churchill was quick to oppose the measure, partly because he felt that there was a link between alien restriction and Tariff Reform, and partly because his father's old friend, Lord Rothschild, took up the case of his co-religionists and pointed out that the proposals involved the establishment in Britain of 'a loathsome system of police interference and espionage, of passports and arbitrary power'.[43]

Churchill wrote to Nathan Laski, a leader of Manchester Jewry, to say that he would strongly oppose a measure 'which, without any proved necessity, smirches those ancient traditions of freedom and hospitality for which Britain has been so long renowned'.[44] Churchill was one of the critics of the bill who, by the vigour of their opposition, caused the government to postpone legislation on the subject until 1905. The Manchester Jewish voters, many of whom resided at Cheetham within Churchill's constituency, could be expected to show their approval of this attitude at the general election.

As he became more hostile to Conservative attitudes, so Churchill began to hit still harder at the leaders of his former party. His weapon was not quite the rapier of ridicule that his father had employed, but rather a bludgeon of invective – albeit a bludgeon that he wielded only after his customary careful preparation. A good example of his style is provided by a speech he made in the Commons in July 1905, after Balfour had refused to resign although the government had been defeated on a snap vote. Churchill said, among other things, that he 'had a great respect for the intelligence of the Prime Minister – almost as great as for the character of the Home Secretary'; and he concluded that by staying in office Balfour had 'flouted the traditions of Parliament and dishonoured the service of the Crown'.[45] Balfour's reply was not unjust: 'It is not, on the whole, desirable to come down to this House with invective which is both prepared and violent.... If there is preparation there should be more finish, and if there is so much violence there should certainly be more obvious veracity of feeling.'[46] Even one of his new Liberal colleagues, the Master of Elibank, felt impelled to write to him to urge him to moderate his abuse of the Conservative leaders.[47]

Churchill had already found that loyal Conservatives resented the tone of his speeches, for when he applied in 1904 to join the Hurlingham Club as a polo-playing member he suffered the almost unheard-of indignity of being blackballed.[48] It is significant, too, that when Campbell-Bannerman visited Manchester late in 1904 he found that the Liberal leaders there were doubtful whether this young convert from the Conservatives was 'quite the sort of man to capture the quiet non-party voter' who had been prepared to support the sitting Conservative MP for the division.[49] Temporarily, it seemed, Churchill's impatience with a government that refused to resign got the better of his customary good humour. He seems to have felt that his life was slipping away without positive achievement in his chosen career, for he was already two-thirds the age of his father at his death in 1895, and seemed to think that he, too, was likely to die early. It was with real feeling that he expressed concern about the passing years and about his own retreat from youth.[50]

Churchill belied Disraeli's cynical dictum that 'No man is regular in his attendance at the House of Commons until he is married'. He was assiduous in his parliamentary work, and during sessions of the House lived close to Westminster in the flat which he shared with his brother in Mount Street, Mayfair. He had his relaxations – he played polo when he had a chance, and went hunting on winter weekends from Blenheim. His mother, who was trying to economise by living outside London, had taken a lease on an old house called Salisbury Hall, near St Albans, and this provided a pleasant occasional resort for her son. He took short annual holidays on the Continent, and in December 1902 returned to Egypt as the guest of Sir Ernest Cassel in order to attend the opening of the Assouan Dam. But it was not easy for him to set aside for any length of time the cares of the political conflicts in which he was involved.

There was, however, one special task on which he had set his mind, and which provided, to a limited degree, a change from the day-to-day concerns in which he was engaged. This was the biography of Lord Randolph Churchill which he had persuaded his father's literary executors to allow him to undertake. His father's papers provided a great deal of the essential material, and his aunt, Lady Wimborne, was able to help him with scrap-books of newspaper cuttings which she had kept assiduously during her brother's lifetime. For the rest, Churchill proceeded to call upon his father's old friends and colleagues for their remi-niscences and for any correspondence which they had preserved. Joseph Chamberlain, of whom he was now a bitter public oppon-ent, helped him generously and even invited him to stay overnight at his home at Highbury. Rosebery perhaps gave him the greatest assistance, and Churchill was frequently a guest at one or other of the ex-Premier's magnificent homes – at Mentmore in Bucking-hamshire, at the Durdens near Epsom Downs, or at Dalmeny on the Firth of Forth. But he also caused Churchill the greatest embarrassment, for he prepared a special memoir of Lord Ran-dolph which he suggested should be incorporated in the biog-raphy. Churchill took exception to Rosebery's description of his father as a 'scug' at Eton – not a complimentary term – and asked Rosebery to take it out. But Rosebery was offended and withdrew his contribution, which was later published separately in a slightly expanded form. Among those who lent papers to Churchill was Wilfrid Scawen Blunt, an eccentric old Radical landowner who was a keen sympathiser with Arab nationalism, and who had known Lord Randolph in the 1880s. Churchill persuaded Blunt to visit him to explain some of the allusions in the correspondence. Blunt recorded in his diary:

> He is astonishingly like his father in manners and ways, and the whole attitude of his mind. He had just come in from playing polo, a short, stocky little man with a twinkle in his eye, reminding me especially of the Randolph of twenty years ago.... There is some-thing touching about the fidelity with which he continues to espouse his father's cause and his father's quarrels.[51]

The first draft of the text was completed in 1904, and in 1905 Churchill was getting Rosebery, John Morley and others to read the draft, which he had had set up in proof. The journalist Frank Harris, another of his father's old friends, undertook to act as his literary agent, and he drove an excellent bargain with Macmillan, who undertook to pay Churchill £8000 (£1000 at once, £1000 when the proofs were passed for the press, and another £6000 on publication day) and also to divide equally with him all the profits after they had made a clear £4000.[52] The book, published in two volumes, was on the scale of *The River War*, and was offered at the same price of 36s. It appeared on January 2nd 1906, just as the general election campaign was beginning, but was nevertheless widely reviewed on publication day. There were, of course, some interesting revelations about events in the Cabinet and relations between ministers and the Queen, which had considerable news value – especially as the events concerned were comparatively recent. But the book contained relatively little about Lord Randolph's private life. The birth of his sons was not mentioned, and the nature of his fatal illness was not disclosed.

The reviewers were almost unanimous in hailing the work as a brilliant one, and they were as much surprised as pleased by the fact that the author had, as the *Spectator* put it, 'avoided the pitfalls of the partisan', while showing a filial devotion to his father's memory.[53] Considering how fully Winston was involved in current political controversy and how much he was at odds with Balfour and Chamberlain and other leaders who figured prominently in the story of his father's career, it was amazing that he was able to avoid the temptation to make some pointed allusions to his own times. But the style and tone of the book were throughout well above the market-place, as if the young Churchill were writing for future generations rather than for the present.

As the historian, A. F. Pollard, wrote, 'Its solid merits raise hopes that Mr Churchill is gifted with greater staying power than his brilliant but neurotic father possessed'.[54] For, on the whole, while the book greatly increased the respect in which Winston was held, it did not convert very many people who remembered Lord Randolph to the view that he had been, as Winston put it, 'the object of powerful and widespread prejudice', especially after his resignation in 1886.[55] Any reader could see, from the evidence that the book presented, that there were elements of serious instability and lack of judgment in Lord Randolph's character throughout his career. But all the same the biography has done much over the years to remind those interested in late Victorian politics of the remarkable ability of Lord Randolph Churchill as a parliamentarian and platform orator, and of the vital role that he played in making his party aware of the need to adapt itself to the era of the mass electorate.

Winston did not have much time to read the reviews of his new book as they appeared. He had just accepted office in the new Liberal government, and was opening his campaign in the general election. Balfour had resigned at the beginning of December 1905, thus forcing the Liberals to form a government before the dissolution of Parliament. The retiring Prime Minister hoped that dissensions in the Liberal ranks would make the process of forming a government a difficult and embarrassing one: but in fact the Liberal leaders soon came to terms with each other, and only Rosebery insisted on remaining outside. Campbell-Bannerman, having completed his Cabinet, invited Churchill to become Financial Secretary to the Treasury, and was rather surprised when he demurred and asked instead for the more junior post of Under-Secretary for the Colonies. Churchill preferred the Colonies because he would have full responsibility for representing the office in the Commons since the new Secretary of State, Lord Elgin, was in the Lords; and also because of his personal knowledge of South Africa.[56]

It was therefore as a junior minister that Churchill fought the general election of January 1906. Just before the end of the old year he and Eddie Marsh, a Colonial Office civil servant of his own age whom he had appointed his private secretary, moved into the Midland Hotel at Manchester for the campaign period.[57] The following fortnight was a hectic round of enthusiastic, crowded meetings. As the *Manchester Guardian* declared just before polling day:

> If Mr Churchill could charge a shilling per head for admission to his meetings ... a small fortune would have been garnered during the last fortnight. He was billed to speak in the Manchester Coal Exchange at three o'clock yesterday. At half past two the hall was packed with a struggling crowd; a second crowd was struggling on the staircase leading to the hall; and a third crowd jostling for standing room on the pavement in the street.

His audiences, the newspaper recorded, greeted him with 'an enthusiasm which finds no parallel in previous political contests in Manchester'.[58] The *Guardian* was supporting Churchill's cause; but this sort of language was not simply the zeal of the partisan. A special correspondent of the Conservative *Daily Mail* reported:

> There is no question about it, the public interest of Manchester in the general election is centred and focused on the personality of Mr Winston Churchill.... Ladies who have been privileged to speak to him are envied of their sex.... He is wearing a new old-fashioned hat, a flat-topped sort of felt hat, and already the hatters are having enquiries for articles of that pattern.[59]

Churchill was greatly aided, of course, by the great tide of support for Liberal candidates that had arisen throughout the country. His mother, who was with him during most of the campaign, noticed the contrast with previous contests: 'I have been to lots of elections but I never saw such excitement,' she wrote to a sister.[60] All the same, her son was the sort of candidate to make the most of the situation; and his fight for a seat which had for so long been a Conservative stronghold appealed to the imagination of the public. The *Manchester Guardian* attributed no small part of his popularity to his knowledge and skill in speaking and to his 'lightness of touch and genuine eloquence'.[61] His opponent, William Joynson-Hicks, a strong churchman but a moderate on the Tariff Reform question, attacked him for his inconsistency in changing sides, and produced a pamphlet recording many of the unkind remarks about Liberalism that Churchill had made in the past. But Churchill dealt simply with this by admitting: 'I said a lot of stupid things when I worked with the Conservative Party, and I left it because I did not want to go on saying stupid things (Cheers and laughter).'[62]

Joynson-Hicks would have done better to concentrate his campaign on those points where Churchill remained loyal to his old beliefs, in spite of having become a Liberal. On Ireland, for instance, he said in his election address that he would 'support no Irish legislation which I regard as likely to injure the effective integrity of the United Kingdom'.[63] Even though the Liberals had pledged themselves not to introduce Home Rule in the succeeding parliament, they were still predominantly a Home Rule party; and anything Churchill was forced to say on this subject was likely to embarrass a section of his supporters. He said, in fact, very little. On social reform, too, he was remarkably vague and even negative; presumably out of loyalty to his party: 'We have got no quack remedies, we have no plan for making the world run itself without human effort and struggle.'[64] A demand for 'votes for women' was put to him by Sylvia Pankhurst, the twenty-three-year-old daughter of the suffragette leader, Mrs Emmeline Pankhurst, who insisted on interrupting one of his meetings; and he was so annoyed at the interruptions that he told her he would henceforth oppose the idea of women's suffrage, to which he had previously been favourably inclined. But when he thought she had left the meeting (in fact she was locked in a side room by the stewards) he admitted that he was not so hostile as he had implied, but 'I'm not going to be hen-pecked (laughter) on a question of such grave public importance'.[65] His mother agreed: 'The female suffrage women are too odious,' she wrote.[66]

Churchill, of course, knew very well that he had to win the support of Conservatives as well as Radicals if he was to carry this predominantly middle-class constituency. He was fortunate in having the assistance of a group of Conservative Free Traders led by a Mr Tootal Broadhurst, a prominent local businessman.[67] Whenever and wherever he spoke, he emphasised that the Free Trade question was the crucial issue of the election:

> What is the great historical issue at this election? What is it you will look back to if you live for another twenty years and say it was approved by the decision of the people in 1906? Free Trade. (applause) Everything else will be forgotten.[68]

Most people agreed with him in this, and also accepted his overall view of the matter; and so, as the campaign went on, a remarkable rapport developed between him and his audience. As the *Daily Mail* correspondent wrote:

> He glories in the crowds; and the cheering, and the frank, unaffected, beaming manifestation of his delight in it all redoubles the interest and exuberance of the crowd.... The harder he works, the fresher and keener and brighter he grows. I have never seen him looking so physically fit.... The pleasure of the fight is the greatest stimulus of all.[69]

Manchester polled early in the election; and all eyes were on the city to see whether Churchill would win his difficult contest and whether Balfour, the ex-Prime Minister, would survive in the working-class Eastern division of the city. The result was a decisive blow to the Conservative Party: Churchill in, Balfour out. The Liberals or their Labour allies won every division of Manchester and Salford. Churchill's own majority was over 1200 on an 88% poll. The figures were:

W. S. Churchill (Liberal and Free Trade)   5639   Elected
W. Joynson-Hicks (Unionist)   4398

As the seat had not been contested in 1900, it is impossible to say what the swing amounted to. But the national swing was 10.3%; for the Lancashire and Cheshire region, with its special industrial and commercial interests in the maintenance of Free Trade, it was 13.1%; and for the Manchester district it was 17.9%.[70] Nobody on the Liberal side could claim a greater part in the Manchester victory than Churchill; and the unfortunate Balfour had to secure return to the Commons by means of a by-election elsewhere – in fact in the City of London.

The new House contained 401 Liberals, 29 members of the Labour Party and 83 Irish Nationalists, as against 157 Unionists. Among those who suffered severely were the Unionist Free Traders – those former allies of Churchill who had remained on the ministerialist side until Balfour's resignation. Lord Hugh Cecil was defeated, and Churchill wrote him a letter of condolence. The letter is of interest because it suggests that Churchill himself still had mixed feelings about the partisan victory which he had helped to achieve:

The Tory Party is powerless. Remember that even in 1832 they were only delivered to the Whigs. Now it is to Radicalism. . . . More than that. There is a potent underslide sweeping us to new chores. Well! This is an odd letter for the full flush of victory. Alas what vanity it all is.[71]

He still felt that he did not quite fit into the party system: he was a Whig in company with a host of Radicals. But at the age of thirty-one a new career, that of government, lay before him. As he wrote to an old Harrow master in reply to a letter of congratulation: 'The office to which I have been appointed is not one of great responsibility, but it possesses possibilities – both towards danger and success.'[72]

93

5. *Colonial Under-Secretary*

As the Liberal government took office in December 1905, Lord Elgin, the new Secretary of State for the Colonies, had misgivings about the prospects of his relationship with his Parliamentary Under-Secretary. 'When I accepted Churchill as my Under Secy', he later wrote, 'I knew I should have no easy task.'[1] Aged fifty-six when he joined Campbell-Bannerman's Cabinet, Lord Elgin was a former Viceroy of India, who had acquitted himself with merit in that high office; but his shyness and complete lack either of oratorical ability or of social grace gravely hampered his reputation. Eddie Marsh, Churchill's private secretary, described him as 'a rugged old thane of antique virtue and simplicity'.[2] He was now to have as his spokesman in the Commons – where indeed the great bulk of hostile criticism of the Colonial Office would have to be encountered – a man who was his junior by a quarter of a century, but who was also already known as one of the most powerful orators of the time. It would have been surprising if there had been no friction between two such very different men; and it was not difficult for the view to gain currency that Churchill was gradually supplanting Elgin as the source of policy at the Colonial Office.

Such a view, however, does less than justice both to the administrative qualities of the Secretary of State and to his subordinate's sense of loyalty and propriety. Elgin was quite prepared to let Churchill take part in all the discussions of policy, but he reserved the final decisions for himself. As he put it, 'I resolved to give him access to all business – but to keep control.'[3] Fortunately they were in substantial agreement on how to deal with the major problems of policy, for they were both, at heart, statesmen in the Whig tradition. Only in liquidating the legacy of the South African War were they obliged to abandon the continuity of policy which most Whigs like to maintain: but this was because Milner's policy of trying to force the pace of Anglicisation in South Africa was profoundly un-Whiggish. The new government had to demonstrate that, unlike its predecessors, it was anxious to reconcile the defeated Boers and to give them an equal status with the South Africans of British descent; and it had also to satisfy its own backbench MPs and its supporters in the country that it was doing all it could to put an end to the employment of Chinese labour in the Transvaal – for this had been an issue of major importance in the general election just concluded.

The first major issue that confronted Elgin was whether to accept the proposed new constitution for the Transvaal, which had been drawn up by his Conservative predecessor, Alfred Lyttelton, or to start afresh. Elgin did not like completely overthrowing the work of the previous administration and thought that the Lyttelton constitution promising representative but not fully responsible government could be modified to suit Liberal purposes. But a powerful memorandum by Churchill, dated January 2nd 1906 – that is, just before his Manchester election campaign – helped to convince the Colonial Secretary that it was desirable to make a clean break with past policy on this matter. Using the military metaphor which throughout his life sprang so readily to his mind, Churchill argued:

> We have ... abandoned one practical and defensible position, viz., Crown Colony Government.... Mr Lyttelton's plan ... does not appear to promise either permanence or stability. When one crest line is abandoned it is necessary to return to the next. Halting at a 'half-way house' midway in the valley is fatal. What is the next defensible position? I submit that it will not now be possible to deny the Transvaal a representative Assembly with an Executive responsible thereto.[4]

Churchill also argued in favour of a fully democratic franchise – 'one man one vote' and 'one vote one value' with single-member constituencies – on the grounds that this would give full weight to the strength of the British element in the country. 'It is not often that democratic principles are helpful in Imperial Administration. When they are they should be cherished.'[5]

Churchill's paper – which must count as the first important state paper that he wrote in his long career in government – was read by the Lord Chancellor, Lord Loreburn, as well as by the Colonial Secretary; and both of them were impressed by his argument in favour of the early attainment of responsible government in the Transvaal. At a Cabinet meeting on February 8th 1906 it was decided to withdraw the Lyttelton constitution and to start again. General Smuts, the Boer leader, who was in London at the time, saw this as a gesture of reconciliation to his fellow-countrymen, and mistakenly assumed that it was the result of his own advocacy. But the documents of the time show that Smuts was still regarded with suspicion even by the Liberal leaders.[6]

Churchill himself regarded the reconciliation of the defeated enemy as a matter of prime importance. Although in private he emphasised the desirability of safeguarding and extending British influence in South Africa, he also regarded it as essential to win over the Boers to the Imperial cause, as the French had been won over in Canada. Speaking in the House of Commons in April, he said:

> There is a profound difference ... between the schools of thought which exist upon South African politics in this House. We think that British authority in South Africa has got to stand on two legs. Hon. Gentlemen opposite have laboured for ten years to make it stand on one. We on this side know that if British dominion is to endure in South Africa it must endure with the assent of the Dutch.[7]

This policy, generous and optimistic as it was in its attitude to the Boers, left little room for the protection of the native African population against the white settlers; but African rights had already been virtually abandoned by the terms of the Treaty of Vereeniging which ended the war in 1902, Article VII of which stated that 'The question of granting the franchise to natives will not be decided until after the introduction of self-government.'

The terms of the Liberal government's Transvaal constitution were announced on July 31st 1906. Churchill explained the details in the Commons, in a speech which ended in an eloquent appeal for the support of the Conservative Party: 'We can only make it the gift of a party; you can make it the gift of England.'[8] The Conservative leadership did not respond to this appeal; but all sections of the Liberal Party approved the proposals, and the drafting of the new letters patent for the constitution proceeded smoothly in the autumn. They were debated in both Houses in December, and Churchill again made an impressive speech on the question, with a peroration strikingly indicative of his generalising power:

> Everywhere small peoples will get more room to breathe, and everywhere great empires will be encouraged by our example to step forward ... into the sunshine of a more gentle and a more generous age.[9]

Meanwhile the question of Chinese labour proved an embarrassment, for although Campbell-Bannerman had announced in December 1905 that the Cabinet had decided to 'stop forthwith so far as it is practicable' the importation of labourers it was discovered that the British government had no power to revoke licences already issued. Elgin and Churchill found themselves on the horns of a dilemma, for on the one hand the Liberal backbenchers were pressing for the early repatriation of all Chinese labour from South Africa, while on the other hand the Transvaal mineowners argued that without the Chinese there could be no speedy return to prosperity on the Rand. As early as February 1906 Churchill told the Commons that the conditions of the Chinese could not be described as 'slavery' without, as he put it, 'some risk of terminological inexactitude'.[10] The phrase led to a good many barbed comments from Conservatives who had suffered during the election campaign from accusations of 'Chinese slavery' by Liberal candidates – though not, indeed, by Churchill himself.

But as against this in March it was revealed that Milner had allowed the Chinese to be disciplined by flogging – which was contrary to law. The revelation stimulated a group of Liberal backbenchers to put down a motion of censure upon Milner, who was now in retirement. It was a mistake on the part of the Liberal leaders to leave Churchill the difficult task of resisting the motion: it was obviously a matter for a senior and experienced minister – perhaps for the Prime Minister himself. Churchill as usual carefully prepared his speech in advance, and rehearsed it on his private secretary, who expressed his approval. But the speech was a failure, and aroused great wrath among the Conservatives. 'The fault', said Marsh, 'was one of manner, not of feeling.... He appeared to be taunting a discredited statesman.'[11] It at least had the effect of achieving its main purpose, which was to rally the majority of Liberals to support the government in rejecting the motion. But the King thought Churchill's remarks were 'violent and objectionable' and wrote to Lady Londonderry, who was distantly related to Churchill, 'the conduct of a certain relation of yours is simply scandalous'.[12]

The Chinese labour question continued to worry Elgin and Churchill for some months after this. A scheme was introduced for voluntary repatriation, but it was not advertised very effectively and few of the labourers took advantage of it. There were complaints from Liberal MPs about 'unnatural vice' among the labourers in their compounds. It was only after the Transvaal constitution came into force in 1907 that the whole question was cleared up. The new Transvaal government – which contrary to expectation turned out to be predominantly Boer – decided not to re-enact the labour ordinance; and so the Chinese were sent home when their contracts expired. An issue which had strangely excited the British electorate was thus finally put to rest.

On questions other than these important and sensitive problems of the future of South Africa, there was not infrequent friction between Churchill and his Secretary of State. Elgin had to face many a harangue from his subordinate on one or another point of policy or some individual case which came up for confirmation. A member of the office wrote that it was not uncommon for Churchill to

> spend perhaps twenty minutes or half an hour with Lord Elgin, walking up and down the room and pouring out his views. Lord Elgin would hardly say a word, and at the end, when Churchill had finished, he would turn round and say, 'I do not agree with you, and I will not do it', and nothing then could move him.[13]

Austen Chamberlain, who as a Conservative frontbencher was no friend of Churchill's, was amused by a story that Churchill on one occasion wrote a long memorandum for Elgin, finishing with the words 'These are my views'. Elgin simply added the words

'But not mine'.[14] The issues between the two men were perhaps less of general political attitude than of personal situation and experience. Churchill knew that he had to answer for the government to the Liberal backbenchers, who were sensitive on matters of principle and on the whole hostile to the colonial governors, whom they were inclined to regard as reactionary mandarins. Elgin, as a former viceroy, looked at matters more from the point of view of the man on the spot who has to take the responsibility of governing a distant territory.

A good example of the sort of clash that could develop is provided by the case of a railway clerk in Ceylon, named Serasinghe, who had been dismissed from his employment on suspicion of having brought false charges against a stationmaster. Churchill thought it very wrong that the governor of the colony, Sir Henry Blake, had ordered the dismissal of a man who had not been found guilty of any charge; but he could not persuade Lord Elgin to agree with him. Churchill maintained that if any MP got hold of the story and raised the matter in the House it would be he, and not Elgin, who would have to bear the brunt of the criticism:

If Mr S. chooses to write to any Member of Parliament – Liberal or Tory – & point out that he has been dismissed by a Departmental Inquiry for frauds on which he was acquitted in the High Court, the brickbats will be about *my* ears; & let me say most solemnly that the Liberal party cares vy much for the rights of individuals to just & lawful treatment, & vy little for the petty pride of a Colonial Governor.[15]

Lord Elgin remained obdurate in the face of this protest, and Churchill wrote him further letters complaining that he was being 'overruled' without adequate reason. Elgin replied very moderately, repeating to him a request that he had made previously that their differences should not be allowed to 'appear on the minutes circulated in the Office', and saying, so far as the substance of the case went,

My view may be coloured by the fact that I also had been a 'man on the spot' – but I cannot see why conviction by a Court should be a *sine qua non* for this class of servant.... I do not think it is fair, in this case, to allege the 'petty pride' of a Colonial Governor. No doubt petty pride exists among them as amongst other men and even in the House of Commons.[16]

This is only one instance of a good many cases where the Secretary of State, although anxious to preserve good relations with his Parliamentary Under-Secretary, insisted on making up his own mind and refused to be bullied into decisions which his experience and character told him were incorrect. But the relationship of the two men never broke down: Elgin was patient, and Churchill was never deliberately disloyal. The ordinary courtesies between the two men were maintained throughout, and it seems that it was with real warmth that Churchill wrote to Elgin at the end of the first year of their association:

> No one could ever have had a more trustful & indulgent chief than I have been most lucky to find on first joining a Government; & I have learned a very great deal in the conduct of official business from your instruction and example which I should all my life have remained completely ignorant of, if I had gone elsewhere.[17]

But it was not only Elgin who felt some strain in working with Churchill. He soon became distinctly unpopular with the permanent officials who had to serve under him. They disliked his habit of rephrasing the replies to parliamentary questions which they had carefully drafted for him; and they found him distinctly overbearing for so young a man. Not that the fault was necessarily on Churchill's side. It would have been a sign of weakness, of laziness or of political insensitivity if so skilful a journalist had been prepared to allow civil servants to determine the style of his public utterances. On this count at least it is possible to exonerate the young and ambitious Under-Secretary for the Colonies in Campbell-Bannerman's government.

The Colonial Office in this period was still responsible for relations with the self-governing as well as with the dependent territories of the Empire. In April and May 1907 a Colonial Conference was held in London at which the prime ministers of the self-governing territories were present. In order to satisfy their feelings of self-respect Elgin announced to the conference that he was proposing to establish a separate department for them within the Colonial Office, to deal with their relations with Britain. The conference itself was thereafter renamed the Imperial Conference and the department within the Colonial Office became known as the Dominions Office.

Churchill was not formally a member of the conference, but

he attended its sessions and perhaps at his own request was invited to deliver an address on the political aspects of Imperial
Preference. He wished to expound to the prime ministers, who
were mostly in favour of Tariff Reform, the nature of the opposition that he felt would persist in Britain even if a British government eventually agreed to join in an Imperial system of fiscal
protection. The higher prices which were bound to result from
the preferences would, thought Churchill, 'accumulate a deep
feeling of sullen hatred of the Colonies and of Colonial affairs
among [the] poorer people in this country'.[18] The argument
seemed rather overstrained, and it provoked Alfred Deakin, the
Australian Prime Minister, into replying rather tartly that the
speech suggested 'the indulgence of a riotous imagination'.[19]
The members of the conference had to agree to differ on the question of Imperial Preference – as indeed they had done at their
previous meeting in 1902, which was before Joseph Chamberlain
had announced his conversion to the idea.

After the conference was over, the immediate major problems
of colonial policy appeared to be out of the way. Churchill began
planning a trip to East Africa, so that he could see for himself
something of the large territories acquired there by the Crown
in the preceding three decades, and form an impression on the
spot of what should be done for their development. Elgin encouraged him to make the trip, hoping perhaps that life would
be quieter in his absence; but it was agreed, in order to forestall
hostile criticism, that Churchill, who wished to do some big-game
hunting as well, should pay his own travel expenses. Churchill
accordingly arranged to write a series of articles about the trip
for the *Strand Magazine*, and reckoned that this would pay the
expenses of his party of four – for he was to be accompanied not
only by Eddie Marsh and a manservant, but also by his uncle by
marriage, Lieutenant-Colonel Gordon Wilson.

It soon proved impossible for Churchill to regard his trip as
in any sense 'private'. At every port of call, beginning with
Malta and Cyprus, he was at once deeply involved in official
business, and soon began to prepare and transmit to Whitehall
long papers about measures which he thought desirable for the
welfare of the colonies concerned. Elgin was alarmed to find that
the 'purely sporting and private expedition' had turned rapidly
into an 'official progress', and he was distressed by the flood of
memoranda, most of which he regarded as 'hopelessly ... un-

practicable'.[20] Churchill reached Mombasa on October 28th 1907 and spent several days discussing local problems, receiving deputations and preparing for his trip into the interior. He attended a dinner in his honour at the Mombasa Club, which began with 'Hors d'Oeuvres Inexactitudes Terminologiques' and ended with 'Joynson-Hicks sur croûte-toast' and 'Glace Blenheim'.[21] From there he proceeded by rail to Nairobi, pausing on the way to hunt and kill a rhinoceros – an exciting and distinctly dangerous experience. At Nairobi he was again beset by lobbyists and petitioners: as he observed, 'Every white man in Nairobi is a politician; and most of them are leaders of parties.'[22]

From Nairobi after three days Churchill and his party went on by the Uganda railway towards Lake Victoria Nyanza and the Uganda Protectorate. Churchill engaged in some pig-sticking on the way to the lake, crossed the lake by steamer, and then entered Uganda, where he encountered the King or Kabaka, a boy of about eleven years who was being educated so far as possible in the English fashion. The Kabaka and his chiefs, according to Hesketh Bell, the Governor of Uganda, behaved with suitable dignity; but Churchill 'was a perfect nuisance, dodging about with his camera all the time, taking photographs'.[23] In view of the fact that his visitor also kept the Governor awake at night by dictating material for his *Strand Magazine* articles to Eddie Marsh from the bathroom, it was remarkable that Bell on the whole enjoyed having Churchill with him: 'He is a difficult fellow to handle, but I can't help liking him.... He sees things *en grand* and appreciates adequately the great possibilities of industrial development that are latent in this remarkable country.'[24]

After this came the most difficult part of the trip – a journey by safari through the jungle to reconnoitre the line of a proposed railway extension to connect Lakes Victoria and Albert. Even with about four hundred native porters the party could only cover twelve to fourteen miles a day; and Churchill must have been uncomfortable much of the time, for he was wearing a topi and 'persisted in muffling himself up like Father Christmas', partly because he had a very sensitive skin, partly because he shared the prevalent belief that the direct rays of the tropical sun were highly dangerous for the white man.[25] To some extent he reduced his exertions by riding a bicycle when the going permitted it, while his companions and the long line of porters went on foot. Each night the party was able to settle down in a *banda* or temporary rest-house which would be specially erected by the local tribesmen; and Churchill regaled his companions with such a flow of talk that even Marsh, who was used to him, was amazed – 'nothing ever pumps him dry'.[26] Eventually the party reached the headwaters of the Nile, and boarded a steamer which had been sent to take them down to Khartoum. It was here that, much to Churchill's distress, his manservant died as a result of food-poisoning. Churchill himself was back in England by mid-January 1908.

The articles which Churchill had written for the Strand Magazine were later published, with a little extra material, as a book entitled My African Journey. The book gives some idea of Churchill's hopes for the development of East Africa. He seemed to think that if communications were improved, in particular by completing the railway link that he had surveyed, the economy of Uganda could be transformed, as a 'practical experiment in State Socialism', by the growing of cotton for the Lancashire market.[27] This was to prove a considerable over-estimate of the immediate potentialities of the region. Elsewhere in East Africa, Churchill's views were less optimistic and more perceptive. He foresaw the danger of racial conflict, for he realised that European and Indian immigration could not go on unchecked without causing serious friction. 'The mighty continent of tropical Africa lies open ... if only we could solve the Sphinx's riddle in its newest form.'[28] As usual, Churchill's journalistic skill made a success of the book and it was well received by the press and public.

While he had been devoting so much energy to the problems of the Empire, Churchill had naturally been unable to pay any close attention to home affairs. But he had not abandoned the positive attitude to social reform which he had developed as a Tory Democrat and as a backbench MP. In the early months of 1906 he wrote a review of Upton Sinclair's novel The Jungle, which was a searing account of the conditions of labour in the Chicago meatpacking industry. In the course of this piece, which was published in T. P. O'Connor's weekly, P.T.O., Churchill declared:

It forces people who never think about the foundations of society to pause and wonder.... The justification of that vast and intricate fabric of Factory Law, of Health Acts, of Workmen's Compensation, upon which Parliament is swiftly and laboriously building year by year and month by month, is made plain.[29]

In October of the same year, in a speech at Glasgow, he articulated a programme of social reform which, although necessarily still vague, provided an outline of suitable legislative action:

> I am of the opinion that the State should increasingly assume the position of the reserve employer of labour. I am very sorry we have not got the railways of this country in our hands. We may do something better with the canals, and we are all agreed, every one in this hall who belongs to the Progressive Party, that the State must increasingly and earnestly concern itself with the care of the sick and the aged, and, above all, of the children. I look forward to the universal establishment of minimum standards of life and labour, and their progressive elevation as the increasing energies of production may permit.[30]

This statement showed the impact of the ideas of the most advanced social thinkers of the time, and particularly of Sidney and Beatrice Webb, the Fabian Socialists, who believed in the idea of the 'national minimum' – eventually to be incorporated in the Labour Party programme after the First World War – and who were trying to persuade the Royal Commission on the Poor Law, which had been set up in 1905, to recommend a complete 'break-up' of the workhouses, and separate arrangements for the state maintenance of the old, children and the infirm. Churchill was not directly in touch with the Webbs as yet, but he could get an idea of the sort of legislation which they supported from their books, tracts and articles – including Sidney Webb's recent piece in the *National Review* outlining a legislative programme for the new Liberal government.[31]

It has been suggested that the interest of the younger Liberals in a policy of social reform was dictated by their desire to win, or at least not to lose, working-class votes. This certainly may have been the motivation of some: but Churchill, at least, does not seem to have thought of social reform as being likely to benefit directly any large proportion of the electorate. In the military imagery which he adopted so readily, he saw the potential beneficiaries of reform as the 'rearguard' of the working-class army and not as its main body. This rearguard, as he said in his Glasgow speech, had to be 'extricated' from difficult ground (shades of the

Malakand Field Force!) 'in the long war which humanity wages with the elements of nature'. 'There is the place for the bravest soldiers and the most trusted generals. It is there that all the resources of military science and its heaviest artillery should be employed.'[32] But clearly, if it was no more than a 'rearguard', its electoral impact might well be very small indeed, especially at a time when large numbers of adult males were still without the franchise. Eighteen months later Churchill was to admit that social reform was liable to make the government unpopular:

> Every reform we attempt makes an enemy, those who have been affected by it, whose privileges are curtailed. They do not forget; and so the life of the Liberal Government, if it genuinely devotes itself to the pursuit of reform, always becomes more difficult in proportion as it does its duty.[33]

In the late summer of 1907, just before he went off on his trip to Africa, Churchill had dinner with Charles Masterman, one of the young Liberal social reformers who had been elected to Parliament in 1906, and who was also a leader-writer for the *Daily News*. Churchill helped him by composing the conclusion for a leader that he was preparing, which was about the prospects before the Liberal Party.[34] The article spoke of the issues that the party had to face, including 'the degeneration of civilised poverty, the harsh excesses of accumulated capital' and 'the awful gaping sorrows of the left-out millions', and asked rhetorically, 'Who among its leaders is ready with the answer to a single one of those conundrums?'[35] The immediate answer, doubtless, was expected to be – none; but Churchill was proposing to fit himself for leadership on this question as on others. A friend who called on him as he was packing for his journey noticed that he was putting in a number of books on Socialism. 'They are going to be my reading on the voyage,' said Churchill. 'I'm going to see what the Socialist case really is.'[36]

As we have seen, Churchill found plenty to do on his trip without investigating the problems of British social reform. But there seems to be no doubt that he did manage to do some reading and thinking on the subject. An officer on the safari with him later recorded that Churchill had given his fellow-travellers both the Liberal and the Conservative views of Socialism, and that 'a timorous request for his own private conception brought forth the most interesting, if possible, dissertation of the lot'.[37]

A rather humdrum letter of political news from J. A. Spender, the editor of the *Westminster Gazette*, provoked him to some significant reflections upon future policy:

> Minimum standards of wages and comfort, insurance in some effective form or other against sickness, unemployment, old age – these are the questions, and the only questions, by which parties are going to live in the future.

As for popular feeling, he saw 'the democracy' as 'patient beyond conception' – an echo of Lord Randolph Churchill's remark about the Irish poor, that they were 'patient beyond belief' – but he thought that there was a general hostility to 'the money power', and that 'this theoretical repulsion will ultimately extend to any party associated in maintaining the *status quo*'. This was as far as he went in arguing that social reform would in the end prove to be a popular policy.[38]

On his way back to England, Churchill resolved to discuss these problems in a speech he was to give at Birmingham late in January 1908. He therefore wrote to Arthur Wilson Fox, the head of the General, Labour and Statistical Department at the Board of Trade, to ask him about the idea of using German experience of state labour exchanges, sickness insurance and so on, which he thought compared favourably with the British 'voluntary private machinery in the shape of friendly & benefit societies, trade unions & the like'. It seems very likely that he obtained the idea of a comparison with Germany from William Beveridge, a young social worker and journalist, who in the previous September had written four articles in the *Morning Post* describing the German system.[39] It was the lack of complete coverage, Churchill thought, which was the weakness of the existing arrangements in Britain:

> The meshes of our safety net are only adapted to subscribers, & all those who are not found on any of those innumerable lists go smashing down on the pavement. It is this very class, the residue, the rearguard, call it what you will, for whom no provision exists in our English machinery. who have neither the character nor the resources to make provision for themselves, who require the aid of the state.

Churchill asked Wilson Fox to advise him on how it might be possible to introduce into Britain something of the German system, so as to 'underpin the whole existing social security apparatus with a foundation of comparatively low-grade state safeguards'. He wanted to know in time for his Birmingham speech, as 'these ideas of minimum standards of life & wages, of security against going to the Devil through accident, sickness or weakness of character, & of competition upwards but not downwards, will be my general theme'.[40]

We do not know how Wilson Fox replied, but probably he was rather discouraging – perhaps because he thought that Churchill would be treading too far on the political preserves of his own master, Lloyd George, who at this time was the President of the Board of Trade. This we may infer from the fact that Churchill decided to confine his remarks at Birmingham to a call for a broadening of educational opportunities:

Is it not a terrible thing that the whole of our educational system, upon which so many millions are lavished, stops short at the age of fourteen, and that boys and girls, just at the age when they ought to receive training and discipline to make them good craftsmen and careful housekeepers, are allowed to slip away from all guidance and control and fritter away priceless years on odd jobs and idleness ... ? Where is there the general and compulsory system of technical and secondary education which alone can sift the clever from the skilled and the skilled from the simply industrious? Where are those broad ladders which ought to stretch from the exit of the board school to the entrance of the university and learned professions?[41]

Thus while Churchill was still at the Colonial Office he was already revolving the problems of social reform, and testing the path ahead, on which he was to travel in the company of Lloyd George. The opportunity for him to take responsibilities on the domestic side was just about to unfold. Campbell-Bannerman, the Prime Minister, had a stroke on February 12th 1908 and although he did not finally resign the premiership until April it became clear in March that he was unlikely to recover. Asquith, who was obviously his successor, began in March to plan his Cabinet, and tentatively offered Churchill the choice of the Admiralty or the Local Government Board. Churchill had no great difficulty about his decision.[42] In spite of the attraction of the Admiralty – one of the senior posts in the Cabinet – he felt embarrassment about replacing Lord Tweedmouth, the present incumbent, who was the husband of his Aunt Fanny (née Spencer-Churchill).

Furthermore, he knew nothing about the navy, and would have preferred, if he were to have a post dealing with external affairs, to take over from Lord Elgin as Colonial Secretary.

Churchill therefore chose the Local Government Board: but as it was a post considerably junior to the Admiralty, albeit in the Cabinet, he felt free to make certain conditions about it. He thought that it should be placed on a par with the Secretaryships of State, and that its powers should be extended to cover a wide area of social reform. At the time, it seemed to be entirely taken up with the routine matters of the administration of the Poor Law and with questions of Rating. Churchill did not want to spend his time tinkering with the Poor Law – as he told Marsh, 'I refuse to be shut up in a soup-kitchen with Mrs Sidney Webb'[43] – but he was by no means unwilling to devote his energies to tackling social problems at their root.

He expounded to Asquith the directions in which he thought policy should be directed: they were much the same as those that he had indicated in his Glasgow speech of eighteen months earlier.

> Dimly across gulfs of ignorance I see the outline of a policy which I call the Minimum Standard.... Youth must be educated, disciplined & trained from 14 to 18. The exploitation of Boy Labour must be absolutely stopped. The Army must be made to afford a life-long career of State Employment to at any rate a large proportion of its soldiers on leaving the colonies. Labour must be de-casualised by a system of Labour Exchanges. The resultant residuum must be treated exactly as if they were hospital patients. The hours of labour must be regulated in different trades subject to seasonal or cyclical fluctuations.

And then came an almost Keynesian proposal, which nevertheless was implicit in the widespread demand that the government should act to prevent unemployment at times of depression:

> Measures must be found by which the State can within certain limits and for short periods augment the demand of the ordinary market for unskilled labour so as to counterbalance the oscillations of world trade.

He then reverted to the points he had already made to Wilson Fox:

> Underneath, though not in substitution for, the immense disjointed fabric of social safeguards & insurances which has grown up by itself

in England, there must be spread out – at a lower level – a sort of Germanised network of State intervention & regulation.[44]

Asquith may have paid little attention to this remarkable outline of the prospects for reform – he was later to describe Churchill's personal letters to himself as 'begotten by froth out of foam'[45] – but he certainly noticed with some surprise that Churchill was lukewarm about going to the Admiralty, and was at least intrigued by the idea of working on the domestic side of government. It turned out, however, that John Burns – the only trade unionist in the Cabinet – was unwilling to leave the Local Government Board where he had been since 1905. Asquith, therefore, offered Churchill the post of President of the Board of Trade, which was being vacated by Lloyd George on his appointment to succeed Asquith himself at the Exchequer. The new Prime Minister also promised Churchill that he would raise the status of the Board of Trade to that of a Secretaryship of State. It was obvious that many of the reforms in which Churchill was interested could be undertaken by the Board of Trade, which had major responsibilities in the sphere of labour as well as of commerce. So in April 1908, at the age of thirty-three, Churchill joined the Cabinet – the youngest Cabinet Minister since Hartington (later the Duke of Devonshire) joined Lord Russell's government in 1866.

6. *President of the Board of Trade*

BEFORE he could settle down as President of the Board of Trade, Churchill had to vacate his parliamentary seat and fight a by-election – indeed as it turned out, two by-elections. The need for certain ministers on appointment to vacate their seats in the Commons was a tiresome legacy of the Regency Act of 1707, which was designed to limit the powers of the Crown to give places to Members of Parliament. Churchill found ranged against him at Manchester North-West not only his Conservative opponent of the 1906 election, William Joynson-Hicks, but also a Socialist of uncompromising views, Dan Irving of the Social-Democratic Federation, a small body which had no links with the Labour Party. Fortunately, the Socialist challenge was not very significant with such a candidate in such a constituency; and H. G. Wells, the distinguished Socialist novelist, went out of his way to publish a long statement urging electors to support Churchill rather than Irving, because he showed 'the spirit of our movement' and moreover was more likely to be able to defeat Joynson-Hicks.[1] But Churchill could not feel confident of success in the contest, for the great tide of enthusiasm for Liberalism and for Free Trade had ebbed somewhat since 1906. The trade cycle had turned downwards, and the resulting depression revived the Tariff Reform agitation – though what success it would have in Lancashire remained to be seen. Of more obvious local significance was the government's Education Bill, which offended both Anglicans and Catholics, for it proposed to cut down public support for denominational schools.

Churchill went down to Manchester in mid-April and at once launched into the vigorous campaign of oratory which his constituents had learnt to expect of him. In his election address he stressed the importance for Manchester of the work he had done at the Colonial Office in the development of African railways, which might lead to a supply of cotton sufficient to break the virtual monopoly of the American South.[2] In the course of his speeches he outlined the policy which he proposed to follow at the Board of Trade: to try to eliminate casual labour, to upgrade the unskilled and to prevent the exploitation of school-leavers in dead-end jobs; to establish state industries, to encourage afforestation and to nationalise the canals.[3] In the hope of winning the votes of the 900 or so Irish electors in the constituency, he persuaded Asquith to allow him to say that the Liberal Party would place the issue of Irish Home Rule before the electorate at the next general election.

Churchill's opponents were not to be outdone on this occasion: and soon all sorts of speakers on behalf of special causes – Socialists, suffragettes, Tariff Reformers, opponents of the government's Licensing Bill and its Education Bill – invaded the constituency. Masterman's description was not far from the truth: 'Manchester ... was in a pandemonium. A kind of intoxication of oratory fell upon its enormous packed population. Wherever a man was holding forth on any conceivable subject there was an assured and sympathetic audience.'[4] And the campaign became bitter as well as animated. Churchill was angered by a letter in the *Manchester Courier*, a Conservative paper, which alleged that he had broken his parole when he was a prisoner in South Africa. He brought a libel action against the editor of the *Courier*, which was settled in his favour long after the election.[5] But it was the Irish vote which proved to be his Achilles' heel on polling day. The greater part of the Irishmen who had voted for him in 1906 followed the advice of the Catholic Bishop of Salford and voted Conservative on the education question. The figures were:

W. Joynson-Hicks (Conservative)	5417	Elected
W. S. Churchill (Liberal)	4988	
D. Irving (Socialist)	276	

There was a swing to the Conservatives of about 8%, which was enough to determine the election in their favour, but, as Churchill later pointed out, nothing like enough to suggest that the former Conservative predominance throughout the city had been re-asserted.[6] Two years later, at the general election of January 1910, Churchill had the satisfaction of seeing Manchester North-West won back by the Liberals – partly at least because the Irish electors returned in most cases to their usual allegiance.

But Churchill was now without a seat in Parliament, and he had to obtain one as soon as possible. His personal popularity stood him in good stead, for many Liberal Associations were only too anxious to have him as their candidate. The Dundee Association, which had a by-election pending, was the most alert; and within a few minutes of hearing the declaration of the poll at Manchester Churchill received a telegram from Dundee offering him the vacancy. Dundee was a two-member constituency which had returned one Liberal and one Labour member at the 1906 election, and the former had just become a peer. The electors were mostly of the working class, engaged in jute weaving, ship-building and other industrial occupations. Here as elsewhere in eastern Scotland, Liberalism was strong and not likely (so it seemed) to be permanently eclipsed by Labour. So Churchill accepted the invitation, and another hurried election campaign followed, interrupted for him by overnight journeys to London to deal with urgent business at the Board of Trade.

Churchill had to face three other candidates – Sir George Baxter, a prominent local industrialist, who was the Unionist standard-bearer; G. H. Stuart, a Labour candidate; and E. Scrymgeour, a Prohibitionist, who as Churchill put it 'pleaded for the Kingdom of God upon earth with special reference to the evils of alcohol'.[7] Churchill had to rally the Liberals as quickly as possible and acquire a degree of local popularity, and this he soon did – in spite of frequent interruptions of his speeches by a suffragette sounding a hand-bell. He dealt courteously with her and also replied skilfully to 'hecklers' – that is, persons who in the Scottish custom asked impromptu questions at the close of the meeting. At this time it was customary in England for questioners to submit their points on paper to the chairman of the meeting, who would pass them to the speaker to answer, if he saw fit, after his address.

Churchill also delivered several set-pieces of oratory to large audiences. One of them, an elaborate comparison of Liberalism and Socialism, aroused enormous enthusiasm. He had started with some touches of humour:

> Translated into concrete terms, Socialist society is a set of disagreeable individuals who obtained a majority for their caucus at some recent elections, and whose officials would now look upon humanity through innumerable grills and pigeon holes and over innumerable counters, and say to them 'Tickets please'.[8]

But soon he launched into a great series of pointed epigrams:

> Socialism seeks to pull down wealth; Liberalism seeks to raise up poverty. Socialism would destroy private interests; Liberalism would preserve private interests in the only way in which they can be safely and justly preserved, namely, by reconciling them with public right. Socialism would kill enterprise; Liberalism would rescue enterprise from the trammels of privilege and preference.

And so he went on, each of his definitions being punctuated by a cheer from his audience; and finally, according to the newspaper account:

> When Mr Churchill wound up with some fine phrases about the Liberal faith not being worn out and about the capacity of Liberal philosophy to respond to the needs of the future, those who were sitting joined those who were standing in a frenzied demonstration of approval.[9]

Heartened by this oratory, the Dundee Liberals, who had been rather demoralised in 1906 by having to share the representation with the Labour Party, rallied to Churchill in strength. The Irish vote, which was numerous here, was safe for the Liberals at this election, for the education controversy at Westminster related only to England. When the polling took place five days later, Churchill was safely returned:

W. S. Churchill (Liberal)	7079	Elected
Sir G. Baxter (Unionist)	4370	
G. H. Stuart (Labour)	4014	
E. Scrymgeour (Prohibitionist)	655	

After a month of almost constant electioneering, the new President of the Board of Trade could turn his mind to the problems of his department. But there were also other, more private concerns, for which he now had more time.

After his defeat at Manchester, Churchill wrote a letter to a Miss Clementine Hozier, which ended:

> How I should have liked you to have been there. You would have enjoyed it I think. We had a jolly party and it was a whirling week. Life for all its incompleteness is rather fun sometimes.
> Write to me again – I am a solitary creature in the midst of crowds. Be kind to me.[10]

Clementine was the daughter of Sir Henry Hozier, a former soldier and, like Churchill, a military writer and war correspondent. He had died in 1907, leaving a widow, Lady Blanche Hozier, who was the daughter of the fifth Earl of Airlie, and three children, of whom Clementine was the oldest. For a long time before his death, however, Lady Blanche had been separated from her husband and, having only a small income, had been forced to bring up the family very quietly. It was due to Lady St Helier who was her great-aunt, that Clementine had a chance of entering London society. Churchill met her briefly in 1904 but did not renew the acquaintance until March 1908, when Clementine was twenty-three. She was generally regarded as a very attractive girl, and Violet Asquith, the new Prime Minister's daughter, wrote that she had 'a face of classical perfection' and a 'finished, flawless beauty'.[11] A newspaper description ran: 'She has fine eyes, a lovely complexion, and quantities of dark hair, parted in the middle of her forehead and softly arranged on either side.'[12] The family had spent a good deal of time in France and she spoke French fluently.

Churchill's interest in Clementine did not lead to a very rapid courtship as Clementine almost immediately went abroad for several weeks with her mother. But by August Churchill's mind was turning towards marriage, especially as the wedding of his brother Jack to Lady Gwendoline Bertie took place that month. For her own part, Clementine's interest in Churchill must have been stirred by a new instance of his astonishing bravado which had occurred only a few days earlier. He had been staying with his cousin, Captain Freddie Guest, at a rented mansion in Rutland, when fire broke out in the middle of the night. The local fire brigades were slow to arrive, and the water supply was quite inadequate; so the house could not be saved. But Churchill did his best, first of all donning a fireman's helmet and directing the efforts of all others; and then playing his part in salvaging the contents of the house. According to a newspaper account, 'He had a most miraculous escape. He had just come out carrying a couple of busts in his arms when the roof fell in. Had he been a second later he must have been buried in the debris.'[13] He was delighted to receive a telegram from Clementine after this episode, and replied 'The fire was great fun & we all enjoyed it thoroughly'.[14]

He had already invited Clementine to spend two or three days at Salisbury Hall, his mother's home. But he now changed the plan and persuaded her to join him at Blenheim instead. Clementine was somewhat taken aback by this, thinking it would be a formal occasion for which she did not have the right clothes. But the Duke, who was separated from his wife, had no large party of guests; and Clementine found that Churchill simply wanted to talk to her. One afternoon he took her for a walk in the park and proposed to her in an ornamental temple not far from the palace, in which they were sheltering from a sudden shower.[15]

Clementine was not the first girl in whom Winston had been seriously interested. There had been Pamela Plowden and, more recently, a girl called Muriel Wilson, of the Hull ship-owning family. He had also vainly sought the affections of the well-known actress Ethel Barrymore.[16] But these had all been unsuccessful approaches. He was somewhat gauche in his attitude to women: he did not care to engage in light conversation, and disliked dancing. The result was that he was thought to be self-centred and even boorish. Clementine took this view of him to begin with; but by the time they met at Blenheim she had changed her mind, and accepted him at once. Lady Hozier approved the match. She wrote of Winston to a sister-in-law: 'His mother and he are devoted to one another, and I think a good son makes a good husband. Clementine is wise. She will follow him and, I hope, say little.'[17] The engagement was announced on August 15th and the wedding took place on September 12th at St Margaret's, Westminster.

The wedding of a Cabinet minister is usually a rare event, but in fact Churchill was the third of the existing body of ministers to be married within twelve months – the others were Reginald

McKenna, the First Lord of the Admiralty, and Lord Loreburn, the Lord Chancellor. Churchill's best man was Lord Hugh Cecil, his former ally as a Conservative Free Trader, and the ceremony was conducted by the Bishop of St Asaph, Dr A. G. Edwards, one of the few Anglican bishops not strongly hostile to the Liberal Party, and by the Dean of Manchester, who was his old Harrow headmaster, J. E. C. Welldon. Although London was 'out of season' in mid-September, fourteen hundred people attended the wedding by invitation, and the streets outside were thronged with sightseers. Before the ceremony began Churchill, who 'wore the orthodox wedding attire – the high hat and frock coat',[18] appeared a little nervous, particularly as his bride was late. He probably knew that she had had her doubts after their blithe betrothal at Blenheim.[19] But he recovered rapidly when she arrived, 'her tall, slim figure being beautifully clad in soft white satin trimmed with Venetian lace lent by Mrs Cornwallis West'.[20] The service, however, was not very satisfactory for the congregation. The Bishop of St Asaph was inaudible beyond the front three pews, and 'a general gloom seemed to settle on everybody'. Eventually the stillness was broken by 'a loud and clear "I, Winston Leonard, take thee, Clementine Ogilvy" and the tension was over'.[21] After signing the register – to which Lloyd George attached his own signature as a witness – the newly wed couple walked together down the aisle 'as if marrying were an every day event for both of them'.[22]

The reception was held at Lady St Helier's home in Portland Place, where the wedding gifts were on display, including a gold-capped Malacca cane with the Marlborough insignia on it, a present from King Edward to the bridegroom. The couple went by train to Blenheim to begin their honeymoon; at Woodstock they were greeted less formally than Lord Randolph and Jennie thirty-four years earlier, but there was cheering in the streets and a 'merry peal' on the church bells – the bells that had saluted Churchill's birth. On the following evening they walked through the park to Bladon to visit the grave of Lord Randolph Churchill, and Clementine stayed for the service in the village church.[23] After a few days they left for Baveno, near Stresa, a resort on Lake Maggiore which Winston had visited and approved a year earlier. After that they had a few days in Venice before returning to London.

It was, by all accounts, a happy honeymoon: but Clementine

obtained a clearer idea of what was in store for her, no doubt, when she found that her husband even talked politics in the vestry (to Lloyd George); that he insisted on working on the final text of *My African Journey* when they were at Blenheim, and wrote long letters about current affairs to his colleagues from Baveno; and that even in Venice he insisted on travelling by motorboat, rather than by gondola, on the grounds that it was quicker and more hygienic.[24]

The Board of Trade was well suited in the early years of the century to act as the instrument of a minister interested in social reform. There was as yet no separate Ministry of Labour, and the functions that were later assumed by that body (now the Department of Employment and Productivity) were, in so far as they existed at all, mostly vested in the Board of Trade. The Home Office was in charge of the task of supervising the Factory Acts, and the Local Government Board, as we have seen, attended to the operations of the Poor Law. But questions of employment and unemployment, and of strikes and lockouts, fell within the ambit of the President of the Board of Trade. His powers in these fields were as yet very limited; but the knowledge at his disposal, which might form the basis of legislation to extend his powers, was improving rapidly. The Board's service of labour statistics, started in 1886, and developed steadily under the control of a civil servant who was also a keen social reformer, Hubert Llewellyn Smith, supplied far better information about the conditions of life and labour than was directly available to the Home Office or the Local Government Board. So Churchill found himself far better placed to carry out some of the reforms that he had mentioned to Asquith than he would have been if he had gone to the Local Government Board. Almost his first act on taking office was to send to the Labour Department for literature about labour exchanges; and Beveridge – who happened to be visiting the department that day – helped the clerks to supply to the minister a body of 'articles, pamphlets and Poor Law Commission memoranda' all written by himself.[25] About ten weeks later Churchill arranged for Beveridge to join the Board of Trade to help him with the preparation of legislation on this subject.

Meanwhile, there was of course much other business for Churchill to deal with. He did not approve of the way in which his predecessor, Lloyd George, had delegated a large proportion of the work to the Parliamentary Under-Secretary, Hudson Kearley. Kearley was a capable businessman eighteen years older than Churchill, and he naturally did not like having to hand over his responsibilities to (as he later put it) 'a comparative youth' – especially if he were to continue to serve as the Board's Parliamentary Secretary.[26] The transition was made somewhat less painful for him by the fact that he had several weeks to tidy up his office, while Churchill was fighting his two by-elections. During this period, he piloted through its second reading a bill to take the London docks into public ownership; and early in 1909 a solution to the problem of his relationship with Churchill was found by his appointment as chairman of the new Port of London Authority, which the Act had established. In this post and with the title of Lord Devonport, he proved a considerable success.

The early months of Churchill's tenure of the Board of Trade were marked by a cyclical depression: unemployment increased markedly, and in many trades employers sought to cut wages. Churchill found his time taken up with attempts to terminate strikes or lockouts which had started when workmen refused to accept wage reductions. The government had no effective strategy to fit this sort of situation: the Conciliation Act of 1896 gave the Board of Trade powers to intervene as a conciliator, but not to act as a determining agent. As one senior official noticed, the new President of the Board of Trade was not personally suited to act as a conciliator: he talked too much.[27] But he was able to take one small step forward by establishing, in September 1908, a panel of approved conciliators in three categories – employers, trade-union leaders, and neutral – which might be drawn upon for the composition of small committees of three or five conciliators for particular disputes. But George Askwith, whom Churchill appointed in 1909 to succeed Wilson Fox as Comptroller-General of the General, Labour and Statistical Departments of the Board of Trade, later argued that 'no great use' was made of the panel system, because the members of the panel were busy men who could not readily take up the task of conciliation at short notice.[28] Later, during the First World War, a system of permanent industrial courts, whose members were immediately available, proved more effective.

The first major piece of legislation for which Churchill was responsible in his new office was not about labour exchanges but about 'sweated labour' – a matter sufficiently akin to factory legislation to be regarded, up to this time, as falling within the concern of the Home Secretary. 'Sweated labour' was labour which, owing to special circumstances in certain industries or trades, was employed under exceptionally unfavourable conditions and poor wages. The 'sweated' workers had no trade unions, and it was widely felt that the State should step in to secure a more reasonable life for them. In Australia and New Zealand, legislation to fix minimum wages in certain industries had been carried in the 1890s; and after a vigorous agitation in Britain, led by the veteran Radical MP Sir Charles Dilke, a Select Committee of the House of Commons had been appointed in 1907. It reported in 1908 in favour of 'tentative and experimental' legislation to establish wages councils in a few appropriate trades – the system to be extended if it proved successful.[29] The Cabinet decided that the Board of Trade, which had so many detailed figures of wages and hours in different trades at its disposal, should take over the responsibility for action from the Home Office; and in March 1909 Churchill introduced a bill on the subject into the House of Commons. It met practically no opposition and soon found its way to the Statute Book. The Trade Boards Act, as it was called, applied to only four trades in the first instance – tailoring, chain-making, paper box-making and machine-made lace and net finishing. But the Board of Trade was empowered to make Orders to extend the number of trades covered by the Act, and this was done in later years. Trade boards – or, as they are now called, wages councils – have become an important part of the machinery of British industrial relations.

Meanwhile Churchill and his officials, including Beveridge, had been working on the question of labour exchanges. In the autumn of 1908 he was endeavouring to overcome the suspicions of many trade-union leaders that the exchanges would work against their interests; for this purpose he invited some of them to breakfast at the Board of Trade, to meet officials of his department. He also invited Sidney and Beatrice Webb, who he knew would help him to convert the unconverted.[30] Churchill accepted Beveridge's view that labour exchanges were an essential preliminary to any further action to deal with unemployment. As he told the Cabinet in December 1908, they would act as 'the Intelligence Department' of labour: they would provide detailed information about the character and extent of unemployment, and this would enable him to prepare and introduce a system of compulsory unemployment insurance.[31]

The idea of introducing compulsory insurance, both for unemployment and for sickness, originated with Lloyd George, who followed in Beveridge's path and visited Germany himself in August 1908 to examine the system in operation there. On his return he spent what Churchill later described as 'two days very memorable to me' explaining to his junior colleague, who was visiting him in North Wales, both the outlines of the 1909 Budget and the principles of compulsory insurance.[32] These ideas ran into conflict with the proposals of the Webbs, who favoured voluntary insurance through the unions, coupled with – for those not insured – a new system of state maintenance and compulsory training. The Webbs' proposals were explained in detail in the Minority Report of the Poor Law Commission, which was published early in 1909. But Churchill and the officials concerned, of whom Llewellyn Smith was the most important, refused to be diverted from their compulsory scheme. The chief disagreement which arose between Churchill and Llewellyn Smith was over the question of payments to those who were unemployed through their own fault – for instance, because of laziness or drunkenness. Churchill took the more liberal view: he felt that the State could not refuse benefits to individuals who had paid their contributions: 'I do not like mixing up moralities and mathematics.... Our concern is with the evil, not with the causes, with the fact of unemployment, not with the character of the unemployed.'[33] Churchill's view did not prevail, and the scheme, while remaining compulsory, was not saved from being somewhat inquisitorial.

But there could be no question of getting unemployment insurance on to the Statute Book in 1909. Unemployment and health insurance had to be taken together, for, as Churchill wrote to Asquith, 'it would never do to exact contributions from masters & men in successive layers'.[34] And Lloyd George was far too busy with his 1909 Budget to be able to make much headway with the preparation of the health scheme, for which he was assuming responsibility. It was agreed, therefore, that Churchill should put through the Labour Exchanges Bill in the 1909 session, but that he should do no more than announce the government's intention to proceed with proposals for unemployment insurance in a later session. The proposals were not for a fully comprehensive scheme covering all occupations, but in the first instance only for workers in industries where, although the average wage was relatively high, the work was subject to serious cyclical unemployment. These industries were building, construction of works and vehicles, shipbuilding, mechanical engineering, iron-founding, and saw-milling. Since labour exchanges had been unanimously recommended by the Poor Law Commission, there was relatively little opposition to Churchill's bill, which became law in September 1909. Beveridge was appointed as Director of Labour Exchanges, and the first exchange opened its doors in February 1910.

Important though this legislation was – and in 1909 Churchill also initiated bills on shipping, electric lighting, and insurance companies – it would not be true to say that it formed a major concern of either Cabinet or country. The questions that excited most political interest in 1909 were, first, the divisions within the government on the programme of naval building, and secondly Lloyd George's Budget, with its proposals for controversial new taxation. As a Cabinet minister, Churchill was much concerned in the discussions on defence expenditure; and as a leading spokesman of the government he found himself also in the forefront of the battle for the Budget, although he was not sufficiently well versed in the financial details to be able to contribute much to its progress in committee in the House.

Within a few weeks of entering the Cabinet Churchill was repeating his father's strategy of attacking the army estimates. In view of his campaign against the War Office in the previous parliament it was not surprising that he should take an interest in military finance. But it was remarkable that only two months after joining a Cabinet whose average age was twenty years older than his he should produce a detailed scheme of reform for a department other than his own and all but persuade the Cabinet to accept it. His idea was that the army could not fight a Continental war, and should not try to prepare for one. For purely colonial purposes, on the other hand, its size was somewhat too large, and savings of over a million pounds a year could, he thought, easily be realised.[35] Haldane, though reduced to an 'agitated and nervous state' by all this,[36] managed with difficulty to hold his own.

But worse was to follow when in alliance with Lloyd George Churchill attacked the naval estimates, and ridiculed the argument that the country was in danger of being plunged into war with Germany. This was at a time when even the Admiralty had only just begun to worry about the threat posed by German battleship building. In 1906 Britain had introduced a new type of battleship, the 'dreadnought', which with its relatively high speed and all-round armament of heavy guns was thought to have made all earlier types of battleship obsolete. The German navy recognised the advantages of the new type and at once began a major building programme of ships of similar design. In December 1908, therefore, Reginald McKenna, the First Lord of the Admiralty, recommended to the Cabinet that Britain should lay down six battleships in 1909–10, instead of four as had previously been planned. This led to immediate opposition from Lloyd George and Churchill, who at once began to worry about the prospects of their social reform proposals, and who were in any case doubtful about the need for what they regarded as 'panic' measures.

Churchill was particularly active in challenging McKenna's detailed statistics about the relative strengths of the British and German navies at future dates. He argued that the older battleships were by no means completely obsolete, and that in any case, some account should be taken of the relative manpower and cost of the two navies. 'The brutal fact remains', he emphasised, 'that with an expenditure of 35 millions a year we are, *it is alleged*, being outbuilt in the essential units of naval strength by a Power whose expenditure is scarcely more than 20 millions.'[37] Asquith and the majority of the Cabinet supported McKenna, and Asquith complained to his wife that Lloyd George and Churchill 'go about darkly hinting at resignation (which is stuff) ... but there are moments when I am disposed summarily to cashier them both'.[38] Finally in February 1909 the Cabinet made a compromise of sorts: four dreadnoughts were to be laid down, but powers were to be taken to lay down an extra four if the need were demonstrated by new evidence. In the upshot, information about dreadnought building by Austria and Italy – both at this time regarded as in some sense associated with Germany – induced the Cabinet to authorise the building of the extra four battleships. Thus the conflict between the supporters of four and the supporters of six had led to eventual agreement on eight.[39]

Churchill took part in the debate not only in the Cabinet but also in public. Sir Edward Grey, the Foreign Secretary, with some difficulty persuaded him not to discuss foreign policy when he was visiting on the Continent, as his father had done;[40] but he could not prevent him from commenting on Anglo-German relations in speeches delivered inside Britain. At Swansea in August 1908 Churchill declared:

> Although there may be snapping and snarling in the newspapers and in the London press, these two great peoples have nothing to fight about, have no prize to fight for, and have no place to fight in.[41]

This strongly suggested that, so far as Britain was concerned, Germany could have a free hand in Europe – which was not at all the intention of Grey's policy. Grey was annoyed and took him to task for 'the fallacies of some of his statements' and even for 'the undesirability of his embarking on questions of foreign policy' in constituency speeches.[42] Churchill wrote an open letter to the chairman of the Dundee Liberal Association criticising the 'dreadnought fear-all school' and declaring that 'in spite of the evil forces we see at work in every land, the foundations of European peace are laid more broadly and more deeply every year'.[43] As *The Times* pointed out in a leader, Churchill's letter was obviously a blow in a battle within the Liberal government – an attempt to convince his own colleagues rather than his political opponents. But the logic of events and the feeling among the majority of the Cabinet bore him down in the end.

It fell to Lloyd George, as Chancellor of the Exchequer, to make the financial provisions for increasing naval expenditure as well as for social reform – in particular, old age pensions, which were not contributory. His proposals at once aroused alarm in influential quarters, for they involved new taxes on wealth and especially on landed wealth. But they served to revitalise the Liberal Party, and – in spite of some criticism, mostly among its own wealthy supporters – to re-unite the main sections of the party which had been falling apart over rearmament. Income tax was to go up from one shilling to fourteen pence in the pound; death duties were to be doubled; and a supertax was to be introduced, though at a relatively modest level – its highest rate was to be no more than one shilling and ninepence in the pound. But the most controversial proposals of all were for new taxes on undeveloped land and on increases in land values. Finally, a Development Fund was to be set up, which was to be used to finance projects such as afforestation or road-building which could be used to provide extra employment at times of cyclical depression. This was in line with Churchill's proposal to Asquith in March 1908, which he had put in even clearer form in a speech at Dundee in October of the same year, when he spoke of the need for 'averaging machinery' to regulate the labour market 'just as easily as you can pull out the stops or work the pedals of an organ'.[44]

The hostility of the Conservatives to Lloyd George's Budget was powerfully expressed. The Opposition in the House of Commons fought the details clause by clause in the course of the late spring and summer, and Churchill had to give what help he could in the debates. In May he delivered a vigorous speech in favour of special taxes on land as distinct from other forms of property. His argument probably had a special appeal to Liberals in Scotland, where the big landlords were particularly influential. He stressed that land ownership implied a position of monopoly, for which there was no direct equivalent in most other forms of wealth: furthermore, land could increase in value without any action on the part of the owner, and there was no parallel to this in the growth in value of a railway or other industrial property.[45]

But the Conservatives remained incensed with the terms of the Budget, and in November they ensured its defeat by using their majority in the House of Lords. This was an action which the Liberals looked upon as unconstitutional – with some justice, for the long-established understanding between the two Houses of Parliament was that the Lords did not reject money bills. The Conservative decision to use the Lords' veto was also a tactical error: it was to the Liberals' advantage to fight a general election on the constitutional issue, and to rally its supporters with the slogan of 'the Peers against the People'. Churchill himself became the chairman of a campaign body called the Budget League, and developed a powerful line of ridicule at the expense of the peers who opposed the measure. This was in spite of the fact that he had been somewhat lukewarm about the actual details of the Chancellor's proposals. Lloyd George even went so far as to suggest privately that 'Winston is opposed to pretty nearly every item in the Budget except the "Brat", and that was because he was expecting soon to be a father himself'.[46]

The 'Brat' was Lloyd George's term for a children's allowance against income tax, which he was proposing to introduce. Churchill had passed on to the Chancellor various complaints from his rich relatives, such as the Duke of Marlborough and Ivor Guest, about particular provisions of the Budget that hit them severely. But this does not mean that he could not see the argument that the money had to be raised somehow, and that direct taxation of the wealthy was a more equitable way of raising it than the imposition of fiscal burdens on the poor.

After the Lords' rejection of the Budget it became of critical importance to rally the country for the election battle. Lancashire and Cheshire, which had swung so heavily to the Liberals in 1906, had to be saved from swinging back to the Conservatives. In the view of the Liberal organisers, this was a task for none other than Churchill. He was soon committed to an intensive series of speeches in Manchester and other north-western towns. As usual, he prepared his speeches with care, securing detailed figures from the Commercial Department at the Board of Trade about Lancashire trade and the way in which it compared with that of foreign countries.[47] He opened his campaign on December 2nd at Preston, where the Liberal candidate was his father's old colleague in the Fourth Party, Sir John Gorst. 'Protection', said Churchill, 'is not merely injurious but fatal to Lancashire. There is no tariff they may devise which will not strike a heavy blow at cotton.'[48]

This theme, and that of the absurdity of the Lords trying to hold up the tide of progress, entered into all his speeches in his ten-day campaign. At Liverpool he spoke of 'The Lords of the backwoods, all meditating on their great estates great questions of government, all studying *Ruff's Guide [to the Turf]* and other blue-books, all revolving the problems of Empire and Epsom'.[49] The Conservative leaders were worried by Churchill's campaign, and Henry Chaplin, one of their frontbenchers, wrote to Sandars, Balfour's secretary, 'Winston is a captivating speaker to working men – and if they are wavering it is of real importance that his mischief should be counteracted.'[50] Churchill found himself being followed around the Lancashire towns by Lord Curzon, a former MP for Southport, recently Viceroy of India, and now a Conservative leader. But Curzon could not equal Churchill as a popular orator. He told the people of Oldham that 'all civilisation has been the work of aristocracies' – a quotation from Renan. Churchill made fun of this as soon as he heard it: 'There is not a duke, a marquis, an earl or a viscount in Oldham who will not feel that a compliment has been paid to him. But it would be much more true to say that the upkeep of aristocracies has been the hard work of all civilisation.'[51]

The Prime Minister was deeply impressed at the reports which he heard of Churchill's campaign, and not least by the fact that he could make so many speeches without constantly repeating himself. He even compared it with Gladstone's Midlothian campaign; and he asked Churchill to speak in his own constituency of East Fife, which was not far distant from Dundee.[52] Meanwhile Churchill was hastily knitting his speeches together into a continuous argument for publication as an election handbook. This was rushed into print and published in time for the closing stages of the campaign in January 1910, under the title of *The People's Rights*.

By this time Churchill was at Dundee, where he had to defend the seat he had won less than two years earlier. There was little doubt about his prospects of success. The Labour Party, realising that the seat held by Alexander Wilkie, a leading member of their parliamentary group, would be put at risk if they put up two candidates rather than one, decided to allow Churchill a clear run against the Unionist opposition. In effect, therefore, Churchill and Wilkie stood in alliance as the two 'Progressive' candidates against two Unionists and the inevitable Prohibitionist, Scrymgeour. The Unionists could make little headway in Scotland at this election, for Scottish opinion was never friendly to the House of Lords. Churchill felt able to take some risks with his own contest: he not only spoke at East Fife and elsewhere during the final stages of the election, but he also went off to play golf at Carnoustie almost every morning – including polling day.[53] Still, he had had a gruelling time during the Lancashire campaign, and needed some relaxation; and there was no doubt about the power and effectiveness of the speeches that he delivered in the afternoons and evenings.

The outcome of the election was that many Liberal seats were lost, but the government was able to survive with the support of the Irish and the Labour Parties. In Britain as a whole there was a swing, by constituency median, of 4.5% from Liberal to Conservative or Unionist; but in Scotland the swing was virtually non-existent (0.2%).[54] At Dundee the result, although not quite as good as the Scottish average, was nevertheless highly satisfactory – a swing of no more than 1.2%. The figures were:

W. S. Churchill (Liberal)	10,747	Elected
A. Wilkie (Labour)	10,365	Elected
J. S. Lloyd (Unionist)	4552	
J. Glass (Unionist)	4339	
E. Scrymgeour (Prohibitionist)	1512	

A large proportion of Churchill's supporters also voted for Wilkie, and *vice versa*, but Churchill had 997 'plumpers' (that is, voters who used only one of their two votes) and Wilkie had only 419.[55] Churchill could also feel some personal satisfaction about the results from Lancashire and Cheshire, where there had been no reversion to the Unionist strength of 1895 and 1900. His own campaign in the region may have played some part in damping down the swing against the Liberals, which was only 2.9%, or 1.6% less than the national average.[56] These local variations were of vital importance in determining the outcome of the election.

After the election was over, Asquith made some changes in his Cabinet. He recognised Churchill's claims for promotion, which were strengthened by the important part he had played in the campaign. At first he tried to persuade him to become Chief Secretary for Ireland: but Churchill did not fancy the post, and asked instead for the Admiralty or the Home Secretaryship.[57] The latter office was now vacant, because Herbert Gladstone was leaving it to become Governor-General of South Africa. So Asquith agreed to make Churchill Home Secretary, and he appointed Sydney Buxton, a man twenty years Churchill's senior, to succeed him at the Board of Trade.

At the Home Office Churchill was less directly concerned with social reform, but he continued to take a close interest in unemployment insurance, and took charge of the measure when in 1911 it was presented to the Commons as Part II of the National Insurance Bill (Part I being Lloyd George's sickness insurance scheme). Since Lloyd George's plans were more controversial, and since as Chancellor of the Exchequer he was the senior minister, it is natural that he has always been regarded as principally responsible for what was the single most important measure of social reform of this period – and perhaps the single most important measure of social reform ever to be carried by Parliament. It is true, as we have seen, that the conception of compulsory insurance was Lloyd George's. But taking the period 1908 to 1911 as a whole, it is clear that Churchill deserves great credit for pressing the whole movement forward and ensuring that it did not collapse after the enactment of old age pensions.

Churchill's commitment to social reform began before he became a Cabinet minister, and he was able to urge on his colleagues a programme of increasing coherence in the course of 1907 and 1908. According to Herbert Gladstone, Churchill was the only member of the Cabinet to support him in pressing for the Miners (Eight Hours) Bill, which was passed in the course of 1908.[58] Five months before Lloyd George visited Germany to look at methods of insurance, Churchill was urging Asquith to favour 'a sort of Germanised network of State intervention and regulation'. And at the end of that year he was again writing to the Prime Minister to urge on him a programme even more ambitious than that which he had agreed with Lloyd George:

> The Minister who will apply to this country the successful experiences of Germany may or may not be supported at the polls, but he will at least have left a memorial which time will not deface of his administration.... Here are the steps as I see them.
>
>   I. Labour Exchanges & Unemployed Insurance:
> II. National Infirmity Insurance etc:
> III. Special Expansive State Industries – Afforestation – Roads:
> IV. Modernised Poor Law i.e. classification:
>   V. Railway Amalgamation with State Control and guarantee:
> VI. Education compulsory till 17.[59]

Of the last three reforms, which Asquith's government did not pass into legislation, the 'classification' or break-up of the Poor Law had to wait for the later 1920s; railway amalgamation was largely achieved after the First World War; but compulsory education to the age of seventeen is still awaited – though few would deny that it will some day be attained.

Of the three items of reform that were carried out in the period we have surveyed, Churchill was directly responsible for the first (labour exchanges and national unemployed insurance) and he also deserves credit for pressing the third (expansive State industries) upon the Chancellor of the Exchequer. He had an increasingly clear idea of how the government could guide the economy by increasing State expenditure as private investment declined, but he had doubts about whether the Treasury was the right organ of government to take the decisions. He told Lloyd George that there should be a permanent Cabinet committee, comparable to the Committee of Imperial Defence, which should conduct the 'war against poverty'; it should use as its instruments not only the Development Fund, but also the programmes of the 'great contracting departments' such as the Admiralty. The statistics of the Board of Trade would be the equivalent of military intelligence on the basis of which the spending strategy would be planned.[60]

Virtually nothing was accomplished to fulfil this vision of a state-regulated economy. The Development Fund remained under the control of the Treasury which, as Churchill foresaw, was not capable of supervising expenditure. But in any case the years 1910 to 1914 were years of good trade and relatively full employment; and in the post-war years Britain faced problems which the Fund and even the proposed Cabinet committee could not have dealt with. As for Churchill himself, in other posts and with new duties he could no longer grapple with social evils as he had done in 1908 and 1909 – at any rate until he became Chancellor of the Exchequer in 1924.

Churchill had talked to Charles Masterman about his hopes of success as a social reformer even before he had joined the Cabinet – in the brief interlude between his return from East Africa and his appointment to the Board of Trade. Masterman, a little unfairly, was inclined to regard him as a Johnny-come-lately in this field: 'Winston ... is full of the poor who he has just discovered. He thinks he is called by Providence to do something for them. "Why have I always been kept safe within a hair's breadth of death," he asked, "except to do something like this? I'm not going to live long", was also his refrain.'[61] It is certainly true, as has recently been pointed out, that the Board of Trade with its equipment of labour statistics, was in a strong position to undertake social reform.[62] Yet if Churchill had died at the age when his father died, and still more if he had finally left office at the age when his father left office, he would more easily be recognised for what he was in those years – a man equalled only by Lloyd George among his contemporaries in his capacity to diagnose and effectively to treat the worst social evils of his day.

7. *Home Secretary*

THE Home Secretary is the senior Secretary of State, and it was a remarkable achievement for Churchill to have attained this office at the early age of thirty-five, much more so indeed than to have entered the Cabinet two years earlier. The Home Office had then as now a strange jumble of responsibilities, for it has usually been entrusted with the supervision of new ventures of state activity in domestic affairs – ventures which sometimes have led to the formation of new ministries. So it was that Churchill found himself answering questions in the Commons quite as varied as those which he had had to answer when he was at the Colonial Office: for instance, on the conditions for the immigration of Italian ice-cream men; on the censorship of stage plays; on proposals for the protection of game birds; and on the regulations as to the mudguards of motorcars. Every night while Parliament was sitting he had to prepare a longhand report on Commons proceedings for submission to the King – a task once performed by the Prime Minister, but now delegated to the Home Secretary.

But apart from all the miscellaneous lesser functions of his office there were some major areas of responsibility on which, as a social reformer, he was likely to concentrate his attention. There was the supervision of the police and the control of the prison system; and there was the administration of the Factory Acts, which was only to be transferred from the Home Office to the Ministry of Labour (now the Department of Employment) in the course of the Second World War. Herbert Gladstone, Churchill's predecessor at the Home Office, summed up his own view of the main features of his task:

Answerable for the safety, health and working conditions of seven million people in factories and workshops, for a million in the mines, for the personal rights of all persons under police jurisdiction, for public decency, for the dark corners of police cells and prisons, the Home Secretary, of all administrators, stands closest to the lives of the multitude.[1]

Gladstone himself, with the aid of an able Parliamentary Under-Secretary, Herbert Samuel, had established an enviable record as a reforming minister. He had secured the passing of a more generous Workmen's Compensation Act, and as a result of three important measures, the Probation of Offenders Act, the Prevention of Crime Act and the Children's Act, he had gone a long way towards sorting out those offences and offenders for which there were more appropriate methods of treatment or punishment than a term in prison. He had also begun to explore the possibility of restricting the practice of placing prisoners in solitary confinement. But he apparently did not regard this matter as requiring urgent action, for on leaving office he told Churchill: 'As regards Prisons it won't be a bad thing to give a harassed department some rest.'[2]

But it was precisely in this sphere that Churchill wished to take action. His experiences as a prisoner of war in Boer hands, although much less harsh than they might have been, had nevertheless given him a considerable sympathy with all those who lost their freedom; and he knew from his father's old friend Wilfrid Scawen Blunt, who had served a term as a political offender in Ireland in the 1880s, that solitary confinement was a very cruel form of detention. When he took office, therefore, he at once telegraphed Blunt for a memorandum on his experiences and proposals for reform. Blunt wrote that he had emerged from Kilmainham Gaol with 'a spirit of revolt against all society', and declared, 'The silence of the place was a systematised oppression worse to my mind than the noisy discomfort of the rude prisons of the East, where men, perhaps in chains, are at least permitted to sit together in the sun and talk, if it is only of their sufferings.'[3] Blunt thought that political prisoners should be treated more or less like prisoners of war – 'honourably, that is, and as opponents whom the law has captured'.[4] This point was particularly relevant at a time when the agitation for women's suffrage had reached the point where offences against the law were frequently being committed, and the number of political offenders, and especially of women political offenders, was rapidly on the increase.

In the immediate aftermath of the general election of January 1910, the Cabinet was doubtful of continued support for its policies from its main parliamentary ally, the Irish Nationalists. Churchill thought the government might fall within a few weeks, but he was determined to take action on prison reform before he left office. He was aided by the fact that informed public opinion was moving strongly in favour of a more generous treatment of offenders. One factor of importance in this movement was the impact of John Galsworthy's current play *Justice*, which drew particular attention to the evils of solitary confinement. Galsworthy thought that the officials of the Home Office were opposed to reform; but as Churchill pointed out to him in private correspondence, this was not true of the key official, Sir Evelyn Ruggles-Brise, the head of the Prison Commission, who already had much liberal reform to his credit.[5] There were, to be sure, administrative difficulties in giving special preference to all political offenders, as they might in some cases have committed far more serious offences than many non-political offenders. With the aid of Ruggles-Brise and other officials, Churchill got round the difficulty by defining a special class of prisoners who were of good previous record and who had not been convicted of offences involving 'dishonesty, cruelty, indecency, or serious violence'. In March 1910 – within a month of taking office – he was able to inform the Commons that he was introducing a more favourable code of treatment for this class of offenders.[6]

In the ensuing months Churchill continued to work hurriedly on other aspects of prison reform. With the assistance of Ruggles-Brise he drew up stricter regulations for the imposition of solitary confinement: except for recidivists, it would now be limited to a period of one month. Galsworthy, who was invited to the Home Office to hear the news from Churchill himself in advance of the public announcement, reckoned that the reform put an end to '4,800 months of suffering a year'.[7] Churchill also introduced arrangements for occasional lectures and concerts for prisoners to attend; and he improved the system of prisoners' aid on discharge, by co-ordinating more effectively the work of the various interested charities. In this work he was powerfully motivated by a sense of the failure of the existing prison system to act as an effective deterrent to crime: for he had discovered that no less than three out of every four long-term prisoners discharged during the years

1903–5 were already back in penal servitude. He explained all the measures to the Commons in July.[8]

At the end of the summer Churchill outlined to Asquith, in one of his powerful memoranda on policy, what he thought should be the direction of future reform: to enforce more fully the terms of the Probation of Offenders Act passed by his predecessor in 1907, especially so as to allow for 'disciplinary probation' rather than imprisonment for the young; to work towards the abolition of imprisonment for debt; to allow people more time in which to pay fines; and to 'classify' the institutions, which would mean having a different type of prison for every main category of offence.[9] These were far-sighted objects, but they needed legislation, and in the press of other parliamentary business in 1910–11 Churchill was not able to secure time for them. He was convinced, however, of their importance, for as he had already put it in his report to the Commons: 'The mood and temper of the public in regard to the treatment of crime and criminals is one of the most unfailing tests of the civilisation of any country.'[10]

For a conscientious Home Secretary it was necessary to spend as much time on the examination of individual cases as in the preparation of measures of reform. The most serious individual cases were, of course, those of prisoners convicted on capital charges, for if the Home Secretary did not advise the King to exercise his prerogative of mercy the prisoners were hanged. About once a fortnight, on average, Churchill had to decide whether a hanging should be carried out or not. He was not in principle opposed to hanging, as a small minority of his contemporaries were, for he thought that for many people it was a less severe punishment than life imprisonment. But he felt a keen concern for justice for the individual, and so he read the cases conscientiously and recorded his conclusions in weighty memoranda. It was the burden of this responsibility that made him declare in a later reminiscence that 'Of all the offices I have held this was the one that I liked the least'.[11]

Churchill also looked into the record of long prison sentences, and discovered some instances of exceptionally heavy punishment for apparently trivial offences. One of these cases was given unusual publicity because it was mentioned in a polemical speech by Lloyd George, who had accompanied Churchill on a visit to Dartmoor.[12] They had encountered an old man called David

Davies, a 'model' prisoner who acted as the shepherd of the flock of sheep at the prison, and who was serving three years penal servitude and ten years preventive detention for stealing two shillings from a church poorbox. The case was not quite as simple as it seemed, for Davies had a long record of burglary and stealing, for which he had already served a total of thirty-eight years in prison.[13] Churchill had him released on probation, and he was placed with a farmer near Wrexham. Much to the delight of Opposition MPs and the Conservative press, he was soon arrested again for house-breaking, found guilty and sent to prison for a further term.[14] Churchill was at least justified in regarding with apprehension the use of long terms of 'preventive detention' for supposed habitual criminals. As he pointed out, 'There is a grave danger of using smooth words for ugly things. Preventive detention is penal servitude in all its aspects.'[15]

The principal piece of legislation for which Churchill was responsible during his tenure of the Home Office was the Mines Act of 1911, which dealt with safety regulations for the pits. Public feeling on this question had been aroused by two major disasters in 1910. At Whitehaven in Cumberland 132 miners had died, and at the Preston Pit at Bolton in Lancashire there was a death-roll of no less than 320 – the heaviest toll of any British colliery accident up to that date. A Royal Commission on the Mines set up in 1906 had published a report in 1909, making various recommendations for improvements in the existing safety code; but the bill which was prepared in the Home Office in 1910 contained various additional proposals as a result of the lessons learned from the accidents of that year. The technical details of the legislation were prepared by Richard Redmayne, the Chief Inspector of Mines. He found Churchill a 'driver'; but he developed a respect for his chief which overbore any hard feelings which this caused: 'He drove himself also (he later wrote), being a demon for work though amazingly quick in the uptake.'[16] These were important qualities for a minister who had to ensure that a long and complicated bill was properly prepared for presentation and adequately defended at all its stages of progress through the parliamentary machine. It should be added that it was Masterman who did the great bulk of the work of defending the bill in committee; it was finally passed only after Churchill had left the Home Office.

The Act laid down detailed regulations for the training and appointment of managers, foremen and examiners in the mines. It set up a strict code of regulation on such matters as the ventilation of pits, the use of electricity and explosives, and the systems of haulage and machinery. To ensure observance of the code, the inspectorate was substantially increased. The provision of ambulance and rescue services was made compulsory. The minimum age of employment for underground work was raised from thirteen to fourteen. Finally, there was a great extension of the powers of the Home Secretary to issue regulations to improve the safety code. All this set a pattern of state intervention which was to be repeated in much of twentieth-century legislation, though it was not invariably to gain as much support from Churchill as it did on this occasion. Ramsay MacDonald, in his official parliamentary report to the Labour Party Conference of 1912, described the Act as 'a boon to our mining community', and Charles Fenwick, the doyen of the miner MPs, said that it would be 'hailed with great satisfaction throughout the country'.[17]

Churchill also introduced a Shops Bill designed to limit the hours of shop assistants. A similar bill had been introduced by Gladstone in 1909, but it had lapsed owing to the dissolution of Parliament. It was Churchill's object to limit weekly hours to sixty, exclusive of mealtimes; and also to ensure that the mealtimes were adequate and that assistants were given a regular weekly half-holiday. But the bill encountered determined opposition from small shopkeepers and special interests, and in the end the hours section of the bill had to be dropped. The assistants at least got their half-holiday; but Churchill regarded the final measure as 'a mere piece of salvage from a wreck'.[18] He might have been able to put up a better fight on behalf of the limitation of hours if he had not been transferred from the Home Office to the Admiralty before the struggle was over. But in any case the Shop Assistants' Union was a weak body compared with other unions, and its political influence did not match that of the numerous small employers in the trade. In the spring of 1914 Churchill declared, 'No bill occupied so much of my time and carried so small a proportion of its original intention to the Statute Book.'[19] As if in compensation for this failure, Churchill accepted the office of President of the Early Closing Association, a shop assistants' pressure group, which he continued to hold until the Second World War.

If the crippling of the Shops Act was a disappointment for him, at any rate he was able to play a major role in the enactment of a measure to which he attached great importance, although it was no longer a departmental responsibility of his. This was the National Insurance Act, Part II of which (Unemployment Insurance) he had helped to prepare at the Board of Trade and undertook to pilot on its course through the Commons. 'There is no proposal in the field of politics', he said, 'that I care about more than this great insurance scheme.'[20] When he gave his Dundee constituents an account of his parliamentary work in the session of 1910–11, he laid his greatest stress upon his role in passing this measure. It provided the liveliest metaphor of his peroration: he pictured unemployment and sickness as two 'unwelcome visitors' in the workman's home, and declared that henceforward 'the workman will be armed to meet his unwelcome visitors by the broad shield of national organisation and the sharp, bright sword of modern science'.[21]

At the end of 1910 and in the course of 1911 Churchill was faced with grave and unprecedented problems of public order, mostly associated with the 'labour unrest' of the period, which developed as a result of relatively full employment and the consequent opportunity provided for trade-union militancy and growth. There was a small minority of trade-union activists who embraced the revolutionary philosophy of 'syndicalism', and this created much concern, as people did not realise how relatively small and uninfluential this minority was.[22]

In November 1910 a serious miners' strike in South Wales led to rioting in the Rhondda Valley which the Glamorgan County police force was quite insufficient to control. Troops were ordered to the area on the initiative of the general commanding the Southern Command, without authorisation from the Home Office. Churchill decided that the best policy was to hold them in reserve and to support the Chief Constable of Glamorgan with reinforcements from the Metropolitan Police.[23] This was a wise decision: for although rioting took place and many of the shops in the town of Tonypandy were wrecked order was restored by the police wielding their rolled-up mackintoshes, and there was no loss of life. According to General Macready, who was in charge of the troops: 'It was entirely due to Mr Churchill's forethought in sending in strong forces of Metropolitan Police directly he was made aware of the state of affairs in the Valley that bloodshed was avoided.'[24]

Yet the cry of 'Tonypandy' was often raised against Churchill in later years, apparently because of the move of troops early in the course of the dispute, and because Churchill had firmly told the Miners' Federation, when they protested about it, that he would not hesitate 'after what has occurred to authorise the employment of the military'.[25]

It was not easy for Churchill to avoid the charge that he enjoyed ordering troops about the country. His own remarkable military career was against him, and new incidents occurred to add to the popular impression of his character. Only a few weeks after 'Tonypandy', in early January 1911, he obtained much publicity, not a little of it of a hostile nature, as a result of his presence at the 'Battle of Sidney Street'. The remnants of a gang of East European revolutionaries, who possessed powerful automatic pistols and had already killed three policemen when interrupted during a raid on a jeweller's shop in Houndsditch, were discovered in a house in Sidney Street, off the Mile End Road in East London. They opened fire again on the police, who surrounded the house and asked for the assistance of soldiers armed with rifles. Churchill at once agreed to the request and then proceeded to the scene, where he was photographed peering at the besieged house from a convenient vantage point. To his surprise, he found that artillery had also arrived; this additional service was not in fact required. Churchill wisely did not attempt to assume control or interfere with the dispositions made by the senior police officer in charge; but he was able to support the officer concerned in his decision to allow the house, which had caught fire with the gunmen inside it, to burn down without intervention from the fire brigade. The decision may have saved the lives of some of the firemen, who were eager to attack the flames. The bodies of two men were found in the embers of the house.

The whole affair was naturally given great prominence in the press, and the photograph of the Home Secretary on the scene of battle was widely published. Arthur Balfour, the Leader of the Opposition, took the opportunity to criticise Churchill's conduct: 'I understand what the photographer was doing, but what was the right honourable gentleman doing?'[26] For although his presence may have given moral encouragement to the police it might have been unfortunate if fresh decisions had become necessary at the Home Office in Whitehall. Charles Masterman, who was Churchill's Parliamentary Under-Secretary, was on holiday at the time; according to his widow, when he returned and demanded 'What the hell have you been doing now, Winston?', 'The reply, in Winston's characteristic lisp, was unanswerable. "Now, Charlie. Don't be croth. It was such fun." '[27]

It was bound to be difficult for the Home Secretary, as the custodian of law and order, to avoid unpopularity with the leaders of labour; but after the Sidney Street affair it was doubly difficult for Churchill to do so. Seven months later, in August 1911, a major crisis arose when a series of transport strikes, beginning with the docks, culminated in a national railway strike. The first local situation that threatened to get out of hand was a general transport strike on Merseyside. Rioting in Liverpool, particularly in the Irish quarter, could not be controlled by the police, and at the request of the Head Constable and the Lord Mayor troops were brought in. Two men were shot and killed when rioters made an attack on police vans conveying prisoners to Walton Gaol. The Lord Mayor of Liverpool thought that a revolution was beginning, and the King, who took the same view, urged Churchill to allow even stronger measures by the troops; but the Home Secretary replied reassuringly, saying, 'The forces at the disposal of the Government are ample to secure the ascendancy of the Law. The difficulty is not to maintain order but to maintain order without loss of life.'[28]

But at this point the situation became much more serious as a result of a decision by the railway unions to start a national strike. Such a strike had never taken place before and it threatened to immobilise the troops and to prevent the movement of food and other essential supplies. The government happened to be facing an acute international crisis at the same time, owing to the attempt by Germany to assert her position in Morocco by despatching a warship to Agadir. It was against this background that Churchill encouraged local authorities to recruit special constables – 'in the first instance ... public-spirited citizens whose position enables them to serve without pay'.[29] This showed an excessive regard for public economy, for it was bound to appear to the railwaymen to be an attempt to establish a middle-class militia hostile to their cause. Two days later, by which time the strike had halted most trains in the North of England, Churchill informed the local authorities that the army would now use its own discretion as to the movement of troops, and 'the Army regulation which requires a requisition for troops from a civil authority is suspended'.[30] He nevertheless issued an optimistic statement to the effect that '... considerably more than two-thirds of the railwaymen are remaining at their posts. Numerous applications are being received by the railway companies for employment'.[31] A report which he sent to the King on the same day conveyed a very different picture of the situation.[32]

Churchill's public statements on this critical day – August 19th – exposed him to severe censure from the Labour leadership. Ramsay MacDonald, the chairman of the Parliamentary Labour Party, spoke of them in the Commons a few days later as 'prejudiced, ill-informed, and inaccurate'.[33] This view was privately shared by Masterman, who told his wife that while he thought Churchill's course of action was 'in the main' right, 'he did it in an amazingly wrong way, issuing wild bulletins and longing for "blood"'.[34] Masterman's role in the crisis, it should be noted, was not really a Home Office role at all. He was not principally concerned, as Churchill was, with the preservation of law and order, but was helping two other Cabinet ministers, first John Burns and then Lloyd George, to find terms on which the successive transport strikes might be settled.

It was fortunate that these efforts at conciliation quickly proved successful. In the case of the railway strike, the main point of contention was the employers' refusal to recognise the unions as bargaining agents, on the grounds, which they had long maintained, that the organisation of a railway required something akin to military discipline. Lloyd George was able to persuade the employers to give way on this point – partly, no doubt, through his exceptional skill as a negotiator, partly because the employers must have been impressed by the solidarity of the strikers, at least in the North, and partly because Lloyd George made a sudden appeal to them not to allow the railway system to remain crippled at a time when war with Germany might break out without warning.

Before the men had all returned to work there was a grave incident at Llanelly, where a train had been halted by the action of rioters. As it lay immobilised, a large body of men began throwing stones, and some soldiers who arrived on the scene opened fire, killing two men, one of whom was apparently merely watching the incident from his own back garden. This was a distressing conclusion to the whole series of strikes, but it was not something for which Churchill had reason to feel personally responsible. He was pleased to receive a telegram from the King saying, 'Feel convinced that prompt action taken by you prevented loss of life in different parts of the country.'[35]

Not that this testimonial would be of much assistance in his future political career. It was perhaps more significant that although he had had the support of the Prime Minister and the Cabinet his actions had by no means fully commended themselves to the Liberal Party outside Parliament. Even the *Manchester Guardian*, which for many years had been his best friend in the press, took him to task for authorising the despatch of troops to towns whose mayors had not requested their assistance. In particular, the *Guardian* was affronted by the arrival of a detachment of soldiers in the middle of Manchester, where without any specific request from the Lord Mayor they had proceeded to occupy the railway stations.[36]

During this time Churchill had continued to play his part in the Cabinet discussions of general policy. So far as domestic affairs were concerned, this meant, above all, the search for a solution to the constitutional deadlock with the House of Lords. The general election of January 1910 had, as we have seen, largely been fought by the Liberals on the slogan of 'The Peers versus the People', and it was a considerable disappointment to the rank and file of the party to discover, after the election was over, that there were still no definite plans on the part of the Cabinet for dealing with the opposition of the Lords, and that the King had given no guarantee to create enough peers to swamp the Conservative majority. The government was also now dependent, not just on its own backbenchers, but also on the Irish Nationalists and the members of the Labour Party; and the Irish Nationalists, who had never liked the whisky tax which was proposed in the 1909 Budget, threatened to vote against the Budget when it was reintroduced and so destroy the government – at any rate, if the government would not give a binding promise to remove the Lords' Veto, which they now saw as the one obstacle remaining to prevent the enactment of Irish Home Rule.

At this point Asquith, who was in uncertain mood himself, was beset by conflicting advice from members of the Cabinet. Both Grey and Churchill were in favour of reforming the House of Lords, rather than simply abolishing its veto. In mid-February Churchill produced a plan for a small second chamber elected by specially large constituencies on a democratic franchise. He proposed that peers should be eligible to sit in the Commons and that ministers should have the right to speak in either House. But Churchill's new Second Chamber was to have a suspensory veto only, and after a delay of over two years the future of a contentious bill was to be decided by a joint session of both Houses.[37] All this was very complicated and had the disadvantage that it had not been the subject of discussion at the general election.

In the end the Cabinet, after much wrangling, decided that it would go simply for the restriction of the veto and not – in the immediate future at any rate – attempt a reform of the Lords. This meant that the King would be asked to give a guarantee that if necessary he would create sufficient peers to override the Lords' existing veto. The Prime Minister seemed to obtain a new lease of life when the decision was made: his announcement of the policy to the House of Commons was a great parliamentary occasion, and there was enthusiasm in the rank and file of the Liberal Party. The Irish, too, accepted the policy and gave their support to the Budget in spite of the whisky tax. The Lords now felt obliged to accept the Budget when it came to them from the Commons for a second time.

There was something of a political lull in the late spring of 1910. King Edward VII died suddenly in May, and as the new king, his son George V, was politically inexperienced, both main parties agreed to hold a constitutional conference to see if they could arrive at a compromise solution of their difficulties without involving the powers of the Crown. Nothing came of the discussions, though they gave time for the King to accustom himself to his new responsibilities. But while they were being conducted, some remarkable secret negotiations took place on the initiative of Lloyd George to form a coalition in order to carry a whole range of reforms which were being held up by the deadlock of the parties. Among these Lloyd George mentioned National Insurance; Federal Home Rule to get round the Irish problem; some form of National Service to strengthen the armed forces; and an impartial enquiry into the desirability of further fiscal reform.[38]

Churchill was quick to see the merits of the plan – he was still more a Whig than a Liberal – and it was probably he who made the first contacts with the Conservative leadership on Lloyd George's behalf, for F. E. Smith, the brilliant young Conservative barrister, was a close friend of his. Smith and Austen Chamberlain became supporters of the proposals, and Balfour himself might have accepted them if he had received the agreement of his former Chief Whip, Lord Chilston; but the latter felt that it would result in a split of the Conservative Party, and so Balfour drew back.[39] It is interesting to notice that the supporters of coalition in 1910 were to be the main stalwarts of the post-war Lloyd George government ten years later.

After the failure of the Constitutional Conference there was nothing the government could do except hold another general election, in order to obtain a mandate for the reform of the House of Lords. Parliament was dissolved in November after a life of only ten months, and the election campaigns and polling all took place before Christmas 1910. The issues were naturally much the same as in the January election, but in the course of the campaign Balfour was persuaded to make a bid for the support of the industrial North by promising to postpone the introduction of Tariff Reform until after a special referendum on the subject. This may have been the main factor in enabling the Conservatives to win more support, and consequently a few more seats, in Lancashire and Yorkshire; elsewhere, however, they lost a few seats, partly owing to mutual withdrawals of candidatures by the Liberals and Labour. The net result of the December election was thus almost exactly the same as that of the previous January: on balance, the Conservatives lost one seat, and the Liberals lost three – the gains going to Labour and the Irish.

Churchill was again called upon to speak in various parts of the country, but the brevity of the entire campaign limited his scope. He was challenged by Bonar Law, who was one of the most prominent Opposition spokesmen, to fight again in Manchester North-West where Law himself was the Conservative candidate. Law also suggested that they should make a gentleman's agreement that the loser should stay out of the succeeding Parliament. But this was altogether too great a sacrifice to ask of Churchill, who now had, as he thought, a completely safe seat at Dundee. All the same, he missed a chance of scoring a great triumph and altering the course of history: for Manchester North-West remained in the Liberal camp and Bonar Law, although defeated there, soon secured a seat elsewhere and in 1911 succeeded Balfour in the leadership of the Conservative Party.

Balfour's acceptance of the idea of the referendum at a late stage in the campaign gave Churchill the opportunity for one of his most scathing speeches, which was delivered at Sheffield, where Tariff Reform had long been a popular cause. On November 30th Churchill had this – and much else – to say:

> What a ridiculous, pitiable spectacle is the route of a great political party! General Scuttle is in command. Frantic appeals for quarter and mercy rend the air; the white flag is hung up over the Tory Club, over many a noble residence, and many a public house. All the colours, tents, baggage, ammunition – all are scattered along the line of flight. England has never witnessed such a spectacle since the days of Naseby and Marston Moor. And at the head of the route what do we discern? In the very forefront of the retreat gleams the white bonnet of their leader.... Mr Balfour, like 'Charley's Aunt', is still running.[40]

In Dundee he took good care to stress the anti-democratic tendency of the Lords' veto and the fact that, if it represented any popular feeling, it was that of the South of England only. These were points that went down well with a Scottish audience, which was likely to regard the House of Lords as an essentially English institution. 'We ask', he said,

> that ... the Free Traders of Scotland and the Free Traders of Lancashire shall not be tabooed and put on a lower political foundation, even when they have a majority in the House of Commons, by the votes of the Jingoes and the Protectionists of Birmingham and Kent.[41]

Churchill made the most of his few days in his constituency, and Clementine helped him, even to the extent of making a short speech on the danger of an increased cost of living if Tariff Reform was introduced.[42] But it was a disadvantage that Sir George Baxter, the popular local industrialist who had stood against him in 1908, was again one of the Conservative candidates. At the other end of the political spectrum, Scrymgeour, the Prohibitionist, was picking up votes that might otherwise have gone to a Liberal candidate. The result was that while the national swing against the Liberals was only 0.4%, and that for Scotland was 1.1%, for Dundee it was 7.0%.[43] The figures were:

W. S. Churchill (Liberal)	9240	Elected
A. Wilkie (Labour)	8957	Elected
Sir George Baxter (Conservative)	5685	
J. S. Lloyd (Conservative)	4914	
E. Scrymgeour (Prohibitionist)	1825	

With this confirmation of its support in the country, the Liberal government proceeded to pass through the Commons a bill to reduce the veto of the Lords to a delaying power: any measure sent up to and rejected by the Lords in three successive sessions was nevertheless to become law, and financial measures were to go through without any delay at all. Churchill, speaking in support of the bill, declared himself 'almost aghast' at the government's moderation. He was in favour of putting as much public pressure as possible on the Lords at this juncture: as he wrote to Asquith, 'If this Bill does not make proper progress we should clink the coronets in their scabbards!' Yet at the same time he hoped for a rapid reconciliation of parties as soon as the measure was put into operation – '*une politique d'apaisement*' as he described it to the Premier, and 'a national & not a sectional policy'. Among other things, it was desirable, he thought, to make a grant of honours to the Conservative leaders, such as the Order of Merit for Joseph Chamberlain (now a retired invalid) and Privy Councillorships for Bonar Law and F. E. Smith.[44]

For a time in the spring of 1911 the political passions of the parties were relatively quiescent. The King's coronation in June had a good deal to do with this. But soon afterwards the Lords returned the Parliament Bill to the Commons in a drastically amended form, and it became necessary for Asquith to ask the King to declare his intention to create peers if necessary to override the opposition of the majority of the existing House of Lords. The King reluctantly agreed, and as soon as this became known the Conservative peers divided into two factions – the 'hedgers', who were for passing the Parliament Bill in order to forestall the new creations, and the 'ditchers', who refused to change their attitude of opposition. On August 10th the dénouement came when the few Liberal peers were joined by a sufficient number of 'hedgers' to pass the bill with a narrow majority – 131 to 114. The crisis was over, and Churchill in his daily report to the King on proceedings in the Commons ventured to offer his congratulations 'upon the conclusion of this long & anxious constitutional crisis'. He added prophetically: 'When the keen feelings of the moment have passed away, the singular moderation of the change that has been effected will be apparent and will gradually be admitted with relief by the Conservatives & with regret by many of the supporters of the Government.'[45]

If the summer of 1911 saw an end to some of the government's preoccupations, it also witnessed the intensification of others. There was not only the succession of transport strikes, culminating in the national railway stoppage; there was also a very serious international crisis, sparked off by the German despatch of a warship to Agadir, in order to assert German claims to a share in Morocco. Lloyd George and Churchill, because they had been the 'economists' in the Cabinet on the subject of military and naval expenditure, were thought to be the British ministers most anxious to avoid a clash with foreign powers. But both of them took the German move very seriously, and it was Lloyd George who on July 21st in his Mansion House speech issued a warning that Britain must not be treated 'as if she were of no account in the Cabinet of nations'.[46] The German reaction to Lloyd George's statement was strong; and Grey was afraid for a time that Germany might make a sudden attack on Britain.

Churchill realised that as Home Secretary he had major responsibilities for national security. Among them was the defence of the reserves of cordite for the big guns of the fleet, which were kept in magazines in the London area. He persuaded the War Office at short notice to post a guard of soldiers for their protection.[47] He also took a close interest in the proceedings of the Committee of Imperial Defence, the permanent Cabinet committee which dealt with war plans; he bombarded the generals with questions about the existing military situation and drew up a memorandum of his own about what he thought would happen if war broke out between Germany and Austria on the one hand and France, Britain and Russia on the other. The memorandum was in fact a remarkable forecast of what did happen in 1914, suggesting for instance that the Germans would cross the Meuse by the twentieth day but that the tide of battle would turn about the fortieth day.[48] But the crisis convinced Churchill that the Admiralty had no proper plans to deal with a war, and moreover were not prepared for any emergency, since, as he pointed out to Asquith, 'they are nearly all on leave at the present time'.[49]

Asquith was also worried about the Admiralty. Although McKenna, the First Lord, had fought vigorously and in the end successfully – against Churchill himself among others – to secure a larger dreadnought-building programme, he had not created a war staff for the navy as Haldane had done for the army. The meeting of the Committee of Imperial Defence showed that the navy had no plans to guarantee the safety of a British Expeditionary Force crossing the Channel to France, and the Admiralty strategy, such as it was, lurked in the recesses of the mind of the taciturn First Sea Lord, Admiral Sir Arthur Wilson. Asquith decided that he must replace McKenna, and while Churchill was spending a few days' holiday with him in late September 1911 at Archerfield, his temporary home on the Firth of Forth, he abruptly invited him to take McKenna's place.[50]

Churchill agreed at once, although it meant difficulty, not only with McKenna himself, but also with Haldane. The latter, having created a war staff at the War Office, had the ambition to do the same at the Admiralty; and when he visited Archerfield to press his case Asquith left him with Churchill to argue it out.[51] Churchill refused to agree that Haldane's claims were stronger than his own; and Asquith saw no reason to change his own views. Haldane had accepted a peerage only a few months earlier, and this was an argument against his transfer to the Admiralty. As Asquith wrote to Lord Crewe a few days later:

> The First Lord ought to be in the H. of Commons, and the Navy would not take very kindly in the first instance to a new organisation imported direct from the War Office. On the whole, I am satisfied Churchill is the right man, & he would like to go.[52]

The outcome was that McKenna and Churchill simply exchanged offices on October 25th. As Churchill later put it: 'Mr McKenna and I changed guard with strict punctilio.'[53] Haldane, with whom Churchill now had to collaborate closely, was soon reconciled to the situation, and wrote to his mother, 'It is delightful to work with him.'[54]

8. First Lord of the Admiralty

ALTHOUGH the Admiralty was the senior service ministry, it did not rank above the Home Office in the hierarchy of the government, and so it could not be said that Churchill was being promoted in becoming First Lord. He was, however, moving to a post where rapid reform was expected of him, and this was as usual to his taste. In short order he was as he put it 'burrowing about in an illimitable rabbit-warren'.[1] He found it necessary to work long hours, either in the Admiralty or on the Admiralty yacht, HMS *Enchantress*. Marsh, who had again followed him as Private Secretary, was placed under the same obligation: he wrote wryly to a friend after the first month:

> Winston stays until at least 8 every day.... Even Sundays are no longer my own, as I have spent 3 out of the last 4 on the *Enchantress*. We have made a new commandment. 'The seventh day is the Sabbath of the First Lord, on it thou shalt do all manner of work.'[2]

Churchill soon found that the main obstacle to the creation of a naval war staff lay in the opposition of the First Sea Lord, Admiral Sir Arthur Wilson. Wilson, who was almost twice Churchill's age, had a fine reputation as a sailor, but he seemed to the new First Lord to be 'dwelling too much in the past of naval science, not sufficiently receptive of new ideas'.[3] Certainly the paper he wrote for Churchill outlining his objection to a war staff showed little understanding of the purpose which such a

147

staff might serve.[4] To replace him, Churchill thought first of bringing back Admiral Sir John Fisher, Wilson's predecessor, a brilliant but mercurial personality who during his six-year period as First Sea Lord had been largely responsible for inaugurating the dreadnought era. Churchill had first met Fisher in 1907 and they had at once struck up a friendship which was the more remarkable because of their difference in age. But there were two grave objections to reinstating Fisher. One was that he would insist on determining policy: as he put it himself, 'I don't care about playing Second Fiddle when for so long I had the First Violin.'[5] The other objection, no less grave, was that Fisher had made a bitter enemy of another leading admiral, Lord Charles Beresford, who was now Conservative MP for Portsmouth, and their quarrel had already done serious damage to the navy, dividing its senior officers into two factions.

Churchill therefore decided not to restore Fisher to office, but merely to use him as a source of advice about naval problems and personalities. The new First Sea Lord was Admiral Sir Francis Bridgeman, but partly on Fisher's advice Churchill brought in Admiral Prince Louis of Battenberg as Second Sea Lord and Bridgeman's prospective successor. Churchill also confirmed Fisher's recommendation of Admiral Sir John Jellicoe as Second-in-Command of the Home Fleet, so that in due course he could take over the most important seagoing command. But it was entirely his own idea to appoint Rear-Admiral David Beatty, at the age of forty the youngest flag officer in the navy, as his personal Naval Secretary. All these appointments took effect within a few weeks of Churchill's arrival at the Admiralty.

In the following January Churchill formally established the Naval War Staff, under the direction of the First Sea Lord and organised in three divisions – Operations, Intelligence and Mobilisation. A staff training course was to be set up at the Naval War College, Portsmouth, and Churchill laid it down that the lessons of history, as exemplified by earlier wars in which Britain had been engaged, should form part of the instruction. The new establishment was to be paid for by suppressing the personal yachts of the commander-in-chief at the Nore, Portsmouth and Devonport, and giving these officers a financial compensation.[6] It was a misfortune that the Naval War Staff did not have more than thirty months to develop before the outbreak of the First World War. There was much prejudice against it among the senior officers, and perhaps as a result it has been suggested that 'the candidates chosen for training were sometimes below average ability'.[7] But several important strategic ideas were evolved by the War Staff and applied at the outbreak of war – notably the policy of the 'distant blockade' of Germany instead of the 'close blockade' which would undoubtedly have been far too costly to maintain.

Churchill's relations with his senior naval advisers were at first far from friendly. Previously the Sea Lords, especially the First Sea Lord, had exercised considerable discretionary powers in executive matters, for the Board of Admiralty, unlike the Board of Trade, was constitutionally a sort of Cabinet with joint authority. This was not good enough for the new First Lord, who issued peremptory instructions to the Sea Lords, and began to alter their responsibilities to fit a new pattern of authority, subordinate to himself. Feeling the need for an experienced civil servant to take charge of purchasing and management, he appointed Sir Francis Hopwood, whom he had known at the Colonial Office, to a new post as Civil Lord. Soon he was at odds with Bridgeman, who thought that his own position as First Sea Lord was being undermined: and after only a year he insisted on Bridgeman's retirement, ostensibly on grounds of poor health, and replaced him with the more amenable and distinctly abler Prince Louis. Admiral Lord Charles Beresford and the other Conservative members, who were looking for an excuse to attack Churchill, took up Bridgeman's case, and initiated a debate on the subject. Churchill was obliged to defend himself by quoting from his private correspondence with Bridgeman about the latter's health, and also from letters from Bridgeman to Prince Louis and to Beatty.

It was undoubtedly an advantage to have Prince Louis as First Sea Lord instead of Bridgeman; but Churchill's reputation among the senior officers did not improve as a result. Rear-Admiral Dudley de Chair, who succeeded Beatty as Naval Secretary at the end of 1912, was shocked by the First Lord's habit of judging the quality of flag officers and captains after a brief meeting; he found him 'impulsive, headstrong and even at times obstinate'.[8] Other senior officers were scandalised by Churchill's behaviour when on tours of inspection. Junior officers and ratings were allowed their say, even if it involved criticism of commanding officers. Sometimes the latter complained to higher authority, and on one occasion, when the matter was taken up by Admiral Sir Richard Poore, Commander-in-Chief, the Nore, Churchill proposed to relieve the

Admiral of his command and was only prevented from doing so by a threat of joint resignation by the Second, Third and Fourth Sea Lords.[9]

Among the junior ranks, however, Churchill's unorthodox methods found more favour. He secured an improvement in the rates of pay, which for the Lower Deck had been almost stationary since the middle of the nineteenth century. He also revised the code of discipline, which contained some old-fashioned absurdities shocking to a former Home Secretary of enlightened views. Among them was the punishment, for minor offences, of being 'stood in the corner' like a child while other seamen were off duty: this was now abolished. Churchill also introduced a channel of promotion, albeit a very narrow one, for exceptional seamen into the commissioned ranks. After he had been in office for a year the editor of the monthly journal the *Fleet*, which acted as the organ of Lower Deck opinion, declared that, 'No First Lord in the history of the Navy has shown himself more practically sympathetic with the conditions of the Lower Deck than Winston Churchill.'[10]

If these reforms made Churchill more popular among the junior ranks, even the senior officers came to see that he was better than McKenna in pressing their claims for more naval building. Faced with the evidence of rapid German naval expansion, the new First Lord threw off his own past as an 'economist' within the Cabinet and campaigned vigorously for higher naval estimates. In February 1912 he made a very frank observation in a speech at Glasgow, to the effect that while a navy was essential for Britain, for Germany it was 'from some points of view ... more in the nature of a luxury'.[11] These remarks were made just at a time when Haldane was visiting Germany on behalf of the Cabinet, to explore the possibility of a mutual understanding about the limitation of naval building. They did not make Haldane's mission any easier, for they were much resented in German naval circles; but Haldane was probably already doomed to failure, and there is no evidence that Churchill's words altered the course of German policy. It was Churchill's view, probably a correct one, that the only way to put a check to German naval expansion was to demonstrate that there was no chance of outbuilding the British navy. In presenting the annual estimates in March 1912 he made it clear that this was in fact his purpose; and although the Emperor of Germany described his speech as 'arrogant' it met with general approval in the British press. *The Times* thought that it was 'perhaps ... the best exposition of naval policy which has been made since Lord George Hamilton's famous statement in 1889'.[12]

The Times was then a Conservative newspaper, and it was of course the Conservative press which had most enthusiastically supported the demand for a strengthening of the navy in earlier years. But not everything that Churchill did to prepare the navy for a possible conflict with Germany commended itself to the Opposition. In the spring of 1912 he proposed a rearrangement of naval squadrons: the Mediterranean Fleet was to be cut in order to strengthen the concentration in the North Sea. This meant that in the event of war in the Mediterranean Britain might at first be unable to hold her own unless she could rely on French assistance. There was a considerable outcry against the plan on the part of Beresford and the Conservatives in Parliament and in the Press; and it became known that it met with little favour either in the War Office or in the Foreign Office. In the end, Churchill was forced to agree to a compromise whereby the fleet in the Mediterranean was maintained at a level at least equal to that of the strongest Mediterranean power, excluding France. Informal naval conversations with the French Admiralty were then initiated, in order to determine the most suitable dispositions in the event of the two powers being simultaneously involved in war with Germany. But Churchill was conscious of the opposition of the Liberal rank and file to any definite alliance with France, and he minuted that the conversations were for mutual information only and involved no commitment on Britain's part to assist France in the event of war. It was essential, he thought, to 'safeguard ... our freedom of choice if the occasion arises, and consequent power to influence French policy beforehand'.[13] This was in accordance with the general line of Grey's foreign policy.

In his insistence on maintaining a general control of the navy's preparation for war, Churchill found himself drawn more and more into the field of technical innovation. One of the most important decisions that he made during his term of office was to authorise the introduction of oil-firing for battleships. Oil was undoubtedly more efficient than coal as a fuel for warships, but the initial costs were higher, and it made the navy dependent upon a foreign source of supply. Fisher was convinced of the need for the change, and he urged Churchill forward. Churchill in turn persuaded Fisher in the summer of 1912 to act as chairman of a Royal Commission on Fuel Oil, which went into the problems of procurement and storage. There were major political difficulties in making the change, owing to the opposition of MPs representing mining constituencies. The Cabinet also had to be persuaded to agree to purchase control of the Anglo-Persian Oil Company at a cost of a little over £2,000,000. This was an investment which as it turned out was to prove extremely profitable for the British government.

In other directions, too, Churchill encouraged rapid technological development. During his tenure of office the Admiralty took the risk of introducing the fifteen-inch gun as the main armament of its newest battleships, in place of the thoroughly tested but much lighter 13.5-inch. The first battleships to be armed with this gun, the *Queen Elizabeth* class, were also strongly powered and had a high speed. They were outstandingly successful and served as the backbone of the fleet for many years. Churchill also gave as much encouragement as he could to the Royal Naval Air Service, which was experimenting with the use of aeroplanes and seaplanes and, to a limited extent, airships. The First Lord assisted the development of flying – still a highly hazardous undertaking at this time – by repeatedly going up in every type of machine, and by taking instruction as a pilot.

Technical progress was expensive and helped to increase the cost of the navy still more. In introducing the 1913 estimates Churchill felt bound to take a somewhat apologetic line, for the Liberal backbenchers were getting very restive. He described the armaments race as 'stupid' and 'wasteful' and suggested that Britain and Germany might agree to a 'naval holiday' or temporary cessation of battleship building.[14] There was no response from Germany, and in the following November Churchill gave a warning that the estimates for 1914 would be considerably larger than those for 1913. But this had not yet been agreed by the Cabinet, still less by the parliamentary party, and it soon became apparent that Churchill would not get his way without a struggle. Lloyd George, who for so long had been his closest colleague, was not prepared to have Churchill dictate the terms of his next Budget: and in an interview published in the *Daily Chronicle* on New Year's Day 1914 he recalled that Churchill's father had resigned rather than agree to what he thought was exorbitant expenditure on armaments. Churchill replied with what in effect was a public rebuke to Lloyd George by telling the press that he made it a rule 'not to give interviews to newspapers on important subjects of this character while they were under the consideration of the Cabinet'.[15]

As both Lloyd George and Churchill marshalled support for their respective points of view, it looked as if the Cabinet conflict would end in the resignation of one or the other. Lloyd George was backed by most of the younger members, who were Churchill's contemporaries and to a certain extent his rivals – Samuel, Runciman, Simon, and, ironically, the former First Lord, McKenna. But Lloyd George at least did not want to force Churchill out and even went so far as to say that it was 'worth a million' to keep him as a member of the government.[16]

In January 1914 Lloyd George and Churchill argued the matter out in what Churchill called a 'polite but deadly' negotiation: after five hours of tête-à-tête talks, concluding in a triangular meeting with the Prime Minister, a compromise was framed. Churchill obtained almost all that he had asked for in 1914–15, but had to undertake to make economies in the estimates for 1915–16.[17] Cuts were made in the programme of building of cruisers and torpedo boats, but the battleships that Churchill wanted were all agreed to. Further, there were to be no manœuvres in the summer of 1914, but instead there was to be a less expensive exercise – a trial mobilisation of the Reserve Fleet. Churchill's speech introducing the estimates in March 1914 as usual pleased the Conservatives more than the Liberals. It was described by the Daily Telegraph as 'the longest, and perhaps also the most weighty and eloquent, speech to which the House of Commons has listened from a First Lord of the Admiralty during the present generation'.[18]

When Churchill was leaving the Admiralty in 1915, Kitchener, who was then Secretary for War, paid him a courtesy call, and told him that he could always take pride in the fact that at the outbreak of war 'you had the Fleet ready'.[19] This was very largely true. There were defects in the design of the big ships and in the ammunition of their guns: but Churchill was not to blame for these. He had failed to overcome red tape in preparing the anti-submarine defences of Rosyth and Scapa, which meant that the battleships had to spend much of their time at sea, with consequent wear and tear to their engines. But the rapid developments in the power and efficiency of the navy in the three years between 1911 and 1914 were in large part due to Churchill's energy and effort. None of those who criticised his career in later years were able to deprive him of the credit for this achievement.

In spite of the intensive work which he undertook to reform the navy and prepare it for war, Churchill could not ignore the other problems that beset the Liberal government in these years. The suffragettes of course refused to allow any minister to ignore their demand for the franchise; indeed they harried most ministers unmercifully, and were drawn to make great efforts to disrupt Churchill's speeches because they were popular and well attended. In 1909 a woman had attacked him on Bristol station with a dog-whip, but he had managed to wrench the whip from her grasp almost at once.[20] In November 1910, as Home Secretary, he was blamed for what became known, at least by the suffragettes themselves, as 'Black Friday'. Some three hundred women who were conducting a demonstration at Westminster, and who expected to be arrested, were roughly handled by the police for some time before a proportion of them were taken into custody; and the latter were released next day without being charged. In fact, the police had failed to observe the instructions which Churchill had given them on how such a demonstration was to be handled.[21] A few days later an indignant young man who sympathised with the suffragettes attacked him, again with a whip, as he was on his way to the restaurant car on a train from Bradford to London. But an alert plainclothes detective seized the assailant before he could use the whip.[22]

Churchill was able to escape the attentions of the suffragettes when at sea or when visiting naval establishments; but they beset him in London and in his constituency of Dundee. In 1912 a Miss Lila Clunas posted herself to Churchill's temporary residence in Dundee by express messenger, and was delivered by telegraph boy; rather uncharacteristically she allowed herself to be rejected at the door by a mere secretary.[23] In early 1914 when a seaplane in which he was flying made an emergency landing at Clacton, suffragettes were at once on the scene and Churchill was obliged to accept some of their literature; more of it was later found inside the plane.[24]

It was not that he was able to oppose women's suffrage in principle, though it may be that he would have liked to. The practical difficulty which worried him and many other members of the government was that if women were accepted on the existing household franchise only the relatively affluent women would in fact qualify, and this would almost certainly be a clear electoral advantage for the Conservatives. When in 1910 a pressure group called the Conciliation Committee produced a bill for women's suffrage on the existing franchise, Churchill, who had at first promised to help the Committee, executed a *volte face* and made a most damaging speech against the bill. 'It is an undemocratic bill,' he said. 'It gives an entirely unfair representation to property as against persons.'[25] His old friend Lord Lytton, who was chairman of the Committee, and whose sister had been imprisoned and forcibly fed when on hunger strike, regarded Churchill's action as treachery and for some time broke off all relations with him – much to the embarrassment of Marsh, who was very friendly with Lytton.[26]

Although Clementine sympathised with the suffragettes, Churchill did not feel that the issue was sufficiently important to rank with the other major problems that the government faced. He was alarmed when late in 1911 it looked momentarily as if it might lead to a break-up of the Cabinet. He thought that it was a matter that might reasonably be settled by a referendum, first of the women and then of the men. 'What a ridiculous tragedy it will be,' he told the Liberal Chief Whip, the Master of Elibank, 'if this strong Government & party which has made its mark in history were to go down on Petticoat politics.'[27] In the end, much to the anger of the supporters of women's suffrage, an attempt to introduce it by way of an amendment to a bill for adult male suffrage was ruled out of order by the Speaker. The record of the years of agitation does not suggest that violent action furthered the cause as it is sometimes supposed to have done.

Meanwhile the Irish Nationalists were demanding payment in full for their support of the Liberal government – and that meant the enactment of a measure to establish a parliament at Dublin for the whole of Ireland. The House of Lords could no longer veto such a bill, though it could prevent its operation for three sessions of Parliament, or a little over two years. Churchill was a late convert to the cause – the Manchester by-election of 1908 having been the catalysing factor – and he was always mindful of his father's sympathy with Ulster in 1886 and his famous declaration,

'Ulster will fight and Ulster will be right.' In 1911 he was trying to raise interest in a revival of the idea of 'Home Rule All Round', partly perhaps as a result of Lloyd George's mention of it in his coalition proposals, partly because he knew that some Conservatives, such as those who belonged to the 'Round Table' group, and also some Irish Nationalists such as his own uncle Moreton Frewen, who was briefly MP for Cork, were in favour of the plan.[28]

He therefore circulated two papers to the Cabinet on this subject, and later expounded the idea in a speech at Dundee.[29] He thought that a federal arrangement for the United Kingdom would involve the creation of separate subordinate parliaments not only for Wales, Scotland and Ireland, but also for a number of regions of England. Obviously, as *The Times* pointed out in a leading article, a division of Ireland into two regions would also be possible under such a scheme.[30] But neither his Cabinet colleagues nor public opinion as a whole responded warmly to these suggestions, and so he let the matter drop. In any case, Churchill was not at all sure that the Protestants of Ulster were as intransigent as they were made out to be. He accepted an invitation from a body called the Ulster Liberal Association to make a speech in Belfast in February 1912.

It seems that Churchill badly misjudged the Ulster situation at this time. The Ulster Liberal Association was an unrepresentative body, more remarkable for its temerity than its strength. When its leaders booked the Ulster Hall – where Lord Randolph Churchill had made his famous utterance in 1886 – a howl of rage went up from the supporters of the Union, and the Unionist Council undertook to occupy the hall in advance in order to deny it to the Liberals. Churchill felt himself under an obligation to visit Belfast, if only to assert the rights of free speech; but he was quite willing to abandon the Ulster Hall and to hold his meeting in a place where Unionist feelings were less likely to be dominant. This meant, in practice, transferring it to the Catholic quarter. As there was no suitably large hall, an enormous tent was brought over from Scotland and erected on the Celtic Park football ground. But the situation in Belfast was so tense that a serious riot was feared: 3500 troops were drafted into the city; and the Liberal Chief Whip, hearing that 'great quantities of bolts and nuts' had been abstracted from the shipyards, strongly advised Churchill not to take his wife with him on the trip.[31]

In spite of this Clementine insisted on accompanying her husband.

The Belfast visit was a major ordeal for the Churchills. Both on the train from London and on the passage to Larne they were rudely disturbed by suffragette demonstrators; but they knew that the more serious threat of violence lay in Ireland. Clementine was afraid, not of being killed, but of being disfigured by broken glass or some other injury.[32] Her husband as usual showed little sign of nervousness, and at the Belfast station 'smilingly raised his hat whenever the crowd groaned'.[33] They broke their journey to the meeting at an hotel in the centre of the city, and this enabled another crowd of hostile demonstrators to growl their disapproval. As they moved off to the meeting in a motor car, they were surrounded for a time by demonstrators, and before the police could reach them their car was lifted eighteen inches off the ground on one side. 'Men pushed angry faces against its windows and hooted with all their might.'[34] As soon as they reached the Falls Road, however, their reception abruptly changed. This was the Catholic district, and it was full of cheering, friendly people. According to *The Times*, 'The whole Roman Catholic community seemed to have turned out to do him honour. There were more black-shawled mill girls than men.'[35]

The meeting itself was something of an anticlimax. Rain fell heavily and seeped through the tent, which was only two-thirds full. Churchill read his speech in a low voice, and the only interruptions came from supporters of women's suffrage.[36] In his peroration Churchill did his best to turn his father's words to his own advantage:

Let Ulster fight for the dignity and honour of Ireland. Let her fight for the reconciliation of races and the forgiveness of ancient wrongs. Let her fight for the unity and consolidation of the British Empire. Let her fight for the spreading of charity, tolerance and enlightenment among men. Then indeed 'Ulster will fight and Ulster will be right'.[37]

After the conclusion of his speech Churchill and his wife were taken to the railway station by a circuitous route, and before the crowds realised it they were on their way to Larne by a special train.

The experience must have served to convince Churchill of the strength of Ulster Protestant feeling, and the sharpness of the

sectarian conflict. He had always been of the opinion that concessions ought to be made to satisfy Protestant opinion, but his
colleagues had told him that it was good tactics to hold such
concessions in reserve until the last moment.[38] Lloyd George had
begun to suggest making special arrangements for Ulster or for
part of Ulster, but had dropped the idea when he met bitter
opposition not only from the Nationalists but also from the
Conservatives, who were hoping to use the Ulster issue in order
to kill Home Rule altogether. Churchill therefore played his part
loyally in helping to put the Home Rule Bill on the Statute
Book. He made a major speech in the Commons introducing the
Second Reading of the measure, and he was active in the bitter
debates that accompanied its later progress. It was in one of these,
just after the Speaker had adjourned the House, that an angry
Irish Unionist, Ronald McNeill, threw a book at him which
bruised his face.[39]

But as time went on Churchill became more and more convinced that the only solution of the problem lay along the lines
of the exclusion of Ulster, as Lloyd George had suggested. In
October 1913, in a speech at Dundee, Churchill struck out on
his own and declared that Ulster's claim for special treatment
was 'very different from the claim to bar and defer Home Rule
and block the path of the whole of the rest of Ireland'. The Irish
Nationalists were worried by this defection, as they regarded it,
of one of their allies in the battle for Home Rule. T. P. O'Connor, who was especially friendly with the Liberal leaders, wrote
to John Dillon, Redmond's closest colleague in the Nationalist
leadership, to say that 'We may be faced with the very perilous
dilemma of either accepting his views – which I think impossible
or repudiating him publicly, which might involve his retirement from the Ministry.' Redmond did in fact reply to Churchill's
speech, but without attacking him personally, by declaring that
'Irish Nationalists can never be consenting parties to the mutilation of the Irish nation'.[40]

Churchill's search for a compromise solution of the Ulster
problem, though wise, honourable, and quite in keeping with his
instinctively Whiggish attitude to politics, increased his difficulties with his Cabinet colleagues at the time of his disagreement
with them over naval expenditure. Some of the latter may have
felt that it would be better to force Churchill to resign over
battleship building than over the coercion of Ulster. Lloyd George

did not fail to question him closely on his attitude to Ireland at the time that they came to a bargain on the estimates. According to Lloyd George Churchill was 'greatly confused and taken aback'.[41] He evidently felt obliged thereafter as a matter of tactics to take a stiffer line on Ireland: as he later put it, 'In order to strengthen myself with my party, I mingled actively in the Irish controversy.'[42] Just as Lloyd George was the most suitable Liberal leader to deliver a solemn warning to Germany, so by virtue of his previously conciliatory attitude to the Ulster Protestants Churchill was the most suitable minister to tell them that the government would not allow them to take the law into their own hands.

At Bradford on March 14th 1914 he said:

> But if there is no wish for peace, if every concession that is made is spurned and exploited ... if all the loose, wanton and reckless chatter we have been forced to listen to all these many months is in the end to disclose a sinister and revolutionary purpose – then gentlemen I can only say to you, let us go forward together and put these grave matters to the proof.[43]

The Times was not far wrong when it interpreted the speech as that of

> a Minister who, having carried the claims of his own Department against a formidable menace from the Radical rank and file, seemed to think it necessary to show that on occasion he could shout defiance with the rest.[44]

But *The Times*, which was of course backing the Unionists, did not bother to acknowledge that Churchill's attempts to find a compromise had so far met with no response from the Unionist side. And his speech met with warm approval, not only from the Liberals of Bradford, but also from the Prime Minister himself.[45]

But by this time Churchill was grappling with the very problem which his speech had discussed – that of preventing a revolutionary *coup* by the Ulster Volunteers, the Protestant army which had been drilling in Northern Ireland and now only needed a supply of arms to turn itself into an effective fighting force. He and his old friend Colonel 'Jack' Seely, who had succeeded Haldane as War Minister in 1912, decided with Asquith's approval on an immediate policy of strengthening the guards on military installations and depots in Ulster, and devised certain precautionary measures to deal with any attempt by the Ulster Volunteers to seize control of civil government. Troops were to move into Ulster from the big camp west of Dublin at the Curragh, and also from stations in Britain. The navy was to provide transport for the troops and if necessary landing-parties of its own, and for this purpose Churchill ordered a squadron of battleships to move from the Bay of Biscay to Lamlash at the mouth of the Clyde.

The whole sequence of manœuvres was, however, frustrated by the so-called 'Curragh mutiny', which was the result of incompetence at the War Office and a strong sense of sympathy for the Ulster Protestants on the part of the army officers, many of whom were themselves Ulstermen. General Sir Arthur Paget, the Commander-in-Chief in Ireland, had been given only verbal orders by Seely, and in discussing the proposed operations with his senior commanders he told them that officers domiciled in Ulster who did not wish to comply with the orders could be given leave of absence, while others who took the same view would have to do their duty or resign their commissions. Thereupon Brigadier-General Hubert Gough of the Cavalry Brigade at the Curragh, who was an Irish Unionist without domicile in Ulster, together with fifty-seven of his officers, gaining the impression that they were being asked to take part at once in an operation to 'coerce' Ulster, submitted their resignations.

The news of the trouble at the Curragh at once aroused the Prime Minister, who now realised that the military movements proposed by the service ministers could no longer proceed without very serious consequences for the armed forces themselves as well as for Ulster. He told Churchill to countermand the orders to the battleships, which had not yet entered the Irish Sea, and he instructed Seely to call off his plan for sending reinforcements to Ulster, and to try to repair the damage at the Curragh. Seely summoned the senior officers concerned to meet him at the War Office, and when they did so he demanded that they should withdraw their resignations. Gough refused to do so unless he received a written guarantee that he would not be required to enforce Home Rule on Ulster. Seely obtained for him a statement authorised by the Cabinet, but then foolishly added two more paragraphs on his own initiative. The upshot was that Gough withdrew his resignation and so did his subordinate officers, but when the Prime Minister refused to accept the two extra paragraphs of Seely's guarantee Seely himself and also his two main military advisers at the War Office all felt obliged to resign.

Naturally the government faced a storm of criticism in the House of Commons. The Conservatives accused it of planning a 'pogrom' against Ulster, and for some time ministers were much on the defensive. Churchill described as a 'diabolic falsehood' the suggestion that it had been the government's intention to provoke a rising.[46] Only a few weeks later, however, it became known that the Ulster Volunteers had secured a large cargo of between 30,000 and 50,000 rifles, together with ammunition, which had been smuggled in through the port of Larne. When a previously arranged Commons debate took place on a vote of censure of the government, it was easy for ministers to use the Larne gun-running as a justification for their own action, and to accuse the Conservative leaders of being implicated in an illegal enterprise. Churchill suggested that the Opposition motion was 'uncommonly like a vote of censure by the criminal classes on the police'.[47] But at the end of his speech he suddenly uttered a new plea for reconciliation between the parties. He appealed in particular to Sir Edward Carson, the Irish Protestant leader who had put himself at the head of the Ulster movement.

Churchill's plea for peace was proffered entirely on his own initiative, and he was delighted to find that it did in fact change the atmosphere, for Carson replied moderately, and the result was the re-opening of negotiations between the two sides. The move was not popular with the Liberal rank and file or with the Nationalists, and Churchill, whose position in his party was still shaky, described it to his wife as 'the biggest risk I have taken'.[48] It is significant that when he spoke in threatening tones to Ulster, it was with the approval of other senior ministers, but when he adopted a conciliatory tone it was entirely on his own account. But it was probably too late for one man to halt the drift towards civil war in Ireland.

While the renewed negotiations were proceeding the government had introduced an amending bill to allow individual counties of Ireland to opt out of Home Rule for a period not exceeding six years. But this concession was not enough to satisfy the Opposition leaders, who demanded the permanent exclusion of the whole of Ulster. On July 20th the King intervened and summoned an all-party conference at Buckingham Palace: it met for several days under the chairmanship of the Speaker of the House of Commons. But no progress was made, and on July 24th the Prime Minister had to report to the Cabinet that the conference had failed to reach agreement. The same Cabinet also heard an important piece of international news: the Austrian government had sent a remarkable ultimatum to Serbia, coldly prepared in the course of the four weeks that had elapsed since the murder of the Archduke Franz Ferdinand at Sarajevo. As Churchill put it,

The parishes of Fermanagh and Tyrone faded back into the mists and squalls of Ireland, and a strange light began immediately, but by perceptible gradations, to fall and grow upon the map of Europe.[49]

9. *Early Married Life*

FORTUNATE in many things, Churchill was especially so in his marriage. But he deserves much of the credit himself for choosing, without regard to hopes of inherited wealth, a wife whose personality was complementary to his own; who could soften the asperities of his bachelor habits and give him a stable and restful home background amidst the vicissitudes of politics and war. Clementine was a Liberal, and on one occasion declared publicly (at Dundee) that she was 'ardently in favour of votes for women'.[1] On another occasion she wrote to *The Times* on the same subject, but discreetly concealed her identity behind initials.[2] Like most Liberals, she was worried by the armaments race and by the prospect of war.[3] But she wisely made no attempt to emulate the wives of some famous politicians, notably in this period the temperamental Margot Asquith, by intriguing behind the scenes as if some of her husband's authority were at her own disposal.

Having married after so brief an engagement, it took the Churchills some time to set up a household in a manner suitable for a Cabinet minister. For the autumn and winter of 1908–9 they 'squatted' in the little house in Bolton Street which Churchill had occupied in his last two years as a bachelor, and here they held a few small lunch and dinner parties for their closer friends and more important political associates.

Apparently the first guests to be entertained to dinner were Admiral Sir John Fisher, then the First Sea Lord, and Lord Randolph's old friend Sir Ernest Cassel, who had given them £500 as a wedding present.[4] Shortly afterwards, on a Friday,

Charles and Lucy Masterman, also newly wed, came to dine: 'Dinner talk did not flow from anyone but Winston, who poured out ideas in an undigested form.'[5] Two days later the Webbs came to Sunday lunch; and Mrs Webb remarked upon her hostess in her diary: '... a charming lady, well-bred and pretty, and earnest withal – but not rich, by no means a good match, which is to Winston's credit.'[6]

In early 1909 Churchill took an eighteen-year lease on No. 33 Eccleston Square, a house in Pimlico close to Victoria Station, and convenient for Westminster and Whitehall. Built in late regency style by Thomas Cubitt, it had four storeys and a basement, and provided ample accommodation for hospitality as well as for the needs of a family. It took some time for the principal rooms to be prepared, as they required various alterations and redecoration. Two rooms on the first floor were converted into a library, where Churchill could display his fine collection of books, considerably augmented by wedding gifts from his friends, such as Coxe's *Marlborough* from Edward Grey, the works of George Meredith from J. M. Barrie, and the works of Sainte-Beuve from Eddie Marsh.

Clementine was now expecting her first child, and Churchill was very solicitous of her health and her ordeal to come: 'I rather shrink from it – because I don't like your having to bear pain & face this ordeal. But we are in the grip of circumstances, & out of pain joy will spring & from present circumstances new strength arise.'[7] The baby was known to its parents-to-be as the 'Puppy Kitten' or 'PK'. This was because they had given each other the pet names of 'Pug' and 'Kat': their mutual correspondence was embellished with drawings of these animals. The child, when born in July (1909), turned out to be a girl and was christened Diana. She had no less than five godparents, all from within the family, and of these the only godfather was 'Sunny', the Duke of Marlborough.[8] Churchill was very proud of Diana, and according to Masterman boasted to Lloyd George that she was 'the prettiest child ever seen'. "Like her mother, I suppose?" said George. "No", said Winston still more gravely, "she is exactly like me".'[9]

In the following months Clementine felt unable to accompany her husband on a trip to France and Germany, and she saw less of him than she would have liked. She began to wonder how loyal to her he really was, but when she mentioned her doubts on paper she received a very indignant reply.[10] It was a tiff that hardly seems to have ruffled the surface of their mutual affection. They were fully re-united in the autumn, and Lord Esher, who was a guest at a small birthday party for Churchill on November 30th, was impressed by their devotion to each other:

> He had a birthday cake with 35 candles. And *crackers*. He sat all evening with a paper cap, from a cracker, on his head. A queer sight.... He and she sat on the same sofa, and he holds her hand. I never saw two people more in love.[11]

At this time Churchill's salary as President of the Board of Trade was £2500, which was only half that of a Secretary of State. Asquith had agreed, in response to Churchill's request, to bring the status and emoluments of the office up to the level of the Secretaryships of State, but Churchill had been more or less obliged to agree that the increased salary should apply to his successor and not to himself. The expenses of his life as an MP and junior minister had gradually eaten away his savings, and now that he was married he was spending all his income. He told Esher that if he left office he would have nothing, but he was 'ready to live in a *lodging* – just two rooms – with Clementine and the baby'.[12] As it was, he maintained an establishment consisting of a cook, two maids and a man. Eleven weeks later, when he became Home Secretary, his salary went up to £5000. It stayed at this level when he became First Lord of the Admiralty, until such time as he should move into Admiralty House, when there would be a deduction of £500 because of the free accommodation. In fact, he was in no hurry to move from Eccleston Square, which he and his wife had so lately arranged to suit themselves; and he was quite satisfied that for the time being the Naval War Staff should be housed in Admiralty House instead of the First Lord's family.

In May 1911 the Churchills' second child, a boy, was born. He was known in advance as the 'Chum Bolly', perhaps a name invented by Diana. He was not christened for five months – the delay probably being occasioned by the Agadir crisis, for one of those who were invited to be godparents was Sir Edward Grey. The others were F. E. Smith, Churchill's friend on the Opposition front bench, and Viscountess Ridley, who was one of Churchill's cousins of the Guest family.[13] Although the baby was given only three godparents, as against Diana's five, he made up for this by having four names: Randolph, after his grandfather; Frederick, after F. E. Smith; Edward, after Edward Grey; and Spencer as the old family surname.[14]

In April 1913 Churchill at last moved his family into Admiralty House – apologising to his wife for the extra work that this would involve for her. He liked the 'spacious' rooms in the Georgian building, some of which, especially the library on the first floor, were much larger than those of Eccleston Square.[15] There were also splendid views from the windows across St James's Park and also, rather surprisingly, of St Paul's Cathedral on the White-hall side.[16] The historical associations of the building with Nelson and other great commanders also gripped him. But his daughter Diana, now almost four, who was encouraged to look forward to ampler accommodation, was at first somewhat disappointed – her comment was, 'It is not as big as Blenheim.'[17] Meanwhile 33 Eccleston Square was let to Randolph's godfather, Sir Edward Grey.[18] But living at Admiralty House seems to have proved more expensive than Churchill expected. It was difficult to keep a control on expenditure, and after a year he was writing to Clementine: 'Our finances are in a condition which requires serious & prompt attention.'[19] He was in the same state of impe-cunious affluence to which he had become accustomed in much of his earlier life.

A minister who worked as hard as Churchill needed to make a habit of getting away from his duties at regular intervals. He had had a pronounced stoop ever since he had grown up; but in 1909 it was also noticed by the press that he was getting fat[20] – and indeed in young middle age he had already assumed the chubbi-ness of figure which he was always to retain: it is clearly indicated in the cartoons of the day as well as in photographs. His old recreations of hunting and polo, though not entirely abandoned, were less practicable for him now, and his most regular exercise came from golf. He had taken up the game not long before he acquired his Scottish constituency and, as we have seen, when he was fighting an election there he would regularly go to play at Carnoustie, where he was a guest of James Falconer, the Liberal MP for Forfarshire. According to an account in the local paper:

Mr Churchill has taken some pains to learn how to hit the ball, and very often gets a long stroke both from the tee and through the green, but he has yet a lot to learn which a professional teacher could in two or three lessons enable him to do. For enthusiasm he has few equals.... Impatient always ... he follows up his ball at a fast pace, which is all right from the point of view of getting the exercise which he is after, but is all wrong when there are other players in front.[21]

When in London, he frequently played at Walton Heath on the North Downs as a guest of George Riddell, who owned the *News of the World* and other newspapers. Riddell was a wealthy man who was eager for social advancement, and he was pleased to entertain the younger Liberal ministers: and the ministers for their part enjoyed the clean, invigorating air at Walton which was less than an hour's run from London. Riddell presented Lloyd George with a house, which he built near the golf course: its completion was delayed owing to its being damaged by a fire caused by suffragettes. Clementine sometimes joined Churchill on the course, and Lloyd George and Masterman often played with him – indeed Masterman decided to lease a house on Riddell's estate. Towards the end of 1911 Riddell reckoned that 'he had usually played golf with Winston twice a week' for a whole year; but this arrangement went astray when Churchill went to the Admiralty and began spending his weekends on the *Enchantress*. Riddell found him very good company – 'never dull, never tedious ... a considerate and loyal friend'.

> He is also kind-hearted. The other day we came across a worm on the golf-course. Winston tenderly picked it up and placed it in the bracken, saying, 'Poor fellow! If I leave you here, you will be trampled by some ruthless boot.'[22]

But the fact was that Churchill was not really very good at golf, especially as he enjoyed the conversation quite as much as the exercise. His principal contribution to the game was to invent a form of foursome known as a 'greensome'. The idea was that both players in a partnership should play tee shots, and that they should then select one of the two balls to be played by alternate partners thereafter. In this way Churchill, by taking a good player as his partner – for instance, the Walton Heath professional James Braid – could get all the exercise he needed and also win a fair proportion of his games.[23] Sometimes, of course, he wished to talk confidentially to a fellow-minister on the course; indeed many of his most intimate conversations with Lloyd George must have taken place at Walton Heath.

Churchill also very occasionally got in a day's shooting, if he was invited to join a party in the country. From the relatively limited experience of shooting hedgerows with Churchill, Wilfrid Blunt formed the impression that he was a good shot, as indeed an ex-soldier practised in big-game hunting ought to have been.[24] In September 1913, as a guest of the King at Balmoral, he shot four stags and 'cd have shot more – but refrained not wishing to become a butcher'; but this was his first shooting that year.[25]

It was about this time that he found a form of recreation which for a time threatened to exclude all others. He took his first flight in an aeroplane in 1912, as a matter of duty;[26] but he found that he enjoyed it, and in 1913 he made repeated ascents and then began to take lessons in managing the controls. The airmen knew that their occupation was very risky and they did not allow him to fly solo. Their own casualty rate was very high – Churchill's instructor at the naval air station at Eastchurch was killed only three days after they had been flying together.[27] Churchill also took lessons at Upavon, the army flying centre, but Colonel Trenchard (later Marshal of the RAF Lord Trenchard) watched his 'wallowing about the sky', as he called it, and decided that he was 'altogether too impatient for a good pupil'.[28] As the flights continued his friends, and still more his wife, became very concerned about the danger. Finally in June 1914, after he had been up nearly 140 times, he promised Clementine that he would abandon flying 'decidedly for many months & perhaps for ever'. He told her that it was quite a sacrifice for him, as, 'Though I had no need & perhaps no right to do it – it was an important part of my life during the last 7 months. I am sure my nerve, my spirits & my virtue were all improved by it.'[29]

For some years after his marriage Churchill continued to go to an annual camp with the Oxfordshire Yeomanry, in which with the rank of major he now commanded a squadron. The camp was usually in the grounds of Blenheim Park, where he was close to his friend 'Sunny' and the comforts of the palace. Out in the sunshine with his squadron, he would soon get rather burnt on the face.[30] It was a change from sitting at a desk, but for a man who had served in so many campaigns it was small beer. He would have liked to command the whole force instead of merely being a sub-

ordinate, because he reckoned that he could organise the manœuvres himself much more successfully than anyone else. As he told
his wife in 1909,

On nothing do I seem to *feel* the truth more than in tactical combinations. It is a vain and foolish thing to say – but *you* will not
laugh at it. I am sure I have the root of the matter in me – but
never I fear in this state of existence will it have a chance of
flowering – in bright red blossom.[31]

It was for this reason that he made a point of attending manœuvres by the regular army whenever he could. In both 1908 and
1910 he watched the exercises on Salisbury Plain, and on the
latter occasion a senior officer noticed that 'Mr Winston Churchill
in a chocolate uniform of rare elegance and the posture of a
Caesar, a solitary figure, watched the proceedings with the concentrated gloom of an acknowledged expert.'[32] His gloom might
have arisen from his experiences of the previous year, when for
the second time he had witnessed the German army manœuvres,
and met the Emperor Wilhelm II. He had noticed a very considerable improvement in the handling of the troops since his first
visit in 1906.[33] It had made him reflect on the danger of a
large-scale war: he wrote to Clementine:

Much as war attracts me & fascinates my mind with its tremendous
situations – I feel more deeply every year – and can measure the
feeling here in the midst of arms – what vile & wicked folly &
barbarism it all is.[34]

It was on the whole more pleasant to visit the battlefields of
old. One of those he saw was Gravelotte, where the French were
defeated in 1870 and where the graves of the soldiers 'are dotted
about in hundreds just where they fell – all are very carefully
kept, so that one can follow the phases of the battle by the
movements of the fallen'.[35] Another battlefield was that of Blenheim, where in spite of many changes of habitation and scenery
it was still possible to trace the topography of Marlborough's
greatest victory. 'Sunny ought to make the pilgrimage', wrote
Churchill to his wife.[36]

For Churchill, as for most people who really enjoy their work,
holidays and professional occupations often merged into one
another. Even if attendance at the French or German manœuvres
did not count as official business for a President of the Board

of Trade, it was obviously important for a Cabinet minister to know about the strength of the Continental armies; and in 1909 Churchill could combine his visit to the German manœuvres with a study of the labour exchanges in towns in Alsace.[37] But at no time in his career were pleasure and business more mixed than when as First Lord of the Admiralty he had at his disposal the 3500 ton yacht, HMS *Enchantress*. In the period of less than three years between his appointment as First Lord and the outbreak of war, he spent no less than eight months on board the yacht.[38]

To be sure, some of his days on the *Enchantress* were not very different from days at Whitehall. During a spell on board the ship at Portsmouth, he developed a routine which he explained to Clementine:

> I stay placidly in my nice cabin working all the morning, walk round the Dockyard in the afternoon & then home to tea & a couple of hours more work before dinner. The papers in files & bags & boxes come rolling in. One never seems to do more than keep abreast of them.[39]

'Walking round the Dockyard' probably involved a good deal of brisk exercise for himself and others. He walked fast and those who accompanied him to discuss some matter of policy often found themselves short of breath.[40] But the more pleasurable part of life on the yacht was when she was at sea in good weather; and best of all was a trip to the Mediterranean, where fortunately the Admiralty had considerable establishments that merited inspection by the First Lord.

When Churchill went to the Admiralty the custom of a First Lord using the yacht to entertain his friends on a Mediterranean cruise was already established. In the spring of 1912 Churchill made up a party for a Mediterranean trip which included Asquith and his daughter Violet; they joined the yacht at Genoa and spent three weeks on board. Apart from a conference at Malta with Kitchener, who was then Consul-General in Egypt, the Prime Minister took a complete rest from his usual work and spent his time visiting the classical sights and museums and mugging up the details from Baedeker. Churchill on the other hand was for much of the time too busy with naval matters to take much interest in sightseeing, which in any case his lack of classical knowledge prevented him from fully appreciating.[41] Even

Admiral Beatty, who was also on board, grew weary of Churchill's talking 'about nothing but the sea and the Navy'.[42] Violet appears to have enjoyed everything, including the company of the First Lord whom she greatly admired.

The following year Churchill arranged a similar cruise; this time they were also accompanied by Asquith's wife Margot (Violet's step-mother) and by Churchill's mother, who had separated from George Cornwallis-West and was feeling rather lonely. (She was to resume the name of Lady Randolph Churchill early in 1914[43].) Violet described these additions to the complement as 'two rather explosive elements both singly and – still more – conjointly'.[44] This time the cruise started at Venice and the yacht visited the Adriatic coast and Greece. The following April (1914) Churchill warned his wife not to 'commit yourself & the yacht unnecessarily to Margot';[45] but in any case the gravity of the crisis over Ireland must have ruled out a Mediterranean cruise in the spring or early summer.

Before he became First Lord, Churchill had already enjoyed an extensive Mediterranean cruise as a private holiday. In the summer of 1910 he and Clementine joined his friend Count de Forest on the latter's yacht, and visited Greece, Rhodes – where he much enjoyed the medieval fortifications – and Turkey, where he travelled inland on the 'cow-catcher' of a locomotive as he had done in East Africa.[46] But in planning their private holidays in later years the Churchills had to think of the needs of their children. Owing to the difficulties of long-distance travel, this meant seaside holidays on the English coast or at Dieppe, which Clementine already knew well from her unmarried days. For the entertainment of a new generation, Churchill resumed his youthful occupation of building sand-castles – or, rather, elaborate fortresses and dykes against the sea.[47] He was with Clementine at Dieppe for a week in October 1911, but thereafter, although Clementine returned with the children, he was usually too busy to go. In the summer of 1914 they took a cottage at Overstrand near Cromer, and Churchill joined his family for the weekend and was on the beach there on the Sunday before the European war broke out.[48]

The Churchill family circle was never a narrowly restricted one. Churchill was very loyal to his relatives and with rare exceptions kept in touch with them even when the press of business might have afforded him an excuse for avoiding them. His cousin 'Sunny', the Duke of Marlborough, gradually became more estranged from him in politics. But this did not interrupt the family courtesies, and every now and then the Winston Churchills with their children visited Blenheim. Churchill had conveyed 'Sunny's' doubts about the 1909 Budget to Lloyd George, and the Chancellor said on one occasion that if he put a special clause in the Finance Bill exempting 'Sunny' Churchill would let him do what he liked at the expense of everyone else.[49] In March 1914, just as Churchill was threatening the Ulster Unionists to 'put these grave matters to the proof', 'Sunny' was attending a dinner of Unionist notables at the Ritz to present a sword of honour to Sir Edward Carson, the Irish Unionist leader.[50] But there were also Liberals among Churchill's cousins. The Guest family changed parties at the same time as he did, largely owing to the influence of Cornelia, Lady Wimborne, who was Churchill's aunt. No less than three of her five sons were Liberal MPs in the pre-war period, and two of them held office – Ivor, the eldest, as Paymaster-General from 1910 and Freddie, who became a Whip in 1912. They would turn up to help Churchill at by-elections and other times of crisis, and in return Churchill would do his best to visit and speak in their constituencies at election time.

Beyond the circle of his relations, Churchill also maintained his association with many of his father's old friends. They were a cosmopolitan group – the remnants of the court circle of Edward VII as Prince of Wales. Conspicuous among them was the rich and generous German–Jewish financier, Sir Ernest Cassel, who had helped Churchill's brother Jack to establish himself as a stockbroker in the City. Another younger friend was Count de Forest, whose foster-father, Baron Hirsch, had advised the Prince of Wales on financial matters as Cassel later did. De Forest had estates in Moravia and, as we have seen, entertained the Churchills on his yacht in the Mediterranean in 1910. He had fought the general election in January 1910 as Liberal candidate for Southport, but although Churchill spoke in his support he was narrowly defeated. Churchill later helped to obtain for him the more strongly Liberal constituency of West Ham, North, where he was elected in 1911.

Wilfrid Blunt, the Radical Sussex squire, had also been a friend of Lord Randolph's, but he was of a different type from Cassel and de Forest. He was an English 'nationalist' in the

Gladstonian sense of supporting the aspirations of other nation-alities than his own. Churchill's ties with him had been streng-thened by the fact that he knew the Hozier family quite well. Churchill enjoyed Blunt's conversation and knowledge of the East, and he and Clementine spent weekends on his Sussex estate where on one occasion in 1912 they hunted deer and then dined together in oriental costume: the company included George Wyndham, the Conservative ex-minister, and according to the host it was 'a true feast of reason and flow of bowl; the secrets of the Cabinet were gloriously divulged'.[51]

But probably the closest of Churchill's friends in this period was a man too young and too provincial in his origins to have known Lord Randolph – although his spectacular career may have remin-ded Churchill of the way in which his father made his reputation. This was F. E. Smith, the brilliant barrister only two years Churchill's senior, who won a Conservative seat in Liverpool in the 1906 election and immediately made his mark as the ablest speaker on the Opposition benches, with the exception only of Arthur Balfour. Churchill's own tribute to 'F.E.' after the latter's death was unique. 'Our friendship', he wrote, 'was perfect. It was one of my most treasured possessions.' He admired him for his range of eloquence, of which he had a professional appreciation, and also for the quality of his personality – 'a gay, brilliant, loyal, lovable being'.[52] It was 'F.E.' who introduced Churchill to the Oxford Union, where they both made impressive speeches in a debate in March 1907.[53] Later on Churchill was able to do his friend a favour by urging on Asquith the proposal to make him a Privy Councillor – a proposal which Balfour, as Conservative leader, accepted only with great reluctance.[54]

In refusing to limit his friendships to those who were on his own side of the political fence, Churchill behaved as his father had behaved; and it was a matter of regret to him that in 1909 and 1910, during the battle over the Budget and the House of Lords, and again in 1914 over Ireland, political partisanship became so fierce that the maintenance of such ties was frowned upon by many. It was as early as 1909 that the Duke of Beaufort had ex-pressed a wish to see 'Winston Churchill and Lloyd George in the middle of twenty couple of dog hounds'.[55]

In the hope of maintaining some sort of friendly social contact and dialogue between political opponents Churchill and 'F.E.' decided in 1911 to form a club, to be known as 'The Other Club', to consist of leading figures of both major political parties or of none. The constitution of the club stated that, 'Nothing in the Rules or intercourse of the Club shall interfere with the rancour or asperity of party politics.'[56] Among the dozen or so members of the club in its earliest days were Lloyd George, Seely, and Buckmaster, later Solicitor-General – all of these from Liberal ranks; Bonar Law, Max Aitken and Northcliffe among Conservatives; and some distinguished figures from outside politics such as General Lord Kitchener, with whom Churchill was now on good terms, and Anthony Hope the novelist, whom he had admired since boyhood.

Churchill's tendency to mix with Opposition leaders was a sign that he did not take the party system as seriously as some of his colleagues did. This attitude grew on him during his time at the Admiralty, and was naturally intensified when war broke out, leading Asquith himself to say that he 'does not inspire trust'.[57] But this comment was very wide of the mark if it implied that Churchill was capable of deceit. Unlike Lloyd George, he was temperamentally unsuited to intrigue: as Lucy Masterman said, 'He is an extraordinarily transparent creature.... I never heard or saw any attempt at intrigue by him that could have taken in a kitten.'[58] There was nothing dishonourable in Churchill's view that defence, and even more, war, were matters which required the enlistment of the nation's talent irrespective of party.

Nor did this view conflict, in peacetime at any rate, with Churchill's loyalty to the Prime Minister himself and to his Cabinet colleagues. For more than six years Asquith led a remarkably able and homogeneous team of ministers. Although in those days the Cabinet was smaller than it now is, no less than eleven of its members, apart from the Prime Minister himself, served continuously from the formation of the government in 1908 until the outbreak of war: among them were Augustine Birrell, John Burns, Grey, Haldane, Lloyd George, Morley and Churchill. It was a remarkable tribute both to Churchill's self-confidence and also to his genuine quality that as soon as he entered this distinguished team he was at once able to assert a right to speak on almost every topic that was on the agenda – and to speak at length. What he said was too often rhetorical in form, and not suitably concise for a committee of busy men.

A good indication of his style is provided in the parody of a

Cabinet meeting which was written by Herbert Samuel and has since been published by his biographer.[59] Birrell clearly did not like listening to him – 'I think we are a very forebearing Cabinet to his chatter,' he said;[60] and the Master of Elibank, who attended as Chief Whip for some time, thought that 'Churchill talks too much at the Cabinets and too loudly, and does not carry the weight there that I would expect'. All the same, he thought that his influence counted for more than that of any other minister except Morley and Lloyd George.[61] As early as 1908 Grey thought that 'Winston, very soon, will become incapable from sheer activity of mind, of being anything in a Cabinet but Prime Minister'.[62] But he also thought that he was 'a genius', and declared shrewdly, 'His fault, that phrases master him, rather than he them. But his faults and mistakes will be forgotten in his achievements.'[63]

Churchill had made an impression of over-confident versatility because when he joined the Cabinet he already knew a lot about colonial affairs, because in any case he had to speak on behalf of his own ministry, the Board of Trade, and because he was encouraged by Lloyd George to resume the economy campaign against Service expenditure which he had begun as a Conservative backbencher. For several years Lloyd George was his most intimate colleague among the members of the Cabinet, and the two men never ceased to be in friendly contact while they were both in office. We have seen how closely they worked together on social policy in the years 1908 to 1912, and how Churchill followed Lloyd George's lead in the preparation of unemployment insurance. Churchill later paid generous tribute to Lloyd George's astonishing powers of persuasion. Using a metaphor that Admiral Fisher had used of Balfour, he said: 'At his best he could almost talk a bird out of a tree.'[64]

In 1911, however, there came a change. Churchill's increasing involvement in the problems of defence brought him into closer touch with Grey. The change appeared to be symbolised by the fact that while Lloyd George witnessed Churchill's marriage in 1908 it was Grey who became godfather to his son in 1911. Grey had found that Churchill's 'high-mettled spirit' gave him comfort during the Agadir crisis; at the end of a trying day they would go to the Automobile Club where, as Grey put it, 'he would cool his ardour and I revive my spirits in the swimming-bath'.[65] In the following year Churchill's work brought him more fully into contact with the problems that beset Grey as Foreign Secretary; and his demands for increased naval expenditure led to friction with Lloyd George at the Treasury. As early as April 1912 Masterman told Riddell that Lloyd George and Churchill were 'not concerting plans as formerly'.[66] At the end of that year Lloyd George complained that 'He is too concentrated on his particular office. He has not got the art of playing in conjunction with others.... When we refuse him anything, he talks of resigning.'[67] All the same, the two men remained friends, and Lloyd George had reason to be very grateful to Churchill in 1913, when he stood by the Chancellor in the Marconi scandal and persuaded Northcliffe not to attack him in the Harmsworth newspapers.[68]

But there were members of the Cabinet, as there were many in the parliamentary party and in the Liberal press, who were distressed by Churchill's change of view on the importance of increasing defence expenditure. Some of them had already noticed with concern his interest in military affairs and his enthusiasm for the memory of Napoleon, of whom he had a bust on his office writing-table.[69] Morley was later to point out to him that Napoleon's career had not been uniformly successful. On another occasion he told Churchill that his own career would probably end on St Helena; but 'he was more flattered than dismayed by the prospect'.[70] John Burns, the trade-union member of the Cabinet, thought him 'patriotic ... but at heart ... dictatorial'.[71] These varying attitudes were indications of differences in policy which were to be fully revealed in the war crisis of July–August 1914.

On Friday afternoon, July 24th 1914, Churchill had heard the news of the Austrian ultimatum to Serbia with the feeling that it presented more danger for Britain than the Ulster crisis. But the navy was uniquely ready for war, as the trial mobilisation of the fleets – decided on in place of manœuvres, as a matter of economy – was still taking place. Some of the Reservists were already being paid off and going on leave, but most were to remain at least until Monday. On Saturday the news came that the Serbians had virtually accepted the Austrian demands. Churchill spent Saturday night at Cromer with his wife and children, and they spent Sunday morning on the beach: 'We dammed the little rivulets which trickled down to the sea as the tide went out. It was a very beautiful day.'[72] But at midday he telephoned to London, and on hearing that the situation still seemed critical he decided to return to London that evening. In the meantime the First Sea Lord, Prince Louis of Battenberg, had already taken the important decision to cancel the arrangements for the dispersal of the fleets on Monday.[73] This decision was confirmed by Churchill when he reached Admiralty House.

During the following week the crisis deepened. The Cabinet met at least once every day to consider what action to take. Grey had suggested a London conference of ambassadors of the powers, to try to settle the Balkan dispute. But Germany refused to agree to this; and on Tuesday (July 30th) Austria declared war on Serbia. Churchill decided it was time for the fleets to take up their battle stations. This did not need Cabinet authorisation, but he informed the Prime Minister before he acted.[74] The First Fleet was ordered to move by night from Portland to its new stations at Scapa and Rosyth. Churchill himself stayed permanently in Whitehall, shuttling between the Admiralty and Downing Street, and deflecting his path only as far as St James's Park, where he inspected a cygnet which had lately been born to a black swan on the lake. He was, however, quite free from the personal distress that beset his Cabinet colleagues at this time. He wrote to Clementine:

> Everything tends towards catastrophe & collapse. I am interested, geared up & happy. Is it not horrible to be built like that? The preparations have a hideous fascination for me. I pray to God to forgive me for such fearful moods of levity. Yet I wd do my best for peace, & nothing would induce me wrongfully to strike the blow.[75]

Most of the members of the Cabinet, although worried about the prospect of war, had not yet decided that it would be right for Britain to participate. When Churchill tried to persuade them to authorise the final acts of naval mobilisation, they would not concur. Grey, who felt that Britain was morally obliged to go to the assistance of France if she was attacked, was worried that a section, perhaps a majority, of the Cabinet opposed his view. Lloyd George was the most powerful voice on the other side, and he was supported by about half the others.[76] Churchill foresaw a possible break-up of the existing Cabinet and the need to form an immediate Coalition: as early as July 30th he got in touch with F. E. Smith, and asked him to sound out Bonar Law, who was now the Conservative leader.[77] Law was suspicious of this approach, which he thought should have come from the Prime Minister if at all; he refused to discuss the question of joining the government, but authorised Smith to tell Churchill that the Opposition favoured full support for France.[78]

On Saturday morning, August 1st, the Cabinet was still resisting Churchill's demand for full naval mobilisation. Asquith described Churchill that day as 'very bellicose'[79] and complained: 'It is no exaggeration to say that Winston occupied at least half the time.'[80] Churchill tried especially hard to win over Lloyd George, and kept passing him notes across the table, reminding him of their years of collaboration and of the work that they could still do if they remained together.[81]

In the evening Churchill had F. E. Smith, Max Aitken (the wealthy Canadian who was now a Conservative MP) and two others to dine with him at the Admiralty. He had invited Bonar Law and also Grey, but Law refused and Grey also then withdrew.[82] After dinner all except Aitken played bridge. Then a despatch box was brought in and Churchill opened it, to find a single paper bearing the message, 'Germany has declared war on Russia'. Churchill left the room almost immediately, leaving Aitken to take his hand at the game. According to Aitken, 'He was not depressed; he was not elated; he was not surprised. He went straight out like a man going to a well-accustomed job.'[83] He crossed the Horse Guards Parade to 10 Downing Street and told the Prime Minister that he was ordering full mobilisation on his own initiative, and would seek retrospective authorisation from the Cabinet. Asquith did not speak: 'He looked at me with a hard stare and gave a sort of grunt. I did not require anything else.'[84] As he left to return to the Admiralty he was accompanied by Grey, who told him that he had promised the French ambassador that Britain would not permit a German naval attack on the French Channel coast.[85]

On Sunday morning the Cabinet met once more, and confirmed these decisions; but one member, John Burns, resigned forthwith. It still remained doubtful whether the Cabinet would agree to authorise British entry into the war. The country was under no formal obligation to assist France and Russia, and Liberals disliked siding with Russia on ideological grounds. In the evening, however, news came that German troops had entered Luxembourg and were on the point of attacking Belgium, whose neutrality was guaranteed by a treaty to which both Britain and Germany were parties. Lloyd George swung over into support of intervention, seeing the effect that this issue would have on British public opinion. Morley, who was bitterly opposed to intervention, attributed his change of view to 'the influence of the splendid *condottiere* at the Admiralty'.[86]

Next morning (Monday August 3rd) the Cabinet authorised army mobilisation and Morley resigned from the government. Simon and Beauchamp did likewise, but Asquith later persuaded them to withdraw their resignations.[87] Churchill was able to instruct British naval commanders to get in touch with appropriate French officers for the purpose of combined action. And Grey made his famous statement in the House of Commons, explaining the moral obligation to France, and pointing to Britain's treaty commitment to Belgium. He was well received, and John Redmond gave a striking pledge of support on behalf of the Irish Nationalists.

War was now imminent; only the formalities remained. Next morning (August 4th) the Cabinet was told that German troops had invaded Belgium, and authorised the despatch of an ultimatum to Germany demanding their withdrawal. The ultimatum was timed to expire at midnight Berlin time, which was 11 p.m. in London. No reply to the ultimatum came in the course of the day; and as 11 p.m. approached ministers and their staffs in Whitehall waited tensely for the moment of war. Churchill was at the Admiralty, with 'a small group of Admirals and Captains and a cluster of clerks, pencil in hand, waiting'.[88] It was a warm night; and as Big Ben struck the hour the sound of cheering and the singing of 'God Save the King' came through the open windows from the direction of Buckingham Palace. The telegrams ordering naval action against Germany were now sent out, and Churchill crossed the Horse Guards Parade once more to inform the Prime Minister. In the Cabinet room at No. 10 another rather despondent group had been waiting: it included not only ministers, but also the Prime Minister's wife, Margot – though soon after eleven o'clock she decided to go to bed. As she was at the foot of the stairs she saw Churchill entering the house and 'with a happy face striding towards the double doors of the Cabinet room'.[89]

10. *Antwerp and the Dardanelles*

IN the crisis that preceded the outbreak of war Churchill had been obliged to stay inside the Admiralty, or close at hand, to meet each emergency as it arose. With the outbreak of hostilities, the need for his presence on almost continuous duty was at first not less great. The constitutional position was that two members of the Board of Admiralty had to concur in any order that was sent to the fleet. Although the junior Sea Lords did not like it, it was easy for Churchill to develop an executive committee at the Admiralty consisting of himself, the First and Second Sea Lords and, for advisory and administrative purposes, the Chief of the War Staff and the Secretary of the Admiralty.[1] In the early weeks of the war this group met every morning to determine policy and action, which involved warship movements in every part of the globe, in order to hunt down the scattered German cruisers and merchantmen which were not in home ports.

An early disappointment for the Admiralty was the failure to prevent the German battlecruiser *Goeben* and the light cruiser *Breslau* from escaping through the eastern Mediterranean to enter Turkish territorial waters. The fact that the two warships were not caught was due in large part to errors of judgment by the Commander-in-Chief of the British Mediterranean Fleet and by the officer commanding a cruiser squadron, who felt that his orders obliged him to refuse action when he sighted the enemy ships; but part of the responsibility for failure lay with the

Admiralty War Staff, whose instructions were, to say the least, confusing.[2] Vice-Admiral Sir Doveton Sturdee, who headed this body, was not really cut out to be a staff officer, and the First Sea Lord, Admiral Prince Louis of Battenberg, should have recognised this. The *Goeben* and the *Breslau* were nominally sold to the Turkish government, which had not yet entered the war; but the two ships retained their German crews, and so had to be 'marked' by a superior British force stationed at the Dardanelles to prevent their escape. Churchill was very unhappy about this turn of events, especially as Turkey was on the verge of entering the war on the German side and the arrival of the two warships encouraged the war party.

Meanwhile the German High Seas Fleet was showing no enthusiasm for action in the North Sea. At first, the enemy's only activity was to send out patrols of destroyers near Heligoland, to prevent British minelaying in the area. There was thus little that the Grand Fleet, now commanded by Admiral Jellicoe, could do but wait. But in the meantime the commanders of light forces on the British side, Commodores Roger Keyes and Reginald Tyrwhitt, laid a plan to cut off these destroyers from their bases; and Beatty, who was in charge of Jellicoe's battle-cruisers, arranged to shadow the British light forces from the North. The operation took place on August 27th–28th. It was not well planned, as many of the British light force commanders were not aware that Beatty's battle-cruisers were approaching the area; and when the German ships came out in greater strength than usual, having obtained some warning from the increased British naval signals, it was more by luck than good management that Beatty's battle-cruisers were able to intervene at the crucial moment. British losses were slight but the Germans lost three light cruisers and a destroyer sunk and other cruisers badly damaged. The moral effect of the engagement was even greater than the material: the German Emperor ordered his naval commanders to avoid offensive action, and in Britain the Battle of the Heligoland Bight was hailed as a notable victory.

Less than a month later, on September 22nd, the Germans got their revenge when one of their submarines succeeded in torpedoing in succession three old armoured cruisers, the *Cressy*, *Hogue* and *Aboukir*, which were on patrol off the Dutch coast. The three ships ignored almost every rule of warfare: they had no destroyer escort, they were not zig-zagging to avoid torpedoes, and when one was torpedoed the others stopped at once in order to pick up survivors. Almost two-thirds of the crews, amounting to 1400 men, were lost. Here again the Admiralty War Staff was partly to blame for allowing such old and slow ships to be on patrol in an area which enemy submarines could easily reach. They had been known to some British officers as the 'live-bait squadron', and when Churchill first heard this expression, only a few days before the disaster, he at once ordered fresh dispositions to be made.[3] His message to this effect was dated September 18th, but Sturdee had failed to act on it in the succeeding few days. The immediate effect of this disaster was to make Jellicoe very anxious about the submarine danger to his fleet. Fearing that Scapa Flow might be penetrated by a skilful U-boat commander, he decided to transfer his battleships to Lough Swilly on the north coast of Ireland. Arrangements for better protection against submarines were not completed at Scapa until the middle of 1915.

Meanwhile the German armies were advancing into Belgium and France, and the great battles to decide the fate of Europe were taking place much as Churchill had expected in his paper of 1911. Brussels fell on August 20th and Namur, reputedly a fortress of considerable strength, was taken on the 23rd. The Germans were free to advance into northern France in the direction of Paris, with no strong defences in front of them. The small British expeditionary force under General Sir John French had concentrated on the Franco-Belgian frontier near Le Cateau, and here it took some of the shock of the German right wing; it then retreated in conjunction with the French as far as the River Marne, where it turned and counter-attacked early in September. The German armies, over-extended by their advance, were now forced into retreat, but they in turn could easily hold the line of the River Aisne, and in late September it became clear that mobile warfare in the main area of conflict between the opposing armies was at an end. But the Belgian coast as far north as Antwerp had not yet been invaded by enemy forces in strength, and its strategic importance only came to be appreciated as the front inland froze into immobility.

The Admiralty was naturally interested in preventing the Belgian coast from falling into the hands of the enemy. Churchill had also assumed responsibility for the air defence of Great Britain – which the War Office was too busy to undertake in the early months of the war – and he had decided that this could best be effected by stationing naval aircraft at Dunkirk, whence attacks could be made on German airships either at their bases or when they were on their way to the English coast. On September 10th, wearing the uniform of an Elder Brother of Trinity House, he paid a hasty visit to Dunkirk and Calais, conferred with the governors of both ports to satisfy himself that they were adequately prepared to face a German attack, and made plans for the protection of the aircraft base he was establishing at Dunkirk.* It was his idea to organise a force of armoured cars – Rolls-Royce motor-cars swiftly adapted for the purpose – and this force was for some weeks very successful in dealing with marauding German cavalry which penetrated towards the coast. At the invitation of the French command, a brigade of marines was also landed at Dunkirk to reinforce the garrison.

At the outbreak of war Asquith had still been acting as Secretary for War, the post which Seely had resigned after the Curragh incident; but he thereupon decided to invite Field-Marshal Lord Kitchener, the country's most distinguished soldier, to assume this responsibility. It was a popular appointment, and Kitchener's reputation was enhanced by many of his early decisions – in particular, his announcement that he expected the war to last for three years and that he was planning recruitment accordingly. Churchill to begin with had great admiration but little personal regard for his new colleague, whom he had criticised for his ruthlessness in the Sudan campaign; but he had established friendly relations with him since becoming First Lord. He had urged Kitchener's appointment on Asquith on August 4th;[4] and he now found him to be a cordial and loyal colleague. But Churchill had closer ties with General French, which had developed when French was CIGS before the war; and he soon found himself in the position of having to try to reconcile French and Kitchener, for French strongly resented interference in operational matters from the Secretary of State, while the latter regarded himself as more of a Commander-in-Chief than a civilian minister. With Kit-

* According to Admiral Oliver, who accompanied him, Churchill was asked by the French general at Dunkirk what uniform he was wearing. 'Churchill replied "Trinity House" and the amazed general ejaculated "Mon Dieu la Trinité" ': – James, *Oliver*, 131. Within a few months the incident appears to have been embroidered. According to Poore, 357, Churchill's statement to the general was 'Je suis le Frère Ainé de la Trinité'.

chener's agreement Churchill visited French from September 26th to 28th to see what the land warfare was like and to discuss co-operation between the army and navy on the left flank of the Allied line, so as to maintain the security of the Belgian coast.[5] This plan was, however, frustrated by the French commanders, who feared that it might lead to a separation of the British troops from their own strategic control.

The need for action on the coastal flank remained urgent, however, and became acute when on October 2nd it was reported that the Belgian government had decided to abandon Antwerp and retire to Ostend. When the news reached London, Asquith was already on his way to a recruiting meeting at Cardiff and Churchill was just leaving for a second visit to Dunkirk. A hastily assembled group of ministers – Grey, Churchill and Kitchener – decided to ask the Belgian government to hold on at Antwerp and to await reinforcements which would be sent to the city direct from Britain. It was agreed that Churchill, who was on his way to France in any case, should go to Antwerp to deliver the message and to see what the existing military position was.

Churchill reached Antwerp by motorcar from Dunkirk, on the afternoon of October 3rd, and at once conferred with the Belgian government. At his request, the Belgians agreed to prolong their struggle at Antwerp for ten days or so, pending the arrival of Allied reinforcements. The marine brigade from Dunkirk arrived next morning, and Churchill at once ordered the despatch of two more brigades which were forming in Britain as part of a projected Royal Naval Division.[6] These units were in large part still untrained, and they were short of much of their essential equipment. It was understood that other British military units and French troops and marines would follow as soon as possible. On the 4th, feeling that it was his duty to stay and co-ordinate the defences of the city, Churchill telegraphed to Asquith offering to resign his post as First Lord if he were given formal military command. Kitchener took this seriously and offered to give him the rank of lieutenant-general; but Asquith seemed to think it was an absurd suggestion. As he put it in his diary,

Winston is an ex-lieutenant of Hussars, and would, if his proposal had been accepted, have been in command of two distinguished major-generals, not to mention brigadiers, colonels, etc., while the Navy were only contributing their little brigades.[7]

The Cabinet greeted the idea with laughter and in the upshot Lieutenant-General Sir Henry Rawlinson was appointed to take command of British troops at Antwerp.

It was only for a very few days, therefore, that Churchill was in charge in the beleaguered city. But it was a unique period in his life: as his old friend Seely, who visited him there on a liaison trip, was later to describe it:

> It was apparent that the whole business was in Winston's hands. He dominated the whole place: the King, ministers, soldiers, sailors. So great was his influence that I am convinced that with 20,000 troops he could have held Antwerp against almost any onslaught.[8]

At first he revived all he met with the news that 'we are going to save the city'.[9] He set himself up in the best hotel, and introduced his usual routine of activity, dealing with incoming telegrams in the early morning before getting out of bed, and making use of Admiral Oliver, the Director of Naval Intelligence, as his secretary. He moved about under heavy shellfire without showing any concern, to the alarm of Oliver who was accompanying him; and he supervised the positioning of the naval brigades on their arrival on October 6th.[10] General Rawlinson also arrived that day, and Churchill left the city for London in the evening. Rawlinson, who agreed with Churchill that Antwerp could be held for some time, accompanied him as far as Bruges in order to organise the relieving forces.[11]

But within a few hours of Churchill's departure from Antwerp, the Belgian government decided to give up the struggle to hold the city. On October 8th the main Belgian army units evacuated their positions and moved rapidly to the south-west. The British naval brigades fell back in confusion, some 2500 men being either captured by the enemy or forced into internment across the nearby Dutch frontier. The capitulation of the city took place on the 10th, probably five days later than it would have occurred without British intervention. Churchill was disappointed by this outcome, and felt for a time that his efforts had not been worthwhile.[12] In the larger picture of the development of the campaign, however, it is apparent that the prolonged defence of Antwerp played an important part in helping the Allied cause.

At this time both sides in the great struggle were trying desperately to marshal their forces for the occupation of the coast. Dunkirk, Calais and Boulogne were at stake as well as the Belgian ports, and the use of the siege artillery which the Germans were employing at Antwerp might well have been decisive if it had been free a few days earlier. The British army was now redeployed on the left flank as Churchill had originally proposed, and with the remnants of the Naval Division joining up with it a stand was made in front of Ypres, just inside Belgium. The defensive positions that had just been established up to the coast were fiercely attacked by the Germans in late October and early November, but they held firm, and became the trench line that was to separate the armies with little change until March 1918. Zeebrugge and Ostend were lost to the enemy; Dunkirk, Calais and Boulogne were saved. In this task Churchill's foray at Antwerp, albeit conducted at short notice with ill-trained and ill-equipped forces, was a factor of considerable strategic importance. King Albert of the Belgians himself recognised this fact: as he later said of the episode, 'Churchill understood the importance of Antwerp. If a stand had not been made there, the Germans would have taken Dunkirk.'[13]

But the apparent failure of the hastily improvised Antwerp expedition, the absence of the First Lord of the Admiralty from his post in Whitehall, and the lack of training and equipment in the Royal Naval Division, all aroused criticism in Britain, and it was readily assumed that the whole thing was an adventure impetuously decided upon by Churchill alone. The *Morning Post*, a Conservative journal which had long been very hostile to Churchill, published a leading article entitled 'The Antwerp Blunder', which held him to blame and advised the members of the Cabinet to 'keep a tight hand upon their impetuous colleague'.[14] Churchill, who had won such popularity by his efficient and prompt action in mobilising the fleet at the outbreak of war, now saw his reputation declining because he was thought to be neglecting the navy and engaging in rash adventures, even though what he had done had been undertaken at the request of his colleagues and on their behalf. But he had enjoyed his brief taste of military command at Antwerp; and he took an early opportunity of letting Asquith know that he would like to give up the Admiralty if he could simultaneously be transferred to a high military command. Asquith recorded a conversation which he had with Churchill at which the latter had raised the question of his own future:

His mouth waters at the sight and thought of Kitchener's new armies. Are these 'glittering commands' to be entrusted to 'dug-out trash' bred on the obsolete tactics of twenty-five years ago, 'mediocrities who had led a sheltered life mouldering in military routine', etc., etc.?[15]

In late October an added complication was the growing campaign against the First Sea Lord, Prince Louis of Battenburg, on the grounds of his German nationality. An agitation led by the London evening paper, the *Globe*, demanded his replacement at an early date by 'an Englishman'.[16] A more sophisticated approach, apparently fed by inside information, was that he was 'played out', and that he had, as the *Morning Post* put it, 'unfortunately assented' to a position subordinate to the First Lord.[17] Churchill himself seems to have thought it desirable to obtain a more vigorous colleague at the Admiralty; he soon made up his mind that he would like to bring back to office the dynamic Lord Fisher, who was now seventy-three years old but still astonishingly fit and active. The Prince was persuaded to offer his resignation after a 'delicate and painful' interview with the First Lord;[18] and there followed a difficult argument with the King, who disliked Fisher and not unreasonably thought him too old for the job. When the King said that he thought the work would kill the old Admiral, the First Lord replied, 'Sir, I cannot imagine a more glorious death.'[19] The appointment was confirmed on October 29th.

Those who had the fullest knowledge of the character of the two men thought that their association in office would not last long. Beatty told his wife that he could not 'see Winston and Jacky Fisher working very long in harmony';[20] and Admiral Wester Wemyss prophesied that they would be 'thick as thieves at first until they differ on some subject, probably as to who is to be no. 1, when they will begin to intrigue against each other'.[21] At least their collaboration began auspiciously. They at once had to avenge a naval defeat which occurred on November 2nd when Admiral Sir Christopher Cradock, the commander of the South American squadron, bravely but unwisely challenged Admiral von Spee's armoured cruisers, the *Scharnhorst* and the *Gneisenau*, to battle at Coronel, off the coast of Chile, and suffered almost complete annihilation.

It is possible that the disaster could have been averted if the Admiralty had responded sharply to a signal from Cradock saying that he was leaving his one and only battleship, the old and slow *Canopus*, at the Falkland Islands. But Cradock's decision was not properly appreciated in time, and for this the Chief of the War Staff, Sturdee, was again primarily to blame.[22] On hearing the bad news Fisher's reaction was immediate: two battle-cruisers were at once to be detached from the Grand Fleet to the South Atlantic, to hunt the German armoured cruisers; and Sturdee was to be sacked. Churchill, however, persuaded Fisher that Sturdee should be given the opportunity to take command of the battle-cruisers, as nobody could deny that he had an excellent record as an officer afloat. The result was an overwhelming victory when von Spee's squadron encountered Sturdee's battle-cruisers at the Falkland Islands. The *Scharnhorst*, the *Gneisenau* and two smaller German warships were sunk without loss to Sturdee's force.

Churchill and Fisher could now settle down to a regular routine at the Admiralty, which Churchill was later to describe.[23] Fisher was in the habit of waking early, at about 5 a.m., and going to bed early, at 9 p.m. or so. Churchill liked to work late at night and he now exaggerated this tendency, so that either Fisher or himself would be available to deal with urgent messages at almost any time of day or night. He woke a little later – at 8 a.m., and worked on papers and telegrams sitting up in bed for an hour or two:

> He presented a most extraordinary spectacle, perched up in a huge bed, with the whole of the counterpane littered with despatch boxes, red and all colours, and a stenographer sitting at the foot – Mr Churchill himself with an enormous Corona Corona in his mouth.[24]

The daily meetings with the First Sea Lord could take place as before, with Admiral Sir Arthur Wilson brought back from retirement as an unofficial adviser, with the new Naval Secretary, Capt. C. M. de Bartolomé in place of the Second Sea Lord, and with Oliver, the former Director of Naval Intelligence, replacing Sturdee as Chief of the War Staff. Churchill now developed a habit which his Private Secretary, Eddie Marsh, introduced him to, of taking a nap after lunch.[25] In the late afternoon and evening there would be further meetings in the First Lord's room, and finally Churchill would retire to bed again at one or two a.m. Even at this hour there would be Admiralty officials, such as the Naval Censor, Admiral Brownrigg, who would waylay him to ask for decisions of one sort or another. Brownrigg later declared: 'I never had anything but pleasant relations with him. I could not help admiring his appetite for work and his pluck in taking decisions.'[26]

It was Oliver who had instituted a cryptographic section at the Admiralty to obtain intelligence from German wireless signals. This office had a great stroke of luck when the Russians were able to provide a copy of the German signals book, which was salvaged from a German warship wrecked in the Baltic in the first month of the war. With this information at its disposal, the Admiralty was able to lay traps for the German fleet when it occasionally emerged on 'tip-and-run' raids. One of these occurred on December 16th, when German battle-cruisers shelled Scarborough, causing some 500 casualties. But although Beatty's battle-cruiser squadron was in a position to cut off the enemy ships from their bases, bad visibility enabled the raiders to make their way home unharmed. It was reported at Westminster next morning that Churchill was 'best left alone this morning, so sick with disappointment was he'.[27] But in January another opportunity occurred, again as a result of the interception of radio signals. A German fleet was encountered at the Dogger Bank and attacked by Beatty's battle-cruisers. In the pursuit that developed the German armoured cruiser *Blücher,* which had bombarded Scarborough, was sunk, and a battle-cruiser severely damaged; but the chase was broken off prematurely owing to a signals mix-up on the British side which occurred when Beatty's flagship was temporarily disabled and forced to drop out of the line.

The appointment of Fisher as First Sea Lord and the victory at the Falkland Isles did much to restore the prestige of the Admiralty, and at the end of the year even the *Morning Post* was forced to acknowledge that 'The Royal Navy may look back upon the record of 1914 with a just pride and forward to the future with an equal confidence'.[28] But Churchill and Fisher were looking forward to the day when the navy could take the offensive in a way which would assist a strategical decision of the whole war. At meetings of the War Council – the wartime successor of the Committee of Imperial Defence – Churchill repeatedly argued that the best means of defence was offence: on November 25th he suggested that the 'ideal method' of defending Egypt against the Turks, who had now entered the war, was by attacking the Gallipoli peninsula, though he acknowledged that this would be 'a very difficult operation involving a large force'.[29] On December

1st he urged that the dangers of an enemy invasion of Britain could best be countered by seizing an island off the German coast as a base, and blockading the enemy ports with submarines, torpedo craft, and aircraft.[30] He was already actively conducting the air defence of England by means of attacks on enemy airship and aircraft bases. At the turn of the year he sent Asquith one of his customary annual memoranda on future policy, and this time it was devoted to war strategy. In a key passage of this very perceptive document Churchill wrote:

> I think it quite possible that neither side will have the strength to penetrate the other's lines in the Western theatre.... Without attempting to take a final view, my impression is that the position of both armies is not likely to undergo any decisive change – although no doubt several hundred thousand men will be spent to satisfy the military mind on the point.... Are there not other alternatives than sending our armies to chew barbed wire in Flanders? Further, cannot the power of the Navy be brought to bear upon the enemy?[31]

At this stage Churchill was thinking primarily of a naval operation in the North Sea – the seizure of the island of Borkum in order to block the German navy's exit from its harbours, to be followed by an assault upon Schleswig-Holstein and the opening of the Baltic. Borkum had figured prominently in Admiralty planning for a number of years; but there were still a number of practical objections to be overcome before an operation could be launched. The alternative was to strike on the opposite flank of the enemy position in Europe, by attacking the Dardanelles and opening the passage to the Sea of Marmora, where the fleet could turn its guns on Constantinople and then link up with the hard-pressed Russians. On January 2nd the Dardanelles proposal was given greater urgency by a message received from the Grand Duke Nicholas, the Commander-in-Chief of the Russian forces, appealing for a 'demonstration' against Turkey to relieve the pressure of the Turkish army in the Caucasus.

In spite of his interest in opening the Baltic, for which he was preparing with a vast programme of construction of shallow-draught battle-cruisers and monitors, Fisher was willing to give favourable consideration to a joint attack by military and naval forces on Gallipoli and the Dardanelles, using British, French, Indian and Greek forces – it being assumed that Greece could be persuaded to enter the war on the Allied side. The naval attack could, he thought, be made by obsolete pre-dreadnought battle-ships which were no longer fit to serve in the North Sea. But Kitchener was not willing to provide any British military support for an early operation in the Mediterranean, and so Churchill began to turn his mind to the possibility of forcing the Dardanelles with naval forces only. He put the suggestion to Admiral S. H. Carden, who was now in command of the fleet in the eastern Mediterranean, and received the reply: 'I do not think that the Dardanelles can be rushed, but they might be forced by extended operations.'[32] Churchill was pleased with this response, and even more pleased when Fisher suggested that the *Queen Elizabeth*, the first battleship to mount fifteen-inch guns, should conduct her gunnery trials by demolishing the Dardanelles forts.

On January 13th Churchill therefore expounded proposals along these lines to his colleagues on the War Council. Maurice Hankey, the Secretary of the Council, has described the reaction of the members of the Council to Churchill's explanation of the possibilities:

> The War Council had been sitting all day.... I suppose the coun-cillors were as weary as I was.... The idea caught on at once. The whole atmosphere changed. Fatigue was forgotten. The War Council turned eagerly from the dreary vista of a 'slogging match' on the Western Front to brighter prospects, as they seemed, in the Mediter-ranean. The Navy, in whom everyone had implicit confidence, and whose opportunities so far had been few and far between, was to come into the front line.[33]

The Council agreed readily to a minute drawn up by the Prime Minister that the Admiralty should 'prepare for a naval expedi-tion in February to bombard and take the Gallipoli Peninsula with Constantinople as its objective'.[34]

In the next two weeks the preparations for the attack went ahead, but Churchill began to find that Fisher was lukewarm to an exclusively naval operation. Fisher persuaded Hankey to help him in drafting a paper which warned of the dangers of reducing the margin of superiority in the North Sea and also complained of the unwillingness of the army to co-operate in the attack on the Dardanelles.[35] He told Churchill that he would not attend the next War Council meeting on January 28th; but Churchill arranged for Asquith to meet Fisher and himself for a short dis-cussion immediately before the War Council assembled. At this encounter, Fisher told Asquith that he preferred the idea of an operation on the German coast in the North Sea, leading to the opening of the Baltic. He 'did not criticise the attack on the Gallipoli Peninsula on its own merits';[36] nor did he give any indication that he would resign if overruled. Under the circumstances, Asquith felt justified in asserting his authority over the First Sea Lord. He declared, 'I am the arbitrator. I have heard Mr Winston Churchill and I have heard you and now I am going to give my decision.... The Dardanelles will go on.'[37]

But when the meeting of the War Council began and the question of the Dardanelles came up, Fisher made as if to leave the room, apparently to disavow any responsibility. Kitchener then quickly got up and spoke earnestly to him, pointing out that he was the only dissentient and that the operation was strongly favoured by the other members of the Council; and Fisher then resumed his seat.[38] The favourable view of the operation taken by other members of the War Council was noticed by Asquith, who recorded that it was 'warmly supported by Kitchener and Grey and enthusiastically by A.J.B.[alfour]'[39] – the latter, although an Opposition leader, having accepted an invitation to serve on the Council.

There was indeed very little reason why anyone should object to the operation, even on technical grounds. The danger of serious losses, either in manpower or in material, was slight. The idea was to proceed systematically through the straits of the Dardanelles, destroying the fortresses by gunfire from the battleships. The *Queen Elizabeth* could easily keep out of range of the enemy guns, and the other battleships that might be required to engage them more closely were all expendable, being too old and slow to have a part to play in a fleet action. Furthermore, the whole operation, if it proved unduly costly, could easily be broken off at short notice and explained simply as a 'demonstration' to aid the Russians and to mislead the enemy about the main intentions of British action in the Mediterranean. But if it proved successful, there would obviously be a need for military action in the Constantinople area, and for that reason Kitchener in mid-February agreed to provide a regular division, the 29th, as the stiffening for an expeditionary force which would also consist of troops from Australia and New Zealand and a contingent from France.[40]

The first bombardment of the Dardanelles forts (apart from a token attack that had taken place in October, shortly after

Turkey entered the war) was delivered on February 19th. The assault was broken off at dusk and owing to several days of gales and poor visibility it could not be resumed until February 25th. But the operations seemed to be going well, and small landing parties from the warships were able to approach many of the guns near the entrance to the straits and complete their demolition. Churchill, although suffering from a mild attack of influenza, was in high spirits at the news. He had already ordered the despatch of the Naval Division, which was now reorganised after its exertions in Belgium and more adequately equipped and trained. The King inspected the Division at Blandford, in Dorset, before it embarked, and Churchill was present at the occasion on horseback, 'glowing with pride' in his little army.[41]

But soon he began to be worried by delays which slowed up the progress of the operation. In the first place, Carden did not press the bombardment with vigour. In early March his efforts were desultory, and although Churchill wrote to Jellicoe on the 9th that 'Our affairs in the Dardanelles are prospering' he was already becoming impatient.[42] The explanation for Carden's weakness soon became apparent: on March 15th he resigned his command owing to ill-health. His second-in-command, Rear-Admiral J. N. de Robeck, took charge of the next major concerted attack, already arranged for the 18th. But this attack suffered from indifferent planning. Since the enemy guns did little damage to the warships, it was obvious that the main obstacle to progress was the enemy minefield; but the only minesweepers in use were civilian-manned trawlers which were easy targets for the enemy. There would have been little difficulty in adapting some of the fleet's destroyers to a minesweeping role, but this was not done.[43] Although some damage was again done to the enemy positions, three battleships, two British and one French, were sunk by mines on this one day, and there was a heavy loss of life on the French ship.

Neither Churchill nor Fisher was dismayed simply by the loss of a few battleships – Fisher indeed had assumed that up to ten would be lost in the course of the engagements between the ships and the forts. Arrangements were therefore immediately made to replace the losses, and de Robeck seemed ready to press on with the attack as soon as possible, pausing only to reorganise his minesweeping force. But by this time some of the troops were arriving, and General Sir Ian Hamilton, Churchill's old friend, whom Kitchener had placed in charge of the military forces, had reached the scene. On March 22nd de Robeck told him that he had decided to delay his next attack until it could be undertaken jointly with a military assault.

Unfortunately, there had also been serious delays on the military side. Kitchener had held back the 29th Division in February and March, thinking that it might be needed for some unspecified emergency on the Western Front. Churchill vehemently remonstrated against this, and insisted that his view should be recorded in the War Council minutes; if a disaster occurred in Turkey owing to insufficiency of troops, he must disclaim all responsibility.[44] It was on this occasion that Asquith described Churchill as 'at his worst.... he was noisy, rhetorical, tactless & temperless – or full'.[45] When Kitchener at last released the 29th Division, it was discovered that the transports had been dispersed; and as a result of this further delay the Division could not be available for service at the Dardanelles until mid-April. Churchill feared that the enemy would make good use of the intervening period by building up the Gallipoli defences, and that casualties would be heavy when the landings took place. He therefore sought to resume the naval bombardment without further delay, and drafted a telegram to de Robeck to this effect. But although Asquith and Kitchener agreed with him, Fisher refused his approval to any attempt to overrule the local commander, and so the telegram was never sent.

It remains a matter of controversy today whether a renewed naval operation would have had any success. Commodore Keyes, who was on the spot, thought that a great opportunity was missed, especially as the Turkish guns were running short of ammunition which could not be replaced. But other competent naval officers disagreed with him, and as the naval attack was never in fact renewed it is difficult to be sure. All the same, de Robeck was in favour of renewing the attack in May – but this time he was overruled by Fisher.[46]

At this point it would have been possible to call off the whole effort and to use the troops for some other operation, such as the support of Serbia through Salonika, or an attack on the Turks at Alexandretta. But Kitchener had now become keen on using troops to follow up the naval attack, arguing that Britain would suffer serious loss of 'face' throughout the East if she acknowledged defeat at the Dardanelles. So the military planning went ahead; but it was not until April 25th that the assault took place, and by this time the peninsula had been well prepared for defence by Turkish troops under the command of the German general, Liman von Sanders. The battleships were now used as artillery to attack strongpoints of these new defence positions, but when the landings took place it was apparent that this had done little to damage the defence. The Turkish soldiers emerged from their trenches to greet the Allied troops with a devastating rifle- and machine-gun fire. Many were killed in the open boats, or on the beaches where they were held up by barbed wire obstacles. At first Hamilton sent optimistic reports to London, but after a few days the news of heavy losses reached England, and also the depressing information that the Turks still held the high ground from one end of the peninsula to the other. Gradually a deadlock developed, as on the Western Front, and it became apparent that the invasion would have to be substantially reinforced if it was to succeed.[47]

From then onwards the Dardanelles became an unpopular operation in Whitehall. At the Admiralty, Fisher's opposition was intensified, and he insisted on the return of the *Queen Elizabeth* to home waters because of the danger of German submarines in the Mediterranean. Churchill could not resist this demand, but after much argument with Fisher he persuaded him to agree to a substantial reinforcement of the Mediterranean fleet by other ships so that it could renew the naval attack on the Dardanelles if de Robeck favoured it once more. Fisher was also criticised by Kitchener at a War Council meeting on May 14th for his sudden insistence on withdrawing the *Queen Elizabeth*. The Admiral replied by saying openly, and for the first time in the presence of his War Council colleagues, that 'he had been no party to the Dardanelles operation'. Kitchener responded that 'If we abandoned the enterprise, there would be a danger of a rising in the Moslem world'.[48]

The old Admiral was now on the verge of a nervous breakdown. He had worked very hard for over five months to develop the Admiralty building programme, with impressive results; but he found it difficult to cope with the stream of instructions, many of them on very detailed operational or technical matters, which came to him from the First Lord for approval or for further discussion. He was constantly being pressed by the *Morning Post* to assert his own views against those of the First Lord and to 'insist on the ancient right of the Board to control the Navy'.[49]

Very early on the morning after the War Council meeting – on Saturday, May 15th – Fisher entered his office to discover a draft order from Churchill listing all the ships which the two men had agreed to send to the Mediterranean, but also including two extra submarines which were not part of their bargain. He decided that this was the last straw, and having written letters of resignation to both Asquith and Churchill he left the Admiralty and went into hiding. The reason that he gave for his action in his letter to Churchill was as follows:

> It is undesirable in the public interest to go into details – Jowett said 'Never explain' – but I find it increasingly difficult to adjust myself to the daily requirements of the Dardanelles to meet your views – as you truly said yesterday I am in the position of continually vetoing your proposals.[50]

It was the end of the Churchill–Fisher partnership. But, as soon became apparent, it was the end of Churchill's tenure of his post as First Lord, and also the signal for the formation of the First Coalition, with all that this portended for the future of British party politics and social change.

As we have seen, Churchill had favoured a coalition government since the days of late July when war became inevitable.[51] He felt that the old issues of peacetime controversy were not merely stilled, but were extinguished, by the outbreak of war. As he put it in a letter to Walter Long, the Conservative leader, on the day after the declaration of war: 'I don't think things can ever be the same again in English politics and I cannot say I am sorry.'[52] He discussed war policy freely with his Conservative friends F. E. Smith and Max Aitken, and provided a room in the Admiralty for Balfour – who was, to be sure, a member of the War Council. All this aroused some suspicion in Liberal circles, and even the Prime Minister was inclined to think it was an indication of dissatisfaction with the existing party system. Asquith noted early in February that his First Lord was 'always hankering after Coalitions and odd groupings, mainly designed (as one thinks) to bring in F. E. Smith & perhaps the Duke of Marlborough. I think his future one of the most puzzling enigmas in politics.' But he did not apprehend any immediate threat to the government from Churchill's restlessness, if only because, as he correctly put it, 'he has no personal following'.[53]

But Asquith's suspicions of Churchill were mild compared with those harboured by other members of the Cabinet and of the party and press outside the government. The War Council had to some extent superseded the Cabinet, and war strategy was determined, as Churchill later explained, 'by the Prime Minister and Lord Kitchener, and me'.[54] This exposed Churchill to jealousy on the part of immediate civil colleagues, such as Lloyd George, who was quite prepared to gossip unkindly at his expense. In November 1914 Lloyd George gave C. P. Scott an account of Churchill's role at the Admiralty which, as Scott noticed, was marked by a 'strong personal antagonism'.[55] Reginald McKenna, who still resented the way in which he had been replaced at the Admiralty, learnt much of the Admiralty gossip direct from Fisher and used it to encourage suspicion in Asquith's mind. In March 1915 the Prime Minister became alarmed by a story from the Liberal journalist, H. W. Massingham, that Churchill was intriguing to replace Grey at the Foreign Office with Balfour; he asked Lloyd George if this was at all likely, and was told that it was.[56] It is against this background that we must judge Asquith's comment at the time that:

It is a pity that Winston hasn't a better sense of proportion, and also a larger endowment of the instinct of loyalty.... I am rarely fond of him, but regard his future with many misgivings.... To speak with the tongue of men and angels, and to spend laborious days and nights in administration, is no good if a man does not inspire trust.[57]

Churchill was not an intriguer: it was foreign to his nature. But if there was any member of the government against whom he had a motive for intriguing it was not Asquith but Kitchener. Asquith, after all, was prepared to back the Dardanelles campaign to the hilt; Kitchener, on the other hand, had refused military support when it would have been most effective, and then had insisted on undertaking the invasion of Gallipoli at a time when the enemy was well prepared for resistance. It was obvious, too, that Kitchener had no idea how to run the War Office, and in particular how to organise the production of munitions, for which the War Office was responsible. Churchill was on intimate terms with French, who still resented Kitchener's interference in his conduct of operations on the Western Front. Early in May he visited French on his way back from some negotiations in Paris about the naval arrangements for the entry of Italy into the war, and probably discussed with French and C. d'A. Repington, the *Times* correspondent, the current shortage of munitions, especially artillery shells, and the War Office's responsibility for this. On May 14th, the day before Fisher's resignation, Repington published a sensational article in *The Times* drawing public attention to the shell shortage and the wastage of British lives which it caused.

There is evidence that McKenna and others blamed Churchill for encouraging Repington to publish the details of the shell shortage, and it is certainly possible that Churchill did so. But to suppose, as one recent historian has done, that Churchill could have been seeking to precipitate the fall of the Cabinet at this particular moment is to venture into speculation of a most implausible kind.[58] Italy was just on the verge of joining the Allies in the war – which indeed was the reason for Churchill's visit to France – and she would only be discouraged from taking the plunge if Britain became absorbed in an immediate political crisis. Repington could have got all the evidence that he required from French alone, who had plenty of motive for wishing to change the management of the War Office. But in any case, the repercussions of the Repington article were not felt until well after Fisher had resigned. It was not until May 19th that the *Daily Mail,* Northcliffe's other major property, called for the resignation of Kitchener for having 'starved the Army in France of high-explosive shells'. But Asquith had decided to form a coalition government as soon as he heard of Fisher's resignation on the 15th.

The sequence of events did not immediately doom Churchill's prospects of remaining at the Admiralty. Asquith tried hard over the weekend of May 15th/16th to repair the damage, in the first place by finding out where Fisher was and ordering him back to his post. The First Sea Lord, who had said that he was off to Scotland 'at once', was discovered at the Charing Cross Hotel, and on Asquith's instructions 'in the King's name' to return he went back to the Admiralty. Asquith held that Fisher could not resign until his resignation was formally accepted; but Fisher refused to see the First Lord and sent messages to say that he was definitely leaving for Scotland on May the 17th. Churchill wrote two long, friendly letters urging him to withdraw his resignation, and also on the 17th sent him a message, conveyed by George

Lambert, the Civil Lord of the Admiralty, offering him a seat in the Cabinet if he would do so.[59] Presumably Asquith was prepared to authorise this proposal, which would have given Fisher something of the prestige if not the actual power of Kitchener at the War Office.

Meanwhile Churchill had had his hand strengthened by the action of Admiral Sir Arthur Wilson, who had served with Churchill and Fisher as a member of the War Council since before the Dardanelles campaign was decided on. Wilson urged the other Sea Lords not to resign in sympathy with Fisher, and when asked by Churchill if he would become First Sea Lord himself agreed to do so. Having obtained this assurance on the Sunday, Churchill at once hurried to Asquith's country home to tell the Prime Minister. He came away with the impression that he was to remain at the Admiralty, and next day, Fisher having refused to respond to his further overtures, he went to the House of Commons intending to announce his new Board of Admiralty. But Lloyd George told him, when he called on the Chancellor in his room at the House, that the Prime Minister had changed his mind and had decided to have a new First Lord.[60] At the same time Asquith wrote to Fisher implying that, as Churchill was leaving the Admiralty, it was not necessary for him to abandon his post as First Lord.[61]

It was evident that Bonar Law had insisted that Churchill must go. He may have been influenced by backbench pressure in making this demand; but certainly he had little personal sympathy with Churchill's plight, as the two men had never developed really friendly relations. The Conservative leader appears to have insisted that Haldane should leave the Cabinet altogether, and that Churchill should leave the Admiralty. Haldane had been the victim of what Churchill described as 'a vile campaign' in the Conservative press because of supposed sympathy with the German cause – although he had done more than anyone to prepare the regular army for its wartime role.[62] Churchill was not to be excluded altogether; and Lloyd George suggested to him, in Asquith's presence, that he should be Colonial Secretary, and in this capacity help to mobilise the manpower and resources of the Empire for the conduct of the war.[63] Churchill seemed to be willing to consider this, and recommended to the Prime Minister that Balfour should be his successor at the Admiralty. Later in the day he sent a letter to Asquith in which he said he could not accept any office except 'a military department'; otherwise he would prefer 'employment in the field'.[64]

The events of the evening of the 17th at the Admiralty may have provoked this change of attitude. The German fleet suddenly emerged into the North Sea, and yet another trap was laid by the Admiralty in the hope of destroying its major enemy. At this critical moment Churchill was at his post, but Fisher was absent. The hoped-for encounter failed to materialise; but the First Sea Lord's desertion of his post was commented on severely within the Admiralty, and Churchill began to sense that it was highly desirable for some continuity of naval policy to be maintained. He wrote yet another letter to Asquith on the 18th, saying he was prepared to accept the Colonial Secretaryship, but pleading to be allowed to stay at the Admiralty.[65]

Fisher, for his part, seemed to think that Asquith was bound to keep him as First Sea Lord, and that he could make his own terms for the withdrawal of his resignation. What he really wanted was a position like that of Kitchener, so that he could be his own First Lord and First Sea Lord as well. He drew up a list of 'conditions' which he sent to Asquith, which included a refusal to serve under either Churchill or Balfour and a demand for a completely new Board of Admiralty.[66] Asquith was shocked by this letter; and Churchill next day was able to report that Admiral Sir Arthur Wilson, who was the obvious alternative First Sea Lord, had declared that he would serve under no other First Lord than Churchill – 'the greatest compliment I have ever been paid'.[67] But Asquith could not encourage any vain hope on Churchill's part. 'You must take it as settled', he wrote on the 20th, 'that you are not to remain at the Admiralty.' He hoped to offer him a post, but could not yet specify what it would be.[68]

The following day, the 21st, was a Friday. Almost a week had been absorbed in the political crisis, and it was still not resolved. The delay was probably caused more than anything else by discussions about the War Office. Asquith recognised that something must be done to improve the administration of the munitions industry, but he did not want to put a Conservative in charge of munitions if he was already putting a Conservative at the Admiralty. Bonar Law seems to have thought of replacing Kitchener altogether,[69] but if Asquith shared this idea it was extinguished by events. On May 19th the *Daily Mail* came out with its demand for Kitchener's resignation; but this produced such an outcry in favour of the injured military hero that offending copies of the *Mail* were actually burnt on the floor of the London Stock Exchange. Asquith acknowledged that Kitchener had to stay; and under the circumstances Fisher became more dispensable. Churchill appealed once more for the rescinding of the veto on his retention of the Admiralty, in letters both to Asquith and Bonar Law. As he saw it, he was pleading not just for himself, but for the continuity of military and naval policy: 'I am clinging to my *task* & to my *duty*', he wrote to the Prime Minister.[70] To Bonar Law he suggested that it was unfair to judge his role at the Admiralty in ignorance of the facts.[71] Clementine Churchill was also aroused by the agony of her husband's position to make an appeal to Asquith:

Winston may in your eyes & in those with whom he has to work have faults, but he has the supreme quality which I venture to say very few of your present or future Cabinet possess – the power, the imagination, the deadliness, to fight Germany.[72]

But Bonar Law would not give way, and on Saturday May 22nd Churchill saw all the heads of department at the Admiralty, one by one, and thanked them for their loyalty, both to him and to the national cause. One of the officers thought this 'extraordinarily dignified, and won him a great deal of sympathy'.[73] But the details of the Coalition Cabinet were agreed only after another three days, on the 25th. Asquith made a compromise with the Conservative leaders whereby Balfour became First Lord and Lloyd George took the new post of Minister of Munitions, handing over the Exchequer temporarily to McKenna. Fisher was succeeded as First Sea Lord by Admiral Sir Henry Jackson, who seemed to Churchill the best man available if Wilson would not serve. The Colonial Office was no longer free as a vacancy for Churchill, as Asquith needed it for Bonar Law, whom he had managed to keep out of any more senior post. Churchill had to be content with the junior Cabinet post of Chancellor of the Duchy of Lancaster, which as Lloyd George put it was '... generally reserved either for beginners in the Cabinet or for distinguished politicians who had reached the first stages of unmistakable decrepitude'.[74] He would not have taken the post if he had not been promised continued membership of the War Council, now renamed the Dardanelles Committee; and it was to supervising, however indirectly, the conduct of the great but so far indecisive operation in the eastern Mediterranean that the former First Lord now sought to devote his exertions.

When a meeting of the Privy Council was held on May 27th for the swearing-in of the ministers of the new government, Sir Almeric Fitzroy, the Council's secretary, noticed that Churchill was looking 'restless and worried'.[75] This was not surprising: he must have been taken aback to find how little support there was for him either in the party or in the press during his imbroglio with Fisher. The Liberal backbenchers seemed to regard him, as the *Times* parliamentary correspondent reported, as a convenient scapegoat for the old government's mistakes and also as the precipitant of that government's final crisis, 'the author of all their ills'.[76] In this situation all the old suspicions of his behaviour that had been harboured by old-fashioned Liberals came to the fore, and it was even remembered against him that he had been a convert from Toryism. In a significant passage in the *Nation*, H. W. Massingham, its editor, once an ally of Churchill's but now evidently an enemy, complained that there was 'no obvious reason why the present end of his own career should entail the ruin of his adopted party'.[77] The sting was in the word 'adopted'. Massingham seemed to have forgotten that at one time even Gladstone had been the 'rising hope of the stern, unbending Tories'.

When the new Coalition Cabinet met for the first time, on the same day as that of the Privy Council meeting, Churchill observed with some quiet satisfaction that although he had now had some eight years' experience of Cabinets, he was still younger than all the newcomers by a margin of at least ten years.[78] That evening, at dinner at Admiralty House which was still his home, he seemed to a young lady guest to be 'dignified and unbitter', and when Clementine said that trouble with Fisher had been inevitable he replied, 'if I could do things over again, I would do just the same with regard to appointing Fisher, as he has done really great organising work'. He also expressed pleasure that Balfour was succeeding him, and described him, rather quaintly, as 'a great luxury'. His freedom from rancour was endearing, and his guest recorded 'I have never liked him so much'.[79]

The relations between Balfour and Churchill were now of course very close. Balfour had been a member of the War Council throughout, had long had a room at the Admiralty and, even more important, shared Churchill's views about the desirability of the Dardanelles operations. Now that Balfour had the power, it was his turn to offer the hospitality of the Admiralty to his predecessor. He told Churchill that he must not feel obliged to leave Admiralty House at once, but could take his time in finding alternative accommodation for himself and his family. This courteous behaviour was frowned upon by many in the Conservative Party, and J. S. Sandars, who had long been Balfour's private secretary, was so offended by it that he used it as a reason for breaking off relations with his distinguished employer just at the moment when he was taking office.[80]

In public, Churchill was determined to look on the bright side. Early in June he went up to Dundee to render a report to his constituents about his own record and to tell them what he thought the future might hold. Of his period in office, 'I have done my best,' he said: 'The archives in the Admiralty will show in the utmost detail the part I have played in all the great transactions that have taken place, and it is to them I look for my defence.' But in any case, although there had been a check at the Dardanelles, the prospects there were still bright: 'The army of Sir Ian Hamilton, the fleet of Admiral de Robeck, are separated only by a few miles from a victory such as this war has not yet seen.' At home, the time had come, he argued, for a far greater war effort, and he warned that this might mean the adoption of conscription:

> Our whole nation must be organised – must be socialised, if you like the word – must be organised and mobilised.... There must be asserted in some form or other by the government, a reserve power to give the necessary control and organising authority and to make sure that every one of every rank and condition, men and women as well, do in their own way, their full share.

The speech, which had started almost conversationally, rose to a climax on this note, and according to the *Times* correspondent aroused his audience to 'high enthusiasm'.[81]

But in the privacy of a dinner party in London the senior member for Dundee was inclined to be gloomy about the immediate prospects. One of the very few newspaper correspondents who were allowed to visit the Dardanelles, Ellis Ashmead-Bartlett, has left an account of a visit to Churchill at about this time, on his return from the Mediterranean. They met at dinner at Lady Randolph's home in Brook Street. Ashmead-Bartlett thought that

Churchill looked 'years older' and that he seemed 'very depressed'. Towards the end of dinner the former First Lord burst into a 'tremendous discourse' on the Dardanelles, directed ostensibly at his mother, who listened 'most attentively'. When the party broke up at midnight Ashmead-Bartlett accompanied Churchill back to the Admiralty. It was an hour at which, a few weeks earlier, Churchill could have had the Admiralty staff busy on many duties, but now the offices were empty:

> The ornate rooms and official papers seemed to mock him; the deserted hall so lately full of sycophants, admirers and place-seekers now only re-echoed with the sound of his own voice. He presented the perfect picture of a fallen Minister. Once again he cried out in the silent night, 'They never fought it out to a finish. They never gave my schemes a fair trial.'

Getting out the maps and plans, he talked to Ashmead-Bartlett until 3 a.m. about what might have been done and about what might yet be done. 'I left him restored to comparative good-humour and looking more like his old self again.'[82]

Certainly, all was not lost at the Dardanelles by the early summer of 1915. If it had been, Churchill would have resigned from the government at once. As it was, he could at least keep in touch with the latest information, which he obtained at the War Office every morning, and then he could urge his colleagues on the Dardanelles Committee to a policy of vigorous action at the earliest possible date. It was very frustrating not to be able to control the levers of power himself – as he later put it to a lady at a dinner party, it was like 'being bound head and foot, and watching one's best girl being – well, I won't say what'.[83] But he did what he could in small ways to speed up the flow of munitions, of which there was a great shortage. We hear of him, for instance, pressing officials at the Ministry of Munitions to try to arrange for an emergency supply of grenades to be sent out within forty-eight hours.[84] But the absence of executive authority made him very unhappy, and time hung heavily upon his hands. Lady Randolph wrote to her sister Clara (Mrs Moreton Frewen): 'I'm afraid Winston is very sad at having nothing to do.'[85] Marsh, his private secretary, admitted that 'The "Duchy" is of course a farce so far as work is concerned.' He wrote to Violet Asquith:

> I am miserably sorry for Winston. You can imagine what a horrible

wound and mutilation it is for him to be torn away from his work there [i.e. at the Admiralty] – and it's like Beethoven deaf.... However he has recovered his serenity.[86]

Churchill himself later described his plight even more vividly:

I knew everything and could do nothing.... Like a sea-beast fished up from the depths, or a diver too suddenly hoisted, my veins threatened to burst from the fall in pressure.[87]

In mid-June Churchill moved from Admiralty House to 22 Arlington Street, Piccadilly, the home of his cousin Ivor Guest, now Lord Wimborne, who had just become Lord-Lieutenant of Ireland. He could not go back to his house in Eccleston Square because he had let it to Sir Edward Grey.[88] His family – now augmented by a second daughter, Sarah, born when he was on his way home from Antwerp – were installed for a time at Hoe Farm, near Godalming in Surrey.[89] One weekend they were joined there by the family of his brother Jack, who was serving on Hamilton's staff at the Dardanelles. Jack's wife, Lady Gwendoline, or 'Goonie' as she was always known, was a keen amateur painter, and watching her Churchill suddenly decided to take up the art himself. He experimented with the paintbox of his nephew John, and when he returned to London he at once (according to Marsh) 'bought up the entire contents of Roberson's colour-shop in Piccadilly – easels, palettes, brushes, tubes and canvases'.[90]

Churchill never did anything by halves; and soon it became one of Marsh's duties to pose for his portrait at his minister's convenience. The result was apparently not very satisfactory, for Marsh was pleased when the canvas later disappeared.[91] But Churchill had enough talent to impress John Lavery, the portrait painter, who coached him in the ensuing months and encouraged him to continue. According to Lady Randolph, Lavery was convinced within a few months that Churchill could make a living as an artist if he chose – 'but of course,' she added, 'he uses it as an opiate'.[92] It was a genuine recreation for him, for as Violet Asquith noticed it was apparently the only activity that so concentrated his mind as to cause him to pursue it in silence.[93] There is an interesting study by Lavery, painted in 1915, which shows Churchill at work on a garden or landscape scene. Wearing a white coat and a Homburg hat and smoking a cigar, Churchill is seen standing with a palette in hand, evidently busily at work.[94]

He now made a habit of taking his easel and paints with him whenever he left London at the weekend. Aitken invited him to his home in Surrey, Cherkley Court, and thought that he himself would be able to get some of his own work done while Churchill was busy painting. But Churchill also brought to Cherkley a red despatch box containing many of his personal papers on the Dardanelles, and insisted on Aitken reading them while he himself was painting on the terrace.[95]

The Dardanelles Committee, set up under the First Coalition government to take charge of the operation from which it derived its name, was a most unsuitable body to conduct such a task. It was too large, consisting of twelve and later thirteen members; and it was too inexpert, consisting almost entirely of politicians. Churchill urged the Committee early in June to carry on the operation with the utmost vigour, arguing that an offensive on the Western Front could lead to no strategic gains, whereas even a few hundred yards on Gallipoli might be decisive.[96] It was in some part due to his arguments that the despatch was authorised, during June or July, of five fresh divisions as reinforcements for Hamilton's army. But the delays caused by the interregnum of government in May and by the disagreements in the War Council and the Dardanelles Committee allowed the Turks to strengthen their defences; and Hamilton was still very short of artillery to prepare the ground for an infantry advance. Since Hamilton and Churchill were close friends, it is just possible that if Churchill had been allowed to visit the Dardanelles in July, as he desired, and as indeed he had arranged with Kitchener, he might have avoided the tragedy that ensued. But his Conservative colleagues on the Dardanelles Committee heard of his project, and interposed a veto.[97]

On August 7th a fresh landing took place on Gallipoli, at Suvla Bay, and this was timed to coincide with attacks from the existing enclaves. But Hamilton's subordinates failed to exploit the advantages of surprise that they had on the first day, and the operations gradually petered out after heavy losses. A final great attack took place on August 21st – again without success and with heavy casualties. Among those killed was Churchill's friend from his Harrow days – Jack Milbanke, now Colonel Sir John Milbanke, wearing the ribbon of a Victoria Cross which he had won in the South African War.

Hamilton had meanwhile telegraphed the War Office asking for another 95,000 men to provide 'the necessary superiority'.[98] Such a large demand for reinforcements, coming after Hamilton's assurances that the five divisions would be sufficient for his purposes, met with strong opposition on the Dardanelles Committee, and this was augmented when Kitchener announced that he had decided to support General Joffre, the French Commander-in-Chief, in a major attack on the Western Front. Churchill's views carried less and less weight with his colleagues, and those who favoured cutting the losses at Gallipoli by an evacuation were further strengthened when Carson joined the Committee. Carson was as Hankey put it a 'veritable Dismal Jimmy', and he at once took up the cudgels against Churchill.[99] Thus at the Committee meeting on August 19th the following interchange took place: '*Mr Churchill* inquired why the losses incurred in Gallipoli were felt so much more, apparently, than the losses incurred in France. *Sir E. Carson* suggested that the reason was that in France the losses were incurred in killing Germans.'[100]

The Cabinet was also severely divided at this time on the question of introducing conscription. Lloyd George, Churchill and Curzon were all strongly in favour, but there was opposition from most of the other Liberal ministers, and also from Kitchener, who was very proud of his recruitment of a great volunteer army. Churchill himself wrote a remarkable memorandum for the Cabinet on the need for conscription as a preliminary to the efficient use of manpower. We could not, he said, 'afford to take men indiscriminately for service as they present themselves, without regard to their individual services or their usefulness in other spheres'.[101] No decision was reached on this matter for the time being. Asquith himself was undecided: Churchill described his position, with biting accuracy, as that of 'the man in the howdah – wherever the elephant [i.e. the Cabinet majority] goes he will go'.[102]

Meanwhile it became clear that the failure of the Allies at the Dardanelles was having unfortunate repercussions in the Balkans. The Bulgarians were preparing to enter the war on the German side, by an attack on Serbia. The only way to save Serbia from being completely occupied by the Germans, Austrians and Bulgarians seemed to be by sending an expeditionary force to Salonika. In view of the competing demands for troops, it became more and more likely that the Dardanelles Committee would decide to withdraw from Gallipoli, especially as the bad weather of winter was approaching and it would be difficult to maintain supplies, let alone to provide the troops with any winter comforts. Churchill urged a further attempt by the navy to force its way through the straits, and this was strongly backed by Commodore Keyes, who returned to England to try to persuade the Committee and the Admiralty to agree. But they had no success; and it became apparent that the evacuation of the peninsula would soon be ordered. On October 14th the Committee took a first step by ordering the replacement of Hamilton. General Sir Charles Monro was sent out in his place, with a free hand to recommend evacuation if he thought fit. On October 31st Monro telegraphed his view that Gallipoli should be evacuated. After some further delays, this course was adopted, but not before Churchill had ceased to be a member of the government.

He had for some time been aware that his influence, weak as it had been since the coalition was formed, was becoming still weaker; and he did not want to be saddled with responsibility for events over which he had no control. 'It is odious to me', he wrote to Seely, 'to remain here watching sloth and folly with full knowledge and no occupation.'[103] In early September he again asked Asquith to give him a field command. He thought that the rank of a major-general and the command of an army corps would be appropriate to someone of his knowledge and experience. The request was embarrassing to both Asquith and Kitchener, who had had to face criticism when Seely, another politician turned soldier, had been given command of a division. Kitchener told Asquith that he 'would like to get rid of Churchill, but could not offend the Army'.[104] Churchill then suggested as an alternative that he should become 'Governor-General and Military Commander-in-Chief in British East Africa'.[105] It seems that he had the idea that he could mobilise an African army to serve in Europe.

Early in November Asquith at last decided that the Dardanelles Committee was no longer serving a useful purpose, and that the best thing would be to reconstitute it as a 'War Committee' with a smaller membership, to supervise the conduct of operations generally. Churchill was not included in the membership of this new body, and as the reason for his continued membership of the government had now disappeared he had no alternative but to resign, even though no other employment had been offered to him by the Prime Minister. Hankey had suggested that Churchill be sent to Russia to organise the despatch of munitions to the Eastern Front; but nothing came of this.[106] On November 12th, the day after the composition of the War Committee had been announced to the Cabinet, Churchill wrote to Asquith saying that he could not stay in a post of 'well-paid inactivity' and that he now proposed to place himself 'unreservedly at the disposal of the military authorities, observing that my regiment is in France'.[107]

There was an epilogue to Churchill's career as a member of the Asquith administration. On November 15th he once again took the corner seat immediately behind the Treasury Bench in the House of Commons, whence his father had made his resignation speech twenty-nine years earlier. He then delivered a personal statement, which could be regarded as an interim defence of his role in the war, principally in the period of his tenure of the office of First Lord. In all the episodes which had led to criticism of his own actions – the sinking of the three armoured cruisers, Antwerp, the Battle of Coronel, and the Dardanelles operation – he showed that he had always had the support of the appropriate naval experts. He put the point clearly and distinctly:

There is no important act of policy, no scheme of fleet redistribution, of movements of ships or of plans of war which have been acted on during my tenure at the Admiralty in which the First Sea Lord has not concurred in writing.[108]

It was an impressive self-defence; but Asquith, who made a brief following speech to acknowledge Churchill's statement and to wish him well, spoke no word to suggest that he himself was as responsible as the former First Lord for the Dardanelles operation, and more so for the Gallipoli landings.

11. *Battalion Commander and Opposition Spokesman*

THE few days after his resignation speech Churchill spent largely in preparing for his departure for France to join his regiment. He was pleased by the reactions to his speech: *The Times* described it as 'an undoubted Parliamentary triumph' and the *Manchester Guardian* lamented his resignation as 'a grave public misfortune'. C. P. Scott, the *Guardian* editor, had visited him a few days previously and had been shown some of the confidential papers about the Dardanelles operation.[1] The Churchill family was now living at 41 Cromwell Road, which they shared with Jack Churchill's family. There were two nurses and two nursery-maids to look after the children, and so it was a large household.[2] On the 16th there was a farewell luncheon party, at which Violet Asquith and her step-mother Margot were present: they arrived to find 'baggage and other military impedimenta' in the hall and on the landings. Churchill was excited at the prospect of going to the front but, as Violet said, 'for most of us it was a kind of a wake'.[3]

There was another day of farewells on the 17th, and Churchill was telling his friends that every morning he felt 'fresh chunks of responsibility' falling away from him.[4] If this pleased him, it distressed his closest friends. That night Aitken called at 41 Cromwell Road, and found the whole household 'upside down':

Downstairs, Mr Eddie Marsh, his faithful secretary, was in tears.... Upstairs, Lady Randolph was in a state of despair at the idea of her brilliant son being relegated to the trenches. Mrs Churchill seemed to be the only person who remained calm, collected and efficient.[5]

Next day (the 18th) he donned his uniform, that of a major in the Oxfordshire Hussars (Territorial Army), and started his journey to join his regiment at St Omer. 'I have no plans,' he wrote to Seely, 'except to remain with them.'[6]

He crossed the Channel in a regular steamer crowded with officers and men returning from leave. It was not the way he had travelled to France on previous occasions during the war. Asquith had noted with some amusement his 'usual regal fashion' of making journeys as First Lord – special train to the coast, a destroyer detailed to the task of making his journey as fast as possible, and then an Admiralty car in France.[7] This time he did not expect to be met on landing, but to his surprise on leaving the ship he discovered that French, the Commander-in-Chief, had sent a car with instructions that he was to be brought to his head-quarters at the château of Blondecque near St Omer. 'We dined together almost alone, and talked long on the war situation on the same footing as if I had still been First Lord.'[8]

Next morning French offered him command of a brigade, and Churchill readily accepted, but said that he must first undergo an apprenticeship in trench warfare as it was now being waged. French invited him to choose an appropriate division to join for this apprenticeship, and he chose the Guards. So Major Churchill shortly found himself with a battalion of the Grenadier Guards which was just moving into the line in front of Merville.

Churchill at first found that the Commanding Officer of his battalion, Lieutenant-Colonel George Jeffreys, was very cold with him. 'I think I ought to tell you', he said, 'that we were not at all consulted in the matter of your coming to join us.'[9] Jeffreys combined strongly Conservative politics with a contempt for would-be soldiers who were not regular Guardsmen; to make matters worse, he was an Etonian.[10] Churchill also found that the battalion, including its officers, were living in great discomfort, as there were no communication trenches and they had to live on the kit that they carried with them 'over the top' into the line. He nevertheless soon settled down, and asked to accompany the Colonel on his twice-daily rounds of the trenches. Gradually, Jeffreys' attitude towards him began to soften; and when the battalion's Second-in-Command went home on leave, Churchill was invited to take his place. He later said that he regarded this as 'one of the greatest honours I had ever received'.[11]

There was in Churchill's view one serious drawback about the battalion: its headquarter mess, on Jeffreys' orders, was 'dry'. He therefore asked if he could further develop his knowledge of warfare by living with a company in the trenches. Jeffreys agreed and he moved to join the company commanded by Edward Grigg, a young officer whom he had known before the war. In spite of the alternation of frost and rain and the dangerous condition of the trenches, which had to be repaired under enemy fire, he was impressed by the 'indomitable good temper' and 'inflexible discipline' of the Grenadiers.[12] It seems that he really enjoyed his month with them. In a letter to Curzon on December 8th he wrote: 'I do not know when I have passed a more joyous three weeks.... It is a jolly life with nice people; and one does not seem to mind the cold and wet and general discomfort.'[13] He might have mentioned the danger as well as the discomfort. He had a particularly narrow escape when the frail sandbagged shelter which was his temporary home received a direct hit from a 'whizz-bang' or artillery shell – fortunately for him, at a time when he had been called out of the line.[14]

Trench warfare was regarded, rightly, as a gruelling experience that required constant reliefs. Every few days the front-line troops were withdrawn for a 'rest' period, usually equivalent in length to their period in the trenches. It was in the first of his 'rest' periods that Churchill sat down to compose one of the most important of his State Papers – a paper which, although written by one no longer in the government, was printed and circulated by the War Committee. It was called 'Variants of the Offensive', and contained proposals for the use of caterpillar vehicles, a number of which he had bravely authorised to be built under the title 'landships' out of Admiralty funds when he was still First Lord.[15] The idea had really developed from the use of armoured cars to protect the naval airmen at Dunkirk; the armoured cars were very successful until the enemy began to dig trenches across the roads. For a time Churchill thought the solution would be a form of steamroller; but Capt. Murray Sueter, the Director of the Admiralty Air Division, had persuaded him by a demonstration on the Horse Guards Parade in February 1915 that the solution lay in the use of caterpillar track.[16] Now Churchill elaborated the tactical implications of the new weapon: it would be able not only to crush barbed wire and to run down the enemy trenches but also to bring enfilading fire to bear on their defenders. More than any other single person in high office, Churchill was responsible for developing the tank, which was the one weapon which seemed capable of restoring mobility to the battlefield.

Churchill had completed his apprenticeship with the Guards by mid-December, and Jeffreys had reported favourably upon his keenness and progress.[17] French recalled him to his head-quarters, and arranged that he should have a brigade in the 19th (Western) Division, whose commander, General Tom Bridges, he had known in the South African War. But this appointment was no sooner agreed than it was countermanded. It appears that French had mentioned it to Asquith when he was on a visit to London, and Asquith had strongly advised against its confirmation.[18] The Prime Minister was probably still afraid of the political repercussions if Seely's rapid military promotion was repeated in Churchill's case. It was as it happened just at this point that French was replaced as Commander-in-Chief by General Douglas Haig – who was much less inclined to look with special favour upon a politician turned soldier. Haig's view was that Churchill could not be made a brigadier until he had 'shown that he could bear responsibility in action as C.O. of a battalion'.[19] So Churchill found himself appointed to the command of the 6th Battalion, the Royal Scots Fusiliers, which was in the 9th (Scottish) Division, part of Kitchener's 'New Army'.

The 6th Royal Scots Fusiliers was mostly composed of Lowland Scots who had volunteered for service in the early days of the war. They had lost heavily in French's offensive at Loos in the autumn of 1915, and were now rather short of their full complement. The officers were nearly all volunteers; but Churchill managed to secure the appointment to his battalion of a regular officer whom he had known in pre-war days. This was Sir Archibald Sinclair, a twenty-five-year-old Guardsman and aristocrat – fortunately also a Scot – who had been a keen pioneer airman and was now ADC to General Seely. Sinclair became Churchill's second-in-command. The battalion was engaged in reorganisation and re-training when Churchill joined it; and his first act, after meeting the officers, was to insist on a de-lousing operation: 'War is declared, gentlemen, on the lice.' Three or four days were spent in frenzied but successful scrubbing, and soon there was a 'manifest smartening-up' of the battalion.[20] In spite of the effort involved, the men were delighted to have so distinguished a commanding officer. The officers also gradually succumbed to his charm at dinner in the HQ Mess, where he talked freely about politics. 'Regarding Mr Asquith at that time he was somewhat bitter.'[21]

In January 1916 the battalion moved into the line at Ploeg-steert, or 'Plug Street' as it was called by the soldiers – a place just inside the corner of Belgium that was still in Allied hands. Churchill worked hard to look after his troops, visiting the line three times a day and insisting on careful sandbagging and equally careful positioning of sentries to prevent their being exposed unnecessarily to enemy fire. He allowed himself a few luxuries which the men could not share: among these was a French military helmet, which was more comfortable than the clumsy British version; and also a tin bath for personal hygiene, which however he was prepared to loan to his fellow-officers.[22] He carried a pocket Shakespeare with him to read when he had time; but he encouraged Eddie Marsh to write to him as often as he liked, as he said that he did little reading except of letters that he received.[23]

On the whole, the front was inactive while Churchill was serving with his battalion. This may have bored him a little, as he was never more pleased than when in the midst of a hail of bullets and shells. He could, however, conjure up his own 'war', as the commander of the divisional artillery, Brigadier-General H. H. Tudor, was an old friend of his and would respond to a request for a bombardment of the enemy trenches in Churchill's sector – and this, of course, would lead to a counter-bombardment.[24] Churchill also had many distinguished visitors call on him when they visited the front. F. E. Smith, the Attorney-General arrived without an official pass and was arrested and taken to base on the orders of the Adjutant-General – an incident that caused some ill-feeling for a time.[25] Other visitors included General Seely, who sang a song at a soldiers' concert, playing his own accompaniment. The most popular thing Churchill did, however, so far as his troops were concerned, was to insist on his visitors making a tour of the trenches, where their elegant service-dress ran the risk of getting torn on the wire and their highly polished boots became covered in mud.[26]

Early in March Churchill secured a week's leave, and he

returned to the Commons to take part in the debate on the Navy Estimates. He was unhappy about the loss of vigour at the Admiralty since he and Fisher had left it, and after Balfour had made his statement as First Lord, and with Fisher 'sitting in the gallery like a sphinx',[27] he uttered what he described as 'a jarring note, a note not of reproach, nor of censure, nor of panic, but a note in some respects of warning'.[28] He urged the need for a still larger programme of ship-building in order to be sure of keeping well ahead of Germany. If he had left it at that, his speech would have been regarded as a valuable corrective to Admiralty complacency, and a major step on the way to the re-assertion of his own position in the House. But he concluded with a very unexpected demand for the recall of Fisher as First Sea Lord. Since it was little more than nine months since his quarrel with Fisher had led to his own fall and also a change of government, observers could not understand his motive and supposed it was due to some intrigue.

Balfour had little difficulty in showing the inconsistency of Churchill's attitude. The fact was that Churchill had no hard feelings against Fisher and genuinely believed that his talents were required in order to push ahead the shipbuilding effort that seemed to be called for. But his error lay in supposing that this was an appropriate moment for him to urge the restoration of Fisher to office, and that Fisher's chances of being restored would be improved thereby. He had some excuse for not properly assessing the political situation – for he could not easily gauge Westminster opinion from 'Plug Street' – but he was badly advised by those he consulted, who included Fisher himself and the editors C. P. Scott and J. L. Garvin. Repington of *The Times* heard that Churchill had been 'up until 4 a.m. with Garvin before his Navy speech' and commented, 'This accounts for the mess he made of it.'[29] The general reaction to the speech was very hostile, and Churchill again became the object of attack, not of course in Scott's *Manchester Guardian* or in Garvin's *Observer*, but in much of the rest of the press. The *Spectator* declared:

He has played the part of a political adventurer, and played it with a skill and audacity, but also with a want of scruple and want of consideration for public interests and with a reckless selfishness, to which our political history affords no parallel, or affords it alone in the political life of Charles James Fox.[30]

It was perhaps remarkable that such a harsh view of Churchill could gain credence; even more remarkable that Lloyd George should speak of the *Spectator*'s words to a friend as 'on the whole very true'.[31]

But in spite of the need to live down this disfavour Churchill became increasingly convinced that there was a strong case for his early return to Westminster. It was evident that the government was in serious difficulty, because its leading members were divided about policy, and especially about conscription. There was widespread impatience with Asquith's lack of leadership, and Lloyd George was on the verge of resigning and going into opposition with the object of effecting a change. Under such circumstances, Churchill would obviously have a major role to play; and not only Fisher and Scott but also Aitken, who was in close touch with politics at the highest level owing to his association with Bonar Law, urged him to leave the army and return to life at Westminster. Churchill did not take the advice at once: but he went back to France in an unusual state of irresolution. He wrote to Aitken a few days later:

> The problem wh now faces me is vy difficult: my work out here with all its risk & all its honour wh I greatly value: on the other hand the increasingly grave situation of the war and the feeling of knowledge & of power to help in mending matters wh is strong within me: add to this dilemma the awkwardness of changing and the cause of my I hope unusual hesitations is obvious.[32]

Shortly afterwards, a change in his military status helped to make up his mind for him. In April he was told that owing to the shortage of manpower his battalion, the 6th, was to be merged with the 7th Battalion the Royal Scots Fusiliers. The Commanding Officer of the 7th Battalion, who was senior to him, would take command of the new unit. Hence Churchill was now free to say that 'he had not left his battalion, because his battalion had left him'.[33] With this news he returned to England on further leave and began to plan to 'form a strong opposition' in alliance with any others who would join him.[34] He found the government on the point of collapse on the conscription issue, with Lloyd George threatening to resign if a definite decision was not made. Eventually the crisis was settled by a compromise, much to the disappointment of Churchill, who saw Lloyd George and tried to persuade him to come out and lead the opposition.[35]

Churchill returned to France to tidy up his affairs and those of his battalion. One last generous endeavour of his was to visit other units – indeed he 'borrowed motor cars and *scoured* France'[36] – trying to fix up his officers in suitable posts. His adjutant, Capt. A. D. Gibb, a Scottish advocate, was very sorry to see him go: 'I am firmly convinced that no more popular officer ever commanded troops. As a soldier he was hard-working, persevering and tough.... He loved soldiering: it lay near his heart and I think he could have been a very great soldier.' Gibb recalled particularly Churchill's remark that 'War is a game to be played with a smiling face.' 'Never', he said, 'was precept more constantly practised than this.'[37] On May 9th 1916 Churchill was back in London and that day he issued a statement to say that he was 'on leave of absence' and intended to 'resume his Parliamentary and political duties'.[38] Three weeks later the *London Gazette* announced that Major the Rt Hon. W. L. S. Churchill, Oxfordshire Yeomanry (Territorial Army), had relinquished his temporary rank of Lieutenant-Colonel. His active military career was over.[39]

On his return to political life Churchill had two main problems to face. He had to safeguard his financial position by earning a living for himself and his family; and he had to restore his reputation in the face of criticism of his conduct as First Lord of the Admiralty. The first of these problems was much the easier to deal with. As a journalist of the first rank and as an ex-minister of rare experience he could command an exceptional price for articles in the press. Newspaper magnates who opposed his return to government were quite willing to use his services to attract new readers to their journals. In July 1916 he wrote four articles for the *Sunday Pictorial*, for which he was paid the sum of £1000. At this rate, he reckoned that he could earn £5000 a year without difficulty – and this would equal his salary as First Lord and exceed that which he received as Chancellor of the Duchy.[40] The articles were about the outbreak of war and its opening phases: after the first had been published, the editor was able to announce that the circulation of the paper had reached almost 2½ million copies, which was a record.[41]

There followed a series of monthly articles on current developments in the war which was published in the *London Magazine* from October 1916 onwards until March 1917. They were paid for at £500 apiece, and were enough by themselves to enable Churchill to attain his financial target.[42] The *London Magazine* was owned by Northcliffe, who at the end of 1915 had instructed the editor of the *Daily Mail* not on any account to 'puff' Churchill: 'We got rid of the man with difficulty and he is trying to come back. "Puffing" will bring him back.'[43] But it was a different matter if Churchill's name could be used to improve the sales of a Harmsworth newspaper. Since Churchill also sold a few occasional articles to the American press his financial situation must if anything have benefited from his loss of office. And he still had time for a good deal of painting.

The remedy for his unpopularity in political circles, however, was less easily found. He did not enjoy having his speeches interrupted with the cry 'What about the Dardanelles?'[44] He was therefore anxious – as were, for different reasons, many other backbenchers in Parliament – that the government should publish the papers about the Dardanelles and Gallipoli as soon as possible. It was with no little satisfaction that he heard Bonar Law's announcement on June 1st that a decision had been made in favour of this course.[45] But Hankey was at once upset about the revelations of confidential information that this would involve, and wrote a long memorandum to the Prime Minister explaining how awkward it would be.[46] Asquith realised, however, that he could not entirely resist parliamentary pressure; and in the upshot it was agreed that a commission should be set up to hear evidence and to present a report on the operation. A similar commission was decided on for the Mesopotamia expedition, for which Churchill had had no responsibility at all, but which had also ended in disaster, though on a smaller scale.

The Dardanelles Commission was presided over by Lord Cromer, the former pro-consul of Egypt who had helped Churchill in his research for *The River War* seventeen years earlier. Cromer was now old and poorly, and the task of presiding over the Commission in its early stages was his last service to the State. He thought that his colleagues – who included several MPs – were 'harsh in judgment': but at least he persuaded them to produce an agreed first report.[47]

The Commission began to hear evidence in September 1916, and Hankey, who presented the case for the government, was an early witness. Churchill prepared an extensive statement of his own for which he secured the aid of both Hankey and F. E. Smith

– the latter as a personal friend rather than in his office as Attorney-General. It was not an easy task to tell the story in such a way as to justify his own position without throwing blame directly on others: but Churchill aimed to do this as far as possible, as he had made up his mind not to indulge in recriminations. He told Fisher 'no single word shall escape me' to the latter's detriment;[48] and when he began his evidence on September 25th he announced to the Commission:

> I am here to defend those by whose professional advice I was guided and those who carried out the operations. This includes all, without exception. Therefore, in what I am about to say I do not seek to transfer responsibility to any officer serving under the Admiralty.[49]

His principal object in his testimony was to show that the forcing of the Dardanelles was a plan which had the support of his competent naval advisers at the time that it was authorised, and that nothing was done by him which did not have the approval of the appropriate naval experts. Above all, he asserted that Fisher on January 28th had 'definitely consented' to undertake the Dardanelles attack: 'I state this positively. Well I state everything positively, but I state this super-positively.'[50] As for the fact that the operation was in the end a failure: 'It is idle to condemn operations because they involve hazard and uncertainty. All war is hazard. Victory is only wrested by running risks.'[51] In any case, responsibility for the vastly more expensive operations by the army was carried by Lord Kitchener, and this was symbolised by the transfer to his command of the Royal Naval Division.

Churchill was examined on his evidence at the next meeting of the Commission, on October 4th, and then three weeks later he was allowed to examine witnesses himself, which he did on three successive days. He showed a complete mastery of the evidence, and although many of the Admiralty witnesses professed to have been more lukewarm about the operation than Churchill had ever realised, much of what he said was confirmed by Fisher who in a letter to the Commission paid him a special tribute: 'I backed him up till I resigned. *I would do the same again!* He had courage and imagination! *He was a War Man!*'[52] Fisher also entertained the Commission by asserting that the warmest supporter of the operation was Balfour, Churchill's successor as First Lord:

The one man ... whose influence carried the day absolutely, was Mr Balfour. He was beautiful! He has got the brain of Moses, and the voice of Aaron. He would talk a bird out of a tree, and they were all carried away with him. I was not, myself.[53]

The Commission's First Report, signed in January 1917, dealt with the origins and inception of the enterprise, and naturally covered the whole of the entirely naval operation, where Churchill's responsibility was direct. The report criticised him in its conclusions only for not ensuring that 'the views of the Naval Advisers were clearly put before the [War] Council'.[54] It was felt that he had been 'carried away by his sanguine temperament and his firm belief in the success of the operation which he advocated'.[55] But the main criticism of the Commissioners fell upon Asquith as Prime Minister for holding no meeting of the War Council between March 19th and May 14th, and also for 'the atmosphere of vagueness and want of precision which seems to have characterised the proceedings of the War Council'.[56] There was also some censure of Kitchener for having failed to make use of his General Staff, which resulted in 'confusion and want of efficiency';[57] and also for delays in authorising the despatch of troops – delays which Churchill had correctly protested against. But Kitchener escaped relatively lightly, because he could not be examined by the Commission, having died by drowning on the way to Russia in June 1916.

Churchill was moderately pleased with the Report when he first read it in February, having obtained an advance copy from Lloyd George.[58] Hankey, who saw him at the time, asked him what he thought of it: 'He said he was satisfied, but the tone of his voice indicated disappointment.'[59] No doubt he was disappointed not to be more fully rehabilitated: but as he came to realise when it was published in March the Report disposed of many of the accusations against himself, and also directed attention to the faults of the Asquith government's methods of control, for which, of course, the Prime Minister was principally to blame. Although he could see that the narrative of the Report was by no means perfect – indeed he described it in private as 'curiously careless and inaccurate'[60] – nevertheless, as he told the Commons when it was debated, he regarded it as 'an instalment of fair play'. So far as his personal responsibility was concerned, he said, 'The burden that I have hitherto borne alone is now shared with the most eminent men which this country has produced within the lifetime of a whole generation in Parliament, in the Army, in the Fleet.'[61]

Meanwhile Churchill had been serving, somewhat intermittently, as an Opposition Front Bench spokesman, sometimes making very powerful speeches in criticism of the government, but sometimes failing to attend the House for long periods. He was not, of course, opposed to the prosecution of the war; on the contrary, he wanted it prosecuted more vigorously and efficiently. His criticism was therefore always constructive in character. To begin with, much of it derived from his experience in the trenches and the attitudes that he encountered among the troops there. A speech which he delivered on the manpower question within a few weeks of leaving the army reflected this most strongly. His view was that the front-line soldiers suffered severely from what he described as 'One of the clearest and grimmest class distinctions ever drawn in this world, the distinction between the trench and the non-trench population.'[62] The two elements were kept so completely separate that for long periods at the Dardanelles and in France fighting units would be well below strength after suffering casualties, while all the support units would be at full strength. This was very un-economical and could be remedied if the War Office would only look more critically at its use of able-bodied men behind the lines: 'We hear a good deal ... about "comb this industry" or "comb that", or "comb this Department or that", but I say to the War Office, "Physician, comb thyself".'[63]

He wanted to see the resources of the Empire as a whole brought into fuller use, whether to fight or to work, and urged a more active policy of recruitment in India and Africa. This was a point which Repington, the *Times* military correspondent, urged upon him in the frequent discussions about military affairs which they had in these months when Churchill was out of office.[64] He reminded the House of what was in fact happening to British soldiers every day of the year:

Nearly a thousand men – Englishmen, Britishers, men of our own race – are knocked into bundles of bloody rags every twenty-four hours, and carried away to hasty graves or to field ambulances.[65]

It was no wonder that society ladies who met him at the dinner-table or at the weekend parties that still took place, albeit on a reduced scale, found that he was inclined to be glum at times and that he would hardly ever talk about anything except the war – unless it were to describe his one recreation of painting, in which he continued industriously to develop his technique.[66]

In July there began the great offensive on the Somme, in which Kitchener's volunteers were thrown against the enemy lines in a sustained attempt to secure a breakthrough. Churchill was doubtful from the start about the chances of success, and when the news began to filter back of catastrophic losses in return for tiny morsels of enemy-occupied territory, he felt it necessary to prepare a paper on the folly of this type of warfare. His statement was designed to show that far from wearing down the enemy's forces by inflicting heavier casualties than were received, which was what Haig and his staff thought they were doing, the British losses exceeded those of the Germans by a factor of about three to one.[67] Churchill showed the paper to his friend 'F.E.', now the Attorney-General, and 'F.E.' took the responsibility of circulating it to the Cabinet.[68] Churchill underestimated the German losses, which probably came to about two for every three British, owing to the German commanders' insistence on counter-offensives to recover lost ground.[69] But he was certainly correct in his general assumption that offensive action was more costly than defensive. These arguments did not, however, carry weight with ministers, many of whom still felt that he was to blame for Gallipoli and that as an 'amateur' he was not likely to be wiser than the professionals of Haig's staff.

This issue was not one that could be thrashed out in open session of Parliament. To do so would have been to endanger both military and civil morale, and Churchill was not prepared to do this. He could, and did, raise questions in the House about the rapid return of wounded men to the trenches as soon as they were adjudged fit once more; he thought this unjust, and urged that older men who had not yet served should be called up to serve instead.[70] He demanded the promotion of men of talent who had joined as volunteers early in the war; and he urged a more generous policy of awarding medals and decorations to those who had behaved with exceptional courage in the face of the enemy.[71] He also pointed out that British trenches were much less elaborate, comfortable and secure than those of the enemy, and he urged that greater efforts should be made to improve their quality, and that a system of light railways should be set up to improve mobility and supply. He argued that British night flares were by no means as good as German, and that there was still a shortage of steel helmets.[72] All this was a formidable agenda for the new Secretary for War, Lloyd George, who had now succeeded to the administrative responsibilities somewhat imperfectly borne in preceding months by Kitchener.

At sea, the greatest naval battle of the war was fought at the end of May 1916, in what became known in Britain as the Battle of Jutland. The German fleet did not risk more than a few relatively brief encounters with the British, but in the exchanges of fire that took place heavy losses were suffered by Beatty's battle-cruisers, owing to explosions in the powder magazines after direct hits on the gun-turrets. Three British battle-cruisers were sunk, as against one German battleship and one battle-cruiser. In total tonnage and manpower the British losses were twice as great as those of the enemy. The Germans announced a victory, and the first British Admiralty statement, made before Jellicoe's report was complete, was by no means reassuring. Admiral Brownrigg, the Naval Censor, hit on the idea of inviting Churchill to look at the official reports and to draft a statement for the press, to be published under his own name.[73] This was a most unusual step, although it was a remarkable tribute to the former First Lord's journalistic skill. Churchill demurred for a time, but then agreed to undertake the task if he was personally asked to do so by Balfour. Balfour then made the request, and Churchill produced his statement, in which he pointed out that the enemy had lost a larger proportion of his forces than Jellicoe had done. The statement undoubtedly did go some way to reassure public opinion; but the use of an unofficial and indeed in the eyes of many a discredited commentator seemed to put the Admiralty itself in a very poor light. Churchill later said that if he had wished deliberately to bring the Admiralty into disrepute he could hardly have done it more effectively.[74]

Churchill was still so unpopular with the press, and particularly with the Northcliffe press, that he found he could make little impact on the country by making speeches in the Commons. In August he made an urgent demand for state control of shipping, to keep down freight charges, and he urged the introduction of food rationing as an alternative to the restriction of consumption solely by rising prices which he thought 'the most cruel and the most unfair manner of dealing with a great national and economic problem'. 'In time of war, particularly,' he argued,

> ... you should have regard for the broader claims of social justice.
> A war with all its evils should at least be a great equaliser in these
> matters. If we are to look upon the whole nation as an army, on
> our men and women as an army struggling for a common purpose,
> then they are all entitled to their rations. . . .[75]

This was a strong call: but it evoked little response even in
Liberal and Labour quarters – except in the *Manchester Guardian*, which under C. P. Scott was his most loyal ally among a
predominantly hostile body of commentators. Not long after this
Churchill decided to spend less time in the Commons and to seek
to influence opinion more directly by himself writing articles for
the press about the immediate issues of public policy. The *Sunday
Pictorial* was prepared to serve as the vehicle of his views, and to
pay him, not £500 per article as before, but at any rate £250.[76]

Meanwhile Lloyd George was taking very much the same line
as Churchill's in discussions on policy within the government. He
wanted to see an intensification of effort, to secure the 'knock-out'
of the enemy which he had demanded in a public speech at the end
of September. It was difficult for him to make any move against
Asquith's leadership unless some strong manifestation of discontent took place outside the government. Early in November this
took the form of a division on the question of the government's
policy with regard to enemy assets in Nigeria – a matter of very
little general interest, but one which gave an opportunity of
assessing the personal popularity of the Colonial Secretary, Bonar
Law, who was also Leader of the Conservative Party and primarily
responsible for the party's participation in the Coalition under
Asquith's leadership. The government carried the vote, but only
by 231 votes to 117, and no less than 65 Conservatives went into
the opposition lobby. Bonar Law was at once advised by his close
friend Aitken to re-establish his hold on his party by turning
against Asquith; but he was naturally reluctant to give way so
quickly to a backbench revolt, and when he visited Aitken a few
days later and found himself subjected to a fierce tirade against
the Coalition from Churchill, who happened to be visiting and
had also voted with the Conservative rebels, he abruptly threatened him with a general election, which Churchill regarded as
'the most terribly immoral thing he had ever heard of'.[77]

There was in fact no need for a general election. Lloyd George apparently took the Nigeria vote as a green light for him to put pressure on Asquith for a drastic reorganisation of the government, including the establishment of a small committee to run the war. In the end, Asquith refused to permit any transfer of power from his own hands, and when Bonar Law supported Lloyd George the Prime Minister was forced to resign. To Asquith's surprise, Lloyd George, when invited by the King to form a government on the evening of December 6th, rapidly proved able to do so. He formed a War Cabinet consisting only of himself, Bonar Law, Curzon and two newcomers to the top leadership – Lord Milner, who had not held office since he ceased to be High Commissioner for South Africa in 1905, and Arthur Henderson, the Labour Party chairman, who owed his promotion to Lloyd George's desire to detach his party from its previous position of loyalty to Asquith. Carson, who had led the Conservative rebels, became First Lord of the Admiralty, outside the War Cabinet; he was, however, to join the War Cabinet in 1917.

Although Churchill had not yet received his partial exoneration from the Dardanelles Commission, he confidently expected to be restored to office when Lloyd George, who shared his attitude to the war, became Prime Minister. He did not realise how hostile many of the Conservative leaders still were to the idea of his reappearance in the government. Four of them, indeed, who were acting together at the time – Curzon, Lord Robert Cecil, Austen Chamberlain and Walter Long – made it a condition of their adherence to Lloyd George's government that he should refuse office to both Churchill and Northcliffe.[78] Lloyd George accepted this condition, and asked Max Aitken to convey a hint to Churchill that he could not expect office. Aitken did so when they met at dinner at F. E. Smith's that evening: but Churchill was furious when he realised what he was being told, and burst out roughly to his host: 'Smith, this man knows I am not to be included in the new Government.' Angry words then passed between him and Aitken and without further ado Churchill gathered up his hat and coat and left the dinner-party, pursued into the street by 'F.E.' in a vain attempt to persuade him to return.[79]

On December 10th Lloyd George sent a more deliberate message of apology to Churchill through the medium of their common friend George Riddell. Churchill told Riddell, 'His conscience will tell him what he should do', and asked him to convey that message back to Lloyd George and to say that in the meantime he

(Churchill) would not allow his freedom of action to be restricted.[80] Churchill could not believe that Lloyd George had had
no option but to leave him out of the ministry. He told C. P.
Scott in March that the Prime Minister 'professed that he had
tried [to reinstate him in office] but the Tories would not let him.'
Churchill's view was that Lloyd George 'did not behave well to
me'.[81] There was nothing for it but to speak his mind on policy,
either in the House or in the *Sunday Pictorial,* and to carry on
painting.

Churchill's new series of articles in the *Sunday Pictorial* was
more effective in dealing with current problems than his earlier
series in the *London Magazine* had been, because there had always
been a lapse of several weeks between the submission of his copy
to the *London Magazine* and its appearance in print. Churchill
took up several topics of immediate political importance in his
new series. Early in April he demanded a more scientific use of
manpower, and pointed to the need to strike a balance between
the requirements of industry and the forces: 'Machines may be a
substitute for men.... Mechanical devices of all kinds augment
the power of the human hand and shield the sacred chalice of
human life.'[82]

Late in the same month he urged the appointment of Smuts,
the South African Prime Minister, to the British War Cabinet,
so as to make the latter the nucleus of an Empire Cabinet:
Lloyd George was later to follow this course.[83] In May he hailed
the entry of the United States into the war, but declared that
although this guaranteed an eventual victory it did not mean that
there were not serious difficulties still ahead: 'We have got to
hold on.'[84]

Meanwhile, as we have seen, the Dardanelles Commission had
reported and had largely exonerated him from the great weight
of the Dardanelles failure. He now found that there was more
sympathy for his utterances in Parliament;[85] and he demanded
that Parliament itself should 'watch with severe attention the
course and management of the war'. He deplored the fact that
the Press had assumed 'altogether disproportionate power' as a
result of the 'abdication of Parliament' and the absence of party
politics and elections. He once more demanded a Secret Session,
so that matters which could not be stated publicly, albeit not
necessarily highly secret, could be effectively discussed.[86] He put
this demand formally to the government through the Chief Whip,

and although it was not backed by Asquith and the rump of Liberal ex-ministers who now sat on the Opposition benches it was acceded to by Lloyd George.[87] When the Secret Session opened, on May 10th, Churchill was the first to speak. He argued that the military position was far more grave than the public realised, owing to the failure of a new Allied offensive planned by General Nivelle, the new French Commander-in-Chief. He asked pointedly, 'Is it not true that the French have suffered a great disappointment? Is it not true that our offensive has been brought to a standstill?'[88] Lloyd George replied with an able debating speech, but it was apparent that Churchill's contribution to the debate had impressed the House.

Since the publication of the Dardanelles Report Lloyd George had been seeking some means of bringing Churchill back into the government. He no longer felt Churchill to be a personal rival, as he had done in the early months of the war; and his attitude softened accordingly. He also wished to strengthen the Liberal element in the Coalition. He first asked Christopher Addison, the Minister of Munitions, if it would be practicable to put Churchill in charge of tank production; but Addison demurred, on the grounds that 'a man like Winston' could not be put into 'a minor post like that: it would be sure to lead to trouble'.[89] Addison promised to see if there was any other post that Churchill could suitably fill: but nothing had been found by the time of the Secret Session. However, the debate had shown so clearly that Churchill was the outstanding man among the government's critics that Lloyd George no longer hesitated to promise him an early return to office. He had a word with him immediately after the debate, and nine days later Churchill lunched with Lloyd George at the latter's house at Walton Heath.[90]

There were still grave difficulties in the Prime Minister's path before he could fulfil his promise. The supporters of the government in the Liberal Party were not likely to object to Churchill's return to office, and the new government's Chief Whip, Freddie Guest, was Churchill's cousin and, as ever, his loyal friend. Guest argued strongly for Churchill's reinstatement, so much so indeed that some of the Conservative leaders complained about his enthusiasm.[91] Lloyd George had first thought of making Churchill Minister of Munitions, and had mentioned this possibility to him; but in late May and early June he toyed with a proposal to make him Chairman of the Air Board, a body which co-ordinated the air effort of the War Office and the Admiralty. He asked Smuts – who still had no official position in Britain – to find out whether Churchill would accept this office, and Smuts reported that he would, provided that he could 'control the higher patronage in the Air Service'.[92] But mention of this possibility in the press led to strong protests from leading Conservatives, including Curzon and Sir George Younger, the party chairman.[93] There was also an obstacle of a different kind: Lord Cowdray, the industrialist who held the post at the time, was reputed to be a successful minister.

Lloyd George decided to try again, but to divide his enemies and then to act quickly, making several new appointments simultaneously. He first found official duty for Northcliffe, Churchill's principal persecutor. Northcliffe was entrusted with a mission to the United States, which had just entered the war, and was despatched to Washington. Then in July, having ascertained that Churchill preferred the post of Minister of Munitions to that of Chairman of the Air Board, Lloyd George decided to go ahead and act. Among other appointments he put Addison, the existing Minister of Munitions, in charge of studies of post-war reconstruction; and without even consulting Bonar Law, he announced that Churchill would take the vacant post.[94] Churchill's exile from office, after twenty months, was over at last.

12. *Munitions*

WHEN Churchill's appointment as Minister of Munitions was announced on July 17th 1917, there was an immediate outcry both in Fleet Street and at Westminster. The *Morning Post* was, predictably, especially hostile in its comments: it suggested that the appointment showed that 'although we have not yet invented the unsinkable ship we have discovered the unsinkable politician. ... We confidently anticipate that he will continue to make colossal blunders at the cost of the nation.'[1]

But more serious than this was the reaction of Conservative politicians. Lord Derby, the Secretary for War, at once threatened to resign;[2] and Walter Long, who was Colonial Secretary, wrote to the Prime Minister that it was 'extremely difficult to many of my friends to continue their support'.[3] A business committee of Conservative backbenchers met hastily, to the number of about sixty, to express their strong disapproval. Some forty of them went in a deputation to see Bonar Law, to complain about several matters, but principally about Churchill's appointment.[4] As Lloyd George himself was to say in his memoirs, the hostility to Churchill 'swelled to the dimensions of a grave ministerial crisis which threatened the life of the Government'.[5] But Bonar Law, although sore at Lloyd George's failure to consult him in advance of the appointment, felt that this was not an issue on which to end the Coalition. He defended the Prime Minister's right to make the appointment if he thought it would help the war effort. In the face of Bonar Law's loyalty the cries of protest gradually died away. But the furore had been an eye-opener for Churchill himself. He had not realised how unpopular he still was; and he now acknowledged that Lloyd George had been speaking the truth when he had told him that it would have been impossible to re-admit him to the government immediately after the fall of Asquith. Hankey, the Cabinet Secretary, found him in 'a chastened mood' a few days after his return to office.[6] But he was, of course, delighted to be back at work. Repington described him a few weeks later as 'looking a different man ... I never saw anyone so changed, and to such advantage, in so short a time'.[7]

As in 1908 on his appointment to the Board of Trade, Churchill had to resign his seat at Dundee and submit himself for re-election. He hoped to escape without a contest, for there was an election truce between the main parties, and the Dundee Conservatives announced that they would not oppose his return. But Edwin Scrymgeour came forward once more on behalf of his Prohibition Party, and claimed also to speak for Labour and in general for opposition to the war. Churchill had to combine his campaign with urgent work at his Ministry, but he made several speeches in Dundee and found himself being heckled frequently both on his own record and on that of the government. The workers of Dundee had some reason to be in a critical mood, owing to rapid price-rises which the government had failed to curb. Revolution in Russia and the heavy losses in France added to the feeling of unrest. Churchill could only announce himself a believer in the vigorous prosecution of the war: 'If ever there was a time in the history of this island when Britain should be a rock, it is now.'[8] He asked for all who accepted this view to support him, and not to be diverted by issues such as that of prohibition. 'My opponent', he declared, 'proposes to seek peace with Germany in order to suppress the liquor traffic in Scotland.'[9]

There was little election literature or canvassing, but when Churchill had to return to London he left Clementine to address meetings on his behalf, and she was helped by a mixed group of supporters from outside the constituency, including his loyal friend Alexander MacCallum Scott, Liberal MP for Bridgeton, Glasgow, and Bandmaster W. Robertson who had served under Churchill in the 6th Battalion of the Royal Scots Fusiliers and was prepared to speak warmly of his popularity with the soldiers.[10] In spite of the assistance of these friends, Clementine had the unpleasant experience of being shouted down at one of her meetings;[11] and it was obvious that Scrymgeour would obtain a fair proportion of the vote. In the end Churchill was quite safely re-elected on a small poll of only 43% – the register being three years out of date – but Scrymgeour had reason to feel satisfied that he was making more and more impact on his fellow-citizens of Dundee. The figures were:

W. S. Churchill (Liberal and Coalition)	7302	Elected
E. Scrymgeour (Prohibitionist and Labour)	2036	

In his new post Churchill was not a member of the War Cabinet, and so he was in theory at least only an executant of high policy and not a formulator of it. As he told Repington he was 'a shop-man at the orders of the War Cabinet'.[12] But he was a shopman who kept busy a remarkably large sector of British industry. The Ministry of Munitions of War, created in the spring of 1915 and for over a year presided over by Lloyd George himself, had developed a whole host of departments dealing with different areas of supply, each of them headed by a business man who had no great knowledge of Whitehall and who paid scant attention to what the other departments of the Ministry were doing. By the time Churchill took over, two more Ministers – Edwin Montagu and Christopher Addison – had come and gone; neither of them had managed effectively to control and co-ordinate the depart-ments; each became involved in 'tedious and unimportant detail';[13] and the confusion became increasingly serious as short-ages of raw material and labour began to intensify. Although there was a staff of some 12,000 housed in the central London offices of the Ministry, many of them in Northumberland Avenue, adjoining Whitehall, there was no effective civil service control and little proper check on financial expenditure. As one of the Ministry's officials put it, the older Departments of State were like 'a row of Queen Anne houses' peering with astonishment at this 'insecure skyscraper' which had come into existence for war purposes.[14] When Churchill moved into his office at the Hotel Metropole in Northumberland Avenue – accompanied as usual by Eddie Marsh whom he had summoned back from the Colonial Office – he knew already that it would be his first task to reorganise the administration, to tighten the system of financial control, and in general to consolidate a structure which had expanded far too quickly in the preceding two years. And all this had to be done while the Ministry was still rapidly developing the production of munitions, which were so urgently needed for the war.

Churchill had been forewarned by his old friend George Riddell, and probably by others as well, that the Ministry of Munitions needed drastic changes. Riddell understood that most of the 'leading men' in the Ministry were 'in a state of mutiny' and that it would be necessary to create some sort of Executive Board, consisting of a limited number of officers, to control all the fifty departments.[15] It did not take the new Minister very long to come to the same conclusion. Churchill decided that he wanted a committee like the Board of Admiralty – though of course without the constitutional limitations which, at any rate in theory, had restricted the power of the First Lord.[16] He established a body which he called the 'Munitions Council', consisting of ten to a dozen members, most of them business men, each of them in control of a group of departments. The Council, which was to meet daily under his chairmanship, was also to have a proper secretariat. To undertake the reorganisation Churchill secured the services of Sir Graham Greene, the former Secretary of the Admiralty; and James Masterton Smith, who had been his Private Secretary (in addition to Eddie Marsh) at the Admiralty, was brought in to take charge of the Munitions Council Secretariat. On August 18th, just a calendar month after taking office, Churchill issued a statement about the changes. He first of all described the need for a new system in the light of developments in the war, and concluded:

> Recourse at this juncture to a Council of business men already closely associated with the development of the department together with the strengthening of the Official Secretariat, should enable the Ministry, in spite of the increasing difficulties and strain of the war, to continue to render good and remarkable service to the State.[17]

With these new arrangements in operation Churchill found that he still had a great deal of work to do, but he was not submerged in detail as his predecessors had been. He wrote to Lloyd George in early September:

> This is a very happy Department: almost as interesting as the Admiralty with the enormous advantage that one has neither got to fight Admirals nor Huns! I am delighted with all these clever business men who are helping me to their utmost. It is very pleasant to work with competent people.[18]

There were, however, some remaining difficulties of organisation, though they were external to the Ministry. Churchill was responsible for munitions for the army only. The Admiralty retained control of its own supply, including all shipbuilding, which by decision of the War Cabinet had the highest priority. This meant that there were, as Churchill put it, 'two Ministries of Munitions, serving separate interests, competing and clashing with each other in an ever-narrowing field of labour and materials'.[19] Churchill realised that the building of new merchant ships was very important, to make good the losses due to submarine attacks in the intensifying war at sea. But he saw little point in the further enlargement of the battle fleet, which already had an overwhelming superiority over the enemy and which could now be reinforced by the American navy. Churchill, of course, had the technical knowledge to support his criticisms of Admiralty policy. On the other hand the First Lord of this period, Sir Eric Geddes, was a newcomer to naval affairs. He was touchy about his position and he threatened to resign when he heard that Churchill was advocating the building of smaller destroyers for anti-submarine work and the removal of heavy guns from obsolete battleships for use on land.[20] His ruffled feelings were soothed by Lloyd George and Hankey, but it seems that they both thought that Geddes was largely to blame. But no sooner was this difficulty overcome than Derby, the Secretary for War, complained that Churchill was urging that Haig should give up some of his howitzers for transfer to the Russian front. Derby also criticised Churchill for voting at a War Cabinet meeting to which he had only been invited in order to state a case.[21]

Obviously Churchill had to some degree exceeded his authority, and Lloyd George probably directed a few blunt words of advice to him on his future conduct as a minister below War Cabinet level. But relations between the Ministry of Munitions and the Admiralty were bound to cause continuing difficulty. A War Priorities Committee of the War Cabinet was set up under the chairmanship of General Smuts to determine the allocation of materials and shipping between the competing departments. There were also serious disputes over labour questions between the Ministry of Munitions and the Admiralty, because the Minister of National Service, whose task it was to organise the redeployment of labour, did not have the authority or the executive power to transform the existing employment policies of the supply departments. The Admiralty took advantage of the priority that it had been given by the War Cabinet, and at one time Churchill found that skilled men were being sought for making potato-peeling machines for the navy when they were being withdrawn from making range-finders for anti-aircraft guns.[22] The Admiralty also failed to make much effort to release workers for service in the armed forces, whereas Churchill with his strong views on the importance of keeping up the army's manpower found as many recruits as he could from his factory labour force. Between March and November 1917 the Ministry of Munitions provided 53,000 men, whereas the Admiralty yielded only 700.[23]

Munition workers' wages also caused disagreement between members of the government. Before Churchill returned to office there had been much unrest in industrial districts, and a series of official commissions of enquiry examined the reasons for discontent in different parts of the country. The commissions found that the erosion of the wage differential between the skilled and the unskilled was much resented by the skilled men. There were also complaints about the 'Leaving Certificates' which prevented men from leaving jobs in key factories without the consent of their employers.[24] The War Cabinet agreed that it was advisable to abolish the certificate system; but this was likely to lead to a drain of skilled men from the key factories unless something was done about their wages. It was for these reasons that Churchill, on the authority of an advisory committee of employers and trade-union leaders, asked for and secured the War Cabinet's approval for an increase of wages of $12\frac{1}{2}\%$ for skilled men on time rates.

Unfortunately for the government, this did not end the matter, for the bargaining power of the unskilled had increased rapidly during the war years, and they now felt that the differential was too large. In the end, substantial increases had also to be granted to piece workers, and the original problem which the $12\frac{1}{2}\%$ increase had been intended to solve reappeared. In January 1918 George Barnes, the Labour leader who had replaced Arthur Henderson in the Cabinet when the latter resigned, in a public speech in Glasgow blamed Churchill for 'butting in' with the $12\frac{1}{2}\%$ increase at a time when the grievances of the skilled workers had been 'very largely adjusted by other means'.[25] This criticism of Churchill's action was a grave breach of Cabinet solidarity and loyalty between colleagues, especially as Barnes had not merely participated in the decision to grant the increase, but had actually widened the original schedule which Churchill had proposed.[26] But it was probably true that Churchill was the strongest proponent of a course which the government later recognised to have been a mistaken one, although it must have helped to maintain relatively peaceful industrial relations in the munition factories in the critical early months of 1918.

On the whole, in spite of foreboding at the time when he was appointed, Churchill's record of achievement in the sphere of labour relations was not a bad one. On the side of welfare, his wife may have been able to give him some useful advice: for Clementine had been engaged for some time in welfare work for the YMCA at munition factories, and in 1918 was awarded the CBE for her efforts.[27] W. C. Anderson, a Labour MP who was a persistent critic of the government, paid Churchill the compliment late in 1917 of saying that he had brought 'courage and a certain quality of imagination to the task of dealing with labour questions', with the result that 'the situation has perceptibly improved'.[28] Certainly in the last year of the war there were relatively few serious stoppages in the factories.

But even in mid-1918 there were problems of industrial relations which severely tested the resources of the Minister of Munitions. At the works of the Alliance Aeroplane Company in London, a strike began in June owing to the dismissal of a shop steward who had held a meeting in the factory. Churchill decided in this case that the management was at fault, because its attitude to the shop-steward movement was not 'instructed or sympathetic'.[29] He therefore ordered that the firm should be taken out of private hands and run directly by his officers. This order did not need to be carried out, however, for the management rapidly changed its policy and came to terms with the men.[30] Shortly afterwards a still more serious stoppage developed among skilled engineers at Coventry, and this rapidly spread to other districts. It was caused by the Ministry's own embargo on the engagement of skilled labour by firms in the neighbourhood which were not expanding their output of munitions. The men thought that these firms were being encouraged to use unskilled men for skilled work: and Churchill's Trade Union Advisory Committee, having discovered that this was not the case, urged the men to return to work. It looked as if they were going to stay out, and so Churchill with the authority of the War Cabinet announced that their protection from conscription would be terminated if they did not report for work on July 29th – a week after the strike had begun.[31] This threat was immediately effective: of the 10,000 men who had left work in Coventry only about fifty failed to return, and of these 'several had telephoned regretting their absence and saying that they were making their way back'.[32]

Churchill set himself to get on good terms with the War Office and with the army in France, whose needs he had to supply. He realised that he could not develop the munitions programme according to his own strategic whim, and he accepted the need to replace Alfred Stern, the Director of Mechanical Warfare at the Ministry, because his advocacy of tanks had been so zealous that his relations with the generals had become very strained.[33] Stern was sent off to develop a joint programme of tank construction with the Americans. So far as general strategic policy was concerned, Churchill had now become something of a 'Westerner'. It was not that he had changed his view that offensives on the Western Front, at any rate if they took the traditional form of an artillery bombardment followed by an infantry assault, were a needless waste of manpower and munitions, unless an exceptional superiority of force were obtained. It was rather that he recognised, after the United States had entered the war, that the obvious German strategy was to attack in the West and hope for a decision before American troops could be brought to France in large numbers.

The principal offensive on the British front in France in 1917 was that at Passchendaele. It was not quite as costly as the Somme offensive in 1916, but it was nevertheless a terrible drain on the army's manpower, with no resulting strategic gain. The battlefield became a quagmire of mud, as the weather was bad and the drainage of the land had been destroyed. As Churchill put it, the generals 'wore down alike the manhood and the guns of the British Army almost to destruction'.[34] He himself had wished to witness the opening of this offensive, for he had been in France at the time, but General Sir Herbert Plumer, the Second Army Commander, forbade him to visit the front. As it turned out, the divisional commander whom he had intended to visit, his old friend 'Tom' Bridges, was seriously wounded by shellfire at the time when Churchill would have been with him, and had to have a leg amputated.[35]

Churchill had thought, as did Lloyd George, that it would be better not to make a major attack on the Western Front in 1917, but to remain on the defensive and to send some reinforcements to the Italian front, which was by no means strong. But Haig responded to French pressure to take the offensive, and so the Italian front was left to the Italians. The results of this were on the one hand the Passchendaele offensive, and on the other hand an Italian disaster at Caporetto in October. Although Churchill was not in the War Cabinet, Lloyd George did not hesitate to consult him informally, especially at a crisis: he knew that as always he would find him a counsellor of courage and resource. On Saturday October 27th the Prime Minister had Churchill to visit him at his home at Walton, and as in pre-war days they played golf together. They played 'appallingly badly, everyone's mind being pre-occupied with the Italian affair'.[36] British and French divisions had to be sent to stabilise the position, and Churchill had to supply munitions direct to the Italian army.

Churchill frequently visited British General Headquarters in France, and Haig's attitude to him gradually softened as he observed his efforts to increase the flow of munitions. In September 1917 the Commander-in-Chief recorded:

> I have no doubt that Winston means to do his utmost to provide the Army with all it requires, but at the same time he can hardly help meddling in the larger questions of strategy and tactics; for the solution of the latter he has had no real training, and his agile mind only makes him a danger.[37]

But by November Churchill was urging, in a paper circulated to the Cabinet, something which Haig strongly favoured – an increase in the manpower of the armies in France by a reduction of the large forces which were still retained in Britain.[38] When General Sir William Robertson, the Chief of the Imperial General Staff, reported this to Haig, it naturally improved still further his opinion of the Minister of Munitions.[39] There were good reports of the supply situation, and in January Haig recorded that 'Churchill is really doing very well, and has quite stirred up his office.'[40] Meanwhile Churchill was sufficiently alarmed about the way in which Haig was being starved of manpower to write directly to the Prime Minister:

> The imminent danger is on the Western Front: & the crisis will come before June. A defeat there will be *fatal*. Please don't let

vexation against past military blunders (wh I share with you to the full) lead you to underrate the gravity of the impending campaign, or to keep the Army short of what is needed. . . . The Germans are a terrible foe & their generals are better than ours. Ponder, & then *Act*.[41]

Lloyd George may have pondered, but he did not act; and when the German offensive began on March 21st it encountered a thinly-held line, especially at the southern end of the British front where a sector had just been taken over from the French. Churchill himself had been at the front on the day before the attack began, and he left next morning as the enemy bombardment was hammering at the British positions: well before daylight he was woken by the guns and watched as 'the enormous explosions of the shells upon our trenches seemed almost to touch each other'.[42] He had been visiting the division in which he had previously served, the 9th Scottish, now commanded by its former artillery chief, General Tudor, under the command of the Third Army south-east of Arras. Although in that sector the front held firm against the first enemy attacks, further south the Fifth Army was driven back in disorder, and a general retreat was ordered. The enemy captured 70,000 prisoners and over a thousand guns, and large stores of munitions were engulfed in their advance.[43]

Churchill was back in London on March 24th, and that night Lloyd George and General Sir Henry Wilson, who had replaced Robertson as Chief of the Imperial General Staff, dined with him and Clementine at 33 Eccleston Square, which they were again using as a London home now that Grey had given up his tenancy. 'I never remember', Churchill said later, 'in the whole course of the war a more anxious evening.'[44] At least there were plenty of troops available to be sent to France, and the reserves of munitions were adequate to replace all that was lost. A few days later, at a meeting between Haig, Wilson and the French leaders, the co-ordination of Allied strategy along the entire front was at last entrusted to one man – Marshal Foch. Meanwhile Churchill announced a temporary speed-up of munitions production in Britain, and called upon the two-and-a-half million workers in the factories to forego their Easter holidays if necessary. The response was so good that later in the year he was able to claim that this extra time more than made up for all the time lost by strikes since he had become Minister of Munitions.[45]

No sooner had Churchill made these emergency arrangements

than he was asked by Lloyd George to call upon the French Prime Minister, the seventy-six-year-old Georges Clemenceau, and persuade him to order an attack to relieve the hard-pressed British troops. Churchill found this an embarrassing mission, but he was speedily reassured about the general strategic situation by Clemenceau and Foch, and Clemenceau then took him on a visit to the front. This was one occasion when Churchill encountered a statesman even more ebullient and energetic than himself. After an excursion to the British lines, in the course of which they came under shellfire, Churchill reproved Clemenceau for venturing into danger, but the old man replied simply, 'C'est mon grand plaisir.'[46]

As was usual in offensives, the attack had suffered more casualties than the defence. But the pressure was very great for many weeks, and it was exerted on many sectors of the front. On April 12th Haig issued his famous 'backs-to-the-wall' appeal to his troops, but for some time there was fear of a breakthrough to the Channel Ports. In May the enemy pressure gradually weakened, and for the first time American troops entered the lines to assist the exhausted British and French. In the early summer the Germans still held the initiative, and in July launched a new offensive on French troops either side of Rheims; but this attack was halted without loss of ground. The prospect of a German victory in 1918 – or later – had now disappeared.

Meanwhile Lloyd George had had to defend himself from bitter criticisms for his attempt to starve Haig of troops in the winter of 1917–18. General Sir Frederick Maurice, who had been Director of Military Operations at the War Office, in a letter to the *Morning Post* early in May accused the government of misleading Parliament about the manpower of the British army in France. Asquith and his Liberal colleagues decided to take advantage of this to attack Lloyd George; but their temporary alliance with the professional soldiers was not cemented by any collaboration on the details of the charge. When the debate took place on May 9th Lloyd George replied skilfully, and the government was upheld by 293 votes to 106. The minority did not include a single Conservative; and Lloyd George was later to use the division list as a means of deciding which Liberal members he wished to see re-elected to Parliament in the first post-war general election. Churchill, however, had taken good care not to speak in the debate. Since he was not a member of the War Cabinet, he felt no obligation to defend a policy which he had opposed and which he had not helped to formulate. As he put it to Lloyd George, 'I will never accept political responsibility without recognised & regular power.... I shd fail in the frankness wh our long & intimate friendship required were I not ... to make my position clear.'[47]

During his period as Minister of Munitions, indeed, the House of Commons saw Churchill very little. When he was not at his desk at the Hotel Metropole, he was visiting munition factories or – more likely – conferring in Paris or at the front on the future needs of the armies or actually watching the fighting. He later said that, 'The view which I took of my own work made it necessary for me to keep continually in touch with the actual conditions of the fighting line.'[48] In any case, he reckoned that he needed to spend about a fifth of his time either in Paris or at British GHQ in France.[49] Some observers were doubtful whether this was strictly necessary, and wondered why he did not make more use of Sir Charles Ellis, who was in charge of the Ministry's permanent office in Paris.[50]

But if Churchill had not been in France a great deal he could not have kept abreast of the developments of military technique which were taking place all the time. Although he was not supposed to be advising the government on matters of military strategy, his department needed decisions by the War Cabinet on the country's future armament needs, and this provided him with the opportunity of presenting memoranda on what he thought should be the course of the war in 1918 and 1919. He was for staying on the defensive in 1918 and building up all the most scientific weapons of war – aeroplanes, tanks, machine guns and gas – for a new type of offensive in 1919. As he put it in a paper of March 5th 1918,

We should create, in order to attack the enemy in 1919, an army essentially different in its composition and methods of warfare from any that have yet been employed on either side.[51]

Sir Henry Wilson on the whole agreed with his arguments, especially after the success of tanks at Cambrai in November 1917; and the War Cabinet approved his proposal to manufacture 4000 tanks by April 1919. But Haig thought that the plan was too ambitious, as it would probably not be possible to find sufficient crews.[52]

Churchill kept in close touch with the French Minister of Armaments, Louis Loucheur, and with the United States Supply organisers, especially Edward Stettinius and (by telegram only) Bernard Baruch. The Americans were more helpful with raw materials than with munitions, for their industry was slow to adapt to military needs. But Churchill was pleased when they agreed that the allocation of world production of nitrates should be centralised in London, and he boasted later of having been the 'Nitrate King' for the remainder of the war.[53] For purposes of liaison with the British forces in the field Churchill had a headquarters allocated to him by Haig at the Château Verchocq, in the Pas de Calais between Étaples and St Omer. The Château was not large, but it had a magnificent avenue of trees, which Eddie Marsh thought was rivalled only by that at Savernake.[54] If he was in a hurry, Churchill would fly across the Channel – a method of travel still not without its hazards. In August he heard in Whitehall of a projected British tank attack near Amiens, and so he 'decided to get into my aeroplane and take a couple of days' holiday'.[55] When he got there, the attack had already proven a success; the roads were crowded with German prisoners, and he reported to Lloyd George, 'It seems to me this is the greatest British victory that has been won in the whole war.'[56]

He sent his congratulations to Haig, and was rewarded with the latter's thanks and a kind reference to the 'energy and foresight which you have displayed as Minister of Munitions'.[57] A few days later, probably after a further visit to France, he almost lost his life when the aeroplane taking him home suffered a temporary engine-failure over the Channel. After changing planes on the French side, he set off once more, but the engine again failed, though fortunately over England. The pilot made a forced landing and Churchill missed an appointment in London.[58]

In September Churchill visited General Lipsett of the 3rd Canadian Division in the First Army, which had just broken through an important line of enemy fortifications east of Arras. He saw how easily the infantry had advanced when they were assisted by tanks, though there were plenty of casualties where they had to go forward on their own.[59] Haig was now confident of early victory as evidence mounted of declining morale among the enemy troops, and he co-operated with Foch in continually harassing the retreating Germans. At the end of September the German High Command realised that resistance could not be prolonged, and persuaded the Kaiser to authorise a change of government. Prince Max of Baden took office to negotiate a peace settlement on the basis of the 'Fourteen Points' enunciated by President Wilson in a speech of January 1918.

Soon afterwards Churchill undertook a tour of munitions factories in Scotland and Northern England to see how they were preparing themselves for the great increases in production required for the 1919 fighting campaign. It began to look as if these efforts might not be required; but for the time being he could only point out that the war was not yet over, and that if the Allies were to agree to an armistice, they were bound to require, as he said at Leeds, 'effective guarantees' to ensure that the enemy could not resume fighting when it suited him.[60] On October 13th he interrupted his tour to join the Prime Minister at Riddell's house, Danny Park, Sussex, where a group of ministers met to discuss the proposed armistice and to agree that its terms must indeed be stern, in view of the strategic advantage which the Allies had now secured.[61] Not all the War Cabinet was present on this occasion, and it became a source of grievance against Lloyd George on the part of the absentees, and particularly Curzon, that important decisions had been taken in their absence.[62] But it was with full knowledge of government policy at the highest level that Churchill returned north to resume his tour. On October 15th, speaking at Manchester, he emphasised that though Britain would expect safeguards there was no question of demanding the complete prostration of the enemy:

> We are not asking for the unconditional surrender of the German nation. It would not be right to rob any nation – any great branch of the human family – of a reasonable assurance of its future position in the world. We do not seek to ruin Germany.[63]

In late October, accompanied by Marsh, Churchill was again in France, touring the front and meeting several old friends – Archibald Sinclair, who was to become a liaison officer between the army and the Ministry of Munitions; his own brother Jack, who was serving with the Australian Corps; Reggie Barnes, who had been with him at Sandhurst and on the expedition to Cuba and who was now a major-general. At Lille, in the company of Millicent, Duchess of Sutherland, who had been running a hospital in Flanders, he witnessed the ceremonial entry of British troops into the newly liberated city.[64] Undeterred by his earlier scare, he flew back to England at the end of the month. In the early days of November he made some preliminary plans for the first few days after an armistice. To prevent disorganisation, the policy would be, as he announced it on November 7th, 'Carry on at reduced speed until you receive further orders.'[65]

On November 11th just before 11 a.m. Churchill was at the window of his office in the Hotel Metropole looking towards Trafalgar Square. 'I was conscious of reaction rather than elation.'[66] There were so many problems to be faced in halting the work of his ministry and in transferring the munitions workers to peacetime occupations. At the stroke of eleven the streets filled with excited people and work stopped in all the offices. A few minutes later Clementine, although in an advanced stage of pregnancy, arrived to be with her husband at the moment of victory. Together they made their way by car to Downing Street to offer their congratulations to the Prime Minister. Enthusiastic crowds surrounded their car as it slowly made its way through Whitehall, and some people even climbed on the roof. Churchill was moved to remember similar demonstrations in Whitehall in August 1914:

> It was with feelings which do not lend themselves to words that I heard the cheers of the brave people who had borne so much and given all, who had never wavered, who had never lost faith in their country or its destiny, and who could be indulgent to the faults of their servants when the hour of deliverance had come.[67]

Throughout the summer and autumn of 1918 Lloyd George had been pondering the desirability of an early general election, so as to capitalise on the popularity of himself and his government, and to provide a firm government for the transition to peace, based upon the suffrages of the new electorate as extended by the Franchise Act of 1918. He had been thinking that the election should be held before the war was over; but early in November, when immediate victory appeared likely, he was for holding it as soon after the armistice as possible. He therefore sounded out Churchill and Edwin Montagu, his two senior Liberal colleagues in the government, on the idea of fighting by his side on a Coalition platform. Montagu has left an amusing account of the discussion, which took place over lunch after a meeting of the War Cabinet:

Winston began sulky, morose, and unforthcoming. The Prime Minister put out all his weapons. He addressed him with affection as 'Old man'. He reminded him of their old campaigns.... Finally, in a torrent of turgid eloquence, Winston exposed his hand. Never, he said, would he allow any personal consideration to weigh with him.... And he then began his usual arguments against the great men in the present Cabinet, the impossibility of the present machinery, the degradation of being a Minister without responsibility for policy, and so on.

When Lloyd George replied that he had made up his mind to bring the War Cabinet system to an end, and to have instead 'a Gladstone-like Cabinet of something between ten and twelve', Churchill's hostility turned to enthusiasm. 'The sullen looks disappeared, smiles wreathed the hungry face, the fish was landed.'[68]

Montagu himself asked some questions about policy, but was fairly soon satisfied; and then, with his principal colleagues apparently secured, Lloyd George widened the circle of consultation among the Coalition Liberals. He held a dinner to discuss the details of policy, and invited not only Churchill and Montagu but also several lesser Liberal ministers – Addison, H. A. L. Fisher, Sir Gordon Hewart, Robert Munro – and also Lord Reading, the Lord Chief Justice who had served in Asquith's Cabinet, and Freddie Guest who was Chief Whip of the Coalition Liberals. They decided that they could accept some infringements of Free Trade, such as fiscal arrangements to protect key industries, to provide Imperial Preference, and to prevent 'dumping' of foreign goods below cost, provided that in return the Conservatives agreed to Irish Home Rule, excluding only the Protestant counties of Ulster.[69]

Churchill did not like giving up his old ideas about 'dumping', which, he argued, was beneficial to the economy of the country where the goods were 'dumped'. But he appeared at the time to be prepared to accept the terms. Next day, however, he wrote to the Prime Minister to ask him to clarify, not the details of the programme, but the question of the composition of the new Cabinet.[70] Lloyd George was irritated by this apparent backsliding and took it as a threat of withdrawal from the Coalition in advance of the election.[71] But in reality Churchill merely wanted a guarantee of a 'seat at the Council table' and some information about the 'balance of parties' in the new government.[72] He had not forgotten how harshly he had himself been treated by several of the Conservative leaders in the preceding years of war. He was mollified by the Prime Minister in time for the election campaign, which began briskly at the end of November.

The idea of carrying on the Coalition was congenial to Churchill's mind, for he believed that the immediate problems of peacemaking and restoring the peacetime economy required a non-party approach. The concessions which he agreed to with regard to Free Trade were probably no greater than those which he would have made under the terms of the proposed Coalition of 1910. The war had seen the emergence of new forces in British politics and society, particularly the power of organised labour; but he thought that labour could be satisfied by a generous housing programme, as was envisaged by Lloyd George himself, by railway nationalisation which he had regarded as desirable ever since his days at the Board of Trade, and by heavy taxation of war fortunes. During his period at the Ministry of Munitions he had realised that 'profiteering' was a source of grievance to the workers, and he had urged the introduction of a 100% Excess Profits Tax;[73] now that the war was over, he thought that some way should be found of getting the money back for the State. He urged Lloyd George to refer to the matter in the election manifesto:

The old Tories have nothing to fear from it & everybody else except the profiteers will be enchanted. Why should anybody make a great fortune out of the war? ... I wd reclaim everything above say £10,000 (to let the small fry off) as reduction of the War Debt.[74]

But Lloyd George could go no further than his Conservative colleagues would allow, and the final draft of the manifesto not only omitted any reference to the taxation of war fortunes, but also eliminated the commitments to railway nationalisation which had been in the draft that Churchill had seen.

The election campaign was a most unusual one, fought in exceptional conditions with great confusion on all sides. The Coalition agreement between the Lloyd George Liberals and the Conservatives ensured that these elements would work together, and Conservative candidates were asked to withdraw from constituencies where Lloyd George Liberals were defending their seats. But Liberals who were not regarded as Lloyd George's supporters, and so did not get his endorsement ('the coupon' as Asquith called it), were faced with Conservative candidates, endorsed by Lloyd George as well as by Bonar Law. These Liberals, who looked to Asquith as their leader, had no real policy differences with the

Coalition and it was difficult for them to show cause for the electors to support them rather than the candidates favoured by the Prime Minister. As the Liberal paper in Churchill's constituency, the *Dundee Advertiser*, put it: 'Asquithites and Lloyd Georgites are separated on the question of Mr Asquith's personal dignity and absolutely nothing else.'[75]

It was only the outright opponents of the war – a handful of Liberal and Labour MPs – and, to a lesser extent, the Labour Party as a whole, which had come out of the Coalition and was now demanding a more radical policy of reconstruction including a capital levy, who could really be said to have distinctive attitudes; and it was obvious in any case that the outright opponents of the war were likely to suffer a severe defeat at the hands of a still predominantly 'patriotic' electorate.

Churchill's position at Dundee was a very strong one. He had retained his seat in 1910 in informal alliance with a Labour member, Alexander Wilkie of the shipwrights, who was not a Socialist and who had been a loyal supporter of the Coalition during the war. Both the Liberal and Conservative associations decided that they could not try to improve on Churchill and Wilkie, and it was only the local Labour Representation Committee which, to Wilkie's annoyance, insisted on putting up another Labour candidate, James S. Brown, also a shipwright and a man who had opposed at least the final stages of the war. Labour Party headquarters in London endorsed both Wilkie and Brown, but they fought their campaigns quite independently. Since Scrymgeour, the Prohibitionist, entered the lists once again, and declared himself a friend of Labour and of the Conscientious Objector, the campaign became one between Churchill and Wilkie on the one hand and Brown and Scrymgeour on the other. Wilkie advised his supporters to divide their votes between himself and Churchill, and Churchill called upon the electorate to return 'the Old Firm' once again.[76]

Churchill's speeches in Dundee were designed to rally all who had supported the war and the Coalition government. He denounced the 'pacifists, faint-hearts, defeatists, Lansdowne letter-writers, Stockholm excursionists' who had advocated different policies. But so far as he could he resisted the pressure for excessive reparations or for reprisals – though as he later admitted he was 'constrained' against his better judgment to support the idea of putting the Kaiser on trial.[77] He called for the avoidance of militarism in British life, for the establishment of a League of Nations to prevent future war, and in general for the reassertion of 'the broad principles of justice and freedom, of tolerance and humanity'.[78] His election address stressed the need for social reconstruction: 'We can make a new Britain so prosperous and so fair that our dead will not have died in vain.'[79] He also gave a pledge that the new government would nationalise the railways – not realising that this had been dropped from the Coalition's programme at Bonar Law's insistence.[80]

But the *Dundee Advertiser* was not unjustified in saying that from the tone of his campaign Churchill would be 'the Prime Minister's strongest lieutenant on the progressive side of his administration'.[81] When he described the Asquithians as trying to leave Lloyd George 'marooned' among the Conservatives, Asquith described such a picture of the political situation as the work of a 'post-impressionist' who 'lacks finish';[82] but Churchill refused to be drawn into an exchange of raillery with his old chief. He knew that it was best to keep the debate within the Liberal Party to grounds of policy, and not to indulge in personal acrimony. And certainly on grounds of policy no Liberal who had supported the war had any reason to fail to vote for him in this election.

Owing to the delay in collecting the votes of electors serving in the forces, the count was held up for a fortnight after election day, and the result was declared only after Christmas. Churchill and Wilkie were easily re-elected, but the two anti-war candidates, and especially Scrymgeour, had secured a creditable proportion of the poll. The figures were:

W. S. Churchill (Coalition Liberal)	25,788	Elected
A. Wilkie (Labour)	24,822	Elected
E. Scrymgeour (Prohibitionist)	10,423	
J. S. Brown (Labour)	7769	

The proportion of the electorate which actually voted was no more than 47%, and this low figure – which was not untypical – is to be explained by the fact that the election was rushed, and that there was little opportunity for the new voters (many of them women) to make up their minds how to vote. The servicemen's vote was very light, for very often they did not know how to fill in their ballot papers and get them witnessed. The analysis of the poll reveals that no less than 20,752 voters split their votes between Churchill and Wilkie, and a further 4625 split between Scrymgeour and Brown. There were only 1885 who voted for both the Labour candidates.[83] The disarray of Labour at the end of the war is something that historians omit to mention when they point to the damaging effects of the war upon the unity of the Liberal Party.

It is true enough, however, that the 1918 general election was especially harmful to the Asquithian Liberals. Of more than 250 candidates, only 29 were returned. The Lloyd George Liberals, on the other hand, as a result of their alliance with the Conservatives, were nearly all returned – 136 out of 159. The Coalition Conservatives secured 333 seats, and thus constituted a majority of the new House of Commons. Labour won 57 seats, but this success, although a considerable improvement on the party's previous strength, was marred by the fact that all its more prominent leaders such as Henderson, MacDonald and Snowden were defeated. In Ireland, the Irish Nationalists were reduced to a mere handful of seats owing to the successful competition of a more extreme party, the Sinn Fein, who refused to go to Westminster and established themselves as an Irish Parliament at Dublin. Thus, although the Coalition government had quite as large a majority as its leaders had hoped, there were two disturbing features about it for Lloyd George and for his Liberal colleagues: the Conservatives alone could exercise a veto on government policy by virtue of their control of the Commons; and the old forces of the moderate Left, the Liberal and Irish Nationalist parties, were being eroded by two new parties, both of them intransigent in their different ways – Labour and Sinn Fein. The war was over, but it did not look as if the pattern of British politics in peacetime would be more tranquil than it had been in the bitter pre-war years.

13. *Secretary of State in the Post-war Coalition*

At Christmas after the Armistice Churchill and his family, and also his brother Jack and F. E. Smith and their families, all went to stay with the Duke of Marlborough. There were delayed twenty-first-birthday celebrations for the Duke's son and heir: illuminations were put up, a firework display took place, and a whole ox was roasted. There was also 'a gigantic bonfire on top of which was placed an effigy of the Kaiser'.[1] On the morning of December 29th Churchill was back in London and had an interview with the Prime Minister, who was planning the reconstruction of his government after his success in the general election. Before Christmas Churchill had understood that he was probably to become Secretary of State for War; but now Lloyd George offered him either that post or the Admiralty, with the Air Ministry thrown in as a bonus whichever he chose. Churchill retired to Blenheim to consider the matter, but sent his reply later on the same day: he favoured the Admiralty, as he knew it so well already and as 'any claim I may be granted in public goodwill rests on the fact that "the Fleet was ready"'.[2]

But Lloyd George, who had been busy negotiating with other colleagues in the meantime, had already decided to withdraw his offer of the Admiralty, and so it was to the War Office and Air

Ministry that Churchill was appointed on January 10th. He took with him, as usual, the faithful Eddie Marsh as his Principal Private Secretary. The press was distinctly hostile to the appointment and especially to the fact that it gave Churchill a double responsibility. As the *Times* leader put it: 'One horse, one man; we doubt even Mr Churchill's ability to ride two at once, especially two such high spirited and mettlesome creatures.'[3] Churchill did his best to appease the critics by saying at once that the Air Ministry would continue to be a quite separate organisation. He persuaded Lloyd George to agree to the appointment of Seely as deputy head of the Air Ministry, with the title of Under-Secretary of State. Seely had, of course, once been a full Secretary of State; but he was a close friend of Churchill's, and if any two men could make the new arrangement work it was likely, Churchill thought, to be himself and Seely.

The most immediate problems of both ministries were concerned with demobilisation. Millions of men, having seen the war through to its conclusion, were thinking of little else but of returning to their homes and families and re-establishing their civilian lives. A War Office scheme for demobilisation had been drawn up in 1917, after consultation with the civil departments. It took account of the needs of industrial reconstruction, and laid down that men regarded as most valuable for the revival of trade should be the first to be released. This scheme unfortunately paid no regard to the feelings of the servicemen themselves, and it deeply offended their sense of justice. Soldiers who had volunteered early and suffered much saw others who had only lately joined them being released at once owing to the needs, real or supposed, of industry or trade. This led to a rapid collapse of army morale: mutinies began to occur, both in France and in Britain, and insubordinate troops demonstrated in the streets.

Churchill knew at once that he had a critical situation to face. There was a gap of four days between the announcement of his appointment and his actual assumption of the seals of office, but he spent the time studying the situation and deciding what action to take. On January 14th he went to Buckingham Palace to kiss hands; next day he held a conference, to which the whole Army Council, as well as representatives of certain civil departments, and also the Commander-in-Chief in France, General Sir Douglas Haig, had been summoned. He announced that he was proposing to scrap the existing demobilisation scheme and to substitute one which was based upon age, length of service, and wounds. Haig declared himself well pleased with the proposals and such opposition as there was came from the civilians, especially Sir Robert Horne, the Minister of Labour, who thought that it would cause trouble with employers and trade unions. Churchill said that he was quite prepared to face this.[4]

One major difficulty with the proposals, however, was that they also involved a continuation of conscription in order to tide over the period between the demobilisation of the existing army and the reconstruction of a volunteer force of pre-war character. To be sure, those who were not demobilised at once could be appeased to some degree by an increase of pay, which was one of Churchill's proposals. But the trouble was that those who had been recruited to fight in the war could not be retained beyond 'the duration' – that is to say, the period of the war itself. It was bound to embarrass the government to have to bring in a conscription bill, even for a limited period, because Coalition candidates at the election had been authorised to pledge themselves against any such measure.

Churchill immediately entered into consultations with ministers who were in London, in order to obtain their support. But he could not discuss the question in detail with the Prime Minister, for he was in Paris for the Peace Conference. In fact Lloyd George heard of the proposals for the first time through members of the Cabinet Secretariat, and at once became alarmed about drastic measures being formulated behind his back.[5] Churchill had to tell him bluntly by telegram that this was an emergency: 'A few more weeks on present lines and there will be nothing left but a demoralised and angry mob, made up of men left behind on no principle that they consider fair and without the slightest regard to military formation.'[6] Major Sir Archibald Sinclair, who was acting as one of his private secretaries, was sent over to Paris with a copy of the new proposals; and Churchill followed shortly afterwards and discussed it with the Prime Minister over breakfast on January 24th. Lloyd George gave his assent, and five days later the Army Orders were issued, outlining the new policy and indicating the new rates of pay. Meanwhile Churchill had written a frank explanation of the principles which henceforth were to govern the order in which men were to be demobilised, and this was published in the newspapers on January 27th.

The worst incidents of indiscipline took place just as these new arrangements were being announced. At the end of January a mutiny of Ordnance and Transport units took place at Calais. To the number of three or four thousand, the men took possession of the port, and held it for some days until two divisions of front line troops arrived to overawe them into submission. A week later there was an alarming incident very close to the War Office itself. About three thousand armed soldiers returning from leave had been caught by a tube strike while passing through London and, having missed their train from Victoria, had been left overnight without food or accommodation. In the morning they decided to demonstrate in Whitehall, and soon they were assembled on the Horse Guards Parade. Churchill arrived hastily at the War Office and after consultations ordered detachments of the Grenadier Guards and Household Cavalry to cordon them off and then to escort them to Wellington Barracks. Fearing a clash, he sat in his office for some time 'a prey to anxiety', but all passed off quietly, and no serious disciplinary action was taken.[7]

After this incident army morale steadily improved as the new demobilisation scheme was understood and accepted as reasonable and fair. Churchill summed up the policy as 'to let three men out of four go, and to pay the fourth double to finish the job'.[8] This meant the release of about 2,600,000 men and the temporary retention of some 900,000 to provide armies of occupation and garrisons abroad while the peace treaties were being negotiated. The Conscription Bill was accepted as necessary by the supporters of the government and passed through the Commons with large majorities, although it was bitterly opposed by both the Asquithian Liberals and by the Labour Party. Its period of operation was limited: it was to lapse in April 1920, by which time, it was hoped, an adequate supply of volunteers would have been recruited and trained to assume the role of the normal peacetime regular army.

These plans were fulfilled much as Churchill had intended, and he was justly praised for his wise and decisive action in this emergency.[9] When he introduced the Army Estimates in February 1920 he was able to report that a new volunteer army of 220,000 was available to take over from the last of the conscripts.[10] After the signature of the Versailles Treaty with Germany, only 16,000 men were required for the Occupation Zone on the Rhine and for the temporary work of supervising plebiscites to determine the destiny of certain disputed districts on the German frontiers. More substantial forces were still needed for the Middle East, as there was a temporary occupation of Constantinople and the Dardanelles, pending a peace treaty with Turkey, and as the ex-Turkish provinces of Mesopotamia and Palestine, which were in British occupation, were still awaiting decisions about their future government. But Churchill hoped that these commitments could soon be drastically cut. As for Ireland, the serious trouble there was engaging large numbers of extra troops, but they were all drawn from establishments in Britain and did not involve any additional call on military manpower.

One problem which engaged Churchill's attention for much of his time in his first year at the War Office was that of British and Allied intervention in Russia. After the Bolshevik Revolution at the end of 1917 British, French, Japanese and American forces had all entered Russian territory to prevent German seizure of port facilities or munition dumps and to try to re-establish the Eastern Front, so as to discourage the Germans from transferring the great bulk of their forces to the battles in France. The British troops in Russia, although not numerous, were widely scattered. The largest contingents were at Murmansk and Archangel, where an Allied force of about 30,000 altogether was under the command of Brigadier-General Edmund Ironside. Few of these were first-class fighting troops, but they could not readily be evacuated as the ports were ice-bound during the winter. There were also a couple of British battalions which had penetrated into the interior of Asia from the port of Vladivostock, and had made contact with the anti-Bolshevik or White Russian army of Admiral Kolchak.

These British interventions had taken place before the war ended, and before Churchill moved from the Ministry of Munitions to the War Office. When he came into direct contact with the problem, the Cabinet had already decided to do what it could to support the White Russians and the anti-Bolshevik governments which had appeared on the Baltic coast – not necessarily by active warfare, but certainly with supplies and munitions. Arrangements were being made to send British troops to hold the railway running from Batum, on the Black Sea, to Baku, on the Caspian; and contact was being established with General Denikin, the White leader in South Russia.[11]

Churchill later said that he approached the subject in early

1919 with 'no strong and vehement convictions ... as to what it is right and proper for the country to do' with respect to Russia.[12] But he had already suggested to the Imperial War Cabinet at the end of 1918 that it would be best either to withdraw from Russia as soon as possible or to intervene more effectively 'with large forces, abundantly supplied with mechanical devices'.[13] He declared his own preference for the latter course, but the Dominion prime ministers disagreed, and so did Lloyd George himself, arguing that British troops would not be available for a new war and that intervention by foreign powers to overthrow the Bolshevik regime would only enable it to win patriotic support.[14]

Thereafter, however, it soon became apparent that British policy towards Russia had to be determined within fairly narrow limits. On the one hand, it was very difficult to make peace with the Bolsheviks without appearing to favour their cause against that of the anti-Bolsheviks – a course which the Conservative-dominated House of Commons refused to accept. This policy was attempted by Lloyd George, who initiated the idea of a conference of representatives of Allied powers and of both sides of the Russian Civil War at Prinkipo, on the Sea of Marmora. It was, in fact, the anti-Bolsheviks who wrecked the proposal by refusing to attend. But, on the other hand, it became quite clear that in Britain the general public and particularly the soldiers, war-weary as they were, were very hostile to the idea of a large-scale campaign fought in Russia. A War Office questionnaire sent to commanding officers of units in Britain elicited the information that their men looked upon the prospect of serving in Russia with great reluctance, principally (it was reported) because they were afraid of the cold, but also at least in part because they did not wish to become involved in a war the objects of which they could not understand.[15]

The difference of policy towards Russia between Lloyd George and Churchill therefore boiled down to a difference between a policy of disentangling Britain from association with the anti-Bolshevik forces and a policy of supporting those forces with more supplies and perhaps with volunteer specialist advisers, and also trying to encourage the other Allied countries and the newly independent nations in eastern Europe to form a co-ordinated battle-front against the Bolsheviks. The Prime Minister could not prevent his Secretary for War from proceeding some way with this more active policy, partly because his own time was so much taken up with the work of peace-making with Germany, and partly because other members of the Cabinet were half-way towards supporting Churchill's position and because there was much sympathy for it in the Commons, and especially in the Conservative Party.

In February 1919 Churchill was already urging that plans for more effective intervention in Russia should be drawn up by some sort of inter-Allied council. Lloyd George, who was temporarily back in London, knew that President Wilson of the United States was hostile to intervention, as the American troops in Europe were quite as keen to return home after eighteen months of war as the British forces were after four years. He therefore felt that no harm would come if he allowed Churchill to go over to Paris and to put his proposals before the Supreme War Council, which was continuing to meet in his absence. Churchill did so, and just managed to catch Wilson before he left Paris for a few weeks' break in the United States. Wilson, although anxious to get away, listened to Churchill with courtesy and then rather surprisingly declared that while he personally was against intervention he would accept the decision of the other powers with respect to the preparation of joint plans. Thus encouraged, Churchill next day set forth a proposal for a new inter-Allied body to prepare what Hankey called 'a definite war scheme'.[16]

Lloyd George was much taken aback at this turn of events. His impatient colleague, instead of receiving a snub from the President as he had hoped, had been encouraged to go ahead and make plans for a vigorous inter-Allied campaign against the Bolsheviks. The Prime Minister told his friend Riddell: 'Winston is in Paris. He wants to conduct a war against the Bolsheviks. That *would* cause a revolution!'[17] Through Philip Kerr, his private secretary, who was still in Paris, he sent a telegram to Churchill saying that the Cabinet had not authorised any such action, and he asked Kerr to give a copy of the telegram to Colonel House, the President's adviser and deputy. This indication of Lloyd George's distrust of himself pained Churchill, but he replied coolly enough:

> You need not be alarmed about the phrase 'planning war against the Bolsheviks'. We are, as you pointed out at the Cabinet, actually making war on them at the present moment. All that is intended is to assemble possible means and resources for action in a comprehen-

sive form and to submit this report to the Supreme War Council.[18]

It soon became apparent to him, however, that the Americans were opposed even to the making of plans; and so he abandoned the project, and returned to Whitehall.

In the course of the spring and summer of 1919 the War Office tried to organise the withdrawal of British troops from Russia in such a way as not to place the anti-Bolsheviks at a disadvantage and not to abandon friendly Russians to a savage fate at the hands of the Bolsheviks. At the same time, it sought to sustain the main White Russian armies with munitions and specialist assistance. The British battalions in Siberia were withdrawn, and it was decided that the bulk of the military aid should go to Denikin in South Russia. Murmansk and Archangel were to be evacuated, but as the existing British force was of poor quality and morale and hardly capable of defending itself authority was given to raise a volunteer force of 8000 men to join them and to act as a rearguard.[19] Churchill later sponsored a plan for this force to thrust forward into the interior, in order to join up with Kolchak and thus ensure the transfer of the territory the British troops were leaving to a substantial White Russian army. This plan was later abandoned, as Kolchak was forced into retreat; but the British forces under Ironside did fight a battle which effectively covered their own withdrawal. The whole affair was on a small scale and British fatal casualties in north Russia from the German armistice to the evacuation amounted to less than two hundred.[20]

The quantity of munitions and supplies sent to Denikin in the South was nevertheless very considerable, amounting as it did to enough for a force of a quarter of a million men. Partly as a result of this aid, Denikin's army advanced rapidly in the late summer of 1919, and high hopes were raised that he would overturn the Bolshevik regime. Churchill told Sir Henry Wilson, the Chief of the Imperial General Staff, that if Denikin took Moscow he would be prepared to go out 'as a sort of Ambassador' to 'help Denikin mould the new Russian constitution'.[21] He discussed the matter with Lloyd George, who apparently 'strongly dissuaded him' from such a course.[22] But the opportunity never arose, for in the late autumn the tide of battle changed decisively. The Bolsheviks struck at Denikin's over-extended columns and threw them back. Once in retreat, they rapidly disintegrated. By the spring of

1920 Denikin controlled only the Crimea, and it was obvious that the Civil War was nearing its end.

Denikin's first reverses provided Lloyd George with an opportunity to call a halt to British participation, even by way of supplies. In a speech at the Lord Mayor's Banquet at the Guildhall in November 1919 he declared: 'We cannot, of course, afford to continue so costly an intervention in an interminable Civil War.'[23] This speech took all his colleagues, including Churchill, by surprise; but events justified his attitude, and in the following February, when Churchill complained in the Cabinet that the government had no Russian policy, Lloyd George, according to the deputy secretary of the Cabinet, Tom Jones, gave him a 'dressing down', telling him that the government's policy was 'to try to escape the results of the evil policy which Winston had persuaded the Cabinet to adopt'.[24] Soon it was a question of deciding whether or not to provide some assistance for anti-Bolshevik refugees. Churchill was distressed in November 1920 when the Cabinet decided not to evacuate any refugees from the Crimea other than those of British nationality. Characteristically loyal to those who had been his allies, he formally dissociated himself from the decision which he felt would almost certainly 'lead to a massacre of the civilians in the Crimea'.[25]

It was undoubtedly the issue of intervention in Russia which swung Churchill into sympathy with the Conservative Party and which lost him the respect of the Labour Party and the trade unions. The *Morning Post* began to speak of him with friendliness, while the *Daily Herald*, a newspaper of the Left, resurrected all the old charges against him from Sidney Street to the Dardanelles. A Labour Party delegation to Russia in 1920 brought back a captured White Russian document which gave an account of an interview between Churchill and a White Russian emissary, General Golovin, in May 1919, in which Churchill promised to give every possible assistance including volunteer forces to support the anti-Bolshevik cause, and declared, 'I am myself carrying out Kolchak's orders.'[26] Ramsay MacDonald wrote at the time: 'If Mr Churchill had been an unlimited monarch, he could not have spent the money and lives of the nation with more unstinted generosity. . . . If the Labour Party can't fight this, it can fight nothing.'[27]

Posterity has judged Churchill's policy towards Russia in this period to have been mistaken. It was based upon an erroneous view of the existing degree of support for the Bolsheviks in Russia, and of the prospects of success for the anti-Bolshevik armies. Lloyd George's view was wiser: he held that Allied intervention would only provide the Bolsheviks with increased support within Russia just as foreign invasion had strengthened the Jacobins in revolutionary France.[28] Churchill did not accept the historical analogy, pointing out that it was by no means precise as the intervention of Allied troops in Russia had taken place before the end of the war with Germany, and was intended to help Russia against her traditional enemy. But the most striking feature of Churchill's thought at this time was the strength of his hostility to Bolshevism, so soon after the end of a long and exhausting war against a different enemy, Imperial Germany. In April 1919, for instance, Churchill could declare that 'Of all tyrannies in history the Bolshevik tyranny is the worst, the most destructive, and the most degrading.'[29]

There have been various attempts to explain the strength of Churchill's anti-Bolshevism. Such an attitude might have been expected of a Conservative, or even of an old-fashioned Liberal, but not of one who had seen the need for radical social policies even in Britain. Lloyd George thought that 'his ducal blood revolted against the wholesale elimination of Grand Dukes in Russia';[30] but there seems to have been rather more to it than that. Churchill's temperament was always more Whiggish than Radical; and he was keenly alive to the realities of power – so that when Germany collapsed he was the first to plead for generosity towards the beaten enemy, but also the first to recognise that Bolshevism, with its international claims, was now the most dangerous enemy of the victorious powers. Already in February 1919 he outlined to the Cabinet his fear of 'a great combination from Yokohama to Cologne in hostility to France, Britain and America'.[31] Never war-weary himself, he could hardly imagine that his fellow-countrymen, having defeated Germany, would be unwilling to make the relatively small effort necessary to consolidate their success throughout Europe. It seems, moreover, that his sense of loyalty to comrades and allies was stronger than that of Lloyd George. He did not like the way the Cabinet threw over the White Russians as soon as the tide of war went against them; and he dedicated his history of the Eastern Front during the war – the fifth volume of *The World Crisis* – to: 'Our Faithful Allies and Comrades in the Russian Imperial Armies'.

Lloyd George complained to Churchill in August 1919 that his absorption with Russia was preventing him from grappling with the problems of reform and retrenchment at the War Office and the Air Ministry.[32] Churchill replied by pointing out that retrenchment was held up by the delays in making peace at Paris: the treaty with Germany had only recently been signed, and that with Turkey was still awaited. The future of Palestine and Mesopotamia, which were occupied with substantial forces, had still to be decided. There were also temporary extra military commitments as a result of unrest in India, Egypt and Ireland, and the civil power even in Britain expected soldiers to be held available in large numbers for fear of disturbances. Churchill did, however, complain of being much overworked, saying that 'the daily routine business in volume exceeds several times the greatest pressure known before the war'.[33]

Seely, the Under-Secretary at the Air Ministry, had already told the Prime Minister that the Royal Air Force suffered most as a result of Churchill's many occupations. He wrote to say that combination of the two ministries in one man's hands was leading to 'a feeling of unrest and uncertainty throughout the Air Force'.[34] Lloyd George took the matter up with Churchill when the latter, accompanied by the CIGS, General Sir Henry Wilson, paid a visit to his home at Criccieth a few days later. Churchill suggested that the best solution would be to appoint a Minister of Defence, with four departments under his authority – the War Office, the Admiralty, the Air Ministry, and the Ministry of Supply. Lloyd George seemed interested in the proposal; and on his return to Whitehall Churchill drew up a list of names to head the four departments under his own suzerainty as Minister of Defence. The list did not include Seely's name: Churchill now regarded him as an embarrassing subordinate, especially as he had previously served as a Secretary of State.[35]

It soon became apparent, however, that the political obstacles to the establishment of a Ministry of Defence were too strong to overcome. Lloyd George probably realised that the Conservatives would not be prepared to accept the change, the more so as Churchill was the only obvious candidate for the post. Churchill himself came to accept that the integration of the services could take place only gradually. The first step would be to build up a cadre of officers with experience of all three services, which could be done by the creation of a united staff college. In the meantime it was desirable, he thought, to abolish the Ministry of Supply – the former Ministry of Munitions – and to distribute its departments to the appropriate service ministries. This was because there was no longer the same need as had existed in wartime for the organising of a vast flow of munitions.[36]

Seely's complaints about the neglect of the air force therefore went unsatisfied; and the problem of his own subordination to Churchill continued. In November 1919 he gave up his post, and explained to the Commons his view that although he and Churchill were the best of friends their relationship was an impossible one: 'The War Office is a whole-time job ... and the duty of the Secretary of State for Air ... is a whole-time job too.'[37] On a later occasion Seely told the House that the amount of time in each week that Churchill spent at the Air Ministry was about one hour. Churchill in reply had to point out that Seely's attitude had discouraged him from setting foot in the Air Ministry very often, but that he spent very much more than an hour each week on its affairs and problems.[38]

It was in fact very important for the Royal Air Force that Churchill was concerned with its future in this period, and that he was subjected to the vigour of the arguments put forward on its behalf by General (later Air Marshal) Trenchard, the Chief of Air Staff. Trenchard had to establish the case for an independent air force against all those who sought to throttle the new service. He had to face, not only the combined opposition of the two older services, but also the Treasury's insistence upon economy, which could so easily be met by preventing the RAF from having a separate establishment of its own. He struck a responsive chord in Churchill's mind when he said that if the other services absorbed the air force, the pilots would be 'mere chauffeurs for the army and navy'. Asked to elaborate his case on paper, Trenchard argued for an organisation which '... will encourage and develop airmanship, or better still, the air spirit, like the naval spirit, and ... make it a force that will profoundly alter the strategy of the future'.[39]

Once convinced, Churchill could be a powerful advocate for an independent air force in the reconstituted peacetime Cabinet which, in belated fulfilment of his promise before the election, Lloyd George brought into existence in the autumn of 1919. It also served the interests of the air force that Churchill as Secretary of State for War could acknowledge that 'the first duty of the Royal Air Force is to garrison the British Empire' and then, ignoring the opposition of Sir Henry Wilson, the CIGS, could re-examine the War Office's responsibilities to see which of them could be handed over to the RAF.[40] An experiment in work of this type was carried out in Somaliland early in 1920 when a punitive expedition against the so-called 'Mad Mullah', consisting of a single bomber squadron with two battalions of Camel Corps and King's African Rifles and a native levy, was able to defeat the Mullah without delay and force him into exile in Ethiopia, where he was killed shortly afterwards. The total expenses for the expedition amounted to £77,000, and Churchill reckoned that if the army alone had been employed for the task it would have cost between six and seven million pounds.[41] He had little doubt thereafter that this was the way to maintain peace in the desert country of Mesopotamia, or Iraq as it came to be called, which was to become henceforth a permanent responsibility of the British government under a mandate from the League of Nations. As he told the Commons, he proposed 'to invite, as it were, competitive tenders from the Air Staff' for the maintenance of order in the Empire.[42]

Thus Churchill did much to secure the future of the RAF at a critical period of its early life. He and Trenchard had to concentrate on essentials, at a time when every form of government expenditure came under increasing scrutiny. They had to accept that the government would not provide a subsidy for civil aviation – a matter which naturally caused much distress to General Sir Frederick Sykes, who was Director of Civil Aviation at the Air Ministry.[43] But Trenchard was happy to have had Churchill as his Secretary for Air in these critical years. He told Bonar Law that in spite of also being Secretary for War Churchill had been a successful Air Minister, and had 'enormously assisted in the formation of the Air Service on an economical basis'.[44]

Permanent arrangements for governing Iraq and other parts of the Middle East were, to begin with, held up by the delay in making a settlement with Turkey. It was only in 1920 that the boundaries of the mandated territories were decided, Syria being allotted to France and Palestine and Iraq to Britain. The British government had promised during the war to 'recognise and support the independence of the Arabs', in return for their assistance in the struggle against Turkey; but the fulfilment of this promise in its entirety had been compromised by the Balfour Declaration of 1917, which authorised the establishment of a Jewish National Home in Palestine. After the war the Arabs found that the French would not tolerate Arab self-government in Syria, but insisted upon the centralised regime characteristic of other French colonies. All this led to serious unrest throughout Arabia. The British government also found it difficult to make decisions for the future because the responsibility for policy was divided among so many different departments. The administration of Iraq was supervised by the India Office, that of Palestine by the Foreign Office, and other Arab territories such as Aden were under the Colonial Office. The War Office had to provide the troops, and already in May 1920 Churchill was complaining to the Cabinet of the 'vicious system' in Iraq whereby 'the department calling the tune has no responsibility for paying the piper'. His solution did not entirely get over this difficulty, but it promised considerable economies in the long run. The Colonial Office, he thought, should be in charge of all the new territories, and the responsibility for keeping the peace should go to the Air Ministry.[45] His paper was accompanied by a scheme drawn up by Trenchard for an RAF garrison of Iraq.

For most of 1920 there was no decision on this question, as both Curzon, the Foreign Secretary, and Montagu, the Secretary for India, were against giving up their respective responsibilities: but the burden of military expenditure was so great that in the end Lloyd George persuaded the Cabinet to act in the direction that Churchill had indicated. At the end of the year he asked Churchill himself to take over the Colonial Office, from which the now ageing Milner had decided to resign, and to assume in addition the task of supervising the Middle East mandates and attempting a permanent settlement of their political and military problems. Churchill confessed to the Prime Minister that he had some misgivings about taking on 'the burden & the odium of the Mesopotamia entanglement', but he was also 'deeply sensible of the greatness of the sphere you are confiding to my charge'.[46] He decided that it would be necessary for him to visit the Middle East to meet all the British administrators responsible for its problems, and to make decisions on the spot.

Churchill moved to the Colonial Office in mid-February, taking with him not only Eddie Marsh, who had accompanied him throughout his ministerial career, but also, among others, Major Sir Archibald Sinclair. On his arrival at the Colonial Office in Downing Street – where, thirteen years earlier, he had made his first acquaintance with public administration – the incumbent civil servants soon noticed that 'an unfamiliar, unmistakable wind blew through the Office'. The new minister read few papers to begin with, but made the personal acquaintance of all the members of the 'First Division' – that is, of the administrative grade. Then he discussed the policy of each of the departments in turn, in the presence of its principals and assistant principals.[47] Soon, however, it was the plans for the new Middle Eastern Department, which formally only came into existence as a department of the Colonial Office on March 1st, which absorbed most of his time. 'He will be under an irresistible temptation', Curzon wrote unkindly to Samuel, the High Commissioner in Palestine, 'to proclaim himself King in Babylon.'[48]

The most important thing was to plan the conference which Churchill had now decided to hold in Cairo, and to outline the general policy which those attending would be expected to accept. If the Royal Air Force was to act as the garrison of Iraq, the day-to-day administration of the country could be left to an Arab regime. Churchill recruited to his new department T. E. Lawrence, the complex former archaeologist who had played so large a part in the Arab revolt during the war, and who, having taken up a Fellowship at All Souls, Oxford, had lately been agitating for the fulfilment of Britain's wartime promises to the Arab leaders.[49] Lawrence recommended, and Churchill agreed before the conference met, that the most suitable candidate for the throne of an Arab kingdom of Iraq would be the Emir Feisal, a son of the Sharif of Mecca.

Churchill was still Air Minister as well as Colonial Secretary, and he was accompanied to the Cairo conference by Trenchard, as well as by Lawrence and by Archibald Sinclair. The future of Egypt was not on the agenda of the conference, as this was a matter for the Foreign Office, but Churchill had publicly described the country as an integral part of the British Empire, and so he was given a very hostile reception by Egyptian Nationalists, who attacked his party with stones and other missiles whenever they had the opportunity.[50] For his own safety his train was stopped several miles from Cairo, and he proceeded to the Semiramis Hotel, where the conference was held, by car.[51] The hotel was soon reported to be 'a scene of feverish bustle' as governors and high commissioners arrived from Mesopotamia, Palestine, the Persian Gulf, and even British Somaliland.[52]

The conference had its formal banquets and exchanges of hospitality with Lord Allenby, the High Commissioner in Egypt; and Churchill had to pay his respects to King Fuad at the Royal Palace. He also visited RAF detachments and inspected their married quarters, which he found inadequate and unworthy of the service.[53] But the main business of the visit was to determine the future of Iraq. Sir Percy Cox, the High Commissioner, accepted Churchill's plans and undertook to arrange for Feisal to be invited to Iraq by the local population, so that he should at least appear to be a democratic choice. The new regime would then control its own defence and budget and would enter into a treaty relationship with Britain, whereby an RAF base would be maintained at Habbaniyah but other British forces would be withdrawn. Feisal's willingness to accept these arrangements had already been secured by Lawrence.[54]

The Times referred to the conference rather sarcastically as a 'Durbar', but it was undoubtedly a success as it enabled the British authorities in all the Arab countries to hear an exposition of the government's policy, and to discuss with the minister in charge and also with each other the ways in which it could best be put into effect.[55] The problems of Palestine, however, seemed to require the minister's personal intervention, and the party therefore proceeded by train to Jerusalem. Greeted en route by shouting Arab crowds, Churchill waved cheerfully, no doubt being gratified that at least they were not throwing stones; but according to Lawrence they were uttering imprecations against the Jews, whose aspirations to settle in the country they regarded as a threat to their way of life.[56] Churchill firmly reasserted in public the government's policy of allowing the establishment of a Jewish National Home in Palestine, and he planted a tree on Mount Scopus, near the site of the new Hebrew University, as a gesture of his association with the Zionist cause.[57] But he also received Moslem and Christian Arab delegations and told them that the British government would ensure that they did not suffer as a result: 'Great Britain is the greatest Moslem state in the world, and is well-disposed to the Arabs and cherishes their friendship.'[58]

One major change of policy, to the advantage of the Arabs, resulted from Churchill's personal negotiations with the Emir Abdullah, elder brother of the Emir Feisal, who was seeking to challenge French authority in Syria and who might at any time challenge his brother's position in Iraq. Churchill wanted Abdullah to act as governor of Transjordania under the suzerainty of the British High Commissioner for Palestine. But Abdullah insisted that Transjordania should be independent of Palestine and should not be regarded as a land for Jewish colonisation. Churchill agreed, and told Samuel rather quaintly that 'The same latitude must be given to him in speeches that he makes as would be given to a Member supporting the Government but with a shaky seat.'[59] In this way a new Arab principality came into existence.

Churchill's dispositions for the future of the British mandated territories met with remarkable success in the ensuing years. It proved possible rapidly to reduce the cost of the British garrison in Iraq; and even in Palestine, where the hostility of Arab and Jew was bound to persist, there was comparative peace throughout the 1920s. Feisal died peacefully in possession of the throne of Iraq, and his brother's family remains in Transjordania – or Jordan, as it is now called – to the present day. Considering that even a decade is a long time for an Arab regime to stay in power, the arrangements made in 1921 can be considered to have been justified by events, particularly from the point of view of the British government, whose prime concern at this juncture was to secure British supremacy in the area at the minimum of expense.

Having made these important dispositions in the Middle East – for which he secured the Cabinet's approval by telegram – Churchill returned to Whitehall to supervise the more regular work of the Colonial Office. He had hopes of promotion to the Exchequer, which had been the object of his ambition since his youth, for Austen Chamberlain had left that office vacant when he succeeded Bonar Law as Lord Privy Seal and Leader of the Conservative Party on the latter's temporary retirement. But Lloyd George felt that the Exchequer must be left in Conservative hands, and so he promoted Sir Robert Horne, a relatively insignificant figure, to take Chamberlain's place. Churchill was reported by Lord Beaverbrook (the former Max Aitken) to be 'very-very-very-very-angry' over this.[60]

Churchill was now relieved of the Air Ministry, Freddie Guest having been appointed to succeed him in April; and for some months he had only the business of the Colonial Office to absorb his energies. This, however, was in itself quite substantial, as there was a backlog of papers to read, and in addition an Imperial Conference was due to take place in June. For some weeks Churchill did not see his Under-Secretary, Edward Wood, the son of Viscount Halifax and a Conservative MP. When Wood complained, however, Churchill at once made amends, and treated him courteously enough, although he did not provide him with very much to do.[61] Eventually he arranged for Wood to visit the West Indian colonies and report on their condition, as he himself had reported on East Africa in 1908.

Churchill would have liked as Colonial Secretary to bring to fruition some of the plans for the economic development of East Africa which he had conceived on his African trip thirteen years earlier. He could not help contrasting the fertility of the lands he had visited there with the barren wastes of the Arab territories which he had just seen. As he told a meeting of the British Cotton-growing Association in Manchester,

In Africa the population is docile and the country fruitful; in Mesopotamia and the Middle East the country is arid and the population ferocious. A little money goes a long way in Africa and a lot of money goes a very little way in Arabia.[62]

Churchill would much have liked to loosen the Treasury purse-strings in order to provide credit for ambitious projects in the colonies. There would have been the additional advantage that the work would have helped to relieve the unemployment in Britain, which had become serious after the collapse of the post-war boom in 1920.[63] But successive chancellors of the exchequer – Austen Chamberlain and then Sir Robert Horne – pursued deflationary policies, and consequently showed no enthusiasm for such ideas. In the absence of financial help from Britain, the colonies had to be left to manage their own affairs as best they could, under the control of their respective governors. The role of the Colonial Office in this situation was bound to be a limited one as Churchill acknowledged in a speech to an audience of colonial civil servants:

It would not be possible to govern the British Empire from Downing Street. We do not try. Downing Street attempts to supervise the action of responsible governors who are expected to act in accordance with the conditions which are associated with the personality of an English gentleman.[64]

There were occasions, however, when the 'English gentleman' had to be offered some guide-lines of policy by the Secretary of State in Downing Street. One matter which caused trouble owing to the absence of an agreed policy was that of the rights of Indian immigrants in East Africa. Churchill had been aware of the tensions caused by racial rivalry when he had visited Kenya in 1908; and he decided to make some concessions to both European and African opinion. In January 1922 he announced that although the British government acknowledged 'the principle of equal rights for all civilised men' it recognised the need for stricter regulations upon Indian immigration. He also renewed a pledge given by his predecessor, Lord Milner, to safeguard the position of white settlers in the Kenya Highlands by preventing Indians from purchasing land there. He remarked in the course of his speech that 'The democratic principles of Europe are by no means suited to the development of Asiatic and African people.'[65]

Such views were common enough in Conservative circles at home, as well as among colonial civil servants and European settlers. But they did not commend themselves to the Indian nationalist élite, nor to Liberal opinion at home – and Montagu, the Secretary of State for India, was a much more convinced Liberal on such matters than Churchill. Montagu raised the matter of Churchill's speech in the Cabinet, and eventually it was agreed that the future of the Indian community in Kenya should be thrashed out by the Under-Secretaries of the two departments involved. The Wood–Winterton agreement which resulted, and which made some concessions to the Indian standpoint, so infuriated the Europeans in Kenya that late in 1922, when the Coalition government fell, they were on the verge of revolt.[66] Their intransigence on this question was strengthened by the knowledge that the South African government was also hostile to full citizenship for Indian immigrants. At the 1921 Imperial Conference it proved impossible to obtain South African support for a very mild resolution saying that it was 'desirable' that the claims of Indian immigrants to citizenship should be recognised.[67]

*   *   *

267

At this time the Colonial Office was still fully responsible for relations with the self-governing Dominions, and Churchill was expected to play the part of impresario at the Imperial Conference, even though the leading roles would be taken by the prime ministers, and especially by Lloyd George. The 1921 meeting did not turn out to be one of the more important Imperial Conferences, as no major constitutional decisions were taken; and while Lloyd George enjoyed the role of acting as host to his old colleagues in the Imperial War Cabinet Churchill found himself taking the chair at a number of minor committees dealing with such details as Imperial Patents and Condominium Control of the New Hebrides. He could not even enjoy the social side of the conference, as his mother had died and he was in mourning.

Much more important than the conference, however, was the work in which Churchill was increasingly engaged – that of finding a solution to the Irish question. He had long favoured an attempt at negotiation with Sinn Fein; but as Secretary for War he had had to order the reassertion of British control of the island by military force. The brutality of the warfare that developed between Sinn Fein on the one side and the army, the police and especially the auxiliary police or 'Black and Tans' on the other, is still a bitter memory. Churchill felt obliged to ask the Cabinet to allow 'authorised reprisals' against Sinn Fein in order to restore army and police morale and to check the unauthorised action which had already begun to develop in response to terrorism.[68] But he had become Colonial Secretary before this new policy came into operation.

In May 1921 Lloyd George felt that the time had at last arrived when public opinion in Britain and even in the Conservative Party in Parliament would be prepared to come to terms with Sinn Fein, provided that the six counties of Northern Ireland were exempted from the agreement and provided that Ireland remained an integral part of the Empire. He therefore invited Eamon de Valera, the Sinn Fein leader, to enter into negotiations for this purpose. A truce was proclaimed in July, and in October 1921 a conference began at 10 Downing Street, at which five representatives of Sinn Fein – not, however, including de Valera himself – met Lloyd George and several of his colleagues, including Austen Chamberlain, Lord Birkenhead (the former 'F.E.') and Churchill in direct negotiation across the Cabinet table.

The leader of the Irish delegation was Arthur Griffith, an intellectual of the Sinn Fein movement, and among its other members was Michael Collins, a burly thirty-year-old clerk who was the leader of the Irish Republican Army. Churchill did not play a major part in the negotiations, which on the British side were largely conducted by the Prime Minister himself. But he was able to observe the behaviour of the Irish delegation and to decide that they were sincerely attempting to come to terms. After some weeks had passed without agreement, Lloyd George, being harassed by opposition from within the ranks of the Conservative Party, and fearing that Bonar Law, who had withdrawn from the government owing to ill-health, might re-emerge as his rival for the Premiership, began to talk of resignation. He apparently thought that Bonar Law would be unable to form a government, or that if he did he would inevitably lose a general election. But Churchill warned him against such a course, pointing out brutally but realistically:

> Most men sink into insignificance when they quit office. Very insignificant men acquire weight when they obtain it.... The delusion that an alternative government cannot be formed is perennial.[69]

It was no doubt his father's experience which led him to this view.

Gradually the members of the two delegations began to develop a measure of mutual trust. Churchill came to recognise both the 'high integrity' of Griffith and the 'elemental qualities and mother wit' of Collins.[70] Collins visited him at his house in Sussex Square, and Churchill showed him the Boer proclamation of 1899 offering £25 for his own head. When Collins said there had been a price on his head, Churchill replied: 'At any rate it was a good price – £5000. Look at me – £25, dead or alive. How would you like that?'[71] The feelings of mutual goodwill which animated the leading delegates may have been of great importance when early in December Lloyd George felt it necessary to call the negotiations to a halt. He presented the Irishmen with the stark choice: acceptance of Dominion status, or a resumption of the civil war. After an adjournment of a few hours, to the relief of the British leaders they announced their willingness to accept the terms.

Once the treaty was signed it became Churchill's responsibility as Colonial Secretary to take charge of the transfer of power in Ireland. The work was delayed and complicated by the refusal of a large section of Sinn Fein, led by de Valera himself, to accept the terms negotiated in London. Units of the Irish Republican Army took up arms again, and there was bloodshed both in Belfast and on the new border between the two Irish states. Churchill for his part was faced with the difficult task of persuading the backbenchers of the Conservative Party to accept the agreement, which was embodied in the Irish Free State Bill. He argued that British relations with her other Dominions and with the United States had long been embittered by the feud with Ireland, but that this would now cease to be the case:

> When the Sinn Fein ideal is realised – 'Ourselves Alone' – though they may wish to follow their own way of life in Ireland, as they have a right to wish, the power to stand in the path of the British Empire and to obstruct our world-wide policy will have absolutely departed.[72]

This was a skilful speech, as was widely recognised;[73] and in the end there were only about sixty 'die-hard' MPs who resisted the settlement in the division. But thereafter this group formed the nucleus of a potential Conservative revolt against Lloyd George's leadership of the Coalition. If the Irish settlement was the greatest of the Coalition's achievements, it was also the most important factor in its eventual collapse.

This was partly because Ireland for some time obstinately refused to be pacified by the enactment of the terms of the treaty. The divisions within Sinn Fein itself became still more acute, and a group of extremists, in defiance of the Provisional Government, seized the Law Courts in Dublin and proclaimed the Republic. Then in June 1922 Sir Henry Wilson, now a field-marshal and lately retired from the post of Chief of the Imperial General Staff, was assassinated by two Irish gunmen on the steps of his home in Eaton Square, in the West End of London. Churchill, who had been trying to persuade both Collins and Craig, the Ulster leader, to discipline their extremists, was forced to utter a grave public warning to the Provisional Government about terrorism:

> If either from weakness, from want of courage, or for some other even less creditable reasons, it is not brought to an end, and a very speedy end, then, it is my duty to say ... that we shall regard the

Treaty as having been formally violated ... and that we shall resume full liberty of action.[74]

This did not stop Bonar Law from making a menacing speech about the British government's own weakness, and from quoting, not without irony, Churchill's own phraseology at Bradford in March 1914: 'Much time cannot elapse before these grave matters – to quote a saying of the Colonial Secretary – are brought to the test.'[75]

The Cabinet's reaction was now to order General Sir Nevil Macready, who was in charge of the British army in Ireland, to undertake the eviction of the extremists from the Dublin Law Courts. Macready, who detected Churchill's hand in this, realised at once that it would only unite the factions of Sinn Fein against his troops; and so, finding or appearing to find that he did not have enough ammunition to undertake the task without some delay, he despatched to London a vigorous protest against the order.[76] It was duly countermanded; but in the meantime Collins, goaded by Churchill, had at last decided to assert his government's authority. Borrowing artillery from the British forces, he broke down the wall of the Law Courts; and, although fighting continued for several days, in the end the extremists were defeated and the authority of the Provisional Government was upheld.

There followed a new civil war in Ireland – a war between the two factions of Sinn Fein. Collins himself was killed in late August; and as Arthur Griffith, the other principal Irish signatory of the treaty, had died of heart failure only a few days earlier it seemed as if the Provisional Government was leaderless. But into the gap stepped the unspectacular figure of William Cosgrave, who became the new leader of the government; and Churchill hastened to assure him of Britain's 'co-operation and support'. Cosgrave went on to win the civil war and to survive for a decade as the Prime Minister of the Irish Free State. As it turned out, it was Lloyd George's government, rather than Cosgrave's, which was mortally wounded by the treaty – as Churchill later pointed out, it was by no means the first British government to have fallen over an Irish issue, but it was the first to have offered something like a solution to the everlasting problem of the relationship between the two islands.[77]

When Churchill joined Lloyd George's government during the

war he told his Dundee constituents that he remained 'a believer in party politics',[78] and he certainly expected that Britain would return to something like the pre-war pattern after a limited period of recovery from the war. Already by mid-1919 he was trying to decide what the future character of party politics would be. The Coalition Liberals could have little future if they were to try to fight elections independently; but on the other hand they were by no means without bargaining power in the existing situation. Churchill discussed the matter with Lloyd George when he visited him at Criccieth in July, and shortly afterwards he made a speech to a gathering of a 'Centre Group' of Coalition MPs as a *ballon d'essai* to determine the amount of sympathy there was for the creation of a 'Fusion Party' out of the various elements of the existing Coalition.

In this speech Churchill revealed to the public for the first time the efforts Lloyd George had made in 1910 to establish a Coalition of the two main political parties. He argued that efforts to achieve a common platform were fully justified by the absence of real differences between the standpoint of most Conservatives and most Liberals. Some people had thought that these two parties might find a serious cause for divergence over the issue of the nationalisation of industry; but this was not really the case:

> Every one of us is a collectivist for some things, an individualist for others. Everybody agrees that there must be some services organised nationally, and that others should be left to private enterprise and ownership. It is impossible to make a cleavage of principle upon a point like that.[79]

The speech caused a good deal of discussion, but no action followed. It was perhaps premature, for only a few months had passed since the preceding election, and MPs did not feel the compelling need to examine their prospects of re-election.

But Churchill remained an advocate of the Fusion policy. In January 1920 he declared to a Coalition rally at Sunderland that the break-up of the alliance of forces behind the existing government could only have the result of 'pushing the Labour Party into power at a period in their development when they are quite unfitted for the responsibility of government, and when through their incompetence they would come hopelessly to grief at our expense'. He returned to the idea of Fusion: 'Why should it not be possible to combine the patriotism and stability of the Conservative Party with the broad humanities and tolerances of Liberalism?'[80] In the following month, at Dundee, he spelt out his reasons for regarding the Labour Party as still 'unfit to govern'. It was because its members had deliberately made of it 'a class party', and because they had no 'useful or helpful solutions of the difficult problems which are in front of us', other than nationalisation as a general principle, and self-determination for all peoples, which might mean that Ireland would be free to ally herself with Germany.[81]

Lloyd George himself now felt that the time had come to take the initiative in the direction of Fusion. He decided to address a Coalition Liberal conference to this effect; but before he did so he took the precaution of summoning the Liberal ministers of his government, twenty-five in all, and inviting their comments on the idea. He found that many of them were critical. Churchill, to be sure, was in favour, and advocated 'a definite stand against the Labour Party on the lines of his recent speeches'. But it was pointed out by others that Coalition Liberals sitting for Scottish constituencies would almost certainly be abandoned by their local associations if they joined a Fusion party.[82] Lloyd George therefore changed his plans and did not raise the matter at the ensuing conference. The doubts expressed about feeling in Scotland were largely confirmed by the proceedings at a conference of the Scottish Liberal Federation in Glasgow at the end of April. Liberalism had always been relatively strong in Scotland, and there was a general view among Scottish Liberals that the 'coupon' election of 1918 had given far too many Scottish seats to the Conservatives, and so had done their own cause a grave disservice.[83] Churchill ventured to attend and to speak at the Glasgow conference, but he was coolly received, and his demand that the Annual Report of the federation, which was Asquithian in tone, should be referred back was defeated, on a show of hands, by about 200 to about 70.[84]

Up to 1920 Lloyd George's reputation in the country was so high that the Conservatives would probably have accepted the idea of Fusion without much hesitation. Afterwards, however, and especially in 1922, this ceased to be the case. The concessions made by the government over Ireland, the collapse of the post-war boom and a host of minor discontents caused many of the Conservative backbenchers to wish to break away from the Coalition and form their own government. Lloyd George himself sensed this mood, and also the growing support in the country for the Labour Party, but planned to win back prestige for his government by a final diplomatic success in the economic sphere. He sponsored a conference of the powers at Genoa in April 1922, at which he hoped to scale down the international war-debt payments, to make an agreement with Germany about reparations, and to bring Soviet Russia into the comity of nations.

But these plans soon ran into difficulties. In the first place, the reduction of the war-debt payments depended on concessions by the Americans, the principle creditor-nation; and the United States government refused to attend the conference. Secondly, there was backbench Conservative opposition to any attempt by Lloyd George to give official recognition to the Soviet government, and on this issue, as was to be expected, Churchill sided with the anti-Bolsheviks. Lloyd George complained angrily to Austen Chamberlain, saying that the Cabinet must choose between them;[85] but Chamberlain in reply warned the Prime Minister that Churchill was 'doubly dangerous to me and my colleagues if he parts from us on a question where he would have the sympathy of a large section of Unionist opinion'.[86] C. A. McCurdy, who had succeeded Guest as Lloyd George's Chief Whip, had already told him that there was a danger that if Churchill went over to the Conservatives he would take a good many of the Coalition Liberals with him.[87]

Lloyd George therefore went to Genoa with relatively little freedom of manœuvre. But the conference was doomed to failure for other reasons as well. There was no unity of purpose between Britain and France; and as a result the German and Russian delegations, realising that they had little to gain from the Western Powers, met separately at Rapallo and made an economic agreement between themselves. Lloyd George returned to Britain in May, virtually empty-handed. Fearing that he intended to re-open the question of the recognition of the Soviet government, Churchill warned him solemnly in July that he felt it to be 'quite impossible'. He reminded the Prime Minister that he had once said that he (Churchill) was 'a branch that creaked before it broke' – and he strongly implied that this issue was, for him, a breaking matter.[88]

Over the years of the Coalition's life it had been surprising how well Churchill had been able to carry on under Lloyd George's leadership, considering the differences that separated them on important questions of the time. In their correspondence Churchill always replied courteously to the Prime Minister, even when the latter was most ill-tempered, but he did not fail to make clear his own disagreements with Lloyd George's policy or with that of the Cabinet. In March 1920 he told Lloyd George in a personal letter: 'since the armistice my policy wd have been "Peace with the German people, War on the Bolshevik tyranny". Willingly or unavoidably you have followed something very near the reverse.'[89] They also clashed over policy towards Turkey. Here their roles appeared to be reversed: Churchill was as sympathetic towards the revolution effected by Mustapha Kemal as he was hostile to that of the Bolsheviks in Russia, and pointed out to Lloyd George that 'an attempt to enforce a peace on Turkey ... wd require great & powerful armies & long costly operations & occupations. On this world so torn with strife I dread to see you let loose the Greek armies....'[90] But Lloyd George had a remarkable pro-Greek bias, and he encouraged the Greek government to indulge in aggrandisement far beyond its capacity – a policy that led only to disaster in the ensuing months.

On these issues of foreign policy the other members of the Cabinet usually held the balance between their two most versatile and determined colleagues, and helped to keep them in uneasy partnership. Churchill was not of course as powerful as Lloyd George; but the fact that his views tended to coincide with those of many of the Conservative rank and file in Parliament gave them a weight in the Cabinet which they would not otherwise have had. On domestic affairs, the situation was quite different: here Churchill's views were more radical, and here he found more common ground with the Prime Minister than with the Conservative members of the Cabinet. But because the Treasury was always in Conservative hands, and because the temper of the House of Commons and of public opinion (aided by an 'anti-waste' campaign in the Northcliffe press) was strongly on the side of economy, nothing could be done to prevent the operation of an increasingly orthodox financial policy.

Churchill's discontent with the government's domestic policy is manifested to the historian in a sequence of recorded disagreements at the Cabinet and in private letters of complaint to the Prime Minister. We have already seen that he had advocated the nationalisation of the railways during his election campaign, not having been aware that this had been cut out of the Coalition

manifesto at Bonar Law's insistence. He also favoured the imposition of a capital levy, so as to force the war profiteers to dis-
gorge some of their (as he saw it) ill-gotten gains. When in June
1920 the Cabinet finally declared against the proposal, Churchill's
dissent was recorded in the minutes.[91] Then in the autumn of
1921, on paying a visit to Dundee, Churchill was shocked to find
widespread distress due to unemployment, with 'some men in
bare feet & some children obviously in a savage & starving condition'.[92] The distress was aggravated by the government's abrupt
decision to abandon its housing subsidies, which left the Town
Council with a number of prepared sites on which it could no
longer afford to build. Churchill therefore wrote a Cabinet Paper
criticising the 'austere Bankers' policy' which had been accepted
by the Chancellor of the Exchequer and by the Cabinet.[93] When
Lloyd George replied saying that 'recrimination will not help',
Churchill appealed to him to apply his mind to the problem systematically; he admitted that he personally could not offer a solution, but he thought that close study under the Prime Minister's
direction could 'get to the bottom of it & frame a definite policy
... wh wd carry us through the temporary & baffling fluctuations
wh are affecting us so violently at the present time.... We are
drifting about in a fog without a compass.'[94]

But Lloyd George seemed to be at the mercy of the economists,
to a degree which had no parallel when he was Chancellor of the
Exchequer himself in the pre-war years. In so far as he personally
sought an answer to the depression, it was in the sphere of international diplomacy, for it was generally believed that world trade
was suffering from the burden of reparations and war debts and
from the severance of normal economic links with Russia. In
1921, in the face of demands for the reduction of government expenditure, he agreed to appoint a committee of businessmen,
under Sir Eric Geddes, to examine the entire national expenditure and to recommend ways in which it could be reduced. When
the committee reported, he appointed three groups of ministers
to see how far the recommendations could be accepted.

Churchill was put in charge of the group examining the Service
departments, but he did not feel that there were great economies
still to be made. It was, after all, he himself who had in 1919
invented the idea of the 'Ten Year Rule', by which the estimates
were drawn up on the assumption that there would be no major
war until at least 1929.[95] Nevertheless he made a personal study

of naval expenditure, and his old friend Beatty, who was now First Sea Lord, had to defend the Admiralty administration against the criticisms of his former chief. On the whole Churchill was inclined to sympathise with the Admiralty against Geddes, so much so indeed that Beatty was able to tell his wife that Churchill had 'supported us nobly'.[96] The 'Geddes axe' was prevented from cutting deeply into the naval estimates at this time – although there were of course substantial savings made in naval construction as a result of the 1922 Washington Treaty with the United States and Japan, which eliminated the threat of battleship building rivalry between the leading powers.

In the end it was a foreign-policy question on which the Coalition government fought its last battle, and here in spite of past differences Lloyd George and Churchill found themselves united in deciding what to do. Mustapha Kemal, the Turkish Nationalist leader, had refused to accept the Treaty of Sèvres dictated by the Allies in 1920, whereby a large section of Asia Minor was handed over to the Greeks. In 1922 he attacked the Greek forces and threw them back to the Aegean. By September of that year he was advancing towards Chanak on the Dardanelles, where there was a small British occupation force, and he threatened to storm its positions and to close the Straits once more to the western powers. Churchill had foreseen this turn of events, and, as we have seen, had long been beseeching Lloyd George to abandon his encouragement of the Greeks, whom he could not support with military strength. But the balance was now swinging too far the other way, and he agreed with the Prime Minister and other leading members of the Cabinet that Kemal had to be prevented from overrunning the British zone and assuming full control in the area.

On Friday September 15th a solemn warning was sent to Kemal that he must on no account enter the British zone, and at the same time telegrams were sent to the Dominion governments asking them for their support and, if necessary, for contingents of troops to help reassert the British control of the Straits. Unfortunately the Dominion prime ministers did not have their telegrams deciphered very quickly, and in the meantime a communiqué, drafted by Churchill at Lloyd George's request and held up for only a few hours before release, had appeared in newspapers all over the world. Reaction in the Dominion capitals, and especially in Canada, was not therefore initially friendly; and public opinion in Britain was also largely unprepared for the threat of war. Yet in spite of these adverse repercussions the action taken was decisive. Tension continued for several weeks, and at one point the British general in charge was ordered to move against a small Turkish infringement of his zone. But he wisely held his hand, as Macready had done in Dublin; and in mid-October Kemal came to terms and undertook to respect the zone occupied by the British troops. Greek forces in the region were allowed to retire unmolested into Thrace. It was an important diplomatic victory for the Coalition government at last, but not one that a war-weary and distracted mass electorate could very easily recognise as such.

The Coalition government had now held office for almost four years since the 1918 general election, and its life was already in serious danger from its own supporters. Lloyd George had decided to dissolve Parliament before the next meeting of the National Union of Conservative Associations in November, because he feared an attempt would then be made to disavow his leadership. He still had the backing of the principal Conservatives in the Cabinet, with the exception of Lord Curzon, who was already moving into opposition, and it was they who brought matters to a head by summoning a meeting of the parliamentary party at the Carlton Club on October 19th, with the intention of obtaining a vote of confidence. The opponents of the Coalition mostly consisted of backbenchers, and they needed a prominent Commons spokesman to serve as an alternative prime minister if they won the vote. They therefore pressed Bonar Law to take up their cause, and it was of crucial importance that in the end he agreed to do so. Stanley Baldwin, the President of the Board of Trade, was the only Cabinet Minister to speak on the rebel side; but the vote against the Coalition was unexpectedly decisive – 185 to 88.[97]

This was the end of the road for Lloyd George. All his Conservative colleagues felt obliged to resign their offices, and immediately, on the same day, Lloyd George went to Buckingham Palace and tendered his own resignation. Bonar Law was then hastily elected leader of the Conservative Party in place of Austen Chamberlain, and having already been invited to form a government, he kissed hands as the new Prime Minister on October 23rd. It was the end of an era.

14. *Out of Parliament, 1922-4*

THE decisive events of October 19th 1922 – the meeting at the Carlton Club, and Lloyd George's visit to Buckingham Palace to resign the Premiership – took place while Churchill lay on a sickbed. He had fallen ill on the 15th, and on the 16th it was announced that he had 'acute gastro-enteritis'.[1] But the diagnosis soon changed to acute appendicitis, and an operation for the removal of the appendix was performed on October 18th. Bonar Law did not formally become Prime Minister until five days later, when he had been elected Leader of the Conservative Party; but Churchill, expecting an immediate general election, had already dictated a statement about his own position in politics. He would stand, he said, 'as a Liberal and a Free Trader, but I shall ask the electors to authorise me to co-operate freely with sober-minded and progressive Conservatives'.[2]

By the time Bonar Law had formed his government and a dissolution of Parliament had been announced, Churchill had despatched Lord Wodehouse, who was one of his private secretaries, to Dundee to prepare the ground for his campaign. This prompt action may have been of some value in discouraging the Dundee Conservatives from putting up a candidate against him and against D. J. Macdonald, a local engineer who, in view of Wilkie's retirement, had been adopted as Churchill's running-mate as a Coalition Liberal – or rather as a National Liberal, for the group had changed names. It was obvious that a strong challenge would come from Labour, which was in no mood to share the representation with Churchill as in the past. E. D. Morel, the powerful propagandist who had run the Union of Democratic Control during the war, was adopted as a Labour candidate in 1920.[3] The only other candidate with whom Morel was prepared to co-operate for electoral purposes was Edwin Scrymgeour, the Prohibitionist, who was once again in the field. There was also a standard-bearer of the newly formed Communist Party of Great Britain – William Gallacher, a Clydeside factory worker; and an Asquithian Liberal, R. R. Pilkington, a London barrister who entered the lists without much local support.

Dundee was a city much dependent upon foreign trade, and its predominantly working-class population had suffered severely in the post-war depression that had begun in 1920. As we have seen, Churchill had been shocked by the obvious signs of poverty that he had seen in the city in 1921, and had urged his Cabinet colleagues to take more effective remedial action. But little was done; and his remonstrations within the Cabinet naturally did not enable him to escape from the local political consequences of the distress, which were to transfer support among the electors from himself to Morel, Scrymgeour, and to a lesser extent Gallacher. The 'patriotic' Labour element which had supported both Churchill and Wilkie in 1918 had virtually disappeared; and the Irish vote, which had not been properly organised in 1918, was now much more effectively marshalled in opposition to Churchill and Macdonald.[4] To cap all this, there was the fact that the two local papers, one Liberal and one Conservative, were now both owned by one proprietor, D. C. Thomson, a man of decided views and an opponent of the Coalition. In an acrid correspondence earlier in 1922 Churchill had threatened Thomson with the establishment of a rival newspaper if he did not show more favour to the government; but Thomson had refused to make any concession.[5]

In the face of all these adverse factors, Churchill was almost powerless. He could issue statements to the national press from his bedside in London, but he was too weak to enter the early stages of the campaign in Dundee itself. His colleague Macdonald was of little use, and soon lost his voice in attempts to shout down his opponents.[6] Clementine arrived in the constituency ten days before polling, carrying a baby in her arms – her fifth and last child, later to be christened Mary.[7] Accompanied by Churchill's most faithful political supporter, MacCallum Scott, and by J. W.

Pratt, another National Liberal MP, she endeavoured to conduct a regular campaign on behalf of her husband. She did her best to revive the issues of the 1918 election, reminding the electors of Morel's opposition to the war; but this seemed to be largely a dead issue, and she had to face constant interruptions from her audiences, which often silenced her altogether, and on one occasion upset her by the use of sneezing-powder.

Churchill himself, 'frail and pale-looking', arrived for the last four days of the campaign. He was still too weak to walk, and had to be carried into the Caird Hall, the scene of some of his earlier oratorical triumphs, on an improvised sedan chair. The content of his address, which he delivered sitting down, was not below his usual standard: it had been composed during his enforced leisure after the operation. He defended himself and his colleagues for taking a risk of war over Chanak: 'It is true a risk was run. Risks are run every time a lifeboat goes into a storm, but such risks have never deterred men, aye and women too, of British blood from doing their duty.' And then in a reference to the saving of Greek lives in Constantinople and Thrace as a result, he said: 'Never in the history of the world was there a rescue organised on so gigantic a scale and resulting in the salvation of such vast numbers of human beings.'* Churchill rose to his feet for a final sentence in which he exhorted his audience to abhor the political extremes and to 'tread the sober middle way'.[8]

But the audiences that he was addressing were not at all the same as those which had listened respectfully to him in 1908 and 1910. Apart from the shift of feeling from Liberalism to Labour, there was a Communist element which did not believe in free speech, at any rate for non-Communists. Two days before polling day Churchill was held up by a chorus of young men singing 'Tell me the old, old story'; after a time, weak as he was, he lost his temper with them and called them 'young reptiles'. This section of the 'audience' responded with the Red Flag and cheers for the Irish Republic.[9] Gallacher, the Communist candidate, later claimed credit for doing 'all the fighting' in the election, while Morel and Scrymgeour 'just lay back and took it easy'.[10]

But Morel and Scrymgeour were conducting their campaign more effectively than Gallacher, and their informal alliance

---

*Compare the more famous sentence uttered in August 1940: 'Never in the field of human conflict was so much owed by so many to so few.'

brought them complementary advantages. Their success on polling day was so great that neither Churchill nor Macdonald could have secured election even if Pilkington had stood down. The figures were:

E. Scrymgeour (Prohibitionist)	32,578	Elected
E. D. Morel (Labour)	30,392	Elected
D. J. Macdonald (Nat. Liberal)	22,244	
W. S. Churchill (Nat. Liberal)	20,466	
R. R. Pilkington (Liberal)	6681	
W. Gallacher (Communist)	5906	

Two-thirds of those who voted for Scrymgeour also voted for Morel, and three-quarters of those who voted for Macdonald also voted for Churchill. But Scrymgeour had over 5000 'plumpers', and Churchill was beaten into fourth place because many of those who voted for Pilkington also voted for Macdonald.[11]

This was a massive defeat for Dundee Liberalism. It could not be explained by abstentions, for there was a turn-out of 81%. It is difficult to see the transformation in terms of 'swing', as in 1918 Churchill had run in virtual alliance with a Labour candidate. But it was evident that in Dundee as elsewhere the sympathies of the majority of working men and women could no longer be relied upon by the Liberal Party. The Dundee result did not increase the size of the Labour Party at Westminster; and in the London papers it was taken as more of a personal defeat for Churchill than as a symptom of the break-up of Liberalism. Asquith, writing to Venetia Montagu, was inclined as he put it to 'gloat over the corpses which have been left on the battlefield', prominent among whom he listed Churchill.[12] But this was meagre compensation for the fact that of the more than three hundred candidates who had stood as Asquithian Liberals more than five-sixths had been defeated. The Conservatives secured a clear parliamentary majority and the National Liberals and Asquithians combined numbered distinctly less than Labour, which was over twice as strong in the new House as in 1918.

After the event, Churchill was philosophical about his defeat. As he wrote to H. A. L. Fisher, one of his former colleagues, 'If you ever saw the kind of lives the Dundee folk have to live, you wd admit they have many excuses.'[13] But he now found himself, as he later put it, 'without an office, without a seat, without a party, and without an appendix'.[14] One consolation was that he had been made a Companion of Honour in Lloyd George's final distribution of honours – a more positively merited award than many that Lloyd George had made during his term of office. He also had a sense of relief at being quit of his heavy responsibilities and being free to take a long holiday to recuperate from his existing state of physical exhaustion.

For a period of six months after the election Churchill was absent from the public scene. He went to the south of France early in December and except for a brief visit to London at the beginning of February he stayed on the Mediterranean coast throughout the winter and early spring. He had rented a villa at Cannes, and used that as his base. He did not, however, allow himself to be forgotten in Britain, for in February *The Times* serialised the first volume of his *World Crisis*, which he had found time to put together despite being continuously in office since 1918. It dealt with the coming of the war and his own work at the Admiralty from 1911 to the end of 1914. As usual, it was written in a vividly attractive style, and it had the additional advantage of revealing a great deal of secret information, often in the form of extensive quotation of state papers not previously published. There were complaints about this in the House of Commons, and Bonar Law in reply gave the impression that he believed Churchill to have breached his Privy Councillor's oath.[15]

Churchill could not accept this at all. In a letter to the Prime Minister he pointed out that George Arthur, Kitchener's biographer, had already been allowed to publish official documents, including one of Churchill's Cabinet Papers of 1915. Jellicoe, Fisher, and others had also published memoirs which included confidential material, and Churchill did not see why Privy Councillors should be precluded, by reason of their oath, from doing the same.[16] Hankey, the Cabinet Secretary, when shown this letter told Bonar Law that he felt that there was a good deal of force in the argument, and it was agreed that a Cabinet Committee should look into the matter.[17]

In the meantime Churchill proceeded to publish his work precisely as he had intended. It appeared in April, and by then its author was hard at work on a second volume covering the year 1915. This in turn was serialised in *The Times*, the extracts beginning on October 8th 1923 and the book being published on October 30th.

During these months the political situation had been changing rapidly. In May 1923 Bonar Law, suffering from cancer of the throat, had been forced to resign the Premiership; he was to die within a few months. After consultations with leading members of the Conservative Party the King chose Stanley Baldwin as Bonar Law's successor. This was a remarkable promotion for a man who had entered the Cabinet for the first time only two years previously; but there was no other serious contender except Curzon, and he, for all his experience, had the disadvantage of being a member of the House of Lords. Baldwin, in forming his government, was still unable to call upon the Conservative leaders who had been most prominent in the later years of the Coalition – in particular Austen Chamberlain, Horne and Birkenhead. The Cabinet was thus inevitably as much a 'second eleven' as Bonar Law's had been. In casting round for a means to reunite his party, therefore, Baldwin decided that his best course was to revive the campaign for Tariff Reform – the campaign that had proved so disastrous to the party before the war, but which in the existing state of unemployment and distress might prove popular with the electorate. In October he made a speech at Plymouth describing unemployment as 'the most crucial problem of our country' and saying, 'I cannot fight it without weapons'.[18] This drew him immediate support from Austen Chamberlain and his associates. In mid-November he dissolved Parliament, and the country found itself once more plunged into a general election.

These developments brought Churchill back into the political arena. They took him by surprise, for he had assured McCurdy, the former National Liberal Chief Whip, that 'his knowledge of Conservative psychology' made him sure that the government would run its full term.[19] Still a devoted Free Trader, he felt that he had no alternative but to resist Baldwin's policy; and so he sought adoption as a Liberal candidate, acknowledging once more the leadership of his former chief, Asquith. He was not alone in this: for the reunion of the Conservatives, which Baldwin had hoped for, had been accompanied by a reunion of Liberals. Even Lloyd George, who had been on a tour of America, agreed on his return to make common cause with his old leader. On

November 11th Churchill issued a personal statement on Tariff Reform:

> I deplore the raising of this issue. I have taken no part in opposing the Conservative Government nor in disparaging the new ministers. I should have been perfectly content to remain for a much longer period in private life. But an aggressive attack has been levelled needlessly and wantonly at the foundations of the people's livelihood.[20]

Churchill's thoughts must have turned back to the great campaigns for Free Trade which he had fought in Lancashire in 1903-6 and again in 1909-10. The Free Trade Union returned to its pristine vigour and once more invited him to be its champion at a mass meeting in Manchester, and he accepted the invitation. Lancashire, after all, was still the great exporting county, and its interests were bound to suffer if tariffs were introduced. The meeting, which was held on November 16th at the Free Trade Hall, was attended by a full house of 3000 people, and there was an overflow meeting almost as large to whom the speech was relayed. 'Once again,' said Churchill, 'it is within the power of Lancashire to decide the policy of Britain. No tariff can be imposed upon the people if you say "No".' Recalling a joke from Surtees – favourite reading of his father's – he poked fun at Baldwin:

> You will remember how Mr Jorrocks, the famous fox-hunter, was sleeping at an inn with his huntsman, James Pigg, and was eager, if the weather would allow him, to hunt the next day. You will remember how Pigg got up, walked round the room in the dark, missed the window, and opened a small cupboard, and reported to his master: 'It's as dark as pitch and smells of cheese.' (Laughter) Well, Mr Baldwin's revelation or discovery was rather on this level, and at Plymouth he produced from the depths of his consciousness the following murky gem: 'The only way of fighting unemployment is by protecting the home market.'[21]

Churchill was invited to contest a seat in Lancashire, but he was also offered Leicester West, a working-class constituency captured by Labour in a three-cornered contest in 1922. The latter was not a particularly good prospect for him, unless the Conservatives decided to withdraw and allow him a straight fight against Labour. Churchill had reason to believe that this was more than a possibility.[22] Furthermore, there were signs of disagreement in the Labour camp, as the Boot and Shoe Operatives regarded the constituency as one where they were entitled to nominate the Labour candidate; but the local Labour Party had adopted a Socialist intellectual, F. W. Pethick-Lawrence.[23] So Churchill accepted the Leicester invitation and was soon engaged in a vigorous local campaign. He was soon disappointed to find that he had a Conservative opponent after all; and Baldwin, predicting his defeat, described him as 'the proudest statesman who has entered Leicester since Cardinal Wolsey came to lay his bones in the Abbey'.[24]

In many respects Churchill's campaign was an easier one for him than that at Dundee had been, for he was again fit and well and could cope good-humouredly with the heckling. It was tiresome, to be sure, that the theme of many of the interruptions was 'What about the Dardanelles?' – but it was agreeable that at least one man who had served there, Lieutenant A. P. Herbert, who was a Conservative, came to his rescue on this issue.[25] As at Dundee, the Liberal cause lacked a newspaper of its own; and it was therefore arranged to distribute free to all households a daily sheet called the *Leicester Liberal Elector* – though unfortunately it had to be printed in Nottingham, which was not very pleasing to the more parochially minded Leicester voters.[26]

Nationally the election was mainly fought on the issue of Tariff Reform, and once again the voters rejected the Conservative Party's favourite proposal. Both the Liberal and Labour Parties gained votes and seats at the expense of the Conservatives. Churchill found to his disappointment that the electors of his constituency behaved very similarly to those elsewhere. Pethick-Lawrence did not suffer at all from the disgruntlement of the Boot and Shoe Operatives; and he had an excellent constituency organisation, which had been built up by Ramsay MacDonald in the days when he represented Leicester before the war.[27] So Churchill was again defeated:

F. W. Pethick-Lawrence (Labour)	13,634	Elected
W. S. Churchill (Liberal)	9236	
Capt. A. Instone (Conservative)	7696	

It is not practicable to calculate the swing from the result of the preceding general election, as in 1922 there had been no candidate calling himself a Conservative; but it was undoubtedly a serious disappointment for Churchill to have increased the Liberal vote by only 3.6% of the total poll. The figure was better than the average for Liberal candidates in English borough constituencies, but only by a small margin.[28] He drew some consolation from the fact that the successful candidate, Pethick-Lawrence, who was three years older than Churchill, and was entering the House for the first time, shared his views on the need to maintain Free Trade.

Meanwhile the party leaders faced an awkward constitutional situation. The Conservatives, although they lost their Commons majority as a result of the election, were still the largest of the three parties, with a total of 258 MPs. The Liberals numbered 159, which was a considerable increase since 1922. Many of their gains were in Lancashire – for instance, they now held five of the ten Manchester seats, whereas in 1922 they had won none of them. Churchill now realised that he would probably have won if he had fought a Lancashire constituency. But the main feature of the election was the continued growth of the Labour Party, which kept well ahead of the Liberals and had a total of 191 seats. Asquith as Liberal leader decided that the experiment of a Labour government, supported from outside by the Liberals, must now be tried. It was his view that since it would be dependent on Liberal votes, 'it could hardly be tried under safer conditions'.[29]

Churchill was shocked by this prospect, and tried to avert it by expressing his views to the Liberal leader through the latter's daughter, Violet, now Lady Bonham-Carter, with whom he had been so friendly before the war. He urged Asquith to form a government of his own, with the support of the Conservatives. On this basis, he thought, it might be possible to create a firm anti-Socialist alliance – which had been his object since 1918.[30] He issued a statement to the press to say that 'The enthronement in office of a Socialist Government will be a serious national misfortune such as has usually befallen great states only on the morrow of defeat in war.'[31] But Asquith refused to be deflected from his purpose; and Churchill resolved to abandon him as leader, and to strike out in independence from the Liberal Party if necessary.

The first Labour government was formed in January 1924, with Ramsay MacDonald as Prime Minister. Churchill discovered that there were very few out of the Liberal parliamentary party who refused to sustain Asquith's policy with their votes. Even Freddie Guest supported the move to put Labour in office, though he repented of it shortly afterwards.[32] From outside Parliament, Churchill could at first do little to rally the Anti-Socialist cause. But he was greatly encouraged when in February Baldwin announced that in accordance with the verdict of the electorate he would abandon the policy of Tariff Reform. This decision was endorsed by the Conservative Party in Parliament and by the Central Council of the constituency organisation. Churchill therefore wrote a letter in support of a Conservative candidate who was standing at a by-election at Burnley, and was engaged in a straight fight with a Labour candidate.[33] And he himself looked for a constituency where he could stand as an Anti-Socialist, with the support of the Conservatives.

The opportunity seemed to be immediately available in the Abbey division of Westminster, where the sitting member, J. S. Nicholson, a Conservative, had died not long after his unopposed return at the general election. Churchill got in touch with the Chief Agent of the Conservative Party, Colonel Stanley Jackson, to enquire if the party leadership would oppose him if he stood as an Anti-Socialist and secured the backing of the local Conservatives. Jackson, almost certainly after consulting Baldwin, replied in the negative, and pointed out that the matter of the party label should not worry the local association as it was in fact called the 'Constitutional' and not the 'Conservative' Association.[34] Unfortunately, however, this body was very dependent upon the Nicholson family for its finances, and it decided in the end to invite O. W. Nicholson, the nephew of the previous member, to contest the seat on its behalf. This led to serious disagreement within the Constitutional Association itself, and Churchill decided to force the issue by fighting as an independent.

The by-election, which took place in March 1924, aroused great interest, especially as Churchill, lacking the support of any party machine, was nevertheless warmly backed by the national press. *The Times* was not far from the truth when it described the contest as 'a match between "the Press Trust" and the "Machine"' – the former being the Rothermere and Beaverbrook newspapers (Northcliffe having died in 1922) and the latter the tightly controlled local constituency leadership.[35] It is true that there was a Labour candidate, Fenner Brockway, a leading

Socialist intellectual, and also a Liberal, Scott Duckers. They had both been conscientious objectors during the war, and although this might not have mattered in an industrial constituency it was not thought that they could get much support in such a relatively wealthy district as Westminster.

The question was, rather, what impact could Churchill make upon the traditional Conservative vote? He appealed to Baldwin 'not to fire upon the reinforcements I am bringing to your aid',[36] and Baldwin did his best to respond to this by discouraging Cabinet ministers from supporting either candidate. When one minister, Leopold Amery, insisted upon publishing a message of encouragement to Nicholson, Baldwin released a letter which Balfour had written in support of Churchill, but which he had authorised Baldwin to use at his discretion.[37] For the rest, it was up to Churchill to make the best of his campaign. He was helped by 'a young man with flaming red hair and sparkling eyes ... who treated his chief as a god'.[38] This was Brendan Bracken, a twenty-three-year-old City man of somewhat mysterious origin – in fact he was born in Ireland and largely educated in Australia. Bracken had a flair for organisation and publicity, and he helped to arrange some spectacular 'stunts' for Churchill's campaign, notably a tour round the constituency with a coach-and-four and a trumpeter. Churchill had a Conservative MP to head each of his nine ward committees, and the outdoor campaign was in the hands of James Seddon, a former Labour MP and ex-chairman of the TUC. It was of still greater significance that he had the active support of several members of the Constitutional Association.

But the campaign only lasted ten days, and Churchill felt it was hardly enough time for him to make a full impact on the constituency. All the same, great interest was aroused among the electors of every social class, and the chorus girls of Daly's Theatre were sufficiently enthusiastic to stay up all one night addressing envelopes in the Churchill cause. He later described the campaign as 'incomparably the most exciting, stirring, sensational election I have ever fought',[39] and for Churchill this really meant a lot. In his speeches he hammered away at the danger of Socialism, arguing that the mildness of the existing Labour government was deceptive:

How well the Socialist Government is doing! How moderate and general they are! ... I say there is no correspondence between this glassy surface and the turbulent currents we know are flowing underneath.[40]

It was his case that the Socialist challenge could only be met by a united Conservative Party 'in co-operation with a Liberal wing on the lines of 1886':

> Such a Liberal wing would modify Conservative policy in proportion to its numbers and strength, and with progressive Conservatives and those who sit for great working-class constituencies, would afford the nation the guarantee which it requires against retrogression. Thus, and thus alone, will a line be formed strong enough and broad enough to resist the increasing attack of the Socialist Party, with all its old heresies and new prestige. I have chosen for the Westminster election the watchword, 'Union and Freedom.'[41]

Meanwhile Brockway, the Labour candidate, was surprised by the amount of support he was receiving – some of it from a working-class district near the Horseferry Road, some of it from intellectuals and artists who either resided or had property in the constituency. He received an amusing letter from Bernard Shaw saying that he would have liked to vote for Churchill because he 'thought Gallipoli a good idea', but he could not support a man who had spent '£100,000,000 of our money in trying to put the clock back in Russia to his own feudal date'.[42] Churchill was exonerated from blame over Gallipoli by another of Brockway's supporters, Major C. R. Attlee, the Under-Secretary for War in the Labour government, who said at a meeting in the constituency:

> I was in some of Mr Churchill's shows. I was in Sidney Street as a spectator and believe that perhaps it was the escape of Peter the Painter that sent Winston off on his anti-Russian mood (Laughter). I was in Gallipoli, but will give the devil his due and say that I think Mr Churchill was right about Gallipoli.[43]

When polling day came there was a relatively heavy turn-out of voters – at 61.6% it was the highest proportion of any election in the constituency's existence. But Churchill's hopes were dashed by a narrow margin. The official Conservative candidate scraped home with a majority of 43:

O. W. Nicholson (Conservative) 8187 Elected
W. S. Churchill (Independent Anti-Socialist) 8144

The relative success of the Labour candidate and the pitiful weakness of the Liberal performance were also noteworthy features of the election.

Churchill had had high hopes of winning; and for a moment he thought he had won, as there was a report during the count that he was the victor. But this was soon contradicted, and the news came, though still unofficially, that he was just defeated. Brockway observed him closely at this moment of disappointment: 'He began to tramp the length of the hall, head down, body lurching, like a despairing animal.'[44] He had now lost three elections in a row, and there was talk in the House of Commons of arranging a dinner of MPs who had defeated him in parliamentary contests: Runciman, Joynson-Hicks, Scrymgeour, Morel, Pethick-Lawrence, and now Nicholson.[45] The trouble was that electorally he had none of the local organisation and support which Joseph Chamberlain had had in 1886. He had no real following in the country, and although he was popular in Lancashire, just as his father had been, he had failed to capitalise upon this fact at the 1923 election.

Clearly if Churchill were to rejoin the Conservative Party he would have to do so as an individual. But he wished to do so gradually and honourably, without in the short run sacrificing his independent status. The transition, if it could not be like that of 1886, should at least resemble his own move to the Liberal Party in 1903–6. In the late spring of 1924 he turned to the idea of forming 'Conservative and Liberal Unions' in the constituencies, which would provide a basis for an Anti-Socialist front. The obvious place for such bodies would be working-class constituencies where the Labour vote was already strong. It occurred to him to get in touch with Sir Archibald Salvidge, the Conservative leader at Liverpool, who had sympathised with the Fusion proposals in the Coalition years. He therefore wrote to Salvidge to ask if he would arrange for 'a meeting on a joint platform under your presidency'.[46] Salvidge was doubtful about the idea of a joint Conservative–Liberal meeting, but he was anxious to help, for two of the Liverpool seats had been won by Liberals at the 1923 election. He therefore visited Churchill in London, and persuaded him to address what would be an exclusively Conservative rally. Churchill agreed, and the meeting was arranged for May.

Clementine accompanied her husband to Liverpool and for the first time found herself sitting on a purely Conservative platform. After the speeches were over, Churchill told his hosts at supper at the Adelphi Hotel: 'She's a Liberal, and always has been. It's all very strange for her. But to me, of course, it's just like coming home.'[47] He was a bit disappointed with his speech, which he had given in advance to the London newspapers and rather wished that he had been freer to improvise. But he cheered up in the course of supper, gave an interview to reporters after midnight, and kept one his hosts awake until after two in the morning by reciting to him the speech which he now felt he should have delivered at the meeting.[48]

In the course of his public speech Churchill had indicated that he did not object to the McKenna duties – the thin end of the wedge of Tariff Reform, as it appeared to Free Trade purists, which had been introduced during the war principally as a tax on foreign luxuries such as motorcars, clocks and watches. He also accepted the principle of Imperial Preference to benefit the Colonies and Dominions. These statements indicating the flexibility of his fiscal views made him generally more acceptable on Conservative platforms; and he now received an invitation, which he readily accepted, to address Scottish Conservatives at Edinburgh.[49] More important still, the officers of the Conservative Association of a middle-class residential constituency near London – Epping, one of the divisions of Essex – approached him with a view to his being adopted as their candidate. The constituency had a sitting Conservative MP, but he was retiring. Although not an entirely safe seat, the threat to the Conservative hold came from the Liberal Party and not from Labour: so Churchill would be a good candidate if he could pull in some of the Liberal voters as well as the Conservatives.

Churchill's adoption by the Epping Conservative Association took place in September. The Association could not allow him simply to stand as an 'Independent' for fear of defections from Conservative die-hards; nor could Churchill as yet consent to be called a 'Conservative'. The compromise suggested by the officials of the Epping Association was that he should come forward as a 'Constitutionalist' – perhaps they obtained the term from Colonel Jackson, who had suggested it as suitable for Churchill's candidature at Westminster. Churchill also agreed to attend a meeting of the Council of the Association, which was held, to suit his convenience, in London. He was then adopted as candidate by the members of the Council, not unanimously, but by an overwhelming majority.[50] It only remained for another general election to provide him with a new opportunity for returning to Parliament.

The fall of the Labour government was not long in coming. In the course of the summer J. R. Campbell, the acting editor of a Communist newspaper, had been charged with incitement to mutiny for publishing an article urging soldiers not to fire on their 'fellow-workers'. But the case was withdrawn in August, and the government at once came under attack by both Conservative and Liberals for dropping the prosecution. When Parliament met at the end of September, the Liberals decided to insist on a select committee of enquiry. The Labour Cabinet, realising that a select committee would reflect the proportions of the parties in the House of Commons, which would put their own supporters in a minority, decided to resist the move. The issue was debated on October 8th and the government was defeated by 364 votes to 198. Next day Parliament was dissolved, and the third general election in two years took place before the month was out.

At Epping Churchill faced both Liberal and Labour candidates. He had little to fear from the Labour challenger, J. R. McPhie, a science master at Tiffin's School, Kingston, and a newcomer to the constituency. But the Liberal, Granville Sharp, an able young barrister, had fought the constituency before and in 1923 had come within 1600 votes of victory. Churchill at least had the personal advantage that Clementine was well known at Waltham Abbey for her welfare work for munition workers there during the war. As was now customary with him he left nothing to chance during the campaign: he spoke at four meetings every day and showed once again his remarkable capacity to say something new on each occasion. For the most part it was practicable for him to strike at both his opponents by criticising the Labour government, which the Liberals had supported. He argued that it had 'utterly failed to deal with unemployment', had, by abandoning the proposal to build a base at Singapore, 'deprived the British Navy of the power of defending Australia and New Zealand', and, in its action on the Campbell case, had 'tampered with the clean and impartial administration of justice'.[51]

All this was reasonable criticism; but in his election address and later in the heat of the campaign he advanced some very strained arguments about Labour which bore little relation to reality. For instance:

> The eagerness with which the Socialist Party grasped at the chance of ruling in a minority, their reluctance to yield up this unwholesome power, show clearly the undemocratic nature of their minds.[52]

So, too, the Churchill who before the war had denounced 'sentiment by the bucketful; patriotism and imperialism by the imperial pint' must surely have been restless at hearing his later self perorating at Woodford:

> Let Britannia cast off the ridiculous and dishonourable disguises and rags made in Germany and made in Russia with which the Socialists seek to drape her. Let her reveal herself once again, sedate, majestic on her throne, grasping the trident with determination, and displaying on her shield not the foul Red Flag of Communist revolution, but the Union Jack.[53]

At any rate his Woodford audience seemed to enjoy this: there were 'loud and prolonged cheers' as he sat down. Baldwin, too, was impressed by the speeches he made, which were generously reported in the national press. After a message of support early in the campaign he sent a second letter saying: 'You have given a splendid lead to moderate men of all parties.... We shall warmly welcome your assistance in the House, where your great Parliamentary talents have been much missed.'[54] Churchill also had the support of the two previous Conservative MPs for Epping and even of a former independent Labour candidate, J. Conoley. On polling day he reverted to his Westminster by-election stratagem of touring the polling booths with a coach-and-four. It seemed an appropriate way of travelling across a constituency which was still in large part agricultural, providing dairy produce for the London market. And as at Westminster, the impact of his personality apparently helped to encourage a heavy poll. Altogether 78% of the electorate registered their votes – the largest proportion at any contest while the constituency was in existence. And Churchill's majority was almost 10,000, which was a considerable improvement on the Conservative performance in 1923. The figures were:

W. S. Churchill (Constitutionalist)	19,843	Elected
G. G. Sharp (Liberal)	10,080	
J. R. McPhie (Labour)	3768	

It was in high good humour that Churchill a few days later addressed those who had helped him in the campaign. He announced that he proposed to give each of them a medal, inscribed with the words 'Union and Victory'. He felt that there was much to be said for the people of the Epping division:

> I am very happy to find that after some ups and downs – quite as many downs as ups – and many vicissitudes, I have at length found myself among a large, powerful and intelligent community of citizens with whom I am in the most natural and hearty accord.[55]

So Churchill was back in Parliament; and he was on the side of the majority, for his allies in the Conservative Party proper had a clear majority over all other parties. The feature of the election was the defeat of the Liberals, who were reduced to only forty seats and henceforth could not be counted as a major force in parliamentary politics. All this was now acceptable to Churchill, and he was very pleased to be an MP once more. But the question that now arose was whether Baldwin would offer him a suitable post in his government. What was he to do if the Prime Minister's best offer was something that he felt to be beneath his talents? Churchill was never very good at playing his own hand in circumstances of this sort; and so he consulted Beaverbrook, who had shown himself a wise counsellor in 1916. Beaverbrook always enjoyed the role of a political *éminence grise*, and he advised Churchill not to accept outright any offer from Baldwin unless it was exceptionally good.[56] After all, Churchill was the spokesman of a large body of formerly Liberal electors, now voting Conservative for the first time; some dozen candidates, Liberals or ex-Liberals, had followed his lead in calling themselves 'Constitutionalists', and altogether seven, including three in Lancashire, had been elected. This was not an organised party, as the Liberal Unionists had been in 1886 and for long afterwards; but it was a symptom of feeling in the electorate, and if treated wisely it might be of crucial importance in encouraging further movement of Liberal electors into the Conservative ranks.

In forming his Cabinet Baldwin first of all made his peace with the former Coalition leaders, Austen Chamberlain and Birkenhead in particular, who had not been in his previous government. Austen Chamberlain became Foreign Secretary and Birkenhead was also to have Cabinet office. Baldwin thought of making Neville Chamberlain, Austen's half-brother, his Chancellor of the Exchequer; he had held this post briefly before and Baldwin had found him the most congenial of his colleagues. As for Churchill, Baldwin thought he would be 'more under control in than out'. He seems to have wanted to avoid giving him a post on the home front, as he thought him 'anti-Labour'; and he considered him first for Secretary for India.

But before finally deciding Baldwin consulted Tom Jones, the Deputy Secretary of the Cabinet; and Jones thought that it would be awkward to have Churchill responsible for India, where harsh measures might be required, which would be attributed to Churchill's impetuosity. Jones warned him that Churchill was indeed impetuous, and said, 'I have seen him lose his head at critical moments in the Irish business.'[57] Baldwin now talked of giving him the Admiralty, or perhaps the Ministry of Health, where he could develop the system of national insurance with which he had been so closely associated before the war.

But to Baldwin's surprise, Neville Chamberlain did not want to return to the Exchequer: the fruits of that office had turned sour for him when Tariff Reform was disavowed. He preferred to go to the Ministry of Health, and he urged Churchill as Chancellor of the Exchequer in his place. Baldwin thought there would be a 'howl' from the party at this, but Chamberlain doubted if it would be worse than if Churchill returned to the Admiralty.[58] Baldwin had to see Churchill immediately after Neville Chamberlain left him; and he made up his mind rapidly to accept the latter's advice.

According to Baldwin's official biographer, he asked Churchill if he would serve 'as Chancellor': ' "Of the Duchy?" Churchill asked. "No, of the Exchequer", said the Prime Minister. Tears came into Churchill's eyes.'[59] No contemporary evidence is quoted for this brief exchange, but it is clear from what Churchill later told Duff Cooper that he at first thought he was being offered the Duchy.[60] Baldwin told Tom Jones that Churchill was 'greatly surprised' to be offered this high office, and 'showed it by his emotion'.[61] He pledged his loyalty to Baldwin, adding 'You have done more for me than Lloyd George ever did.' That night (November 8th 1924) Churchill dined with Beaverbrook and Birkenhead, and although Clementine had made him promise not to tell Beaverbrook – for the matter was still secret – he could not forbear to reveal the news.[62] It was the office his father had held at the pinnacle of his career, and the object of his own ambition since he was a schoolboy.

Churchill did not forget the friends who had helped him on his rapid upward climb on the Conservative side of politics. The election workers of Epping got their medals; and early in December Churchill went to Liverpool to speak at a victory celebration at which Salvidge was the guest of honour. Salvidge had been one of Lord Randolph Churchill's allies in his declining years; and in thanking him for 'extending ... the hand of help and friendship' to himself Lord Randolph's son spoke of it as 'not only a personal but a filial duty' to be present on that occasion. He reflected on the 'extraordinary transformation' which had led him from a position of political isolation only a few months earlier to one of the highest offices of state, and justly said that it reminded him of Disraeli's remark that 'the vicissitudes of politics are inexhaustible'.[63]

15. *Chancellor of the Exchequer*

THE office of Chancellor of the Exchequer is in practice, if not in formal precedence, the highest post at the disposal of the Prime Minister, and for most prime ministers of the early twentieth century – Asquith, Lloyd George, Bonar Law, Baldwin – it had been the last or almost the last stepping-stone on their path to the highest office of all. Churchill had good reason to be delighted by his promotion, which had long been the object of his ambition, and which gave him the opportunity of wearing the Chancellor's robes worn by his father, and 'kept in tissue paper and camphor' for over thirty years by his mother.[1] But if the Exchequer was the most eminent it was also the most difficult post he had yet occupied. Many years of administrative experience lay behind him, but he knew little of economics or finance; and although he had a formidable team of advisers at the Treasury in the last resort it was he who had to take responsibility for policy, and to defend it before Parliament and the country.

As usual, Eddie Marsh accompanied Churchill to his new post, and so did Lord Wodehouse, who had served him in office since 1919. But Marsh had to share the post of Principal Private Secretary with P. J. Grigg, who had served successive Chancellors since 1921 and was becoming 'almost as much a part of the Chancellor's office as the William and Mary inkstands and the Georgian chairs and board-room table'.[2] On first encounter Churchill found Grigg far from pliant and apparently tried to secure his removal, but he was persuaded to retain him for a trial period, and soon they came to understand each other.[3] Grigg was given the task of helping Churchill in all financial and administrative matters, while Marsh looked after the political and personal aspects of his master's public life. Another Treasury official, J. Donald Fergusson, acted with Wodehouse as an Assistant Private Secretary, bringing the membership of the Chancellor's private office up to four. In addition Churchill had a Parliamentary Private Secretary – first, Major Sir Clive Morrison-Bell, and then, when he retired at the end of 1926 in order to make some money on the Stock Exchange, a much younger MP, Robert Boothby. Both were Conservatives.

Grigg has described Churchill's normal methods of working when he was Chancellor. He lived at No. 11 Downing Street while Parliament was sitting, but although this was very close to the Treasury he did not arrive at his office until half-way through the morning. He liked to work in bed before getting up, and arranged for a box of official papers and correspondence to be supplied to him by his private office late at night. He would dictate minutes on these papers, or on any other matters that took his interest, before dressing for the day. On his way by an internal passage through No. 10 Downing Street to the Treasury, he would frequently have a few words with the Prime Minister. The rest of the day would be filled with consultations with his Treasury advisers, attendance at the House of Commons for questions and debates and visits to the smoking-room, and other political meetings.

Cabinets were held less frequently than in the Coalition period, Wednesday being the regular day. But there would also be various meetings of *ad hoc* Cabinet committees; and Churchill continued to take a regular interest in the Committee of Imperial Defence, and did not often miss a session. As before, he drafted his own speeches, and, Grigg tells us, 'would never accept from officials the draft of any pronouncement or important letter or Cabinet paper without distilling it entirely through the alembic of his own literary genius'.[4] In addition, as Boothby records, Churchill was always holding forth vigorously to his friends, colleagues, and subordinates, wherever he was: 'In the drawing room, the dining room, the bedroom, the bathroom, the garden, the car, the train, or in his room at the House of Commons, the flow of his "private" oratory, which was in fact great literature, never ceased.'[5] Grigg was puzzled that a man of such fluency should prepare in advance the complete text of all his speeches, reduced in length only by his customary abbreviations: but, as we have seen, this was a habit which Churchill had learnt by trial and error in the course of his first Parliament early in the century.

The first major decision that Churchill had to take was whether Britain was to return to the Gold Standard at the pre-war rate – the rate which had prevailed in peacetime, with little interruption, since the early eighteenth century. Montagu Norman, the Governor of the Bank of England, had been working towards such a restoration since the end of the war, and it was largely his influence which had persuaded successive Chancellors from 1920 onwards to adopt deflationary policies, with damaging results on the level of employment in industry, but with considerable success in reducing prices. Against the dollar, sterling rose from 3.40 in February 1920 to $4.63\frac{1}{2}$ at the end of 1922.[6] Some fluctuations ensued, but by the beginning of 1925 the Governor was preparing for the final move to the level of 4.86 which would enable the country to attain the Gold Standard at the pre-war level. If this could be done in 1925, it would avert the need for further legislation to retain control over the export of gold, for the existing powers were due to expire at the end of that year.

In 1924, during the period of the Labour government, a committee had been appointed under the chairmanship of Sir Austen Chamberlain – himself a former Chancellor – to consider, among other financial questions, that of the restoration of the Gold Standard. Although the committee heard some adverse views on the matter – notably from the Cambridge economist J. M. Keynes and from the former Liberal Chancellor, Reginald McKenna, now the chairman of the Midland Bank – it reported unanimously in favour of an early return to the Gold Standard. But in view of the domestic 'inconveniences' of deflation – that is to say, the probable increase of unemployment – it advocated waiting for twelve months in the hope that a rise in American prices would reduce the gap that had to be bridged between the major currencies.[7] The general election of 1924, with its decisive result presumably terminating the period of almost annual general elections which had preceded it, encouraged the Treasury officials, in particular Sir John Bradbury and Sir Otto Niemeyer, and the

Governor of the Bank himself, to urge immediate measures to return to gold. By early December Norman had talked to the new Chancellor and had decided to visit New York to arrange a stand-by credit in the event of difficulties immediately after the announcement; Churchill had accepted Norman's views, and told Baldwin:

It will be easy to attain the Gold Standard, and indeed almost impossible to avoid taking the decision, but to keep it will require a most strict policy of debt repayment and a high standard of credit. To reach it and have to abandon it would be disastrous.[8]

Norman duly visited New York and arranged for a facility of $500,000,000 to be put at his disposal. Soon after his return to London, however, he found that Churchill was beginning to wobble on the question. At the end of January a fierce attack on the return to gold was made in Beaverbrook's paper the *Daily Express*.[9] Churchill was upset, and began to re-examine the whole question. His own views only a year earlier had been that there should be an expansion of British credit, for economic development both at home and in the Empire.[10] He now prepared a paper setting out in his own words the arguments which he thought would be deployed against the return to gold. In this paper, which became known in the Treasury as 'Mr Churchill's Exercise', he argued that there was a danger of a 'very serious check' to trade and employment and suggested that

The whole question of a return to the Gold Standard must not be dealt with only upon its financial and currency aspects. The merchant, the manufacturer, the workman and the consumer have interests which, though largely common, do not by any means exactly coincide either with each other or with the financial and currency interests.[11]

It has been suggested that Churchill did not hold these views himself but merely wished to challenge the Treasury advisers into explaining the fundamentals of their thought.[12] But there seems to be no doubt that he was genuinely hesitating over policy at the time, and contemplated the possibility of making a change in the direction of a less deflationary course. His impressions of the unhappy results of deflation at Dundee in 1921–2 must have remained in his mind. Niemeyer wrote to Frederick Leith-Ross, a junior colleague who was abroad at the time: 'Gold is excessively active and troublesome. None of the witch-doctors see eye to eye and Winston cannot make up his mind from day to day whether he is a gold bug or a pure inflationist.'[13]

It is not clear who Niemeyer meant by the 'witch-doctors'. At any rate he, Bradley and Norman all vigorously countered Churchill's main contentions in well-argued papers. Furthermore, McKenna made a speech acknowledging that a return to gold was inevitable in the prevailing state of financial opinion. Austen Chamberlain personally urged on Churchill the need for an early revaluation, and Philip Snowden, the Labour ex-Chancellor and Churchill's principal antagonist in the Commons on financial questions, wrote in the *Observer* on similar lines. Of the experts, only Keynes remained fixedly opposed to the return to gold, warning Churchill in an article in the *Nation* that there were serious dangers in being linked rigidly to Wall Street.[14] But Niemeyer gave the Chancellor a rebuttal of Keynes's views, and there seemed no alternative but to act as both the Bank and the Treasury required and expected of him. Churchill's reluctance to accept his advisers' views is recorded in his letter to Niemeyer, after reading the latter's views on Keynes's article:

> The Treasury has never, it seems to me, faced the profound paradox of what Mr Keynes calls 'the paradox of unemployment amidst dearth'.... On the other hand I do not pretend to see even 'through a glass darkly' how the financial and credit policy of the country could be handled so as to bridge the gap between a dearth of goods and a surplus of labour; and well I realise the danger of experiment to that end. The seas of history are full of famous wrecks. Still, if I could see a way I would far rather follow it than any other. I would rather see Finance less proud and Industry more content.[15]

A final decision had to be made in March. Churchill arranged a dinner party at No. 11 Downing Street, to which he invited not only Bradley and Niemeyer, but also McKenna and Keynes. Grigg was also present and later recalled the main lines of the discussion.[16] Keynes's view was that the gap that still had to be bridged by reducing the price-level was larger than the Treasury officials thought – something in the region of 10%. This, he thought, might well cause unemployment and strikes. The Treasury officials stuck to their view that the short-term disadvantages, which they thought Keynes was exaggerating, would be counterbalanced by the long-term advantages to banking, shipping and insurance. McKenna still had his doubts, but could see no way out. Churchill accepted the view of the majority: and shortly afterwards, at a meeting with the Prime Minister attended by the Governor of the Bank, it was agreed that the return to gold should be announced as part of the Budget speech in April. For Montagu Norman it was, as Churchill put it, his 'greatest achievement', although also 'only the final step without which all those efforts and sufferings [i.e. in the years since 1920] would have gone for nought'.[17]

The annual ritual of Budget day focuses the limelight of public attention upon the Chancellor of the Exchequer. Churchill found this by no means uncongenial. As usual he took the utmost pains over his speech, so that even if the Budget itself was unexciting its presentation was likely to be interesting and even dramatic. However, he was determined that the contents of his first Budget should also be of major importance. He wished at the outset to undertake some large social schemes of the type which Lloyd George had undertaken, and which already had a place in the Conservative programme. The difficulty was that current financial policy required, as we have seen, a stern attitude of economy and a strict insistence on debt repayment rather than new expenditure. And so far from being able to make immediate cuts in military expenditure, as he had hoped, Churchill found that there were existing plans for a rapid increase in both the Admiralty and the RAF estimates in the succeeding years.

He therefore warned Baldwin within a few weeks of taking office that something would have to be done to keep the Service estimates in check.[18] With his exceptional knowledge of naval questions, he was at once able to put W. C. Bridgeman, the new First Lord of the Admiralty, on the defensive. Bridgeman described in his diary how he was plunged into 'desperate fighting in the Cabinet' on behalf of the navy.[19] Beatty, the First Sea Lord, wrote to his wife: 'We have suffered a severe blow from this Government ... actually behaving worse to us at the Admiralty than the Labour Party. Of course it is all Winston as Chancellor. He has gone economy mad.'[20] But the conflict could not be fought to a finish before March, when the naval estimates had to be presented to Parliament; and so it was agreed that the whole question of new naval construction should be left over for the time being, for investigation by a Cabinet committee and, if necessary, for the promulgation of additional estimates for the new financial year.

It was not to be expected that Churchill could make sweeping tax reductions in his first Budget. But he was determined to make a gesture to show his new colleagues of the Conservative Party that his heart was in the right place, and he therefore took sixpence off the income tax, thus reducing it to four shillings in the pound. He balanced this partly by an increase in death duties, partly by the imposition of a number of indirect taxes – an entirely new duty on silk and artificial silk and the restoration of the war-time McKenna duties on expensive manufactured goods from abroad such as motorcars, clocks and watches. This was, of course, the thin end of the wedge of Tariff Reform; but Churchill and many other Liberals had accepted the McKenna duties as desirable during the period of the wartime and post-war coalitions; and when Snowden removed them in 1924 he had declared that he was in favour of their restoration.

In addition, he announced in his Budget speech proposals for a contributory scheme of pensions for widows and orphans, and the provision of old-age pensions at sixty-five instead of seventy, as hitherto. These proposals were not Churchill's own idea, but they had been included in the Conservative election manifesto at the instance of Neville Chamberlain. Naturally, Chamberlain did not entirely relish having his policies appropriated by Churchill and announced in the Budget speech as if they were the Chancellor's own; but he had to acknowledge that they would probably come to fruition earlier as a result. 'In a sense', he wrote in his diary, 'it *is* his scheme. We were pledged to something of the kind, but I don't think we should have done it this year if he had not made it part of his Budget scheme, and in my opinion he does deserve special personal credit for his initiative and drive.'[21] Churchill took the opportunity to revive the military metaphor about social welfare that he had first used eighteen years previously. It was not, he argued, the average, healthy, employed workman and his family who needed help, but the family suffering from 'exceptional misfortune': 'It is not to the sturdy marching troops that extra rewards and indulgences are needed at the present time. It is to the stragglers, to the exhausted, to the weak, to the wounded, to the veterans....'[22]

The speech, which lasted two and a half hours, was as Chamberlain said a 'masterly performance'.[23] It drew from Philip Snowden, his immediate predecessor as Chancellor, the immediate comment that it was a 'great rhetorical and argumentative triumph'.[24] But of course the protective taxation was bound to be regarded by all Free Traders as a betrayal of their cause by one who had previously been one of their most prominent champions; and the simultaneous reduction of the income tax, which was largely for the benefit of the middle and upper classes, enabled Snowden to describe the Budget as 'the worst rich man's Budget that was ever proposed'.[25] The widows' and orphans' pensions, he pointed out, would be paid not by the State but by contributions from employers and workmen, which would be a tax on industry; and the new duty on artificial silk would be a duty not on a luxury but on everyday clothing. But Snowden was as orthodox in financial policy as Churchill, and on the restoration of the Gold Standard he had no hostile comments to make.

Since Churchill has suffered much criticism in later years for his return to gold, it is desirable to emphasise that his action in this respect was supported in the first instance by the leading financial spokesmen of all three political parties. Sir Alfred Mond of the Liberal Party was the only important critic of the move in the course of the Budget debate; and several weeks had passed before Lloyd George began to argue that it was exacerbating the difficulties of the export industries, and particularly coal. Churchill was annoyed by this *volte-face* on the part of his old colleague, and replied rather tartly in a speech at a Conservative fête in his constituency:

> I never heard any argument more strange and so ill-founded, as that the Gold Standard is responsible for the condition of affairs in the coal industry. The Gold Standard is no more responsible than is the Gulf Stream.[26]

It was true enough that the return to gold could not yet have added much to the existing difficulties of the coal industry, which were due partly to the loss of export markets as a result of changes in the pattern of international demand and the competition of oil, and partly to the deflationary policies followed by successive governments before Churchill became Chancellor. Any further alterations which took place in the course of 1925 in the competitive position of British coal were probably due more to the revival of exports from the Ruhr mines, which had been closed by the French occupation in 1923, than to any other single factor. But to suggest, as Churchill did, that a financial change involving a revaluation of the pound would have no effect at all upon the coal industry was clearly a mistake, and Keynes not unjustly described it as a remark 'of the feather-brained order'.[27] Looking back to the 1920s from the vantage-point of half a century, we can now see that the return to gold was an error of policy, for it increased the difficulties of British industry at a time when it already had severe problems of adjustment to a changed world trading pattern. Nor can there have been much advantage to the country's international financial interests, for the restored Gold Standard did not survive for very long, as Britain was ignominiously driven to devalue again in 1931.

But if Keynes's criticism of the Gold Standard policy has been justified by results, it is also fair to say that Churchill himself has received far too much of the blame. This was partly due to the title of Keynes's brilliant pamphlet, *The Economic Consequences of Mr Churchill,* which was really an attack, not upon the Chancellor of the Exchequer, but upon the policy of the Bank of England under Montagu Norman. Yet even if the Bank's policy was mistaken, as most people would probably now agree, it should not be forgotten that the main difficulties of the British economy in the inter-war period were not financial, but were due to excess capacity in the staple export trades. As Sir Alec Cairncross has put it,

> Granted that the return to gold was a mistake, how big a mistake was it, seen against the background of the period as a whole with all the structural and deflationary pressures released by Britain's changed position in the world economy?[28]

Meanwhile Churchill had no alternative but to pursue the path of economy in government expenditure, to provide the background of austere governmental financial policy which the return to gold necessitated. The question of naval construction, which threatened to produce a serious increase in the naval estimates, was being examined by a committee under his friend Lord Birkenhead, who was in the Cabinet as Secretary of State for India. Birkenhead's committee first heard the full Admiralty case for the building programme, which was based on the need for the replacement of obsolescent cruisers and other craft. Churchill then put his criticisms, which were to the effect that there was no foreign power with which the navy had any reason to contemplate future hostilities. The German navy had been destroyed, and strict limitations imposed upon its future development; the American navy was not regarded as hostile to the interests of the British Empire; there remained only Japan, until recently formally allied to Britain, and a war with Japan was not, in Churchill's opinion, a possibility of either the near or the distant future. He had already told Baldwin that in his view naval expenditure should be recast 'on the basis that no naval war against a first-class Navy is likely to take place within the next twenty years'.[29] He now urged that the idea of basing a fleet at Singapore should be dropped – although previously, when the Labour government had proposed to adopt this course, he had made it grounds for the charge that it had 'flouted the Dominions' and 'deprived the British Navy of the power of defending Australia and England'.[30]

It was Bridgeman who pointed the way for the Birkenhead Committee to resolve the dilemma. If in fact the navy did not need to prepare for a war against any major foreign power, then, he said, it was for the Committee of Imperial Defence to give it an instruction to that effect. Birkenhead's Committee therefore recommended that the CID should be consulted afresh on the prospects of hostilities taking place in the foreseeable future with some or other great power. The CID's conclusion went some way to confirm Churchill's diagnosis: war with Japan was not, it thought, a reasonable contingency of the next ten years.[31] This was to extend the Ten Year Rule, which as we have seen had been applied in 1919, but which had not been reconsidered in more recent years.

This decision of the CID put both Bridgeman and Beatty in difficulty. The reputation of both men depended upon their success in maintaining naval strength, and if the naval building programme was simply abandoned it would be obvious to all that they had been defeated. In July 1925 Bridgeman was being strongly pressed to make concessions, but he refused to do so, and both he and Beatty appeared to be on the brink of resignation. They were, however, in a stronger position than they at first realised. Churchill, who was not yet even a member of the Conservative Party, could carry little weight among the backbenchers if he chose to resign. Gradually the balance swung the other way as it became evident that Conservative MPs would not stand for the abandonment of the naval building programme. The Whips and the National Agent warned Baldwin that there would be serious repercussions if the First Lord was forced to resign, and so Baldwin was obliged to try to find some line of compromise between his rival Cabinet colleagues.[32] On July 22nd he announced that he had decided to impose his own solution. Much of the building programme was to be accepted, but economies were to be effected in various ways, such as by reducing the size of the new cruisers, by laying them down late in the financial year, and by other minor economies.

The RAF was also asked to curtail its programme of expansion, and here Churchill was able to get greater co-operation from the minister in charge, Sir Samuel Hoare, because the preliminary work on aerodromes and equipment was already lagging behind schedule. Even Air Marshal Trenchard was content to see a slowing down of the supply of new aircraft, because he thought that any rapid growth in the air force would reduce the quality of the pilots. As Hoare later put it, 'Trenchard's prevailing fear was that ... we should endanger the high standard of his *corps d'élite*.'[33]

So by the late summer of 1925 Churchill could be moderately satisfied with economies which he had imposed upon the armed forces – economies which would at least enable him to maintain his four-shilling income-tax and his adherence to the programme of debt repayment which post-war Chancellors had laid down as the mark of orthodox economic policy.

But at the very time that the battle of the naval estimates was reaching its climax inside the Cabinet and in the Conservative Party, another grave threat to the Chancellor's budgetary plans began rapidly to emerge. Whatever the factors responsible, it was obvious that the coal industry was experiencing serious financial difficulties. Exports were badly down, and many of the mining districts were reporting heavy financial losses on their operations. On June 30th the owners gave notice that they wanted to end their existing agreement with the miners, and they demanded wage reductions unless the men were prepared to return to working eight hours a day instead of seven. Such a change might have cut costs a little, but it was bound to increase unemployment; and the Miners' Federation of Great Britain, the miners' union, at once prepared for a national strike, and called upon the General

Council of the TUC for assistance. The General Council, which was at this stage in a militant mood, strongly sympathetic to the miners, called a special meeting of leaders of the railway and other transport workers to co-ordinate plans for joint action. Clearly, a general strike was imminent.

Under this pressure, the government had to decide whether it was prepared to face a general strike or whether it would provide a temporary subsidy to tide the mining industry over the next few months while a solution to the problem of costs and wages was sought. On July 30th, the day before the existing agreement was due to expire, the Cabinet decided to pay a subsidy for a period of about nine months, during which time a commission of enquiry was to investigate the industry's difficulties and recommend a course of action to bring them to an end. It is clear that Baldwin was in favour of this course, because he was most anxious to avert a general strike; and he was quite prepared to pay the cost of the temporary subsidy, which was estimated in the first instance at £10,000,000, but later turned out to involve total charges amounting to about £23,000,000. But there was opposition in the Cabinet to what some ministers regarded as a surrender to force, and the subsidy was not approved unanimously.[34]

Although it was Churchill who had to find the money, and although he was never a man to give way to pressure, on this occasion he sided with the Prime Minister at an early stage in the discussion. Like Baldwin, he sympathised with the miners in their difficulties with the owners; and he must have realised, from his discussions on the Gold Standard, that financial policy over the long term was partly responsible for their plight. It has been suggested that the concession was made because the government did not yet have any adequate plans for coping with the maintenance of essential services during a general strike. But the evidence in the Cabinet Papers of the period indicates that the plans were in fact ready, although it is true that they were modified and improved in detail in later months.[35]

So, for the time being, the miners continued to earn their existing wage and work their seven-hour shifts; and in the meantime a commission got down to work on the problems of the industry under the chairmanship of Sir Herbert Samuel, the Liberal leader. Churchill had to pursue still more relentlessly his search for economy in government expenditure. A Cabinet committee which had already been exploring the subject came up with proposals for reducing government contributions to health and unemployment insurance, on revised and rather optimistic expectations of what would happen in the future, and these proposals were embodied in an Economy (Miscellaneous Provisions) Bill which went through Parliament early in 1926. There was strong criticism from members of the Labour Party who described the Chancellor as a 'robber', but, as Churchill ironically pointed out, to one who had frequently been called a 'murderer' by members of the Opposition this was 'a sort of promotion'.[36] Further economies in the defence departments were also sought by means of a committee under Lord Colwyn, which set about the task of securing savings, particularly in naval expenditure. The Board of Admiralty responded to this by demanding to take over full control of the Fleet Air Arm, which, it argued, would result in overall savings. This led to bitter in-fighting between the Admiralty and the Air Ministry, but it did not save the navy from having to bear the brunt of the Colwyn Committee's pressure.[37]

When Churchill presented his second Budget in April 1926 the period of the coal subsidy was coming to an end, and there was a serious danger of renewed industrial strife. But he was determined to take an optimistic line, and he shaped his proposals on the assumption that any calamity such as a general strike or a prolonged coal strike would be averted. He described the existing picture of the national economy as '... not black. It is not grey. It is piebald, and, on the whole, the dark patches are less prominent this year than last.'[38] He increased revenue, not by restoring his cut in the income tax, but by introducing a betting tax, by increasing the taxation of heavy vehicles, and by a number of ingenious expedients of a temporary nature. He raided the Road Fund for £7,000,000, and claimed henceforth a third of its income, though he promised that the expenditure on roads would continue to rise. He also reduced the period of credit allowed to brewers for the payment of beer duties, thus obtaining extra revenue in the ensuing financial year only. He amused the House by describing these latter changes as 'windfalls produced not only by the wind but by a certain judicious shaking of the trees'.[39]

The Budget speech was again a brilliant success: Lloyd George spoke of the 'conspicuous clarity of the statement and the charm and fascination with which the Chancellor of the Exchequer has entertained the House';[40] but there was perhaps not much that could be said in favour of the changes that he had announced, except that they were an ingenious way of finding the money for the coal subsidy. Snowden's description of the Budget as that 'of a profligate and a bankrupt' need not be taken seriously.[41] The weak point of the proposals was the betting tax, which aroused unreasoning opposition on the part of puritanically minded people as well as from the bookmakers and their friends, but which came to grief because it encouraged illicit bookmaking. This tax had to be modified in later Budgets and was finally rescinded in its entirety by Churchill himself in 1929.

Meanwhile the Samuel Commission had made its report upon the problems of the coal industry. The Commission rejected the owners' proposal that the miners should be obliged to increase their hours of work, but it recognised that wages must fall if the industry was to be competitive. For the long term, it recommended the amalgamation of mines so as to enlarge the scale of production; and it urged the development of better welfare arrangements for the miners. But it provided no satisfactory short-term solution for the industry's difficulties, and when negotiations between miners and owners were resumed they rapidly came to a deadlock. The owners insisted, not merely on cuts in wages, but also on district agreements, thus threatening the very basis of the Miners' Federation of Great Britain. The miners, on the other hand, refused to accept any reduction of pay: their militant secretary, A. J. Cook, summed up their attitude in the slogan 'not a penny off the pay, not a minute on the day'.

In April 1926 the complete breakdown of negotiations within the industry led to the renewed intervention of the General Council of the TUC, which began to prepare for a general strike, meanwhile calling upon the government to solve the dispute. Baldwin tried hard to find a formula which would reopen negotiations, but without success. In the end, a complete rupture between government and TUC took place on the night of May 2nd/3rd when it was reported that printers at the *Daily Mail* had refused to set up type for an editorial criticising the threatened strike. Churchill was not on the Cabinet negotiating committee, and there seems to be no evidence to sustain the idea that he was among a 'war party' within the Cabinet, which was pressing Baldwin to call the unions' bluff. Sir Samuel Hoare, who was Secretary for Air, later recorded that 'There were no divisions amongst ministers and it is incorrect to say that a Churchill-Birkenhead section were determined upon a fight to a finish.'[42] Lord Eustace Percy, who was also in the Cabinet, made the same point in his own memoirs.[43]

Once the strike had begun, though, Churchill was all in favour of defeating it as quickly as possible. This could only be done, he thought, by putting the government's case to the nation, and by ensuring that all essential services were maintained. He and Birkenhead joined the Supply and Transport Committee, a body which under the chairmanship of Joynson-Hicks, the Home Secretary, had already made detailed plans for the emergency. The credit for the thoroughness of the preparations must go to Sir John Anderson, the Permanent Under-Secretary at the Home Office, and one of the ablest civil servants of his generation. But Churchill and Birkenhead upset the smooth working of the committee and irritated Joynson-Hicks by demanding more energetic preparations to deal with the violence which they seemed to expect from the strikers.[44] As the printing workers at the London newspaper offices had almost all left work, there was also need for some improvised form of government newspaper, and Joynson-Hicks was probably relieved when Churchill began to take special interest in this particular problem, which naturally aroused his journalistic instincts.

The newspaper proprietors had held talks to discuss the possibility of their producing one joint newspaper, but these discussions had ended in failure. H. A. Gwynne, the editor of the *Morning Post*, was the first to place his premises at the disposal of the government; and as a result Churchill, accompanied by Samuel Hoare and by J. C. C. Davidson, a junior minister, visited the *Morning Post* offices in the Strand on the evening of May 3rd, and stayed until 3 a.m. planning the production of a new official daily.[45] Churchill's idea was that it should be a vigorous, hard-hitting journal with popular appeal. As he explained it to Geoffrey Dawson, the editor of *The Times*:

> Large numbers of working people feel quite detached from the conflict; and they are waiting, as if they were spectators at a football match, to see whether the Government or the trades union is the stronger.[46]

It was given the name *British Gazette*, and after its first issue appeared on May 5th it was published every day, except Sunday, until May 13th, when it was able to announce that the TUC had called off the stoppage. Its circulation rose from 232,000 to two and a half million – a figure far exceeding that of any other newspaper at that time in any part of the world.[47]

Churchill has often been described as editor of the *British Gazette*. In fact, his responsibility was less than that of Davidson who had direct authority from Baldwin and who did not hesitate to censor or reject articles even from the pen of the Chancellor of the Exchequer. It was, however, Churchill who insisted that the *Gazette* should not be a dull information sheet but should be a vigorous journal putting forward the government's cause to the people. When he was at the printing office he interested himself in all aspects of the production, and in Davidson's view he 'rattled ... very badly' the little band of compositors working on unfamiliar machines. Davidson wrote angrily: 'He thinks he is Napoleon, but curiously enough the men who have been printing all their life in the various processes happen to know more about their job than he does.'[48] According to Tom Jones, the Deputy Secretary of the Cabinet, Gwynne sent several messages to the Prime Minister urging that Churchill should be kept away from the printing office: 'He butts in at the busiest hours and insists on changing commas and full stops until the staff is furious.'[49]

Churchill also tried to treat the BBC as 'an offshoot of the *British Gazette*', but with Davidson's approval the Managing Director, John Reith, refused to agree.[50] Churchill was angry about this, and took the matter to Cabinet level, but got no satisfaction. All the same, Davidson had a veto on the BBC's news bulletins and on its daily 'appreciations', and so its freedom was far from complete.

Davidson could hardly have acted as he did if he had not been fully in the Prime Minister's confidence. He had served for a time as Baldwin's Parliamentary Private Secretary and had developed a close association with his master – so close that he and his wife used regularly to join the Baldwins on their annual holiday at Aix-les-Bains. After the strike was over Davidson retained as souvenirs 'about ten or twelve galley proofs of leading articles written by Winston', which he had refused to publish.[51] He also kept a number of drafts by Churchill which had been heavily blue-pencilled. Unfortunately, all were destroyed during the Second World War. But this explains why it is impossible to identify articles in the *Gazette* which show clear signs of the Churchillian style.

The tone of some of the censored material may be indicated by Grigg's comment to Tom Jones that on the night of May 6th/7th Churchill had dictated 'a wild article about embodying the Territorial troops', which he had persuaded the Chancellor to 'sleep over' before submitting to the *Gazette*.[52] It seems that Churchill believed in intimidating the strikers with a show of force, while Baldwin, Joynson-Hicks and Davidson all felt – correctly as it turned out – that the strikers were anxious to keep the peace and that a show of force would only be regarded by them as provocative. In fact, the Cabinet did agree on May 7th that it would be desirable to encourage the Territorials to volunteer in their units to serve as a Civil Constabulary Reserve, armed only with truncheons and wearing civilian clothes with armbands rather than uniforms.[53] Churchill was put in charge of a sub-committee to make the arrangements, and according to Major Ismay, a staff officer of the Committee of Imperial Defence who acted as secretary of the sub-committee, he produced a ready-made plan which was soon accepted by his colleagues and which was announced to the public that night.[54] If there had been any disturbance beyond the control of the police, the force might well have served a useful purpose in maintaining order without resort to troops with rifles.

Further, although Davidson disagreed with Churchill's point of view he admitted that Churchill made an important contribution to the success of the *Gazette*, which he later said was in the end 'a fair compromise'.[55] It was certainly an effective organ of the government while it lasted. Naturally it came under heavy fire afterwards from the Opposition in the House of Commons. Labour MPs accused its direction of lack of impartiality, but Churchill was able to defend it to the satisfaction of the government side of the House by saying, 'I decline utterly to be impartial as between the fire brigade and the fire.' He warned the Opposition, with a touch of the *gaminerie* which often disarmed his opponents,

I have no wish to make threats or to use language which would disturb the House or cause bad blood, but this I must say: Make your minds perfectly clear that if ever you let loose upon us again a general strike, we will loose upon you – another *British Gazette*.[56]

Kingsley Martin, a young left-wing journalist who wrote an able account of the role of the press during the strike, thought that the *British Gazette*, with its partial reporting and omission of certain items of news – in particular, an appeal from the Churches which implied that both sides were equally to blame— had 'discredited' Churchill in the eyes of the public, and that he had grown 'daily less popular'.[57] This was certainly not Churchill's personal experience, for when he went to the Empire Theatre on the evening of the day when the strike was called off he was greeted with cries of 'We want Winston!' and 'Good old Churchill!' Such a demonstration was somewhat embarrassing, as the performance, which was of the musical *Lady Be Good*, had already begun. But the audience insisted on stopping the show, and Adèle Astaire, Fred Astaire's sister, who was on-stage, called upon the audience to give three cheers for the Chancellor, who then 'bowed his acknowledgements'.[58] But Kingsley Martin would not have regarded a London theatre audience as a cross-section of the British public. As the Gallup Poll had not yet been founded, the question of whether Churchill lost popularity as a result of his role in the strike must remain open.

Although Churchill was for taking a strong line to terminate the General Strike, which he saw as a threat to constitutional government, he took a relatively detached view of the issues at dispute between the miners and their employers, and was in favour of taking 'the utmost pains to reach a settlement in the most conciliatory spirit'.[59] He was distressed that after the end of the General Strike, the miners' strike dragged on for month after month, causing far greater damage to the economy than that occasioned by the nine days of stoppage in other industries. Already in June he was urging the Prime Minister to take action to bring the strike to an end.[60] Baldwin attempted various approaches, but without success; he was clearly exhausted, and on medical advice went off for his usual summer holiday at Aix-les-Bains on August 19th. Churchill was left in charge of the task of trying to solve the dispute.

Churchill first brought his persuasive powers to bear upon the miners' leaders. Sir Arthur Steel-Maitland, the Minister of Labour, who was present at his talks with them, thought that he showed himself a little too friendly with them: 'The miners were nearly down and out & ready to agree to anything.... As it

was Winston jumped in too readily and it was impossible to stop.
... Of course the miners have in turn stiffened a lot.'[61] Baldwin
seems to have taken Steel-Maitland's view, for he had written to
Churchill on September 5th that so far as negotiations with the
miners were concerned, 'I am a great believer in paying out rope
to the last'.[62] But Tom Jones, who was helping and advising
Churchill at the time, thought that he was doing well – so well,
indeed, that there was a danger of his getting all the *kudos*
for a settlement while the Prime Minister was on holiday.[63]

Churchill had in fact secured concessions from the miners'
leaders as to the terms upon which they would re-enter negotiations, and he had used Ramsay MacDonald as an intermediary
for this purpose. But though the miners were prepared to abandon their refusal to consider wage reductions they stood out
against the owners' demand that negotiations should be conducted
at the district level. Churchill saw the spokesmen of the mineowners on September 6th, but he could not get them to agree to
national negotiations, and they parted on rather bad terms:
Steel-Maitland thought he bullied them 'in a way that put their
backs up'.[64] Tom Jones described the encounter between Churchill and Evan Williams, the owners' chief negotiator, as 'an acute
and at times acrimonious debate'[65]: but Williams did not give
way, though he promised to put Churchill's arguments to his
colleagues. The owners refused to change their unyielding attitude, and the strike continued.

The only chance of an early settlement now seemed to lie in
the exercise, or at least the threat, of statutory intervention.
Churchill was getting more and more concerned about the repercussions of the strike on Britain's economic life, and he urged
Baldwin, who was due to return shortly, to take action as soon
as possible: 'I do hope that a little employers' agitation will not
prevent H.M.G. from advancing with courage & conviction
against both the detractors of the public interest.'[66] But this was
an area where Baldwin, for all his desire to conciliate, was anxious
to avoid state responsibility if at all possible. He knew, in addition, that there were powerful forces in the Conservative Party
which would construe any coercion of the employers as a form of
surrender to the Miners' Federation. Accordingly, from September 15th onwards, when Baldwin returned from holiday, the
government began to withdraw from any positive role in the
dispute. All that Baldwin was prepared to promise the miners

was the appointment of a National Appeal Tribunal to supervise district agreements, after the men had gone back to work.

This was much less than Churchill wanted. He was prepared, as Tom Jones wrote in his diary, 'to go to great lengths in the way of legislation on hours, wages and conditions – which terrified his colleagues'.[67] But he did not get his way; and Herbert Smith, the miners' leader, rebuked him for shifting his ground in obedience to the caution of his colleagues. Smith told a meeting of miners' delegates:

> We said to Churchill, 'We understood you were a man of courage, but you have broken down at the first fence! You have dismounted. Have you been doing wrong while the masters have been away; and got reprimanded?' He did not like it.[68]

And so the strike dragged on. Apparently only Churchill continued to press within the Cabinet for government action to end what he called 'the really frightful injuries to national wealth and character'.[69] The owners knew they were in a strong position as the men were getting desperate. In November and December the resistance in the coalfields gradually crumbled, and the men drifted back to work on the owners' terms in one district after another. The loss of coal output in 1926 amounted to about half the normal annual total; and in addition to the miners' loss of production, it was reckoned that over half a million other workers had been laid off as a result.

The repercussions of the industrial strife for Churchill's next two Budgets were severe. When he presented his third Budget in April 1927 he had to report a deficit on the financial year of £36½ million, of which £32 million was due to the strikes, caused partly by extra expenditure and partly by loss of revenue. A further loss of revenue amounting to about £18 million would, he thought, occur in 1927–8. The 'consuming power of the masses' had, he reported, been little affected: at any rate, sugar and tobacco consumption were up, bread and meat had shown no decrease, and only beer and spirits were down. Nevertheless, it was essential to seek some £35–40 million of new revenue.

The House of Commons feared the worst, and listened with astonishment as Churchill proceeded to find this large sum without increasing any major taxes. He put a duty on imported motor tyres, and increased taxation on wines, matches and tobacco; but none of these changes were of a substantial nature. He then proceeded to a number of temporary expedients of the type which he had undertaken in the previous year. He raided the Road Fund for another £12 million; he took another month off the brewers' credit period, which provided another £5 million; and he made Income Tax under Schedule A (Property) payable in one instalment instead of two, which meant a gain to the Exchequer of £15 million in the succeeding financial year. With all this, he admitted, as well he might, 'I am at the end of my adventitious resources'.[70] It was an astonishing series of conjuring tricks, accompanied by a very entertaining speech, and Lloyd George described him as 'the merriest tax collector since the days of Robin Hood'.[71] Snowden commented rather sourly on the 'jugglery and deceit' involved,[72] but in general the reception was good, as most people were very relieved to find that there were no swingeing increases in taxation.

But Churchill was not satisfied simply to be conducting a holding operation with the national finances. He felt that the Chancellor of the Exchequer ought to be able to do something to assist the recovery and expansion of industry. A chance remark by the young 'progressive' Conservative MP for Stockton-on-Tees, Harold Macmillan, probably in 1925, put into his head the idea of relieving manufacturers of the burden of excessive rates.[73] In June 1927 he put to Baldwin a proposal for a 'large new constructive measure' which might well also have an encouraging effect on the party's election prospects. The plan was to abolish rates on both industry and agriculture. He thought he could do this if he had 'what in wartime parlance would be called "a mass of manœuvre"' of some £30 million. Half of this could come from a tax on petrol, and half from economies, particularly in naval expenditure.[74]

These proposals had to be examined by other members of the Cabinet, and in particular by the Minister of Health, Neville Chamberlain, who was responsible for the oversight of local government. Chamberlain was fully aware of the problem of heavy rates in the poorer parts of the country, and he wanted to deal with it by a system of block grants from the Exchequer, taking the place of the existing percentage grant system. At first he reacted unkindly to Churchill's 'new and I fear fantastic plan', especially as his own proposals involved Exchequer assistance on a much more modest basis of perhaps £3-4 million, designed to give assistance where it was most needed. Churchill persisted, however, and in the autumn wrote to Chamberlain: 'I see no reason why yr plans and mine shd not be interwoven.... You really must not expect me to produce 3 or 4 millions a year for a partial scheme of modest dimensions.'[75] Chamberlain did not want to see industry completely freed from its existing association with local government, and so he opposed the idea of total exemption from rating. He was also critical of giving relief to utilities such as the railways, which Churchill also favoured. The argument continued throughout the winter, and in late March Chamberlain was on the point of resignation. But in the end there was a compromise: industry was not to be entirely de-rated, but was to continue to pay a quarter. Chamberlain gave way over the railways, finding that feeling within the Conservative Party was against him.[76]

Churchill expounded his scheme to the House of Commons in his Budget speech of 1928, which ran to about three and a half hours. He pointed to the 'obstinately chronic' state of depression in the staple industries, with a million people unemployed; and he showed how the rates 'fall the heaviest on industry when it is most depressed'.[77] He then announced that with the aid of a tax of fourpence a gallon on oil, three-quarters of the rates on productive industry would be remitted from October 1929 onwards, and agriculture would be completely freed. Almost as an afterthought, he added that there would be an increase of children's allowance on income tax – 'another example', as he put it humorously, 'of our general policy of helping the producer'.[78]

With the enactment of the 1928 Budget, coupled with Chamberlain's Local Government Act, which abolished the Poor Law Unions and the Boards of Guardians and transferred their powers to the counties and county boroughs, the whole scheme came into operation in 1929. Churchill's last Budget, in April 1929, was by comparison of little intrinsic importance, though it was delivered with his usual aplomb and was described in the *Sunday Times* as 'the most brilliantly entertaining of modern Budget speeches'.[79] Its main feature was the abolition of the duty on tea, which Snowden at once described as 'election bribery'.[80] But Snowden had described the tea duty only a year earlier as 'crushing the bent backs of the working classes',[81] and Churchill was disappointed, if not surprised, that Snowden could not give at least this item of the Budget a more cordial welcome. By this time, however, the party leaders had their eyes on the forthcoming election, and Churchill's Budget speech contained some obvious campaign jibes, such as his description of the policy of the Liberal 'Yellow Book' – which advocated increased expenditure on roads and other measures in order to create employment – as 'paying the unemployed to make racing tracks for well-to-do motorists to make the ordinary pedestrian skip' and 'the policy of buying a biscuit early in the morning and walking about all day looking for a dog to give it to.[82]

In 1928 Churchill was optimistic about the election prospects of the government. He thought his own big scheme of de-rating would impress the public, and that unemployment was largely confined to certain parts of the country which would go against the government in any case. But he seems to have changed his mind about the prospects over Christmas – always a time when he devoted himself to long-term meditation. Beaverbrook found him 'plunged in despair' as a result.[83] In February he discussed with Lloyd George the possibility of collaboration between the Conservative and Liberal Parties if the election result was similar to that in 1924, with no party winning a clear majority. Lloyd George said that the Liberal terms would be: electoral reform, to redress the 'grievance' of the third party under the existing 'first-past-the-post' system; no tariffs on iron, steel, wool, or any other commodity; and changes in the existing Cabinet. Churchill expressed his own sympathy with these conditions and undertook to tell Baldwin about them.[84] His doubts about the Conservative election prospects remained, in spite of a general cheerfulness among other ministers as the time for the campaign approached. Hoare recorded that at Philip Sassoon's weekly lunches 'we found everyone, except Winston, in a happy mood'.[85]

Although Churchill would have favoured an electoral pact between the Conservatives and the Liberals, this was clearly impossible, whatever might be done after the result. Aided by the Lloyd George Fund which had been built up during the Coalition period, the Liberals put up more candidates than at any election since 1906. In Churchill's own constituency there was again a strong challenge by Granville Sharp, his principal opponent in 1924, and it was lucky for Churchill that there was also as before a Labour candidate, this time the former Communist MP for Motherwell, J. T. W. Newbold. The electorate had

grown by over half since 1924, as the result of the building of
new suburbs, and Churchill could not regard his own re-election
as a certainty.

He engaged in his usual strenuous campaign, and spoke repeatedly each evening. There was a shortage of large halls in
the constituency, and so he arranged for two large tents to be
erected, one at Woodford and one at Wanstead. Although each
could hold four or five times as many people as any of the halls,
they were still crowded at his meetings.[86] This time, too, he
could make use of more extensive backing from his family. At a
women's meeting at Wanstead, his son Randolph, now almost
eighteen, made a short speech, while Clementine acted as chairman.[87] Diana, who had been a débutante in 1928, also took part
in the campaign. The Epping result was as follows:

> W. S. Churchill (Conservative)   23,972   Elected
> G. G. Sharp (Liberal)   19,005
> J. T. W. Newbold (Labour)   6472

Churchill this time had no clear majority of those voting; and
while the labour vote had increased from 11.2% to 13.1% of
the total poll, there had been a swing from Conservative to Liberal of 9.4%. Owing to the changes in his constituency, it is
difficult to compare Churchill's experience with that of his party
as a whole; but the average percentage poll of opposed Conservative candidates dropped by 12.5% between the two general elections, partly of course because of the increase of Liberal
candidates.

The Epping count did not take place on the night of the polling (May 30th), and so Churchill was able to join Baldwin at
10 Downing Street, where the early borough results came in on
a tape-machine. Churchill had thought that the Conservatives
would still be the largest party, but

> As Labour gain after Labour gain was announced, Winston became
> more and more flushed with anger, left his seat and confronted the
> machine in the passage; with his shoulders hunched he glared at
> the figures, tore the sheets and behaved as though if any more
> Labour gains came along he would smash the whole apparatus.
> His ejaculations to the surrounding staff were quite unprintable.[88]

Baldwin took his defeat more quietly, but he was even more disappointed as he had had a successful election tour, and on the basis of the calculations of the Central Office he thought the Conservatives would win a clear majority.

By the afternoon of the next day (May 31st) it was apparent that, as in 1924, the Liberals would hold the balance. The final results were: Labour 288, Conservatives 260, Liberals 59. Baldwin retreated to Chequers to consider whether he should meet Parliament. Churchill and Austen Chamberlain visited him there and declared themselves in favour of this course. But they were old friends of Lloyd George, whereas Baldwin was the man who, more than any other, had accomplished his downfall in 1922 – and thereby secured his own rise to power. Baldwin took the weekend to make up his mind, but he does not seem to have had much doubt as to what he should do. On Monday June 3rd he held a meeting of Cabinet ministers at Downing Street, and told them that he proposed to resign.[89] Apparently the majority of them agreed with him, and next day he went to Windsor to see the King, who was recuperating from an illness. Three days later at the King's request the Cabinet ministers all put on frock coats and travelled to Windsor by special train to hand in their seals. Next day it was the turn of MacDonald's new appointees to go there and collect them again.

Churchill had already written an article for *John Bull* on 'Why We Lost'.[90] He blamed, first, 'the natural desire for change'; secondly, the 'prolonged campaign of disparagement' in the popular press – by which he principally meant the Rothermere and Beaverbrook newspapers; and thirdly the 'cold-blooded use of the Lloyd George Fund to sabotage as many Conservative seats as possible'. But he held out a hand once more in the direction of the Liberal Party by saying that he agreed that they had a just grievance over the working of the existing electoral law. For although the Liberals had polled, on the average, more than a quarter of the votes in every seat that they had contested, they had won less than one-tenth of the seats in the House. He promised a vigorous opposition from the Conservative Party, which, he declared in a final flourish, stood as 'the armed and vigilant sentinel, guarding the title-deeds of British freedom and the treasures of our island home'.

The Conservative government of 1924–9 had been, as its leaders had wished, a notable social reforming government, but its greatest failure – one which must have weighed with the electorate more than Churchill at first had assumed – was that it had not dealt with the intractable problem of unemployment. For this failure, the Chancellor of the Exchequer could expect to bear a large share of the responsibility. Yet, as has been suggested, it is unfair to criticise Churchill severely for failing to resist the joint pressure of his Treasury advisers and the Governor of the Bank. The orthodox financial policy that he adopted was a mistake, but it was a collective mistake made by the whole 'establishment' of British finance. By 1927 Churchill, who was relatively quick to learn, had recognised the error in private, though he could not admit it in public. He quite frequently implied as much to Montagu Norman, and relations between the two men became distinctly strained as a result.[91]

Because Churchill was responsible for the return to gold, and because he also resisted the General Strike with greater vigour than that shown by his colleagues, it is sometimes assumed that he was particularly hostile to labour and insensitive to the tribulations of the striking miners and the unemployed. But this was not true at all, and his efforts to end the miners' strike on terms far short of complete defeat for the union side reveal his true attitude. He favoured stricter trade-union legislation, and thought – as did many Conservatives and Liberals – that the Labour Party got an unfair advantage from the political levy; but on more than one occasion he expressed the hope that any legislation on the subject would be coupled with State payment of all candidates' election expenses, so that the Labour Party would not be put at a financial disadvantage as a result.[92] He had the generosity of the natural aristocrat, and was too kind-hearted to play the part of Scrooge. Snowden, who was well read in Dickens, regarded him, perhaps most justly, as a combination of Mark Tapley and Mr Micawber.[93]

Similar characteristics were revealed in Churchill's behaviour towards the European countries which owed war debts to Britain. Britain owed less to the United States than she was owed by her European ex-allies, even excluding Russia, and since the Americans expected Britain to pay up it was obviously in her interest to get all she could from her own debtors, so as to offset the payments to America. Leith-Ross, who accompanied Churchill in several of the debt negotiations, found him 'unfamiliar with technical matters', and on the whole quite willing to leave the details to his subordinates. But he was also 'easily swayed by appeals to his generosity by our former allies', and Leith-Ross thought that the result was often much more favourable to the foreign government than to the British Treasury:

> The negotiations with the French and Italians were conducted throughout by Winston and we found out afterwards that in both cases their governments had authorised their representatives to offer substantially more than what Winston had accepted.[94]

Grigg took the same view: 'Winston wasn't a good dun. He hadn't the qualities which make a man capable of driving hard bargains.' He got impatient, and could usually be defeated by 'an antagonist who was prepared to spin out negotiations'.[95] All the same, he was able to show, at the end of his period as Chancellor, that the Treasury's payments to America were just about balanced by the income from German reparations and foreign debtors. Not that it made much difference in the long run, as the whole system broke down in the international financial crisis that ensued.

Those who thought Churchill most flint-hearted were the spending departments of the government, and especially the Service departments. This was partly because he had such an excellent knowledge of the working of these departments, had been in charge of each of the Services for a period of years, and could argue powerfully against their present spokesmen. His attitude may also have derived to some degree from a desire to emulate his father's enthusiasm for cutting down the Services when he was Chancellor of the Exchequer in 1886. It may be noticed in passing that there were many similarities between Lord Randolph's projected Budget for 1887 and the changes in the fiscal system actually made by his son, such as the reduction of income tax, the increase of death duties, the cut in the tea duty, and the re-organisation of the system of financing local government from the centre.[96]

The criticism has been made that Churchill was responsible for disarming the nation to a dangerous degree in these years, so that it would have been difficult to recover in the 1930s even if the will to re-arm had then existed. As we have seen, this criticism can hardly apply to the RAF, in view of the ease with which Churchill was able to come to terms about financial cuts with both Hoare and his Service chief, Trenchard. Nor can it apply to the army, which suffered little from fresh cuts in this period, having already been reduced to its pre-war level, and which was in fact being urged by Churchill to increase the speed with which it transformed its cavalry regiments into armoured units.[97]

In the case of the navy, however, it would certainly have been damaging if the replacement of obsolete warships had been prevented, as building programmes had to be pursued over a period of many years. It has sometimes been forgotten that Churchill did not really get his way in this matter. Sir Warren Fisher, who was then head of the Civil Service, later argued that the government of 1924–9, in 'reducing our naval forces to a skeleton', had brought the country to a state of 'military impotence'.[98] Yet the total defence budget, which in 1923 had been £105 millions, was in 1929 £113 millions, and this in a period of declining prices. Nor was Churchill's desire to postpone cruiser construction unjustified at a time when the admirals themselves could not make up their minds what type of cruiser they required.[99] On the other hand, Churchill's view, expressed in private letters to Baldwin, that war with Japan could be ruled out 'in our lifetime', or 'in the next twenty years', was far too sanguine.[100] Such a degree of prevision was never acceptable to the Committee of Imperial Defence, which went no further than to adopt a moving Ten Year Rule in 1928.[101] Even this was risky, and, as it turned out, although war did not occur until 1939 it very nearly broke out in 1938. Yet we must allow for the climate of the time, and especially for the high hopes held out by the Treaty of Locarno of 1925, which seemed likely to lead to the pacification of Europe. At the time of Churchill's last Budget, he was being castigated in the *Economist* for the fact that defence took up about 3% of the national income, as against 2% in the latter half of the nineteenth century.[102]

When the government fell the retiring Chancellor gave his senior Treasury advisers 'a very cheerful farewell party at Buck's Club'.[103] None was more sorry to see Churchill go than Grigg, who was coming to regard him as 'the most brilliant and versatile individual who has lived in our age'.[104] It was also a sad parting for Eddie Marsh, who now became Private Secretary to J. H. Thomas, the new Lord Privy Seal: it would have been sadder still if Marsh had realised that Churchill would not be back in office for over ten years, by which time he himself had retired from the Civil Service.

16. *Private Life and Public Critics, 1918-29*

At the time of the Armistice in 1918 Churchill was already almost forty-four years old. When he ceased to be Chancellor of the Exchequer in June 1929, he could look back on ten years of hard work, punctuated by vigorous recreation of a type not usually persisted in by men in middle age. Physically, he changed relatively slowly: he already looked somewhat middle-aged before the war, for his hair had become rather thin and his figure was chubby. In this period his baldness increased, but what was left of his hair had not lost all its sandy colour. And exercise, in the form of polo, boar-hunting and even brick-laying helped to keep his weight down. He needed spectacles for reading and writing, but not for other purposes.

Clementine's fourth child, a daughter, was born only four days after the Armistice. She was christened Marigold Frances, the two names being taken respectively from her godmothers, Lady Sinclair, the wife of Sir Archibald Sinclair, and Lady Horner, a much older friend of the family. But in August 1921, to the great distress of her parents, Marigold died of complications following a septic throat, before reaching the age of three. Clementine's last child, another daughter, was born on September 15th 1922 – at the moment of crisis over Chanak. She was given the name of Mary, perhaps because Maryon Whyte, a cousin of Clementine's, was a godmother.

Marigold's death was not the only family loss the Churchills experienced in 1921, for in June Lady Randolph died after an injury which should not have proved fatal. Still only 67, and far more active than most women of her age, she developed an infection in her foot after breaking an ankle. This led to an amputation, from which she was apparently recovering when she collapsed and died. In reply to a letter of sympathy from Lloyd George, Churchill wrote that she 'had the gift of eternal youth of spirit, & never have I felt this more than in these weeks of cruel pain'.[1] It was a heavy personal blow for him, as she had shared many of his pleasures and sorrows even when he had been adult, and her example in many ways shaped his own attitude to life. She was buried at Bladon, by the side of her first husband; and her elder son wrote afterwards to the Duke of Connaught, who had expressed his condolence: 'She looked beautiful yesterday in her coffin.... Thirty years had rolled from her brow and one saw again her old splendour of features and expression, without a wrinkle or trace of pain or weariness.'[2] Asquith's comment on her death was apt: 'An amazing reservoir of vitality and gay, unflinching courage. I call her the last of the Victorians.'[3] She had always lived up to her income, and indeed beyond, and there was virtually nothing for her sons to inherit. The net value of her personal estate was £2480.[4]

The older Churchill children had spent the latter part of the war outside London at Lullenden Farm, an Elizabethan house near East Grinstead in Sussex. They did not see a great deal of their parents, for Clementine was helping the YMCA in organising factory canteens and her husband was much preoccupied by work in Whitehall and by visits to the front in France.[5] In the summer of 1918 Churchill sold the lease of 33 Eccleston Square: the purchaser, curiously enough, was the Labour Party, which was looking for office-space reasonably close to Whitehall and Westminster.[6] The Churchills moved slightly further west to what was now a more distinctly residential neighbourhood: they bought the lease of 2 Sussex Square, a tall mid-nineteenth-century house at Lancaster Gate with a good view south across Hyde Park.

In September 1919 Churchill sold Lullenden Farm to his old friend General Sir Ian Hamilton, but it was not his intention to remain without a place in the country for himself and his family.[7] In 1920 Lloyd George acquired an estate at Churt, in Surrey, and commissioned the architect Philip Tilden to build him a house. This fired Churchill's imagination, but he seems to have been inclined to wait for a time until his financial situation was more secure. Ministerial salaries were not worth as much as before the war, and his best chance of having a substantial sum of money at his disposal was by obtaining advance royalties for his memoirs. He was already working on the first volume of *World Crisis* while he was at the War Office, and by early 1921 he had contracts worth several thousand pounds, and reckoned that he was being paid something like half-a-crown a word.[8]

Just at this time, however, he received an unexpected windfall in the form of the inheritance of a valuable Irish estate, which came to him on trust under a settlement made by his great-grandmother, the wife of the third Marquess of Londonderry. The estate had been in the hands of his distant cousin, Lord Herbert Vane-Tempest, who was killed in a railway accident in January 1921.[9] It consisted principally of rural property in County Antrim, not far from Larne; there had been a mansion known as Garron Tower, but this had been destroyed by fire in 1914. Churchill seems to have visited the estate only once, in March 1926, and then only in the course of one day. But it was probably worth several thousand pounds a year in the 1920s.

In September 1922 Churchill bought the Chartwell Manor and Estate near Westerham, in Kent. The house had been built in Henry VII's reign, but substantially altered and extended in the Victorian period. It was dark and decayed, and would need much alteration to become a comfortable residence. Churchill was nevertheless attracted by the promise of the site and its surroundings. It had good views across the Kentish Weald, though well protected from the north; and the 300-acre estate contained a pleasant valley with a stream and a lake.

He commissioned Philip Tilden to rebuild the house, and sometimes drove him down to Chartwell in a two-seater car that he owned at this time. Tilden found this an alarming experience on one occasion in winter when the road was icy and 'we skidded down Westerham Hill from top to bottom'.[10] In due course he produced drawings which Churchill approved, and the builders moved in. The Victorian additions had to be almost entirely removed, as they were suffering from damp and fungus, but the old Tudor structure was largely sound. Churchill repeatedly visited the scene, and frequently demanded changes of plan. He said afterwards that it was difficult to judge a building from drawings, and that it would have been cheaper to have a scale model constructed, even if it cost £100.[11] The total cost of the alterations and additions worked out at nearly £18,000, although the manor and estate had originally been bought for only £5000.[12] The house was not ready for occupation until the spring of 1924, but in the summer of 1923 Churchill rented a house in Westerham called Hosey Rigge, where the family could live while he was directing operations at Chartwell.[13]

It was the extent of the Conservative victory in the 1924 election, as well as Baldwin's decision to make Churchill his Chancellor of the Exchequer, that determined the future of 2 Sussex Square. Churchill now became entitled to occupy 11 Downing Street, next door to the Prime Minister's house; and foreseeing a reasonable tenancy in Whitehall he decided to sell the leasehold of the now superfluous residence at Lancaster Gate. The previous incumbent of 11 Downing Street was J. R. Clynes – not the Chancellor of the Exchequer, but the senior member of the Labour government after MacDonald himself. Clynes was a little slow to leave, having let his own home for the remainder of the year; but early in 1925 it was announced that Churchill was in residence at Downing Street,[14] and there he was to live while Parliament was in session until the election of 1929 brought defeat and the end of his Chancellorship.

During the early post-war period Churchill was working so hard that for some time he could take no real holiday. Instead, he combined business with pleasure in various ways whenever he could. As Secretary of State for Air he could easily continue flying; and when he had occasion to visit France during the Paris Peace Conference he usually went by air. His pilot was Colonel Jack Scott, a skilful veteran, but there was a dual control on the plane and thus Churchill could enjoy acting as pilot himself for at least part of each trip. On one occasion fire broke out, but Scott managed to put it out with an extinguisher, although the machine temporarily went out of control. On another occasion the plane somersaulted on take-off at Bec Airport, Paris, owing to running into a concealed ditch; it was a write-off, but there were no injuries to pilot or passenger.[15] But an incident in July

1919 put an end to flying for pleasure, so far as Churchill was concerned. He took off from Croydon aerodrome with Scott, intending to return after a couple of hours as he had a dinner engagement in London. He completed the take-off himself, but then found, according to his own account, that the controls were not functioning properly. Scott tried to take over, but the machine had gained little height – about ninety feet – and he could not prevent it from plunging to the ground. Churchill's belt took most of the pressure of his body weight, and he escaped with a scratched forehead and severe bruising of the legs. But Scott was knocked unconscious and had both legs broken. Churchill was able to attend his dinner, which was for General Pershing, who had commanded the American troops in France during the war. But he felt responsible for Scott's injuries, and decided to give up flying except when it was absolutely essential. For ten years or more he averaged only about one flight a year.[16]

Churchill now turned back to a recreation which he had largely given up before the war, owing to lack of opportunity. This was polo, which was a sport regularly indulged in by his cousins Lord Wimborne and Freddie Guest, the former at his home at Ashby St Legers near Rugby, and the latter at Templeton, Roehampton. One of Churchill's private secretaries at the War Office, Lord Wodehouse, was an expert player – indeed he later wrote a book on the subject – and so Churchill did not lack for fellow-enthusiasts. Polo matches began to appear so frequently in his engagement diary that Eddie Marsh decided to substitute the mystifying term 'collective equitation', which he understood to be an expression used for the sport in the French army.[17] Churchill took his family down to Freddie Guest's house for some months in late 1919 so that he could play polo while still within easy reach of London; and in the summer of the following year he rented the headmaster's house at Rugby with a similar purpose, for this was close to Ashby St Legers.[18] In April 1922 he was severely bruised and shaken by a fall when at polo practice with the Duke of Westminster at Eaton Hall, the Duke's home near Chester.[19] He told his friend 'F.E.' that he had 'never had a worse fall'.[20] He lay in bed for a week, consoling himself with the knowledge that he was entitled to claim from various insurance schemes run by newspapers for their subscribers, which he had made a point of joining.[21] After this he played polo less often. He was a member of a House of Commons team which defeated the House of Lords in 1925, and he played his last match at Malta in 1927 – at the age of fifty-two.[22]

From 1923 onwards most of Churchill's physical recreation was obtained in work on the Chartwell buildings and estate. But he enjoyed swimming when on holiday, and on several occasions went boar-hunting with the Duke of Westminster in France. The Duke had a château at Mimizan, north of Biarritz, which he used as a base for this sport, and Churchill was a guest there in 1920. But the supply of boars at Mimizan began to decline, and the Duke moved his *équipage* to St Saens in Normandy, an hour's drive from Rouen.[23] Churchill went boar-hunting for a few days every year at St Saens in the late 1920s, and his son Randolph joined in the sport when he grew up.[24]

A different form of recreation was afforded by the hobby which Churchill had taken up for the first time in the depths of his despair over the mismanagement of the Gallipoli operation – painting. Two features of this hobby were particularly agreeable to him. First, his work was distinctly promising, for although he could not draw very well he had a very good sense of colour. Claude Lowther, in a cottage on whose Sussex estate the Churchills had spent a few weeks in the summer of 1916, noticed these characteristics at once: 'He has taken to painting – draws badly – but has just a touch of genius! His colouring is wonderful & his grasp of atmosphere almost uncanny for a novice.'[25] Secondly, Churchill found painting to be a completely absorbing occupation. This meant that he could forget about his political and administrative chores for a time and obtain complete relaxation. 'Sometimes,' he told his cousin Clare Sheridan (*née* Frewen), who was a sculptress, 'I could *almost* give up everything for it.'[26]

Of the pictures that he painted in this period probably only a minority survive, and even fewer have been catalogued. He told the journalist Philip Gibbs that he regarded a day as ill-spent if he had not painted two pictures. ' "My dear Mr Churchill," I expostulated, "the professional painter is more than satisfied if he paints two pictures in two months." '[27] The known works of his from the early 1920s include scenes of sunset at Roehampton; of the lake and trees at Mimizan; and several views of the pyramids and of Jerusalem, done in the course of his Middle East tour in 1921.[28] One of the latter was put up for auction in aid of the fund for the Dundee unemployed.[29] Several pictures were completed in Sir John Lavery's studio; others were done at

Lympne or at Trent, the houses of Sir Philip Sassoon, a rich Conservative MP who owed his minor office in the government almost entirely to his munificence as a host. The brightest canvases, however, were derived from holidays on the Mediterranean coast, where on one occasion he fell in with some disciples of Cézanne, who gave him the idea of pointillism – providing an impression for the eye by crowding the surface of the canvas with small spots of various colours.[30]

When Churchill was out of office he was able to devote much of his time to writing and journalism, and at first he needed to do so in order to maintain a satisfactory income for himself and his family. But we have already seen that a great deal of the work on the first volume of *World Crisis* was accomplished when he was still serving in Lloyd George's Cabinet. It was a yet more remarkable feat to be able to continue the series, to the extent of three more large books, while he was Chancellor of the Exchequer. Two of them appeared as the two parts of Volume III, covering the years 1916–18: they were published in March 1927. Volume IV, intended to be the last, and entitled *The Aftermath*, came out almost exactly two years later. The whole work was highly profitable. Thornton Butterworth, the publishers, gave the author an advance of £4000 on the first volume, against a royalty of $33\frac{1}{3}\%$, the retail price of the volume being thirty shillings. For later volumes the advance was reduced, and the royalty fell slightly to 30%. Volume III, in its two parts, sold at forty-two shillings.[31]

The success of the series was guaranteed by the fact that it presented a vivid account of events still very imperfectly understood, from the standpoint of an exceptionally well-informed observer and participant. The daily newspapers all devoted columns to each volume on publication day, for they contained much that was entirely new to the general public as well as much that was retold in a fresh and interesting manner. There was a general chorus of praise for the author's lucidity and power of description, and even the most hostile critics had to concede that the narrative was brilliantly readable. Churchill's rhetorical style was displeasing to some – the text had of course been dictated rather than composed – and a reviewer in *Blackwood's* picked out some of the more strained passages in the first volume, such as the description of the pre-war world as 'a world of monstrous shadows moving in convulsive combinations through vistas of fathomless catastrophe'.[32] H. M. Tomlinson, himself a former war correspondent, wrote that there was 'a hectic flush to the words which gives the reader the chilly fear that Mr Churchill will, in his excitement, step right over the footlights and finish up his remarks on the big drum'.[33] But most reviewers were willing to forgive him the occasional purple patch for the sake of the larger whole. As W. P. Crozier put it in the *Manchester Guardian*, 'He cannot be dull in writing any more than in action.'[34]

It was in volumes II and III that the main outline of Churchill's views on the conduct of the war became clear. His contention was that for the most part the professional soldiers and sailors were wrong about strategy, while the professional politicians were, sometimes at least, right. No nation had a 'King-Warrior-Statesman' who might from a combination of military and political experience have been able to deal thoroughly with the problems that war brought forward. The result was the appalling policy of 'attrition' on the Western Front, which led to the wastage of soldiers' lives by the generals on both sides. The failure to exploit the opportunity of the Dardanelles operation – Churchill's own scheme at the beginning – dominates Volume II and gives it a sombre tone; and the account of the Battle of the Somme, with its terrible casualties for the British army, is the main feature of Volume III. In spite of the power of his general indictment, Churchill rarely criticised specific individuals, though he allowed himself a shaft at General Sir Charles Monro, who went out to Gallipoli in the autumn of 1915 and at once ordered the evacuation: 'He came, he saw, he capitulated.'[35]

There were of course those who could easily take offence at his judgements – particularly among the now-retired generals and admirals who had helped to plan the operations concerned. A number of critics of the work got together in 1927 to produce a book of their own. It was entitled *The World Crisis: A Criticism*, and contained a series of essays taking up particular points, many of them of a rather technical nature.[36] General Sir Frederick Maurice, Director of Military Operations at the War Office for most of the war, devoted a chapter to the Battle of the Marne, where he thought Churchill had gone badly wrong; Sir Charles Oman, the Oxford historian, found fault with his figures of the Somme casualties which he held were proportionately much heavier on the German side than Churchill had allowed; and

Admiral Sir Reginald Bacon castigated errors in his treatment of the tactics of the Battle of Jutland. The criticisms were too detailed and particular to do any serious damage to Churchill's main contentions, except for those of Sir Charles Oman; and on the whole more recent research has tended to confirm Churchill's figures, rather than Oman's attempted corrections.[37]

The volumes had many admirers. Among them was a man who had no reason to be especially sympathetic towards their author – J. M. Keynes; and it is perhaps appropriate to quote the conclusion of his review of *The Aftermath* in the *Nation*:

> The chronicle is finished. With what feelings does one lay down Mr Churchill's two-thousandth page? Gratitude to one who can write with so much eloquence and feeling of things which are part of the lives of all of us of the war generation, but which he saw and knew much closer and clearer. Admiration for his energies of mind and his intense absorption of intellectual interest and elemental emotion on what is for the moment the matter in hand – which is his best quality. A little envy, perhaps, for his undoubting conviction that frontiers, races, patriotisms, even wars if need be, are ultimate verities for mankind, which lends for him a kind of dignity and even nobility to events, which for others are only a nightmare interlude, something to be permanently avoided.[38]

For much of the war and the early post-war period Churchill had been so busy that he had seen less of his family than he would have wished. He had always enjoyed playing with the children – there was still plenty of the schoolboy in his own make-up – and one popular game at Hoe Farm and at Lullenden had been 'gorilla', in which he lurched about making grunting noises like a gorilla and trying to seize the children, who did their best to hide.[39] He always liked dressing up and acting charades – the children's equivalent of fancy-dress balls, which he also enjoyed.[40] He also encouraged the children to organise their own entertainment, and he built a house in a tree for them at Chartwell, as he had done for himself at Salisbury Hall.[41] After the murder of Sir Henry Wilson, when there was fear of further assassinations of public figures, he had three detectives to follow him around; and on a family holiday at Frinton in 1922 he employed them to help him and the children in massive stream-damming operations on the beach.[42] But Diana and Randolph were in their teens in the mid and late 1920s; and they began to be absorbed into their parents' intellectual life, and were encouraged, as Winston had been by his mother, to take part in general conversation with guests. Tom Jones, who visited Chartwell for a short visit in 1926, thought that 'Nothing could be more charming than Winston's handling of the children'.[43]

Randolph went to Eton at the age of twelve, having been given the choice by his father of going either there or to Harrow. 'I thought it very civilised of him to give me the option,' he wrote many years later: 'I went down and inspected both institutions. It seemed that there were fewer rules and less discipline at Eton than at Harrow; accordingly I opted for Eton....'[44] From about that time onwards the children often accompanied their parents on holiday on the Continent. Their customary form of travel was by road, in the family car which was a Wolseley limousine. But early in 1927 Randolph accompanied his father on a rather grander vacation, not unmixed with high politics. They went overland to Italy and then by sea to Malta, where Churchill was the guest of Admiral Sir Roger Keyes. They then embarked with the Mediterranean Fleet and watched naval manœuvres before landing at Athens, where a semi-formal visit was made to ministers of the Greek government. Returning to Italy, Churchill and his son called upon the Pope at the Vatican and Churchill also visited the King of Italy and paid a call on Mussolini.[45]

Meanwhile, Churchill had become more and more absorbed in the development of Chartwell. In late 1924 he had 'a little band of workmen' to build a dam in the valley, so as to provide a new lake for swimming.[46] This did not turn out to be satisfactory, however, as it was too muddy and weedy, and so another dam was built and another pool created.[47] In 1925 he was at work on a rockery, which was to have a waterfall as well.[48] As he told Baldwin, he spent the whole of August 1928 'building a cottage & dictating a book: 200 bricks & 2000 words per day'.[49] He also worked off and on at the construction of a high wall round a kitchen garden.

His prowess as a bricklayer came to the notice of James F. Lane, the Southern Counties divisional secretary of the Amalgamated Union of Building Trade Workers, who decided to recruit the Chancellor of the Exchequer as a member of his union. He therefore sent him an invitation to join, which Churchill cautiously announced himself prepared to accept:

Would you mind letting me know whether there is any rule regulating the number of bricks which a man may lay in a day; also, is there any rule that a trade unionist may not work with one who is not a trade unionist; and what are the restrictions on overtime? I may say that I shall be very pleased to join the union if you are of the opinion that it would not be unwelcome to your members. I take a high view of the dignity both of craftsmanship and of manual labour.[50]

These questions were satisfactorily answered, and Lane attended at the Treasury to initiate the new member, to address him as 'Brother Churchill' and to give him his membership card. Unfortunately the more militant members of the union would not accept him as one of their colleagues. One of the Manchester branches passed a resolution of protest, describing the incident as 'bringing upon the organisation public contempt and ridicule'. The Executive Council met and decided that Churchill was not eligible for union membership. His cheque in payment of fees had not been cashed, and so it could be reasonably maintained that he never had been a member – in spite of the initiation ceremony in the Treasury, and a certificate of membership which Churchill retained for his own satisfaction.[51]

Before the war, Churchill had had an exceptionally wide range of political friendships, spreading right across the parliamentary spectrum from Radicalism to High Toryism. His association with colleagues in the Cabinet and in the Liberal Party was balanced by his family ties with the Conservative aristocracy and by his personal friendships with 'F.E.', with Beaverbrook, and with the deliberately mixed membership of the Other Club. Only the Labour Party was largely missed out, although Churchill had links among the Socialist intelligentsia. He knew H. G. Wells personally and had long admired his work, and of course he had exchanged hospitality with the Webbs.

But this catholicity of association largely came to an end with the war. Churchill did not deliberately sever his relations with his Asquithian former colleagues, but inevitably they drifted apart, and he saw less of them. His ties with Lloyd George were, of course, exceptionally close during the period of the post-war Coalition. Although the two men sometimes disagreed violently on questions of policy, Churchill's loyalty as a 'lieutenant' of the Prime Minister was absolute, and Lloyd George knew that he could rely upon Churchill, however awkward a subordinate he was in other respects, never to intrigue against him. Their intimacy was marked by the regularity with which they shared their leisure, at innumerable weekends in the country or even at Continental resorts. This association had been weakened after 1920, but it only came to an end with the fall of the Coalition government. Afterwards they rarely met in circumstances which allowed the re-establishment of their old intimacy; but Churchill's respect and admiration for his former chief survived through their political differences. After Lloyd George had visited him at 11 Downing Street one evening in the late 1920s to discuss passages in *The Aftermath*, Churchill told his Parliamentary Private Secretary, Robert Boothby: 'Lloyd George hadn't been in this room for three minutes before the old relationship was completely re-established – the relationship of master and servant.'[52]

Politically speaking, however, Churchill's range of friendships became more limited when he joined the Conservatives. The move naturally strengthened his concord with his aristocratic relations, such as the Duke of Marlborough and the Marquess of Londonderry, and with other people of rank and wealth, such as the Dukes of Sutherland and Westminster and Sir Philip Sassoon. He enjoyed visiting their great houses, partly for the sake of the opportunities they afforded for recreation in pleasant surroundings, partly because he wished to take advantage of their fine landscapes for his painting. But his closest friendship was still with 'F.E.', with whom he could relax more easily than with any other friends. He found Beaverbrook's company almost equally agreeable, but their relations were marred by Beaverbrook's newspaper campaigns against the government and even against the Chancellor's fiscal policy. The path of reconciliation, Beaverbrook discovered, could be smoothed by gifts, and in December 1926 Churchill was the recipient of a refrigerator which kept his champagne cool and enabled him to abandon his existing habit of diluting it with ice.[53]

The corollary of this was that he became increasingly out of touch with the new forces in British politics on the Left. The Labour Party had become the chief opposition party, but its leaders were relatively poor men and they could not move in the social circles which Churchill frequented. They would have felt out of place in the Other Club – even though that dining group was set up in order to bring together persons of contrasting political opinions. It seems that one of the few members of the club

337

who belonged to the Labour Party was Colonel Josiah Wedgwood, who may have been elected when he was still a Liberal.[54] On one occasion Churchill invited Snowden to dine with him at 11 Downing Street[55]; but a courtesy such as this, although not uncharacteristic of Churchill, was an exceptional event. It was not that, in other respects, Churchill did not have a great variety of social contacts. One not infrequent visitor at Chartwell, who otherwise shunned society altogether, was T. E. Lawrence, now serving in the ranks of the RAF. Lawrence would suddenly appear at Chartwell on his motor-cycle, and then Churchill 'would make haste to kill the fatted calf'.[56] Lawrence displayed a keen admiration for the *World Crisis*, and when Churchill described the third volume to him as 'a pot boiler' he wrote to Eddie Marsh, 'Some pot! and probably some boil, too' – a form of expression which Churchill may have cherished in his mind for future oratorical purposes.[57]*

A much more regular visitor at Chartwell, at least from 1926 onwards, was Professor F. A. Lindemann, whom Churchill first met briefly in 1921 but really got to know through 'F.E.'. Lindemann was Professor of Experimental Philosophy – which in fact meant physics – at Oxford University, and he often visited 'F.E.' at his home at Charlton in Oxfordshire, where he was known as 'the Prof.'.[58] Churchill obtained his advice about the hydraulics of his Chartwell water-supply, and Lindemann, who was of Alsatian origin, also gave valuable assistance on the question of comparative British and German war casualties on the Somme, which as we have seen was of controversial importance at the time.[59] But the Oxford scientist was so reactionary in his political views that Churchill expressed gratitude to Tom Jones for 'expounding the democratic faith' to his son Randolph at dinner at Chartwell, as Randolph seemed to be falling under Lindemann's influence.[60] It was Lindemann who persuaded his college, Christ Church, to admit Randolph as a freshman in January 1929, when he was still less than eighteen, although in many ways precocious.[61]

Before the war the Churchills had been keen theatregoers, and were well up in the latest works of Galsworthy and Shaw. During the war Eddie Marsh, who, thanks to his private income was already a distinguished patron of the arts, saw to it that his minister

* For the context of the expression 'Some chicken! Some neck!', see WSC, *WW2*, iii, 602.

met many of the younger literary figures of promise, such as Rupert Brooke, who died while serving in the Royal Naval Division, and Ivor Novello and even Siegfried Sassoon – a cadet member of the wealthy Conservative Jewish family, but one who reflected in his poetry a deep disillusionment with war as an instrument of policy.[62] Sassoon and Churchill had little in common on this question, but Churchill as a former front-line soldier and as one fully conscious of the terrible cost of 'attrition' could understand Sassoon's feelings, and he admired his war poems, many of which he learnt off by heart. There was less of this cultivation of the poets in the 1920s, partly perhaps because Marsh was less closely in touch with the post-war generation.

But if Marsh could no longer introduce Churchill to the *avant-garde*, there were other important literary services which he could render to his master. He undertook the revision of the text of each of Churchill's books when they were in typescript or proof.[63] His careful scrutiny of style and grammar almost certainly prevented many faults upon which the critics would have pounced with relish. It was Beaverbrook, however, who drew Churchill's attention to the inappropriate character of a quotation from Julian Grenfell's rather brash poem 'Into Battle' which was placed at the opening of the chapter on the Battle of the Somme in the *World Crisis*. 'Surely this is a piece of irony?' he asked.[64] It was not: but Churchill had the good sense to replace it with a fittingly sombre couplet from Siegfried Sassoon.

A journalist's assessment of Churchill's standing at the close of the war contained this passage: 'At thirty-seven men looked upon Mr Churchill as a statesman of some achievement. At forty-seven he is discussed as a politician of considerable promise.'[65] Apart from the error of 'forty-seven' for 'forty-three', it is apparent that these two sentences are not far from the truth. After the fierce controversy that centred around Gallipoli, Churchill had to remake his reputation, and had certainly not completed the task when he ceased to be Minister of Munitions. His success as an administrator was, of course, known to those inside the government, but some of his immediate colleagues disliked his tendency to encroach upon their own spheres, whether in word or deed – Curzon and Montagu being particularly bitter at times.[66] When he became Chancellor of the Exchequer in 1924, the appointment was resented by many of the Tariff Reformers in the Cabinet, and his position both as a Free Trader and as a recent convert from Liberalism was relatively weak. He resumed his formal membership of the Conservative Party only in late 1925, and lunched at the Carlton Club in his own right for the first time on November 2nd.[67] But the resentment against his Free Trade views continued. As late as November 1928 Amery was complaining in his diary of the Chancellor's 'hopelessly negative' attitude on fiscal policy, and was even looking forward to a Conservative defeat in the forthcoming general election as a way of 'getting that "old man of the sea", Winston, off our shoulders'.[68] Such attitudes help to explain how it was that Bridgeman, a comparative lightweight as a politician, was able to defeat Churchill over naval expenditure. Not that these differences in the Baldwin Cabinet led to personal hostilities of any serious character. Bridgeman himself described Churchill as 'the most indescribable and amazing character of all my colleagues.... With all his peculiarities and irritating methods, one cannot help liking him – and his ability and vitality are enormous'.[69]

A great deal of Churchill's reputation as a leading politician rested on his ability to master the House of Commons. There is no doubt that his ministerial statements, distinguished as they were for their clarity of exposition and generosity of vision, impressed friend and foe alike. In February 1920, when he presented the army estimates, the Liberal Opposition spokesman, F. D. Acland, said that he 'invariably illuminates every subject he touches, and has a wonderful power of inducing in his audience the belief that the subject with which he happens for the moment to be identified, is more vital than any other'.[70] On occasion he could convert a hostile Commons within the hour to acquiescence in government policy. An example occurred in July 1920, when Montagu aroused the anger of Conservative backbenchers by a truculent speech about General R. F. H. Dyer, who had been put on half-pay after the massacre of Indian civilians at Amritsar. Churchill expounded the government's case against Dyer with great moderation in what Leopold Amery described as 'a masterly performance for its purpose and for its audience'.[71] His capacity to understand the sort of argument which would appeal to a predominantly Conservative House was never more needed than in early 1922, when he had to pilot the Irish Free State Bill through the House; but his success was remarkable. He could fairly say several years later that 'the session of 1922 was the most prosperous I have ever had as a minister in the House of Commons.[72] If he did not carry quite so much weight in the later 1920s, nevertheless his Budget speeches were a delight to the whole House, and as Harold Macmillan has recalled 'no one could withhold admiration for the wit, humour, ingenuity and oratorical skill which he displayed'.[73]

So far as the wider public was concerned, his great qualities as a platform speaker counted for less than they had done before the war, for the new electorate was less prepared to sit through long formal speeches. The supporters of the extreme Left delighted in shouting down their principal opponents, and Churchill found this opposition disruptive of his set speeches – although he could deal with a single heckler easily enough. His type of formal oration, carefully prepared, and containing long and elaborate sentences, building up gradually to a climax, was less suitable for the 1920s than Baldwin's more casual and conversational style. One young Liberal who heard Churchill speak in a by-election thought that he was 'detestable as anything but a humorous comic entertainer.... He is such a preposterous little fellow, with his folded arms and tufted forelock and his Lyceum Theatre voice.'[74] This was a woman's view; and it is noteworthy that Churchill for his part did not think much of the new women voters, and tried to prevent the extension of the franchise to women aged between twenty-one and thirty when it was being debated in the Cabinet in 1927.[75]

But at the same time he was well aware that methods of public communication were changing. He deplored the fact that his speeches – and those of other political leaders – were inadequately reported in the popular papers, and he attached all the more importance to the new medium of radio. When arrangements were made to broadcast a speech of his from the Annual Dinner of the Engineers' Club in October 1925, he was very disappointed to find that John Reith, the General Manager of the British Broadcasting Company, expected him to avoid political controversy in his remarks. Churchill did not live up to this expectation, and Reith had to defend his staff against angry critics who thought he should have been cut off in the middle of his speech.[76]

During the General Strike, as we have seen, Churchill showed clearly enough the importance that he attached to broadcasting as a means of political communication. Then in February 1928, when arrangements were made to broadcast his speech from the annual Civil Service dinner, Churchill was reminded that political controversy was not permitted, but he took the opportunity to criticise this ruling:

> Why, controversy is the soul of British life, and I really do not see why politicians should not be allowed to express their controversial views through the agency of the broadcasting apparatus. Of course they are no longer allowed to do so through the Press. The newspapers ... only go prowling about looking for the wrong tit-bits.[77]

He had evidently forgotten that the ruling had been made by the Cabinet, and when this was pointed out to him he apologised to his colleagues. But the incident had a positive result, for it led to the revocation of the ban for 'an experimental period'.[78] After his Budget of that year, Churchill was allowed to make what was supposed to be a non-controversial statement about it: but Reith thought that it was not non-controversial, and Beatrice Webb, who also heard it, described it as a 'vividly rhetorical representation of his own case'. She was impressed: 'Except that his voice is harsh he is a first-rate broadcaster.'[79]

But the possibilities of the medium, so far as Churchill was concerned, still lay largely in the future. In the meantime, he was more or less debarred from recovering any wide degree of popular acceptance, at any rate on the Left. He was widely distrusted within the labour movement for his well-publicised enthusiasm for intervention against Russia in 1919–20, and throughout the 1920s it was easy for Labour leaders, and for Socialist intellectuals such as H. G. Wells, to criticise him as a dangerous man who should not be trusted with public office. Churchill had a sharp exchange of views with Wells in late 1920, when he attacked Wells's plea for an understanding with the Bolsheviks by calling him a 'philosophical romancer'.[80] But Wells got the better of this encounter by describing him in turn as an adventurer 'closely akin to the d'Annunzio type', and by saying:

> Before all things he desires a dramatic world with villains – and one hero.... Bolshevism is a substitutional enemy with him. It is not the Communism of Moscow and its ineffectual propaganda he assails, but the steadfast movement of the west towards a collectivist society, which will call the rich man to account.[81]

Some time in 1921 and 1922 Wells decided to make rather more of this line of criticism, and he wrote his *Men Like Gods* (pub-

342

lished early in 1923), in which he depicted a Socialist Utopia
being rudely disturbed by the arrival of a group of ordinary
mortals including one 'Rupert Catskill', who at once became
discontented and organised a revolt. 'Catskill' had all the Churchillian characteristics; and Lloyd George sent a copy of the
book to Balfour with the observation that the lampoon of their
former colleague was 'killing'.[82] But in fact there was another
character in the novel called 'Cecil Burleigh' who was an even
more precise caricature of Balfour himself.

Criticism of Churchill by members of the Liberal Party took
a rather different form. There was a tendency on their part to
emphasise his special unreliability and opportunism in twice
changing his party. When he became Chancellor of the Exchequer the *Manchester Guardian*, his old ally, commented
sourly: 'Mr Churchill for the second time has – shall we say? –
quitted the sinking ship, and for the second time the reward of
this fine instinct has been not safety only but high promotion.'[83]
Sir John Simon not long afterwards described him as

> a meteor in the political sky of whom it can safely be said that he
> will not very long remain in a fixed position. Mr Churchill is very
> fitly included in the Conservative Government, the watchword of
> which is tranquillity and stability (Laughter). There is a new piece
> of jazz music now being played which has been called 'the Winston
> Constitution'. You take a step forward, two steps backward, a side
> step to the right, and then reverse (Loud laughter). You can see
> that the piece is well named.[84]

Almost four years later Sir Herbert Samuel was still hammering
away at the theme of Churchill's opportunism and comparing
him to the Vicar of Bray.[85]

Of course this was fair comment, but it was not a true representation of Churchill's mode of thinking. Those who knew him
best realised that it was not by any Machiavellian scheming that
he had managed to jump from Cabinet to Cabinet. J. A. Spender,
the former editor of the *Westminster Gazette*, thought that there
was 'some luck' in the way in which he was able to 'catch the
tides of opinion which the more scientific calculators seemed to
miss'. But in Spender's view his ready accession to office was
principally due to the fact that he was such a very formidable
parliamentarian and platform speaker: 'For ten years or more it
was almost a formula with Tories and Coalitionists that Winston
must on no account be left loose in opposition.'[86]

Such a calculation had weighed with Lloyd George as Prime Minister, and no doubt it did to some extent with Baldwin; but the latter was also worried by the fear that Churchill's accession to a Conservative Cabinet would only alienate Labour still more, and so damage his chances of reconciling all classes in the community. Edward Wood, Churchill's former Under-Secretary at the Colonial Office, took the same line and added in conversation with Neville Chamberlain that 'he feared Winston Churchill would play a part similar to that of Carson in the old days – one of embitterment between those who might have otherwise worked for the good of the country'.[87] Ministers who urged Baldwin to take Churchill in, such as Cunliffe-Lister and, probably, Hoare, were less concerned about this side of Baldwin's policy. Baldwin was also worried about the company that Churchill kept, for he regarded both Birkenhead and Beaverbrook as vulgarly ostentatious and immoral. This view was shared by others – for instance, by the anonymous author of a book of short political biographies entitled *The Mirrors of Downing Street*, who said that 'His character suffers ... from association with second-rate people.'[88]

Some time in 1923, however, Baldwin decided that he could manage Churchill as a colleague. Churchill's response justified Baldwin's decision, and as early as the end of the 1924–5 parliamentary session a commentator was writing in *The Times*:

> Except in a class war, Mr Churchill could never lead England, but his immense intellectual fertility and vigour, his discriminating and insatiable *goût des grandes choses*, the reach, variety and weight of his debating and oratorical gifts make him the ideal complement to the deeper moral power of his leader.[89]

It was a combination which, as we have seen, continued to work well, though it was not to outlast the 1920s.

In the new world of the 1930s, things were very different: but in 1929 Churchill could look back on a political career whose success, in terms of both duration and range, exceeded that of any of his contemporaries.

17. *Out of Office: Indian Affairs*

CHURCHILL was disappointed with the result of the 1929 general election and the formation of another Labour government; but it was not without an agreeable sense of release that he exchanged office for opposition. Clementine had to undergo a throat operation in July, but once she was on the path of recovery her husband set off on a tour of Canada and the United States, accompanied by his son Randolph and also by his brother Jack and Jack's son Johnnie, who like Randolph was an undergraduate at Oxford. 'What fun it is', Churchill wrote to Beaverbrook, 'to get away from England, and feel one has no responsibility for her exceedingly tiresome and embarrassing affairs.'[1] The party spent most of August on the journey across Canada, travelling luxuriously in a special coach on the Canadian Pacific Railway and pausing at large cities for speeches and at selected beauty spots for sightseeing. In early September they moved into California and then travelled east to New York. On October 19th Churchill paid a courtesy call on President Hoover at the White House, and two weeks later he set out on the return trip from New York to Southampton so as to be present at the autumn session of Parliament. He had enjoyed his tour well enough, but he had been disturbed by the widespread opinion that he had encountered in both Canada and the United States that Britain was in decline, because so many of her people were living on the 'dole', and because a 'Socialist' government was in office.[2] On the latter point he tried to reassure the audiences he addressed by pointing out that Ramsay MacDonald's position as Prime Minister of a minority government depended on 'good behaviour' and willingness to put aside the 'silly nonsense' spoken during the election campaign and earlier.[3]

Meanwhile the Conservative Party, in a mood of recrimination after its defeat, was plunged into dissension on questions of policy and leadership. Baldwin was assailed vigorously by the newspaper barons Beaverbrook and Rothermere, who launched in concert a 'United Empire Crusade' in order to win the party for a full-blooded policy of Tariff Reform (including food taxes) and Imperial Preference. Churchill could not approve of this: he had returned to the Conservative Party only when it disavowed a thorough-going tariff policy; and he still hoped for a Conservative/Liberal combination, which could not be achieved if the Conservatives swung still further away from Free Trade. Immediately after the election he had tried to persuade Baldwin to open negotiations with Lloyd George, impressing upon the former his fears of a 'Lib–Lab block';[4] and at the first meeting of Parliament in July 1929 he had declared his hope that 'the floor will prove to be broader than the gangway' – that is, that the Liberals, who sat below the gangway on the Opposition side, would see their way to collaborate with the Conservatives rather than with the government.[5] This annoyed Amery, the Conservative Party's leading Tariff Reformer, who urged, on the contrary, that the party should be more friendly to Labour than to 'doctrinaire Liberalism'. According to Amery, Baldwin was 'well content that Churchill and I cancelled each other out'.[6] But this did not take into account the pressure from Beaverbrook and Rothermere.

At Christmas Tom Jones reported Churchill to be 'restive and would much prefer to be running in double harness with L.G.'.[7] He was still of the same mind in January 1930 when Beaverbrook made an attempt to win him over to the Empire Crusade. As usual when out of office, he was becoming out of sorts: according to Harold Nicolson, who was present at the meeting of the two old friends, Churchill was gloomy and looked 'incredibly aged'. He disagreed strongly with Beaverbrook's fiscal programme, but said that he felt 'too old to fight it'. He rejected altogether the idea of food taxes, and complained 'pitiably': 'But Max, Max, you are destroying my party.'[8] They separated without agreement, and in February Beaverbrook and Rothermere announced the

formation of a United Empire Party, open to individual membership. Receiving a favourable response from the public, they
decided to choose fifty candidates to contest Conservative constituencies in southern England – among them, Churchill's Epping.
Meanwhile unemployment grew; the Labour government clearly
had no policy to cope with the situation; and Sir Oswald Mosley,
who had made some constructive proposals, resigned from office
in despair when they were rejected.

The result of this was to push Baldwin into fuller compliance
with the wishes of his Tariff Reform wing. In March he went so
far as to agree to accept any proposals for inter-imperial fiscal
arrangements which were agreed to by the Dominions, even if
they involved food taxes – though he qualified this by saying that
any such proposals must be accepted also by a national referendum. This statement met with Beaverbrook's approval, but
Rothermere was not appeased and took over sole direction of the
United Empire Party. Two months later, however, Beaverbrook
and Baldwin were again at odds when Baldwin made it clear
that he did not propose to make an issue of food taxes at the
next general election.

In September a by-election at Bromley showed that a considerable proportion of Conservative voters were prepared to support
a candidate of the United Empire Party against an official Conservative. An Imperial Conference assembled in London in
October, and the Dominions prime ministers declared themselves in favour of Empire Preference – a policy which did not
immediately commend itself to the Labour government, but which
naturally strengthened the hand of Beaverbrook and Rothermere.
Baldwin had to accommodate these new developments, and in
October he issued a statement accepting the idea of Empire Preference, and advocating an immediate tariff on all imported
manufactures. Agriculture, he thought, could be assisted by a
'quota' system, which would obviate the need for any increase
in the cost of food. This did not now satisfy Beaverbrook and
Rothermere, but it evoked a cry of warning from Churchill:
'I cannot consent to the protective taxation of staple foods....
Let me add that in my opinion, if you had not been subjected to
so much ill-treatment & intrigue this year, you would have been
able in 1931 to lead our party into as great a victory as 1924.'[9]

Baldwin was in such difficulty with the Tariff Reformers that
he was obliged to regard Churchill's possible defection as no more

than a relatively minor misfortune. He replied coolly, therefore, telling Churchill that he was under heavy pressure to move still further towards Tariff Reform, and that if Churchill was forced to make a break with him on this question 'I hope and believe that nothing will disturb a friendship which I value.'[10] He had in fact been advised by Robert Topping, the Principal Agent of the Conservative Party, to 'risk the loss of Winston, because in exchange you will get the support of many'.[11]

Baldwin's eyes were now upon a by-election at South Paddington, where the official Conservative candidate was opposed by a supporter of Beaverbrook's Empire Crusade – who, indeed, eventually won the contest. Churchill wondered whether he should intervene with a statement expressing his own views – as he put it to his cousin Freddie Guest, whether he should 'lay an egg'. Guest replied: 'When in doubt whether to lay an egg, don't lay it.'[12] This was wise advice: for in any case the ensuing months were to see a still further rise in unemployment and the acceptance of Tariff Reform even by a large section of the Liberal Party – which removed much of the force of Churchill's argument for holding the Conservative Party from a thoroughgoing commitment. Only a few months later Churchill himself had swallowed the entire Tariff Reform programme, food taxes included.

But it was on quite another issue that the rift took place between Baldwin and Churchill. This was the issue of Indian constitutional reform, which came to the fore owing to an initiative taken by Lord Irwin, the Viceroy, shortly after the Labour government was formed. Irwin is better known as Lord Halifax – a title to which he succeeded a few years later: as Edward Wood he had been Churchill's Under-Secretary at the Colonial Office in 1921–22. He was a close friend of Baldwin's, and believed like him that so far as possible imperial questions should be treated in a bipartisan fashion as between Conservative and Labour. As early as 1917 a promise had been made by the Lloyd George government that the ultimate goal of British policy in India was the achievement of Dominion Status; but the Statutory Commission of British parliamentarians, which was sent out by the Baldwin government in 1928 under Sir John Simon to draw up a programme of constitutional advance, was not instructed to do more than to prepare for provincial self-government. It was boycotted by the Indian Congress Party, the predominantly Hindu nationalist organisation led at this time by Gandhi and the two Nehrus, father and son.

Irwin felt in 1929 that it was necessary to improve the political atmosphere in India by reaffirming the goal of Dominion Status and by arranging for a conference in London at which Indian opinion would be able to make itself heard on the findings of the Simon Commission. This was agreed to by Ramsay MacDonald and his Cabinet, and also by Baldwin, who was consulted when on holiday and without the means of referring the matter to his colleagues. The Viceroy's statement about Dominion Status and the news of the forthcoming 'Round Table Conference', as it was called, were published simultaneously on October 31st 1929. But they received a very mixed reception from other political leaders in Britain. Birkenhead, who had been Secretary of State for India when the Simon Commission was appointed, strongly attacked the Viceroy's declaration; and in the Commons Lloyd George criticised it vigorously, arguing that it was taken to be a new commitment and not just a reaffirmation of an earlier one, and that it should not have been made while the Simon Commission's report was still pending. Churchill, just back from America, did not speak; but he disconcerted Baldwin's more loyal followers by cheering Lloyd George 'very loudly' in the course of his speech.[13] He also wrote an article for the *Daily Mail* criticising the view that India could achieve Dominion Status in any foreseeable future:

> Dominion Status can certainly not be attained while India is a prey to fierce racial and religious dissensions.... It cannot be attained while the political classes of India represent only an insignificant fraction of the three hundred and fifty millions for whose welfare we are responsible.[14]

It has been argued by some critics of Churchill's behaviour that he abandoned earlier and more liberal views of imperial development to find a convenient means of attacking Baldwin, thus winning the support of the Conservative backbenchers, and so becoming party leader. There is, however, a distinct continuity in his attitude to nationalist movements within the imperial sphere which can be traced back to the early post-war period. Although he supported the Irish Treaty, he felt that Britain had gone to the very limit of the safeguards that she required, and he was thereafter very hostile to any talk of the erosion of the Treaty terms.

349

During the Coalition government he had shown strong opposition to any British recognition of Egyptian independence, arguing that there must be no diminution of 'the King's Dominions, whether in Egypt, Ireland or India', although there might be advance towards 'the broad ideal of full self-government'.[15] When Edwin Montagu had been Secretary of State for India, Churchill had done his best to defend him in public, as in the Amritsar debate; but in private he had been annoyed by the personification of Indian opinion – 'she' feeling 'upset' and so on – which Montagu pressed on his Cabinet colleagues in matters where Indian interests impinged on British.[16] When Birkenhead was Secretary of State for India, the two friends found themselves in basic agreement on the need for firm government combined with the discouragement of any expectation of rapid constitutional change. And with a minority Labour government holding office Churchill saw no case at all for Conservative approval of a change in policy – especially when the Liberals were expressing concern and disapproval.

Policy towards India was not Churchill's personal responsibility. His duties in the Conservative Party's 'Business Committee' – a term used at this time for what we should now call the Shadow Cabinet – were to deal with finance and to 'mark' Snowden who had replaced him as Chancellor of the Exchequer. Irwin was upset by the degree of intervention in Indian affairs which Churchill had already made in public utterances, and in a letter to Lord Salisbury, the Conservative leader in the House of Lords, he asked him to do what he could to 'curb Winston', whom he regarded as 'doing not a little harm'.[17] It was not so much that he disagreed with Churchill about the difficulties of an early approach to Dominion Status; it was rather that he regarded it as unwise to say so, for fear of inflaming Indian nationalist opinion. He wrote directly to Churchill: 'Please don't think that I am ever likely to forget the point of view that you and others have been putting, or indeed that I differ from it.... Half the problem here is psychological and a case of hurt feelings.'[18] Churchill's reply was a warning that in his view the political situation in Britain did not justify Irwin's attitude: 'However matters may be settled, it is the duty of the Conservative party to act both as a brake upon and a counterpoise to the Socialist party. In this we shall certainly be joined, though from a somewhat different angle and in a lesser degree, by the Liberal party.'[19]

But Irwin was not to be put off his policy of trying to reconcile Indian nationalist feeling. He did not have much success at first, for the Indian Congress Party refused to take part in the Round Table Conference, and embarked on a campaign of civil disobedience which led to the imprisonment of Gandhi and both the Nehrus. But the plans for the Round Table Conference went ahead, and Churchill grew more and more unhappy about the prospects. His old friend Birkenhead was seriously ill and could take no further part in the criticism of Indian policy: indeed, to Churchill's deep sorrow, he died at the end of September, a victim of cirrhosis of the liver due to alcohol poisoning. Earlier that month Churchill had decided that it was now his duty to lead the resistance to the MacDonald–Baldwin–Irwin policy, and he began to marshal his forces. He put out a feeler to Beaverbrook to see if he would join in a campaign to maintain the Empire 'splendid and united', but he virtually excluded the tariff issue by adding 'Of course we must gather the Liberals to us.' This was no use to Beaverbrook, who replied bluntly, 'I am only interested in a single issue.'[20]

Churchill's decision to fight on India was not, however, dependent upon the formation of political alliances. He was firmly convinced that his action was necessitated by the facts of the situation. Almost simultaneously he wrote to Baldwin to tell him that he 'care[d] more about this business than anything else in public life'. He had been receiving, as a result of speeches on the question in July and August, 'streams of letters from our people in India' imparting to him their anxiety about the Irwin policy.[21] Churchill was still hoping that Baldwin would abandon his support for India, but there was no real prospect of this, and in mid-November Baldwin, who had read Churchill's *My Early Life* in proof during his summer holiday, wrote to his confidant Davidson that his colleague had 'become once more the subaltern of Hussars of '96'.[22]

By this time the Round Table Conference was in session, and a new organisation to resist drastic constitutional change in India had been set up under the title of the Indian Empire Society. It was composed of Conservative 'die-hards' and retired officials of the Indian Civil Service, and although Churchill was not among its officers or on its committee he was the principal speaker at its first meeting in London on December 12th. He declared that he believed Dominion Status to be still a distant goal, as immediate self-government would mean 'either a Hindu despotism ... or a renewal of ... ferocious internal wars'. These were hard words; still harder was his statement that 'Ghandi-ism and all it stands for will, sooner or later, have to be grappled and finally crushed. It is no use trying to satisfy a tiger by feeding him with cat's-meat.'[23] The speech aroused an immediate storm in both Britain and India, and Ramsay MacDonald described it as

> mischievous from beginning to end ... expressive of nothing except an antiquated relationship between Imperial authority and the people who come under its sway, blind to every modern movement in politics, stiff-necked regarding the handling of people whom we ourselves have enlightened in political affairs and aspirations.[24]

After this, the final break with Baldwin and the Conservative leadership could not be long in coming. When the Commons debated the proceedings of the Round Table Conference in January 1931, Churchill uttered a solemn warning that the government's policy could lead only to a complete separation of Britain and India. It was a gloomy speech, for he had begun to realise that this was not an issue on which public opinion in Britain could easily be aroused:

> They are all worried by unemployment or taxation or absorbed in sport and crime news. The great liner is sinking in a calm sea. One bulkhead after another gives way; one compartment after another is bilged; the list increases; she is sinking; but the captain and the officers and the crew are all in the saloon dancing to the jazz band. But wait till the passengers find out what is their position![25]

But Baldwin committed the Conservative Party to support of the Labour Government's policy, and compared Churchill to 'George III ... endowed with the tongue of Edmund Burke'.[26] Churchill's standpoint had found virtually no support from other speakers in the course of the debate; but it did not follow that the backbenchers were not worried about Indian policy – indeed Topping, the Principal Agent, in a memorandum to Neville Chamberlain argued that many of the parliamentary party sympathised more with Churchill than with Baldwin on the question, though they did not want a change of leadership on this ground.[27] The day after the debate Churchill formally wrote to Baldwin resigning from the party's Business Committee. He was now free to try to mobilise the backbenchers and the party outside Parliament for a change in policy – and perhaps in leadership.

Churchill's secession came at a bad time for Baldwin, who was facing a renewed threat to his leadership on the question of fiscal policy. But there could now be no possibility of Churchill making common cause with Beaverbrook and Rothermere on Empire Free Trade, and Baldwin was able to turn aside from the major threat to his leadership to deal with the minor. In January 1931 Gandhi, the Nehrus and other Congress leaders who had been arrested were released from prison so as to be able to take part in the discussions in India about the Round Table Conference; and a few weeks later, after a meeting between Irwin and Gandhi, the Congress Party agreed to terminate its campaign of civil disobedience in return for the removal of certain government restrictions. Churchill was shocked by the idea of negotiations between the Viceroy and a lately released prisoner: he said in a speech in his constituency that it was 'alarming and also nauseating to see Mr Gandhi, a seditious Middle Temple lawyer, now posing as a fakir of a type well-known in the East, striding half-naked up the steps of the Viceregal Palace'.[28]

A debate in the Commons on the subject of the Viceroy's action took place shortly afterwards, and this provided Baldwin with an opportunity to rally his supporters on the issue. It was one of his most effective speeches. He quoted from Churchill's Amritsar speech of 1920, without naming its author, to support his view that India could not be governed without the co-operation of Indians and the consent of the Indian people. A few days later, at a meeting of the Unionist Indian Committee, his attitude was approved by 'a very large majority'.[29]

Meanwhile Baldwin was also preoccupied with his major opponents, the newspaper barons. He intervened in a critical by-election then being fought at St George's, Westminster, where an official Conservative was opposed by an Independent backed by Beaverbrook, and said at a meeting in Queen's Hall: 'What the proprietorship of these papers is aiming at is power, and power without responsibility, the prerogative of the harlot through the ages.'[30] The phrase 'the prerogative of the harlot through the ages' was an unusual one for a Conservative leader to use at this period or at any period: it had been suggested to him by his cousin Rudyard Kipling. The official candidate, Duff Cooper, won the contest with a substantial majority, and thereafter much of the steam went out of the attack on Baldwin's leadership. But Beaverbrook was henceforward an enemy for life.

One reason why Baldwin's position improved in the succeeding months was that the Labour government became very shaky, and its fall seemed imminent. Economic depression meant that revenue was contracting, at a time when heavy unemployment required increasing government expenditure in the form of the 'dole'. In March the Cabinet was forced to agree to the appointment of a committee under Sir George May to look into the prospects of reducing public expenditure along the lines of the Geddes Committee of 1921. At the end of July the committee reported that in the existing situation the national finances were deteriorating so rapidly that the next Budget would show a deficit of £120 million. This revelation seriously weakened the international standing of sterling, and in August there developed a heavy run on the pound. A sub-committee of the Labour Cabinet prepared a series of economic measures to deal with the budgetary deficit, but the Cabinet as a whole failed to accept them, a minority objecting in particular to a proposal to reduce unemployment benefits. The prospects of tiding over the crisis depended on getting support for the pound from bankers in New York, who were insisting on the acceptance of the entire programme of cuts as a condition. Having failed to obtain the agreement of his colleagues, Ramsay MacDonald had no alternative but to resign; but the King, after consulting Baldwin and Herbert Samuel, the Liberal Deputy Leader, urged MacDonald to form a 'National' government of all parties to undertake the unpopular measures of economy.

Churchill had been expecting some such development, and in July he had discussed with Lloyd George and Oswald Mosley the possibility of providing an alternative coalition to that which might be formed by MacDonald and Baldwin.[31] But the initiative was not in their hands, and the discussion was necessarily in vague terms. Moreover, at the critical moment in August Lloyd George was seriously ill, and could take no part in concerting counter-measures. MacDonald's National Government – which was at first assumed to be only a temporary affair – was supported not only by Baldwin and the Conservative Party as a whole, but also by virtually all Liberal MPs in two main sections under Samuel and Sir John Simon. Churchill was not invited to join the new Cabinet, which contained only three Conservatives besides Baldwin himself; but, as he told his Epping constituents, 'In view of my differences in public with him [Baldwin] on this India question I have no complaint to make that he has not invited me to assist him at the present time.'[32] When Parliament met in September he moved from the front Opposition bench to a seat below the gangway on the ministerial side, which showed that he was not proposing to make any direct attack upon the new government;[33] but in newspaper articles at the time he urged that MacDonald should visit Lloyd George at Churt, where he was lying ill, in order to negotiate an enlargement of his basis of support: 'Unless the formal and official support of two out of the three great parties is gathered to the Government, it cannot display the title-deeds of national authority.'[34]

MacDonald did in fact decide to visit Lloyd George at Churt and was probably disappointed to find him well on the way to recovery, for he had found Samuel and Simon much easier to deal with while the ex-premier had been on his sick-bed. Lloyd George was anxious only that there should be no general election, and that he should have a chance, after returning to Westminster, of reasserting control over the fragments of the Liberal Party. But it was already too late for that: within a few days Samuel gave way to the insistence of MacDonald and Baldwin that there should be an early dissolution. Henceforward Lloyd George was a leader without a party, a lone figure brooding on the back benches. Churchill, in believing that his former colleague had a major role to play, had evidently backed the wrong horse.

Meanwhile there was a general election to be fought. Churchill took his stand with his party in support of the National Government, but was disappointed to find that in his constituency he still had to face opposition from a Samuelite Liberal as well as a Labour candidate. Fortunately, the events of the summer had at least eliminated the competition of the Beaverbrook–Rothermere Independent. The Liberal, A. S. Comyns Carr, who was a leading land lawyer and a King's Counsel, sought the suffrages of the electorate as a Free Trader, as a moderate on India policy, and as a critic of Churchill's return to the Gold Standard in 1925.[35] But Churchill had the general tide of opinion on his side, and lost few votes on these various counts. He had now abandoned all his former Free Trade convictions, and told his constituents that he had 'thrown off for ever' the 'Treasury Cobdenism' which was still influencing the government.[36] As for the Labour candidate, James Ranger, a company secretary who was new to politics, he stood no chance at all. Churchill's majority was enormously increased, and was twice as large as it had been even in 1924:

W. S. Churchill (Conservative)	35,956	Elected
A. S. Comyns Carr (Liberal)	15,670	
J. Ranger (Labour)	4713	

Similar swings occurred throughout the country, but comparisons are difficult owing to the withdrawal of many candidates. The Labour Party was reduced to a pathetic remnant of only 46 members. The nominal supporters of the National Government numbered no less than 554, of whom 473 were Conservatives. It was obvious that, contrary to all Churchill's expectations, Baldwin had emerged as the master both of the new government and of his opponents within his own party.

Churchill naturally regarded the National Government with mixed feelings. He was impressed by the great tide of enthusiasm in the country which had swept into Parliament so many of its candidates who stood in constituencies normally held by Labour; but he had no great regard for the Prime Minister, Ramsay MacDonald, whom he had described early that year as 'the boneless wonder'.[37] MacDonald, he complained, had attacked him during the general election, and Sir Herbert Samuel, who held Cabinet office in the new government, had actually sent a message of support to his Liberal opponent. Consequently, Churchill felt free to say in the Debate on the Address that his attitude to the government would be no more than one of 'discriminating benevolence'. He stressed the urgent need for the introduction of Tariff Reform, and reminded Baldwin that when they were working together in the 1924–9 government Baldwin had always impressed on him his 'abhorrence of coalitions'.[38] It was a warning to the Conservative leader that what had happened to the Lloyd George Coalition in 1922 could happen to a new peacetime coalition with a Conservative-dominated House of Commons.

But for the time being the National Government was safe enough after its electoral victory; and in December Churchill went off to the United States for a lecture tour which had been postponed from the autumn. He had the misfortune to be knocked

Lord Randolph Churchill:
a cartoon by Spy.

William Gordon Davis

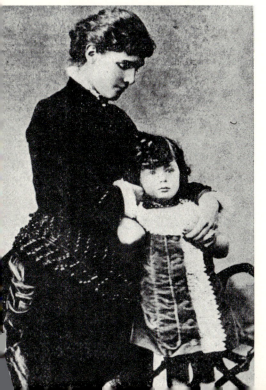

Winston at two years old, with
his mother.

Popperfoto

With his mother and younger
brother John, *c*.1889.

William Gordon Davis

In full-dress uniform as a
subaltern in the 4th Queen's
Hussars.

William Gordon Davis

In tropical kit at
Bangalore, India,
in 1896.

The Times

£ 25.—.—

(vijf en twintig pond stg.)
belooning uitgeloofd door
de Sub. Commissie van wijk V
voor den Specialen Constabel
dezer wijk, die den ontvluchte
Krygsgevangene
Churchill
levend of dood te dezer kantor
aflevert. —

Namens de Sub- Comm.
wijk V
Oaode Haas
Sec.

A Boer proclamation
offering a reward for
Churchill's recapture,
1899.

William Gordon Davis

Churchill revisits the wreck of the armoured train, 1900.

Popperfoto

As a young MP: a cartoon by Spy.

The Times

In east Africa in 1908.

William Gordon Davis

With Clementine not long after
their marriage.

Popperfoto

With his mother in 1911.

Press Association

With Lloyd George on Budget Day 1910.

Mansell Collection

UNDER HIS MASTER'S EYE.

Scene—*Mediterranean, on board the Admiralty yacht "Enchantress."*

Mr. Winston Churchill. "ANY HOME NEWS?"
Mr. Asquith. "HOW CAN THERE BE WITH YOU HERE?"

With Asquith on a Mediterranean cruise: *Punch* cartoon of May 1913.

Punch

With the Kaiser at the German army manœuvres, 1913.

Popperfoto

Churchill arrives at Portsmou[th]
by air, 1913.

Press Association

Wearing a French army helme[t]
in the company of French
officers, 1916.

The Times

The Cairo conference in 1921. On Churchill's right is Herbert Samuel;
behind his left shoulder, wearing a dark suit, is T. E. Lawrence
(Lawrence of Arabia).

William Gordon Davis

'The Recruiting Parade', October 1924.

Cartoon by David Low by arrangement with the Trustees and the London Evening Standard

Churchill and Lloyd George: cartoon of March 1926.

Punch

The Old Fox. "WHAT A SHOCKING SIGHT! I WONDER WHO TAUGHT THAT WICKED YOUNG CUB TO ROB HENROOSTS?"

Bricklaying at Chartwell, *c.*1930.

Popperfoto

Painting in France, 1933.

Popperfoto

With his son Randolph at the Wavertree by-election of 1935.

Popperfoto

THE MANIKIN AND THE SUPERMAN; OR, "IF I WERE DOING IT."

(After an engraving entitled "Malbrook" in the Bibliothèque Nationale, Paris.)

Churchill and Sir Thomas Inskip: cartoon of July 1936.

Punch

In Trinity House uniform, 1937.

The Times

As First Lord of the Admiralty, giving a radio broadcast in March 1940.

Associated Newspapers Group Limited

Churchill and the War Cabinet: cartoon by Illingworth in the *Daily Mail*, October 1940. Left to right: Churchill, Attlee, Greenwood, Halifax, Beaverbrook, Anderson, Bevin, Kingsley Wood.

Associated Newspapers Group Limited

May the many owe much to these few. —by Illingworth.

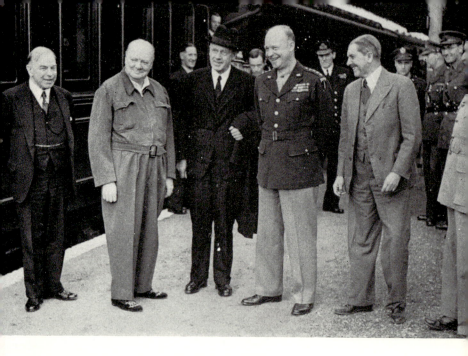

With General Eisenhower and Dominion prime ministers, May 1944. Left to right: Mackenzie King (Canada), Churchill, Peter Fraser (New Zealand), Eisenhower, Sir Godfrey Huggins (Southern Rhodesia), General Smuts (South Africa).

Mansell Collection

With General de Gaulle at the tomb of the Unknown Soldier in Paris, Armistice Day 1944.

Mansell Collection

Churchill, Roosevelt and Stalin at Yalta, February 1945.   *Popperfoto*

Brendan Bracken, Beaverbrook and Churchill: cartoon by Zec in the
Daily Mirror, July 1945.   *Syndication International*

've got a figurehead, we've got an admiral, and if nobody notices we haven't got a
, we shall be O.K." *Having forced the General Election, the Tory Party, with Brendan Bracken and Lord
erbrook as its mouthpieces, tried to make up for its lack of policy by using Churchill's prestige.* **(July 19, 1945)**

At a Conservative rally in
Bedfordshire, May 1955.

Popperfoto

On his last annual visit to
Harrow, November 1961.

Keystone

down by a taxicab in New York, and as a result of his injuries he had to postpone his lectures. The result was that he did not return to England until mid-March. He was soon absorbed in journalism and in research for a life of Marlborough, and for the time being he spent most of his time at Chartwell. Consequently he took his place in the Commons only when he wished to speak, and he made little attempt to cultivate the new members. On one occasion in May 1932 he entered the House in the evening during the committee stage of the Finance Bill. Discovering that the question in which he was interested – that of beer duties – had already been passed over without discussion, he rose to 'report progress', so as to revert to this topic. He was thereupon roundly denounced by George Lansbury, the Leader of the Opposition, for his discourtesy: 'He usurps a position in this House as if he had a right to walk in, make his speech, walk out, and leave the whole place as if God Almighty had spoken.... He never listens to any other man's speech but his own.'[39] Lansbury's outburst was well received, not only on the Labour benches but also on those of the government: it appeared that the House much enjoyed hearing Churchill reprimanded in this way. But his attendance in the House did not improve as a result; and in the autumn he was absent for several weeks as a result of contracting paratyphoid while visiting Marlborough's battlefields in Bavaria.

In 1933 the question of Indian constitutional reform again became prominent, owing to the publication of the government's proposals in a White Paper in March. The White Paper outlined plans for the establishment of an elected Federal Government as soon as half the governments of the Indian states, weighted on a population basis, had given their promises of support. A Joint Select Committee of Lords and Commons was to examine and report on the proposals before legislation was drafted. Churchill naturally took part in the Commons debate on the White Paper, but his speech, elaborately prepared as usual, lost much of its force because when challenged he could not substantiate a charge he had made that British officials were promoted on the basis of their sympathy with government policy rather than on a basis of merit. Sir Samuel Hoare, the Secretary of State, wrote and told the Viceroy, Lord Willingdon, that it was 'a most surprising crash'.[40] It was probably a tactical error on Churchill's part to follow this up by refusing, in concert with the other leading rebels,

357

Lloyd George and Sir Henry Page Croft, to serve on the Joint Select Committee, on the ground that it was too heavily biased in favour of the government. A Commons move to remove the six members of the ministry from the Joint Select Committee of thirty-two was defeated by 209 votes to 118. This was the largest vote so far recorded against the government since the 1931 election, and suggested that the India rebels were growing in strength.

It now became apparent that while the Joint Select Committee was holding its meetings the rebels would do their best to mobilise opinion in the country, and particularly in the extra-parliamentary organisation of the Conservative Party. With two important newspapers on his side – the *Daily Mail* and the *Morning Post* – Churchill was quite capable of conducting a campaign similar to that conducted by his father, Lord Randolph, to force the party leadership to make concessions. In February the rebels had shown unexpected strength at a meeting of the Central Council of the National Union, being voted down only by 189–165. Hoare's Under-Secretary, R. A. Butler, thereupon set to work to establish a pressure-group to act as a counter to the Indian Empire Society. This came into existence in May as the Union of Britain and India, which like the Indian Empire Society had a number of ex-officials and other former members of the British community in India among its officers, and which likewise issued propaganda on the subject of the White Paper.[41] Churchill and his friends replied by creating yet another body for their own cause – the India Defence League, which was really a development of an India Defence Committee of rebel Conservative MPs. The Indian Empire Society, with its membership of distinguished former members of the Indian Civil Service and Indian Army, continued to exist, but its membership never exceeded two thousand.[42] The India Defence League was aimed at the rank and file of the Conservative Party: like the Primrose League it sought a wide membership, who would wear its badge as an emblem of solidarity.[43]

In May the rebels won two subsidiary successes, both of them with the assistance of the Churchill family. Randolph helped to win a vote against the White Paper at a conference of the Junior Imperial League, and Clementine spoke at a meeting of the Central Women's Advisory Committee of the National Union, which also registered its disapproval.[44] Less success attended the rebels' efforts at a meeting of the General Council of the National Union in June 1933, when a resolution was moved by Lord Lloyd to 'view with grave anxiety proposals to transfer at the present time responsibility at the centre of Government in India, and to place control of the judicial system and of the police in the hands of ministers responsible to elected Provincial assemblies'.[45] Baldwin attended this meeting in order to repulse the onslaught on the government, and he spoke effectively in reply to Churchill. An amendment approving the policy of the White Paper was carried by 838 to 356. The proceedings were on the whole good-tempered, and Churchill himself appealed for mutual respect, pointing out that after this is over and settled ... we shall have to stand in line together again'.

But the rebels had no reason to feel that they were losing ground, as the India Defence League, which numbered Churchill among its vice-presidents, had now secured the adherence of 57 MPs.[46] At the annual conference of the National Union in Birmingham early in October, the rebels were defeated by a very similar figure – 737 to 344.[47]

It was obvious that if a central government was established in India the Lancashire cotton trade would lose the last vestige of its influence through Whitehall upon Indian fiscal policy – an influence to which, as Churchill knew, the Lancashire electors had at one time attached considerable importance. By the 1930s much of the London control of Indian fiscal policy had gone, and the Indian government had imposed tariffs on cotton manufactures imported from Britain, under the guise of revenue duties. The Indian Congress Party also operated a boycott on British goods, and this, combined with the duties and the effects of the economic depression, reduced British cotton exports to India from 778 million square yards in 1930 to 389 million in 1931 and 599 million in 1932.[48] Churchill, who had so often before been able to rouse the people of Lancashire in defence of their trading interests, spoke to a large audience in the Free Trade Hall at Manchester in May 1933, but there was no tremendous enthusiasm as in the days of his Free Trade campaign. The Manchester Chamber of Commerce, which might have taken the lead in attacking the new Indian constitution on the grounds that Indian fiscal autonomy threatened Lancashire's trade, preferred instead to send a mission to India to explore the possibility of coming to terms with the Indian manufacturers.

Churchill discovered that the Manchester Chamber had in fact prepared evidence for the Joint Select Committee which embodied a protest against constitutional change on the grounds of the damage it would do to Lancashire trading interests; but after its leaders had attended a dinner party at the invitation of Lord Derby, at which the Secretary of State for India, Sir Samuel Hoare, had also been present, they had withdrawn their evidence and changed its character. Churchill thought that Derby and Hoare had brought improper pressure to bear upon witnesses before the Joint Select Committee, and in April 1934 he raised the matter as a breach of parliamentary privilege.[49] The Speaker ruled that a *prima facie* case had been established, and it was referred to the Committee of Privileges. Much to the annoyance of Hoare, this meant 'a kind of eighteenth-century impeachment', involving several weeks' delay in the work of the Joint Select Committee, several of whose members had to attend the Committee of Privileges.[50]

Two months later the Committee of Privileges reported that although the facts were much as Churchill had stated them, there was no breach of privilege, as the Joint Select Committee was not a judicial body and anybody could properly try to persuade its witnesses to change their evidence. Furthermore, it was the apparent success of the mission to India, rather than the views of Hoare and Derby, which was decisive in persuading the officers of the Manchester Chamber to change their views. When the report was debated by the Commons, Churchill aroused some hostility by impenitently repeating his charges, and when Amery described his policy as 'If I can trip up Sam, the government's bust' there was much laughter.[51] The attack on Lord Derby annoyed the Lancashire Conservative MPs, several of whom were sympathetic to the rebel cause, and they boycotted a mass meeting which Churchill addressed at the Free Trade Hall in Manchester in June. According to the *Times* reporter – perhaps a hostile witness – 'The hall was respectably filled, but was not crowded.'[52] But Churchill's speech, and articles which he wrote for a Manchester paper, the *Sunday Dispatch* ('My Fight for Lancashire'; 'Our Last Chance'), helped to put additional pressure on the Manchester Chamber of Commerce, which decided in the end to press Parliament for constitutional safeguards for the cotton trade.[53]

Nobody could regard the Manchester Chamber's second change of attitude very seriously; and for the most part the struggle to alter the policy of the Conservative Party had to proceed without much help from Lancashire. In 1934 the rebels were still a powerful and dangerous minority, and on occasion they almost had their way in the voting after critical debates in the National Union. But they never won an important division. In March a proposal to defer further discussion until the Joint Select Committee had reported was carried at the Central Council by only 419 to 314; and in October, at the annual conference at Bristol, in Churchill's absence the rebels lost by their narrowest margin – 543 to 520.[54] But in November the Joint Select Committee reported by a majority of 19 to 9 – the latter being both left-wing and right-wing sympathisers – in favour of a scheme closely resembling that of the White Paper; and with the weight of its distinguished members mostly thrown against the rebels the principles of the proposed reforms were endorsed at a great meeting of the Central Council of the National Union by 1102 to 390.[55] This was another full-dress debate, in which both Baldwin and Churchill spoke. But it was virtually the end of the prolonged struggle in the extra-parliamentary party.

There was a further reason why the rebel cause lost support within the ranks of the Conservative Party. In February 1935 Randolph Churchill, who was now making a career for himself as a journalist, and who was nothing if not a 'die-hard' in his views, decided to fight a by-election at Wavertree as an Independent Conservative. This meant challenging the official candidate of the party just as the Empire Crusaders had done. Churchill himself did not approve this action by his son. 'He has taken this step', he said, 'on his own responsibility and without consulting me.'[56] But out of family loyalty he supported him at the hustings, and the India Defence League followed suit.[57] In the event Randolph – 'The Young Chevalier backed by the Old Pretender,' said *The Times*[58] – secured a vote almost as large as that of the official candidate, but as a result of the splitting of the Conservative vote the seat was won by Labour. This led to much ill-feeling within the Conservative ranks throughout the country, and even at Epping, where Churchill had previously had steady support from his Association, local branches began to pass resolutions criticising his attitude.[59]

There remained the final struggle in Parliament. In December 1934 a Commons debate on the Joint Select Committee's Report resulted in its being endorsed by 410 votes to 127. The minority included both the Labour Party and the Conservative rebels, who numbered about 75.[60] Although this was a higher figure of opposition than before, it was obvious that the government would get its way. In February, during the Second Reading debate, Churchill said that if anything could prevent 'lasting bitterness' among the government's opponents it would be a full opportunity to thrash the matter out in Parliament.[61] This sounded like a recognition of inevitable defeat; and the figures on the division were much the same as in December. There followed a long struggle in Committee, and after that a Third Reading debate, marked by a gloomy farewell speech from Churchill in which he admitted his failure to 'arouse the people of Lancashire'.[62] Amery, who had rendered much service to the government by replying to Churchill's speeches as soon as they were made, rose immediately after Churchill sat down to say, 'Here endeth the last chapter of the Book of the Prophet Jeremiah.'[63]

In a period when the government had a quite negligible party opposition to face in the House of Commons, Churchill's India campaign presented a formidable challenge to Baldwin's leadership and to the whole basis of the alliance headed by Ramsay MacDonald. The Parliamentary Conservative Party did not like the government's India policy: in the spring of 1934 Hoare admitted to the Viceroy that not thirty were 'genuinely keen to go on with the bill'.[64] But many of them knew that they owed their seats to non-Conservative electors, and this inclined them to be more moderate than the Conservative MPs of 1929–31. And Baldwin had other great advantages in the struggle. He held the loyal support of *The Times* under Geoffrey Dawson, who had visited India while Irwin was Viceroy and entirely agreed with his policy.[65] Baldwin also controlled the Conservative Central Office and was loyally backed by the Chief Whip, Captain David Margesson, to whose efficiency Churchill paid rueful tribute in his Third Reading speech – slightly misquoting Thomas Gray: 'I do not know whether you can say of the Chief Whip that he was a flower to blush unseen, but certainly he has not wasted his fragrance upon the desert air.'[66]

Churchill would have liked to appeal to the national electorate by radio, but he was allowed to do so only once, and that at a very late date in the struggle – January 1935. The BBC had accepted that political broadcasting should be arranged in agreement with the party whips, and this meant that for long periods Churchill was heard only when he promised to restrict himself to non-controversial subjects.[67]

The failure of the India Defence League to win a mass membership meant that MPs felt no strong pressure on them to support Churchill against the government. Although the League claimed 'many thousands' of members it did not publicise its strength in precise figures, which no doubt it would have done if it had been really successful.[68] Churchill would also have done better if he had assiduously cultivated the many new Conservative members elected for the first time in 1931. In practice, he seemed incapable of studying their feelings. One new member, Robert Bernays, thought Churchill behaved very badly when he (Bernays) was delivering his maiden speech: 'Mr Churchill had strolled into the House in an absent-minded way and sat in front muttering disagreement – not realising it was a maiden speech ... – and after five minutes of it, he could bear no more and strolled out again.'[69] When on another occasion he accused Sir John Wardlaw Milne of 'acting the bully' by interrupting him during a speech, the House roared, for, reported Bernays, 'if there is a bully in the House it is Mr Churchill'.[70]

Bernays was, to be sure, a loyal supporter of the government's India policy. But another Conservative MP more sympathetic to Churchill – Vyvyan Adams – has left us a similar impression of his behaviour: 'If it is necessary for him to stay and listen to important speeches by others in authority he will fidget about on the central seat that he always occupies. He will gossip away in a series of half-audible grunts.'[71] His conduct over the India Bill, thought Adams, 'smacked of cantankerousness'. He seemed to be 'more interested in embarrassing Baldwin and company than in serving the highest interests of the British Commonwealth'.[72]

Such an impression was almost certainly unfair: in the long run Churchill did far more damage to his own reputation by his India campaign than he did to Baldwin's. His success in resisting the bill was remarkable enough – especially as he had so little personal experience of conditions in India, not having been there for over thirty years. His lack of detailed knowledge was brought out when he gave evidence to the Joint Select Committee in October 1933. His written statement was a powerful apologia of

363

the general case against Indian nationalism: it started off by pointing out that

> India is not a country or a nation; it is rather a continent inhabited by many nations. The parallel to India is Europe. But Europe is not a political entity. It is a geographical abstraction.... Such unity of sentiment as exists in India arises entirely through the centralised British Government of India as expressed in the only common language of India – English.[73]

But instead of recognising the need for a high degree of local autonomy, Churchill proposed that there should be a central inspectorate to check upon the misuse of powers delegated to the provinces. Under cross-examination he was unable to satisfy the Committee that this was a workable scheme. He was also questioned about his utterances on Dominion Status for India when he was Colonial Secretary in 1921–2, and he had considerable difficulty in explaining that he had not really changed his views, and that he then meant by 'Dominion Status' not constitutional advance but weight of influence within the Empire. *The Times* was not unjustified in saying of his evidence that 'It was good-humoured, entertaining, embellished with a familiar exuberance of resonant adjectives, but it was a little too irresponsible.... It furnished no basis for constructive discussion.'[74]

Of course there was much justification for Churchill's jaundiced view of the prospects of Indian nationalism. He foresaw all too clearly the dangers of conflict between the great religious communities of the sub-continent when British power was withdrawn – dangers which culminated after the partition in the communal bloodbath of 1947, and led eventually to the war between the two countries and the dreadful plight of Bangladesh in the early 1970s. But in the 1930s, in the face of an ever-growing Congress Party representing the majority of the politically active middle class, there were only two choices for the British government: repression or concession. It is difficult to believe that repression could have served as a satisfactory long-term policy, however successful it might be for a few months or years.

The effects on India of Churchill's long-fought resistance to constitutional reform are difficult to assess. It certainly held back the enactment of the new constitution by several months, stiffened its safeguards against majority rule, increased the hostility of the Congress Party as a result, and yet encouraged the princes to doubt the wisdom of accession to the Federation. This all made it more difficult to bring an elected Central Government into existence before war broke out in 1939. We may, however, keep an open mind on whether the type of constitutional system envisaged by Hoare and Irwin would ever have worked. In their memoirs they both said that they thought it would have preserved a united India, and they blamed Churchill for the opportunity that was missed.[75] More recently, Lord Butler has expressed doubts about whether the system would ever have satisfied the Muslims – doubts that are on the whole sustained by recent academic research.[76]

For Churchill himself and for the history of his own country, the results are perhaps more measurable. They were certainly momentous. His gloomy predictions of the probable results of Irwin's policy of 'appeasement' (the word was used by Birkenhead, if not by Churchill himself)[77] may have had much long-term justification, but in the short term they seemed exaggerated. Their effect was to reduce the force of his similarly gloomy warnings about the danger of appeasing the rising power of Hitler's Germany, for a man who cries 'wolf' too often ceases to be credible to other people. As for Baldwin – who succeeded Ramsay Mac-Donald as Prime Minister when the latter retired in May 1935 – he had made up his mind not to risk such an awkward person as his colleague again. At the age of sixty, it looked as if Churchill's ministerial career was over and done with.

18. *The Road to War*

ALTHOUGH Indian policy was the main topic of Churchill's political activities in the years of the 1931 Parliament, foreign affairs and rearmament were matters of increasing concern to him as the European situation was transformed by the rise of Hitler. In 1930 he expressed his support for the idea of a 'United States of Europe', which had been put forward by a Hungarian aristocrat, Count Coudenhove Kalergi: but he thought that Britain should encourage the idea from outside, as her own destinies lay rather with the Empire and the English-speaking world.[1] At the end of 1931 he was still convinced that there was no prospect of war in Europe, at least 'for many years'.[2] But in 1932 he became disturbed by the revival of the 'war mentality' in Germany. In his visit to Bavaria in the summer of that year to see the battlefields of Marlborough's campaigns, he gained an unpleasant impression of 'bands of sturdy Teutonic youths, marching through the streets and roads of Germany, with the light of desire in their eyes to suffer for their Fatherland'.[3]

In view of the dangers, he believed that the pursuit of a new disarmament agreement, which was a major object of policy for Ramsay MacDonald's government, was a will-o'-the-wisp. Better, he thought, to remove genuine territorial grievances, such as that of the Polish Corridor for Germany, or that of Transylvania for Hungary, than to encourage disarmament for its own sake: 'Here is my general principle. The removal of the just grievances of the vanquished ought to precede the disarmament of the victors.'[4]

When Hitler came to power at the end of January 1933, Churchill for all his hostility to Communism was one of the first to denounce the evil character of the new regime:

> We watch with surprise and distress the tumultuous insurgence of ferocity and war spirit, the pitiless ill-treatment of minorities, the denial of the normal protections of civilised society to large numbers of individuals solely on the grounds of race.[5]

Under such circumstances, he argued, other peoples in Europe might well feel alarmed, and be the more grateful for the fact that, for the time being at least, Germany was militarily weak *vis-à-vis* her neighbours, particularly France: 'There are a good many people who have said to themselves, as I have been saying for several years: "Thank God for the French Army."'[6]

Churchill later recalled the 'look of pain and aversion' which appeared on the faces of his fellow-MPs when he made this remark.[7] Blunt truths about the danger of a new war with Germany found no welcome in Britain at this time. In 1933 hopes of peace through all-round disarmament were still strong. There was a distinct increase in the number of out-and-out pacifists, though Churchill was probably wrong in supposing that this creed animated any large proportion of those Oxford students who supported the famous resolution of their Union 'That this House will in no circumstances fight for King and Country'. His son Randolph made things worse by returning to Oxford, which he had left two years earlier after only eighteen months' formal residence, to move that the offending resolution should be expunged from the Society's records: he was overwhelmingly defeated. Yet eighteen months later a resolution in support of 'full military measures' in support of the League of Nations was carried by a large majority.[8] This was more in line with Churchill's thinking; yet many of those who voted for the earlier resolution could also have supported this one without inconsistency.

Collective security, rather than pacifism, was the watchword of the Left in the early 1930s. It was the official policy of both the Labour and Liberal Parties. But the trouble was that the leaders of both parties believed that Britain could fulfil all her obligations under a system of collective security without spending more money on armaments. They seemed not to realise how much of the burden of resisting an aggressor would fall upon Britain, with her world-wide commitments. In 1933 the acid test of the authority of the League of Nations seemed to be whether it could do anything to help China, which had appealed for assistance against a Japanese invasion of her northern provinces. Churchill did not think that the British government should press for League action in this situation: neither the United States nor Russia belonged to the League, and without their assistance it was hopeless to attempt to coerce Japan. In any case, he was not at all sure that the Chinese peasantry were not better off under Japanese rule than at the mercy of rival warlords and Communist rebels. He had been reading Pearl Buck's description of the life of the Chinese peasantry in her novel *The Good Earth*.[9] His view, in short, was:

> It is in the interests of the whole world that law and order should be established in Northern China.... I do not think that it is any use expecting too much from the League of Nations. I have a great respect for the League and think it is a valuable instrument in Europe.[10]

Even for Europe, however, Churchill's view of the possible role of the League of Nations was still vague. He did not envisage Britain making any contribution to collective security on the Continent, beyond her existing obligations under the Locarno Treaty; and he told a London audience at a meeting in November 1933 that it was 'our business, our wisdom to detach our country as much as possible from the vehement conflicts which are gathering on the continent of Europe'.[11] Britain could not do this, he thought, if she encouraged Germany's neighbours to disarm. For the rest, he urged that Britain herself should be strong: deficiencies in the national defences should be made good, and in particular, the government should accept 'the principle of having an Air Force at least as strong as that of any Power that can get at us'.[12]

Churchill had not been particularly worried in earlier years by the knowledge that the Royal Air Force was much weaker than the French air force, and that in fact it was only the fifth strongest in the world. But now that it was obvious that Germany was rearming in defiance of the Versailles Treaty he felt it essential to act at once in order to ensure that the RAF was as large as any force constructed by Hitler. He thought that the increased expenditure budgeted for in the 1934 air estimates – £130,000 – was derisory. He did not conceal his reasons for concern: 'I dread the day when the means of threatening the heart of the British Empire should pass into the hands of the present rulers of Germany.'[13] He made a special appeal to Baldwin to see that Britain secured air parity as soon as possible: 'he is tonight the captain of the gate'.[14] Baldwin was not the Prime Minister, but as the leader of the Conservative Party, which had always asserted a special concern in maintaining the country's military strength, he could not ignore his responsibility. In his reply to the debate he promised that British air power would no longer be 'inferior to any country within striking distance of our shores'.[15]

In July the government announced an accelerated expansion of the RAF over a five-year period; but this did not satisfy Churchill that Britain was keeping up with the momentum of German rearmament. In November he was joined by several other senior Conservative backbenchers, including Leopold Amery and Sir Robert Horne, in moving an amendment to the Address to the effect that 'the strength of our national defences, and especially of our air defences' was 'no longer adequate'. In his speech – the main points of which he had indicated to Baldwin in advance – he spoke of the dangers of air attack on cities, especially if incendiary bombs were used, and he demanded an urgent study of means to devise proper defences. He asserted that the new German air force would be as strong as the home-based element of the RAF by the end of 1935 and a year later would be 50 per cent stronger.[16] Baldwin, in reply, described these calculations as 'considerably exaggerated': he reckoned that in the autumn of 1935 the home-based RAF would still be nearly twice as strong as the German air force.[17]

On the details of the argument, it seems that Baldwin was nearer to the truth than Churchill. The German air force, which in any case was being built for military co-operation rather than for strategic bombing, had to start from a very rudimentary basis early in 1934 and was not able to achieve much operational strength before 1936. The total German production of combat aircraft from the beginning of the new air force up until the end of 1935 was only 2663 machines – whereas the RAF had more than that number *in service* in March 1935.[18] Allowing for wastage, the RAF evidently had a formidable lead. But of course Churchill was right in principle in supposing that German rearmament would gather momentum, and thus leave

Britain well behind. And by a curious irony as early as the spring of 1935 Baldwin became convinced that Churchill had been right in detail also, because of information that the government received directly from Hitler himself. In March 1935 Sir John Simon, the Foreign Secretary, who was visiting Berlin, was told by the German Chancellor that his country had already achieved parity with Britain; and Baldwin, seeing no reason to suppose that Hitler had deliberately deceived his guest, at once revised his figures. On May 22nd he told the Commons that, although he had correctly stated the relative strengths of the two air forces in 1934, 'Where I was wrong was in my estimate of the future. There I was completely wrong.... We were completely misled on that subject.'[19] Hitler indicated that it was his intention to achieve parity with France, and so Baldwin accepted that Britain should do likewise. This meant attaining a front-line strength of about 1500 machines, or (allowing for the usual lavish margin of reserves) roughly doubling the existing target. Planning a new programme for this purpose was immediately begun.

Meanwhile Churchill had been warned by Lindemann that there appeared to be a complete absence of scientific research on the problems of defence against air attack. Baldwin himself was on record as a pessimist on the subject: in 1932 he had said that 'the bomber will always get through'.[20] In September 1934, while travelling through France, Churchill and Lindemann broke in upon Baldwin's rest at Aix-les-Bains to urge the establishment of a high-powered committee to look into the subject with expert advice.[21] Some correspondence ensued, and eventually Londonderry, the Air Minister, asked Lindemann to submit his ideas to a new Air Ministry committee under Henry Tizard, a scientist and former colleague of Lindemann. But Lindemann, probably after consultation with Churchill, demanded instead the formation of a new body directly responsible to the Committee of Imperial Defence. He decided to appeal directly to the Prime Minister, Ramsay MacDonald. Churchill's relations with the latter were so frosty that the two men decided to invoke the aid of another senior Privy Councillor: and so Lindemann's case was put in a letter signed jointly by Austen Chamberlain and Churchill.[22] After some misunderstanding, apparently due to the fact that MacDonald did not know about the Air Ministry Committee already in existence, the plan which Lindemann had advocated was agreed, and a new committee was set up as a sub-committee of the Committee of Imperial Defence. It had the title of the Air Defence Research Committee. By this time the Tizard Committee had been active for some months, and it had already decided to concentrate research upon the radio-location of aircraft – a field which was to prove of vital importance.

In June 1935 Baldwin succeeded MacDonald as Prime Minister. One of his first acts was to replace Londonderry as Air Minister with Sir Philip Cunliffe-Lister; and he and Cunliffe-Lister decided at once to invite Churchill to join the Air Defence Research Committee. Baldwin assured Churchill that if he accepted the appointment there would be no restriction upon his right to criticise general defence policy: 'My invitation was not intended as a muzzle, but as a gesture of friendliness to an old colleague.'[23] Churchill agreed to serve, but asked that Lindemann should be added to the Tizard Committee, which continued in existence and reported to the Air Defence Research Committee. This was done, and Lindemann asked Tizard to look into a proposal of his own, which was to develop a system of aerial mines, floating from balloons or drifting with parachutes. But Tizard did not feel that this was an urgent field for research. As a result, Lindemann complained to Churchill, and Churchill attacked Tizard at the Air Defence Research Committee, of which Tizard was also a member. This led to much ill-feeling: there was a breach of relations between Tizard and Lindemann, and before the end of 1936 the Tizard Committee was dissolved and then reconstituted without Lindemann.[24] All in all, apart from drawing Baldwin's attention to the matter in 1934, it is by no means clear that Churchill was able to assist significantly in the technical development of air defence. But he undoubtedly learnt a good deal himself while serving on the Air Defence Research Committee, and this was to help him considerably in understanding the strategy and tactics of the Battle of Britain and the Blitz.

The closing stages of the India controversy were enacted, as we have seen, in the spring of 1935, and Churchill had indicated that as soon as the legislation was passed he would be willing to close ranks with his fellow members of the Conservative Party. He had declared that he would not fight the next election as a supporter of the government if Ramsay MacDonald was still Prime Minister;[25] but in June 1935 MacDonald retired, and Samuel Hoare succeeded John Simon as Foreign Secretary. Baldwin briefly toyed with the idea of bringing Churchill straight back into the Cabinet, and discussed it with Dawson, the editor of *The Times*; but Dawson advised him against such a course, not only on the grounds of the remaining ill-feeling within the party, but because Churchill would be 'a disruptive force especially since foreign relations and defence will be uppermost'.[26] For the time being, therefore, Churchill knew that he had to be content with membership of the Air Defence Research Sub-Committee.

But there was now far less at issue between Churchill and the government than there had been in earlier years. Neville Chamberlain, the Chancellor of the Exchequer, was making large sums available for defence, and the new Foreign Secretary, Samuel Hoare, showed a surprising willingness to assert the authority of the League of Nations – this time on behalf of Abyssinia, which was threatened with attack by Italy. Churchill did not think that Abyssinia was a very reputable independent state: he regretted that it had even been admitted to the League. He also thought that it would be 'a terrible deed to smash up Italy'.[27] But he was becoming increasingly favourable to the idea of asserting the League's power to resist aggression, and so he decided that he must endorse the government's attitude to the dispute. At the annual conference of the National Union early in October, he went out of his way to speak generously of Baldwin: 'In the Prime Minister we have a statesman who has gathered to himself a greater fund of confidence and goodwill than any other man I recollect in my long public career.'[28] When Baldwin wrote to thank him, he replied with further encouragement:

> If yr power is great, so also are yr burdens – and yr opportunities. I think you ought to go to the country at the earliest moment, & I hope you will do so. . . . I will abide with you in this election, & do what little I can to help in the most serviceable way.[29]

Baldwin had probably already decided to call an election that autumn. Parliament was dissolved shortly afterwards, and voting took place on November 14th. The government appealed for support on a programme of collective security through the League of Nations – a programme designed to take the wind out of the sails of both the Opposition parties. This suited Churchill well enough, and his own manifesto differed from Baldwin's only in its refusal even to mention the hope of a new disarmament agreement and in its emphasis on the need for co-operation with the United States.[30] As usual at Epping, there were both Liberal and Labour candidates, Comyns Carr, who had been the Liberal candidate in 1931, did not renew the contest, but his place was taken once more by Granville Sharp, who had fought the seat four times before. James Ranger was for the second time the Labour candidate.

The constituency had again grown considerably; it had had 43,000 electors in 1924 and by 1935 the total had more than doubled – to over 87,000. But Churchill had more voluntary workers than ever, and he was really hindered only by the lack of halls large enough to house the audiences prepared to attend his meetings.[31] In the late autumn, the problem could not be solved by erecting tents, as had been done in 1929. Churchill was helped as usual by Clementine, and his godson, the second Earl of Birkenhead, also spoke on his behalf.[32] But Randolph was away fighting his own contest, as official National Conservative candidate for West Toxteth, Liverpool. Churchill went north to speak on his son's behalf, but the constituency was normally less Conservative than the other Liverpool seats, and it could not be saved from Labour.

There was bound to be something of a reaction against the National Government as compared with the exceptional victory of 1931. All the same, the swing was by no means so great as to destroy its majority. The Labour Party probably won back the supporters it lost in 1929, but it could make little appeal to those independent electors who might be attracted by superior leadership. For one thing, it had no obvious potential Prime Minister: Lansbury had retired only a few weeks before the election and had been replaced on a temporary basis by Major C. R. Attlee, the deputy leader – a *locum tenens*, as Churchill described him.[33] Furthermore the country was recovering from the depression, and the level of unemployment had dropped markedly. When all the results were in, the National Government still had 432 seats; Labour had gained 108 as compared with the last election and now numbered 154; and the Liberals had lost ground once more, returning with a mere 21 seats. The prospect of a change of government was postponed for several years.

Although attacked by both his opponents for ignoring the case for disarmament, Churchill was one of the few retiring members of the government side actually to increase his majority.

This success was due partly to the increase in the size of the electorate and partly to the fact that his leading opponent was a Liberal, who in accordance with the national pattern of voting lost some support to the candidates of each of the other main parties. All the same, it was evident that Churchill had suffered no penalty for his independent behaviour in the preceding Parliament, and that he was able to poll the full Conservative vote:

W. S. Churchill (Nat. Cons.) 34,849 Elected
G. G. Sharp (Liberal)   14,430
J. Ranger (Labour)   9758

When the results were in, there was talk of a reconstruction of the government, and Churchill had some hope of being invited to rejoin the Cabinet. At a time when the navy might have to be employed against Italy, he would have liked to be appointed once again to the Admiralty.[34] But no call came from No. 10, for Baldwin had decided to make only minor changes. On December 9th Churchill therefore went on a Mediterranean holiday that he had been planning for some time. He spent a week in Majorca and then went over to French Morocco, returning only in late January. By the time he returned, Britain had a new Foreign Secretary and (by the death of George V) a new King.

By December 1935 it had become apparent to Sir Samuel Hoare that the limited sanctions imposed on Italy by the League powers would not prevent her from conquering Abyssinia. He was aware that the French government was even more reluctant than he was to alienate Mussolini and to push him into alliance with Hitler. He therefore agreed with Pierre Laval, the French Foreign Minister, to sponsor a compromise plan whereby Abyssinia would be partitioned between Italy and its legitimate ruler, the Emperor Haile Selassie, who was now desperately fighting to hold a section of his country. As Churchill later said, this was 'a very shrewd, far-seeing agreement' – but it could not honourably be made by Samuel Hoare, who was fully committed to the policy of sanctions against the aggressor.[35] There was an immediate wave of anger in Britain, not least among Conservative MPs who had promised at the recent election to stand by the League. Baldwin decided that Hoare must resign, although the Cabinet as a whole had endorsed his plan. He was replaced by Anthony Eden, who at the age of thirty-nine was exceptionally young for this senior post, but was already well known for his strong support for the League.

There was no doubt that Baldwin lost much prestige over this unhappy episode. It was, indeed, in large part due to his easy way of running the government. He allowed individual ministers great freedom in running their departments, and acted only as a chairman of the Cabinet. A few weeks later he had an opportunity to tap fresh sources of strength for his government, when it was decided to appoint a minister to co-ordinate the defence programmes of the three service departments. There was speculation that Churchill would be appointed to this post, in view of his immense experience, or if not Churchill then perhaps Amery or even Hoare. Austen Chamberlain both in private and in public declared that Churchill was the obvious choice.[36] There was general astonishment when Sir Thomas Inskip, the Attorney-General, was appointed. Inskip had no knowledge of service administration at the higher levels, and although he was already over sixty years of age he had not served the in the Cabinet before. Clearly, it would be difficult for him to establish any effective control over the policies and plans of the Admiralty, the War Office, and the Air Ministry. Baldwin and his colleagues were indeed afraid of a strong personality in this post, and Neville Chamberlain and David Margesson, the Chief Whip, both favoured Inskip for the appointment because he was 'the safest man'.[37]

The decision to appoint Inskip was only arrived at after a new international crisis had developed, owing to Hitler's sudden reoccupation of the demilitarised Rhineland, on March 7th 1936. There is, in fact, some evidence that this made it easier for Baldwin to rule out the idea of appointing Churchill, on the grounds that he might have strong views on how to deal with Hitler's *coup*.[38] No doubt Churchill would have supported a vigorous French response, such as a re-occupation of the Rhine bridgeheads by the French army; but no such response took place. The French army commanders appeared to be unwilling to move, and the French Cabinet was divided, although Paul-Étienne Flandin, the Foreign Minister, spoke sternly about the dangers of doing nothing. Eden sensed the lack of decision in Paris and, since Britain could contribute no immediate military support, not unnaturally advised caution.[39] He acknowledged, however, that for the future Britain and France would have to draw closer together, and he therefore promised that the British government would initiate staff talks with France and Belgium. The House of Commons did not welcome this course, but Churchill, who during the crisis had rallied his fellow-MPs by talking to them of 'funk versus national honour and our duty to generations yet unborn',[40] now expressed his appreciation of Eden's attitude and called for concerted action, under League auspices, either to come to terms with Hitler or, if he did not agree, to confront him with a collective alliance.[41]

In the course of 1936 Churchill seemed to his fellow-parliamentarians to be in a much more constructive mood than hitherto, and they listened to him with patience and growing appreciation. He was no longer at odds with the government over major issues of policy, but on the contrary provided valuable support in a number of important debates, especially on foreign affairs. He approved the lifting of sanctions in June, after they had obviously failed in their purpose.[42] When the Spanish Civil War broke out shortly afterwards, he agreed with Eden that it was essential for Britain to preserve her neutrality in the struggle. 'It is of the utmost consequence', he wrote in August, 'that France and Britain should act together in observing the strictest neutrality themselves and endeavouring to induce it in others.... This Spanish welter is not the business of either of us. Neither of these Spanish factions expresses our conception of civilisation.'[43]

On rearmament Churchill was naturally impatient that progress still seemed to be very slow, but he had to allow Inskip a period of grace before he started criticising him; and in the meantime he supplied him privately with his own proposals for the establishment of a Ministry of Munitions Supply, which he thought essential for a large rearmament programme.[44] In May 1936 he happened to be passing the old headquarters of the Ministry of Munitions, the Hotel Metropole in Northumberland Avenue, where he had presided eighteen years earlier. He noticed that the hotel furniture was being removed, so that the building could serve as temporary accommodation for a government department which was being rehoused. The sight encouraged him to believe that even the physical surroundings of the old Ministry of Munitions could easily be reconstituted.[45] At Inskip's request he also prepared a memorandum about the relations between the navy and the RAF and the Fleet Air Arm, which provided a blueprint for a later government statement.[46] He and a number of senior Conservative backbenchers, including Austen Chamberlain, Robert Horne and Earl Winterton, began to meet at each other's invitation at the weekends, to discuss rearmament. In May 1936 one of these meetings, at Winterton's home in Sussex, was noticed by a reporter, and the popular press described the occasion as a meeting of the 'Anti-Baldwin Shadow Cabinet'.[47] Baldwin seemed to think that his leadership was again under attack, and declared that it was 'a time of year when midges come out of dirty ditches'.[48]

But what emerged from the conversations of the backbenchers was a request for a meeting with the Prime Minister, at which major problems of rearmament could be discussed seriously and in secret. The meeting took place on two successive days, July 28th and 29th. Churchill did most of the talking on behalf of the backbenchers; Baldwin gave a general reply, and Inskip answered some detailed points. Churchill produced the latest French intelligence estimate of the strength of the German air force, which credited it with a first-line strength of 1236 machines. He said emphatically: 'We are facing the greatest danger and emergency of our history.'[49]

Baldwin, in reply, was distinctly apologetic. He acknowledged that Britain had fallen behind in armaments, but explained his own inaction and that of the government in terms of popular feeling:

It was a question in 1934 whether if you tried to do too much you might not have imperilled and more than imperilled, you might have lost the General Election when it came.... The one thing in my mind was the necessity of winning an election as soon as you could and getting a perfectly free hand with arms.[50]

He rejected Churchill's idea of all-out emergency action. He had discussed the possibility with the Chancellor of the Exchequer, Neville Chamberlain, but the latter had pointed out that it 'might throw back the ordinary trade of the country, perhaps for several years'. He was sorry that the French had made a treaty with Russia, because 'If there is any fighting in Europe to be done I should like to see the Bolshies and the Nazis doing it.'[51]

The Prime Minister's confession naturally did not satisfy the delegation, and when Parliament met in the autumn Churchill, with several of the others, put down an amendment for the Debate on the Address demanding a Select Committee to investigate the progress of rearmament. Churchill's speech elicited another frank confession from Baldwin, this time in public: he described how the East Fulham by-election of October 1933 – when a Labour candidate had won a previously held Conservative seat with a substantial swing – had convinced him that the country was adamant against rearmament at that time. He felt that 'a democracy is always two years behind the dictator'.[52] This was, as Churchill said, a 'deplorable utterance', implying as it did that leadership had no place in a democracy.[53] It was also largely inaccurate, for the issue of disarmament and peace was only one of several issues in the Fulham by-election, and possibly not the most important.[54] If the years 1934 and 1935 were, in Inskip's phrase, 'the years that the locust hath eaten', Baldwin could not avoid a heavy share of the blame.[55]

As the year 1936 drew to a close, it appeared that Baldwin's reputation was seriously in decline. Chamberlain was his obvious successor within the Cabinet, and had in fact been doing much of the day-to-day running of the government, as in August Baldwin had to take three months' rest on doctors' orders. But Chamberlain's knowledge of foreign affairs was not rated very highly, and there was a distinct movement of opinion among all parties in favour of Churchill. Many Liberals now recognised the need for rearmament; trade-union leaders were ahead of intellectual Socialists in coming to the same conclusion; and Conservatives with League sympathies increasingly saw Churchill as a champion of their cause.

Churchill had in fact shown increasing interest in collective security through the League. In June he became President of a body called the New Commonwealth Society, which advocated an international police force and tribunal of justice.[56] He already belonged to a little group of public men and women who had formed themselves into the 'Focus in Defence of Freedom and Peace' – better known simply as 'Focus'. Among them were Violet Bonham Carter, his old friend of the pre-war days, who was still active in Liberal politics; Wickam Steed, a former editor of *The Times*; and Sir Norman Angell, the author and former Labour MP. The group's finances were provided by an émigré Jewish businessman called Eugen Spier.[57] After holding a number of luncheon meetings the group decided on the theme of 'Arms and the Covenant'. The campaign was to start with a meeting in the Albert Hall early in December, with Sir Walter Citrine, the secretary of the TUC, in the chair and Churchill as the principal speaker. As it turned out, however, the occasion was sadly mistimed: it took place just at the height of the crisis caused by Edward VIII's proposal to marry Mrs Wallis Simpson; and consequently it obtained much less than its fair share of coverage in the newspapers. The same crisis also proved immensely damaging to the reputation of the very man that the campaign was designed to boost – Churchill himself.

Mrs Wallis Simpson was an American lady who had been divorced once and was now endeavouring to secure a divorce from a second husband. The King had grown increasingly fond of her, had spent a Mediterranean holiday in her company, and had begun to include her as a guest when he invited ministers and their wives to dine. Yet until December 1st, by an extraordinary act of self-denial, the British newspapers virtually ignored her existence. Suddenly next day, as a result of a public statement by the Bishop of Bradford, they burst out into a flood of comment. The idea that the King should marry a divorced person was disconcerting to many, for his father had refused to allow such persons even to attend the Court. Baldwin by this time had already asked the King what his intentions were and, on being told that he intended to marry Mrs Simpson, had warned him that this would probably mean abdication.

Churchill was much upset by these developments. He had been on friendly terms with the King since as Home Secretary in 1910 he had stood beside him at the ceremony proclaiming him Prince of Wales; later they were often together on public occasions, and Churchill gave the Prince some tips on the technique of after-dinner speaking.[58] The King's legal adviser, Walter Monckton, consulted Churchill about Mrs Simpson as early as June, and Churchill urged that she should be recommended not to divorce her second husband, Ernest Simpson, and not to appear in the King's company at Balmoral or on formal occasions. But when the King refused to follow this advice Churchill saw no reason to condemn him.[59] Not being a churchman himself, and having been brought up in a moral atmosphere that was far from strict, Churchill was more sympathetic to Edward VIII than were most of his contemporaries. Above all, he could see no grounds for a hasty act of abdication. Mrs Simpson's *decree nisi*, awarded late in October, would take six months to become final, and so the King could not marry at once.

Churchill had no direct contact with the King during the greater part of the crisis. But he discussed developments with Beaverbrook, who saw the King on several occasions in November. Beaverbrook was animated by an ardent desire to remove Baldwin from the Premiership, and for him, as Lloyd George was in the West Indies, Churchill was the only possible alternative Prime Minister. By November 27th the Cabinet had obtained the impression, apparently from Beaverbrook, not only that Churchill sympathised with the King but that under certain circumstances he would be prepared to form a government on the King's behalf.[60] On December 3rd the King asked Baldwin if he could consult Churchill as an old friend, and Baldwin 'unenthusiastically' agreed.[61]

This was an awkward moment for Churchill, for his Albert Hall meeting was due to take place that evening. It was arranged that he should see the King next day, but that on leaving the Albert Hall he should call at Stornoway House, Beaverbrook's London residence, in order to see a draft radio address which the King was proposing to deliver. Churchill therefore went to the Albert Hall with his thoughts more on the constitutional crisis than on European politics, and he told Citrine when he arrived that he proposed to make a statement at the close of the meeting expressing his sympathy for the King. Citrine, supported by the other platform speakers, refused to allow this, saying that it was completely irrelevant and would only lead to the expression of differing views. So the meeting went ahead as it had originally been planned. It was a crowded and enthusiastic occasion, but some of the platform party had the impression that Churchill's speech was not as impressive as they had hoped.[62]

Churchill then made his way to Stornoway House, to read the King's proposed radio address. The King's idea was then to go abroad for a time while the constitutional crisis was discussed by Parliament and public opinion. Churchill and Beaverbrook decided that this would be a mistake, for it would leave the situation entirely in the control of Baldwin and the Cabinet. Next day Churchill visited the King at his residence at Fort Belvedere, in Windsor Great Park. He found him in a state of 'mental exhaustion', unable at times to follow the thread of the conversation.[63] According to the King's later account of the meeting, Churchill argued for delay:

> If the Prime Minister persisted with his importunities, he suggested I should claim a respite from strain, adding half whimsically that I should retire to Windsor Castle and close the gates, stationing at one my father's old doctor, Lord Dawson of Penn, and at the other my recently appointed Physician-in-Ordinary, Lord Horder.[64]

The King pondered over this advice, but it did not take him long to reject it. He could not face the coronation ceremony, which was due to take place in the spring of 1937, without some decision about his freedom to marry. Delay would not in any case have altered the outcome of the crisis, for Baldwin had already sounded the Opposition leaders and the Dominion prime ministers, and all were with him in seeking the King's abdication if he insisted on marrying Mrs Simpson. The House of Commons, too, was almost united behind Baldwin, and an attempt to found a 'King's Party' in the country would only have discredited its sponsors. That night (December 4th) the King decided to abdicate at once, and notified the Prime Minister accordingly.

Next morning – a Saturday – Beaverbrook, who had learned of the King's decision, told Churchill 'Our cock won't fight'.[65] But Churchill could hardly believe this to be the case. He had already written a note to Baldwin telling him that it would be a 'cruel and wrong thing to extort a decision from him in his present state'.[66] He now issued a statement to the public saying:

> I plead for time and patience.... We are in the presence of a wish expressed by the Sovereign to perform an act which in no circumstances can be accomplished for nearly five months, and may conceivably, for various reasons, never be accomplished at all.[67]

When the House of Commons met on Monday December 7th it was apparent that members had taken the pulse of their constituencies, and had found that the King had little support. Churchill had not done this: he had been at Chartwell, where Boothby, who was his house-guest, found him 'silent and restless and glancing into corners', like a dog about to be sick.[68] After Baldwin had made a statement, Churchill rose and asked for an assurance that 'no irrevocable step' would be taken before the House had an opportunity to discuss the matter. To his astonishment he found as he later said that it was 'almost physically impossible to make myself heard'.[69] He was shaken by the hostility of the House, and on his way out he told J. C. C. Davidson, whom he happened to meet in the corridor off the lobby, that 'his political career was finished'.[70]

There was nothing to stop the abdication now. The drafting of the necessary legislation took place rapidly, and on December 11th King Edward's reign came to an end. On that day he again invited Churchill to Fort Belvedere to say goodbye and to consult him on the draft of his farewell broadcast. Churchill arrived for lunch, and while they were at table the final stages of the Abdication Act were completed and Edward ceased to be King. Churchill contributed several fine phrases to the radio speech – among them 'bred in the constitutional tradition by my father' and 'one matchless blessing, enjoyed by so many of you and not bestowed on me – a happy home with his wife and children'. As Churchill left, the ex-King noticed that there were tears in his eyes, and later recorded:

> I can still see him standing at the door, hat in one hand, stick in the other. Tapping out the solemn measure with his walking stick, he began to recite, as if to himself:
> He nothing common did or mean
> Upon that memorable scene.[71]

Certainly by his decision to accept his Prime Minister's advice, and not to prolong the crisis Edward saved his country from an extra period of grave political uncertainty and perhaps some civil strife. He also saved Churchill from doing further damage to his reputation, which might have led to the fatal results which he had already begun to fear.

There was no doubt in any case as to the principal political beneficiary of the Abdication Crisis. Baldwin won almost universal praise for his skill in securing the transition to the new reign in the smoothest possible way, without damage to relations with the Dominions and without serious domestic conflict. His position as Prime Minister, shaky as it had been in November 1936, was now completely restored, and he was able to preside over a relatively peaceful political scene until after the Coronation of George VI. He finally retired on May 28th 1937, still some months short of his seventieth birthday. The Chancellor of the Exchequer, Neville Chamberlain, succeeded him without challenge. Chamberlain, although six years younger than his half-brother Austen (who had died in March), was only nineteen months younger than Baldwin, but he seemed much fitter and far more active. Three days later Chamberlain was formally elected leader of the Conservative Party. His election was proposed by Lord Derby and seconded by Churchill – the latter having become, since the death of Austen Chamberlain, the senior Conservative Privy Councillor in the Commons. 'There is no rivalry,' said Churchill. 'There are no competing claims. Mr Chamberlain stands forth alone.'[72]

If Churchill felt obliged to support Chamberlain for the Premiership and party leadership – and he certainly approved of his success as Chancellor of the Exchequer in restoring a fair degree of prosperity to the nation's trade – he was even more enthusiastic about Eden's performance as Foreign Secretary. In July he told his constituents:

> During this last year we have grown in strength and in reputation. We have more friends in the world; we are more closely united to our old friends; we have not abandoned the principle of the Covenant of the League of Nations; we never have been on terms of greater goodwill and understanding with the United States. The vital thing now is not to change our policy.[73]

In August both Eden and Churchill were on holiday in the south of France, and they 'saw a good deal of each other'.[74] In September, when Italian submarines, pretending to be part of General Franco's navy, began to attack and sink international shipping off the Spanish coast, Eden acted promptly to arrange a conference of the powers at Nyon in Switzerland and to organise a system of international naval patrols to prevent the incidents recurring. Churchill warmly encouraged this vigorous action and wrote to Eden to say that he had also secured the approval of Lloyd George.[75]

In October Churchill attended the annual conference of the National Union, this time at Scarborough – but for once it was not with the intention of attacking the party leadership. He told the conference: 'I thought it would be only right that I should come here when we are all agreed.' After praising Eden's performance as Foreign Secretary, he went on to show his appreciation of the government's efforts to improve the national defences:

> At present the government is making a great effort for rearmament. ... It is our duty to support His Majesty's Government in its policies of defence and world peace by every means in our power. Party unity is indispensable.[76]

Nor were these compliments limited to a brief season after Chamberlain took over the Premiership. Almost three months later Churchill wrote an article on British rearmament for the *Evening Standard*, in which he declared:

> Money for defence is certainly pouring out in all directions in Britain. The friends of political and democratic freedom in Europe need not therefore look upon the sombre year now opening [1938] with undue despondency and alarm.[77]

In this period of good relations between the government and its most formidable backbench parliamentarian, Chamberlain could easily have brought Churchill back into office if he had wished. He was in fact urged to do so by Leslie Hore-Belisha, the War Minister. But Chamberlain was afraid that Churchill would prove too strong a force in the Cabinet. He told Hore-Belisha: 'If I take him into the Cabinet he will dominate it. He won't give others a chance of even talking.'[78]

Chamberlain, it should be realised, liked to exert a much stronger control over his ministers than Baldwin had done. He expected to be able to control any field of policy that he chose, using the departmental minister concerned as temporarily merely an assistant. It was indeed this characteristic which brought him into conflict with Eden, who was endeavouring to conduct foreign policy with the freedom traditionally accorded to the Foreign Secretary and his advisers. And this, in turn, led to the shattering of the period of good relations between Churchill and the Chamberlain government. On the night of February 20th 1938 Churchill, who was at Chartwell, received a telephone call to say that Eden had resigned his post. He already knew that there was some friction between him and the Prime Minister, but when he heard the news he was gravely disturbed: 'My heart sank, and for a while the dark waters of despair overwhelmed me.' Always a regular sleeper, for once he stayed awake all night, 'consumed by emotions of sorrow and fear', and next morning 'I watched the daylight slowly creep in through the windows, and saw before me in mental gaze the vision of Death.'[79]

Eden's resignation opened a new period of conflict between Churchill and the government, largely occasioned by Chamberlain's policy of actively 'appeasing' the dictators, in the hope of averting future conflict or at least reducing the number of Britain's enemies. The Chiefs of Staff had advised the Cabinet that Britain was in no condition to fight a war against Germany, Italy and Japan simultaneously. If Germany was the most threatening of these three powers, nevertheless Japan had the most powerful navy; and if Russia intervened on the side of Britain and France this might bring Japan in on the side of Germany and Italy, and thus would be 'in fact an embarrassment rather than a help'. The value of the Russian army was also in doubt as a result of Stalin's purges.[80] As for the United States, popular feeling there in favour of isolation and neutrality appeared to be as strong as ever, and so, as Chamberlain observed, 'he would be a rash man who based his considerations on help from that quarter'. Consequently Britain had to recognise that France was her only possible major ally; and for the rest it was essential to take 'political or international action ... to reduce the number of our potential enemies'.[81]

Eden felt that it was very difficult for him to take the initiative to reduce the number of Britain's potential enemies. Germany, Italy and Japan all had ambitions to fulfil which were likely to cut across Britain's interests. He preferred instead to try to establish closer links with obvious friends – France, Belgium and if possible the United States.[82] It was in fact an American move that brought his differences with the Prime Minister to a head. In January 1937 President Roosevelt consulted Chamberlain alone among European leaders about a proposal that the United States might summon an international conference to discuss the problems of world peace. Eden thought that the proposal should be warmly welcomed, but Chamberlain was anxious only to turn it down.

Chamberlain was hostile to Roosevelt's intervention because he thought that the United States would be most unlikely to throw any real weight into the achievement of a European settlement; and such a conference as was proposed would only delay his own plans for the restoration of friendly relations between

Britain and Italy. Chamberlain wished to accord *de jure* recognition to the Italian conquest of Abyssinia, and this was a step that the American government was not yet prepared to take. Eden for his part saw no point in making concessions to Italy until there were signs that Italy would make mutual concessions to Britain. His own policy of firmness, as exemplified by the success of the Nyon Agreement, had so far paid off well, and he did not wish to reverse it.

So serious a dispute between Prime Minister and Foreign Secretary had to be discussed in detail by the Cabinet. But there Eden found himself without much support, and so he resigned, as did his Under-Secretary, Lord Cranborne. Chamberlain sent Halifax (formerly Irwin) to the Foreign Office, and made R. A. Butler Under-Secretary. Two months later, on April 16th, an Anglo-Italian agreement was signed, by which Britain conceded the *de jure* recognition of the conquest of Abyssinia, in return for vague assurances of Italian friendship. Meanwhile President Roosevelt, disappointed by the cold reception that Chamberlain had given to his proposal for a conference, abandoned the initiative altogether. Yet the international situation was continuing to grow more serious. In March Hitler invaded and annexed the hitherto independent state of Austria. Apart from its intrinsic significance of his bad faith – for the invasion broke solemn promises that he had made in earlier years – the annexation of Austria to Germany meant that Czechoslovakia, a Slav country with a German-speaking minority, was now surrounded on three sides by Nazi territory.

In the House of Commons Churchill was obviously in opposition to the government once more. When Eden and Cranborne made their resignation speeches, Churchill, sitting two benches behind them, according to another member 'cheered so loudly that the scars of his motor accident showed in deep ruts upon a purple countenance'.[83] Henceforward in major parliamentary divisions Churchill ceased to vote for the government, but abstained, usually in the company of at least twenty other MPs on the government side. But there was no distinct group accepting his leadership: his personal supporters numbered only three or four. For the rest, some twenty MPs gathered around Anthony Eden, who rather deliberately kept aloof from Churchill, apparently to show that there was nothing factional about his attitude. Eden's group, including as it did several of the younger MPs, was nicknamed the 'Glamour Boys'.[84] Among them were Harold Macmillan and Harold Nicolson.

Outside Parliament, Churchill was markedly more popular, and as in 1936 he was beginning to gather support from people of all parties. The discreet lunches organised by 'Focus' were still taking place, and in March 1938 Kingsley Martin in the *New Statesman* argued for 'a broadly based government which includes Mr Eden, Mr Churchill and the Labour and Liberal leaders'.[85] In May and June Churchill spoke at several public meetings in large provincial centres under the auspices of the League of Nations Union. These meetings had in fact been arranged by his friends of 'Focus'. He declared that he wished to see what he called a 'Grand Alliance' of powers interested in maintaining the peace. In his view, it was desirable that Britain should join France and Russia in declaring support for Czechoslovakia. France already had an alliance with Czechoslovakia, and Russia had promised her support if that alliance came into operation. At the same time, Churchill realised that the German minority in Czechoslovakia had a definite grievance. Their case had been put to him by Kurt Henlein, their leader, when he visited London in May. He therefore made no objection when in July Chamberlain persuaded the Czech government to receive a British mission headed by Lord Runciman with instructions to advise on a compromise solution to this problem.

But there was a serious conflict of view between Churchill and the government over what to do when the Runciman mission failed. It was quite apparent that although the Czechs were prepared to agree to all that Henlein had demanded in May this was not enough to satisfy Hitler. Churchill wrote to Halifax on August 31st urging that Britain should join with France and Russia in sending a collective warning to Germany, expressing 'interest in a peaceful solution of the Czechoslovak controversy', but also giving notice that any invasion by German troops would 'raise capital issues'.[86] A few days later Churchill received information from Ivan Maisky, the Russian Ambassador, about an exchange of views between Litvinoff, the Russian Foreign Minister, and the French Ambassador in Moscow, on the subject of assistance to Czechoslovakia. He passed this on to the Foreign Office, evidently hoping that the discussion of joint action could become a tripartite affair.[87] But co-operation of action with France and Russia was precisely what Chamberlain did not want, as he had decided already not to support Czechoslovakia against Germany if it involved a risk of war, and his aim was only to secure a means of releasing France from the obligation which she had accepted.

By mid-September the crisis was sufficiently acute for Chamberlain to put into operation a plan which he had previously decided upon. This was simply that he himself should visit Hitler in Germany. Hitler could hardly refuse to see the British Prime Minister, and so they met at Berchtesgaden, Hitler's retreat in the Bavarian Alps, on September 15th. In the meantime Henlein, who was now in Germany, was demanding not just self-government for the Germans in Czechoslovakia but the cession of the predominantly German areas to Germany. This demand was put to Chamberlain by Hitler, and he returned to London with the intention of persuading both the British and the French Cabinets to agree. They did so readily enough, and it only remained to force the Czech government also to accept the terms. Naturally the Czechs were bitterly hostile, for the cession of the German territories meant the loss of the only defensible frontier line, as well as the severance of many of the country's natural lines of communication. But Édouard Daladier's Cabinet threatened that if Czechoslovakia did not agree France would abandon her guarantee under the Franco-Czech Treaty. Under this harsh and dishonourable constraint the Czech government agreed to the dismemberment of their country.

Churchill was shocked by the way the crisis had developed. On September 20th he visited Paris to see his closest friends in the French government, Paul Reynaud and Georges Mandel. Both ministers, he later recalled, were 'in lively distress and on the verge of resignation'. He urged them not to leave the Cabinet, as they would thereby forfeit what remaining influence they had; but on his return to London he published a statement declaring that the Anglo-French proposals meant 'the complete surrender of the Western Democracies to the Nazi threat of force'.[88] On the 22nd he visited his closest friend in the British Cabinet – Duff Cooper, who was now the First Lord of the Admiralty – 'in a state of great excitement and ... violent in his denunciation of the Prime Minister'.[89] Duff Cooper's wife, Diana, later recalled the vision of 'Winston ... stamping to and fro amongst the Admiralty's dolphin furniture, flaming his soul out with his impatience to flout the aggressor in his own way'.[90] It was not the first time that Admiralty House had witnessed such a scene.

When Chamberlain returned to Germany to see Hitler at Godesberg, he found the German dictator more intransigent than ever. So far from agreeing to the modest conditions which Chamberlain felt would satisfy the British Cabinet, he now demanded the immediate occupation by his troops of the predominantly German territories of Czechoslovakia. Chamberlain, although angry at Hitler's behaviour, returned to London determined to secure acceptance of his demands by the Cabinet. On September 25th the Cabinet debated the terms, and, to Chamberlain's distress, Halifax urged their rejection. His conscience had been troubled by the attitude of his Foreign Office advisers, and in the course of a sleepless night he had changed his views. Churchill called on the Prime Minister next day, and again urged his policy of a joint statement by Britain, France and Russia. He found that Halifax, who was also present at the interview, was largely in agreement with him.[91] The upshot was a unilateral statement from the Foreign Office saying that if France went to the aid of Czechoslovakia, Britain and Russia would 'certainly stand by France'. A state of emergency was now declared; the Auxiliary Air Force was called up; and the fleet was mobilised.

On the afternoon of September 28th Chamberlain addressed the House of Commons to explain what had happened so far. The House was crowded, and the atmosphere tense. After the Prime Minister had spoken for an hour, giving a bare recital of events, he was interrupted to receive a note, and suddenly, as Harold Nicolson reported, 'His whole face, his whole body, seemed to change.... He appeared ten years younger and triumphant.'[92] He announced that Hitler had agreed to postpone mobilisation for twenty-four hours and to meet him, Daladier and Mussolini at a conference in Munich. The House burst into cheers and gave him a standing ovation. There were a few isolated individuals who failed to join in: Harold Macmillan noticed 'one man silent and seated, with his head sunk on his shoulders, his whole demeanour depicting something between anger and despair'.[93] Eden walked out; but Churchill picked himself up and went to shake Chamberlain's hand before he left, uttering the barbed comment: 'I congratulate you on your good fortune. You were very lucky.'[94]

Next day the four leaders assembled at Munich – Chamberlain being accompanied only by Sir Horace Wilson, formerly of the

Ministry of Labour, and by relatively junior advisers – Lord Dunglass, his PPS (later Sir Alec Douglas-Home), Ashton-Gwatkin of the Runciman Mission, and William Strang of the Foreign Office. Churchill realised clearly that there was a danger of the Prime Minister, virtually on his own, making further concessions that the Cabinet would not have authorised. That day he attended a meeting of 'Focus' at lunch in a room at the Savoy. The principal Opposition leaders were there – Attlee as well as Sinclair – and also several leading Conservative backbenchers – Eden, Lloyd and Robert Cecil of the League of Nations Union. Churchill urged that they should all sign a telegram to Chamberlain insisting that there should be no surrender of Czech security. But one by one his companions declared that they could not allow their names to be used – Eden for fear of appearing hostile to Chamberlain, Attlee because he had not consulted his Labour Party colleagues, and so on. According to Violet Bonham Carter, who was also present, 'When we parted there were tears in Winston Churchill's eyes.'[95]

When Chamberlain returned to London and the terms of the Munich Agreement became known, it was clear enough that Czechoslovakia had been savagely mauled in order to purchase a temporary peace. But a great wave of relief swept through Britain, and Chamberlain knew that, for a time at least, he had won great popularity. When the Commons debated the agreement, however, it was apparent that the opponents of Chamberlain's policy were more vociferous than before, and moreover were gaining fresh recruits. Duff Cooper had resigned from the Cabinet, and spoke out vigorously against Chamberlain. But as so often, the most effective speech came from Churchill. He summed up the course of events at Berchtesgaden, at Godesberg and at Munich in brilliant fashion:

£1 was demanded at the pistol's point. When it was given, £2 were demanded at the pistol's point. Finally the dictator consented to take £1.17s.6d. and the rest in promises of goodwill for the future.

And he concluded with a solemn warning:

Do not suppose that this is the end. This is only the beginning of the reckoning. This is only the first sip, the first foretaste of a bitter cup which will be proffered to us year by year unless by a supreme recovery of moral health and martial vigour, we arise again and take our stand for freedom as in the olden time.[96]

The division at the end of the debate saw a more convincing demonstration than before that the opposition to Chamberlain within the ranks of his own supporters was at last beginning to solidify. By a pre-arranged plan the critics abstained from the vote by sitting in their seats in the Chamber. They were a distinguished, if not very numerous company – besides Churchill, there were three former Cabinet ministers, Eden, Amery and Duff Cooper, and over twenty others. As Harold Nicolson, who was also one of the group, recorded in his diary, 'It is not our numbers that matter but our reputation.... The House knows that most [of us] know far more about the real issue than they do.'[97]

For a time there was a sharp cleavage of opinion between the supporters and the opponents of Munich in the country. The pro-Munich Conservatives were angry when they learnt of attacks upon their leader from fellow-Conservatives, and sought to take counter-measures. Churchill again encountered unrest within his constituency association, as he had done in the later stages of the controversy over the Indian constitution. He had to threaten to resign his seat and fight a by-election if a resolution of censure was carried. His supporters narrowly carried the day: the Central Council of the West Essex Unionist Association, meeting privately, passed a compromise resolution thanking Chamberlain for his efforts for peace but regretting that the government had failed to make the country's defences as strong as Churchill had demanded in the past.[98] Hitler himself sought to widen the split within British public opinion by denouncing Churchill, Eden and Duff Cooper as 'war agitators'; but his party newspaper *Angriff* spoilt the effect of this by even grosser exaggeration, suggesting that Churchill, Eden and Attlee were accomplices in the murder of a German embassy official in Paris who was shot by a Jewish youth.[99]

In the winter of 1938–9 it gradually began to sink in that Hitler had not been effectively 'appeased', as Chamberlain had hoped, but that he was as much of a danger as ever, and probably worse. Even the actions of the Chamberlain government itself strongly suggested this conclusion: for there were further moves to accelerate rearmament, and to improve the preparations against air raids, which had been so obviously lacking in the days of tension in September. Yet most people still thought Chamberlain had been right to avoid the catastrophe of war in September 1938; and the information we have from the earliest opinion polls conducted in the autumn and winter suggests that Chamberlain still had majority support.[100] The government did quite well in the autumn by-elections, apart from that at Bridgwater, where Vernon Bartlett, the journalist, secured election as an independent Progressive; and when in December the Duchess of Atholl, who sat for Kinross and West Perthshire, resigned her seat and stood as an independent against an official Conservative she was defeated, albeit narrowly. Churchill had sent her a message of support, and had telephoned her almost daily to offer encouragement and to obtain news.[101] Meanwhile Churchill had had to terminate his contract to write regular articles on political affairs for the *Evening Standard*, apparently because Beaverbrook felt that his insistence upon the danger of war was bad for sales.[102]

The worst pressure upon Churchill came from a renewal of the opposition to his attitude from within the Conservative ranks in his constituency. In the Chigwell branch there was a 'clean sweep' of Churchillians at the annual election of officers, all of them being replaced by Chamberlainites; shortly afterwards the Theydon Bois branch declared its complete support for Chamberlain; and dissension arose in the Epping branch.[103] At a meeting at Chigwell on March 10th which the local branch had refused to sanction, Churchill put his case, but it was not without making some concessions to his opponents. He said he would 'cordially support the Government in the policy they have now adopted'. By this he meant the increased effort in rearmament and in air raid precautions, which he described as 'the laggard section of our air defences'. He refused to withdraw a word of what he had said about Munich, but he acknowledged that 'The fact that the Prime Minister is known to be a sincere worker for peace has had a good effect upon the populations of the dictator countries.'[104]

Three days later, however, the need for such a soft-pedalling of his opinions disappeared. On March 13th Hitler invaded the remnant of Czechoslovakia and declared a protectorate over Bohemia. Churchill's remarks about the worthless character of the Munich settlement now appeared thoroughly justified, and he adopted a very different tone when he again spoke in his constituency on March 14th. He now administered a stern lecture to the Epping Chamberlainites:

> People talk about our parliamentary institutions and parliamentary democracy; but if these are to survive, it will not be because the constituencies return tame, docile, subservient members, and try to keep out every form of independent judgment.[105]

There was now a great revulsion of feeling in the country, and a determination to press for all-out rearmament which gripped even Chamberlain himself and his immediate colleagues. To prevent Hitler at once exploiting his success in central Europe by attacking other neighbours, the government in late March gave an immediate guarantee to Poland, and shortly afterwards extended it to Rumania and to Greece. Churchill thought the guarantee to Poland was ill-judged, as it was difficult to see how Britain could provide early assistance to Poland, with her long frontier even more exposed to German invasion than that of Czechoslovakia. 'I was astounded', he told the House, 'when I heard them give this guarantee. I support it, but I was astounded by it.'[106]

The Cabinet also finally gave in to the demand for a Ministry of Supply – a measure which Churchill had urged three years earlier but which both Baldwin and Chamberlain regarded as unnecessary unless rearmament were to be given priority over all normal peacetime trade. The government now clearly accepted the view that it could no longer plan the services on a 'limited liability' basis, and that even the army, which had been assigned no more than a colonial role in the war planning of 1937–8, should be expanded in order to provide a significant contribution to the Western Front. At the end of March it was decided that the Territorial Army should be doubled, and less than a month later Chamberlain announced that Parliament would be asked to authorise the introduction of conscription – for the first time ever in peacetime.

Churchill's attention now turned to the prospects of securing an alliance of European powers before Hitler struck again. He was worried about the Balkans, and when Mussolini occupied Albania at Easter, he thought that Britain should at once have secured the approval of the Greek government for the stationing of British naval forces at Corfu. He was also alarmed that at this critical time the battleships of the Mediterranean Fleet were 'scattered about in the most vulnerable disorder' – one of them actually being in Naples harbour.[107] Later in the spring, when the Mediterranean tension eased somewhat, he turned his attention to the urgency of an alliance with Russia.[108] It was not until June that an emissary was sent to Moscow to prepare the way for a political agreement, and then it was not a minister but a middle-rank member of the Foreign Office staff – William Strang, who had also been at Munich.

By the summer opinion even among hitherto loyal Conservatives was coming round to the view that Churchill ought to be in the Cabinet. If war was inevitable, then the country's outstanding warrior-statesman was needed. On July 3rd the *Daily Telegraph*, the spokesman of orthodox Conservatism, urged this course in a leading article, describing Churchill as

> a statesman not only schooled in responsibility by long and intimate contact with affairs of State, but possessing an unrivalled practical knowledge of the crucial problems which war presents, especially in the higher strategy.

The article encouraged several prominent people, including the Marquess of Salisbury, one of the Conservative Party's most respected figures, to write and express their agreement. There was even a campaign of placards and posters with the slogan 'Churchill Must Come Back'. On July 12th the *Telegraph* published a letter signed by Violet Bonham Carter and several other prominent Liberals in favour of Churchill's return to high office. This letter had originally been sent to *The Times*, but had been refused publication by Dawson – who was as hostile to Churchill on foreign policy as he had been over India. But Chamberlain still felt that there was a glimmer of hope for peace, and thought that this too would disappear if he gave office to Churchill. As he wrote at the time: 'If there is any possibility of easing the tension and getting back to normal relations with the dictators, I wouldn't risk it by what would certainly be regarded by them as a challenge.'[109]

Meanwhile Churchill was doing what he could to cement the Anglo-French alliance and to provide encouragement for the French army, on which as he saw it the heaviest burden of the war was bound to fall. On July 14th he was in Paris for the Fête Nationale, the special celebrations of the 150th anniversary of the Fall of the Bastille. The British Cabinet had authorised an impressive demonstration of solidarity on this occasion, to the extent of sending detachments of the Royal Marines and of the Guards to take part in the march-past, and RAF planes to fly overhead; but Hore-Belisha was the most senior government representative to attend the parade. Early in August Churchill was in his place in the House of Commons to oppose the government's decision to adjourn Parliament until October – but in vain. A few days later he was back in France to undertake a tour of the Maginot Line. The tour lasted three days, and for much of the time he was accompanied by General Georges, Chief of Staff to General Gamelin, the Commander-in-Chief. On his return to Paris he was greeted by a cheering crowd at the Gare de l'Est, to whom he declared, 'My confidence in your country is more unshakeable than ever.'[110]

Six days later, on August 23rd, the Russo-German Non-Aggression Pact was signed. Churchill was not particularly surprised by this move – he had noted the waning of ideology in Russian foreign policy during the preceding four years[111] – but he naturally deplored the failure of Chamberlain and Halifax to get the Russians committed to the side of the Western Allies. Hitler now increased the pressure on Poland, and demanded the immediate despatch of a Polish plenipotentiary to Berlin in order to discuss his terms for a settlement. But the Polish government remained firm, and no emissary was sent. On the morning of September 1st 1939, German forces crossed the frontier and the first campaign of the Second World War began.

Churchill's criticisms of British foreign policy and of delays in the process of rearmament have been given, in retrospect, a consistency and continuity that they did not have. It is true that from the moment Hitler took office Churchill saw the danger of a revived German militarism, directed by an exceptionally cruel and ruthless leadership. From that moment he became an advocate of the highest possible rate of defence expenditure. All else in his view, however, was in flux. He had no sense of inevitability; he was not, like some of those who sympathised with him, in any degree anti-German; and he was sufficiently open-minded about the merits of dictatorship to think that Mussolini had done much good for Italy, and that Hitler could and might do good for Germany. 'History will pronounce Hitler either a monster or a hero,' he wrote in 1937.[112]

Churchill was indeed an empirical statesman, quick to respond to changes in circumstances abroad, and fertile in expedients to cope with them. So long as Britain did not appear to be directly threatened from the Continent – that is to say, so long as France with her system of alliances was still markedly predominant over Germany – he was hostile to any commitments on Britain's part, other than the limited responsibilities she had already accepted by the League Covenant and the Treaty of Locarno. But soon, when the French preponderance was at an end, he decided that the machinery of the League should be used more effectively to rally a concert of the powers to keep the peace. He was now prepared to make an agreement even with Russia, whose leaders he had so much abhorred in the early years after the Bolshevik revolution. As he said in 1936, 'It would not be a question of Right or Left; it would be a question of right or wrong.'[113] This freedom from ideological commitment enabled him to maintain a strictly neutral attitude throughout the Spanish Civil War. It was only in personal sympathy that he veered somewhat towards the Republican cause in the later stages of the war, on the grounds that German and Italian military assistance was so significant an element in Franco's strength.[114]

There were also marked variations in the attitude that Churchill adopted to the government. He had to make allowance for the fact that he was a member of the Conservative Party, that he had been elected as such, and that he had to seek re-election as such. He knew that his chances of returning to office depended on his adopting a constructive view of the problems with which ministers were faced. Unlike other great statesmen of the modern age such as Lloyd George and Joseph Chamberlain, he had no secure geographical power-base – although he might have had one if he had chosen to return to a Lancashire seat in 1923. Nor did he have the craft and temperament to build up a personal following by wooing his fellow-MPs. As A. G. Gardiner pointed out perceptively in the mid-1920s, he was 'an Ishmael in public life'.[115] Everything had to depend upon his generalised power as an orator, whether in the Chamber of the House of Commons or on the public platform.

These characteristics help to explain the extraordinary fluctuations in his parliamentary and public reputation in this period. His Indian crusade cut him off from many who would otherwise have sympathised with his campaign for rearmament, and it was only with great difficulty that he persuaded them to listen to him in 1934 and 1935. In 1936, the last full year of Baldwin's leadership of the Conservative Party, Churchill was winning over his following more and more, and the *Times*'s parliamentary correspondent could say of the Debate on the Address in November of that year that everything else in it was 'dwarfed by Mr Churchill's duel with the government'.[116] Only a few weeks later, however, there occurred the fiasco of his intervention in the Abdication crisis, and the reaction was immediate. Wilson Harris expressed a not untypical comment in the *Spectator*: 'The reputation which he was beginning to shake off of a wayward genius unserviceable in counsel has settled firmly on his shoulders again.'[117]

In 1937, as we have seen, Churchill had to proceed warily; and with the replacement of Baldwin by Neville Chamberlain he became far less critical of the government's efforts to rearm the country. While Eden was Foreign Secretary, he was also satisfied with the course of foreign policy, and only moved into a position of active criticism after Eden's resignation in 1938. There was still no question of his leading a group of Conservative MPs, other than the two or three who had special personal ties with him – Brendan Bracken, Admiral of the Fleet Sir Roger Keyes, and the young Duncan Sandys, who had married his daughter Diana. It was Eden who collected the wavering backbenchers, including even so senior a personality as Leopold Amery, to form a personal following. In March 1939, when an opinion poll invited the public to say who would be the best choice for Prime Minister if Chamberlain retired, 38% of the sample preferred Eden, as against only 7% each for Halifax and Churchill.[118]

Yet in these years of independence and partial isolation Churchill was establishing his claim to be the leader of his country in the supreme crisis of military disaster. His experience of the problems of war, built up over a period of almost half a century, was modernised by his work on the Air Defence Research Committee and his studies of the growth of German air power. His criticisms of 1935 and 1936 undoubtedly stimulated the pace of rearmament in the ensuing years, which may have been decisive in preserving the country from defeat in 1940. Yet because he was not in the government he held no responsibility for the remaining deficiencies, which in the nature of things were bound to emerge as soon as the fighting began. As he later wrote when describing how he had missed appointment to office under Baldwin, 'Over me beat the invisible wings'.[119]

19. *Private Life: Historian and Journalist, 1929-39*

It was only in retrospect that Churchill felt satisfaction in not having been in office during the 1930s. At the time it had been disagreeable, and became increasingly so as the years passed. Yet he had enjoyed release from the Chancellorship in 1929, for it freed him to make a trip to Canada and the United States in the summer of that year. He had not been across the Atlantic for almost thirty years, and apart from the obvious object of rest and recreation, he wanted to find out what changes had taken place since his last visit.[1]

The party of four – Churchill and his brother Jack, and their respective sons, Randolph (aged eighteen) and Johnnie (twenty) – travelled on the Canadian Pacific liner the *Empress of Australia* to Quebec, and then transferred to a private coach of the Canadian Pacific Railroad lent by a vice-president of the company. It contained 'a dining room, a sitting room, three bedrooms, two bathrooms, four lavatories and kitchen and an observation platform at the back'.[2] The party had its own cook and waiter, and there were also a wireless set and electric fans. Churchill made speeches only at major cities en route, and then (unusually for him) but briefly and with little preparation. At Quebec each of the party was presented with a broad-brimmed Stetson hat for a fishing expedition, and Churchill welcomed this addition to his wardrobe as a way of avoiding the glare of the sun. When they reached the Rockies they left their coach for a few days' sightseeing, and at Emerald Lake near Banff Churchill took out his paints and, with his Stetson on his head, set to work at his accustomed pastime.

Early in September the four travellers entered the United States – somewhat apprehensively, for this was the era of Prohibition. They carried with them a good deal of whisky and brandy, but were relieved to find that the precaution was hardly necessary, as the enforcement of the law was so ineffective. Their progress through the Republic had largely been organised by Bernard Baruch, the able financier who, as Chairman of the War Industries Board under President Wilson, had collaborated with Churchill in 1917 and 1918, and had made friends with him by telegram. Baruch persuaded William Randolph Hearst, the proprietor of the isolationist newspaper the *Chicago Tribune*, to act as host to the party in California. Considering the difference in their political views, Churchill got on surprisingly well with his host. The party spent four days at Hearst's home at San Simeon, and then visited the Hollywood film studios to meet the stars: here Churchill struck up a friendship with Charlie Chaplin and told him he wanted him to play the part of Napoleon in a film for which he was going to write the scenario. He also went on an expedition to catch swordfish, and managed to land one of 188 pounds.

On their trip overland from Los Angeles, they again had private coaches on the railway, arranged by Baruch. They visited the Grand Canyon, the stockyards at Chicago and various other sights before reaching New York. Randolph and Johnnie were due back at Oxford early in October and had to return separately; but Churchill took his brother with him to visit the battlefields of the American Civil War at Gettysburg and Richmond and spent a few days also in Washington, where he met not only the President but also the Senate Foreign Relations Committee and other members of Congress.

In the summer of 1929 the United States economy was at the height of its boom. Churchill was immensely impressed with the buoyancy of American life and with the optimism that he encountered everywhere. 'The people in the streets, in the shops, in the hotels; the lift man, the bell-hop, the telephone operator, all are gay.'[3] This picture had to be somewhat modified when he was in New York at the end of his tour, for the sudden collapse of the New York stock market took place at the time, and 'Under my very window a gentleman cast himself down fifteen storeys and was dashed to pieces, causing a wild commotion and the arrival of the fire brigade.'[4] But this volatility of feeling did not unduly disturb Churchill. To some extent his own mental make-up was similar. He foresaw a great future for Anglo-American collaboration, for the British, he thought, could contribute a solidity and obstinacy which the Americans lacked: 'The Americans in their millions are a frailer race with a lighter structure. ... It is in the combination across the Atlantic of these ... complementary virtues and resources, that the brightest promise of the future dwells.'[5]

In spite of the Depression Churchill continued to be optimistic about America, and late in 1930 he was making plans to undertake a lecture tour of the United States in the following autumn, which he understood would bring him a clear £10,000, above expenses, in return for forty lectures.[6] The tour did not go to plan, first because Churchill had to postpone his visit owing to the political crisis and general election in Britain, and then because, when he did arrive in New York in December, he was knocked down by a motorcar and badly bruised.

The accident happened as follows. On December 13th, after dining at his hotel, the Waldorf-Astoria, he telephoned his friend Baruch and received an invitation to the latter's home on Fifth Avenue. He thereupon took a taxi, but having mislaid Baruch's precise address he instructed the driver to put him down at a point which he thought reasonably close. He then crossed the road on foot, but being used to the British left-hand driving system he failed to look in the correct direction for oncoming traffic. He was hit by a car driven by a young unemployed truck-driver of Italo-American parentage, Mario Contasino. No bones were broken, but he suffered severe shock and concussion and heavy bruising on the body, legs and arms, together with cuts on his forehead and nose. A crowd quickly gathered, and Churchill, who though recumbent was still conscious, explained to a policeman that the accident was entirely his own fault, and that the driver was not to blame. He was then hoisted into another taxicab and driven to Lenox-hill Hospital on 76th Street, where he asked for a private room and was soon under treatment.

Churchill took his accident philosophically. He was pleased to find that the imminence of death did not worry him unduly: 'There is neither the time nor the strength for self-pity. There is no room for remorse or fears.... Nature is merciful and does not try her children, man or beast, beyond their compass.'[7] He was also pleased to receive some mathematical calculations from Lindemann, who worked out that if the car was proceeding at 35 m.p.h. he had absorbed in his body some 6000 foot-pounds.

> It was the equivalent of falling thirty feet on to a pavement ... of stopping 10 pounds of buckshot dropped 600 feet, or two charges of buckshot at point-blank range. I do not understand why I was not broken like an egg-shell or squashed like a gooseberry.... I certainly must be very tough or very lucky, or both.[8]

He was in hospital for only eight days, and before Christmas he returned to his hotel, where Clementine and Diana and also his bodyguard, Detective Sergeant W. H. Thompson, were staying. He was obviously still far from well: a caller noticed that 'a deep, livid gash in his forehead gave him the air of a sorely wounded warrior and the droop of his powerful shoulders betrayed a weariness which the jauntiness of his attire could not disguise'.[9] On December 30th he gave an interview to reporters, one of whom described him as 'pale, nervous and shaky'. He admitted that he had not been able to keep up with current affairs; his life, he said, had been like that described in Mark Twain's diary – 'Got up, washed, went to bed.'[10]

Early in January, accompanied by his wife and daughter, he went off on the White Star liner *Majestic* to Nassau in the Bahamas, for a period of convalescence. After a few days at a hotel called Polly Leach's, the family moved into Government House, where a new Governor, Sir Bede Clifford, had just arrived. For some time Churchill had to lie on his back for eighteen hours of the twenty-four, and suffered from what he described as neuritis in the arms. But he was swimming 200 yards daily, and soon made rapid progress in regaining his health.[11] He attended a dinner given by the two Houses of the Bahama Legislature, and listened with pleasure to the affirmations of loyalty to the Crown which were made by politicians of African origin. 'The colour question', he later wrote, 'appears completely solved.'[12]

In late January he returned to New York to resume his lecture tour. He had his misgivings about how he would stand the rail journeys, for there was no private coach this time: but he found the trains 'extremely comfortable'. The atmosphere of the lectures themselves was also congenial to him: he decided that American audiences 'yield to none in the interest, attention and good nature with which they follow a lengthy, considered statement'.[13]

Before leaving America Churchill went to Washington for a time, and stayed at the British Embassy, where he certainly upset the normal routine of the Ambassador, Sir Ronald Lindsay. He insisted on staying in bed for most of the morning, and so the Ambassador had to visit his bedroom to discuss plans for the day.

> These two made the oddest contrast, the immensely dignified diplomat standing extremely ill at ease at the foot of the old-fashioned four-poster and the Peter Pan of British politics sitting up in bed, a cigar in his mouth, his tufts of red hair as yet uncombed, scanning the morning newspapers.[14]

When he returned to England in March he found that his friends, both British and American, had clubbed together to buy him a £2000 saloon car. It was waiting for him alongside the station platform at Victoria. Archibald Sinclair had acted as treasurer of the fund.[15]

In the early years of being out of office Churchill had to develop a new routine. For some time he had no London flat and, as we have seen, he visited the House of Commons relatively rarely. Unless on holiday, he normally lived at Chartwell, where he earned his living by writing articles for the press and by preparing books for publishers. His output was remarkable. In the course of the year 1930, for instance, he wrote forty articles for newspapers and magazines, more than half of them for the *Daily Telegraph*.[16] He delivered the Romanes Lecture at Oxford University in June, on *Parliamentary Government and the Economic Problem*, and this was separately published. In September and October the *News Chronicle* serialised his work of reminiscence, *My Early Life*, which received a warm welcome when it appeared in book form in October. The American edition was called *A Roving Commission*. It certainly showed his various literary skills at their best. As *The Times* commented,

There be few who could play on all these strings – humour, head-long excitement, quiet irony, melancholy regret for vanished customs and glories, love of sport, the pleasures of friendship – with so sure a hand.[17]

Later in his life he agreed with Lady Violet Bonham Carter that it was 'the best book I ever wrote', and there will undoubtedly be many who accept this judgment.[18] As usual, the book's punctu-ation and style had been scrutinised by Eddie Marsh, and, as we have seen, proofs had also been read by Stanley Baldwin, who wrote an appreciative letter.[19]

In 1931 Churchill actually increased his output of articles, and also published, first of all, an abridged and revised version of the *World Crisis*, with an additional chapter on the Battle of the Marne, and then an additional volume of the original series, entitled *The Eastern Front* (or, in America, *The Unknown War*). The latter was described by *The Times* as being 'in interest and literary quality well up to the high standard of the other volumes of the *World Crisis*'.[20] But its account of warfare in eastern Europe, derived as it largely was from secondary sources, lacked the authoritative character that the earlier volumes had possessed. His preoccupation with Indian affairs at this time was marked by the publication of a small volume of his speeches on the subject, under the title *India*, for the price of 2s cloth and 1s paper: its purpose was purely propagandist.

Esmond Harmsworth, the son and heir of Lord Rothermere who now largely controlled the *Daily Mail*, agreed with Churchill about India, and this was the reason why much of Churchill's journalism in the early 1930s was published by the Harmsworth Press. Thus in 1932, although his output was less than previously owing to his accident and illness, most of it was published by the *Mail*. It began with two articles describing his sensations during his 'New York Misadventure', which he must have written before going to the Bahamas. Apparently these articles were sold in the first instance to a New York syndicate for $2500.[21] The year also saw the publication of the best of his work of this character in book form. *Thoughts and Adventures*, published in November 1932 (the American edition was called *Amid These Storms*), contained some reminiscences of outstanding events, such as 'The Battle of Sidney Street' and 'A Day with Clemenceau', and also his Romanes Lecture and some reflections on the future, evidently influenced by the ideas of Lindemann. There was, too, a charming essay on his principal recreation, 'Painting as a Pastime', which was later to be published as a separate work. Churchill was ill when the book finally went to press, and the preface was written, in a clever pastiche of his style, by Eddie Marsh: 'Has there ever been an epoch of such pith and moment?'[22] Marsh also 'ghosted' a series of twelve pot-boiling articles which Churchill undertook for the *News of the World* – 'Great Stories of the World Retold', starting off with *Uncle Tom's Cabin* and ending with *Don Quixote*. They were published weekly in the first three months of 1933.

By this time Churchill was already deeply involved in a major new project – the life of his great ancestor the 1st Duke of Marlborough. Both Balfour and Rosebery had in the past urged this task upon him, and Rosebery had pointed out that Macaulay's savage attack upon the Duke for allegedly betraying the Brest Expedition of 1694 had been effectively rebutted in J. Paget, *The New Examen* (1861), a copy of which he gave Churchill as a present.[23] As early as the summer of 1929 Churchill discussed the project with Keith Feiling, the distinguished seventeenth-century historian who was a colleague of Lindemann's at Christ Church, Oxford; and through Feiling he recruited Maurice Ashley, an Oxford graduate of that year who had secured a First Class in the History School, to work on the manuscripts of the period in the libraries of London, Paris and Vienna, and to investigate those in the possession of his cousin the 9th Duke of Marlborough and his more distant relation the 7th Earl Spencer. Ashley was paid £300 a year to work on a half-time basis.[24] Churchill also secured the assistance of a military expert, Colonel (later General) R. P. Pakenham-Walsh, to examine the details of the military campaigns, and to draw the maps.

The writing of the first volume, covering Marlborough's origins, early life and career up to 1702, was probably begun in 1931-2. But progress was delayed not only by his motor accident, but also by his paratyphoid illness in September 1932, which developed through drinking contaminated water while on a visit to the battlefields of Marlborough's wars in Bavaria and Austria. He visited Ramillies, Oudenarde and Blenheim, which all struck him as being 'bigger than Austerlitz or Gettysburg, and far bigger than Waterloo'. He admitted to being 'deeply moved' and said that, accompanied by Pakenham-Walsh, he 'spent whole days picnicing' on the fields.[25] The first volume was published by Harrap in October 1933 at 25s. It ran to over 600 pages, had many footnotes, and was lavishly illustrated with plates and facsimiles of documents, as well as by Pakenham-Walsh's maps and plans illustrating the military operations.

The original idea was that the work should cover Marlborough's life in two volumes, amounting altogether to about 200,000 words.[26] But the evidence that Churchill found and wished to discuss resulted in an expansion of the original project, and in the end it ran to four volumes of roughly equal length, and a total of about a million words. From 1933 onwards, Ashley was replaced as research assistant by another able Oxford graduate, F. W. (Bill) Deakin. The second volume, covering the years 1702–5 and mainly devoted to military history, including the great march from the Netherlands to the Danube, and the Battle of Blenheim, was published in October 1934; the third, covering 1705–8 and the battles of Ramillies and Oudenarde, came out in October 1936; and the fourth, concluding the life, was issued on September 2nd 1938. Seventeen thousand copies were produced of the first volume and fifteen thousand of the second, but demand fell off somewhat for the third and fourth volumes which were published in editions of ten thousand each only. As usual, the proofs of all the volumes were scrutinised by Eddie Marsh.[27]

Although Churchill had become a stout partisan of his great ancestor, and spent much of his first volume castigating Macaulay for his errors and malevolence, the work was intended to be a scholarly biography, and hence a study of a different character from anything that he had previously attempted. He was naturally pleased when professional historians accepted him as one of their peers. 'An experienced reviewer may say with confidence', wrote Sir Richard Lodge, reviewing the first volume in the *English Historical Review*, 'that few academic historians, dealing with a period of fifty years, have made so few blunders in matters of fact'. But Sir Richard was a little perturbed by the 'incessant denunciations' of Macaulay and by Churchill's insistence that Marlborough was not only a Titan but also a 'virtuous and benevolent being', whose only fault was 'a thrift which verges upon niggardliness'.[28] Lodge also reviewed the second volume and declared Churchill a little weak on diplomatic history, but thought this fault was more than counterbalanced by the high quality of the military narrative. Liddell Hart, the military historian, was especially enthusiastic about this aspect of the work:

> To one who has travelled much in the realm of military history,
> which is mostly a drab expanse with limited views, to come upon
> a book by Mr Churchill is like a sight of the Hill of Cassel rising
> out of the Flanders Plain.[29]

The reviewers were mostly of the opinion that the later volumes
sustained the quality of the first two. Professor Lewis Namier of
Manchester, who had been asked by Churchill for his frank
opinion of the first volume, urged him to subordinate his criticisms
of Macaulay and, as a man of political, administrative and military experience, to expand his own judgments of events: 'Too
much history is written by don-bred dons.'[30] Churchill seems to
have taken the advice to heart, for it was precisely this quality
that Desmond MacCarthy singled out for praise in his review of
the final volume – published in the late summer of 1938:

> ... a sense, educated in the school of experience, of the nature of
> the problem (perpetually recurring) how to get men actuated by
> different motives and ideas, men hostile, lukewarm, uninformed, to
> work towards some common aim in politics and war.... Mr Chur-
> chill's book has an educative value for anyone who proposes to take
> a hand in national affairs, or may some day find himself in a position
> of public responsibility.[31]

Perhaps in retrospect we may regard the greatest value of the
biography as self-educative. To a man who was to be the linchpin
of a great coalition of nations fighting a major war, it was of
the utmost significance to have studied Marlborough's work in
cementing what Churchill calls in Volume I the 'Grand Alliance', in formulating the strategy which he describes in Volume
II as the 'Great Design', and in facing the consequences of what
became in Volume IV a 'Lost Peace' and a 'Darker War'. But
Churchill was too committed, not only to the memory of his
great ancestor but also to England's cause as the Whig tradition had formulated it, to be a great historian in his own right.
As Professor J. H. Plumb, today's leading authority on the period,
has put it, perhaps rather unkindly:

> The freedom-loving English, Parliament the watch-dog of liberty,
> the tyranny of France – the old Whig claptrap echoes in chapter
> after chapter. The confusion of purpose, the haphazard nature of

men's intentions, the totally different nature of institutions in Queen Anne's reign to those which bore the same name in Queen Victoria's – these were never perceived. What dominated Churchill's writing was a sense of the past that was interlocked with history only to distort it.[32]

But believing as he did in the unique destiny of Britain, the Empire, and the English-speaking world it is not surprising that Churchill went on to conceive the idea of a general history covering these topics. He was thinking of the idea already in 1931, and told Ashley that he wished to 'lay stress upon the common heritage of Great Britain and the United States of America as a means of enhancing their friendship'.[33] Early in 1933 he contracted with Cassell, the London publishers, to write a 400,000-word *History of the English-speaking Peoples* in return for an advance of £20,000.[34] As soon as he had finished with Marlborough, Churchill doggedly set to work upon this new project – aided now not only by Deakin but also by a more senior assistant, G. M. Young, the historian of the Victorian age. It was not easy for him to devote himself to the distant past when immediate issues seemed to demand his attention; but he had a remarkable capacity for switching his mind at will from one matter to another. When Hitler annexed Bohemia in March 1939, Churchill was working on the later seventeenth century. After dinner that night he said to Randolph who was also at Chartwell: 'It's hard to take one's attention off the events of today and concentrate on the reign of James II – but I'm going to do it.'[35] By the outbreak of war a draft of some 500,000 words had been prepared, and much of it had been set up in proof.[36] It was then put aside 'for the duration', and was not in fact completed until the later 1950s.

Meanwhile Churchill continued with his journalism, which drew him a more regular income than his books. Undoubtedly his political relations with the big newspaper proprietors affected their readiness to commission articles by him. When he was at odds with Beaverbrook over the Empire Crusade in the early 1930s, he wrote very little for the *Daily Express* or the *Evening Standard*, and when an editorial adviser, Reginald Pound, suggested him as a contributor Beaverbrook said, 'Why Churchill? He's a busted flush.'[37] Later on, however, Pound became literary editor of the *Daily Mail*, with which, as we have seen, Churchill had developed a regular connection in the early 1930s. He received

£180 for each article, and Pound admired his professional attitude to the task: 'I recall his dependability as a contributor. His copy always arrived "clean" and on the appointed day.'[38]

Early in 1936 Churchill did a series of articles for the *News of the World* on 'Great Men of our Time', and this formed the basis of a book published in the following year under the title of *Great Contemporaries*. In 1936, too, when he and Beaverbrook were on better terms, he began a regular series of articles on international affairs for the *Evening Standard*, which was syndicated to no less than twenty-five European papers. The series continued until early 1938, when Beaverbrook terminated them.[39] Churchill thereupon transferred his series to the *Daily Telegraph*. The articles were republished in book form in June 1939 under the title *Step by Step*. His major speeches delivered between 1932 and 1938 on the kindred themes of defence and foreign policy were edited by Randolph Churchill and published in June 1938 under the title *Arms and the Covenant* (or, in America, *While England Slept*).

If the sum that Churchill received from the *Daily Mail* was the average payment for all his articles, his total gross income from this source in the 1930s cannot have been less than £8000 a year. But we know that he made more than this, between £250 and £400 each, for his longer articles for the *Strand Magazine*,[40] and he obtained equally good rates from American magazines, notably *Collier's*, to which he also contributed regularly: a full-length article would bring in $1500, and he would write nothing for less than $1000.[41] Furthermore, many of the articles published first in Britain were republished in the United States and other countries, and *vice versa*, and although the fees for republication were smaller they also went to swell the total. His secretary Phyllis Moir reckoned his average annual income in this period at about $100,000 (say, £20,000).[42] In 1934 he admitted to Baldwin that he was making an 'enormous income' from his writing.[43] Yet in spite of all this he was often short of cash, and would sometimes ask for payment 'if possible, by Monday morning'.[44]

Taking into account his royalties from books as well as the payment for articles, it is obvious that Churchill's income must have been much larger than he would have received as a minister of the Crown; and if he was still drawing an income from his Irish estate it is difficult to understand how he could regard himself as hard up. There were, of course, the expenses of his literary activities – the research assistants for historical work, the payments for 'ghosting' articles (though these cannot have been frequent), the wages of typist-secretaries, of whom he employed several to work on a shift basis,[45] and Eddie Marsh's honorarium for reading the proofs. He was later to admit that he lost much of the publisher's advance for *Marlborough* in the American slump.[46]

For his political work Churchill had several sources of information, but he displayed a marked reluctance to pay for any of them. Many of the sources were official, and in that case the question did not arise. Ralph Wigram, a Counsellor at the Foreign Office, who was in charge of the Central European Department, shared his views about the German danger and supplied much information before depression overtook him and he committed suicide at the end of 1936.[47] The Permanent Under-Secretary at the Foreign Office, Sir Robert Vansittart, also sympathised with Churchill's views on Germany and allowed him to see important official documents on German rearmament.[48] Another informant was Major Desmond Morton, whom Churchill had known during the First World War; he was now engaged in intelligence work, and lived near Chartwell.[49] Among unofficial sources, there was John Baker White, the Director of the Economic League, originally formed to collect information about Communism. White came into possession of details about German rearmament which the government seemed unwilling to receive; he therefore gave the information to Churchill. He found that Churchill was especially affable 'when I made it clear that we did not want to be paid'.[50] Eugen Spier similarly found that there was some difficulty in making the arrangements for 'Focus' until he (Spier) undertook to foot the bills: 'The tension was immediately eased. Churchill seemed greatly relieved.'[51]

So Churchill paid little directly for his political information and activities. But he had expensive personal tastes, and so did the members of his family. Clementine spent a good deal on her wardrobe, and her husband would expostulate with her about the articles he would have to write to pay for her new dresses.[52] His own clothes, although plain, were of the very best quality, and his underwear, socks and shirts were of silk.[53] Randolph, to his father's distress, insisted on curtailing his course at Oxford and became a journalist at the age of twenty. There was a financial saving to his father in this, but whenever Randolph was at Chartwell his expenses must have rivalled his father's, because to the latter's exasperation he was already drinking double brandies at the age of eighteen.[54] It was about this time that Churchill told a visitor to Chartwell: 'Modern young people will do what they like. The only time parents really control their children is before they are born. After that their nature unfolds remorselessly petal by petal.'[55]

Diana, the Churchills' eldest child, was married to John Milner Bailey, the eldest son of Sir Abe Bailey, the South African mining magnate, in December 1932, when she was twenty-three. Churchill's present to the couple was 'a cheque', no doubt a generous one; and the reception was attended by 'a large number of Mr Churchill's constituents'.[56] But the marriage did not last long, and Diana obtained a divorce in 1935. She re-married the same year, her second husband being the young Conservative MP Duncan Sandys, who joined Brendan Bracken as a Churchill supporter in the House of Commons. Sarah was sent to school in Paris to learn French before her début, but her main interest was in dancing, and she was eventually allowed to take this up professionally, although it was late to learn. She became a member of C. B. Cochran's chorus of Young Ladies at the Adelphi Theatre, and at the age of twenty-one upset her parents by falling in love with Vic Oliver, an Austrian-born comedian who had lived in America for some years, and who was appearing in Cochran's revue. Her father was particularly alarmed that she might marry Oliver before he became an American citizen, in which case she might find herself 'married to the enemy'.[57]

As Oliver was Jewish there was not really much likelihood of his being a Nazi sympathiser. Sarah followed Oliver to the United States, and when Randolph also followed to cover the 1936 presidential election, it appeared to the newspapers that his primary object was to save his sister from Oliver's clutches. In the end her parents could only consent to the marriage, which took place on Christmas Eve 1936, at the New York City Hall, after Oliver had become an American citizen. They at once returned to England and Oliver was accepted into the family circle. Only Mary, the Churchill's youngest child, remained entirely with her parents: when war broke out she was still under seventeen, and was a devotee of country life, keen on tennis and riding.[58]

In spite of his devotion to Chartwell, Churchill did not fail to take holidays on the Mediterranean much as he had done in the 1920s. In the summer of 1931 he was at Biarritz, where the attraction was the Duke of Westminster's villa and yacht. In 1933 and in other years he was a guest of Maxine Elliott, the wealthy American actress, at her Château de l'Horizon overlooking the Bay of Cannes.[59] In the summer of 1934 he, Randolph, Diana and Lindemann visited Baldwin at Aix-les-Bains, and Churchill talked earnestly to Baldwin about air defence before proceeding to Chamonix. According to Baldwin, who can hardly have enjoyed this intrusion upon his annual holiday, they arrived for the night in two cars hired at Cannes:

> He had never seen Mont Blanc, so he was going there, letting the mountains have a peep at him, and back to England. . . . He described with flashing eyes how the road from the coast to Grenoble was the very road Napoleon had taken on his return from Elba to Paris, and how he felt he must write a book on Napoleon.[60]

Later that year Churchill went abroad again, visiting Palestine and the eastern Mediterranean. At Rhodes he was impressed by the great improvements in the appearance of the city and its inhabitants which had been effected under the Italian rule.[61] He spent much of December and January 1935–6 in Spain and Morocco. He was 'captivated' by Marrakesh and saw its future as 'a formidable competitor to the Côte d'Azur'. The Arab inhabitants delighted him with their many-coloured robes – 'Every peasant is a picture, every crowd a pageant' – and he admired the progress made by the French administration in improving roads and providing good hotels.[62] Churchill was on the Riviera again in the summer of 1936, and early in 1937 he persuaded Maxine Elliott to offer her château to the Duke and Duchess of Windsor in the early months of their exile.[63] They accepted, and evidently liked the château, for it was there that they met Churchill at dinner in January 1938.[64] Churchill's last real holiday before the war came was at Antibes in January 1939. He did not feel at liberty to go further afield, but while he was at Antibes Clementine was visiting the West Indies on Lord Moyne's yacht.[65]

Yet Churchill obviously enjoyed life at Chartwell, where there were considerable opportunities for his organising power as well as for personal recreation. He continued to spend a portion of his time on bricklaying: he completed a wall round a kitchen garden and also built a cottage. He installed a swimming-pool with a system of heating from a furnace, and was able to invite his guests to swim there even on chilly days.[66] He also established a fishery – trout in one pool, golden carp in another. Waterfalls and rockeries were constructed, and according to his nephew Johnnie, who was seeking to make a career as an interior decorator and was employed by his uncle to decorate a loggia with scenes from Marlborough's battles, 'Monstrous lorries panted in from the depths of Wales carrying colossal chunks of mountainside'.[67] Nor were agricultural activities forgotten. Churchill won prizes for pig-breeding at the Edenbridge Fat Stock Show on more than one occasion.[68]

His daily routine was more or less standard: it has been described by various members of the household.[69] Churchill liked to stay in bed until eleven or so, apart from a trip to the bathroom at 6.30 or 7 a.m. for a wash and to clean his teeth. He then read the newspapers – including even the *Daily Worker* – and this was followed by breakfast in bed 'with a menu that often included beef'. After working in bed for a couple of hours, he got up, took a bath, and strolled in the grounds, perhaps to greet his swans and feed the goldfish, and took a glass of whisky and soda before resuming work. Lunch would be at one, and would be something of an occasion, 'accompanied by champagne and followed by port, brandy and a cigar'. He returned to work after lunch, but there would be a break for 'tea', which really meant another whisky and soda at about 5 p.m., and this was followed by a period of about an hour and a half's rest in bed. Then he had another bath before dinner for which Churchill made a point of dressing. This again was an occasion on the lines of lunch; afterwards he often played a game of backgammon with Clementine. At about 11 p.m. began the main period of dictation which lasted until 2 or 3 a.m. He never slept more than seven hours in the twenty-four. He smoked about fifteen cigars a day, but rarely smoked them to the end; if one went out he did not relight it.

'Work' was primarily a matter of dictation, and not of writing. His research assistants would not be expected to draft chapters, but would provide him with the raw material, together with appropriate books, the relevant passages being marked or even cut out. In dictation, Churchill had a habit of whispering the passages to himself as he coined them before he spoke them out to his secretary. Speeches, articles and books all went through this process, and it is not surprising that the books were often long and somewhat rhetorical in form. The dictated draft of a book would be worked on and, when the author was satisfied, would be sent by the publisher to the printer, who would supply half-a-dozen galleys which Churchill distributed to selected friends and advisers for their view. The draft for putting into page proof would be a much-altered version of the original, and further changes would take place before publication. Churchill had a great respect for accuracy of fact, and was determined that the British edition, if not always the American, should be purged of error to the last possible moment. As he wrote his books very quickly, and often started dictation before the evidence was fully assembled, changes at the proof stage were inevitable. Ashley has described the process of dictation:

> He would walk up and down the room (when I worked for him it was usually his bedroom) puffing at a cigar while a secretary patiently took it all down as best she could in Pitman. Occasionally he would say 'Scrub that and start again.' At times he would stop . . .; at others he would be entirely swept on by the stimulus of his imagination.[70]

This routine was not entirely kept up at the weekend, or when friends were visiting. But Churchill now had fewer of the old associates with whom he had been used to spend long hours in conversation. The greatest blow was the death of 'F.E.' in 1930. He tried to comfort 'F.E.'s' son – then an undergraduate of twenty-two – by saying that perhaps even Marlborough would have done better to die in his prime by 'a cannon-ball at Malplaquet' than to drag out a prolonged existence into old age.[71] But this was not really very consoling to those who had lost a friend. A few years later, in 1935, he mourned the loss of T. E. Lawrence, who died after a motor-cycle accident: spectators noticed that he was in tears at the memorial service.[72] As for making new friends, this was less easy than it had been. During his period as an 'India rebel' the Churchills were invited out very little, and he complained about this on one occasion in the presence of Mrs Wallis Simpson.[73] But it must have been due in part at least to the fact that he spent so little time in London. It was not until 1936 that he obtained the lease of a flat in Pimlico, at 11 Morpeth Mansions, near Westminster Cathedral.

Naturally as he grew older he had to find friends in a younger generation. But there were not many who sympathised with his views or who were prepared to accept his style of life. He saw much of Duff Cooper and his lively, attractive wife Diana, both when Duff was in the government and after his resignation over Munich, which Churchill warmly applauded. For the rest, he became more closely attached to his contemporary Bernard Baruch, as a result of Baruch's help to him when he visited the United States, and also because of his shrewd financial advice which shielded him from some at least of the misfortune experienced by many investors during the depression of the early 1930s.[74] Churchill entertained Baruch on visits to Britain, and also looked after friends of his at times; and Baruch gave him a radiogram as a mark of his thanks.[75]

But increasingly Churchill spent his time with men who were his political dependants. Sunday at Chartwell became known as 'Brendan day' because Brendan Bracken so frequently made an appearance then.[76] He was known by political opponents as 'Churchill's jackal' and was indeed his closest supporter.[77] Churchill also saw much of Lindemann – 'the Prof'. When 'the Prof' had a shot at Parliament, standing as an Independent Conservative at the by-election for the Oxford University seat in 1936, Churchill visited Oxford to speak on his behalf – and described him as 'one of the most attractive and fascinating minds I have ever met with'.[78] But it was to no avail, as Lindemann came third in the election.[79] Churchill also championed Duncan Sandys in the Official Secrets case in which the latter became involved in 1938, as a result of preparing to put a parliamentary question based on secret military information. A. P. Herbert discomfited Churchill, who was a member of the Committee of Privileges, by describing him as seeking to be both 'centre-forward and referee' in the case.[80] But Churchill was nothing if not loyal to his friends. In 1937 he initiated legal action to defend the Duke of Windsor against what he regarded as libel in a book by Geoffrey Dennis entitled *Coronation Commentary*.[81]

In November 1934 Churchill celebrated his sixtieth birthday. It was a moment for reassessment. When he had been young he had thought of such an age as very advanced, probably unattainable for himself as it had been for his father and for his uncle, the 8th Duke. When he reached it, he was mildly surprised to find himself apparently as vigorous as ever: it now seemed to him to be a 'noon-day prime' rather than a period of sunset.[82] He had no intention of retiring from politics: but looking ahead, it seemed to him increasingly doubtful whether he would again hold office. His disappointments at the hands of Baldwin and Chamberlain in the late 1930s were all the more severe.

Churchill now experienced some of the consolations of advancing age. In 1929 he was elected Chancellor of Bristol University,[83] and enjoyed giving honorary degrees to such friends as Admiral of the Fleet Sir Roger Keyes and such worthy political opponents as Philip Snowden. This was a permanent post, altogether better than being Rector of a Scottish university for a brief period as the choice of the students, an honour he had experienced before the First World War. Churchill had noticed and had referred publicly to the 'subversive opinions' of students in 1935[84] and probably he was not surprised to be badly defeated for the Lord Rectorship of Glasgow University in 1937 by Canon 'Dick' Sheppard, the pacifist leader.[85]

In mid-September 1933 he and Clementine quietly celebrated their silver wedding anniversary. They spent the day at Chartwell and then motored in to London to dine at a hotel and to go to a theatre.[86] Their friends marked the occasion by giving them a picture of themselves together at breakfast at Chartwell, specially commissioned from William Nicholson.[87] It was an agreeable gesture, although, of course, they never did breakfast together. A few months later Churchill was invited by the *Daily Sketch* to write a piece on what he thought was the greatest social transformation of the preceding twenty-five years. In his view it was 'the arrival of women in almost every field of activity as the equals, the helpers and the rivals of men.... One must regard it as one of the greatest enrichments and liberations that have ever taken place in the whole history of the world.'[88] This was a generous comment, in view of his resistance to the 'flapper vote' in 1928. At times he was still inclined to think that democracy had gone too far, and that there should be a second vote for householders – which he thought would restore 'that specially responsible political democracy to whose exertions and keen discussions the health and the fame of our pre-war parliamentary institutions were largely due'.[89]

But then he still felt himself to be at odds with the 'political nation' as it was. He admitted: 'When I see the nonconformist conscience and the Primrose League, the Church and *The Times* – all these worshipful forces running in full cry together, my inclinations are to go the other way.'[90] It is not surprising that he did not like the way political controversy was excluded from the radio by the collusion of the party whips; and he referred to the BBC's 'copious stream of pontifical anonymous mugwumpery' with scorn.[91] He had told Reith in 1930 that he was 'not aware that parties had any legal basis at all, or that they had been formally brought into your licence'.[92] In the summer of 1931 he took up with J. H. Whitley, the chairman of the BBC governors, the case for being allowed to broadcast about India, and when he obtained only a promise of later consideration he wrote:

It is a bad cause which cannot afford to face free and responsible discussion and the statements of both sides. I can only regard your refusal as a definite part of the attempt which is being made to lull and chloroform the British people into a fatal decision.[93]

But Churchill found it a struggle to be a prophet of gloom. As he admitted:

I must confess to having a sanguine disposition. Although I see so harshly the dark side of things, yet by a queer contradiction I wake each morning with new hope and energy revived. I believe intensely that the British people are still masters of their own destinies and I have the feeling that time will be given them to repair their past mistakes and negligence.[94]

All the same, even some of his own friends began to notice signs of age and weariness. Duff Cooper discussed with Liddell Hart in January 1936 the suggestion that Churchill might become Minister of Defence, only to dismiss it:

He was not so quick as he had been in grasping points. D.C. went on to reflect that one would have thought that at Winston's present age, and after holding so many high offices, he would have been content to settle down philosophically to become an elder statesman and to devote himself to letters.[95]

But Churchill had shown in the past a remarkable capacity to respond to the responsibilities of high office. As he put it in an article on the Premiership in 1934:

I do not believe in this legend of the intolerable strain of the Premiership. . . . There is an old saying that God gives men strength as they need it. In my own experience there is something in the challenge of a crisis, in knowing that vital issues depend upon him, that draws hidden reserves in a man's nature and makes him rise to the height of a great occasion.[96]

It was the more surprising when early in 1938 it was announced that Churchill was offering Chartwell for sale – and apparently intending to retire to a small cottage which he had built on the estate.[97] His intentions are not clear – it would be puzzling if he were short of money, and it may be that it was his object to relieve Clementine of the burden of running the house. At all events, after only three weeks he withdrew the offer, and announced instead that he merely proposed to sell some of the outlying parts of the estate.[98] And so when war came in 1939 Churchill still owned Chartwell, though he was not to see much of it for a six-year period.

20. *First Lord Again*

On Friday, September 1st, at dawn, the German invasion of
Poland began. The mobilisation of British forces was ordered
in the morning, and in the afternoon Churchill was invited by
Chamberlain to visit him at 10 Downing Street. Chamberlain
invited Churchill to join a small War Cabinet of six ministers,
mostly without departments. He mentioned that he was thinking
in terms of an immediate Coalition of all the major parties, and
that he had sent invitations to both the Liberals and the Labour
leaders, but that while the Liberals were still hesitating it did
not look as if Labour was likely to accept. Even Churchill's
appointment would have to wait until the crisis had resolved
itself; and as the French government was unwilling to declare
war immediately – partly so as to allow time for mobilisation
before having to face air attack – Chamberlain was able to use
the following day (September 2nd) for last-minute efforts to keep
the peace. Churchill had to wait at his flat in Pimlico, whence on
the early morning of the 2nd he wrote to Chamberlain pointing
out that the average age of the six proposed members of the War
Cabinet was sixty-four – 'only one year short of the Old Age
Pension!' He himself was slightly above this average age: 'If
however you added Sinclair (49) and Eden (42) the average comes
down to $57\frac{1}{2}$.'[1] Churchill evidently favoured the addition of these
friends of his to help against the massed weight of the Chamberlainites.

In view of his pending appointment, Churchill was not in a
position to speak in the Commons debate that took place on the
evening of the 2nd. It was clear that the mood of Parliament was

for war, in fulfilment of the obligation to Poland, and that Chamberlain's statement which lacked any indication of the despatch of an ultimatum to Germany was thought very unsatisfactory. Churchill wrote to him again that evening asking to know what the position was: 'It seems to me that entirely different ideas have ruled from those which you expressed to me when you said "the die was cast".'[2] Churchill also asked again for reconsideration of the composition of the War Cabinet. In the meantime he remained in a state of great impatience at his flat in Pimlico, listening to the radio. At 11.15 on the morning of the 3rd (Sunday) he heard Chamberlain's gloomy announcement that a final ultimatum to Germany sent at 9 a.m. had expired at 11, and that the country was at war. Almost immediately an air-raid warning was sounded, and he and Clementine went onto the roof to see a balloon barrage going up into the clear sky. They then made their way to an air-raid shelter a hundred yards down the street, 'armed with a bottle of brandy and other appropriate medical comforts'.[3] After about ten minutes, the 'all clear' was sounded, and Churchill went off to the House of Commons, which met at noon.

In the debate that took place on a government motion to approve the declaration of war, Churchill declared his satisfaction at the way in which the country had come together to face the challenge of Hitler's aggression. Chamberlain asked to see him at the House in the Prime Minister's room, and announced that he had now decided to have the Service ministers in the War Cabinet – with the result that he could now offer Churchill the post of First Lord of the Admiralty. Churchill accepted this readily, and sent word to the Admiralty that he would arrive at 6 p.m. that day – albeit in advance of kissing hands at the Palace, a ceremony which had to wait for two days. The Board of Admiralty thereupon signalled to the Fleet 'Winston is back'.[4] In the meantime, Churchill went off to lunch with the Olivers at their flat in Westminster Gardens. They opened a bottle of champagne and Churchill proposed the toast of 'Victory'.[5] After lunch he took his usual nap before going to keep his appointment at the Admiralty.

During his years out of office Churchill had kept in touch with the progress of the navy, but he still had much to learn when he resumed the post of First Lord. He was familiar, of course, with his office at Admiralty House, and could give instructions for furniture and charts which he knew to be brought out again. But he had to get to know a large number of senior officers who when he had last been First Lord were not more than midshipmen. He appointed Brendan Bracken as his Parliamentary Private Secretary; and it was Bracken who re-introduced him to an officer who was to accompany him a great deal during the war – Commander C. B. Thompson, who had occupied since 1936 the new post of Flag Lieutenant to the Board of Admiralty.[6] He asked Thompson to organise weekly dinner-parties on Tuesday evenings, at which he could meet members of his staff and also senior diplomats and officers of the other services.[7] He also arranged to move into Admiralty House and to occupy a flat above his office as in 1913 – though this did not happen for some days.

Before he moved into Admiralty House Churchill entertained some of his senior colleagues at Morpeth Mansions. On one occasion he was dining with the Admiralty Controller and Third Sea Lord, Rear-Admiral B. A. Fraser, when he was summoned to the telephone to receive a personal call from President Roosevelt.[8] The call was probably about the torpedoing of the liner *Athenia* on the day that war was declared, with the loss of American lives, and it was also a first verbal exchange in what was to be an intimate inter-communication, mostly by telegram, between the American President and 'Former Naval Person', as Churchill was later to describe himself. Churchill had just received from King George VI a detailed account of a conversation between King and President at the latter's country home at Hyde Park, New York State, in the late spring of 1939, from which it was apparent that Roosevelt was willing to do all he could to support the Allied cause.[9]

Churchill also made arrangements to ensure that Admiralty House was properly provided with information. There was to be close to his own private apartments an Upper War Room, with maps on which all naval movements were plotted by a staff under the direction of Commander Richard Pim, RNVR.[10] With the help of Lloyd's, merchant shipping movements were also indicated, and Churchill became very interested in the problem of speeding up the loading and unloading of ships. At Churchill's invitation Professor Lindemann also moved into Admiralty House and with the assistance of statisticians and economists set up a

'Statistical Department', for which there was some precedent in the later years of the First World War. Lindemann's 'S Branch' as it was called built up its strength slowly: he first asked Roy Harrod, his colleague at Christ Church, Oxford, to suggest a promising academic economist, and Harrod suggested Donald McDougall, then a young lecturer at Leeds, and a man who was to have a distinguished career as a public servant. But Lindemann's organisation continued to grow, and at the end of 1939 he persuaded Harrod himself to join.[11]

The First Sea Lord was Admiral Sir Dudley Pound, a strong but silent man whom Churchill, warned by experience, treated warily at first but gradually came to respect more and more. Admiral Fraser, the Third Sea Lord, has recorded his impression of Churchill's first Board Meeting:

> As he once again took the First Lord's chair in the famous Board Room, Churchill was filled with emotion. To a few words of welcome from the First Sea Lord he replied by saying what a privilege and honour it was to be again in that chair, that there were many difficulties ahead but together we would overcome them. He surveyed critically each one of us in turn and then, adding that he would see us all personally later on, he adjourned the meeting. 'Gentlemen', he said, 'to your tasks and duties.'[12]

On the whole, Churchill found the efficiency of the navy to be reassuring. Germany was so far the only enemy, and Hitler had not given priority to naval building – which in any case took years rather than months for the larger vessels. It was true, nevertheless, that the British superiority was in ships which had been laid down in or before the First World War. Churchill made it his business to visit the fleet at its various bases round the coast of Britain. On the night of Thursday September 14th he went north to pay a visit to the Home Fleet, taking with him his old friend Sir Archibald Sinclair, the Liberal leader, whose estates were in Caithness, and also Brendan Bracken and Commander Thompson.[13] He was the guest of the Commander-in-Chief, Admiral Sir Charles Forbes, in his flagship the battleship *Nelson* at Scapa Flow, and in the *Nelson* he visited the rest of the fleet which was hiding on the north-west coast of Scotland at Loch Ewe. His visit to Loch Ewe took place twenty-five years to the day after a similar visit in 1914. He was presented to the officers, and found it an odd experience:

The perfect discipline, style and bearing, the ceremonial routine – all were unchanged. But an entirely different generation filled the uniforms and the posts. Only the ships had most of them been laid down in my tenure. None of them was new.[14]

He discussed the need for greater precautions to protect the fleet against submarine and aircraft attack. Returning to London by train on the night of 18th/19th he was met at Euston Station by the First Sea Lord, who had to report the sinking of the aircraft-carrier *Courageous* by torpedo in the Bristol Channel, with the loss of about 500 men, which was almost half the crew.

It was decided to allow the press to report the sinking immediately, but Churchill felt that there was a need for him to give an early account to the House of Commons on the first weeks of the naval war. On September 26th he made a statement indicating progress in establishing a convoy system for merchant shipping, in arming merchant ships for their own protection, and in actually sinking U-boats. He claimed six or seven already sunk, but this was due to exaggerated claims, for in fact only two were sunk in the month of September.[15] But the statement satisfied the House for other reasons also – because of its clear and vigorous expression and its display of confidence. Churchill referred to the struggle against the U-boats as 'hard, wide-spread and bitter, a war of groping and drowning, a war of ambuscade and stratagem, a war of science and seamanship'.[16] The Opposition leaders greeted the speech warmly: Attlee called it a 'robust, vigorous statement' and Sinclair described it as 'a speech of rare power, a fighting speech from a fighting minister, which is a strong and appropriate tonic for Parliament and the people of this country in wartime'.[17] There was obviously much to be said for letting the Opposition leaders see how the war was being fought.

In mid-October the value of good public relations became still more apparent, for in what Churchill publicly admitted to be 'a remarkable exploit of professional skill and daring'[18] a U-boat succeeded in penetrating the Scapa defences and sank the battleship *Royal Oak* as she lay at anchor. Some 786 officers and men, including the Admiral, perished with the ship as she capsized. As a newly appointed First Lord Churchill was able to escape responsibility for the disaster. Hoare, the Lord Privy Seal, who was inclined to be jealous of him, said that he did it 'by squaring Alexander',[19] and it is true that good relations existed between

Churchill and the Labour spokesman on naval affairs. Early in November Churchill told the Commons:

> I do not intend to embark upon a judicial enquiry with a view to assigning blame to individuals. Such a course would impose an additional burden upon those who, afloat and ashore, are engaged in an intense and deadly, and as may well be thought, not wholly unsuccessful struggle.[20]

Admiral of the Fleet Sir Roger Keyes backed him up by saying,

> In my opinion, and I am sure that it is the opinion of the whole Naval Service, if the Right Hon. Gentleman had been in office for a few months before the war there would have been no question of any state of unreadiness in any of our ports.[21]

But Hoare wrote to Lothian, the Ambassador at Washington:

> Winston has been through a rough sea over the Scapa incidents. Being for the moment the war hero he has won through it fairly well. I shudder to think what would have happened if there had been another First Lord and he had been in Opposition.[22]

To some extent Hoare's attitude reflected the views that he found among the junior ministers on the Home Policy Committee, whom he described in his diary as being 'irritable' because 'Not in the Cabinet and resentment against the service ministers for getting the credit e.g. Churchill on the freedom of the seas and they getting the kicks for restrictions & regulations.'[23]

But it was not all easy going for the First Lord, and at this time the navy had to face a further, more general problem of German ingenuity in the form of the magnetic mine. There was nothing novel in the use of the magnetic principle for mines at sea, but the operating system of the German type had to be worked out by experiments on a recovered sample. In late November one was found on mudflats in the Thames estuary, and as soon as it had been disarmed by a brave and skilful team it revealed its secrets. Arrangements could then be made for the de-magnetising, or 'de-gaussing' as it was called, of British merchant ships.[24]

The story of the magnetic mines had to remain secret for the time being; and Churchill had all the more reason to hope for something like the Battle of the Falkland Islands in the First

World War to re-establish his reputation as First Lord. It was evident that two of the enemy 'pocket battleships' – those built under the restrictions of the Treaty of Versailles – were at large in the Atlantic; and the Admiralty organised 'hunting groups' of aircraft carriers and battleships to track them down. The *Graf Spee*, which was one of the ships concerned, working in the south Atlantic, for some time acted with care and made relatively few attacks on merchant shipping; but on December 13th she was encountered by a patrol force of cruisers employed to protect British shipping at the River Plate – in fact not far from the Falkland Islands. For cruisers to engage a battleship, even a pocket battleship, was a formidable undertaking, and the squadron was weakened by the absence of its most powerful ship, the heavy cruiser *Cumberland*, which was undergoing repairs. Against the eleven-inch guns of the *Graf Spee*, Commodore Henry Harwood, the officer in command, had one cruiser with eight-inch guns, the *Exeter*, and two with six-inch, the *Ajax* and *Achilles*. But he was not deterred from fighting it out, and skilfully manœuvred his three ships so as to confuse the enemy fire. After eighty minutes the engagement was rather surprisingly broken off by the *Graf Spee*, which made rapidly for the neutral port of Montevideo. She had sustained some serious damage, but not proportionately as much as the *Exeter*. Indeed the *Exeter* was obliged to abandon the pursuit, and for some time there were only the two six-inch-gun cruisers maintaining the blockade of the port until the *Cumberland* arrived on the evening of the 14th. It was December 17th when the *Graf Spee* re-emerged from Montevideo, only to blow herself up in the estuary. Her captain then committed suicide.

The remarkable success of the three cruisers in accounting for an enemy battleship was received with great enthusiasm in Britain, and Churchill planned a rousing reception for the crews of the *Exeter* and *Ajax* on their return to home ports in mid-February 1940. (The *Achilles* was a New Zealand ship, and returned to port there.) The two crews were brought to London and inspected by the King, who held a public investiture of officers and men, and they were then entertained to lunch at the Guildhall by the Lord Mayor. To add savour to the occasion, the destroyer *Cossack* by venturing into Norwegian territorial waters had just released 299 prisoners from the *Altmark*, a supply ship which had been working with the *Graf Spee* but which had escaped capture in the south Atlantic. The prisoners were the crews of ships that had been sunk by the *Graf Spee*, and it was an infringement of Norwegian neutrality for the *Altmark* to seek to smuggle them to Germany in such a fashion. But the action to release them was also an infringement of neutrality by the British navy, and Churchill had to 'put a good screw upon the Foreign Office' to obtain authority for it.[25]

Meanwhile as a member of the War Cabinet Churchill was turning his mind to the more general issues of the war. From September 4th 1939 the War Cabinet with few exceptions met daily, and sometimes twice a day. It was a large body of people who assembled for its sessions, consisting not only of the nine official members, but also of Sir John Anderson, the Home Secretary and Minister of Home Security, and Anthony Eden, the Dominions Secretary, both of whom were entitled to attend; and also of the Chiefs of Staff of the Services and several secretaries. Churchill would have preferred to have some meetings at least without outsiders present, so that he could air his views more directly to his colleagues; and towards the end of September he urged this on the Prime Minister. With the aid of the 'S Branch' he also bombarded his colleagues with correspondence on the problems of their departments, and he wrote frequently to the Prime Minister about general policy. Chamberlain did not reply very fully, and as early as September 15th Churchill commented rather tartly:

> I hope you will consider carefully what I write to you. I do so only in my desire to aid you in your responsibilities and discharge my own.

The Prime Minister replied next day:

> All your letters are carefully read and considered by me, and if I have not replied to them it is only because I am seeing you every day, and moreover because, as far as I have been able to observe, your views and mine have very closely coincided.[26]

All the same, it seems to have been mostly pressure from Churchill which persuaded his colleagues to accept the target of an army of fifty-five divisions. This was decided by the Land Forces

Committee of the War Cabinet, which met at the Home Office under the chairmanship of Hoare, the Lord Privy Seal. Churchill felt that it was the least that Britain and her Commonwealth nations could do to assist France on the Western Front.[27]

Churchill was also interested in the idea of a Northern Front. From the earliest days of his return to the Admiralty he began to plan an operation for forcing a passage into the Baltic. The idea was that two or more battleships of the *Royal Sovereign* class should be raised by the addition of caissons so as to enable them to pass the narrows between Denmark and Sweden. Their armour was to be increased so as to protect them more effectively from air attack; and with supporting vessels Churchill thought at first that a fleet could cruise in the Baltic almost indefinitely. The operation was to be known as 'Catherine'. But by January 1940 he was beginning to have second thoughts about the project, as the problem of air attack had not really been solved.[28] He also had two other secret plans, less directly appropriate for the Admiralty, but quite in the tradition that he himself had established in the First World War. One was a powerful excavator designed to cut a way through minefields and other obstacles on land: it was known as 'Cultivator'. The other was a plan for dropping floating mines in the Rhine, known as 'Operation Royal Marine'.[29]

Finally, Churchill wished to put a barrier of mines in the Norwegian 'leads' or coastal waters, so as to prevent shipping from the port of Narvik moving down to German ports with supplies of iron ore from northern Sweden. This would involve an infringement of Norwegian neutrality, and there was opposition from the Foreign Office and also from the Dominions. After a meeting of the War Cabinet on January 15th Churchill complained to a colleague of the 'immense walls of prevention, all built and building' that frustrated any proposal to attack the enemy.[30] For the first time he was invited in early February to accompany the Prime Minister to a meeting of the Supreme War Council in Paris. This gave him an opportunity of experiencing some of the difficulties at first hand, for the French did not want to take any initiative likely to open up the war on the Western Front.[31]

Churchill also found time to see Sumner Welles, President Roosevelt's special emissary to the warring powers, on his visit to

Britain in mid-March. Churchill received him at the Admiralty and according to Sumner Welles's report

> commenced an address which lasted exactly an hour and fifty minutes, and during which I was never given the opportunity to say a word. It constituted a cascade of oratory, brilliant and always effective, interlarded with considerable wit. It would have impressed me more had I not already read his book *Step by Step* (of which, incidentally, he gave me an autographed copy before I left) and of which his address to me constituted a rehash.

Welles was also taken to see the War Room and thought it was 'a demonstration of extraordinary efficiency, and I assume one of the reasons why British shipping losses have not been more severe'.[32] Churchill told him that the Germans had lost 43 U-boats, but this was an exaggeration, since only 22 had been sunk by mid-April.

On the question of the number of U-boat sinkings, Churchill had already come into conflict with his Director of Naval Intelligence, Rear-Admiral John Godfrey. He thought that Godfrey's figures, which were much more conservative, presented a gloomy picture, and he therefore insisted that they should be circulated only to Pound and to Rear-Admiral Tom Phillips, the Deputy Chief of Naval Staff, apart from himself. Godfrey was to begin with invited to attend whenever Churchill was composing a broadcast – in order to check the facts; but not later on. His recollection was of

> a most efficient secretary-typist, a completely silent typewriter, three copies on half sheets of foolscap, two long drinks and two enormous cigars, and Mr Churchill walking up and down dictating, clad in a dishevelled dinner jacket and dropping cigar ash and spilling whisky and soda over his waistcoat.... My interruptions and minor suggestions were welcomed and acted on.... One [copy] was for me to take away and fill in details by 10 a.m. next day. The whole was then reduced to a sort of blank verse, which I have since seen in the BBC records, and it was from this that he addressed the world.[33]

Later on, Churchill's companions on these late-night dictating sessions would be more likely to include Lindemann and Phillips and perhaps Geoffrey Shakespeare, the Admiralty's Parliamentary Secretary. Shakespeare wrote in his memoirs:

> I can see him now in my mind's eye dictating a speech, wearing an old pair of bedroom slippers and padding up and down his room

like a caged lion, hands behind his back, head bent forward. A cigar always protruded from his mouth and through thick clouds of smoke he hissed scintillating sentences at the silent typewriter. He had no prepared notes; he had not even jotted down headlines on the order of his speech. All those distinguished phrases which characterise his speeches came out fashioned spontaneously in the furnace of his imagination.[34]

Meanwhile at the end of November Russia had attacked Finland to secure concessions which would provide a more effective line of defence in the north. The Finns resisted gallantly and succeeded in throwing back the Russian advance; but their success could only be temporary. They appealed to the League of Nations, whose Council and Assembly with remarkable speed both passed resolutions in December denouncing Russia and declaring her to be no longer a member. With a temporary deadlock in the fighting between Russia and Finland the War Cabinet in London began to think of ways of combining assistance to Finland with the original object of cutting Germany off from her supplies of Swedish iron ore. After much argument which extended throughout January and in which Churchill was the leading 'hawk' a plan was put to the French at a meeting of the Supreme War Council; and it was apparent that this was something which they were prepared to approve. Troops were to be put ashore at Narvik under the guise of 'volunteers', and were to make their way through Norway and Sweden; but they were to leave a force near the ore deposits.[35] All the same, the troops would not be ready to sail before mid-March, and in the intervening period the position of the Finnish army became more and more difficult. The governments of Norway and Sweden showed no sign of willingness to let Allied troops through their territory; and so on March 13th the Finns capitulated to the Russians, and the opportunity was lost. One early result was the fall of the Daladier government in France, and its replacement by a new ministry under Paul Reynaud, a man distinctly more congenial to Churchill than Daladier.

The War Cabinet now sought the agreement of the new French government to two simultaneous actions – the mining of the Norwegian leads and the laying of fluvial mines in the Rhine ('Operation Royal Marine'). Both were to take place on April 5th. But the French government, and in particular Daladier – no longer Premier but still a man of power – maintained hostility to 'Operation Royal Marine' for fear of reprisals, and in the end the British decided to go ahead with the mining of the leads only – and this was postponed to April 8th. Meanwhile the Germans had prepared and put into operation a far bolder measure. On the following night (that of April 8th/9th) German troops landed from transports under naval escort at all the main Norwegian ports, including Narvik in the far north. There was a simultaneous invasion of Denmark, largely by land; and as the Danish forces were too weak to offer any effective resistance Copenhagen airport was soon being used by the Germans for flying reinforcements to Norway.

There ensued a period of desperate open struggle between the British and German navies along the coast of Norway. To begin with, Churchill was very optimistic about the 'strategic and political error' which he thought that Hitler had committed.[36] The larger ships of the German navy were deliberately used as a decoy to lead the British navy away from the invading troops – a ruse that was very successful. Bad weather and superior intelligence enabled these German heavy forces to escape detection on their way home. But on the night of April 9th a force of five British destroyers entered the Narvik Fjord, and in spite of having encountered a larger force of enemy destroyers proceeded, with the advantage of surprise, to sink two of them and to damage others. The luck turned against them after a time, however, and they lost two of their ships on the way out.[37] When Churchill reported to the House of Commons on April 11th he did not make a good impression, partly because he was very tired, partly because he had little good news. Nicolson wrote in his diary:

When he rises to speak it is obvious that he is very tired. He starts off by giving an imitation of himself making a speech, and he indulges in vague oratory coupled with tired gibes. I have seldom seen him to less advantage.... He hesitates, gets his notes in the wrong order, puts on the wrong pair of spectacles, fumbles for the right pair, keeps on saying 'Sweden' when he means 'Denmark' and one way and another makes a lamentable performance.[38]

There was better news on April 13th. On that day the battleship *Warspite*, accompanied by a strong force of destroyers, entered the Narvik Fjord and demolished the eight remaining German destroyers without the loss of a single British ship.[39] It now looked as if the enemy hold in north Norway was somewhat tenuous; but their grip on the south was rapidly strengthening. Trondheim, in central Norway, seemed to be the pivotal point; and so the Military Co-ordination Committee of the War Cabinet, of which Churchill was the chairman, decided to send troops to points north and south of this port, in the hope that a pincer movement would lead to its capture. The decision was made in the small hours of the morning on April 14th, and troopships were diverted from a convoy already on the way to Narvik after Churchill and Phillips had called on General Ironside, the Chief of the Imperial General Staff, at the War Office.[40] This occurred in the absence of Oliver Stanley, the War Minister, who went to complain to Chamberlain later in the day. As Ironside put it, 'We cannot have a man trying to supervise all military arrangements as if he were a company commander running a small operation to cross a bridge.'[41]

The Military Co-ordination Committee was a body consisting of ministers and staff chiefs originally under the chairmanship of Lord Chatfield, the Minister for the Co-ordination of Defence; but he had resigned from the government on April 3rd, saying correctly enough that he was 'a fifth wheel to the coach', and Churchill had taken his place as chairman of the committee.[42] As its name implied, it was not a body which could dictate to any particular service – or if it did it was liable to suffer protests such as Oliver Stanley's. After a few more days of trying both to run the committee and to control the Admiralty, Churchill persuaded Chamberlain to take his place as its chairman, and thus to give it his superior authority.[43]

Meanwhile, things were not going well for the Allied cause in Norway. The strength of German air power impressed itself disagreeably upon the British forces. Churchill had thought that well-armoured ships with anti-aircraft guns could hold their own against attacking bombers; but the record of the campaign showed that this was not always the case. He was tempted to interfere in operational matters which were strictly the province of Forbes, the Commander-in-Chief; and he later admitted that in one affair – the cancellation of an intended attack upon the port of Bergen – 'the Admiralty kept too close a control upon the Commander-in-Chief'.[44] More important, however, was the abandonment on April 19th of a proposed direct naval assault on Trondheim, on the unanimous advice of the Chiefs of Staff and their deputies.[45]

It became apparent a few days later that the Allied campaign in central Norway could not succeed. The enemy with good bases in the south was extending his grip inland, and the Allied forces were short of obvious requirements such as artillery and aircraft. In late April, after the troops had been fighting for less than two weeks, orders were given for the evacuation of central Norway – an operation that was undertaken with the navy's customary skill. At the beginning of May Chamberlain agreed that Churchill should resume the chair of the Military Co-ordination Committee, but with increased powers: he was to have direct access to the Chiefs of Staff, the momentary assumption of which had been the object of Oliver Stanley's complaint; he was to have his own staff headed by Major-General Ismay, a Marine officer, who was to be an additional member of the Chiefs of Staff Committee; and he was thus to be a virtual Minister of Defence, so far as operations were concerned.[46] But by this time disappointment at the failure of Allied arms in Norway was rapidly mounting, and this took the form of parliamentary opposition to the Chamberlain government.

The political base of the Chamberlain government was still very narrow. Churchill, although quite able to work with the Prime Minister on matters of policy, was surprised at the extent of his bitterness towards other able ex-minsters, themselves also Conservatives, who had disagreed with him at the time of Munich. In December Chamberlain had decided to replace Hore-Belisha as Minister of War, and Churchill, who was consulted in advance, was in favour of the appointment of Anthony Eden to this post – as were Halifax and Kingsley Wood, though Hoare favoured Archibald Sinclair so as to bring the Liberals in.[47] Chamberlain would not have either suggestion, and appointed instead Oliver Stanley, one of his more faithful followers. The idea of finding a place for Leopold Amery or Duff Cooper was also anathema to the Prime Minister – who undoubtedly in this way encouraged opposition in the Commons.[48] Eden had pointed to the contrast at the top level in government when he dined with his former subordinate at the Foreign Office, Oliver Harvey, early in October: 'He said how inspiring and refreshing Winston was in Cabinet. P.M. still looked at everything personally and would not consider using anybody whom he disliked on personal grounds, e.g. Amery.'[49]

Meanwhile Churchill's personal popularity among the general public was steadily increasing, for people were impressed with the vigour that he showed as First Lord of the Admiralty. His world broadcasts, delivered about once a month, made their mark in Britain also. His description of the navy's enthusiasm for killing U-boats was widely approved: he said they were being hunted, 'I will not say without mercy, because God forbid we should ever part company with that, but at any rate with zeal and not altogether without relish'.[50] At the turn of the year, although the majority of people polled by the Gallup organisation still preferred Chamberlain as Prime Minister, getting on for a third (30%) said that they would prefer Churchill.[51] But this was in answer to a question that deliberately posed the alternatives of Chamberlain and Churchill as Premier. Early in April, the question was put, 'If Mr Chamberlain was to retire, who would you like to succeed him as Prime Minister?' In reply more people chose Eden (28%) than Churchill (25%) – Halifax (7%), Attlee (6%) and Lloyd George (5%) were among the 'also ran'.[52]

There had for some time been a group of anti-Munich Conservative MPs meeting weekly under the chairmanship of Leopold Amery.[53] There was also an All-Party Action Group chaired by Clement Davies, a Liberal member, which met to discuss policy questions behind closed doors.[54] More influential still was a 'Watching Committee' formed early in April by the Marquess of Salisbury, to consist of Conservatives drawn from both Houses of Parliament.[55] The leading anti-Munich Conservatives were able to use this body to see the crystallisation of anti-Chamberlain feeling in late April, after the failure of British operations in central Norway. They did not see Churchill, however, as the obvious successor to Chamberlain. Harold Nicolson, although a warm admirer of Churchill, regarded Lloyd George as a more likely Prime Minister, in spite of his years – he was now seventy-seven.[56] As late as May 6th the *Daily Mail* came out for a change of government with an anonymous politician – in fact, Sir Stafford Cripps – recommending Halifax as Prime Minister.

The critical Commons debate on the Norwegian campaign began next day (May 7th). The Labour Opposition tabled a motion of censure, but at first it was not decided to press it to a division. Clement Davies, however, played a vital role by deciding, after discussion with Amery and others, that this was the moment for a demonstration of feeling by the House, and by urging Attlee to demand a vote.[57] Attlee agreed to the suggestion and with the assistance of his colleague Herbert Morrison persuaded the rest of the Labour Front Bench. Morrison also informed Lloyd George of the importance of the occasion, and asked him to attend, which he did.[58]

The debate, which lasted two days, was full of misunderstandings and misinterpretations. Churchill's faithful friend, Admiral of the Fleet Sir Roger Keyes, appeared in full uniform to deplore the cancellation of plans to send the fleet in at Trondheim, in which he saw a parallel to Fisher's revolt against Churchill over the Dardanelles. Lloyd George also misunderstood Churchill's defence of his own policies and warned him not to 'allow himself to be converted into an air raid shelter to keep the splinters from hitting his colleagues'.[59] Churchill spoke in defence of the government with all his usual vigour – as well he might. He also made a powerful plea for national unity:

> Let party interest be ignored, let all our energies be harnessed, let the whole ability and forces of the nation be hurled into the struggle, and let all the strong horses be pulling on the collar.[60]

But it was probably the direct denunciation of Chamberlain by Amery, the senior Conservative backbencher, that made the greatest impact. He invoked the words of Cromwell to the Long Parliament, concluding 'In the name of God, go'.[61] When the House divided on the evening of May 8th, the Opposition lobby, as Hugh Dalton noted in his diary, 'seemed to be full of young Conservatives in uniform, khaki, Navy blue and Air Force blue all intermingled.'[62] In fact the revolt against Chamberlain's leadership was not as substantial as it might have been: the government's majority dropped from its usual figure of over two hundred to no more than eighty-one. This was accounted for by about forty changing sides, and by perhaps rather more abstaining or being absent.

A government with a majority of eighty-one would not normally be in danger of collapse. But wartime conditions, requiring as they did sacrifices from all sections of the community, were far from normal: as David Margesson, the government Chief Whip, put it, the voting figures made little difference for 'the Government was doomed since a Coalition was impossible under poor Neville'.[63] After the debate Chamberlain decided to explore once more the possibility of persuading the Opposition parties to accept office under his own leadership. Meanwhile on May 9th Churchill lunched with Eden and Kingsley Wood, the latter being a Cabinet Minister who had hitherto been very loyal to Chamberlain. Although lacking in military experience himself, Kingsley Wood sensed that Chamberlain was an unsatisfactory leader for a nation at war, whereas Churchill had the necessary vigour and will to fill the part. He advised Churchill, when he was invited by Chamberlain to give his views on the suitability of Halifax as Prime Minister, to fall silent and thus to refrain from giving any encouragement to the idea.[64]

That afternoon (May 9th) Churchill had the opportunity to put the advice to the test. Chamberlain sent for him and Halifax and also for Margesson. He told them that he was going to resign and he asked Margesson to say who should be his successor. Margesson, however, refused to choose between Churchill and Halifax, and Churchill himself said nothing. As he put it in his *Second World War*, 'Usually I talk a great deal, but on this occasion I was silent.' There was 'a very long pause', and then Halifax said that as a peer it would be awkward for him to become Prime Minister.[65] It was evident that this was no more than an excuse and that Halifax simply did not want the job – at any rate in wartime. He realised that Churchill would be 'running the war anyway' and that he (Halifax) would soon be only a sort of honorary Prime Minister.[66] Churchill then realised that the responsibility was passing to himself, and said that he 'would have no communication with either of the opposition parties until I had the King's Commission to form a Government'.[67] In this curiously negative fashion he indicated his acceptance of the highest office in the land.

Meanwhile the long-awaited German attack on the Western Front was about to begin. Early on the morning of May 10th the assault began – first, it appeared, on Holland and France only, but within a few minutes also on Belgium. Chamberlain began to think his government should continue in view of the emergency; and also that the priority that he had given to the Western Front had been justified by events.[68] But Kingsley Wood took the responsibility of urging him to give way at once; and so Chamberlain decided to wait only for the formal reply from the leaders of the Labour Party, who had gone down to Bournemouth for their party conference, about whether they would join the government and, if so, under whose leadership. He did, however, make a last bid to get Halifax to agree to be Premier, and he asked his Parliamentary Private Secretary, Lord Dunglass (later Sir Alec Douglas-Home) to telephone the Foreign Office to ask the Under-Secretary there, R. A. Butler, if he could persuade Halifax to change his mind. But Butler could do nothing in the short time that was available, as Halifax had slipped out to the dentist.[69]

At 5 p.m. Attlee telephoned from Bournemouth, where the National Executive of the Labour Party had been in session, to say that 'The Labour Party are prepared to take their share of responsibility as a full partner in a new Government, under a new Prime Minister, which would command the confidence of the nation.'[70] The words 'under a new Prime Minister' look as if they had been inserted as an afterthought, and Dalton says in his memoirs that this was in fact the case, and that he had inserted them, wishing to make it entirely clear that the party was hostile to joining a Chamberlain government.[71] Chamberlain took the sense of the message as a definite instruction to quit:

> The Prime Minister said that, in the light of this answer, he had reached the conclusion that the right course was that he should at once tender his resignation to the King. He proposed to do so that evening.[72]

At about 6 p.m., therefore, Chamberlain went to the Palace to resign and to advise the King to send for Churchill. About half an hour later Churchill was in his turn summoned to the Palace; according to his own account the King

> looked at me searchingly and quizzically for some moments, and then said, 'I suppose you don't know why I have sent for you?' Adopting his mood, I replied, 'Sir, I simply couldn't imagine why.' He laughed and said, 'I want to ask you to form a Government.' I said I would certainly do so.[73]

It seems, from the King's own account of the meeting, that he accepted Churchill's reaction as genuine surprise, and believed that he really did not know why he had been summoned to the Palace.[74] But, as we have seen, Churchill was well aware of the political situation, though of course he wished to have the King's formal invitation to form a government.

436

Churchill now returned to the Admiralty, where he took the first measures to set up his War Cabinet. He left a message at 10 Downing Street for Attlee and his deputy, Arthur Greenwood, who were on their way back from Bournemouth, asking to see them at the Admiralty; and when he saw them at about 9.30 p.m. he invited them to join his War Cabinet of 'five, or it might be six' members.[75] He also indicated that various other appointments would be made from the leadership of the Labour Party and the Trades Union Congress; and Attlee and Greenwood, who were careful to follow the strict rules of their party about joining a government, telephoned the outline of the proposals to the National Executive in Bournemouth – with Dalton acting as the messenger.[76] Attlee and Greenwood resisted a proposal that Chamberlain should return to his old post of Chancellor of the Exchequer – a proposal that Churchill probably did not put to Chamberlain personally – and also that Chamberlain should be not only Lord President but also Leader of the House. The latter appointment had already been offered to Chamberlain and accepted, but on the insistence of the Labour leaders it was withdrawn before publication.[77] Halifax was to continue as Foreign Secretary.

After the Labour Party Executive had agreed to the terms, this list of ministers – five in all, including Churchill himself – was submitted to the King; and Churchill himself assumed the title of 'Minister of Defence' as well as Prime Minister. When he retired to bed in the small hours of May 11th it was, as he has himself said, not so much with a feeling that he had assumed a new burden but rather 'conscious of a profound sense of relief'.[78] He could now give directions over the whole field of government, and he 'felt as if I were walking with destiny, and that all my past life had been but a preparation for this hour and for this trial'.[79]

Churchill's accession to the premiership has been seen by some as a triumph of popular feeling over traditionalism. Mr A. J. P. Taylor has written, 'in the last resort he succeeded by calling in the people against the men at the top'.[80] It is true enough that the 'men at the top' wished Halifax to succeed Chamberlain if a change had to be made. Chamberlain and the Chamberlainites preferred him because he was after all a closer colleague of theirs than Churchill, and one also committed to the Munich settlement;

the Labour leaders thought Halifax was sounder from their point of view on the question of constitutional change in India; and the King remembered that Churchill had been a partisan of his brother Edward in the Abdication crisis.[81] But Halifax simply would not serve: when Chamberlain suggested that he might take his place he developed 'a bad stomach ache'. He realised that Churchill would in any case be 'running Defence', and he felt that his own position would then soon be like Asquith's *vis-à-vis* Lloyd George.[82] Thus the highest responsibility passed to Churchill by default.

Yet even the closest of Churchill's own political associates thought that his 'lack of judgment' would rule him out. As early as the end of October 1939 Eden was expressing himself as very dissatisfied with Churchill's attitude to matters which concerned him as Dominions Secretary: he said he was

> most disappointed with Winston's attitude over Eire – latter wishes to seize the ports and drive Eire out of the Empire! ... Winston's attitude over India is just as bad.... AE is beginning to doubt whether Churchill could ever be PM so bad is his judgment in such matters.[83]

His broadcasts were winning him support in some quarters; but Harold Nicolson, after listening to him on the wireless in January 1940, decided that he was 'too belligerent for this pacifist age'.[84] The opinion polls showed that at the turn of the year his principal support was among 'those in the lower income group, those aged between 21 and 30, and among men'.[85] But even at the beginning of April he was, as we have seen, somewhat less generally popular than Eden; and some of his closest friends were still thinking of Lloyd George as the best alternative to Neville Chamberlain. All the same, Chamberlain commanded majority support until the Norwegian campaign; only afterwards was his famous remark that Hitler had 'missed the bus' widely quoted against him.

For those in the higher reaches of the Civil Service there was much concern at the prospect of Churchill taking the reins of government – concern that was not reduced at all by the fiasco of the Norwegian campaign. According to Jock Colville, Chamberlain's Assistant Private Secretary, the thought of Churchill as Premier 'sent a cold chill down the spines of the staff at 10 Downing Street'. Ismay had told them about the 'confusion' that

Churchill had caused on the Military Co-ordination Committee. Colville adds:

> Our feelings at 10 Downing Street were widely shared in the Cabinet Offices, the Treasury and throughout Whitehall.... Seldom can a Prime Minister have taken office with the Establishment ... so dubious of the choice and so prepared to find its doubts justified.[86]

Finally, there was a voice from the past. Lady Oxford, otherwise Margot Asquith, called upon the Chamberlains at the house she knew so well, 10 Downing Street, on the evening of May 10th. She wrote to her friend Geoffrey Dawson, the editor of *The Times*, next day: 'I looked at his spare figure and keen eye and could not help comparing it with Winston's self-indulgent rotundity.'[87]

21. *The Finest Hour*

In the beautiful weather of the Whit weekend – which in France was being exploited to the full by the German army and air force – Churchill set about the construction of his ministry. By Saturday (May 11th) the first list of ministers had been agreed, and after being approved by the Labour Party's National Executive meeting at Bournemouth was published: there were the five members of the War Cabinet, Churchill himself and his two former senior colleagues, Chamberlain and Halifax, and also Attlee and Greenwood for the Labour Party; and there was one representative of each party at the Service ministries – A. V. Alexander (Labour) as First Lord of the Admiralty, Anthony Eden (Conservative) as Secretary for War, and Sir Archibald Sinclair (Liberal) as Air Minister. The Service ministers formed a group which Churchill thought congenial to himself, and willing to serve as his subordinates. They were not to be members of the War Cabinet, although Sinclair, in his capacity as Liberal leader, was to attend when important political matters were discussed.[1] Sinclair was of course an old friend of the Prime Minister, who had no doubt that the arrangement would work satisfactorily.

Churchill gave instructions that there were to be no moves of residence among the ministers for a month.[2] He continued for the time being, therefore, at Admiralty House:

There, after dinner, Ministers, military chiefs and officials would begin to assemble, using the drawing-room with its dolphin furniture ('the fish room' as Churchill called it) as a promenade, while

440

the new Prime Minister popped in and out, first through one door and then through another....[3]

As early as the 11th he held two meetings at the Admiralty with Chamberlain and Halifax and various staff officers to take emergency measures, including the arrest and internment of enemy aliens in the South-East and Eastern Counties.[4] Late on Sunday evening, May 12th, a further meeting also at the Admiralty agreed on action to make open spaces in Britain unusable for gliders, so as to prevent the Germans from flying in troops as they had done in Holland.[5]

Meanwhile the new Prime Minister had been filling the other ministerial posts. Herbert Morrison of the Labour Party was invited to be Minister of Supply; Sir John Simon, who was retiring from the Exchequer, was to become Lord Chancellor as a peer; Lord Lloyd, Churchill's old ally on the India question, was to be Colonial Secretary; and Ernest Bevin, the Secretary of the Transport and General Workers' Union, was brought in from outside Parliament as Minister of Labour. Sir Kingsley Wood was rewarded for his betrayal of the Chamberlainites by becoming Chancellor of the Exchequer, though not in the War Cabinet as yet; and Sir Andrew Duncan, a non-party man, was to carry on as President of the Board of Trade. After much pressure, Lord Beaverbrook was persuaded to take the new post of Minister of Aircraft Production – evidently a key responsibility.[6] Hugh Dalton, who was attending the Labour Party Conference at Bournemouth, was telephoned and invited to be Minister of Economic Warfare, a post which he coveted.[7] Emanuel Shinwell, on the other hand, who was also at Bournemouth, refused an invitation to become Parliamentary Secretary to the Ministry of Food, which he thought inappropriate to his abilities.[8] It seems that Attlee was closely consulted about the Labour appointments, for Dalton noted in his diary (on May 18th):

I think he [Attlee] has made his selections and omissions for Government posts very well. A[ttlee] says that he left out Pethick [Lawrence] because too old, [H.B.] Lees-Smith because too slow, W[edgwood] Benn because too recent [a convert], and Phil [Noel-Baker] because too unbalanced in his judgments.... Also a balance had to be maintained between bourgeois and working-class MPs.[9]

On Whit Monday, May 13th, the House of Commons met,

441

and in the early afternoon Churchill was to be seen on the government front bench, flanked by Chamberlain on one side and by Attlee on the other.[10] Attlee had just come up from Bournemouth that morning after moving a resolution on the opening day of the conference to approve the party's action in taking office.[11] Churchill made a short speech declaring the new government's policy, and asking for the approval of the House. He declared: 'I have nothing to offer but blood, toil, tears and sweat.' He added:

> You ask, What is our policy? I will say: it is to wage war, by sea, land and air, with all our might and with all the strength that God can give us: to wage war against a monstrous tyranny, never surpassed in the dark, lamentable catalogue of human crime. That is our policy. You ask, what is our aim? I can answer in one word: Victory – victory at all costs, victory in spite of all terror, victory, however long and hard the road may be; for without victory there is no survival.[12]

There were echoes here, as *The Times* was quick to point out, of Garibaldi ('hunger, thirst, forced marches, battles and death') and of Clemenceau ('Je fais la guerre').[13]

There were not many speeches in the debate, but Lees-Smith, who, albeit 'slow', was to be the spokesman of the Labour MPs not in office, reported the outcome of the Bournemouth debate – a majority on a card vote of 2,400,000 to 170,000 in favour of joining the government.[14] Lloyd George offered his old colleague his congratulations and best wishes, speaking of his 'glittering intellectual gifts, his dauntless courage, his profound study of war, and his experience in its operation and direction'.[15] Only James Maxton of the pacifist Independent Labour Party spoke out clearly in opposition, and insisted on dividing the House; but the task of acting as tellers absorbed the entire membership of his party, and when the voting figures were announced it was found that the new ministry had been approved by 381 to none.[16]

On Whit Sunday Halifax had written in his diary about the new Prime Minister: 'I have seldom met anybody with stranger gaps of knowledge, or whose mind worked in greater jerks. Will it be possible to make it work in an orderly fashion? On this much depends.'[17] He need not have worried. Jock Colville was one of those at No. 10 who 'viewed with distaste the arrival of his [Churchill's] myrmidons, Bracken, Lindemann, and Desmond

442

Morton, to take the place of such well-liked colleagues as Horace Wilson, Captain Dugdale and Lord Dunglass'; but he soon changed his mind about the efficiency of the new Prime Minister:

> Within a fortnight all was changed. I doubt if there has ever been such a rapid transformation of opinion in Whitehall and of the tempo at which business was conducted.... A sense of urgency was created in the course of a very few days and respectable civil servants were actually to be seen running along the corridors. No delays were condoned; telephone switchboards quadrupled their efficiency; the Chiefs of Staff and the Joint Planning Staff were in almost constant session; regular office hours ceased to exist and weekends disappeared with them.[18]

Brendan Bracken was not in fact formally appointed as the Prime Minister's Parliamentary Private Secretary. He preferred to function informally as a close political colleague, and Churchill showed his confidence in him by appointing him to the Privy Council early in June – a decision that left the King 'much surprised and not a little disturbed'.[19] Major Morton and Professor Lindemann were both formally appointed as personal assistants to the Prime Minister. Of the Civil Service aides, the Principal Private Secretary was Eric Seal, whom Churchill brought over with him from the Admiralty; and there were four other Private Secretaries, three of whom had already been at No. 10: Anthony Bevir, John Peck, Jock Colville, and Miss E. M. Watson.[20] Miss Watson's special responsibility, which she had undertaken for previous prime ministers, was correspondence from the general public.[21] It was apparently she who first described Churchill's late-night sessions as 'the Midnight Follies'.[22]

On Whit Monday, the day of his policy speech to the Commons, Churchill was still undecided about whether the Germans had yet launched their main thrust. He was also hostile to any suggestion of using the main bombing force for a purely tactical purpose – as he put it,

> It is important not to waste our aircraft in France on unprofitable attacks on German tanks, which have given a very good account of themselves against air attack. German tanks should be met by our own tanks and artillery.[23]

On this he was opposed by Eden, but supported by Sinclair, who thought that bombers would not be able to find targets 'in the immediate battle zone'; and the Air Marshals agreed. But next day (14th) the German break-through in the Sedan area began to assume a threatening aspect, and cries of alarm came from the French command and from the French Prime Minister. Reynaud sent a message that day to the effect that the French army was unable to cope with the combination of tanks and dive-bombers, and asking for ten more squadrons of fighters from Britain, to add to the squadrons already supporting the Expeditionary Force, which were rapidly being eroded.[24]

The War Cabinet was unwilling to accept this request straight away. Churchill thought that:

> We should hesitate before we denude still further the heart of the Empire. A penetration of the lines by mechanised units will not be decisive against a large army unless heavily reinforced from the rear. The columns of motor vehicles will require petrol. The essential point is probably to support the coming counter-attack.[25]

With this in view it was decided to prepare to send the ten squadrons, but to delay the final decision about six of them while finding out more about the actual situation.

Early next morning (the 15th) Reynaud became more desperate and telephoned Churchill to say, 'We have been defeated.... We have lost the battle.'[26] This was indeed true: the French Ninth Army, which had covered the front in the Ardennes, was collapsing, and German tanks were driving some sixty miles beyond their original positions. But the situation was not clear as yet to the British War Cabinet, and Churchill decided to fly to Paris to see the French leaders. He took with him General Dill, the Vice-Chief of the Imperial General Staff, and also General Ismay, the head of the Military Wing of the War Cabinet Secretariat. The party reached the Quai d'Orsay at about 5.30 p.m., to find that the ministries were already burning their archives for fear of a German occupation of Paris. In the presence of Reynaud and Daladier they received an explanation of the military situation from General Gamelin, the Commander-in-Chief. After the General had finished, Churchill asked 'Où est la masse de manœuvre?', but the answer was, 'with a shake of the head and a shrug ... "Aucune"'.

As Churchill later wrote, 'What was the Maginot Line for? It should have economised troops.... I admit this was one of

444

the greatest surprises I have had in my life.'[27] Gamelin asked for more British fighters, and Churchill, who was able already to promise four of the ten squadrons earlier requested, now asked Ismay to telephone to London to ask for the further six. 'It would not be good historically if their requests were denied and their ruin resulted.'[28] Before midnight the British government agreed to Churchill's request, and after conveying the news to Reynaud and Daladier in person Churchill slept at the British Embassy and flew home to London in the morning. But in fact the squadrons, though assigned to the battle, did not move to French airfields, where they would have been without radar cover and so especially vulnerable.

By this time it was becoming clear that the object of the German drive was Abbeville and the Channel coast, rather than Paris itself in the first instance. This meant cutting off a section of the French army, and also the whole of the British and Belgian forces. (The Dutch army had already capitulated on the night of May 14th.) By May 19th General Gort, the British Commander, was beginning to think that he would have to retreat to the coast and undertake an evacuation by sea. This was because he obtained no clear orders from the French command, which seemed incapable of decision. Meanwhile Reynaud had decided on a reconstruction of his government: he himself assumed the Defence portfolio from Daladier, whom he put at the Foreign Ministry; and he persuaded the veteran Marshal Pétain, the defender of Verdun in the First World War, to enter his Cabinet as Vice-Premier. He also replaced Gamelin with General Weygand, who although older than Gamelin – he was aged 73 – was reckoned to be more vigorous and effective. It was to see Weygand and to discuss the military position that Churchill again visited Paris on May 22nd. The meeting was held at Weygand's headquarters at the Château de Vincennes. Weygand appeared 'resolute, decisive, and amazingly active',[29] and outlined a plan whereby the French First Army and the British Expeditionary Force were to advance southwards and link hands with other French troops who would attack northwards from south of the Somme. Things seemed more manageable than they had done on Churchill's previous visit, and he spent a fairly comfortable night at the British Embassy before flying back to London next morning.

But events prevented the plan from being put into operation.

The attack from the south of the Somme failed to materialise, and Gort's position on his northern flank was endangered by the collapse of the Belgian army. Gort realised that the only hope for his army was a retreat to the coast at Dunkirk, and to facilitate this by guarding his southern flank orders were sent from Whitehall on the evening of May 26th to the British forces at Calais to fight to the end. Churchill was upset by having to take this decision: 'he ate and drank with evident distaste' and said to Ismay, 'I feel physically sick'.[30] But the Dunkirk evacuation, or 'Operation Dynamo' as it was called, proved remarkably successful: from May 26th, when it began, to June 4th, over 338,000 troops, British and Allied, were brought to England – without their heavy equipment, to be sure, but most of them at least with their rifles.

A meeting of the Supreme War Council was held in Paris on May 31st, and Churchill again flew to attend, accompanied on this occasion by Attlee as well as by Ismay. Also on the British side was Major-General E. L. Spears, a Conservative MP and a friend of Churchill's, who had the additional qualification of speaking French fluently, and whom consequently Churchill had appointed as his personal representative with Reynaud. The meeting agreed to the evacuation of Narvik, which was proposed by the British largely for the sake of saving shipping and anti-aircraft guns. Plans were also made for a combined naval and air attack on Italy as soon as she entered the war – an event which now seemed imminent. But Churchill also had to allay suspicions that French and British troops were not being evacuated from Dunkirk in roughly equal numbers. He insisted that he was in favour of them leaving Dunkirk, as he put it, 'bras dessus, bras dessous' – that is, 'arm-in-arm'. He broke down when he said that orders had been given to allow the unwounded precedence over the wounded, so as to ensure that fresh forces could readily be constituted in Britain. On the French side, it was apparent that the degree of cordiality and enthusiasm for a continuation of the struggle varied considerably. Reynaud responded warmly, but the new Vice-Premier, Marshal Pétain, seemed aloof and hostile. Churchill and Spears went up to the Marshal after the formal proceedings were over, and when someone suggested 'a modification of French foreign policy' Spears said to the Marshal, 'That would not only mean blockade, but bombardment of all French ports in German hands.'[31]

On June 4th Churchill addressed the Commons to report the success of the Dunkirk evacuation, and to indicate the course of future British policy. He warned that 'Wars are not won by evacuations'. But he added at once, 'there was a victory inside this deliverance, which should be noted. It was gained by the Air Force.... All of our types ... and all our pilots have been vindicated as superior to what they have at present to face.' He ended with an expression of resolve:

> We shall fight on the beaches, we shall fight on the landing-grounds, we shall fight in the hills; we shall never surrender, and even if, which I do not for a moment believe, this island or a large part of it were subjugated and starving, then our Empire beyond the seas, armed and guarded by the British Fleet, would carry on the struggle, until, in God's good time, the New World, with all its power and might, steps forth to the rescue and liberation of the Old.[32]

On June 10th the French government left Paris, and when next day a further meeting of the Supreme War Council was held it had to take place at the Château du Muguet, near Briare on the Loire. Churchill again flew to attend, and was accompanied on the trip by Eden as well as by General Dill, who had succeeded Ironside as Chief of the Imperial General Staff, and also by Ismay. Before breakfast next day Reynaud told Churchill and Eden that he had made a mistake in admitting Pétain to his government, as his attitude was defeatist. Tentative plans were made for the establishment of a military redoubt in Brittany; but it seemed clear that French resistance would not be much prolonged.[33]

In fact, the French agony was now reaching its climax. On June 13th Churchill, having only returned to Britain on the previous day, again made his way to France – this time to Tours, where the French government had moved. He took with him on this flight Halifax, Ismay and Beaverbrook: there was no one to meet the party on its arrival and it was with difficulty that they obtained luncheon.[34] When they met Reynaud, they found him in an indecisive state – anxious to make peace, yet still asserting his solidarity with the agreement not to do so arranged three months earlier. According to the record:

> Mr Churchill said that in no case would Britain waste time and energy in reproaches or recriminations. That did not mean that she would consent to action contrary to the recent agreement. The first

step ought to be M. Reynaud's further message putting the present position squarely to President Roosevelt. Let them await the answer before considering anything else. If England won the war France would be restored in her dignity and in her greatness.[35]

Meanwhile Roosevelt replied in a sympathetic fashion to a message of Reynaud's sent on the 10th, but, to the disappointment of the French Premier, he was unwilling to allow his words to be published. On June 14th General Brooke, who was commanding the 150,000 men of the new British force in northern France, persuaded Churchill to order his release from French command and his withdrawal across the Channel. On the 16th the British War Cabinet agreed to France's seeking an armistice provided the French fleet was sailed forthwith for British harbours. But General Charles de Gaulle, a junior member of the French government who was in favour of continued resistance, had meanwhile been in London shaping, along with Vansittart, Desmond Morton and others, a Declaration of Union for Britain and France.[36] After approval by the Cabinet, the text of this was telephoned to Reynaud; and Churchill prepared to visit him once more, taking with him Attlee and Sinclair, the leaders of the two other political parties, to put the case for it. This time they were to travel by cruiser; but the journey did not take place, as Sir Ronald Campbell, the British Ambassador, warned him before he started that the French government was in crisis and that Reynaud had resigned that evening. On the 17th Spears flew home from Bordeaux, bringing with him General de Gaulle, who then made an address to the French people over the BBC urging them to fight on.

Churchill was not to visit France again for a period of four years. On June 18th he spoke to the Commons:

What General Weygand called the Battle of France is over. I expect that the Battle of Britain is about to begin.... Let us therefore brace ourselves to our duties, and so bear ourselves that, if the British Empire and its Commonwealth last for a thousand years, men will still say: 'This was their finest hour.'[37]

It was a moment for stern action to assert national survival. On July 3rd Churchill personally supervised from the Cabinet Room the operation of a plan to seize the French warships in British ports and to immobilise those elsewhere. No great difficulty arose over the ships in British ports or those at Alexandria; but at the north African port of Oran, where there was an important squadron, the French Admiral rejected an ultimatum by Vice-Admiral Sir James Somerville, of 'Force H', and suffered a brief bombardment and an attack from naval aircraft which destroyed three of his battleships and damaged another, with the loss of almost 1300 lives. 'Force H' was virtually undamaged.[38]

On July 4th Churchill explained to the Commons the reasons which had led the government to decide on this drastic action – including the failure of the French to ensure that some 400 German pilots, shot down in the earlier fighting by the RAF as well as by the French air force, were retained in captivity by being sent to Britain. Churchill then told the story of the battle at Oran, and concluded with a message which he was circulating to government servants, urging them to maintain 'a spirit of alert and confident energy'. The message asserted the government's belief that an invasion, if attempted, would fail:

> The Royal Air Force is in excellent order and at the highest strength yet attained. The German Navy was never so weak, nor the British Army at home so strong as now. The Prime Minister expects all His Majesty's servants in high places to set an example of steadiness and resolution.[39]

After this speech Churchill received a remarkable ovation from the whole House, which on all sides stood to cheer as he sat down. As he recorded in his memoirs,

> Up till this moment the Conservative Party had treated me with some reserve, and it was from the Labour benches that I received the warmest welcome when I entered the House or rose on serious occasions. But now all joined in solemn stentorian accord.[40]

This was not an indication of anti-French feeling but rather a mark of approval for a decisive act to maintain the supremacy of the British navy at a moment of crisis.

For some time in the late spring and early summer there were signs of recrimination among politicians, and also a special hostility to the Chamberlainites outside Parliament. The soldiers returning from France and Belgium were bitter about shortages of equipment, not realising that rearmament had deliberately concentrated on the navy and the air force; and those who escaped from Dunkirk did not appreciate how far their escape was due to the success of air force protection.[41] But Churchill was conscious of his dependence upon the support of Chamberlain and his followers, who still dominated the Commons. In late May he made overtures to Lloyd George, inviting him to join his Cabinet on the understanding that Chamberlain would have to agree, but Lloyd George made Chamberlain's presence a reason for refusing, and wrote to Churchill on May 29th: 'Several of the architects of this catastrophe are still leading members of your Government, and two of them are in the Cabinet that directs the war.'[42] Churchill replied: 'Like you, I have no Party of my own. I have received a very great deal of help from Chamberlain. His kindness and courtesy to me in our new relations have touched me. I have joined hands with him, and must act with perfect loyalty.'[43]

Considering that Lloyd George seemed to be rather doubtful in his enthusiasm to fight the war through, it was perhaps as well for Churchill that he refused to join the Cabinet. Within that body, there had already been some differences of opinion about the policy to be adopted towards Italy, which was on the verge of joining the war. Reynaud wanted Britain to take the initiative in buying off Italy by offering to neutralise or demilitarise Gibraltar, Malta and Suez; and Halifax was somewhat attracted by the idea, saying that he 'attached perhaps rather more importance than the Prime Minister to the desirability of allowing France to try out the possibilities of European equilibrium'.[44] But this was in the early days of the Dunkirk evacuation; and Churchill said that 'It is best to decide nothing until we see how much of the Army we can re-embark from France.... This will afford a real test of air superiority.'[45] With the support of Attlee and Greenwood his view prevailed. Churchill also formed the view that the Chiefs of Staff were exaggerating the relative size of the Luftwaffe: 'It is quite misleading to say that the Germans have a superiority of 4 to 1 over us.'[46] This was a perceptive statement, although it contradicted Churchill's own previous views on the question.

Churchill felt it essential to prevent any sort of witch-hunt against any of his colleagues in the Cabinet, and he declared in his Commons speech of June 18th:

Of this I am quite sure, that if we open a quarrel between the past and the present, we shall find that we have lost the future. Therefore, I cannot accept the drawing of any distinctions between the Members of the present Government. It was formed at a moment of crisis in order to unite all the parties and all sections of opinion.[47]

Chamberlain for his part saw journalists about ten days later to tell them that there were no differences within the government and that no section of the Conservative Party favoured suing for peace: 'If I disagreed with the Prime Minister I would resign and go into opposition, but intrigue – never!'[48] There is evidence to suggest that Chamberlain spoke to Margesson, the Chief Whip, to ensure that the Conservative Party in the Commons should indicate its approval of the Prime Minister at the end of his speech on July 4th.[49]

Nevertheless, outside Parliament the hostility to the Chamberlainites smouldered on, and was indeed fanned by the publication early in July of a book by three Beaverbrook journalists entitled *Guilty Men*. A Gallup Poll published about the same time reported that more than three-quarters of those who held opinions on the matter thought that Chamberlain should leave the government, and more than half also thought that Simon, Halifax and Kingsley Wood should go.[50] To some extent the position was eased when Chamberlain fell ill with cancer in late July, and had to undergo a major operation. But Churchill could not but feel that this was a serious loss to his government, as Chamberlain had presided very efficiently over committees dealing with domestic affairs – so much so that he had favourably impressed former political opponents such as Attlee and Greenwood.

Meanwhile the German armed forces were reorganising for an invasion of Britain, plans for which did not exist before July. It was only on July 16th that Hitler issued a directive for the invasion, 'Operation Sealion' as he called it, to take place not earlier than mid-August.[51] At about the same time he made a final offer of peace – an offer that was decisively rejected in a broadcast speech by Halifax three days later. Hostilities with Italy had existed since June 10th, and on July 12th it was announced that Britain had decided to close the Burma Road for three months – an act of appeasement of Japan which the uninformed public naturally attributed to the influence of Halifax, but which was in fact much more the decision of Churchill himself, who as Halifax put it was 'not unnaturally anxious about risking another war'.[52]

By mid-August the efforts of the British Cabinet and of the

Chiefs of Staff to prepare the country to meet an invasion were bearing fruit. It is arguable that the system of high command was unsatisfactory. It seems clear that if invasion had begun Churchill would have taken personal control of the resistance. In late May he invited his old colleague Air Marshal Trenchard to assume the post of GOC, Home Forces, but when the latter demanded the full powers of a generalissimo and Deputy Minister of Defence Churchill drew back, evidently fearing the revival of the 'frocks v. brass-hats' controversy of the First World War.[53]

In spite of this, the work of preparation seemed effective. Beaverbrook, who was appointed to the War Cabinet in early August, was working ruthlessly and successfully to increase the number of aircraft in the hands of Fighter Command: the total of Spitfires and Hurricanes, which was only 331 after Dunkirk, rose to 620, and the reserves rose from 36 to 289.[54] The navy had withdrawn most of its destroyers from escort duties in order to provide raiding parties to deal with an invasion; mines had been sown on approaches, and possible landing-beaches had been provided with obstacles. General Ironside, who had been the army's Commander-in-Chief, Home Forces, since late May, had prepared static lines of defence in the form of anti-tank ditches and concrete pill-boxes: but in mid-July he was replaced by General Alan Brooke, who had distinguished himself in France in May and June, and who shared Churchill's view that there should be mobile forces to hit directly at the invader at his point of landing. Artillery and rifles had come in from the United States in July, to arm the Local Defence Volunteers, or Home Guard as Churchill preferred to call them, who had first been recruited in mid-May and whose number topped the million mark in July.[55]

Churchill himself began a series of visits to the areas of possible invasion. He saw an exercise by the Canadian Division in Kent, and one by the 3rd Division (under General Montgomery) in Sussex. He urged that Montgomery should be allowed to requisition buses so as to increase the mobility of his troops.[56] He inspected the defences of Harwich and Dover, and wrote several minutes demanding the provision of heavy guns for shelling the French coast.[57] He also went up to the north-east coast, and as the *Times* report said:

In one village through which he passed the people about quickly recognised him, and raised their hats or waved their hands. Mr Churchill, who seemed to be in the best of spirits, acknowledged their greeting and smiled.... If Mr Churchill's smiles were a measure of his satisfaction he was indeed satisfied.... The Prime Minister also visited a North-East England shipyard. He spent an hour there, and was quickly recognised and loudly cheered.... Workers' wives gathered at the gates of the shipyard, and Mr Churchill, impressed by the warmth of his welcome, shouted 'Are we downhearted?' The women-folk responded with a roar, 'No'.[58]

When Churchill travelled some way from London he made use of a special train which was equipped for the purpose, in a way suggested to him by his American tours. The train, consisting basically of two 'semi-Royal' coaches, if in a vulnerable area could usually be shunted overnight into a stretch of tunnel to afford protection against air raids; but its telephone could be easily plugged in through any convenient wire to the White-hall exchange. This made the problems of security very much more manageable.[59]

As the summer wore on, it became apparent that the enemy's preparations for invasion were posing a threat to the south coast rather than to the east, which the Chiefs of Staff had originally thought to be the area of principal danger. An invasion fleet was assembling in ports between Havre and Ostend; and the German air force was also concentrating there. On September 7th the threat seemed to be so immediate that the code-word 'Cromwell', meaning 'invasion imminent', was issued to the Home Forces:[60] but the fleet had not yet sailed, and RAF bombers were still vigorously attacking the assembled barges in their har-bours. On September 11th Churchill warned the Commons that 'the next week or so' would be 'a very important period in our history', ranking with 'the days when the Spanish Armada was approaching the Channel'.[61] Six days later he gave more details of the threat in a Secret Session of the House.

But two days earlier – Sunday September 15th – the climax of the danger had been reached, in the battle between the rival air forces. It was witnessed by Churchill himself at the key point in the defence – the headquarters of No. 11 Group, Fighter Com-mand, RAF at Uxbridge, which Churchill could visit easily when en route between Chequers and London. The Operations Room there was a fascinating place: as one observer put it,

The ceaseless, orderly activity of this nerve centre, with the plotters moving their discs to and fro on the table, the Army liaison officers passing information about the anti-aircraft units in action, and the winking of the red and white lights on the far wall, created an instant sense of drama.[62]

Air Vice-Marshal K. R. Park was in command, but the Duty Controller at the time was Group Captain Lord Willoughby de Broke. Broke in fact had to order up all the squadrons, and none was left in reserve as the last German aircraft headed for home. Churchill was much affected by the tension of the occasion. It was a month earlier that he had visited the same headquarters and, as he left with Ismay by car, had evolved the phrase which, in a slightly different form, was to echo round the world – 'Never in the field of human conflict has so much been owed by so many to so few.'[63]

On September 15th the losses of the Luftwaffe were at first reckoned at 183 machines, but later the official total had to be scaled down to 56.[64] All the same, the rate of attrition was high enough, in combination with the damage done a few hours later to the invasion fleet by RAF bombers, to cause Hitler to postpone the date of invasion indefinitely. With the autumn change in the weather, the German strategy perforce changed from one of attempting to destroy the RAF directly to one of wearing down the country's defences over a longer period, principally by night attack on London and other major cities.

Pre-war plans for dealing with air raids had been prepared with great thoroughness, and there were arrangements in existence for the removal of the government from London to the Midlands. But probably as a result of his experience of the disorganisation that followed the French government's move from Paris Churchill decided that any substantial move out of Whitehall would have more disadvantages than advantages.[65] Yet 10 Downing Street itself was a very vulnerable old building, and in the first few weeks of his premiership, while he was still at Admiralty House, a shelter was built in the garden and a small dining-room and sitting-room were furnished in the basement, ceilings being shored up as well. The work was still not complete when the month's wait was over, and Churchill stayed for a time in a suite at the Carlton Hotel in the Haymarket.[66] But it was decided that even with the alterations No. 10 remained dangerous for permanent residence; and so offices for the Prime Minister were established in the so-called Annexe at Storey's Gate – a building specially constructed with the dangers of air raids in mind. The Annexe also contained a room where Cabinet meetings could be held.

Churchill chose to alternate his attendance in the two places, spending the daylight hours at No. 10 and the nights at the Annexe, where he also enjoyed watching the battle from an observation post on the roof.[67] But for some time in the autumn he used at night, not the Annexe which was not ready, but an underground office of the Railway Executive at Piccadilly.[68] At the weekend he went to Chequers or, in the event of a full moon, to the somewhat remoter home of Ronald Tree, a Conservative MP, at Ditchley in Oxfordshire.

Full moon was a dangerous time because the method of air attack engaged in by the enemy was now in the form of night raids. The 'Blitz', or night air-raid offensive against London and other cities, began on September 7th: it thus overlapped with the Battle of Britain. In fact the transfer of the struggle to London was a strategic error by the enemy, as the task of destroying the RAF stations and radar installations in front of the city was then neglected. Of course the night raids imposed a burden upon the morale of the civilian population and upon the services of the local authorities; however, it was not in fact a 'Blitzkreig' or lightning war but rather a prolonged campaign to wear down popular resistance – and it had the disadvantage to the enemy that people in a sense got used to it and discovered how to take effective precautions against anything short of a direct hit. Churchill thought it worth emphasising, in his Commons speech of October 8th, that at the existing rate of attrition it would be ten years before half of London had been destroyed, and 'after that, of course, progress would be much slower'.[69]

But at the same time it was essential not to minimise the personal loss that people experienced when their homes were destroyed. Churchill made a point of visiting some of the scenes of damage, and on one occasion early in September he was quickly on the scene at an 'incident' in the London Docks, and was moved to tears by the sight of the damage and by the spontaneous enthusiasm of the people for himself. Ismay later wrote:

'Good old Winnie', they cried. 'We thought you'd come and see us. We can take it. Give it 'em back.' Churchill broke down, and as

I was struggling to get him through the crowd, I heard an old woman say, 'You see, he really cares. He's crying'. Having pulled himself together, he proceeded to march through dockland at breakneck speed.[70]

It was partly as a result of an earlier experience at Margate in August, when Churchill saw the misery of the proprietor of a small restaurant that had been hit, that arrangements were made by the War Cabinet to introduce a more generous scheme of air-raid compensation. It was also Churchill himself who insisted on the use of sections of the London Tube as air-raid shelters. At the same time, he thought that too much dislocation of factories and offices was taking place as a result of people taking cover whenever the sirens sounded; and he therefore introduced a second stage in the alarm system to be notified by roof spotters, or 'Jim Crows' as he called them.[71] He also persuaded the House of Commons to adapt its sittings to the new situation – to meet in the daylight hours and not to advertise its sittings in advance. Whitehall was certainly a major target: and one day in mid-October, only minutes after Churchill had told the kitchen staff at No. 10 to take shelter, a bomb fell on the Treasury offices and blew in the plate-glass windows of the kitchen.[72]

Although the devastation caused by the air raids was not as bad as had been expected before the war, it was serious enough to have a powerful impact on feeling in other countries, and especially in the United States. Churchill had expected this: Ambassador Joseph Kennedy reported him to Roosevelt as believing in May that 'with the bombing of well-known places in England the United States will come in'.[73] Churchill had also impressed upon Lord Lothian, the British Ambassador in Washington, that the President should realise the danger that if a German invasion of Britain were successful the fleet would become a bargaining weapon for 'some Quisling government'.[74] If Roosevelt did not immediately bring the United States into the war, he nevertheless gave clear indications of his sympathies. On June 10th, in a speech at Charlottesville, Virginia, he denounced the intervention of Italy as a 'dagger ... stuck into the back of its neighbour', and he pledged both American aid to the Allies and the re-armament of his own country.[75] On June 19th he appointed two new Cabinet officers, both of them from the Republican Party, and both of them known sympathisers with the Allied cause:

Colonel Frank Knox as Secretary for the Navy and the veteran Henry Stimson as Secretary for War. Stimson was one of the few prominent war-leaders who were older than Churchill, having served as a Cabinet minister before the First World War.

Churchill's personal links with Roosevelt, by means of the 'Former Naval Person' correspondence, were already close enough for him to consult the President about the attack on the French fleet and obtain his approval.[76] As early as mid-May he had asked Roosevelt to furnish Britain forty to fifty obsolete destroyers as a supplement to the navy;[77] and at the end of July he repeated this request with great emphasis: 'Mr President, with great respect I must tell you that in the long history of the world, this is a thing to do *now*.'[78]

The matter was discussed at a Cabinet meeting called by Roosevelt on August 2nd, and it was agreed that legislation was required, that Roosevelt's Republican opponent for the forthcoming presidential election, Wendell Willkie, should be persuaded to support Roosevelt's attitude, and that Churchill should reaffirm his commitment not to allow the British navy to fall into German hands.[79] But opinion in the United States was still moving towards the Allied cause; and early in September Roosevelt decided after all to proceed without legislation and to provide the fifty destroyers on his own executive authority. What clinched the deal was the willingness of the British government to provide ninety-nine-year leases for American bases on islands in the West Indies, at Bermuda and in Newfoundland. On August 20th Churchill outlined the arrangements in a speech to the Commons:

> Undoubtedly this process means that these two great organisations of the English-speaking democracies, the British Empire and the United States, will have to be somewhat mixed up together in some part of their affairs for mutual and general advantage. For my own part, looking out upon the future, I do not view the process with any misgivings. I could not stop it if I wished; no one can stop it. Like the Mississippi, it just keeps rolling along. Let it roll. Let it roll on – full flood, inexorable, irresistible, benignant, to broader lands and better days.[80]

As it turned out, the fifty destroyers were not of much material value to the British navy. They were supposed to fill a gap in the British naval building programme between the summer of 1940 and the spring of 1941; but as late as the end of December

457

1940 only nine of them came into service with the navy, owing to the need for refitting.[81] The psychological importance of the agreement was its most important element: it committed the United States to the assistance of Britain in the war, to an extent not previously envisaged.

Late in September it became apparent that Chamberlain was dying of cancer. He resigned his office in the government and also his post as Leader of the Conservative Party. Churchill appointed Sir John Anderson, the distinguished former civil servant and now Home Secretary, to succeed him as Lord President, and to take charge of the committees on the domestic side; Herbert Morrison became Home Secretary in Anderson's place; and Kingsley Wood, the Chancellor of the Exchequer, and Ernest Bevin, the Minister of Labour, were admitted to the War Cabinet, which now numbered eight.

At about the same time, Churchill himself was invited to become Leader of the Conservative Party. A few months earlier this would have seemed an impossible development. As *The Times* put it, 'Time weaves "eternal artistries in circumstances", and from the political history of recent years no more unlikely pattern of events would have been predicted.'[82] The new factor in the situation was the Prime Minister's astonishing personal popularity, based upon his evident vigour and energy in the national cause and on his freedom from all responsibility for the existing weak state of British armaments. Through his broadcasts he could appeal to the general public in a fashion not open to his predecessors, and the BBC Listener Research Section reckoned that his broadcast on July 14th was heard by over 64% of the adult population.[83] This interest had been earned by the intrinsic quality of the statements themselves. Vita Sackville-West, the novelist and poet, wrote to her husband, Harold Nicolson, in June:

> I think that one of the reasons why one is stirred by his Elizabethan phrases, is that one feels the whole massive backing of power and resolve behind them, like a great fortress: they are never words for words' sake.[84]

By early August Churchill's popularity was confirmed by a Gallup Poll, published in the *News Chronicle*. Asked whether they approved or disapproved his leadership, 88% of the sample replied in the affirmative, and only 7% were hostile and 5% doubtful.[85] The proportion of approval was far higher than anything that Chamberlain attained.

Under the circumstances, the Conservative Party was keen to associate itself with Churchill's name and reputation; but he for his part might well have felt, in view of past events, that he would prefer to remain independent of what was after all only a section of his supporters. On the other hand, the Conservatives still had a considerable majority in the House of Commons; and if Churchill refused the leadership he might well be putting himself at the mercy of whoever accepted it – probably Halifax, for whom he had much respect but from whom he differed markedly in temperament. It was with these thoughts in mind, which he virtually admitted in his acceptance speech, that Churchill agreed to take the leadership.[86] The party meeting was held in the Caxton Hall, Westminster, and Churchill's name was proposed by Halifax and seconded by Sir George Courthope, a senior backbencher. According to *The Times*, when Churchill entered the hall he was 'given a tremendous reception, the meeting rising to its feet and cheering enthusiastically'.[87]

Although there was no doubt of the national approval of Churchill at this time, it was reinforced by echoes of support from abroad, and especially from English-speaking countries. There was a general election in Australia in September, and both main parties identified their case with the name of Churchill, the United Australia Party using the slogans 'Menzies stands with Churchill' and 'Back the Government that is backing Churchill'.[88] Menzies won the election but late in September he sent Churchill an indignant message about the 'Dakar incident', of which his government had had no advance notice.

An expedition had been sent to Dakar, on the Atlantic coast of French Africa, in the hope of assisting General de Gaulle to assume control by a *coup de main*, but the operation did not succeed. Churchill refused to make any detailed public explanation and told Menzies, 'I thought indeed that from the way my name was used in the election quite a good opinion was entertained in Australia of these efforts [i.e. of the Churchill Government].'[89] Ambassador Kennedy, in a despatch to the American Department of State, described the Dakar failure as 'the first real break in the Churchill popularity',[90] but this was a view held only by a tiny minority. It certainly made no difference to Churchill's election as Conservative Leader, which took place shortly afterwards, and was carried 'nem. con.' and perhaps unanimously.[91]

And on the day when *The Times* published the story of the Conservative Party meeting it also carried a comment by the *New York Times* on Churchill's remark in his Commons speech of October 8th that 'Death and sorrow will be the companions of our journey; hardship our garment; constancy and valour our only shield'. According to the *New York Times*,

> This is the kind of leadership a free people deserve. It is one of Mr Churchill's supreme gifts to democracy that he has put furtiveness and concealment aside in dealing with his countrymen. He has refused to treat his people like children, and they are responding gloriously with all they have and all they are.

22. *The Expanding War*

On September 17th Hitler postponed 'Operation Sea Lion' – the plan for the Channel crossing – 'until further notice', and on October 12th he gave orders that it was definitely not to take place before the spring, but that an appearance of preparation was to be maintained 'as a means of exerting political and military pressure on England'.[1] The British government was not to know, therefore, of the change of plan; but of course it drew its own conclusions from the worsening weather in the Channel. The First Sea Lord told the War Cabinet as early as September 2nd that the use of barges and small fishing craft would become impracticable after about September 21st, owing to the equinoctial gales.[2] In the same period, daylight bombing tailed off, and the Luftwaffe developed the practice of regular night attack on London. There was no doubt about Churchill sharing the danger where it was greatest, at least during the week, for Westminster was one of the five London boroughs which in October–November recorded the heaviest proportion of high-explosive bombs.[3] This was at a time when London was suffering far more than the provincial cities – though the turn of the latter was to come. On November 14th a new pattern emerged with the concentrated attack that night on Coventry, which suffered severe damage to its old centre by both high-explosive and fire bombs. Damage to the factories of the town was not severe, but the cathedral was reduced to a shell, and photographs of the damage were released to the press almost immediately, so as to influence opinion abroad, especially in the United States.

The importance of the United States as a factor in the calculations of the British leaders became increasingly marked after the fall of France, for it seemed clear that without American aid Britain could not possibly expect to win the war, even if she could survive an invasion. In the summer of 1940 large orders for munitions were placed by the British Purchasing Commission, but under the 'cash-and-carry' legislation of the American Congress they could only be paid for by drawing heavily upon relatively limited gold reserves and dollar assets, and it was apparent that these would run out after a few months. But there was an increasing tendency to believe that the American government would help Britain financially. As early as September 5th the War Cabinet agreed to endorse the larger of two possible purchasing programmes for American aircraft on the assumption that 'No United States Government would dare to call a halt to this great expenditure, once it was firmly on the way, and to assume responsibility for the ensuing economic slump.'[4]

Churchill was, of course, uniquely qualified to persuade Americans that they should assist Britain in her difficulties, as he was uniquely qualified in defying Hitler. He was half-American himself; he had visited the United States for long periods within the decade; and his books and journalism were almost as familiar to American readers as to British. For many years, and particularly in the closing stages of the First World War, he had been in demand as a speaker at Anglo-American functions, at which he spoke with enthusiasm of the prospects of co-operation between the 'English-speaking peoples'. In late August he faced the problem posed by Kingsley Wood, the Chancellor of the Exchequer, to the War Cabinet:

> The problem ... is to hold financially until the United States Government are in a position to take their major decisions of policy, i.e. until well into November, in the case of a Democratic victory, or until the 20th January, when the new President would take office, in the case of a Republican victory.[5]

The Prime Minister thought that a suggestion to requisition 'wedding rings and other gold ornaments', which would in any case not produce more than about £20 million, was 'a measure to be produced at a later stage, if we wish to make some striking gesture for the purpose of shaming the Americans'.[6] He thought that it would be a great mistake to cut back on orders for American munitions: 'After all, the greatest economy would be to shorten the war. Nothing could be more extravagant than to shape our course in such a way that we had to fight a prolonged war in a broken-backed condition.'[7]

Roosevelt's opponent for the Presidency, Wendell Willkie, also approved of aid for Britain but, as Kingsley Wood had indicated, it was clear that if he were elected there would be greater delay in organising assistance for Britain. Consequently, Churchill and his colleagues were relieved when early in November Roosevelt was re-elected for a third term. On September 27th the aspect of international affairs had been altered by the signature in Berlin of the Tripartite Pact between Germany, Italy and Japan; this made the existing conflict seem much less parochial in character.[8] In mid-November there came the German raid on Coventry, which shocked American opinion with its brutality; and early in December the President went on a cruise in the Caribbean, to look at some of the sites for American bases which had now been leased by Britain. In the course of his trip he received a long letter from Churchill describing the war situation as he saw it and asking for various forms of assistance, including finance, to enable the struggle to continue.

> The moment approaches [wrote Churchill] when we shall no longer be able to pay cash for shipping and other supplies. While we will do our best, and shrink from no proper sacrifice to make payments across the exchange, I believe you will agree that it would be wrong in principle and mutually disadvantageous in effect if, at the height of this struggle, Great Britain were to be divested of all saleable assets, so that after the victory was won with our blood, civilisation saved, and the time gained for the United States to be fully armed against all eventualities, we should stand stripped to the bone.[9]

Shortly after his return to Washington, on December 17th, Roosevelt held a press conference at which he outlined the solution as he saw it. This was to get rid of the 'silly, foolish, old dollar sign'; and to indicate the way this could be done the President used the analogy of a neighbour's house on fire, and the garden hose which one would at once lend without haggling about the price.[10] Twelve days later, in a broadcast, he spoke of the United States as assuming the role of the 'arsenal of democracy'.[11] This was the idea behind the Lend-Lease Bill, which was passed by Congress in March 1941 and which enabled not only Britain but also Greece and China to draw upon credits provided by the American government.

Meanwhile Lord Lothian, the British Ambassador, had died suddenly early in December, and Churchill had rapidly to find a suitable replacement for this key responsibility. He seems to have thought that it was desirable to appoint not an ordinary diplomat but someone of special authority. His first idea was to approach Lloyd George, and the latter took the suggestion seriously enough to consult his doctor. But he was now 78, and not in good health, and his doctor was not encouraging.[12] Churchill then thought of his colleague Halifax, who was very reluctant to go, and brought his wife Dorothy to argue with the Prime Minister against it: but Churchill could not be gainsaid, and eventually Edward and Dorothy Halifax agreed to undertake the task as a matter of duty.[13] Churchill appointed Eden to succeed Halifax as Foreign Secretary, and – as if to demonstrate that it was not his wish to eliminate the Chamberlainites – he brought in David Margesson, the Conservative Chief Whip, to succeed Eden as Secretary for War.

Meanwhile there was also an interregnum at the American Embassy in London as Joseph Kennedy had resigned, and it took time to get a successor appointed and approved by Congress. Kennedy had been unpopular, as he took a pessimistic view of Britain's prospects. In the meantime Roosevelt chose to send a personal representative to London. This was Harry Hopkins, his former Secretary of Commerce and a close confidant. Hopkins flew the Atlantic early in January by way of Lisbon, and called on Churchill at 10 Downing Street:

> His Man Friday, Brendan Bracken ... led me to a little dining-room in the basement – poured me some sherry and left me to wait for the Prime Minister. A rotund – smiling – red-faced gentleman appeared – extended a fat but none the less convincing hand and wished me welcome to England. A short black coat – striped trousers – a clear eye and a mushy voice was the impression of England's leader.[14]

Hopkins in spite of his poor health soon made his mark, and established a close rapport with Churchill. He spent twelve evenings with him in his first fortnight in Britain, and accompanied him to Scapa Flow where Halifax was embarking for America in the new battleship *King George V*. It was at Glasgow, on the way south from this engagement, that Hopkins made in Churchill's presence his impressive statement of identification with the British cause – 'Whither thou goest I will go ... even to the end.'[15] Hopkins wrote to Roosevelt on January 14th, in a letter that accompanied Halifax on the *King George V*:

> *Churchill* is the govt in every sense of the word – he controls the grand strategy and often the details – labor trusts him – the army, navy, air force are behind him to a man. The politicians and upper crust pretend to like him. I cannot emphasize too strongly that he is the one and only person over here with whom you need to have a full meeting of minds.[16]

Hopkins was staying at Claridge's, which he found comfortable, but at the weekends he joined the Prime Minister's party at Chequers, and this he thought 'the coldest house I have ever visited'. Churchill himself kept cosy in his 'siren suit' – an adaptation of the boiler suit that he had worn for bricklaying – but Hopkins had to keep his overcoat on and found that the only room which had any apparent form of 'central heating' was the downstairs bathroom, and there he settled to read newspapers and despatches.[17] The main impression that he obtained from his talks and his reading was, as he put it, that

> Most of the Cabinet and all of the military leaders here believe that invasion is imminent. They are straining every effort night and day to meet this. They believe that it may come at any moment, but not later than May 1. They believe that it will certainly be an all-out attack, including the use of poison gas and perhaps some other new weapons that Germany may have developed.[18]

Hopkins flew home in mid-February, having spent about twice as long in Britain as he originally intended. On March 8th the Lend-Lease Bill passed the Senate, and shortly afterwards Roosevelt put Hopkins in charge of aid for Britain.

Meanwhile John G. Winant had been appointed American Ambassador in London, and after meeting Hopkins in New York in February he flew over by way of Lisbon and Bristol, being met by the Duke of Kent on arrival in England and then being received by the King at Windsor – a compliment which matched Roosevelt's exceptional courtesy to Halifax when the latter arrived on the *King George V*.[19] Winant, like Averell Harriman who was in charge of the administration of Lend-Lease, was an impressive figure, both physically and intellectually. They both accompanied Churchill on a visit to some of the provincial cities which were being bombed: in April they toured Swansea and then Bristol, and in the latter city they received honorary degrees at the university from Churchill as Chancellor. For this occasion Churchill wore the gown which had been made for his father as Chancellor of the Exchequer; and Winant noticed that the University dons wore their robes over uniforms 'nearly all still soaked from their labours' in dealing with the night's air raids. The Australian Prime Minister Robert Menzies was in the party and was also the recipient of an honorary degree.[20]

In the strategy agreed with the French before war broke out, it had been taken for granted that Italy was the weaker element of the Axis, and that if both Germany and Italy entered the war it would be easy for the British and French to take the offensive against the Italian forces in Africa. But Italy did not enter the war until France was on the verge of collapse, and the plans had to be reconsidered. Early in August the British military commander in the Middle East, General Sir Archibald Wavell, visited Britain, and it was agreed, in spite of the needs of home defence, to reinforce him at once with several battalions of tanks and other equipment. But Wavell did not have a great deal to say for himself; and Eden and General Sir John Dill, the CIGS, were concerned to find that Churchill did not trust him, but regarded him as 'a good average colonel' suited to be 'a good chairman of a Tory association'.[21] In October Eden went out to the Middle East to see for himself; and after his return in November Churchill suggested that he (Eden) should take command – a proposal that Eden firmly rejected.[22]

In mid-December Wavell's troops successfully took the offensive against the Italian army on the borders of Egypt, swiftly capturing Sidi Barrani and moving along the coast into Libya to take (in January) Bardia and Tobruk and (in February) Benghazi. A total of 113,000 Italian soldiers were taken prisoner. The weakness of the Italian military machine was also revealed by the failure of an invasion of Greece, attempted from Albania in late October but thrown back by the Greek army in the ensuing weeks. Then in November an attack on Taranto harbour by aircraft from a British aircraft-carrier put three Italian battleships and a cruiser out of action for several months.

In February it became apparent that a German sweep through the Balkans was impending, and that Greece might then be overrun. By a joint Anglo-French guarantee of the spring of 1939 Greece was entitled to call upon British assistance, though Britain was entitled to argue that the fall of France had rendered the guarantee invalid. But the War Cabinet was concerned about the need to create some sort of barrier to Axis expansion in the Balkans, and encouraged Eden, the new Foreign Secretary, and General Sir John Dill to pay a visit to Cairo, Athens and also the Turkish capital, Ankara, to see what could be done. Churchill was anxious that the emissaries should not think that he was exerting pressure in favour of intervention, and so informed them by telegram;[23] but they both took an optimistic view of the prospects of holding the Germans in Greece, thinking also that the decision to intervene would have an encouraging effect on Turkey and Yugoslavia.[24] Wavell was of the same view.

On March 27th there was a *coup d'état* in Yugoslavia which installed a new government favourable to resistance. The *coup* was at once hailed by Churchill ('Early this morning the Yugoslav nation found its soul') and he envisaged a Balkan front of seventy divisions (including those of Turkey) against the thirty divisions of the German army.[25] But the new Yugoslav government was still hesitating about the idea of a military agreement with Britain and Greece when both Yugoslavia and Greece were invaded by the Germans. The strength of the German armies was soon evident: the Yugoslavs capitulated after eleven days, and shortly afterwards the British troops in Greece were forced to evacuate the country. Nearly 50,000 of the 62,000 British Commonwealth force were successfully withdrawn, many of them to Crete.

The Italian navy had suffered a further serious defeat at the battle of Matapan at the end of March, when in a night action three heavy cruisers had been sunk without loss to the British. But the Germans were not deterred from making an assault upon Crete, using airborne forces as well as seaborne. The battle began on May 20th, and it saw very heavy casualties inflicted on the invaders, who nevertheless gradually won possession of an airfield and thereby secured their grip. In spite of heavy losses the British navy again evacuated the great bulk of the defending troops, most of whom were Australians or New Zealanders. Churchill was convinced that Wavell might have saved the island if he had only committed a few more tanks to the defence of the airfields.[26]

It seemed that the German strategy was to leapfrog across the eastern Mediterranean into Iraq – and a change in regime there looked like the prelude to such a move. Churchill asked Amery, the Secretary of State for India, to get the Viceroy and the Commander-in-Chief to forestall this by despatching some troops from India to Basra; and this was promptly done. Speaking of Auchinleck, the general who commanded the troops in India, Churchill as he later said was 'gratified by his forward mood' whereas Wavell 'only obeyed under protest'.[27] The situation in Iraq certainly responded rapidly to the prompt action that was taken. By the end of May an armistice had been signed and a new and friendly government had been established. Then, prodded by Churchill and the Chiefs of Staff, Wavell undertook the invasion of Syria, where the French colonial regime was loyal to Vichy. This advance, which was begun on June 8th and was assisted by some of General de Gaulle's Free French forces, involved some hard fighting, but it proved successful, and an armistice was signed on July 12th.

In order, as they hoped, to guarantee success in the main battle against the Germans in the Western Desert of north Africa, Churchill and the Chiefs of Staff had sent a large convoy of tanks directly through the Mediterranean instead of round the Cape of Good Hope. The battle in which they were employed had the code-name 'Battleaxe' and started on June 15th. But the German commander, General Rommel, acted with great skill in fighting a defensive battle with the use of 88mm guns whereas, as Churchill says, on the British side there was a 'failure to make a sortie from the Tobruk sally-port an element in the plan'.[28] Consequently this battle proved unsuccessful and had to be called off by Wavell.

Churchill had set much store by the success of 'Battleaxe'. 'I remember', his wife later said, 'terrible anxiety and even anger at Chequers on several Sundays because the newly-arrived tanks could only come into action so slowly.'[29] During the battle itself, while waiting for news, Churchill had gone down to his old home at Chartwell, shut up as it was, and had wandered about the valley there. Now he resolved to replace Wavell. In this he overbore his own CIGS, General Dill, who wrote: 'The fault was not Wavell's, except in so far as he did not resist pressure from Whitehall with sufficient vigour.'[30] Churchill made Wavell change places with Auchinleck, who was Commander-in-Chief, India. He also decided on the appointment of a political adviser for the

Middle East Command, and for this post chose Captain Oliver Lyttelton, whom he had known since childhood and had had as a colleague since October 1940 as President of the Board of Trade. Lyttelton was given the title of Minister of State and appointed to membership of the War Cabinet. The new post was largely the result of a suggestion to Churchill from his son Randolph, who was serving in the Middle East at the time.[31]

Meanwhile evidence had begun to accumulate that it was Hitler's intention to attack Russia. His decision had in fact been made before the end of 1940, but it was not until April that Churchill became convinced that it was desirable to warn Stalin of the danger; and it took some days for Sir Stafford Cripps, the British Ambassador, to find a suitable opportunity to pass the message on. Although the message was delivered in plenty of time to enable the Russian government to take the necessary precautions, it seems that little was done. When the attack began on June 22nd the Russian armed forces were taken by surprise: the troops had no clear orders to fire back, and many aircraft were destroyed on the ground. The British government did not expect the Russian forces to resist very effectively in any case: a Joint Intelligence Committee Report reckoned that the occupation of the Ukraine and the capture of Moscow could be accomplished in three to six weeks.[32] Thereafter it was thought that Hitler might rapidly revert to the idea of an invasion of Britain, and orders were issued for preparations to deal with the threat to be 'at concert pitch' by September 1st.[33]

But the campaign did not go as well as Hitler hoped and the British staff feared. Although the Russians suffered heavy losses, they kept on fighting; and the Germans, who had expected to face in all about two hundred divisions, found themselves confronted with a total of 360.[34] In spite of fierce fighting they continued to advance, and by October government departments were being evacuated from Moscow to Kuibyshev.

It was incumbent upon the British government to make efforts to assist Hitler's new victims. On the day when the invasion of Russia began Churchill, who had been thinking over how he should respond, made a broadcast in which he made his attitude clear. At a War Cabinet meeting on the preceding Thursday, the question had been raised, and Churchill had said that 'Germany should be represented as an insatiable tyrant, that had attacked

Russia in order to obtain material for carrying on the war.[35] On the following day he was with his secretary Jock Colville on the croquet lawn at Chequers when, in reply to a comment of Colville's about the embarrassment that a German invasion of Russia would be to him, he declared: 'If Hitler invaded Hell, I would at least make a favourable reference to the Devil in the House of Commons.'[36]

This set the tone of official British reaction; and in July an Anglo-Soviet agreement was made whereby the two countries undertook not to make a separate peace with Germany. It was arranged that two squadrons of RAF Hurricanes should be despatched to Murmansk to protect the northern shipping route, and also that troops should be sent into Iran to organise supply routes there and to prevent any German thrust to the oilfields. An Anglo-American Supply Conference in London in September decided to allocate to Russia various categories of munitions which had previously been destined for Britain. Churchill also instructed the Chiefs of Staff to examine the possibility of effecting a landing in Europe, for instance in the Normandy peninsula or in Norway; but after exhaustive discussion it transpired that shortage of landing-craft and lack of convenient bases to ensure air superiority rendered the idea impracticable. Churchill pressed the CIGS very hard, but in the last resort he felt he had to give way.[37]

There was nothing for it but to maintain the campaign in north Africa. Dill wrote to Auchinleck in October to stress the 'clamour, which grows, that we should do something for Russia' and the 'more dangerous' fact that the external press campaign was being backed up within the Cabinet by Beaverbrook, who he thought might 'stage a resignation on the grounds that he cannot continue to be a member of a government which has so signally failed to help Russia'.[38] When Auchinleck definitely committed himself to an attack in November, the Prime Minister responded with a warm message to the troops saying that they might well 'add a page to history which will rank with Blenheim and with Waterloo'.[39] But the British tanks were still outgunned by the enemy, and the fighting ended inconclusively. The whole of Cyrenaica was retaken and Tobruk was relieved, but there was no question of Rommel's forces being destroyed. Furthermore, his strength was enhanced by an increase in German air power in the Mediterranean and by the movement of a number of U-boats from the Atlantic. Malta came under heavy blockade, and the British naval squadrons at each end of the Mediterranean suffered serious damage.

Apart from these Mediterranean commitments, the navy was heavily engaged in the task of maintaining the sea-routes across the Atlantic. Hitler had intensified his submarine and air attacks on British shipping in the later months of 1940, and the monthly average of sinkings, which had been less than 100,000 tons, rose to about 250,000. On March 6th Churchill issued a directive giving the highest priority to defeating 'the attempt to strangle our food supplies and our connection with the United States'.[40] The action to be taken involved the bombing of enemy submarine and aircraft bases, and improved air cover and anti-aircraft defence for convoys and for ports. Efforts were also to be made to speed up the turn-round time of ships in dock both at home and overseas.

Enemy surface raiders usually claimed little of the regular monthly toll of shipping, but there was grave concern in May when the new German battleship, the *Bismarck*, thought to be the most powerful ship in the world, moved through Norwegian waters into the North Atlantic and sank the battle-cruiser *Hood*, for many years the pride of the British navy. After eluding pursuit for some hours the *Bismarck* was however brought to bay off the west coast of France by a combination of air attack, gunfire and torpedoes from a naval task force. The Prime Minister heard of the loss of the *Hood* on the Saturday morning of a weekend at Chequers, and there followed a period of acute suspense and attention to the charts, until on Monday morning the *Bismarck* was located and then later in the day brought to a standstill by damage inflicted by torpedoes. But she was very well constructed and was not sunk until after Churchill had completed a statement to the Commons about the incident on the Tuesday morning. He was able to give the news to the House, as it was brought in to him by Brendan Bracken.[41]

In August Churchill and Roosevelt decided to have their meeting, which they had postponed from the spring partly owing to the President's involvement in the legislative programme and partly as a result of Churchill's preoccupations with Greece and Crete.[42] They met on board ship off the coast of Newfoundland – at Argentia, Placentia Bay, where an American naval base was being built. Churchill arrived on the *Prince of Wales*, the newest British battleship, which had just been refitted after the battle with the *Bismarck*; Roosevelt appeared on the heavy cruiser *Augusta*. The two leaders were accompanied by their Chiefs of Staff and by a senior adviser apiece on foreign affairs – Sumner Welles, the Assistant Secretary of State, and Sir Alexander Cadogan, the Permanent Under-Secretary at the Foreign Office; Harry Hopkins, Harriman, Beaverbrook, and Cherwell (the newly ennobled Professor Lindemann) were also there.[43]

The importance of the meeting was more symbolic than actual. Roosevelt and Churchill made each other's acquaintance, virtually for the first time, and began to understand each other's mind. The Chiefs of Staff also had an opportunity to get to know each other; and there was much mutual good-feeling in their attendance together at a Church Parade service on the Sunday morning on the *Prince of Wales*. The service was also attended by a contingent of American sailors as well as by the ship's company of the *Prince of Wales*. Churchill's own account of this occasion deserves quotation:

> I chose the hymns myself – 'For Those in Peril on the Sea' and 'Onward, Christian Soldiers'. We ended with 'O God, Our Help in Ages Past', which Macaulay reminds us the Ironsides had chanted as they bore John Hampden's body to the grave. Every word seemed to stir the heart. It was a great hour to live. Nearly half of those who sang were soon to die.[14]

The two leaders discussed their possible reactions to a German invasion of Spain and Portugal, and to Japanese aggression in the Far East. Churchill thought he had pinned Roosevelt down to a strong warning to Japan positively threatening war, but later on this was watered down by the State Department. They did, however, agree to publish a joint statement of principles which became known as the 'Atlantic Charter'. This incorporated minor amendments for the benefit of the British War Cabinet which during the conference was hastily summoned to a meeting in Whitehall to consider the draft before it was finally agreed. Churchill's colleagues asked him to mention in the text of the Charter the ideals of 'social security' and 'freedom from want', and this was done. Churchill also persuaded Roosevelt to agree to a phrase about the 'establishment of a wider and more permanent system of general security', which involved a degree of commitment to some form of international organisation. The

American Secretary of State, Cordell Hull, on the other hand, who was neither present nor consulted, was pained by the mention of 'due respect for existing obligations' in the paragraph dealing with the post-war economy, and tried subsequently to obtain clarification in the form of a British undertaking to abandon imperial preference – an undertaking that he was unable to secure. The incident certainly implied that the British machinery of government was a good deal more coherent than the American.[45]

For the rest, the trip gave Churchill a chance to relax in congenial surroundings. At Placentia Bay he took exercise by going ashore in his 'siren suit', clambering over the rocks and rolling boulders down a cliff.[46] The need for wireless silence prevented him from working at his usual pace, and he was able to read a historical novel lent him by Oliver Lyttelton – C. S. Forester's *Captain Hornblower R.N.*[47] – and to attend a succession of films in the evenings. He saw *Lady Hamilton* for the fifth time and was again moved to tears.[48] On the return journey the *Prince of Wales* encountered a large convoy of some 72 ships in several columns, proceeding at about 7 knots. According to Cadogan it was 'a beautiful and inspiring sight.... The forest of funnels looked almost like a town.'[49] Churchill also paid a visit to Iceland and reviewed British and American troops there. He received a warm welcome from the people of Reykjavik, whose hot springs he specially admired. The most substantial achievement of the meeting was probably Roosevelt's commitment to 'Plan IV', whereby the United States navy assumed the responsibility for convoying fast merchant ships as far east as Iceland. This would be a considerable easement of the burden being shouldered by the British navy in respect of convoy work.[50]

It was not to be expected that the degree of political unity in Britain achieved in the summer of 1940 would persist throughout the following year – and especially not after the failures of the campaigns at Dakar, in Greece and in Crete. Early in May 1941 the Commons debated a motion of no confidence, and this occasion saw the emergence of various critics of the government, including the leader of the previous wartime Coalition. Lloyd George argued that Churchill had surrounded himself with 'yes-men' rather than with 'absolutely independent men, men of experience' such as Lloyd George had employed in his Cabinet in the First World War.[51] Churchill replied vigorously, and compared Lloyd George to Marshal Pétain. Although Lloyd George himself, and also a leading Labour backbencher, Emanuel Shinwell, abstained from voting, the division at the end of the debate resulted in an overwhelming vote of confidence for Churchill – 447 to 3, the minority, together with the two tellers, consisting of one Communist, one 'crypto-Communist' and three pacifists. As A. J. Cummings, the *News Chronicle* commentator, wrote:

> The War Debate was well worth while.... It revealed to friend and foe alike, and to all the people of the British Empire, the unassailable authority of the Prime Minister. It revealed to the Prime Minister himself the critical alertness of a House of Commons which, in spite of its many C3 characteristics, declines the status of a passive rubber-stamp acquiescence.[52]

In the later spring Churchill grappled with the problem of reorganising his Cabinet so as to deal more effectively with areas of government that had been specially criticised – notably matters of production and of information. On July 1st Beaverbrook became Minister of Supply and was thenceforward responsible for production of tanks, as he had previously been responsible for production of aircraft. Beaverbrook attended the Atlantic meeting in order to develop liaison with American leaders on questions of supply to Russia; and afterwards he went on to Washington, and on his return to London reported unfavourably on the prospects of any early American participation in the fighting war.[53] All the same he thought that the British army should take advantage of the desperate fighting on the Eastern Front, perhaps by a raid by tanks in brigade strength on the Cherbourg peninsula.[54] But Churchill found that the Chiefs of Staff felt this to be impossible. Late in August Churchill had voiced to Hopkins his disappointment at the outcome of his meeting with Roosevelt, especially in the light of the President's assurances to American journalists that the United States was 'no closer to war', which had caused 'a wave of depression' in the British Cabinet and in informed circles; he told Hopkins that he would be 'grateful if you could give me any kind of hope'.[55]

In some respects, in spite of Roosevelt's remarks, the United States was closer to war. There was, for instance, the extension of the role of the United States navy, which resulted in clashes with German U-boats and consequent American casualties. On October 17th a US destroyer, the *Kearney*, was hit by a torpedo not far from Iceland, and suffered eleven fatal casualties. On October 30th another destroyer, the *Reuben James*, was torpedoed and sunk, with the loss of 115 lives. Yet even this failed to precipitate a declaration of war. Hitler for his part was evidently not anxious to provoke another enemy, and Roosevelt felt that Congress – which he recognised was 'not truly representative of the country' – was not yet fully committed to the cause.[56]

The sense of passivity was partly occasioned by the critical character of American–Japanese relations. In Japan the Cabinet of Prince Konoyé fell on October 16th, and a new government was formed by the less moderate General Tojo. Tojo continued to negotiate for an agreement with the US government, but he also prepared an assault upon the US naval base at Pearl Harbor and a simultaneous invasion of Hong Kong and Malaya. At first Roosevelt was prepared to agree to an arrangement whereby the Japanese would be permitted to hold not more than 25,000 troops in French Indo-China – the so-called *modus vivendi* – but when on November 26th the US State Department received news of further Japanese troop movements to the south the *modus vivendi* was abandoned.[57]

There was now an acute threat to the British possessions in the Far East – Hong Kong, Malaya and Singapore in the first instance, and Australia and New Zealand thereafter. It had long been accepted by the British Chiefs of Staff and the Committee of Imperial Defence that the defence of Singapore was even more important than that of the Suez Canal: this was for the sake of Australia and New Zealand, whose governments would not otherwise allow their troops to serve in distant theatres of war.[58] Churchill did not accept this view of Empire strategy: he could not attach, he later wrote, more than one-fifth the importance to Singapore that he did to the Canal. But he conceded that it was 'a tragic issue, like having to decide whether your son or your daughter should be killed'.[59] When Anglo-American staff talks were held in Washington in February–March 1941 the British tried hard to persuade the Americans to undertake a commitment to defend Singapore, but this they refused to do.[60] Consequently, Dill, the CIGS, was for sending reinforcements to the Far East in the spring;[61] but Churchill, believing in the light of Chinese resistance that the Japanese forces could not be very efficient, opposed the idea.[62] Churchill also took the Foreign Office view that the Japanese were unlikely to enter the war until Russia had

475

been defeated.[63] In addition, he mistakenly believed that Singapore was a fortress capable of all-round defence.[64]

Consequently the arrangements for the defence of Malaya and Singapore were distinctly inadequate. The aircraft, which were American-built Buffaloes, were inferior to the Hurricane and not even the equal of the Japanese Zero. The land forces available consisted of two Indian divisions and one Australian, none trained in jungle warfare. There were no tanks; and no arrangements had been made to raise local labour battalions to prepare defences, because the War Office would not pay for them.[65] There was no central control of the three services. In July Churchill, wishing in any case to make a change at the Ministry of Information, sent Duff Cooper to Singapore to make a report on the state of the defences;[66] but this was a very belated effort to improve matters. He later arranged to despatch two of the finest capital ships of the navy – the battleship *Prince of Wales*, on which he had lately travelled to visit Roosevelt, and the older battle-cruiser the *Repulse* – both under the command of Admiral Sir Tom Phillips, the former Vice-Chief of Naval Staff, to the Far East to act as a deterrent against a Japanese invasion of Malaya. Even this arrangement went wrong, as the original idea was that the ships should be accompanied by an aircraft-carrier, the *Indomitable*, but she went aground in the West Indies before she was due to sail and no substitute could be spared.[67]

On the evening of Sunday December 7th Churchill was at Chequers in the company of Winant, the American Ambassador, and Harriman, the Lend-Lease administrator. He had with him a small portable radio which Harry Hopkins had given him, and he turned it on for the news at 9 p.m. The announcer said something about 'the Japanese attacking the Americans', and Churchill and his companions 'all sat up'.[68] The statement was then confirmed by Churchill's butler, Sawyers, who heard it on another set. Churchill at once rose and telephoned to Roosevelt in Washington. He obtained a confirmation of the event, though not of the details – of the eight American battleships at Pearl Harbor four had been sunk and another three badly damaged. But he was now in charge of the Foreign Office, as Eden had set out to visit Stalin, so he then telephoned the Foreign Office to arrange the preparation of a declaration of war. His reaction was one of 'the greatest joy.... So we had won after all!' His confidence in the power of the United States was great; and he recalled a remark of Edward Grey's more than thirty years earlier – that the United States was like 'a gigantic boiler. Once the fire is lighted under it there is no limit to the power it can generate'. With this thought he went to bed and slept 'the sleep of the saved and thankful'.[69]

In the fourteen months leading up to Pearl Harbor Churchill drove himself with little relaxation or recreation – except for the trip to meet Roosevelt in August. It is true that meetings of the War Cabinet were no longer held daily as they had been in the summer of 1940; they normally took place twice a week, and from November 1941 the second meeting of the week, on Thursdays, was to assemble without the Chiefs of Staff or the range of ministers not in the War Cabinet who had got into the habit of attending regularly.[70] But all the same, in view of the numerous sessions of the Defence Committee (Operations) and the informal meetings, at all hours, that Churchill held with the Chiefs of Staff, it could hardly be said that he was taking things easily.[71]

Yet Churchill was very fit – probably fitter than he had been when out of office in the later 1930s. The effect of sustaining the national morale was evidently good for his own. Having a full-time job, he lived well and had a hearty appetite. In June 1941 he was reported – by 'Chips' Channon of all people – as living 'luxuriously . . . a most lavish lunch and grand train' on a special visit to Shoeburyness to see tanks and new anti-aircraft guns and devices.[72] Two months later Alec Cadogan was amazed to find that he could put down, without ill effect, first benedictine and then brandy on the train south from Scotland on the return journey from the Atlantic meeting; and the next morning he could consume cutlets and bacon for breakfast.[73] Barrington-Ward, the new editor of *The Times*, was invited to lunch by Churchill on December 1st 1941 and found him 'at 67 very fresh and young and spry . . . a different man altogether from the rather bloated individual whom I last saw (close to) before the war'.[74]

Churchill evidently enjoyed having a meal out with specially close friends, such as Eden or Beaverbrook. On such occasions he was quite prepared to discuss the most serious political questions. In July, at dinner with the Edens, he raised the question 'What can we do to show the Russians we are in earnest?' and added:

Remember that on my breast are the medals of the Dardanelles, Antwerp, Dakar and Greece, and I cannot support any more adventures or expeditions like that. I do not believe our generals could manage a major raid. They have not got beyond Crécy and Dettingen.[75]

He liked talking over the events of the First World War with Beaverbrook, and early in September he took him and Eden to the Ritz for 'a very good dinner, oysters, partridge etc. and good talk'.

Winston at the top of his form. Talk much of past events, some long past. Winston said that he would like best to have FE back to help him. Not FE of last years, but FE about '14 or '15. Next he would like AJB[alfour].[76]

It seems as if Churchill rather longed for people who were his intellectual equals and contemporaries, in the sense in which those who had been Lloyd George's colleagues were. Diana Cooper, the wife of Duff Cooper, an old colleague and friend but hardly of this stature, sensed the difficulty on a visit to Ditchley in February 1941: 'There is ... a new reverence for so great a leader, and that creates an atmosphere of slight embarrassment until late in the evening.'[77] To some extent this was inevitable, as he had to surround himself with secretaries and military staff and allied leaders, who were bound to take a subordinate place at his table. Brendan Bracken undoubtedly continued to hold his end up vigorously against Churchill, though he described Churchill to others as 'my Master' even after he had become Minister of Information in succession to Duff Cooper in July 1941.[78]

As for the family, Randolph, whose son and heir, Winston, had been born at Chequers in October 1940, served with the army in the Middle East from 1941, and Mary, who was the only one of the children actually living at home, joined the ATS on her nineteenth birthday in September 1941.[79] Sarah (Mrs Oliver), who had continued her work on the stage, joined the WAAF in October of the same year.[80]

Churchill kept his usual close watch on the newspapers, recalling from personal experience in the previous war how much they could influence the political scene. The Communist *Daily Worker*, which had closely followed the line of Soviet policy, in spite of its twists, since before the war, and which had sponsored a so-called People's Convention in January 1941 (which was supposed to represent over a million workers all demanding peace), was suppressed by the Home Secretary under the defence regulations issued the previous summer. But the circulation of the *Daily Worker* was only in five figures, and its suppression did not appear to be a major infringement of the liberty of the press.

But shortly afterwards Churchill took what seemed a long step further, and wrote to Cecil King, an executive of the *Daily Mirror*, to complain about what he took to be an 'offensive story'. Later on he denounced more generally 'a spirit of hatred and malice against the Government, which is after all not a Party Government but a National Government almost unanimously chosen'.[81] A few days later he saw King at 10 Downing Street, and gave him a fuller explanation of his views. He pointed out that the Chamberlainites in the House of Commons had a majority of 150, and said, 'I am not going to fight them as they are too numerous.'[82] King was then virtually forgiven, and lunched at No. 10 shortly afterwards, in a mixed company presided over by Clementine.[83]

We have seen that Churchill secured a remarkable vote of confidence from the Commons in May, in spite of having to listen to much detailed criticism of his policies. This was confirmed by the successive Gallup Polls held to test the popular reaction to his leadership. In February those who answered affirmatively the question 'Do you approve or disapprove of Mr Churchill as Prime Minister?' numbered 85%. In March the proportion was 88%; in June 87%; in October it had slipped back, but not by very much, to 84%.[84] On the other hand, the proportion of those who described themselves as 'satisfied with the government's conduct of the war' in October 1941 was only 44%, as against 58% shortly before the invasion of Crete and 59% in February 1940.[85]

There was in fact a tendency for people to be restive, and to criticise the government and the Commons without having any alternative Prime Minister to propose. Churchill was upset by the result of a by-election at The Wrekin in late September, when a Conservative candidate was given a close run by an independent candidate who advocated a policy of air reprisals. Churchill argued to his colleagues in the War Cabinet that the result gave 'an entirely false impression of the degree of support which the National Government has in the country'. He therefore urged, and the Cabinet agreed, that in future government speakers should play an active part in by-elections.[86]

In the following month Cecil King caused trouble again, for the *Sunday Pictorial*, which was closely associated with the *Daily Mirror*, referred to the Commons in what Churchill thought to be 'the most offensive terms'. It said that

> Five out of every ten of the whole 615 were elected six years ago to see that Baldwin gave us 'Safety First' and no aeroplanes. And the bulk of the others either bought their seats for cash or had them freely handed over for services.[87]

The Home Secretary was instructed to look into the question of whether the *Pictorial* could be prosecuted for this: but in the end nothing was done. It would have been a serious matter to prosecute a newspaper with a circulation of millions.

Although Churchill was usually jealous of the privileges of Parliament and its members, there were occasions when he could lose his temper with backbenchers who sought to snipe at his closest colleagues. In November 1941 he was annoyed by a Parliamentary Question put down by a senior Conservative, Sir Waldron Smithers, implying criticism of the former Professor Lindemann, now Lord Cherwell.[88] He answered it rather abruptly, and when he encountered Sir Waldron in the Smoking Room afterwards he gave him a vigorous telling-off, saying, 'Don't you know that he is one of my oldest and greatest friends?' As 'Chips' Channon, who reported this story, commented, 'Winston's blind loyalty to his friends is one of his most endearing qualities'.[89]

23. 1942, The Critical Year

BEFORE Pearl Harbor, Churchill had regarded the war as essentially a European struggle – even though he had called the power of the United States to the aid of Britain and her Continental allies. After Pearl Harbor, he realised that it was a wider conflict, in which, as he calculated, 'four-fifths of the population of the globe were ranged against the dictator powers'.[1] He saw it as the British task to weld this coalition together, and to ensure that the strategy pursued was the best to accomplish the downfall of the enemy. He himself, like Marlborough or the younger Pitt, had to be the linchpin of the axle for the whole movement. There was a danger that the strategy of the war would lose coherence, as the Americans, in their fury at the success of the first Japanese onslaught, might insist on concentrating all their power on the Pacific War, to the neglect of previous commitments to help Britain and Russia. Russia had not been attacked by Japan, and was therefore not directly involved in the Pacific War. Churchill consequently determined to propose an immediate visit to confer with Roosevelt, meeting him either at Bermuda or in Washington itself.[2]

The President said that he felt obliged to stay at home for the time being, but that he would be pleased to entertain Churchill at the White House. So Churchill, with a party of about eighty, crossed the Atlantic in mid-December 1941 on the battleship *Duke of York*. The party included all the Chiefs of Staff except

General Sir Alan Brooke, who had lately been appointed to succeed General Sir John Dill. The latter was just on the point of reaching retiring age, and Churchill, who found that he was too quietly spoken for his own liking – the 'family solicitor' as he dubbed him[3] – was happy to take this opportunity of releasing him. But all the same he took Dill, who of course knew the background, with him on the trip to Washington.

The *Duke of York* was a modern battleship, in fact the sistership of the *Prince of Wales* on which Churchill had made his last transatlantic trip. But the trip was a less happy one for Churchill, not only because of bad weather, but because the *Prince of Wales* and the *Repulse* had just been sunk by Japanese torpedo-bombers off the coast of Malaya, where they had been endeavouring to intercept and harass enemy troop landings. Admiral Tom Phillips, Churchill's old colleague on the Board of Admiralty, had been lost with eight hundred and forty men. As we have seen, luck had played a part in this disaster: it had been intended that the ships should be accompanied by an aircraft-carrier, but the only available carrier had suffered accidental damage, and there was none to take her place.[4]

The sinkings were a highly inauspicious start to the battle for Singapore, and in themselves a cruel blow, but they did not deflect Churchill and his Chiefs of Staff from the view that Germany remained the principal enemy. The journey provided time for Churchill to prepare three papers summing up the British view of future strategy. Each paper was closely considered by the Chiefs of Staff, but Churchill was pleased to discover what he later called 'our usual harmony on principles and values'.[5] The papers emphasised the significance of 'Hitler's failure and losses in Russia', and spoke also – too optimistically as it turned out – of 'the impending victory of General Auchinleck in Cyrenaica'.[6] For 1942, Churchill argued for Anglo-American concentration on winning French North Africa, so as to clear that continent altogether and to free the Mediterranean for Allied shipping. American troops, he hoped, would soon come to Northern Ireland, and American bombers to bases in England from which Germany could be attacked.

The Pacific War, Churchill thought, might for 1942 be seen mainly in terms of a revival of Anglo-American sea and air power, with aircraft-carriers, rather than battleships, forming the backbone of the fleet. But 1943 would be the year in which it would be possible to take the offensive against Germany. Landings should be made in Europe 'by armoured and mechanised forces capable of disembarking not at ports but on beaches'.[7] This was a remarkable forecast of what was in fact to happen, though not as early as he hoped; but at this stage he also believed that the conquered people of Europe would be able to play an important role: 'If the incursion of the armoured formations is successful, the uprising of the local population, for whom weapons must be brought, will supply the corpus of the liberating offensive.'[8]

In Washington, Churchill was accommodated in the White House itself, and was thus in constant touch with the President. On his first night there, December 22nd, he suggested joint Anglo-American intervention in French North Africa. He recognised that the Americans would be more welcome to the Frenchmen on the spot than the British would be. As he put it in his report to the War Cabinet, 'I emphasised immense psychological effect likely to be produced both in France and among French troops in North Africa by association of United States with the under-taking.'[9] These views were in general warmly greeted by the President, who had already indicated his sympathy with such a strategy in conversation with Attlee on the latter's visit to America in the autumn.[10] It was also specifically agreed that American troops should shortly move to Northern Ireland, thereby relieving more fully trained British troops for other duties; and that American bombers should join the offensive against Germany.

After two days the conversations were interrupted for Christmas festivities. Churchill was with Roosevelt at the lighting of a Christmas tree in the White House grounds, but he had to spend some of Christmas Day itself preparing a speech for delivery to both Houses of Congress on the 26th. This was a unique occasion, at least for Churchill, as he had never previously addressed a foreign parliament.[11] He opened on a quiet note, saying that he wished that his mother, 'whose memory I cherish across the vale of years', could have been there for the occasion. He added: 'I cannot help reflecting that if my father had been American and my mother British, instead of the other way round, I might have got here on my own.' The speech was on the whole warmly received, particularly when, speaking of the Japanese attack, he said, 'What kind of a people do they think we are?' In his perora-tion he dwelt on his faith in the future: 'In the days to come the British and American peoples will for their own safety and for the good of all walk together side by side in majesty, in justice and in peace.'[12] As he left to return to the White House, he was accorded a standing ovation by his audience.

He had been working at very high pressure for many weeks, and the War Cabinet had insisted on his being accompanied on the trip by the distinguished Harley Street physician, Sir Charles Wilson. On the night after his speech he found his room hot and stuffy, and got up to open the window. It was stiff, and he had to use, as he later put it, 'considerable force'. He then experienced some disagreeable sensations, which he reported to Wilson next morning: 'I was short of breath. I had a dull pain over my heart. It went down my left arm. It didn't last very long, but it has never happened before. What is it?'[13] Wilson realised that this was a slight heart attack, but he did not want to worry either Churchill himself or his colleagues and the general public. He therefore simply warned him to avoid exertion, and mentally resolved to 'take him to Parkinson, who will hold his tongue'.[14] Dr John Parkinson was a distinguished London cardiologist.

So Churchill carried on with his programme of discussions. He accepted Roosevelt's proposal that there should be a united command in the south-west Pacific under a single officer. The officer whom the President had in mind was General Wavell, at the time serving as Commander-in-Chief, India; he was to have a staff drawn from all the nationalities represented in his command. It was also agreed that an Anglo-American Combined Chiefs of Staff Committee should be established in Washington, and General Sir John Dill was appointed to serve on this as the senior British representative. These were concessions to American views, justified by Churchill in view of the degree to which British strategic ideas had already prevailed. As the official historians of American strategic planning have put it, 'It appeared at the time to the American staff that the British thoroughness had a decisive influence at the conference.'[15]

Churchill then briefly visited Canada, and addressed the Canadian Parliament as he had addressed the American Congress – though this time he also spoke a few sentences in French. He returned to Washington overnight on New Year's Eve. At midnight he gave a toast to the newsmen who were accompanying him. It was couched in cautious terms: 'Here's to 1942. Here's to a year of toil – a year of struggle and peril, and a long step forward towards victory.'[16] On New Year's Day he and Roosevelt signed a declaration, later adhered to by Russia and the other Allied nations, proclaiming what was rather optimistically called the 'United Nations' – a grouping of powers at any rate all at war together and all now pledged not to make a separate peace with the enemy. Meanwhile Beaverbrook had been impressing on Donald Nelson, the Executive Director of American War Production, the need as he saw it for establishing still higher targets for war supplies.

Early in January Churchill had a few days' rest in Florida, where Edward Stettinius, the President's Administrator of Lend-Lease, lent him a villa near Palm Beach. On January 15th he left Washington for Bermuda, where the *Duke of York* was waiting to take him home, but on the spur of the moment he decided to fly the Atlantic on the Boeing Clipper which was flying him to Bermuda, and which he found comfortable. This was still a rare and brave thing to do, but it brought him back to London a week earlier than otherwise.[17]

On his return to England Churchill found that public opinion was restive, principally about the loss of the *Prince of Wales* and the *Repulse*, but also partly about the sudden success of Rommel's attack in the Western Desert. He therefore decided to have a Commons debate on a vote of confidence. He opened the debate himself, on January 27th, with a speech in which he announced that nearly two-thirds of Rommel's army were 'wounded, prisoners, or dead': but he paid tribute to Rommel as 'a very daring and skilful opponent ... and, may I say across the havoc of war a great general'.[18] He also spoke of the supply of arms and material to Russia and of the decisions made in Washington – the formation of the Combined Chiefs of Staff and the creation of the Combined Command for the South-West Pacific. Harold Nicolson's account of the speech suggests that it was very successful:

> One can actually feel the wind of opposition dropping sentence by sentence, and by the time he finishes it is clear that there is really no opposition at all – only a certain uneasiness.... When he feels that he has the whole House with him, he finds it difficult to conceal his enjoyment of his speech, and that, in fact, is part of his amazing charm. He thrusts both his hands deep into his trouser pockets, and turns his tummy now to the right, now to the left, in evident enjoyment of his mastery of the position.[19]

Those who spoke in the debate were many of them sympathetic critics – that is to say, they announced their willingness to continue their support of the government; but some pointed out, by way of parallel, that the Americans had already held an official enquiry into the Pearl Harbor disaster and had decided that certain officers were to be punished by suspension from duty. Pethick-Lawrence, the Labour spokesman who had defeated Churchill at Leicester in 1923, voiced the left-wing view that the Asiatic population of Britain's eastern empire should be associated more fully with their own defence, and that in particular India should be promised full self-government:

> India with its immense potential energy remains dormant and needs to be awakened. Like the princess in the fairy tale, it is only the magic touch of the prince that can kindle it into pulsating life. For the purpose of this analogy the Prime Minister is that prince. He alone, partly because of his past associations with India, partly because he is the Prime Minister at the present time, and partly because of his wonderful command of words, has the power to touch India in a way no other man in this House or outside can possibly do.[20]

There was also some rather confused criticism of the existing system of government at the top. There was a demand for a War Cabinet of men without departments, on the analogy of Lloyd George's War Cabinet of the First World War; but there was also a call for the creation of a Ministry of Production, apparently on a grander scale than the old Ministry of Munitions. The Prime Minister was personally criticised for being both Prime Minister and Minister of Defence. The debate lasted altogether for three days, and on the last day Churchill spoke for a second time, and announced that, as the United States had a minister who was in effect a Minister of Production – in Donald Nelson – he also would appoint one.[21] This concession may have won over some waverers; and when the House divided, the vote of confidence was carried by 464 votes to one – the single opponent, and two tellers on his side, being members of the pacifist Independent Labour Party.

Such a success in a vote of confidence might have been expected to give the government new strength; but as it happened the news from the war fronts got worse, and it was on this that the government's reputation now largely depended. The situation was different from that of 1940, when Churchill could claim to be free of responsibility for the existing state of the defences. Rommel went on to recapture Benghazi; and, worse still, in the Far East the Japanese invaded Singapore Island itself and on February 15th forced the garrison to surrender. Some 60,000 men yielded to a considerably smaller body of invaders; and Churchill himself later described the event as 'the worst disaster and largest capitulation in British history'.[22] As it happened, another event closer to home upset people to an equal degree – as Churchill thought, unreasonably. This was the movement of the two battle-cruisers *Scharnhorst* and *Gneisenau* and the cruiser *Prinz Eugen* through the English Channel from Brest, apparently without damage from British attack. In reality this was a defensive move on Hitler's part, as he feared a British assault on Norway to bring assistance to the Russians. The failure of torpedo attack from the air was probably due in large part to the despatch of the main force of torpedo bombers to reinforce the Mediterranean Fleet, which was weak at that time owing to the success of Italian frogmen in Alexandria Harbour, where the two remaining British battleships had been temporarily immobilised; and the *Scharnhorst* and *Gneisenau* were later found to have been damaged by mines. But such of these facts as were already known could not be revealed to restore the government's credit.[23]

The only thing Churchill could do to allay distress was to undertake a substantial reconstruction of his government. Sir Stafford Cripps, the former Labour minister who had been ambassador in Moscow, had now returned to Britain and was an obvious candidate for office: in January Churchill had invited him to be Minister of Supply, but Cripps had refused, evidently being reluctant to serve in a position subordinate to Beaverbrook, who was a member of the War Cabinet. In early February Beaverbrook formally became Minister of War Production, but serious problems arose in defining the functions of his ministry, particularly in its relationship with the Ministry of Labour, whose Minister, Ernest Bevin, was to say the least jealous of his powers. Beaverbrook was also suffering seriously from chronic asthma, and late in February he resigned, to depart on what Churchill himself describes as a 'vaguely defined mission to the United States', which was really designed as an opportunity for him to rest.[24] Churchill brought in as Minister of Production another personal friend, Oliver Lyttelton, who had been serving as Minister of State at Cairo.

The changes made in the War Cabinet were not very startling. Its numbers were reduced from eight to seven; and as so many other ministers attended its meeting for particular items of business the appearance of change was slight. As Sir Alexander Cadogan, the Under-Secretary at the Foreign Office who was a 'constant attender', reported in his diary for February 23rd: 'New Cabinet at 6. Looks very much like the old!'[25] Cripps had entered as Lord Privy Seal and Leader of the House of Commons. Attlee had been re-styled Deputy Prime Minister and had also taken on the Dominions Office from Cranborne, who now went to the Colonial Office, again outside the Cabinet. Arthur Greenwood, the Deputy Leader of the Labour Party, who owed his prominence to his position in the party and not to any administrative ability, left the government altogether; and Kingsley Wood was asked to leave the War Cabinet, but not the Chancellorship, to maintain a party balance. Lyttelton, the new Minister of Production, was to be replaced at Cairo by Richard Casey, whom Churchill had met in Washington where he was serving as Australian Minister; and Casey later pointed out that the War Cabinet, of which he attended meetings when visiting London, rarely divided on the lines of political partisanship.[26]

Churchill had been distinctly embarrassed by having to make changes in his government under pressure of public opinion; and he sought to avoid painful interviews with the retiring ministers by notifying them by letter only.[27] But at least the changes seemed to produce the desired effect on public opinion. The parliamentary correspondent of *The Times* reported even before the end of February that there was 'a marked change in the mood of the House of Commons, as was made evident both by the cordiality of the Prime Minister's reception yesterday and by the tone of the debate.'[28]

But the news on the war fronts did not show much improvement. In early March Rangoon fell to the Japanese, and the troops there under the command of General Harold Alexander had to fight their way out to the Indian border – which they did with hardihood and skill. The German submarine war made serious inroads into Allied shipping, especially near the coast of the Americas, where, as Roosevelt admitted to Churchill in a letter of mid-March, 'My Navy has been definitely slack.'[29] So much had changed so quickly that Churchill began to think that it was desirable for him to have another meeting with Roosevelt.

He wrote to him on April 1st: 'Perhaps when the weather gets better I may propose myself for a weekend with you and flip over. We have so much to settle that would go easily in talk.'[30]

One thing that Churchill may have thought needed 'settling' was the increasing American interest in the progress of constitutional reform in India. Roosevelt had appointed a personal representative in India, Colonel Louis Johnson, and although Churchill chose to regard his functions as purely 'technical', that is, to expedite the despatch of war material, Roosevelt's message of appointment sent to the Viceroy was phrased more generously, if more vaguely.[31] Johnson was certainly a man of political importance in the United States, and was later to serve as Truman's Secretary of Defense.

But the opportunity for Johnson to intervene in Indian politics would not have arisen if the British War Cabinet itself had not been deeply divided on Indian constitutional issues, with Cripps's appointment tipping the balance in favour of a new attempt to solve the problem. Early in February Attlee wrote a memorandum for his colleagues arguing that, with the military successes of the Japanese, the dogged character of Chinese resistance, and the remarkable performance of the Russians (whom he described as 'semi-oriental'), 'the East is now asserting itself against the long domination of the West'. He distrusted the 'mental attitude' of the Viceroy, Lord Linlithgow, and advocated a mission similar to that by which a century earlier 'Lord Durham saved Canada to the British Empire'.[32] The result of this was the creation of a special War Cabinet Committee on India: Churchill took the chair at its first meeting, and it also included – besides Amery, the Secretary of State – Attlee and Simon, who had both been on the India Commission of 1929, and also John Anderson and James Grigg, who had both served in the government of India. In March it was decided that Cripps should go out to India to put to the political leaders an offer for Dominion Status after the war: it was hoped that this would win them over to support of resistance against the threatened Japanese invasion, especially as Cripps was a friend of both Gandhi and Nehru, the Congress leaders.

But it soon transpired that Gandhi and Nehru were not interested in post-war promises – which Gandhi was said to have described as 'a post-dated cheque on a crashing bank'.[33] They demanded an immediate reconstruction of the Indian government, so as to make the Viceroy no more than a figurehead. In particular, they wanted control of the defence portfolio; and they persuaded Cripps to modify the proposals which he had brought with him, which he did in collaboration with Colonel Johnson. Churchill could not accept these new ideas, and telegraphed to Cripps: 'It was certainly agreed between us all that there were not to be negotiations but that you were to try to gain acceptance with possibly minor variations or elaborations of our great offer.'[34] Cripps was now obliged to break off the talks with the Indian leaders, although Roosevelt sent Churchill a personal telegram asking him to keep them going. To this Churchill replied in a strongly worded message:

> You know the weight I attach to everything you say to me, but I did not feel I could take the responsibility for the defence of India if everything has to be thrown into the melting-pot at this critical juncture.... Anything like a serious difference between you and me would break my heart, and would surely deeply injure both our countries at the height of this terrible struggle.[35]

So the Cripps Mission was allowed to fail, and the system of government in India remained unchanged for the duration of the war. In mid-June Amery reported to the Viceroy on Churchill's attitude to Indian constitutional change:

> The Cripps Mission ... has by now receded far into the background of his mind. For him, the main thing about it has been the good effect in America; for the rest, he isn't interested, really disliking the whole problem as much as ever before. The main difference perhaps is that he now looks upon me as a steady and supporting influence and not as a dangerous innovator![36]

But of even greater importance in the story was the fact that the danger of Japanese invasion of India by sea rapidly receded in the summer of 1942. This was a result of the sinking of four Japanese aircraft-carriers by the American navy at the battle of Midway on June 4th. Although Midway Island was a very long way from India, being in fact halfway across the Pacific, the battle's effect upon the whole course of the war against Japan was of decisive importance.

Meanwhile, no firm decisions had been made about Allied

strategy for a 'Second Front' in Europe, to relieve some of the German pressure on the Russians. In May the Russian Foreign Minister, Molotov, visited Britain to discuss this and also the question of a long-term alliance with Britain. He wanted the recognition of the Russian frontiers of 1941, but he found Churchill and Eden unable to give way on this point, which would contravene not merely the British guarantee to Poland but also the Atlantic Charter. Eventually he agreed to sign a twenty-year alliance, with no mention of frontiers. Churchill then gave Molotov a statement which implied, without giving a definite promise, that a Second Front would be opened some time in 1942. Actually, his mind was still not yet made up on the question, and he was hoping that British and Canadian forces might assault the north of Norway and gradually 'roll the map of Hitler's Europe down from the top'.[37] But this idea, although thoroughly discussed, found no favour with the Chiefs of Staff and the operational planners and had to be dropped.

It seemed more practicable to postpone the assault on Europe itself until at least 1943 and to revert to the idea of a joint Anglo-American descent upon French North Africa. This would lead to the clearing of enemy forces from the Mediterranean, with considerable advantages for the navy, for shipping in general, and for the air forces. It was to discuss these prospects and other possibilities that Churchill crossed the Atlantic in mid-June, accompanied by General Sir Alan Brooke and by General Sir Hastings Ismay, his Chief of Staff as Minister of Defence.

Churchill made this a briefer trip than his visit over Christmas had been, and his staff was much smaller. He flew both ways by the same Boeing Clipper flying-boat that had brought him home in January. He left England on June 17th, and after a brief rest at Washington went on to visit the President at his family home at Hyde Park, in New York State. While they were there, the two leaders made an agreement for the development of work on the atomic bomb, which had hitherto been in the phase of scientific investigation but now needed the construction of large factories. It was agreed that this should be done in the United States rather than in Britain, where resources were scarce and where the enemy might gain some idea of the work in progress by photographic reconnaissance. But the subject was so secret that nothing was put on paper, and the agreement was virtually forgotten about for some months.[38]

For further discussions with the military leaders Churchill returned to Washington with the President by train on the night of June 20th; and next day at the White House he was suddenly shocked to receive the news, in a message from the President's own hands, of the fall of Tobruk to the enemy, with the loss of twenty-five thousand men taken prisoner. It later turned out that the number of prisoners was still larger – in fact thirty-three thousand. Churchill was touched by the President's immediate response to his obvious distress: 'What can we do to help?' he inquired; and after General Marshall had first proposed to send an American armoured division, it was arranged that 300 Sherman tanks which were just being issued to this division, and also 100 self-propelled guns, should be sent out.[39] This was a vitally important decision, as it turned out; but the further question of the direction of the main Anglo-American military effort was not decided. At least Churchill and Brooke had a valuable opportunity of getting to know Stimson, the Secretary of War, and General Marshall, his Chief of Staff; and at Stimson's and Marshall's urgent request they spent a day at Fort Jackson, South Carolina, where various military exercises were staged, including a parachute descent by over 600 men.

Churchill and some of his party flew home in the Clipper on the night of June 26th and were greeted with the news that Maldon, a previously safe Conservative seat in Essex – not far from Churchill's own constituency – had returned a left-wing independent candidate, Tom Driberg, against the official nominee. He also discovered that a leading Conservative backbench MP, Sir John Wardlaw-Milne, had put down a motion expressing 'no confidence in the central direction of the war'. Churchill had no doubt that it was the fall of Tobruk that had prompted both these manifestations of hostility to his government. He was quite prepared to face the renewed parliamentary challenge, which took place on July 1st and 2nd.

This debate marked the high peak of parliamentary criticism of Churchill's wartime Coalition. But it also showed clearly how weak the critics were when it came to producing a constructive alternative. Wardlaw-Milne, in opening the debate, took Churchill to task once again for being both Prime Minister and Minister of Defence; but he then went on to urge, for the latter post, the appointment of the King's brother, the Duke of Gloucester. The suggestion was thought to be absurd; as Harold

Nicolson recorded in his diary, 'A wave of panic-embarrassment passed over the House. For a full minute the buzz goes round, "But the man must be an ass" Milne pulls himself together and recaptures the attention of the House, but his idiotic suggestion has shaken the validity of his position and his influence is shattered.'[40] The motion was seconded by Admiral of the Fleet Sir Roger Keyes, Churchill's old ally of the Gallipoli days. Keyes had lately been removed from his post as Chief of Combined Operations on the recommendation of the Chiefs of Staff, and it was against them that his wrath was really directed. Unlike Milne, he thought that Churchill interfered with the service planners too little, and not too much. There was thus an obvious inconsistency in the critics' case.

Next day there was an able but bitter speech by Aneurin Bevan, but his capacity for holding the House and producing wounding epithets was not equalled by any strategic grasp. He declared that 'the Prime Minister wins debate after debate and loses battle after battle', and he criticised the army for being 'ridden by class prejudice'.[41] He maintained that if Rommel had been in the British army he would still have been a sergeant – an odd idea in view of Rommel's middle-class background. In his reply Churchill did not attempt to explain the fall of Tobruk, which he admitted he had not expected, but he made much of his opponents' inconsistencies and mistakes and he called upon the House to show loyalty in the face of foreign interest and concern. When the House divided, the motion of no confidence was defeated by 475 to 25. Curiously enough, the figure of 25 was the same as that mentioned by Walter Elliot, one of the Prime Minister's supporters in the debate, as being the highest total of critics that could be mustered to vote against the younger Pitt in the black year of 1799.

Meanwhile Auchinleck had taken personal control of the Eighth Army and had decided to retreat far into Egypt, establishing his line of defence at El Alamein, two-thirds of the way back from the frontier to Cairo. At this point the Qattera Depression, impassable for tanks, was only thirty-five miles from the coast, and so there was valuable flank protection for a defensive stand. When Rommel arrived on the scene, Auchinleck engaged in vigorous counter-attacks, and took several thousand prisoners. Although there had been something of a panic in Cairo early in July, by the end of the month the situation seemed more stable, and the knowledge that substantial reinforcements were on the way encouraged the army to hold on.

Churchill wanted to go out to Cairo early in July to see things for himself, and he was with difficulty restrained from this by Eden, Bracken and Alan Brooke.[42] Later that month, Roosevelt sent Hopkins, General Marshall and Admiral King to London together to try to decide the question of future strategy. Of the three, Marshall was the only one who was really set on an early Second Front in Europe; King gave some support to Marshall's view, arguing that if there was to be no early attack on France, the best alternative lay in putting resources into the Pacific War. But the British Chiefs of Staff adhered solidly to their view that no attack on Europe was possible in 1942, and when this view was relayed to Roosevelt he declared for the assault on French Africa. The date of the decision for this course was July 25th.[43]

A week later Churchill, with Alan Brooke, was on his way by air to the Middle East, in order to see the Eighth Army for himself and make any necessary changes in its command. He proposed to combine this trip with a visit to Stalin, to inform the latter about the decision regarding the Second Front. Smuts also appeared in Cairo, at Churchill's request, to assist him in making changes. Churchill knew that Smuts shared his concern about morale in the Middle East;[44] and he welcomed his advice as a colleague and a contemporary. Senior officers noticed that Smuts was one of the relatively few people who were prepared to engage Churchill in general conversation, and not just allow the Prime Minister to develop a monologue.[45] With the assistance of Smuts and Brooke, Churchill decided to appoint General Sir Harold Alexander to succeed Auchinleck, and to place Lieutenant-General W. H. E. Gott, one of the Eighth Army's Corps Commanders, in charge of the army. Alan Brooke had preferred Bernard Montgomery for the latter post as he felt that Gott was too tired; as it happened he got his way almost at once since Gott's plane was shot down shortly afterwards and he was killed.[46]

Churchill then flew on to Moscow, stopping one night en route at Tehran. On his arrival at the Moscow airport he was received with full military honours and taken to a luxurious villa outside the city. That evening (August 12th) he called on Stalin at the Kremlin and at once informed him that there would be no Second Front in 1942. According to his account, Stalin looked 'very glum' at this news.[47] But Churchill went on to speak of the bombing offensive by the RAF and also to expound the prospects of the assault on French North Africa (Operation Torch, as it was called), and Stalin at once saw the strategic advantages of this course. As Harriman reported to Roosevelt, Churchill drew a picture of a crocodile, pointing out that it was as well to strike the soft underbelly (the Mediterranean) rather than the snout (northern France).[48] After their long discussion they parted amicably, and this, Churchill thought, was a gain for his personal diplomacy: 'He now knew the worst, and yet we parted in an atmosphere of good will.'[49]

The good will was not to last, however, for next day Stalin submitted an aide-mémoire complaining about the absence of a genuine Second Front; the day after that (August 14th) Churchill replied, also on paper. But that evening there was an official dinner at the Kremlin, punctuated by many toasts and speeches. Churchill found himself being outdone in late-night 'follies' and, as he informed the War Cabinet at home, 'I left about 1.30 a.m., as I was afraid we should be drawn into a lengthy film and was fatigued.'[50] At this point, relations between Churchill and Stalin were very strained.

On the 15th the two leaders did not meet until Churchill visited the Kremlin at about 7 p.m. to say goodbye. Stalin was now in friendlier mood and invited him to stay for snacks. After midnight this developed into a full-scale dinner, in the course of which they talked over various episodes of recent history, including the Nazi–Soviet Pact and the RAF's bombing of Berlin while Molotov was there. It seems that Churchill restored good relations partly by promising a Second Front in Europe by 1943 and partly by proposing a joint attack with the Russians on Norway in late 1942.[51] He had no sleep that night as he was due to leave the airport on the return flight at 5.30 a.m. He did, however, sleep through the morning as the plane took his party back to Tehran. On his return to Cairo he spent a few days visiting troops and establishments. He encountered what he described as 'a sense of the reviving ardour of the Army'.[52] He flew home, as he had come, by Liberator, accepting somewhat unwillingly the tight security restrictions made to conceal his departure and also his stay overnight at Gibraltar.[53]

Meanwhile the detailed planning for Operation Torch was going ahead. Churchill arranged a weekly lunch at 10 Downing Street with General Dwight D. Eisenhower, the American officer who was designated by Roosevelt to command the expedition. Eisenhower had no experience of battle, but he was thought to be a good leader of a heterogeneous team. It had been decided that the Americans should assume control and should also provide the first landing parties, in the hope that this would discourage opposition, as the United States was still in diplomatic relations with the Vichy regime. Churchill accepted this arrangement, but he did not conceal his disgruntlement that the early planning allowed for landings only at Casablanca and Oran and not also at Algiers and Bône, whence there would be more chance of a rapid advance into Tunisia, so as to cut the line of approach for German and Italian reinforcements. In the end a compromise was agreed whereby Algiers but not Bône was included among the landing-points.[54]

The dual assault in north Africa went ahead in late October and early November. The attack by Montgomery's army at El Alamein was originally designed for thirteen days before the beginning of Operation Torch, but Torch was delayed by four days without any serious consequences for the co-ordination of the two operations. On October 23rd, after a vigorous artillery bombardment, the infantry advanced into the minefields that protected Rommel's positions, to clear a path for the tanks. It was a set-piece operation, in which the tanks remained in reserve for several days to take their turn in the advance, like cavalry in the old days. It was not until November 2nd that a breakthrough was effected by the British armour, and the German and Italian forces were thrown into full retreat. The 'British armour', of course, included the Sherman tanks that Roosevelt and Marshall had assigned to Egypt just after the fall of Tobruk.

The Allied landings in French North Africa began on November 8th. There was fierce resistance in places, but Algiers was taken on the first day and Oran on the 10th. The Moroccan commander succumbed on the 11th, but only on orders from Admiral Darlan, the Vichy Second-in-Command, who happened to be in Africa and whose authority was recognised by Eisenhower as a temporary expedient. In retaliation, Hitler ordered the German occupation of that part of France which remained unoccupied, and this led in turn to the scuttling of the French fleet at Toulon.

*　　　*　　　*

For the first time since the church bells of Britain had been silenced in order to become the signal of invasion, they rang out in celebration of a victory – that in Egypt – on Sunday November 15th. (Churchill had delayed the celebration over the preceding weekend in case things went wrong with Torch.)[55] On Tuesday 10th Churchill had spoken at the Lord Mayor's luncheon at the Mansion House, and his speech had reflected his cheerfulness following the victory. As he put it, 'The bright gleam has caught the helmets of our soldiers, and warmed and cheered all our hearts.'[56] He felt that this was a turning-point in the war – 'not ... the beginning of the end, but it is, perhaps, the end of the beginning'.[57] Considering how small the El Alamein battle was in relation to the great conflict in Russia (there were only 50,000 German troops facing the Eighth Army on the eve of the battle),[58] it was remarkable how quickly Churchill hardened his attitude towards the future of British imperial responsibilities:

I have not become the King's First Minister in order to preside over the liquidation of the British Empire. For that task, if ever it were prescribed, someone else would have to be found, and, under democracy, I suppose the nation would have to be consulted.[59]

24. *From Alamein to Overlord*

In his war memoirs Churchill was to risk the generalisation: 'Before Alamein we never had a victory. After Alamein we never had a defeat.'[1] There was much truth in the statement, but the main factors leading to the change in the character of the war were the success of the Russians in wearing down the German army, and the ever-increasing weight of American arms production. In mid-November Russian forces attacked the flanks of the German Sixth Army, which had been endeavouring to capture Stalingrad, and encircled it. Attempts at relief proved unavailing, and on February 2nd 1943 the pocket was eliminated, with the loss of 90,000 prisoners, nearly all German. The main American military achievement was against the Japanese, in the campaign in the Solomon Islands: after a naval victory at Guadalcanal in mid-November the Japanese were forced to evacuate that island in February. In north Africa, the Americans were at the same time just coming into contact with German forces: Eisenhower's advance was at first held up by heavy rain, and German reinforcements poured into Tunisia. Meanwhile Montgomery was pursuing Rommel's remaining troops along the Libyan coast, and by the turn of the year it became apparent that Rommel would have to retire into Tunisia to secure his supply-lines there.

Roosevelt and Churchill again felt the need for an early conference to discuss strategy for 1943. They hoped to do so in the company of Stalin, but the latter declared himself unable to leave Russia during the winter owing to 'major operations'.[2] Left to make their own arrangements, the two western leaders met in mid-January in a suburb of the Moroccan city Casablanca, in agreeable surroundings by the sea. Harold Macmillan, whom Churchill had appointed as Minister-resident at Eisenhower's headquarters, described in colourful terms the 'curious mixture of holiday and business' that accompanied the conference. Churchill, he wrote,

> ate and drank enormously all the time, settled huge problems, played bagatelle and bezique by the hour, and generally enjoyed himself. ... The whole affair, which lasted for nearly a fortnight, was a mixture between a cruise, a summer school, and a conference. The notice boards gave the time of the meetings of the various staffs, rather like lectures, and when they got out of school at five o'clock or so, you would see Field-Marshals and Admirals going down to the beach for an hour to play with the pebbles and make sand castles.[3]

When the Combined Chiefs met, it was apparent that the British were more united than the Americans. The British were clear that the most favourable theatre for operations was the Mediterranean, with the object of knocking Italy out of the war and perhaps bringing Turkey in.[4] Of the Americans, Admiral King's interest was, very understandably, largely focused on the Pacific, and it was only General Marshall who doggedly maintained the idea of a cross-Channel operation in 1943. Since there was a shortage of shipping and since there were now so many Allied troops in north Africa, logic dictated, as Marshall was forced to agree, that the next step was an attack somewhere in the Mediterranean. It was decided that the first operation to follow the elimination of the enemy from north Africa should be an invasion of Sicily. Meanwhile, the US Air Force in England was to begin a bombing offensive on Germany, complementing the RAF's own attacks. These decisions were arrived at by staff conferences which neither the President nor the Prime Minister normally attended, though of course they followed their progress and approved the outcome. As late as mid-December 1942 Churchill had in fact still been an advocate of a cross-Channel invasion in the 1943 season, and had only been converted to the Mediterranean strategy by General Sir Alan Brooke, his CIGS, at that time.[5]

The political leaders took a more direct part in seeking a

political settlement for French North Africa. This meant trying to reconcile General de Gaulle, who was with great difficulty persuaded to fly out from England, with General Giraud, who with American approval had succeeded Admiral Darlan in command of French North Africa after the latter's assassination in late December. On arrival, de Gaulle was still recalcitrant and was only just persuaded to talk to Giraud; but in spite of this Churchill could not help admiring his attitude:

> Always, even when he was behaving worst, he seemed to express the personality of France – a great nation, with all its pride, authority, and ambition. It was said in mockery that he thought himself the living embodiment of Joan of Arc.... This did not seem to me as absurd as it looked.[6]

There had been criticism both in Britain and in America of Eisenhower's acceptance of Admiral Darlan as the authority for the occupied area; and Churchill had had to make a long speech justifying the decision at a Secret Session of the House of Commons in mid-December.[7] Darlan's assassination made things somewhat easier for the Allies; and it was partly with the object of providing reassurance for domestic critics, and partly for the sake of allaying Russian suspicions, that Roosevelt, at his joint press conference with Churchill, spoke of 'unconditional surrender' as the object which the Allies would insist upon before making peace. Roosevelt later claimed to have used the phrase spontaneously; but the records show that Churchill had consulted his colleagues of the War Cabinet by telegram about the use of the phrase: their only qualification was to say that it should be applied to Italy as well as to Germany and Japan, as Churchill had originally suggested.[8]

On January 24th the conference broke up, but Churchill persuaded Roosevelt to spend a day with him at Marrakesh, which was within five hours' driving distance. Churchill of course knew Marrakesh from before the war, and was keen to show the President the magnificent view of the Atlas Mountains as the sun was setting. That night they had a family party together, and a sing-song: Randolph Churchill and Hopkins and his son Robert were there. Next morning Churchill saw Roosevelt off at the airport, but he got up so late that he had to appear in his dressing-gown, embroidered with red dragons. Churchill stayed on at Marrakesh for two more days, and took out his paints for the only time during the war. The picture that he painted, of the twelfth-century Katoubia Mosque dominating the city against the background of the snow-capped Atlas Mountains, he presented to the President.[9]

For Churchill, this was not a complete respite from his cares, as he had to argue with the Cabinet at home the case for his paying a visit to Turkey. He got his way and flew off eastwards, first to Cairo, and then to Adana, just inside Turkey near the Syrian border, where he met President Inönü in a special train. He offered the Turks modern equipment for their armed forces, and hoped that in return they would agree to enter the war on the Allied side. But the Turkish President, while accepting the equipment, showed distinct unwillingness to consider the idea of entering the war. Churchill had been warned by the Foreign Office to expect this reaction, and resolved to accept it with good grace. He went on to spend a night and a day in Cyprus, where he inspected his old unit the 4th Hussars, now an armoured formation, and then he returned to Cairo. Shortly after, he flew to Castel Benito in Tripolitania, which Montgomery's Eighth Army had lately captured and where he could meet senior officers and review the victorious troops. Addressing soldiers of the army headquarters at Tripoli, he said: 'It must have been a tremendous experience driving forward day after day over this desert which it has taken me this morning more than six hours to fly at 200 miles an hour.... In the words of the old hymn, you have "nightly pitched your moving tents a day's march nearer home".'[10]

On the night of February 6th Churchill flew home to Lyneham in Wiltshire. The change in climate may have upset him, for a week later he developed a cold in the head and a sore throat. On the 16th his temperature went up and Sir Charles Wilson diagnosed pneumonia. It was not a severe attack, but to be on the safe side Wilson called in Dr Geoffrey Marshall of Guy's Hospital, and started issuing bulletins. Later Wilson was to argue that Churchill took it all rather too solemnly, perhaps because he had never been seriously ill since 1922 when he had his appendix out.[11] But the new 'M & B' drug made pneumonia a much more manageable illness than before, and although Churchill was obliged at the behest of his doctors to slow down the tempo of his work, and to read a novel – he chose Defoe's *Moll Flanders* – he was able, as he put it, to 'follow attentively all the time what was happening in Parliament, and the lively discussions on our home affairs when peace comes'.[12]

The 'lively discussions on home affairs' were largely the result of the publication of the Beveridge Report at the beginning of December 1942. Sir William Beveridge, the former civil servant whom Churchill had recruited for the Board of Trade as an expert on unemployment in 1908, had been invited by Arthur Greenwood, when Greenwood was in charge of reconstruction studies, to take the chair of a committee of officials looking into the consolidation of the social services. The report contained not merely a survey of the existing situation, but also – Beveridge having shed his official colleagues – radical recommendations for reform. Beveridge was determined to make a crusade from within the government: as he put it, 'a revolutionary moment in the world's history is a time for revolutions, not patching'.[13] The revolution came, therefore, in Beveridge's assumptions about the extensions of the social services that would appear in the post-war pattern, rather than in the details of contributions and benefits that he proposed. He took it for granted that the government would accept the need for family allowances, for a national health service, and for the maintenance of full employment – which last, however, he set at a maximum unemployment rate of 'about $8\frac{1}{2}\%$'.[14]

Beveridge was not a modest man, and he thought highly of his own achievement in preparing the report. He was quite prepared to exceed the boundaries of normal civil-service etiquette to ensure its success. Brendan Bracken, the Minister of Information, reported to the Cabinet on November 16th that 'There are indications that he is already working up a political campaign on this question.'[15] But there was bound to be considerable interest in so far-reaching a document, published as it was just two weeks after the ringing of the bells to announce the first important British military victory – the war having already lasted over three years. Cherwell, who saw an advance copy, warned Churchill that if it were accepted it might prove difficult to obtain an extension of Lend-Lease after the war, as Americans might think 'they were being asked to pay for social services in the U.K. far in advance of their own'.[16] Then in mid-January, some weeks after the report had been published, Kingsley Wood circulated to the Cabinet a Treasury Paper entitled 'Financial Aspects of the Social Security Plan', in which stress was laid on the other charges which were likely to fall on the Exchequer at the same time, such as the cost of maintaining armaments in the post-war world.[17]

Churchill was impressed by these warnings, and himself circulated a memorandum advising against 'dangerous optimism': 'Ministers should, in my view, be careful not to raise false hopes as was done last time by speeches about "Homes for Heroes", etc.'[18] He decided to take no part in the debate on the report, which was scheduled for mid-February. As it happened, the debate coincided exactly with the worst phase of his illness, so that he could not intervene even had he wished to. It is quite possible that if he had made a speech similar to the one that he made on the radio a month later (March 21st) envisaging a 'Four Year Plan' of post-war reconstruction the revolt of the parliamentary Labour Party would never have taken place. But, as it was, Anderson, who had to make the government's case in the debate, sounded so much like the civil servant that he had so long been, that even in the process of accepting most of the assumptions of the report – which were surely its essence – it appeared as if he was being very lukewarm about it indeed. Next day Kingsley Wood, following the Treasury brief, sounded even worse; and so the Labour Party backbenchers held a meeting and decided to put down an amendment to the original motion, directly criticising the government.

In the upshot some 119 MPs supported the amendment, as against 335 who were loyal to the government. Of the 119, 98 were members of the Labour Party, and the others were Liberals or Independents. It was the most important Commons revolt in the course of the Churchill Coalition, particularly as it was the result of an official decision by Labour's parliamentary party. Numerically, though, it was hardly worse than a right-wing revolt against Ernest Bevin's Catering Wages Bill, which had passed its second reading a week earlier against the votes of 116 Conservatives.

The fact was that MPs, like their constituents, were now thinking less about the war, which they readily believed was on the way to being won, and more about the peace that was to follow. Although the Labour Party as a body was loyal to the electoral truce, and did not put up candidates in by-elections for seats formerly held by Conservatives, it found itself being threatened with replacement by a rival left-wing organisation called Common Wealth, which had been founded in 1942 by Sir

503

Richard Acland, formerly a Liberal but now an Independent MP. Common Wealth had a Socialist programme and undoubtedly won the Labour vote in constituencies which it fought during the electoral truce. In April 1943 it actually won a seat – at Eddisbury, in Cheshire – and it polled well elsewhere. There was evidently a strong swing to the Left in British politics: a Gallup Poll published in the *News Chronicle* in the late spring of 1943 showed that when people were asked how they would vote 'if a general election were held tomorrow' Labour had a big lead over the Conservatives amounting to over 10%.[19] Yet at the same time Churchill's personal popularity had reached its highest level: it was reported that 93% of those polled had said that they approved of Churchill as Prime Minister.[20] The significance of this dichotomy of the public mind, showing a strong swing to the Left while putting Churchill above party politics and almost in the position of a constitutional monarch, was something that escaped almost all contemporary observers.

In February the German forces in Tunisia, which had poured in from Italy, were able to counter-attack against the Americans and regain some ground. This was a warning that the war was by no means yet won. But arrangements had been made at Casablanca to unite the two Allied armies in north Africa: while Eisenhower took overall command, Alexander was to be his deputy in charge of the co-ordination of strategy for the different contingents. In March Rommel went home to Germany on sick leave; he was not to return. By the end of that month the Eighth Army had forced the Mareth Line in southern Tunisia, and soon the enemy was confined to the tip of the country around Tunis and Bizerta. After a final assault the enemy forces capitulated on May 12th and 13th. It had taken longer than expected, but this was because Hitler had decided to send reinforcements that were badly needed by his armies in Russia. In the end the victory was numerically comparable with that at Stalingrad, for almost a quarter of a million prisoners were taken, of whom over half were German.[21]

It was only in mid-April that Churchill became conscious that the invasion of Sicily would rule out entirely any possibility of a cross-Channel attack in 1943.[22] This was owing to the shortage of landing-craft, which were in great demand for Admiral King's operations in the Pacific, as well as for the difficult operations in

Europe. Churchill had already had to tell Stalin about the delays in the completion of the north African campaign, and about the need to interrupt the Arctic convoys for the sake of mounting the Sicilian invasion. He hesitated about this extra disappointment. There was, too, an awkward breach between the Soviet government and the London Poles, for which to be sure the Western Allies were in no way responsible. The Germans had claimed the discovery of a mass grave of 10,000 Polish officers in the Katyn Forest, near Smolensk; and the Poles, who felt that the Russians might well have been responsible for the murders, supported a call for the International Red Cross to investigate. But this in turn led the Russians to break off their already tenuous relations with the Polish government in London. Churchill tried hard to persuade both parties to retain diplomatic contact, but he felt that the evidence strongly favoured the Polish interpretation of events.[23]

Before the conclusion of the north Africa campaign – and the second official ringing of the church bells, which he had ordered – Churchill had decided that there was a need for fresh consultations with Roosevelt; and as his doctors strongly discouraged him from flying he went by sea on the *Queen Mary*, the great Cunard liner which was serving as an Atlantic troop-carrier for the Americans. On the outward journey, in addition to his own large party of about 150, there were some 5000 German prisoners of war, and also some private passengers including Sir William Beveridge.[24] Churchill felt obliged to invite Beveridge to lunch one day, but there was no love lost – according to Sir Charles Wilson's diary, 'the atmosphere was correct without being unduly cordial'.[25] For the rest, the Prime Minister spent most of his time with the Chiefs of Staff sorting out policies to present to their American counterparts, to ensure as far as possible a continuation of operations in the Mediterranean. He regarded the collapse of Italy as 'a great prize', and thought that, like the fall of Bulgaria in the First World War, it might precipitate the collapse of 'the whole enemy structure'. At any rate, he felt, it would probably bring Turkey into the war.[26]

But when he reached Washington he found that the American Chiefs of Staff did not look at things in quite the same way. They favoured the earliest possible cross-Channel attack, even if it meant that the armies would do virtually nothing in 1943. It seemed that they were all the more inclined to be obdurate because they had given way to the British point of view at Casablanca. In the end a compromise was arrived at. It was agreed that Churchill and General Marshall should visit Algiers together to decide, in conjunction with Eisenhower and Alexander, whether the invasion of Italy should be attempted. At the same time the British conceded that Japan should be subjected to 'unremitting pressure', and not just held in restraint, while the European war was completed; and the need to aid China and keep her in the war was also recognised.[27]

Late in May, therefore, Churchill with General Marshall flew from Washington to Algiers, where Eden was also summoned to help in the task of reconciling de Gaulle and Giraud. Both Churchill and Eden soon found, however, that there was not much for either of them to do. Eisenhower refused to agree to attack Italy until he saw how successful the Sicilian invasion was, and this was not due to start until July 10th. Eden for his part found that the French leaders were able at last to agree among themselves, and a French Committee of National Liberation was formed. Churchill and Eden could therefore relax: they showed themselves to the troops in an agreeable atmosphere of victory and self-congratulation.[28] But they also pondered the question of whether there should be a visit to Stalin to tell him about the postponement of the 'Second Front' until 1944. Eden hotly opposed the idea of Churchill's going, on grounds of health, and it was agreed to send the information by telegram. Stalin took the news badly, and for some weeks the personal correspondence between the two leaders lapsed altogether.

Churchill has been both praised and blamed for preferring a Mediterranean or Balkan strategy to an early cross-Channel attack. It has been argued that this was traditional British policy based upon the use of sea-power for 'peripheral' assault; and it has even been maintained that if Churchill had had his way the post-war Anglo-American position *vis-à-vis* the Russians would have been stronger than it was.[29] But this latter view, dating from the period of the 'Cold War', mistakes the feelings that animated leaders at the time – the desire above all to deal with existing enemies rather than to prepare to deal with hypothetical future ones. In any case, Churchill did not propose to intervene in the Balkans with Allied troops, but rather to supply arms for local patriots – many of whom, as it happened, were Communists. As the official historian of British war strategy in this period has put it,

> It was the spirit of the chase, and not any dedication to 'peripheral strategy' – much less any calculation of post-war political advantage – which led the British now to urge impatiently that their recent victories in North Africa should be exploited to the full.[30]

Churchill was also anxious to employ Allied forces to the maximum degree in the 1943 fighting season. As he put it to Smuts in mid-July: 'I will in no circumstances allow the powerful British and British-controlled armies in the Mediterranean to stand idle.'[31] So far from staking a claim against the Russians in some hypothetical future conflict, it seems that this policy was effective in providing the Red Army with immediate assistance, even before the Sicilian campaign was over. Italian morale had already appeared to be shaky; and after the early success of the landings on the island, in fact on July 13th, Hitler called off his offensive at Kursk on the Russian front, although it had only begun on July 11th.[32] He hastily sent reinforcements into Italy and Sicily to secure the front against the Allies and to make sure of making an effective takeover of Italy in case of an Italian surrender.

The same event – the early success of the Allied landings in Italy – encouraged Churchill to urge that there should be a similar attack some way up the Italian coast. On July 13th he wrote: 'The question arises why we should crawl up the leg like a harvest-bug from the ankle upwards? Let us rather strike at the knee.'[33] But now the case hardly needed arguing even with General Marshall, who swung round to acknowledge the value of an early operation against the Italian mainland. The Combined Chiefs of Staff accepted this view and urged on Eisenhower 'a direct amphibious landing operation against Naples'; and he readily agreed.[34] Then on July 26th it was announced that Mussolini had been overthrown and placed under arrest. A new Italian government was formed under Marshal Badoglio, which made secret contact with the Allies with the intention not merely of seeking an armistice, but also of changing sides in the war. In mid-August the Combined Chiefs of Staff, in session at Quebec at a new meeting of the Allied leaders, agreed that terms should be offered to enable this to occur. The Italian Command was to send the fleet to Allied ports and to release all Allied prisoners of war.

The terms were signed by an Italian general representing Badoglio on September 3rd – the day that British troops first landed on the toe of the Italian mainland, and also the fourth anniversary of the day when Britain entered the war. A period of political confusion followed, during which tentative plans were made, and then abandoned, for an American airborne division to land in Rome and take over the city: the Germans were too much in evidence to allow this to be attempted. On September 8th both Eisenhower and Badoglio announced the Italian surrender; the Italian fleet duly sailed out to Malta, and most of the prisoners were released. But the German reaction was swift, and the British and American troops who landed at Salerno in an attempt to hasten the enemy retreat found that opposition was stiff and that the surrender seemed to have made little difference.

In the midst of the excitements of the Italian collapse Churchill and Roosevelt were meeting at Quebec. The Canadian government had agreed to be host without insisting on a place at the conference table; and Churchill, who arrived on the *Queen Mary* in mid-August, was accompanied by a larger party than ever. It included his wife Clementine, their daughter Mary, now a subaltern of the ATS, and the eccentric Brigadier Orde Wingate, who had commanded a force in the Burmese jungle behind the Japanese lines, and whom Churchill regarded as the Second World War equivalent of T. E. Lawrence. The party landed at Halifax and went on to Quebec, where Churchill was accommodated in the Governor-General's residence with a magnificent view of the St Lawrence river. A few days were to elapse before the conference began, and Churchill employed them on a visit to Hyde Park, the President's home in New York State. On this trip he showed his daughter the Niagara Falls, which he himself had previously visited in 1900.[35]

The staff conference was notable for some sharp disagreements, largely because the Americans suspected that the British were altogether hostile to the cross-Channel project. Stimson told the President that Churchill and Alan Brooke, because of 'the shadows of Passchendaele and Dunquerque', would give the project only 'lip service', and that an American commander for the invasion was essential.[36] It was in fact true that Churchill now favoured the invasion of Italy and its exploitation well beyond Rome, and also what he called 'Jupiter, prepared under cover of Overlord' – that is, an assault on Norway, with a pretence of an assault on France. He had been led to this view, however, mainly by the events of that summer – the Italian collapse and 'the extraordinary fighting efficiency of the German Army'.[37] His own Chiefs of Staff did not agree with him about Jupiter, and preferred Overlord, which was now being planned by a special staff under Lieutenant-General Sir Frederick Morgan, who also attended the conference. The British Chiefs of Staff thought that Overlord, if agreed on, might yet be delayed a few weeks from the target date of May 1st 1944; but their American colleagues insisted that seven divisions, both British and American, must be moved from the Mediterranean to England on the expectation of the earlier date being maintained.

So far as the Far East was concerned, the Americans were anxious to clear the Burma Road in order to sustain China and build up air bases there for the assault on Japan. Churchill knew well enough how strongly American public opinion felt about China. He had reported to the War Cabinet on his previous trip to America that 'It is almost true to say that the American public would be more concerned if China fell out of the war than if Russia did so.'[38] He did not like a campaign in the Burma jungle, which he saw as 'munching a porcupine quill by quill'. His view of the strategy of the Japanese war was that it was desirable to strike directly at the Japanese main islands from Russian Asia. With a vigorous mixture of animal metaphor, he asserted:

> The only way to kill an octopus is to strike at the centre, not to cut off the tentacles one by one. . . . When we start bombing Japan from Russia I will sing
> > Ladybird, ladybird, fly away home,
> > Your house is on fire and your children are gone.[39]

But Russia was not in the Japanese war; and, perhaps partly under Wingate's influence, Churchill now accepted the need for a forward move in Burma under British control, with Vice-Admiral Lord Louis Mountbatten, the relatively young Chief of Combined Operations, in the new post of Supreme Commander of the South-East Asia Command. Finally, an agreement was signed by the two leaders for the mutual exchange of information about the atomic bomb, pledging both countries not to use the weapon without the other's consent.[40]

After the conference Churchill spent a few days at a fishing-lodge at Snow Lake, not far from Quebec. On September 1st he went on to Washington, where he was again the President's guest at the White House during the critical days of the negotiation of the Italian surrender and the Salerno invasion. On September 6th he visited Harvard to take an honorary degree, and made a speech proposing a common citizenship for Britain and the United States.[41] This was agreeable enough to a Harvard audience but was not really practical politics in the United States. On the night of September 11th he set off for home on the battle-cruiser *Renown*, and he reached the Clyde on the morning of the 19th.

As Churchill recognised, the German High Command had certainly made the best of the collapse of their ally. A German occupation of north and central Italy took place, and both the King and the Badoglio government were forced to flee to the south. Mussolini was rescued from captivity by German airborne troops and was set up in the north as the head of a new Fascist regime. But all this was at the cost of slackening German strength on the Eastern Front; and Stalin could at last see that he was getting some relief from the efforts of his allies, and his messages to both Churchill and Roosevelt became distinctly warmer.[42] Not that the relationship was consistently warm: in mid-October Stalin sent a note to Churchill on the subject of the arrangements for the Arctic convoys that so enraged the Prime Minister that he simply returned it to the Russian Ambassador.[43] But Stalin had now indicated that he was prepared to discuss both strategy and post-war policy with the Western Allies; and at the same time a meeting of Foreign Ministers was taking place in Moscow, at which important decisions were taken. Agreement was reached on the establishment of a European Advisory Commission to meet in London and to determine the post-war policy for Germany; and declarations were accepted about the future independence of Austria and about the treatment of Germans who committed atrocities. Arrangements were also made for a meeting of heads of government in late November at Tehran, the capital of Iran.

Before the Tehran Conference Churchill and Roosevelt agreed to have a preliminary meeting at Cairo, to determine joint operations and also to consult with General Chiang Kai-shek about policy for the war in the Far East. Churchill again travelled in the battle-cruiser *Renown*, and this time took with him his daughter Sarah (Mrs Oliver), who was in the WAAF as an interpreter of air photographs, and was commissioned as a section officer. Churchill was not feeling well: he had a heavy cold when he set out, and was upset by his inoculations.[44] After a brief stop at Malta he reached the villa near Cairo where he was to stay for the first conference. Although he was favourably impressed by both General Chiang and his wife – the latter was both attractive and fluent in English – he could not convince himself that it was an advantage to have their influence exerted at his conversations with the Americans. As he put it in his war memoirs, 'The talks of the British and American Staffs were sadly distracted by the Chinese story, which was lengthy, complicated and minor.'[45]

At this time Churchill's interest was in persuading the Americans to commit themselves more fully to Mediterranean operations, in the few months before Overlord took place. He wanted sufficient landing-craft to ensure the early capture of Rome and the seizure of Rhodes, and the opening-up of the supply routes to the Yugoslav Partisans under Marshal Tito. Roosevelt would not agree to this. He was in any case contemplating the appointment of a Supreme Commander for all operations against Germany, both 'from the Mediterranean and the Atlantic'. Churchill and the British Chiefs of Staff for their part could not accept such a sweeping concentration of power in the hands of one commander.[46] This matter, as well as other points of joint concern, was left for decision after the meeting with Stalin. On the evening of November 25th, which was Thanksgiving Day, Roosevelt invited Churchill and Sarah to join him at dinner – a 'family affair' he called it, for he had his son Elliott and his son-in-law Major Boettiger with him. There was dance music from records, but as Sarah was the only woman Churchill himself had to dance with the President's old friend and ADC, General 'Pa' Watson.[47] At dawn on November 27th they flew off to meet Stalin at Tehran.

Considering the importance of this first meeting of the 'Big Three', as they were called, and also the fact that Stalin had arrived a day in advance, thereby indicating the meeting that was to come, the security arrangements for Churchill's arrival were very poor. He was in fact held up in a traffic block for three or four minutes just outside the British Legation. But once inside the grounds of the legation all was well, for the Soviet Embassy was close at hand, and the Russians in fact persuaded Roosevelt to move into their own Embassy because of a plot which they claimed to have unearthed.[48]

The formal work of the conference was largely concerned with the explanation, discussion and determination of future operations. Stalin declared himself in favour of the earliest possible date for Overlord – May 1944 – and a co-ordinated attack on southern France. He undertook to launch an offensive in Russia to prevent German forces being transferred from east to west. He also said that he was in favour of Turkey being pressed to join in the war, and promised to declare war on Bulgaria if that state should attack Turkey. Meanwhile, the 'Big Three' were exchanging hospitality and exploring each other's minds. On the evening of November 29th Stalin was host at dinner and spoke cheerfully of shooting some 50,000 officers of the German officer corps at the end of the war. Roosevelt took this as a joke, but Churchill, probably thinking of Katyn, felt that the remark was serious: he rose abruptly from the table and passed into the next room, whence he was shortly recalled by Stalin who had come to apologise and to say that he was only joking.[49] Earlier, there had been a solemn ceremony at which Churchill had presented to Stalin a Sword of Honour which the King had decided to have made and given to commemorate the defence of Stalingrad.

The final stages of the conference were more consistently cordial. On the evening of November 30th Churchill himself was host at dinner, pointing out to his colleagues that this was his birthday. There were many toasts and speeches, and Churchill, who was now not feeling his cold so badly, went to bed 'tired out but content, feeling sure that nothing but good had been done'.[50] Next day the 'Big Three' lunched together and discussed some outstanding problems. One, about which Stalin evidently did not feel very strongly, was the question of persuading Turkey to join in the war. Another was that of the future frontiers of Poland: it was agreed that these should all move towards the west – that is to say, the Curzon Line on the east side, the River Oder on the west. There was also some talk of the future of Germany: Churchill suggested that the important thing was to separate the southern sections of the country from Prussia, arguing that 'the root of the evil lies in Prussia, in the Prussian Army and the General Staff'.[51] He favoured, for southern Germany and other related areas, a 'Danubian Confederation', but Stalin demurred, and the three leaders adjourned their final meeting without decision on this question.

On December 2nd both Churchill and Roosevelt flew back from Teheran to Cairo, where they had to fill in the details of the policies that they had agreed with Stalin, and for that matter with Chiang. Churchill was pleased when Roosevelt accepted his view that it was not worth while to mount an amphibious assault on the Andaman Islands in the Indian Ocean; but Roosevelt would not divert any landing-craft for the attack on Rhodes that Churchill favoured unless Turkey could be persuaded to enter the war, and this proved impossible, although President Inönü did consent to visit Cairo to discuss the question. Roosevelt now accepted the British view about the desirability of having two separate Supreme Commanders, one for the Mediterranean and one for Overlord. It was for him to choose the Overlord commander owing to the fact that in the build-up of the operation the majority of the troops would be American: he chose, not General Marshall as had been expected, for he felt that he was invaluable at Washington, but General Eisenhower, who had proved his quality in North Africa. For the Mediterranean, where the bulk of the troops were British or British-controlled, the choice of commander was Churchill's, and he selected General Maitland Wilson.

On December 12th Churchill and his party flew to Tunis, to be guests of General Eisehower for one night before paying a visit to the Italian front. But at Tunis he felt so poorly that he decided to stay for a rest. His doctor, Lord Moran (as Sir Charles Wilson had now become) realised his condition was serious, and ordered up an X-ray team: he shortly diagnosed pneumonia, and put his patient on 'M & B' again. This was a grave illness, and Churchill suffered a fibrillation of the heart which made Moran think that he might easily collapse altogether.[52] This time Churchill himself apparently did not regard the illness as so serious, although he noticed the discomfort: as he wrote, 'fever flickered in and out'.[53] But he did not lose touch with events, and he telegraphed Roosevelt about his choice of new commanders, not just Maitland Wilson but also Montgomery, who was to command all the troops in the early stages of Overlord. He did, however, slacken the tempo of his work, and read another novel, or rather, he had it read to him by Sarah: it was Jane

Austen's *Pride and Prejudice*. His wife Clementine flew out to join him, and she was escorted by Jock Colville, who was re-joining his personal staff.[54]

On December 27th he felt well enough to start a convalescence at Marrakesh, although this involved a somewhat hazardous flight over the Atlas Mountains. Various factors now served to improve his morale. One was the sinking in a fleet action of the German battle-cruiser *Scharnhorst*, which had sought to attack one of the Arctic convoys. Another was that the Americans agreed to a delay in the despatch of landing-craft from the Mediterranean to England for Overlord, so that it became possible to mount a new amphibious landing on the Italian coast in January, this time at Anzio – a 'cat-claw', as Churchill called it.[55] Finally, to cheer him he heard from his brother Jack, who was looking after his personal affairs in London, that there had been an agreeable Christmas party at Chequers, where Roosevelt had sent a tree from his estate at Hyde Park, and where Churchill's three grand-children, Randolph's son Winston and the two Sandys children, had assembled.[56]

While at Marrakesh Churchill remained for much of the time very weak, and felt quite unable to do any painting as he had hoped. But he was mentally alert, and he held conferences with visitors in which he mingled business with pleasure by going out for picnics. Among those who visited him were Generals Alexander and Montgomery, President Beneš and General de Gaulle. To the latter he spoke French, and he made such good headway that he told Duff Cooper in a stage whisper during the party: 'Now that the General speaks English so well he understands my French perfectly.'[57] It was mid-January when Churchill left Marrakesh for Gibraltar, whence the battleship *King George V* carried him to Plymouth. He was keen to be home before the Anzio operation began.

The Anzio landing began on January 21st, and was a complete surprise to the enemy.[58] Two divisions, one British and one American, were put ashore within forty miles of Rome under an American general, J. P. Lucas. But Lucas failed to exploit his initial advantage, and the German reaction was swift. The bridge-head consequently became a liability to the Allied cause, rather than an asset: as Churchill said, he 'had hoped that we were hurling a wild cat on the shore, but all we have got is a stranded whale'.[59] The main forces trying to break through from the south were held up in bitter fighting at Monte Cassino, and four weeks after the first landing the bridgehead was subjected to a vigorous counter-attack, which was only held with difficulty. Churchill consoled himself – and the House of Commons – with the argument that Hitler's policy of fighting it out without withdrawal in Italy was not without advantage elsewhere. 'We must fight the Germans somewhere, unless we are to stand still and watch the Russians. This wearing battle in Italy occupies troops who could not be employed in other greater operations, and it is an effective prelude to them.'[60] And General Alexander, the Commander-in-Chief of the Allied Armies in Italy, writing to Churchill, had words of praise for the German paratroops defending Monte Cassino against both bombs and shells: 'I doubt if there are any other troops in the world who could have stood up to it and then gone on fighting with the ferocity they have.'[61]

The real difficulty for Alexander was that a great many of his best troops had been ordered back to England to prepare for Overlord, and thus he had no marked preponderance over the enemy in Italy. For some weeks in March and April his forces were bogged down by mud, with the Anzio beachhead having to be supplied by sea. It was not until mid-May that he was able to renew his offensive. This time his multi-national army was at last successful: Monte Cassino was captured by Polish troops, and what was called the Adolf Hitler Line, with strong fortifications, was breached by the Eighth Army on the right flank. The troops in the Anzio beachhead also took the offensive, and were able to break out and link up with the main front. On June 2nd enemy resistance in front of Rome fell away, and two days later American troops entered the capital. This was a signal encouragement for the Allied troops, who were just about to embark on the still greater amphibious operation, Overlord.

Although before Overlord the armies of the Western Allies, compared with those of Russia, engaged only a relatively small proportion of the German land forces, there was no comparable disparity so far as navies and air forces were concerned. The war against the U-boats was a constant struggle for the British navy, made still more difficult by the need to maintain the Arctic convoys to Russia. Early in 1943 the sinkings were as heavy as in April 1917, at the worst period of the First World War, and the number of U-boats was still rapidly increasing.[62] But in the course of the year Allied counter-measures gradually became effective. Very long-range aircraft – among them the American-made Liberators and Catalinas – were based on Iceland and Newfoundland, and also, from October onwards, on the Azores, where in September facilities were granted by the Portuguese government. The increased use of escort carriers also helped, and the planes themselves, equipped with ten-centimetre radar, could find the U-boats before being evident to them.[63] In the latter months of 1943 the German surface fleet was also seriously depleted. In September the only heavy battleship, the *Tirpitz*, suffered major damage in a midget-submarine attack, and in late December, as mentioned above, the battle-cruiser *Scharnhorst* was sunk in a fleet action.

So far as the air was concerned, the attacks on Germany by RAF Bomber Command early in the war had been found to be seriously inaccurate: a study by Cherwell in August 1941 revealed that only a third of the bombers dropped their bombs within five miles of their targets. Cherwell thereupon worked out a plan for destroying German morale by area bombing and thus 'de-housing' the industrial workers, and this was accepted in February 1942 as policy for the RAF's night attacks.[64] Air Chief Marshal Sir Arthur Harris, the Commander-in-Chief of Bomber Command, put this policy into effect as well as he could, but he was short of heavy bombers, as the construction programme did not make its planned progress. All the same, in May 1942 he managed to stage a raid by one thousand bombers on Cologne, as a demonstration of what could be achieved. Churchill himself, though sometimes revolted by photographs or films of the damage, accepted the policy as the only way in which Britain could provide direct military assistance for the Russians.[65] His letters to Stalin in 1942 and 1943 usually made a point of mentioning the larger air attacks on German cities; and he himself wore RAF uniform at the Tehran meeting.

At the Casablanca Conference, as we have seen, it was decided to step up the air offensive on Germany. The American Eighth Air Force consequently added its strength to that of Bomber Command of the RAF. Its methods, however, were different: trusting to its 'Flying Fortress' bombers, it ventured to attack in daylight. This was not at first a success, and increasingly heavy casualties caused it to switch its attack to the elimination of the German fighter force – which, however, fought back well and actually increased its strength in the winter of 1943–44.

In late 1943 and early 1944 the two Allied bomber forces were increasingly diverted to two other important tasks, in both of which they were more successful. One was the destruction of enemy bases for the despatch of pilotless aircraft or rockets (Operation Crossbow as it was called), and the other was the systematic attack on the French transport network, so as to prevent the rapid movement of German reinforcements during the early stages of Overlord. It was in April 1943 that Churchill had been invited by the Chiefs of Staff to appoint a minister to investigate reports of a German 'secret weapon', and the name of his own son-in-law, Duncan Sandys, who was Joint Parliamentary Secretary to the Ministry of Supply, was put to him and met his ready concurrence. On Sandys' recommendation the German experimental station at Peenemunde on the Baltic was heavily and successfully bombed, with resulting delay to the German programme; and a number of 'ski-sites' in northern France, which were evidently launching-platforms, were located and in most cases damaged by air raids.[66]

The proposals for an attack on French transportation worried the War Cabinet in the spring of 1944 owing to the danger of civilian casualties and the fear that this would alienate the French population. The point was argued most strongly by Eden, the Foreign Secretary, and Churchill agreed to consult Roosevelt about it.[67] The President, in reply, took a robust line: he said he was '... not prepared to impose from this distance any restriction on military action by the responsible commanders that in their opinion might militate against the success of Overlord....'[68] This was accepted as final, and in the event the casualties were far lower than had been feared, and French support was not seriously undermined.

On his return from Marrakesh in January, Churchill decided that preparations for Overlord should now take priority even over the struggle against the U-boats which seemed to be virtually won. He gave orders that there should be a weekly committee meeting, over which he would himself preside, to consider the impact of Overlord on British life, and that this should take the place of the Anti-U-boat Warfare Committee, which could be put 'on a two-monthly basis'.[69] He looked at the details of the 'Mulberry' plans – that is, the construction of artificial harbours on the Normandy beaches, for use before a large natural harbour was captured; he also tightened up the plans for the airborne drop and for the naval bombardment. In March he wrote to General Marshall in Washington to say that he was 'hardening very much on this operation ... in the sense of wishing to strike if humanly possible'.[70]

Certainly by this time the commitment was becoming almost inescapable. Elaborate plans were being made to mislead the enemy about the precise direction and date of the landing, as part of what was called Operation Bodyguard. This derived its name from Churchill's remark at Tehran that 'truth ... should always be attended by a bodyguard of lies'.[71] It was decided to try to persuade the enemy that the main landing would come not in Normandy but in the Pas de Calais: and in the event this was very successful. But there was little reliance placed upon the support of popular resistance movements in the European countries, which in the early part of the war had been regarded as an essential element, perhaps even the main element, in the liberation of their territories. In June 1943 General Morgan in his plan had written that 'The assistance of the [resistance] groups should ... be regarded as a bonus rather than an essential part of the plan.'[72] This continued to be the view of those who completed the task of preparation.

In the first half of May 1944 there was a conference of Dominion prime ministers, at which the progress of the war was reviewed, and there was some discussion of the post-war world. Eden gave an exposition of his views which, he was pleased to discover, proved entirely satisfactory to his audience, except in some respects to his own Prime Minister who subjected him to 'frequent interpellations'. Churchill was keen on a plan for regional councils within the United Nations, but Eden demurred, and the Dominions prime ministers supported Eden on this.[73]

Soon Overlord began to cast its shadow more directly over Britain. On May 15th both the King and the Prime Minister attended Montgomery's presentation of his assault plans at St Paul's School in London, and Churchill also took some of the Dominions prime ministers to visit the invasion troops in Sussex. The King asked Churchill where he intended to be as the operation began, and Churchill confessed that he had made arrangements to watch the assault from a bombarding cruiser, HMS *Belfast*. At first the King thought of accompanying his Prime

Minister, but later, on reflection and after consulting his Private Secretary, Sir Alan Lascelles, he decided that neither he nor Churchill should cross the Channel in this way. 'D-day', the day of the landing, was already fixed for Monday June 5th, and the King had not obtained a reply from Churchill by the time Churchill's special train had departed at the weekend for Droxford, near Portsmouth, where it was stationed beside Eisenhower's headquarters. But Churchill did obey the King's insistent injunction not to go, although it would have been out of character if he had done so without great reluctance.[74] In his train at Droxford Churchill had with him, apart from his personal staff, two close friends – General Smuts and Ernest Bevin. Eden visited the train, but did not stay, because there was only one bath and one telephone and, as he put it, 'Mr Churchill seemed to be always in the bath and General Ismay always on the telephone.'[75]

A major crisis in foreign policy suddenly emerged owing to General de Gaulle's refusal to accept the *fait accompli* of the Overlord arrangements, made, for the sake of security, without consulting him. Churchill greeted de Gaulle warmly, as he arrived to visit him at the train; but de Gaulle's response was cold. He disliked the currency already printed for the use of the troops and threatened, not merely not to broadcast to the French population in support of Overlord, but also to withdraw the French liaison officers who were preparing to land with the troops. The exasperated Churchill finally declared that if he had to choose between supporting the United States and France, he would always side with the United States. Eden commented in his memoirs: 'I did not like this pronouncement, nor did Mr Bevin, who said so in a booming aside.'[76]

Meanwhile Eisenhower had been examining the weather reports to decide if the operation should be postponed. Early on June 4th it seemed that the next morning would be unsuitable owing to an excess of wind, and so Eisenhower decided to postpone the landings for twenty-four hours. Early on June 5th he confirmed that there was an expectation of rather better conditions next day, and allowed the arrangements to proceed. So June 6th 1944 became the day known to history as 'D-day'.

It will be seen that although Churchill exercised great influence within all Allied counsels he was not able to play the complete autocrat and invariably to get his way. In view of Britain's dependence for various types of military assistance, and especially landing-craft, upon the United States, Churchill's strongest card was his close association with Roosevelt – at any rate while Roosevelt was in good health, without an early election impending. But Roosevelt, whom he once described as 'a charming country gentleman', had inadequate business methods, and Churchill acknowledged that he had to 'play the role of courtier and seize opportunities as and when they arose'.[77] He was not always successful. In the autumn of 1943 he failed to persuade the Americans to provide extra landing-craft and transport planes for the little garrisons that Maitland Wilson, at his suggestion, had thrust forward into the Aegean after the Italian surrender: these garrisons were extinguished by German counter-attacks.[78] At Cairo and Tehran it was with concern that Churchill saw Roosevelt in turn play the role of courtier with Chiang Kai-shek and Stalin.

During dinner on the evening of Churchill's birthday at Tehran, Harry Hopkins made a speech in which he said that he had discovered that 'the provisions of the British constitution and the powers of the War Cabinet are just whatever Winston Churchill wants them to be at any given moment'.[79] There was some truth in this remark, but not a great deal. Churchill's influence even over his colleagues of the War Cabinet was powerful but not paramount. There were instances of his being overruled, for example over India in 1942. In 1943 his influence was in some ways restricted by his frequent absences: he was abroad for no less than twenty weeks of the year,[80] and for this reason or because of illness he missed altogether 80 Cabinet meetings out of 176. On one important matter during the year, the occupation of the Azores, he was overborne by his colleagues. Churchill demanded an immediate *coup de main*, but he was restrained by Eden and the Cabinet majority, who favoured diplomacy and an appeal to the ancient alliance.[81] This took time but was certainly a happier solution to the problem.

Halifax thought that Churchill was suffering from 'an amusing form of megalomania' when he appeared in Washington in May 1943 with a party of over a hundred.[82] On later occasions Churchill's party was considerably larger than this, but the fact was that the need for the careful planning of operations and for full integration with the American authorities required many staff contacts. It would have smacked more of megalomania to suppose that the planning could be done by a small party. As for the members of Churchill's private office, they were far less numerous, but even so, working as they did in relays, they were kept busy enough. In compensation, they knew that they were treated by both Churchill and his wife as members of the 'Secret Circle' in which hospitality was shared and business was not unmixed with pleasure. It was a strenuous life, but it was not without its rewards.[83]

25. *From D-day to VE-day*

On June 6th 1944 the great cross-Channel invasion began.[1] The joint landing by British, Canadian and American forces was at first entirely under the operational command of General Montgomery, who had of course previously controlled the landing in Sicily. This undertaking, however, was unique in scope and character. There was an elaborate deception plan to persuade the enemy that the main blow was still to come in the Pas de Calais; and there was unusually heavy preparation by air bombardment, in order to disrupt the communications network of northern France. For the attack itself and its maintenance, the Admiralty calculated that over 7000 craft of all kinds were employed, and the total of aircraft used was of the order of 11,000. The detailed planning had been done by officers working under the direction of General Eisenhower, who was to assume operational control as soon as a substantial part of France had been captured: but the Prime Minister had made one especially important contribution to the preparations, and that was to insist on the construction of components for artificial harbours ('Mulberries') to be used at the open beaches until such time as a major port was captured and restored to working order.

The German forces facing the invasion troops were mostly of no high quality: they included many of miscellaneous nationalities who had been captured on the Eastern Front and then pressed into service by their captors. In some cases they had distinctly inferior equipment – a great variety of types of machine-gun and even horse-drawn vehicles.[2] But they had the advantage of a coastal defence system which, however fiercely attacked by Allied bombers, could not but be a serious obstacle to the landing forces. The Allied troops had the advantage of surprise – their enemy was certainly not expecting an attack that night – and with the assistance of airborne troops on the flanks, the D-day landings proved immediately successful on most of the beaches. Only on 'Omaha' beach, on the American front, was there a failure to make an immediate penetration inland.

Within a few hours of the first assault Churchill made a preliminary report to the House of Commons. Harold Nicolson noticed that his face was 'as white as a sheet', and to begin with feared the worst.[3] Churchill's statement was in fact confident, but it was couched in modest terms, and was evidently designed to encourage the enemy to believe that further landings were still to come.[4] He was keen to visit the beachhead as soon as possible, and after six days Montgomery said that he was prepared to receive a visit. On June 12th, therefore, Churchill set foot in Normandy in the British sector, bringing with him the CIGS, Alan Brooke, and his old friend Smuts. They lunched with Montgomery at his temporary headquarters, a 'château with lawns and lakes', as Churchill later remembered it, in fact at Creully, five miles inland.[5] It was just a day less than four years since Churchill had last set foot on French soil, at Tours. The party examined the little harbours in the bridgehead, to see what use could be made of them, and then returned home by destroyer (HMS *Kelvin*). Churchill particularly enjoyed having the destroyer fire its guns at the enemy-held shore – the only time that he had been on a naval vessel when she had fired her guns 'in anger' – and he then took his usual afternoon nap on board the ship on its journey to Portsmouth.

Although the first crisis of the battle was now over, there was some criticism of Montgomery for failing in one of his early objectives, the capture of the town of Caen. Although Montgomery had certainly intended to capture Caen, he had also planned to let his forces pivot on the town (which was on his left flank) and to enable the Americans on the western flank to cut the Cotentin Peninsula and then to capture the important port of Cherbourg. The tactics were so successful that, at the end of June, of a total of eight enemy *panzer* (armoured) divisions that were now on the Normandy front, no less than seven and a half were facing the British and Canadians, and only half of one division faced the Americans.[6] The American forces had already been able to take advantage of the relative weakness of the enemy divisions opposing them, and although obstructed by the *bocage* country typical of Normandy, on June 17th they severed the Cotentin Peninsula and on June 26th they captured Cherbourg.

On June 23rd the Russians began the offensive that Stalin had promised would coincide with the Allied landings, so as to prevent Hitler switching divisions from the Eastern to the Western Front. They made rapid headway. Before the offensive the Red Army had been roughly on the pre-war frontier of Russia, but in a few weeks it reoccupied the territories that it had gained by the Molotov–Ribbentrop Pact of 1939. Churchill and Stalin now engaged in a mutual competition of congratulation on their respective successes. In the west, Hitler insisted on a stand-up fight without retreat, and it was only on July 10th that Caen, heavily cratered as it was, fell fully into Allied hands.

Meanwhile the Cabinet in London had been concerned about a new type of air offensive to which south-eastern England was being subjected. The V-1, 'buzz-bomb', or 'doodle-bug' as it was variously called, first made its appearance on June 13th. Over 3000 were despatched in the following five weeks, but then the number declined as the Allied armies overran the launching-sites They were pilotless planes, each with a load of explosives. When one had reached a previously calculated distance, the engine would cut out; there would then ensue a short silence which would be followed by the explosion as the plane hit the ground. South London suffered more than most parts of the country, and quite a few fell in parts of Essex and Kent; but the average casualty rate was fortunately not high. All the same, Churchill was 'much upset' by a bomb which fell directly on to the Guards Chapel on Sunday morning, June 18th, killing many distinguished officers and injuring others.[7] His daughter Mary was in action that morning at her battery in Hyde Park.[8] The bombs could be shot down en route, and sometimes were, but it soon became clear that this did little good if they still fell in populous areas. Consequently the guns were moved south, first to the North Downs, and then to the coast. During the first week Churchill had himself presided over the inter-service committee which co-ordinated action against the new weapon (the Crossbow Committee) but after that he passed the chairmanship to his son-in-law Duncan Sandys, who had previously been investigating intelligence reports about German missiles. Both the British and American air forces were instructed to bomb the launching-sites and supply depots in France, but otherwise there was no attempt to alter the character of the Allied offensive on account of the 'buzz-bombs'.

In mid-July Churchill obtained the impression that Montgomery did not wish him to pay a visit, and Alan Brooke had to smooth this out on a visit of his own. The result was that Montgomery wrote a friendly letter to Churchill inviting him to pay a visit at any time;[9] and so Churchill crossed over on July 20th, flying out first by American Army Dakota to an airfield near Cherbourg and inspecting the harbour and also a nearby flying-bomb launching-site. It was evident to him that owing to the German demolitions it would be a long time before the port was fully serviceable. He then travelled by motor torpedo-boat to the British sector, and established himself offshore on the cruiser HMS *Enterprise*, which had reasonably good accommodation and communications for the despatch of his normal London business. From here he could watch the operation of the 'Mulberry' harbour and other landing arrangements. On his third and last day only he went to visit Montgomery, who took him into the bomb-shattered town of Caen. He also surveyed the forward positions from a captured Storch aircraft, and called on some of the air stations. He even plucked up enough courage to visit a field hospital – a thing he rarely did because he could not bear the sight of badly wounded men. That night, July 23rd, he flew home.[10]

Shortly afterwards, on July 25th, began the great break-out of the American forces southward on the right flank. Montgomery turned one American corps of the three into Brittany, and used the other two for a great lunge forward behind the German forces facing the Anglo-Canadian armies. Although Hitler ordered a counter-attack, this was held and only resulted in more troops than otherwise being caught in what was rapidly becoming a trap. Early in August Churchill again spent a day in France, first visiting Montgomery at his headquarters and then touring some of the sectors newly occupied by the army of the senior American general, Omar Bradley. He did not stay the night but returned to England the same evening.[11] By August 20th the highly mobile American divisions had closed the noose of the trap in the neighbourhood of Falaise, and there a dreadful slaughter of the enemy forces took place. Some eight German divisions had been cut off, and many of their troops surrendered. The French Resistance had also been in action, and there was a rising in Paris which enabled General Eisenhower to send a French force to occupy the city – General Leclerc's Second Armoured Division. By the end of August Allied troops were at several points beyond the Seine in their pursuit of the enemy.

Naturally this rapid advance largely put an end to the 'buzz-bomb' offensive, which had been based on launching-platforms in northern France. Already, however, the defences had been securing notable successes, and by far the majority of the V-1s that actually reached the English shore were brought down either by anti-aircraft fire or by fighter attack. But by the end of August the War Cabinet knew well that it had shortly to face another threat from the air – the rocket bomb or V-2. This had a greater range than the V-1 and could be fired at England from Holland. The first to be so despatched fell at Chiswick on September 8th, and thereafter the bombing of London, although intermittent, continued throughout the winter.[12] It was impossible to shoot down the rockets en route, but of course the launching sites in Holland could be and were bombed. The V-2s arrived without warning, and exploded on impact. They were evidently the fore-runners of a far more dangerous form of weapon; but they were less accurate than conventional bombers, and the Germans now had correspondingly fewer of these.

The V-1 and V-2 had arrived on the scene of warfare just a few months too late to make an important contribution to strategy. They were more of nuisance value than anything else. Meanwhile in early August Churchill had been worrying about the arrangements already agreed by the Combined Chiefs of Staff – that is, both British and American – for an invasion of France from the south to supplement that in Normandy. At Tehran this had been favoured by Stalin: but Smuts, after talking to Maitland Wilson and Alexander, had written to Churchill late in June to urge the fuller exploitation of the advance in Italy, so as to open up the possibility of advancing into central Europe through the so-called 'Ljubljana Gap'.[13] This would have had the special advantage, as Churchill later saw it, of enabling the Western Allies to reach Vienna before the Russians did.[14]

But this proposal was not welcome to the American Chiefs of Staff, who continued to favour concentration on the Western Front. The great bulk of reinforcements for the battle fronts were now likely to be American, and among the troops already in Italy there were several French divisions, who of course welcomed the prospect of being transferred to a front on their own soil. In spite of Churchill's insistence, Roosevelt, firmly backed by General Marshall in particular, stood by the existing plans. Then at the last moment, just a few days before the landings were due to take place, Churchill urged a switch of the entire operation to Brittany instead of the Riviera. He thought, as did most Allied planners, that the Riviera attack would be a matter of 'having to force a landing against strong enemy defences'.[15] He saw Eisenhower at his headquarters near Portsmouth and tried to get him to agree. But Eisenhower would not budge; and Roosevelt stood by the arrangements already made.[16]

There were also some political problems concerning Italy and Yugoslavia that Churchill thought required his personal attention in the Mediterranean theatre; and so he flew out to Algiers on August 10th, and from thence to Naples, where General Maitland Wilson had arranged for a conference of the Yugoslavs. The self-styled Marshal Tito appeared, very formally clad, and had some conversation with Churchill before meeting Dr Subasic, the head of King Peter's government. The two Yugoslav leaders patched up a form of agreement on various matters, and while they were talking Churchill went for a daily bathe, visiting among other places the Blue Grotto at Capri, which he had not seen before. On August 14th he flew to Corsica to witness the landing in the south of France, which until so recently he had been trying to divert elsewhere. At dawn next day, he set forth on the destroyer HMS *Kimberley*, then serving as a headquarters ship, to see what he could. The invasion turned out to be somewhat of an anticlimax, however, as it was virtually unopposed; and although the big ships of the Allied navies undertook their arranged bombardments there was no reply even when the troops landed. Churchill must have found it an odd experience to witness a military landing on the beaches which he knew so well from his peacetime holidays. The destroyer took him back again to Ajaccio in Corsica, and he spent the time reading a novel which he happened to find in the captain's cabin.[17] As for the invasion troops, they moved rapidly northwards up the Rhône

Valley, and by early September were able to join hands with the right wing of the troops under Eisenhower, who had taken full operational command of his own forces from Montgomery on September 1st.[18]

Churchill had been making the best of things in Italy, where after all the command was predominantly British and so rather more subject to his control. He had developed much affection for Alexander, whom he found a more congenial figure than the abstemious but ambitious Montgomery. Alexander arranged for him to be established, together with his Private Office, in a 'beautiful but dismantled château a few miles to the west of Siena' – a city which he enjoyed revisiting.[19] There he learnt some of the details of Alexander's plan for an offensive to be launched on August 26th, and on the 19th he went forward to visit units of the American Fifth Army, commanded by General Mark Clark. It was in fact a very mixed command, for there were Black Americans, Japanese Americans and also a contingent of Brazilians. On the 21st he moved to the British Embassy in Rome to deal with the political problems of Italy and Greece.

Greece had suddenly come to the forefront of concern because of the evident German intention to evacuate the country and so shorten their line – as a result of the pressure from the Russian offensive in the Balkans. The question was, should the EAM, the Communist guerrillas in the mountains, who to be sure had provided the strongest resistance to the Germans, be allowed to enter Athens and take over the government? Churchill was determined to avert any such *coup d'état*, and he realised that a British force of some size would be required to assume control in Athens, which was clearly the key to the situation. On August 17th he had asked Roosevelt if he would agree to a British force being sent there, and on the 26th he received a favourable reply. He also talked to leaders of the Italian political parties, and on August 23rd was received in audience at the Vatican. His attitude to the Italians, which had been rather hostile when he first arrived, gradually softened as he saw how warmly they greeted him on his travels within their country.[20]

On the 24th he returned to the château near Siena so as to be near Alexander's troops when they launched their new offensive. He first visited the New Zealand Division, which had fought so many battles from the Western Desert onwards; and then he flew to the battle headquarters of the (British) Eighth Army, now under the command of Lieutenant-General Sir Oliver Leese. Next day he went up to the front line. It was a little bit risky as the Germans were only about five hundred yards away, and his car had to keep carefully to existing wheel-tracks for fear of mines. As he said later, 'This was the nearest I got to the enemy and the time I heard most bullets in the Second World War.'[21] But the dangers of some of his air trips must have exceeded those that he encountered on this occasion. He now flew home to England from Naples by way of Rabat on August 28th, having issued a valedictory proclamation to the Italian people on the practical characteristics of political freedom.

The expectation of an early end to the war had now begun to affect everyone. Churchill himself was not quite so optimistic, and he also felt that Britain was being rapidly overtaken by the enormous resources of both the United States and Russia. The agony of the Warsaw uprising in August upset him very much. The Russian advance had brought that city into the operational zone, and on August 1st its inhabitants came into the open and attacked the German occupation troops. Unfortunately for them, the Russian advance now came to a halt, and it seemed as if Stalin was happy to see the German forces kill off the Polish patriots. The Polish government in London appealed to the Western Allies to help, but it proved almost impossible to send assistance even by air as the Russians were most unwilling to provide landing rights for Allied planes. In the exchange of letters that took place between the leaders, Stalin went so far as to describe the Polish patriots as 'the group of criminals who have embarked on the Warsaw adventure'.[22] Fighting hand to hand in the streets and in the sewers, the Poles continued their resistance until early October, but then had to surrender to the Germans. It is not surprising that in August Lord Moran recorded that Churchill 'never talks of Hitler these days; he is always harping on the dangers of Communism'.[23]

It was late in that month that he circulated to the War Cabinet a penetrating account of life in Russia by Ronald Matthews, who had just returned from Moscow where he had been correspondent of the *Daily Herald* for two years. Matthews's report, sent to Churchill by his editor, criticised the Foreign Office for being too weak in its relations with the Soviet government and quoted General Martel, the head of the British Military Mission, as saying that 'we are licking the Bolshies' boots till we are black in the face'. Matthews also, however, made the interesting point that it was probable that 'the more popular and revolutionary the new Governments of Europe after the war, the less they will fall under Soviet influence'.[24] In support of this view he quoted the custom in Tito's army, which had long been abandoned by the Russians, of discussing tactics between officers and men before and after an operation.

In early September, a three-power meeting apparently not being immediately practicable, Churchill once again visited Roosevelt on the American continent. He travelled with a large staff on the *Queen Mary*, in spite of only lately having recovered from another mild attack of pneumonia. When the two leaders met, Churchill was persuaded to agree – against his own better judgment, and in the absence of Anthony Eden – to a plan presented by Henry Morgenthau, the US Secretary of the Treasury, to pastoralise Germany and thereby eliminate her as an international trading competitor. Churchill's conversion seems to have been the work of Cherwell, who was with him on the trip and persuaded him of its advantages for British exporters.[25] Later both Roosevelt and Churchill thought better of the idea, and its main ill-effect was that it was leaked in the *Washington Post* and provided excellent propaganda for Goebbels in persuading the Germans to continue their resistance.[26]

Since the war fronts in Europe were moving so rapidly, little joint planning could now be done, and attention was largely concentrated on the war against Japan. On the journey westwards Churchill had consulted with the Chiefs of Staff about the transfer of forces from the Mediterranean to South-East Asia; but they came to the conclusion that it was best not to make any early plans to weaken the forces in Italy. Nevertheless, at the conference Mountbatten was instructed to undertake the recapture of Burma; and Churchill, who was afraid that the Americans might later become contemptuous of the British contribution to the defeat of Japan, insisted on the use of substantial naval and air contingents in the Pacific. Roosevelt agreed to this at once, but in the staff discussions it turned out that Admiral King, the US Chief of Naval Staff, was reluctant to agree, and the British Chiefs of Staff had to reassert the point.[27] Churchill was accompanied by his wife and daughter Mary and with them he paid a visit to the Roosevelts' home at Hyde Park before returning home on the *Queen Mary* from New York.[28]

Meanwhile it had become clear that German resistance on the Western Front was gradually stiffening. Eisenhower's forward troops were held up, and although the British Second Army had taken Brussels and Antwerp it was evident that a further strong push forward was required before the Germans would collapse. Montgomery's staff had devised a bold plan to strike northwards into Holland and across the Rhine, with the aid of several airborne divisions (Operation Market-Garden); and Eisenhower authorised this plan, to be executed by the British Second Army with the aid of the First Allied Airborne Army.[29] (Incidentally, there were no other Allied Airborne Armies.) On September 17th two American airborne divisions were dropped ahead of British troops advancing through Belgium and Holland, and the First British Airborne Division was dropped at the Rhine crossing at Arnhem: they were to secure bridges so that the advance could continue unimpeded. But although the land forces relieved the two American divisions fairly quickly enemy resistance was very stiff at the Rhine crossing, there were many casualties, and on September 25th Montgomery had to order the remnants of the First Airborne Division to withdraw. Thereafter, with winter approaching, he had to set about the slower business of clearing the Scheldt estuary, so that the port of Antwerp, which had been little damaged, could be brought into full use for his armies.

It was against this background that Churchill decided to make another visit to Stalin, with whom his personal relations continued to be friendly. It was on October 8th, less than a week after the final collapse of Polish resistance in Warsaw, that he and his party (including Eden) left Northolt on the long trip to Moscow by way of Naples. He wanted to reach some sort of agreement, not only about Poland, where the Russians had established their own government at Lublin, but also about the Balkan countries, including Greece, which were now being released from German control. There could not easily have been a tripartite meeting, as Roosevelt was too much concerned with his candidature for a fourth term in the Presidency to undertake a long journey abroad.

Churchill had a very cordial reception in Moscow, and was given not only a *dacha* or villa outside Moscow in which to reside, but also a 'small, perfectly appointed house' in the capital itself.[30] It was at his first meeting with Stalin that he made out the well-known list of responsibilities for the Balkan countries until the war was fully over:

Romania – Russia 90%, the Others 10%
Greece – Great Britain (in accord with USA) 90%, Russia 10%
Yugoslavia – 50–50%
Hungary – 50–50%
Bulgaria – Russia 75%, the Others 25%

Stalin took this note and put a large tick on it with a blue pencil and then returned it to Churchill, who suddenly felt rather guilty about it.[31] But the idea was not novel: it had been discussed by the Foreign Offices in July.[32] It also took no account of American views; and it touched not at all upon the much more vital problem of Poland. On the 13th Churchill and Eden interviewed in succession the representatives of the London Polish government and those of Lublin. Both British leaders were depressed by the way the Lublin men echoed the Russian view of the future of their country.[33] It was clear that the problems of Poland would not easily be solved.

But all was cordial between the British and the Russians, and on the 14th Stalin and Churchill appeared together in the Royal Box of the Bolshoi Theatre, to what Churchill described as a 'rapturous ovation'. There was a composite programme including some ballet (the First Act of *Giselle*) and some opera; but what Churchill most enjoyed was dancing and singing by the Red Army Choir.[34] After it was over, they adjourned to the Kremlin for a military discussion, and Stalin declared that after the German war was over he would be prepared to intervene against Japan. The party left Moscow on October 19th and returned to Britain by the Mediterranean route again.

In spite of several attacks of fever, one of which came upon him in Moscow much to the alarm of his staff, Churchill was now making more trips abroad than he had made at any earlier period of the war, although they were of somewhat shorter duration.[35] Having Moran with him with supplies of penicillin made him feel safer than otherwise; and he could now make short trips to the battle-fronts in Montgomery's command, which was close at hand: these may have reminded him of his trips in much more hazardous circumstances as Minister of Munitions in the First World War. In the late autumn he acquired a comfortable Skymaster plane, given to him by order of President Roosevelt, and specially fitted out to suit his requirements.[36] One reason why his trips abroad were of shorter duration was because this plane had more speed and range.

Although relations with Stalin seemed quite cordial, the Western Allies, and particularly Britain at this time, were concerned about the possibility of ultra-left-wing governments emerging in the newly freed countries, not only in the Balkans where the Red Army was the 'liberating' force, but also in Western Europe. Major Desmond Morton undertook a reconnaissance of France and Belgium in the early autumn, but found, on the contrary, that 'Everywhere, admiration for Britain and the United States, especially for the former and for Mr Churchill, amounts to veneration.'[37] It was evident also that in France de Gaulle was generally regarded as a national leader; and in October, after further pressure from Churchill, Roosevelt suddenly performed a *volte-face* and agreed to formal recognition of de Gaulle's government. All three major powers acted together on this matter on October 23rd; and the way was now clear for Churchill to pay an official visit to the French capital. The obvious day to be there was November 11th, the anniversary of the ending of the First World War, when he and de Gaulle could be together at the official ceremonies.

The visit, on which Churchill was accompanied not only by his wife and daughter Mary, but also by the Foreign Secretary, began on November 10th. The party was accommodated luxuriously in the Quai d'Orsay, the French Foreign Office, and Churchill was delighted to find that he had a golden bath, which had been installed for Marshal Goering; he was equally delighted that Anthony Eden had only a silver one.[38] On November 11th Churchill joined de Gaulle at the Arc de Triomphe and the two leaders also placed wreaths on the tombs of Clemenceau and Foch. According to Duff Cooper, the new British Ambassador, the cheering was 'the loudest, most spontaneous and genuine' that he had heard.[39] On the 12th Churchill was made a *citoyen d'honneur* of Paris, and next day he went with de Gaulle to visit the army of General de Lattre de Tassigny, which was expected to launch an offensive in the Vosges.[40] But the offensive was postponed owing to bad weather, and although Churchill was not put off from making the trip through snow and ice he was baulked of

533

the opportunity to see any fighting. He was cheered up, however, by learning of the sinking of the *Tirpitz*, the last of the German battleships, by air attack.[41]

If it was at least easy to re-establish friendly relations with France, things were not so easy in Greece. It was not that the people of Athens or Greece as a whole were unfriendly to the British troops who began to land there early in October after the German withdrawal. It was rather that the guerrillas of the EAM in the mountains, who were partly Communist, expected to be able to come down and seize political control in the capital. A recent American study has suggested that at this time 'The EAM was running Greece with efficiency and order and the support of the majority of the population'.[42] In fact this was a period of awkward transition, during which it was impossible to test the nature of popular feeling. As Churchill said in the debate on Greece in the Commons in early December: 'Democracy is no harlot to be picked up in the street by a man with a tommy-gun.'[43] A challenge by a number of backbenchers by moving an amendment on the Reply to the King's Speech was beaten by 279 to 30 – a result which, while not unsatisfactory, suggested a certain amount of abstention on the part of regular government supporters: but it was a Friday, and only a two-line whip had been sent out.[44]

Churchill's difficulties over British policy towards Greece were exaggerated by the leaking into the American press of a telegram that he had sent to General Scobie, the commander of the British force sent to Athens. The telegram, which Churchill later admitted to be 'somewhat strident in tone', included the phrase: 'Do not however hesitate to act as if you were in a conquered city where a local rebellion is in progress.'[45] This was too much not merely for the *Manchester Guardian*, which could be expected to take a liberal stand, but also for *The Times*, whose foreign-policy leaders were now being written by the Socialist intellectual E. H. Carr.[46] As for the Americans, even the State Department, now in the charge of Edward R. Stettinius since Hull's resignation in November owing to ill-health, issued a statement expressing disapproval.[47]

Although both Churchill and Eden were agreed that action must be taken to prevent any take-over in Athens by the EAM, they were not agreed on how the Greek government should be reconstituted. Eden, following the advice of the Ambassador, Rex

Leeper, thought that the King should appoint a regent pending elections. This view coincided with that of President Roosevelt.[48] Churchill, always a royalist, sympathised with the King of Greece who had been a loyal ally throughout the war and who now wanted to return to Athens. In the end Churchill decided to solve the problem by visiting Athens himself to meet the proposed regent, Archbishop Damaskinos, and to see some of the political leaders, including those of EAM. Churchill took Eden with him, and they set out from Northolt at about 1 a.m. on Christmas morning, Churchill travelling in his new Skymaster plane with its comfortable bedroom in the rear.

Next morning, Christmas Day, they were at Athens airport, and Churchill stayed in bed in the plane, conducting business in his usual way. Devoted though they were, his colleagues and staff did not enjoy the first phase of this expedition. Eden hated missing his own family Christmas, especially as his son Simon was on embarkation leave for the Far East.[49] Churchill's own secretary-typist found the going difficult:

> The plane, heated by the running of the engines, began to cool off. ... The table was sloping, the light was bad; the wind howled, and jerked the aircraft up and down; once he stopped and said 'That was cannon-fire'; with cold hands it was hard to type.[50]

Owing to the civil war and the consequent disruption of services it had been decided that the party should move on board the cruiser HMS *Ajax*, which was anchored close by at Phaleron. It was there that Churchill had his first encounter with Archbishop Damaskinos, a formidable figure with black beard and tall hat, who made a favourable impression upon him.[51]

Next day (December 26th) Churchill and his colleagues went ashore to attend a conference of the various political parties at the Greek Foreign Office. Harold Macmillan and General Alexander were also present, with representatives of the other major powers; as there was no electricity they had to use hurricane lamps for lighting. It was bitterly cold, and the whole party kept their overcoats on. Churchill made an introductory speech, shook hands with all the delegates, including those of EAM whose military wing, ELAS, was still shooting in the streets, and then left the conference to discuss the detailed terms for a regency.[52] The terms were soon agreed; all parties had been much impressed by Churchill's readiness to come to Athens at Christmastide; and it only remained to convince the King of Greece of the need to appoint the Archbishop as regent. This took a struggle: in fact, after their return to London on December 29th, Churchill and Eden stayed up until 4.30 a.m., finally securing his agreement by wearing down his resistance.[53]

On November 30th 1944, Churchill celebrated his seventieth birthday. As usual, he enjoyed the fuss and the presents that he received, especially perhaps one from his Map Room Staff – a silver menu-holder with a picture of one of the two 'Mulberry' harbours established in Normandy, that at Arromanches on the British front, and the inscription 'Piers for the beaches. They must rise and fall with the tide.' This was the directive that he had issued in 1942, which had come to fruition in the summer invasion.[54] As for the family circle, Clementine gave him a cigar-case, Sarah a note-case and Mary some Gilbert and Sullivan records. Clementine also arranged a dinner party and there was a birthday cake with seventy candles.[55] Next day Churchill went on a sentimental visit to Harrow to listen to the singing of school songs. Both Clementine and his brother John, as well as several ministers who were Harrovians, accompanied him on this, his fifth annual visit for the occasion.[56] On December 4th he was the guest of the Board of Admiralty at dinner at Admiralty House, and on December 13th he received a presentation from the 1922 Committee of backbenchers.[57]

In reply to a birthday message from Smuts he had admitted that in military affairs 'It is not so easy as it used to be for me to get things done.'[58] This was because of the increasing contribution of the United States to the Allied war effort, and the convention accepted by that country's leaders that political intervention in military decisions should not take place. Montgomery's view that the war could be ended by a single punch by the Anglo-Canadian 21st Army Group in Holland and northern Germany was not accepted by Eisenhower, especially after the failure of Operation Market-Garden. Eisenhower was for moving up to the Rhine on a broad front, so as to have a good defensive position before making further thrusts.[59] The enemy, under Marshal von Rundstedt, was able to recover balance and on December 16th actually launched a strong counter-attack in the Ardennes with several armoured divisions. The counter-attack made considerable initial progress, breaching the front of General Omar Bradley's 12th

Army Group and spreading alarm still more widely. Eisenhower placed the troops north of the breach under the temporary command of Montgomery, who at once took a defensive stance; but the enemy attack soon spent itself, especially when the weather improved and the Allied air forces came in to play their part.[60]

Early in January Churchill sent a message to Stalin asking him to make an early attack on the Eastern Front, and thus create a diversion. Stalin replied that an offensive would begin 'not later than the second half of January'; in fact it began on January 12th.[61] But in any case the Ardennes counter-attack was faltering, and by mid-January it had petered out altogether. Eisenhower caused some consternation to the French for a time by ordering a temporary evacuation of Strasbourg, so as to enable a straightening of the Allied line; but both de Gaulle and Churchill visited his headquarters at St Germains and presented strong political objections to such a course, with the result that he agreed to countermand the order.[62] One upshot of the Ardennes offensive was a very tactless press conference by Montgomery, who implied that he had been brought in to rectify the mistakes made by the American generals. Churchill did his best to put right the damage that this had done to Anglo-American relations in his speech to the Commons on January 18th: 'The United States troops have done almost all the fighting, and have suffered almost all the losses.... According to the professional advice which I have at my disposal, what was done to meet von Rundstedt's counterstroke was resolute, wise and militarily correct.'[63]

One reason for acrimony between the two close allies was the fact that the war, although almost won, was dragging through yet another winter. Although so many of the decisive battles had already been fought, the enemy refused to give in. Churchill, who was at his best when things were bad, now displayed an increased tendency to harangue his Cabinet colleagues without allowing business to proceed. Eden complained in his diary of January 12th of a 'terrible Cabinet' at which 'Everything takes many times longer to decide than is necessary.'[64] Not long afterwards (January 19th) Attlee plucked up his courage and actually wrote Churchill a long letter on 'the method or rather lack of method of dealing with matters requiring Cabinet decisions'. He said that he thought the Prime Minister might at least trust his colleagues' views on civil affairs, which owing to his concentration on war strategy he (Churchill) had been obliged to ignore. The civil committees of the Cabinet contained a careful balance of party representation, and after much discussion they reached agreed conclusions, which Churchill did not read even in outline form. Yet on the other hand 'Not infrequently a phrase catches your eye which gives rise to a disquisition only slightly connected with the subject matter.' Attlee also complained that Churchill relied too much on the views of 'the Lord Privy Seal and the Minister of Information' (Beaverbrook and Bracken), neither of whom was a member of the War Cabinet.[65] Churchill was upset by Attlee's letter but could not find anyone who thought it was really unjust. Three days later (January 22nd) he replied rather curtly, thanking Attlee and saying, 'You may be sure that I shall always endeavour to profit by your comments.'[66]

In spite of their commitments in regard to the Normandy invasion and the V-1 and V-2 launching-sites, the British and American bomber commands had dropped a much heavier load of bombs on German cities in 1944 than in 1943 – 254,666 tons as against 143,578. But the British air marshals were still divided about the best use to make of their shattering strength – Portal, the Chief of Air Staff, favouring an offensive against oil plants, Tedder, who was Eisenhower's deputy, demanding an attack on the enemy communications network; and Harris, the Commander-in-Chief of Bomber Command, still wishing to carry on with the 'area' bombing which Cherwell had converted him to.[67] One remarkable feature of the year, however, was the astonishing resilience of enemy production: in spite of the diversion caused by the effort devoted to the V weapons, German fighter production rose in the most spectacular way in the year 1944 – to 28,926, from a figure of less than 12,000 in 1943.[68]

It was the view of Albert Speer, whom Hitler appointed to control the production of armaments, that the systematic attacks made by the Americans were more effective than the area bombing of the British, which in any case rarely took cities by surprise but consisted of attacks slowly built up from a relatively low level.[69] But Harris, with his headquarters so close to Chequers, had a direct access to the Prime Minister which was unequalled except by Portal. It was, however, when Churchill was away at Yalta that the decision was taken to attack Dresden, at the request of the Russians; and both the Western Allies sent their bombers on successive nights. It has been estimated that 135,000 people died. It was only when news of the devastation became apparent that Churchill late in March wrote to the Chiefs of Staff that 'The destruction of Dresden remains a serious query against the conduct of Allied bombing.'[70] And on April 1st he asked for the 'reviewing' of the policy of area bombing. But by this time the war was virtually at an end.

The Russian offensive which Stalin had announced to Churchill was very successful, owing to the absence of any German armoured reserve. The Red Army rapidly cleared most of what had formerly been Polish territory and penetrated deeply into Hungary and Yugoslavia. By the time of the air assault on Dresden, they were within about fifty miles of that city.

The forward movement of the Russian armies made still more urgent an early meeting of the 'Big Three' – Churchill, Roosevelt and Stalin. The President, who had now been elected for a fourth term of office, announced himself prepared to travel after his inauguration in January to the Mediterranean or even as far as the Black Sea. Stalin, who was still reluctant to make any long journey outside Russia, suggested a meeting at Yalta in the Crimea, and this was agreed. Roosevelt decided to travel most of the way by sea, and Churchill pressed him to stop at Malta and allow the Combined Chiefs of Staff to discuss Western strategy for the remainder of the war. Roosevelt agreed to the staff talks but was unwilling to delay his own visit to Yalta by more than a day, probably so as not to give Stalin the idea that he and Churchill were 'ganging up' against him.

Churchill flew out to Malta on January 29th in time to greet the President on the latter's arrival on board the cruiser USS *Quincy* on February 1st. As his daughter Mary was serving with her anti-aircraft battery in France, he took with him instead Sarah, who had been engaged in air photographic interpretation with the RAF. Next day (February 2nd) both of the large delegations flew on to an airfield in the Crimea, not far from Yalta: Churchill described Roosevelt as looking 'frail and ill' on arrival.[71] The President was housed in the Livadia Palace, a former residence of the Tsar, and for his convenience the sessions of the conference were held there. Churchill and some of his party were allotted the Vorontzov Palace, several miles away, a handsome residence built early in the nineteenth century to the plans of a British architect for a Prince Vorontzov, who served for a few years as Russian ambassador in London. In spite of the grandeur of the buildings and the efforts of their hosts to remedy wartime devastation, the visitors, at any rate those of less senior status, were somewhat upset by the absence of baths, and all were upset by the presence of bugs.[72] At least the weather was mild, and it was possible to tour the Crimea and see the battlefields both of this war and of that of 1854–6. Churchill described the conference area vividly to his colleagues as 'a sheltered strip of austere Riviera, with winding Corniche roads'. He went on: 'The villas and palaces, more or less undamaged, are of an extinct imperialism and nobility. In these we squat on furniture carried with extraordinary effort from Moscow.'[73]

In the formal proceedings he was much struck by a statement of Roosevelt's that he did not propose to allow American troops to stay in Europe for more than two years after the end of the war. Thinking that Britain could not or would not sustain the commitment unaided by any other Western power, he pressed for an occupation zone in Germany for the French. This was agreed, and the three leaders also all accepted the Dumbarton Oaks proposals for the establishment of the United Nations Organisation, with a veto power for the great powers on any action by the Security Council. A Russian demand for the representation in the Assembly of two of the Soviet republics as well as the USSR herself was ceded by the Western powers, partly as a *quid pro quo* for the fact that India, as well as the self-governing British dominions – which the Russians had difficulty in regarding as self-governing anyway – would all have seats as they had done in the League of Nations.[74]

The conference was very cordial, and Stalin proposed a toast to Churchill as a 'man who is born once in a hundred years'.[75] Cadogan described Churchill as 'drinking buckets of Caucasian champagne'.[76] But this did not prevent disagreement over one recalcitrant problem – that of the future of Poland. It was agreed that the Polish frontiers, both east and west, would have to move a long distance to the west – for the benefit of Russia and at the expense of Germany. The eastern frontier was to be the 'Curzon Line', to which the British could hardly object as it had originally been proposed as a fair ethnic frontier by the Foreign Office in 1919. There was some disagreement about the position of the western boundary, however, which the Russians wished to place on the Western Niesse, thus incorporating into Poland a large section of Germany; and also there was a deadlock on the question of the future composition of the Polish government. It was accepted that France should not merely join the occupying forces of conquered Germany but should also have a place on the Control Commission. In addition, there was to be a commission, to meet in Moscow, to discuss reparations; and a conference was to be held in San Francisco in April to establish the new world organisation. The 'Big Three', joined by China and France, would each have a permanent seat, and also a veto on action, in the new body's Security Council.

There has been much argument about the outcome of the Yalta Conference.[77] An American scholar has maintained that Russian attempts to treat Germany harshly foundered on 'the hard rock of Anglo-American solidarity and moderation towards Germany'.[78] But in fact the powers agreed on the dismemberment of Germany, and the Reparations Commission was to take as the basis of its deliberations the figure of twenty billion dollars, which was supported by both Russia and the United States. Stalin showed himself a skilful negotiator, and of the three leaders it was probably Churchill who was most discontented with the outcome, perhaps fearing that too many concessions had been made by the Western powers to the Soviet Union. But at this stage Churchill still trusted Stalin as an ally and colleague. He had not forgotten the Russian silence during his own difficulties over Greece, and he assured the Commons on his return: 'I know of no Government which stands to its obligations, even in its own despite, more solidly than the Russian Soviet Government.'[79]

Roosevelt's attitude to the Russians was still more friendly; and there is no reason to suppose that the President was already too ill to negotiate with care. As Eden, surely an impartial observer on this question, said later, 'I do not believe that the President's declining health altered his judgment, though his handling of the Conference was less sure than it might have been.'[80] But the fact was that the Americans were very anxious to secure Russian participation in the war against Japan, and for that reason were more willing to make concessions elsewhere.

With the conference over, Churchill spent the afternoon of February 13th visiting the battlefield of Balaclava, and saw the valley down which the Charge of the Light Brigade had taken place.[81] Next day he flew to Athens, where the civil war was now over, and where he was greeted by a warmly enthusiastic crowd –

so enthusiastic indeed that he described it to the Commons as 'the high spot of the whole journey'.[82] He made a short speech to a vast crowd in Constitution Square, the centre of the city, and on the 15th flew to Egypt, where he met separately King Farouk, the President of Syria, and the two kings whom Roosevelt had invited to come to see him – Ibn Saud of Saudi Arabia and Haile Selassie of Ethiopia. On February 19th he flew back to England. Just over a week later the Commons debated the Yalta agreements, and a minority of 25, mostly Conservatives, voted against the government for agreeing to the westward movement of the Russo-Polish frontier.[83]

Meanwhile bitter fighting still continued on the Western Front. In the course of February the First Canadian Army (containing many British troops) and the American Ninth Army, both under Montgomery's command, closed up to the Rhine along its length north of Düsseldorf. It now seemed apparent that one final offensive would end the war, by leading to a complete disintegration of the German war machine. Eisenhower's plan was that Montgomery, with the American Ninth Army and also two airborne divisions under his command as well as his First Canadian Army and his Second British, should make the Rhine crossing in force on the northern flank. As it happened, though, at Remagen in the centre of Eisenhower's front a railway bridge across the Rhine was captured virtually intact, and so an immediate crossing was made in that area. Further south, too, a foothold over the Rhine was obtained near Mainz.

All this made Montgomery's last great offensive rather less significant than it would otherwise have been. But Churchill was determined to see as much of it as possible, and he flew to Montgomery's headquarters near Venlo on March 23rd for that purpose. The crossing was made that night, and next day the two divisions of airborne troops were landed behind the enemy's forward positions. Churchill was present as Montgomery interviewed his 'Phantoms' – liaison officers who gave him direct reports of developments on different sectors of the attack; and next day he attended a conference between Eisenhower and Montgomery. Afterwards, when Eisenhower had left, he persuaded Montgomery to allow him to cross the river by launch for half an hour or so. Churchill and Montgomery also visited Wesel, where, evidently to Churchill's satisfaction, they ran into a certain amount of enemy shellfire.[84] But the resistance was now only sporadic, in a few days the Rühr was completely surrounded by American troops, and the British and Canadian armies were moving into north Holland and towards Hamburg.

Now, at long last, the enemy showed signs of capitulation. Late in March there were contacts between some of the German military and officers of General Alexander's command in Switzerland, and although these came to nothing they aroused the suspicions of the Soviet government, in spite of the fact that the Russian Foreign Office had been officially informed and invited to send a representative to see what took place. On March 22nd Molotov gave the British Ambassador a written message which suggested that the Western Allies were negotiating with the Germans 'behind the backs of the Soviet Union, which is bearing the brunt of the war against Germany'.[85] Churchill described this to Eden as 'insulting' and thought for a time that he should postpone the visit to Russia that Clementine was just about to embark upon, by invitation of the Soviet government and in acknowledgment of her work for the 'Aid to Russia' Fund.[86]

Roosevelt reacted to this in the same way as Churchill, but he showed no wish to accept Churchill's other proposal at this time, which was to urge Eisenhower to try to capture Berlin ahead of the Russians, by a swift advance beyond the Elbe. Much to Churchill's annoyance, Eisenhower had already informed Stalin direct that he would send his troops forward on the more southerly axis Erfurt–Leipzig–Dresden and not towards Berlin. Eisenhower stuck to his existing commitment, with the support of Roosevelt and the American Chiefs of Staff, and Churchill decided to accept defeat on this question. As he put it to Roosevelt on April 5th, 'I regard the matter as closed, and to prove my sincerity I will use one of my few Latin quotations, *Amantium irae amoris integratio est.*'[87] The quotation, from Terence, may be translated 'The quarrels of lovers are the renewal of love.'

One week later – April 12th – Roosevelt died suddenly of a cerebral haemorrhage. He and Churchill had been close personal friends over the preceding four years, and on receiving the news Churchill felt 'as if I had been struck a physical blow'.[88] His first impulse was to travel to Washington for the funeral, and for a few days' consultations with Roosevelt's successor, the former Vice-President Harry S. Truman, who was unknown to him and who had been given very little information about the progress of the war at the highest level. Truman also favoured this course, but Churchill was persuaded not to leave London at such a critical moment of the war, and so Eden went instead. Churchill later regretted not having made the journey, perhaps because he had not realised how little information a vice-president received under the American system. But it had been arranged that Eden and Attlee should attend the San Francisco Conference later in the month, and it seemed convenient simply to bring forward Eden's date of departure for the United States.

Eden reported favourably to Churchill on his first meeting with Truman, and there was a general impression that the new President would hold to the policies of his predecessor.[89] But of course there could not at once be the same intimacy between him and Churchill as had previously existed between Roosevelt and Churchill; and Churchill was bound to feel that at a time when the Russians seemed to be defaulting on the decisions made at Yalta, especially in respect of Poland, it was a grave difficulty not to be able to consult his old colleague as he had done in so many crises in the past. It was impossible to find out what was going on in Poland, because the Russians gave no facilities to Allied diplomatic representatives there. All that was known was that sixteen Polish leaders who had emerged from the Underground Army to negotiate with the Russians had simply disappeared, in spite of a formal promise of safe conduct.[90]

But now the formal end of the war in Europe was at hand. A Russian offensive which began on April 16th led to the encirclement of Berlin nine days later, and to contact between American and Russian forces at Torgau on the Elbe. But the first major capitulation took place on the Italian front, where a fresh Allied offensive had begun on April 9th and proved highly successful. General von Vietinghoff, the enemy commander, agreed on April 29th to an unconditional surrender, and this took effect on May 2nd. In the last days of April Mussolini, who had been aiding the Germans in north Italy, made for the Swiss frontier accompanied by his mistress, but both were caught by Italian Partisans and shot. Hitler had decided to stay in Berlin to the end, and on April 30th he and Eva Braun, whom he had just married, committed suicide in the Chancellery. He rather unexpectedly appointed Admiral Doenitz, his naval commander, as his successor; and on May 3rd the Admiral sent an emissary to meet Montgomery to surrender all forces in the north-west, including Holland and Denmark. British troops had reached Lübeck, on the Baltic just beyond the peninsula of Jutland, on May 2nd.

For a few days after this it appeared as if the Germans were playing for time, to enable as many as possible of their troops and people to escape from the path of the Russian armies. But early on May 7th an unconditional surrender was signed by General Jodl, the German Chief of Staff, to take effect at midnight on May 8th/9th. This was confirmed by a formal ratification in Berlin in the early hours of May 9th, at which Marshal Keitel, Commander-in-Chief of the German Army, represented his country and Air Marshall Tedder, Eisenhower's deputy, represented all the Western Allies, with Marshal Zhukov acting for the Soviet Union.

In Britain a war-weary people was waiting to greet the day of victory. On May 7th crowds appeared in Whitehall, and Churchill, though not yet able to make a definite announcement, enjoyed passing through the throng in an open car. It must have reminded him of November 1918. On the 8th he could at last declare the war formally at an end – or rather he could say that all hostilities would terminate at 0001 a.m. next morning.[91] A Commons thanksgiving service took place at St Margaret's and Churchill led the procession over from the Commons accompanied by Greenwood, the acting Leader of the Opposition, immediately behind the Speaker. Later, the Prime Minister was photographed with the King and the Chiefs of Staff. At the invitation of the King he also appeared on the balcony of Buckingham Palace together with the Royal Family.

Thus both May 8th and May 9th were celebrated as 'VE'-days, or the days of victory in Europe. Victory over Japan still lay ahead, and for planning purposes it was generally presumed that this final section of the war would last another eighteen months.[92] In making a broadcast on Sunday May 13th Churchill was at pains to point out: 'We must never forget that beyond all lurks Japan, harassed and failing but still a people of a hundred millions, for whose warriors death has few terrors.'[93] But he could also point to the contrast in the state of British arms in the five years – almost to the day – since he became Prime Minister. He did not fail to acknowledge the contributions to this made by the Russian and American forces, and also the British Dominions, with the exception of 'Southern Ireland', to whose government, under de Valera, he addressed some hostile remarks.

But while the government had lasted for five years the House of Commons had lasted, with annual renewals, for nine and a half. Now that the European war was over, the question of whether to continue the Coalition arose in an acute form. This must form the topic of the next chapter.

The last volume of Churchill's *Second World War*, which covers the events discussed in this chapter, is entitled *Triumph and Tragedy*, and the title indicates Churchill's sense of disappointment at the outcome of the victory. He had been conscious in the last eighteen months of the German war, of course, of the relatively diminishing strength of the British contribution to the 'Grand Alliance' against Germany. With his vivid use of animal metaphor he had told his old friend Violet Bonham Carter after Tehran:

> I realised at Teheran for the first time what a small nation we are. There I sat with the great Russian bear on one side of me, with paws outstretched, and on the other side the great American buffalo, and between the two sat the poor little English donkey who was the only one, the only one of the three, who knew the right way home.[94]

It was still true in mid-1944 that more British troops than American were employed as combatants in Europe; but later in the year the balance swung markedly in favour of the United States, and Churchill complained to some of his junior ministers: 'I cannot take as big a part in running the war now as I used. Now we have got Eisenhower and all these high Generals looking after it.'[95]

As for the Russians, their insistence upon enjoying the fruits of their successful resistance and counter-offensives was only too obvious. Churchill was prepared at first to try what was virtually a policy of appeasement in eastern Europe: Harold Nicolson described him in late February as 'amused ... that the warmongers of the Munich period have now become the appeasers, while the appeasers have become the warmongers'.[96] But his instinct of loyalty to the Poles, on whose behalf Britain had entered the war, soon made him abandon this attitude. On May 12th, just three days after the armistice came into force, he wrote to Truman to express his concern about the future of Europe and to say that an 'iron curtain' had come down to conceal everything that was going on within the Russian sphere – that is to say, virtually all of Europe east of the line Lübeck–Trieste.[97] It was alarming that the Americans were proposing to withdraw their forces so rapidly from western Europe: but at least Truman was willing to react vigorously in one particular instance – when the Yugoslavs occupied the port of Trieste. With Churchill's willing support, he was prepared to instruct Field-Marshal Alexander, the Supreme Commander of the Allied Forces in Italy, to secure the port against all comers.[98]

Churchill had told his two colleagues of the 'Big Three' at Tehran that he was the only one of them who could be suddenly dismissed at the whim of Parliament.[99] The time had now come to renew the mandate of Parliament, and to determine who was to be in charge of the government during the difficult period of 'Stage II', as it was called in Whitehall – the period of the conclusion of the Far Eastern war and of the gradual transition to a peacetime economy.

26. *The Caretaker Government and the Election, May to July 1945*

By the autumn of 1944 most members of the parliamentary parties, who had loyally supported the electoral truce for five years, were beginning to feel that a general election should be fought as soon as the German war was over. In late October Churchill made a statement to the Commons saying that he was personally of this view, and that 'we must look to the termination of the war against Nazism as a pointer which will fix the date of the General Election'.[1] Liberal and Labour MPs were afraid that he would capitalise upon his reputation as the war-winner to have a 'khaki' election; and to allay their fears he spoke of a period of two or three months after the end of the war in Europe, in the course of which suitable preparations could be made. This would allow time for the Liberal and Labour Parties to withdraw from the government and for a 'Caretaker' administration to be constituted by the Conservatives, who had been since 1935 the largest party in the chamber.

When victory came in early May, therefore, Churchill had at once to make up his mind about the date of the election. To avoid the usual holiday period, it had to be either late in June, possibly early July, or to stand over until October. He conducted a straw vote of his Conservative colleagues and found that nearly all were for June, when the strength of gratitude to himself would, they thought, still be strong, thus assisting the Conservative prospects.[2] It was generally believed that Lloyd George, who had died only in late March of that year aged 82, had won the 1918 election because of a similar sense of gratitude: though in fact the two situations were not strictly comparable, as Lloyd George had been fighting with the strength of more than one of the main parties behind him, and against him he had only the Asquithian Liberals and the growing but still small Labour Party. For the same reason the Labour leaders wished to defer the election until October, when, as Herbert Morrison the Home Secretary pointed out, a new register would come into force.

After a few days' thought Churchill decided to offer the Opposition leaders the option of June, or the postponement of the election until after the defeat of Japan. For all government planning purposes, the date when it was expected that Japan would be defeated was still eighteen months ahead of VE-day. But Churchill was worried by the aspect of post-war Europe, and in particular the pretensions of Marshal Tito at Trieste, and felt that 'If there is going to be trouble of this kind the support of men like Attlee, Bevin, Morrison and George Hall is indispensable to the national presentation of the case.'[3] Churchill sensed that both Bevin and A. V. Alexander were sympathetic to his views, and that Attlee at least was prepared to consider the idea. Of the principal Labour leaders, only Morrison appeared to be definitely hostile.[4]

It was still only May 18th – nine days after VE-day, and just before the Whitsun weekend – when Churchill sent Attlee a formal letter inviting him to consider carrying on the Coalition until after the defeat of Japan. The letter had been drafted with the assistance of Attlee himself, so as to make it as acceptable as possible to his colleagues. In this amended form, it read in part: 'In the meanwhile, we would together do our utmost to implement the proposals for social security and full employment contained in the White Papers which we have laid before Parliament.' The letter also contained a suggestion, which evidently emanated only from Churchill's mind, that a referendum might be held on whether to prolong the life of Parliament for yet another year. Copies were sent to Archibald Sinclair, the Liberal leader, and to Ernest Brown of the National Liberals, as well as to Attlee himself.[5]

Attlee was quite prepared to commend the proposal to his colleagues; but the Labour Party Annual Conference was assembling at Blackpool over Whitsun, and this meant a concentration of influence in the contrary direction. When on Saturday May 19th a meeting took place between the Labour ministers and the National Executive for the purpose of considering the letter, it was soon clear that Attlee's view would not prevail. Morrison was strongly in favour of fighting as soon as possible, and Bevin and Dalton, although initially sympathetic to Attlee, changed their minds in the course of the meeting. In the end, only three relatively junior members of the National Executive supported Attlee in his plea for a continuation of the Coalition.[6] The majority decision was greeted enthusiastically at a secret session of the conference on the afternoon of Whit Monday, May 21st, and when a vote was taken only two hands were held up in favour of continuing the Coalition.[7] By this time Attlee, of course, had accepted the majority decision, which, ironically, was soon to make him Prime Minister.

Attlee thereupon wrote to Churchill to say that he and his colleagues could not accept an extension of the Coalition until the end of the war with Japan, but would agree to a prolongation until October, in order to avoid 'a rushed election like that of 1918'. As for the idea of a referendum, he dismissed that as having 'only too often been the instrument of Nazism and Fascism'.[8] This reply was decisive in determining that there should be an early election; and it was a sign that the campaign had already begun that Churchill allowed himself a riposte, in which he declared, 'It is odd that you should accompany so many unjust allegations with an earnest request that we should go on bickering till the autumn.'[9]

On May 23rd Churchill formally resigned, and was at once invited by the King to form a new government. It was announced that the general election would be on July 5th, which meant that there would be altogether six weeks for the campaign – a much more generous allowance than in 1918 when less than five weeks elapsed between Armistice Day and the polling. Churchill's new 'caretaker' government consisted of Conservatives, National

Liberals and a few non-party or 'National' ministers who were prepared to continue in service. Among the latter were Sir John Anderson (Chancellor of the Exchequer), Sir James Grigg (Secretary of State for War) and Lord Leathers (Minister of Transport). Churchill himself continued as Minister of Defence as well as Prime Minister, but he enlarged the Cabinet to a total of sixteen members, and brought in his Service ministers, including Brendan Bracken (First Lord of the Admiralty) and Harold Macmillan (Secretary of State for Air). R. A. Butler was the new Minister of Labour; Viscount Simon, who continued as Lord Chancellor, was to remain outside the Cabinet. On May 28th Churchill held an 'At Home' at No. 10 Downing Street for the senior ministers of the retiring Coalition, and declared, with the tears streaming down his cheeks, 'The light of history will shine on all your helmets.'[10] He added that to ensure continuity of foreign policy in case he lost the election he proposed to invite Attlee to accompany him to the Conference of the 'Big Three', which would be held and perhaps completed before the election results were known.

So far from the election being 'rushed', it was really, as Hugh Dalton admitted in his memoirs, 'very long drawn out'.[11] This was because the date of polling was announced well in advance: Parliament continued in session for several days, and two important measures of social reform were carried with the support of the Opposition – the Family Allowances Bill and the Location of Industry Bill. Parliament was dissolved on June 15th, which still left three weeks before polling; and owing to the difficulty of collecting the postal votes of servicemen in distant parts of the world, the count was to take place only after a further three weeks had passed.

The campaign had begun in late May, and Churchill entered it with all the zest of his earlier elections – perhaps heightened by a feeling that he had yet to establish himself fully as the Leader of the Conservative Party. As early as May 26th he made a tour of his constituency, the borough of Woodford – which was only a segment of his former county division, Epping, now split up owing to the rapid growth of its population since 1918. On June 4th he made a broadcast, the first of four, on behalf of his party's cause in the election. It was a bold attack on the Labour Party, which went so far as to suggest that if its leaders won 'They would have to fall back on some form of Gestapo, no doubt very humanely directed in the first instance.'[12] Most of the newspapers were surprised at the way in which he had changed his tune from that of the national leader to that of the partisan: *The Times* described the transition as 'uncomfortably abrupt'.[13] Attlee replied in a broadcast the following night. His views sounded very reasonable in comparison with Churchill's, but he endeavoured to exonerate Churchill from responsibility for his speech by saying, 'The voice we heard last night was that of Mr Churchill, but the mind was that of Lord Beaverbrook.'[14]

This aroused in listeners' minds the idea of a political scare election, run by a great newspaper proprietor who had tried the same thing before. For some days Opposition spokesmen were able to pursue the theme that Churchill's utterances were no longer his own, and that he was being prompted by an evil counsellor. Not even his second broadcast, on June 13th, was able to remove the idea, although it was devoted primarily to an expression of his views on the need for family allowances, free school milk, national insurance and the building of houses.

On June 15th Churchill found another issue to throw into the election. He had noticed that Professor Harold Laski, who had become chairman of the extra-parliamentary Labour Party, had argued that Attlee was not entitled to attend the conference of the 'Big Three' except as an observer – that is to say, he could not commit the Labour Party in any way to acceptance of its decisions. Laski had also criticised the idea of a continuity of foreign policy between the two governments, if Labour won the election. Churchill therefore wrote to Attlee, in a letter at once revealed to the press, that he wanted him to come as 'a friend and counsellor', and that 'Merely to come as a mute observer would, I think, be derogatory to your position as the Leader of your party, and I should not have a right to throw this burden upon you in such circumstances.'[15]

Churchill had in reality stumbled on a matter of real substance, which exposed the weakness of the Labour Party's structure from the point of view of leadership. The tensions between the parliamentary party and the extra-parliamentary party were to find still more serious form in 1960 in the conflict between Hugh Gaitskell and the Conference over unilateral nuclear disarmament. But in 1945 the issue was largely ignored by the voters, who took it as a 'stunt' of the type of the Zinoviev Letter scare of 1924 and Philip Snowden's talk in 1931 about the effect of Socialism on the Post Office Savings Bank. Beaverbrook increased this impression by making personal appearances on election platforms and saying on June 18th: 'I hereby declare that Laski is aiming at the destruction of the parliamentary system of Great Britain, and that he hopes to set up in its place the dictatorship of something commonly called the National Executive.' This made it all the easier for Attlee to retort by attacking 'Lord Beaverbrook's record of political intrigue and instability' and 'insatiable appetite for power'.[16]

Altogether Churchill broadcast four times, and there were six other broadcasts by his supporters. The Labour Party also had a total of ten broadcasts, but none of its spokesmen appeared more than once. The Liberals were allowed four, and the Communist and Common Wealth Parties were each permitted a brief ten minutes. The BBC reckoned the audience for these broadcasts as very similar among the main parties – 44.5% for Liberals and Labour each and 45.4% for the Conservatives. The latter's exploitation of Churchill was at least justified to the extent that the higher proportion of listeners to Conservative broadcasts was entirely due to his own audience – he scored an average of 49%.[17]

There was a similar contrast in the style of the national manifestos. The main Conservative election address was entitled *Mr Churchill's Declaration of Policy to the Electors*, and was in fact written by Churchill himself. The Labour manifesto was called *Let Us Face the Future*, and although it promised the nationalisation or 'public ownership' of various industries it did not at any point mention the name of the Leader of the party. It was written by Herbert Morrison, and its failure to mention Attlee's name might perhaps be regarded as a sign of jealousy – for Morrison certainly wanted the leadership for himself – if it had not been for the party's hostility to the whole concept of leadership since the so-called 'betrayal' by Ramsay MacDonald in 1931.

There was also a marked difference in the character of the public campaigns of the two parties. Churchill travelled about the country in his special train, which he needed as a mobile communications centre if he were to continue to act as Prime Minister. During the day he would leave the train and fulfil a schedule of meetings, going about in an open car. He was warmly received by crowds of cheering people, and this gave him a false impression of how the election would turn out. It was really only late in the campaign, when he visited constituencies in the London area, that he encountered some hostility, and at Tooting Bec a young man threw a squib at him which exploded almost in his face. At Walthamstow Stadium on July 3rd he was subjected to vigorous heckling, but he 'seemed to be enjoying it enormously'.[18]

Attlee, on the other hand, was driven round the country in an old car by his wife. He did not lack attentive and appreciative audiences, but the very modesty of his behaviour discouraged any great demonstrations, either of support or of disapproval. All the same, in the final stages of the campaign Churchill did something for Attlee's position as Leader by engaging him in vigorous controversy about the nature of the Labour Party's constitution. Attlee made a point of replying to each of Churchill's letters in time for the next day's newspapers. It is very doubtful whether the points at issue were of any interest to the electors. According to a Gallup Poll, the first concern at the time was to determine which party would most effectively deal with housing.[19] The devastation caused by bombing, combined with the almost complete absence of house-building over six years, made this the most urgent problem of the time.

In his last broadcast, which closed the entire series, Churchill again stressed the danger of having a Labour government being dictated to by the National Executive of the extra-parliamentary party, chaired by Laski. He also emphasised, especially for the benefit of service voters abroad, that there was no truth in the supposition that they could vote for any party other than the Conservative Party and still regard themselves as voting for his continuance as Prime Minister.[20] The idea that he was altogether above the parties, like the King, may have developed as a result of his tendency to visit the war fronts in uniform.

So far as his own constituency of Woodford was concerned, Churchill was necessarily absent for much of the campaign. It was the more Conservative part of the old Epping division of Essex, and partly for this reason, partly because they respected Churchill's need to maintain his role as Prime Minister, the Labour, Liberal and Common Wealth parties all agreed not to oppose him. Nevertheless a middle-aged eccentric from Northamptonshire, Alexander Hancock, a shoe-maker turned farmer, decided to stand as an Independent, and so Churchill was obliged to undertake a contest. Clementine acted on his behalf to some extent, and announced in one of her speeches that 'He means to see that the building of houses is treated as a war operation, just as Mulberry Harbour was a war operation.'[21] Churchill himself made a rapid tour of the constituency on polling day, standing in an open car with Clementine at his side, but he did not expect to lose many votes to his opponent, who advocated a one-day working week.[22]

After polling, there was an anticlimax, for the votes were not to be counted for three weeks. A few constituencies in the North were allowed to poll a week late, owing to 'wakes', and in the case of one, Nelson and Colne, the delay was permitted for two weeks.

In the interval before the declaration, Churchill decided to take a holiday. A conference of the 'Big Three' had been arranged to begin at Potsdam on July 15th, but there were several days to spare in the meantime. The Duke of Westminster offered him the use of his hunting-lodge at Mimizan, near Bordeaux, and Churchill, who already knew the place well from before the war, was only doubtful about what had happened to it during the German occupation. His ADC, Commander Thompson, was therefore sent to reconnoitre. He found that the water supply was rusted up and could not be repaired in time.[23]

Fortunately, the new British consul at Bordeaux, whom Thompson had contacted, knew of an alternative, a house which had been offered to himself as a residence. This was the Château de Bordaberry, which was further south, close to the Spanish border at Hendaye. It was owned by a Canadian, General Raymond Brutinel, who expressed himself as favourable to the visit. Churchill therefore flew in to the nearest airport, bringing with him Clementine and Mary and also Lord Moran and his private secretary, Jock Colville, as well as Commander Thompson and the usual two detectives and two typists. He could not forsake business entirely, and papers were sent down to him by way of the Paris Embassy. But after a time he set to work with his paints, and he also bathed on several occasions. The local people were very friendly, and organised an afternoon of Basque games and dancing.[24]

On July 15th Churchill dutifully flew on to Potsdam, where he was joined by Eden and Attlee. Eden had missed most of the election campaigning owing to a gastric ulcer. But Churchill now felt he could not settle any of the big issues of the conference before he knew the election result. At the Château he had said that he would be 'only half a man' until then.[25] On July 16th he made a tour of Berlin, and saw the shattered Chancellery and Hitler's bunker. On the 17th Stimson, the American Secretary of War, told him of the successful experiment with the atomic bomb in the desert of New Mexico two weeks earlier. Next day he lunched alone with the new President, and they explored each other's minds. Truman was very businesslike, and the two men touched on nearly all the outstanding questions at issue between the two nations.

British consent to the use of the bomb against Japan had been given by the Cabinet two weeks earlier and, as Churchill later said, it 'was never even an issue'.[26] Nevertheless this consent was formalised at a joint meeting of Truman and Churchill with their Foreign Ministers on July 22nd (James Byrnes was now the US Secretary of State). A proclamation warning the Japanese of the danger of prolonged resistance in the face of Allied power – but not actually mentioning the new bomb – was drawn up and published a few days later.[27] On July 23rd the Prime Minister entertained Stalin and Truman and the senior officers of the three nations to dinner at what was temporarily called '10 Downing Street, Potsdam'.

On July 25th the three British leaders flew back to England so as to be present when the election results were announced next day. Churchill had already instructed his Map Room staff to set up a diagrammatic representation of the course of events.[28] He was personally fairly confident of victory, as the Conservative Central Office had promised a majority of 56 at least, and the *Daily Express*, with its habitual optimism, thought 'over sixty'.[29] But although he went to sleep that night with a feeling of confidence he woke, as he relates in his memoirs, before daybreak with 'a sharp stab of almost physical pain' and a conviction that the election had gone the wrong way.[30] He then slept on until 9 a.m., and after a time rose to see what was happening in the Map Room.

By lunchtime it was evident that Labour would have a majority of seats in the new Parliament. There was a growing list of Cabinet ministers who had been defeated – Brendan Bracken,

Harold Macmillan, and Leo Amery; also Churchill's son-in-law, Duncan Sandys, and his son, Randolph, at Preston in Lancashire. For a time Churchill himself preserved a cheerful appearance, but he repeatedly telephoned Sir Robert Topping, the General Director of the Central Office, to enquire about the progress of events and to ask why things were going so unexpectedly badly.[31]

Clementine and Mary had gone over to Woodford for the count there, and to their surprise, although Churchill was easily elected, the Independent had polled heavily. The figures were:

W. S. Churchill (Nat. Cons.)	27,688	Elected
A. Hancock (Independent)	10,488	

At luncheon, which was restricted to a few guests, Churchill's distress was evident, and to comfort him Clementine said, 'It may well be a blessing in disguise'; to which he retorted, 'At the moment it seems quite effectively disguised.'[32]

He had already pondered on the possibility that the result of the election might be close. In that event he thought he might continue in power until the Commons met, and wait to be defeated in a vote of the new House. But this was not a close result, but a landslide defeat. Labour won a total of 393 seats, and the Conservatives (including the Ulster Unionists) returned with only 197. There were 2 Nationals and 13 National Liberals – all of these supporters of Churchill – and also 12 Liberals and a few other independents. For the Liberals it was a disappointing result, especially as they secured a total poll of over two millions: on balance, their participation damaged the Labour Party more than it did the Conservatives.[33] Labour secured altogether twelve million votes – not quite a majority of the electorate – and the Conservative and National and National Liberal candidates between them secured somewhat less than ten million. The Common Wealth Party had lost its *raison d'être* with the termination of the electoral truce, and only one of its candidates was elected.

Before the counting was fully completed, Churchill had decided to submit his resignation to the King. He visited the Palace for this purpose at 7 p.m. – it was still May 26th – and advised the King to send for Attlee. 'It was a very sad meeting,' minuted the King.[34] He offered his retiring Prime Minister the Order of the Garter, but Churchill felt it was an inappropriate time for him to accept an honour. He suggested instead that it should be offered to Anthony Eden, but Eden also declined it for similar reasons. At 7.30 p.m. Attlee was summoned to the Palace and invited to form a government: he agreed to do so.

Churchill's last public action at Downing Street on that day was to issue a statement to say that he had resigned, and to thank 'the British people' for their support in the past. He said he was sorry not to retain responsibility for the war against Japan, but 'for this ... all plans and preparations have been made, and the results may come much quicker than we have hitherto been entitled to expect'.[35] Two days later, on the Saturday afternoon, as Attlee and Bevin were winging their way to Potsdam, he spent a final weekend at Chequers. On Monday morning he was back in Downing Street, but that afternoon he went down to Chartwell with his daughter Mary, and spent the night there after walking round the overgrown gardens.[36]

Various explanations have been given for the defeat of the Churchill government in the 1945 general election. The *Manchester Guardian* was inclined to blame Churchill personally for his conduct of the campaign, and in particular his 'attempt to turn the election into a personal plebiscite'.[37] Churchill himself naturally did not accept this interpretation of the defeat, but he also thought that the campaign was important. He pointed out in his memoirs that Conservative constituency organisation was weakened by the absence of many of the officers and agents on full-time war-service, whereas a high proportion of Labour constituency-workers were still at hand, because they were employed in the exempted trades.[38] Such a view must have derived some of its weight from a survey which he had had made by the whips of the two main parties in 1944.[39]

A different interpretation still was offered by the younger Conservatives, particularly those of progressive views, who had since 1943 formed a body called the Tory Reform Committee. Quintin Hogg, for instance, argued that the Conservatives had failed to explain that an economy which was in some degree planned could be reconciled with freedom. This was an immediate reaction to the election result.[40] Many years later R. A. Butler in his memoirs wrote: 'It would have been better if affirmation of post-war policies had not taken a poor third place to the concentrated exploitation of Churchill's personality and a negative attack on the Labour Party.' 'But', he added, 'the election would probably have been lost in any case.' And he then proceeded to argue that 'The forces' vote, in particular, had been virtually won over by the left-wing influence of the Army Bureau of Current Affairs.'[41]

None of these explanations can be regarded as satisfactory. For the very few who had eyes to see, the Gallup Poll had been sampling political feeling from 1942 onwards, and publishing the results in the pages of the *News Chronicle*. These samples were confined to the civilian population, and cannot have been affected by the Army Bureau of Current Affairs. People were asked how they would vote 'if a general election were held tomorrow'. About 9% of the sample normally declared support for the Liberal Party, but Labour had a clear lead over the Conservatives amounting to about 10%. This could be combined with a considerable personal popularity of Churchill as Prime Minister, especially in the period after El Alamein when it was felt that his military strategy was proving successful.[42] If anything, therefore, the actual campaign period in June–July 1945 saw a slight rally by the Conservatives, for in the final result 47.8% voted for Labour or allied candidates and 39.8% for the Conservatives and their allies – a Labour lead of only 8%.

The question then becomes rather different – why, over the long period 1942–5, or even longer, did the Labour Party gain so much ground as against its main electoral competitor? Although the Services vote had no special significance – and was indeed relatively low[43] – the behaviour of two army units stationed in Berlin, as reported by Lord Moran, is not without interest. The 11th Hussars had taken over a barracks previously occupied by the Russians, who had left it in filth and disorder:

> In the first instance they had voted for the Socialists, but since they had met the Russians and seen what they had done, they wanted to vote Conservative. Another regiment did not vote at all. When asked why, they said that now that they knew something about the Russians, their views had altered.[44]

The Red Army did not visit Britain, although the US Army did; and there developed a remarkable schism between public opinion and official opinion about the merits of the two major allies, one of which was the champion of free enterprise and the other (so it was thought) of Socialism. After the invasion of

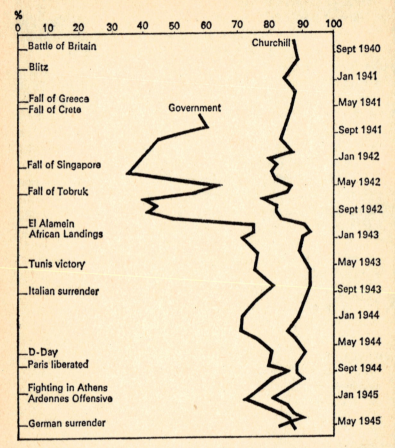

Popularity of the Coalition Government and Prime Minister.
Percentage satisfied in reply to the question 'On the whole, in
general, are you satisfied or dissatisfied with the Government's
conduct of the war?'; and percentage approving in reply to the
question 'On the whole, in general, do you approve or disapprove
of Mr Churchill as Prime Minister?'
Figures by courtesy of The Gallup Poll; drawing by courtesy of
Messrs Collins.

Russia by the German armies in mid-1941, the newspapers were full of stories about the gallant struggle being waged on the Eastern Front; the Americans were not yet heavily engaged, at least in Europe or north Africa; and as early as June 1942 a Gallup Poll asking 'Which country do you think is more popular with the British at the present time, Russia or the United States?' found that 62% answered Russia, as against only 24% for the United States.[45] This was in spite of the increasing dependence of Britain upon Lend-Lease assistance from America – or perhaps in part it was because of it.

It may be thought surprising that many people should see some sort of identity between the Labour Party and the Soviet form of Socialism. Yet it was widely believed that the success of the Red Army on the Eastern Front was due to the fact that, contrary to all expectation on the part of Conservatives, there were forms of Socialism that actually worked. It was a natural supposition that state intervention might be the best way to run British industry, so as to deal with the major outstanding problems of British life. In a Gallup Poll of March 1945, 71% of respondents described themselves as dissatisfied with the government's record in housing, and 59% regarded it as the most important single problem now facing the government.[46] Although no government which devoted most of its resources to winning the war could have satisfied very many people with its record in housing before the end of hostilities, this was a danger signal about popular feeling which Churchill and his colleagues could ignore only at their peril. In fact, Churchill did his best by setting up a committee of the Cabinet in the Caretaker period which he called 'the Housing Squad'.[47] It included his son-in-law, Duncan Sandys, who was Minister of Works. But somehow it was not quite conspicuous enough to the public.

Of course there were other factors determining the course of the election. There was the so-called 'swing of the pendulum' – the reaction against any existing administration, which was bound to be especially strong after a period of ten years. There was the hostility to the 'men of Munich', now allied with Churchill, who were held responsible for the relative unpreparedness of the British armed forces at the beginning of the war. There was the feeling that the Conservatives would not really put into effect the provisions of the Beveridge Report, which the Labour Party had accepted with enthusiasm. There was, too, a feeling that

Churchill, now over seventy, was too old to direct the nation's fortunes in the post-war world. Finally, there was the recollection of what had happened after 1918: great war leader as Lloyd George was, he had somehow failed to run the country effectively in the post-war period. It must have been for a combination of these reasons that the 1945 result was so decisively adverse to Churchill, making him accept the view that the people had spurned him so definitely that he 'did not wish to remain even for an hour responsible for their affairs'.[48]

27. *Leader of the Opposition, 1945–9*

In his *Thoughts and Adventures* (1932) Churchill described the shock of losing executive office at the Admiralty in 1915, in words already quoted in this book: 'Like a sea-beast fished up from the depths, or a diver too suddenly hoisted, my veins threatened to burst from the fall in pressure'.[1] In July 1945 he suffered the same experience, having lost the Premiership in an election which he certainly did not expect to turn out as it did. For a few days there was a good deal of business to be cleared up, but even so he was miserable while this went on. At a final Cabinet meeting on July 27th Eden noticed that he was 'pretty wretched'.[2] Being obliged to leave No. 10 Downing Street, for a few days he took a penthouse at Claridge's Hotel. He was living partly there and partly at Chartwell when Parliament reassembled on August 1st. When he belatedly entered the Chamber with its many new members, the Conservatives greeted him with 'For He's a Jolly Good Fellow'. The effect of this demonstration was, however, at once obliterated when the Labour Party, now of course far outnumbering the Conservatives, responded with the 'Red Flag'. This behaviour upset some of the Conservative leaders considerably. Oliver Lyttelton wrote later that he 'began to fear for my country'.[3]

He need not have been afraid. Ernest Bevin as Attlee's Foreign Secretary retained the continuity of foreign policy, and soon people were saying 'Hasn't Anthony Eden grown fat?'[4] But the course of the war changed dramatically in the next few weeks. The defeat of Japan, which for planning purposes had been expected eighteen months after the end of the German war, took place suddenly in mid-August. This was partly the result of the dropping in early August of the first two atomic bombs, one on Hiroshima and one on Nagasaki. The bombs, which were manufactured under the control of the United States Army, were the product of secret research initiated jointly by Churchill and Roosevelt but carried out for production purposes exclusively in the United States. There was never any question among the Allied leaders of the bombs being used: each one could produce as devastating an effect by itself as the three-day bombing of Dresden, without the hazarding, on the Allied side, of more than the crew of one bomber. The American Secretary of War, Henry Stimson, believed that only a shock such as would be administered by this new and terrible weapon would persuade the Japanese leaders to give up the struggle, and thus avoid the need for an invasion of the main islands of Japan.[5] All the same, it may be that the Japanese collapse owed as much to the Russian declaration of war which took place at this time (August 8th).[6] And so on August 15th Churchill, this time in his role as Opposition Leader, again walked directly behind the Speaker on his way to St Margaret's for a thanksgiving service for victory.[7]

As he was once more a private citizen, and as a parliamentary vacation stretched in front of him, Churchill decided on a holiday before anything else. He had arranged to buy a house in central London – 28 Hyde Park Gate, Kensington – and he had it redecorated at once. Meanwhile, Field-Marshal Alexander lent him a villa on Lake Como in northern Italy, which he had been using as a headquarters. Alexander also assigned to Churchill as ADCs two young officers of Churchill's old regiment, the 4th Hussars. Churchill arrived on September 1st with his daughter Sarah and his doctor, Lord Moran. The holiday was successful in resting him and restoring his morale. The weather was mostly good, and he could spend his time, as Sarah put it, on 'painting and picnics'.[8] He also had his wartime minutes with him, especially those of 1940, to browse through again and to savour: he was beginning to plan the writing of his memoirs. The Italians were friendly, and after a few days of no newspapers or letters 'Alex' arrived with a letter from Clementine, and the two men spent a day together, both painting.[9] After three weeks Churchill left the villa and moved to Cap d'Antibes on the French Riviera for a further two weeks' rest, before returning to England.

Throughout the years of opposition to the Attlee government there were two Winston Churchills – one, the responsible statesman, pointing the way ahead for both Europe and America; the other, the political partisan, denouncing, to the satisfaction of the Conservative rank and file, the 'Socialists' who were encouraging the 'gloomy State vultures of nationalisation' to 'hover above our basic industries'. As Churchill uttered these words to a meeting of the Central Council of the Conservative Party in London in November 1945, he accompanied them with a 'slow flapping of his arms' which amused his audience considerably.[10] But no new general election was likely for some years; and, as it happened, he rather approved of the first measure of nationalisation, which was of the Bank of England, in view of his experiences with Montagu Norman while Chancellor of the Exchequer in the 1920s.

It was not surprising that early in 1946 he decided to absent himself from Parliament for a few months, leaving Anthony Eden in charge of the Opposition. He had accepted an invitation from Westminster College, at Fulton, Missouri, to deliver an address; President Truman undertook to introduce him to the audience; a date was fixed for early March; and so, announcing that Moran had advised him to take a holiday of a month or so in a warm climate, he left England for New York by the *Queen Elizabeth* en route for Florida, on January 9th. Colonel Frank Clarke, of Quebec, had invited him to stay at his home on Miami Beach, and early in February Churchill also went to Havana for several days as guest of the Cuban government.

On March 4th and 5th President Truman took Churchill with him on his own special train on the Baltimore and Ohio Railroad to Missouri, the President's home state. Churchill's speech on this occasion was as usual carefully prepared, and it made a considerable impact, by no means entirely favourable. It was in part a plea for the establishment of a peace-keeping force by the United Nations, consisting in the first instance of air squadrons. But he also argued in favour of the retention by the Western Powers of their 'secret knowledge or experience of the atomic bomb', and for the maintenance of a 'special relationship of the English-speaking peoples', based upon the continuance of military ties –

presumably the Combined Chiefs of Staff. He now spoke out in public about his impression of the tyranny that had descended upon Eastern Europe, in terms which he had used in private correspondence with Truman a year earlier:

> From Stettin in the Baltic to Trieste in the Adriatic, an iron curtain has descended across the Continent. Behind that line lie all the capitals of the ancient states of Central and Eastern Europe.... Police governments are prevailing in nearly every case, and so far, except in Czechoslovakia, there is no true democracy.

He did not suggest that war with Russia was imminent or inevitable; but he argued for a policy of strength and unity in the face of a power which did not desire war, but merely 'the fruits of war'.[11]

At a time when public feeling about Russia was still relatively friendly on both sides of the Atlantic, Churchill's words and his use of the term 'iron curtain' caused a furore. There was an early reaction from Stalin himself, who stated in an interview in *Pravda* that Churchill 'has now adopted the position of warmonger'.[12] Both Attlee and Truman refused to make any public comment on the speech, but Churchill reported to Attlee that Truman had 'seemed equally pleased before and after'.[13] There were, however, some bitterly hostile words spoken in Congress, where a tendency to isolationism was again strong. In 1946 Congress passed the McMahon Act, which deprived Britain of any exchange of information about the atomic bomb – a measure which Attlee regarded as a 'breach of faith'.[14] But Congress also in that session authorised a substantial loan to Britain at a low rate of interest, under an agreement which had been negotiated by Keynes in the autumn of 1945. Churchill, who was in Washington while it was being debated, supported it vigorously at a press conference on March 11th – an act which won him a telegram of thanks from Attlee.[15]

In the course of the next few months, although he was occasionally available for set-piece orations at Westminster denouncing the government, Churchill spent much of his time visiting other countries of Western Europe, receiving honorary degrees, honorary citizenships, medals and gifts. For the theme of his speeches he took the idea, first expounded by him after the war at Brussels in November 1945, of the 'United States of Europe'.[16] This was partly because it was obviously what his audiences wanted to hear in view of the proximity of the Soviet occupation forces; partly because his son-in-law Duncan Sandys was especially keen on the idea, perhaps as a result of his wartime study of new weapons.[17] In August and September 1946 Churchill spent some weeks on holiday in Switzerland as a guest of the Federal government; and when on September 19th he visited Zurich to receive an honorary degree he spoke of the post-war distress in Europe, and of what he saw as the remedy – not only the building of 'a kind of United States of Europe', but also of 'a partnership between France and Germany'.[18]

It was remarkable that so soon after the end of the war, when the trials of Nazi war criminals were still going on, he should publicly urge the early restoration of Germany to a place in the family of nations – and should pick on the crucial importance of Franco-German reconciliation. It appeared, though, that he did not see Britain playing a major role in Europe, except perhaps in some form of external association. As he said in May 1947, at a 'United Europe' meeting at the Albert Hall,

> There is the United States with all its dependencies; there is the Soviet Union; there is the British Empire and Commonwealth; and there is Europe, with which Great Britain is profoundly blended. Here are the four main pillars of the World Temple of Peace.[19]

At this time the British economy at home was running relatively smoothly, with full employment except for a brief breakdown in coal supplies in the harsh winter of early 1947. But the weakness of the European nations created an acute dollar shortage, and Hugh Dalton, the Labour Chancellor of the Exchequer, was confronted by a rapid outflow of the American loan which had so lately been received. In February he had to insist that the Foreign Office give notice to the United States that British aid to Greece and Turkey would shortly be terminated. Although the State Department was aggrieved by the abruptness of the British action, President Truman reacted swiftly to the news, and asked Congress to supply the necessary credits, declaring that it was American policy to 'support free peoples who are resisting attempted subjugation by armed minorities or by outside pressures'.[20] This was retrospective justification, in Churchill's view, for the 'iron curtain' speech, and an indication of the willingness of the United States to undertake the heavy task of 'containment' against the Soviet Union.

General Marshall had now become Truman's Secretary of State, and could bring to bear his great prestige as a war leader against Congressional critics. In June of the same year, 1947, he spoke at a Harvard degree ceremony of the willingness of his country to provide economic aid for Europe as a whole, provided that the countries of Europe got together and made a plan of their own for its use. This speech, which owed something to Churchill's pioneering of the idea of a united Europe, was at once warmly welcomed by Ernest Bevin, and by Georges Bidault, the French Foreign Minister, and there followed a conference of European nations at Paris, from which only Russia, with the states under her control, chose to be absent. The conference proceeded to prepare a 'European Recovery Programme' – also known as the 'Marshall Plan' – which enabled Britain, and of course France and the other nations, to receive further assistance from the United States. The Russian response was to re-establish the Communist International, at least to the extent of founding a Communist Information Bureau or 'Cominform' to expound the view that the world was divided into 'two camps', one of which was 'imperialist' and the other 'anti-imperialist'.

The 'Cold War' between the Western countries and the Russian *bloc* was now clearly under way. It was, fortunately, not a period of open hostilities, at least in Europe; but each side manœuvred for advantages at the expense of the other and engaged in substantial rearmament. In February 1948 a Communist *coup* took place in Czechoslovakia, and in March Jan Masaryk, the prominent pro-Western leader and son of the country's first President, committed suicide. Churchill had known Masaryk well during the war years, and his comment was: 'I am sure we all, especially those who knew him closely, feel a deep respect for Masaryk who has, by his supreme sacrifice, cast a new lustre on an already-famous name.'[21] Only one week later the governments of most of Western Europe – Britain, France, Belgium, the Netherlands and Luxembourg – signed a treaty at Brussels establishing a joint defence pact.

In June 1948 the Soviet occupation authorities closed the ground links used by the Western Powers for supplying their sectors in Berlin. This act was quite legal but smacked strongly of moral blackmail, as nobody in the West wished to take the responsibility for precipitating a world war by forcing a way through the blockade. The solution found was an air lift of supplies, as the Western Powers had established legal rights to air corridors to Berlin. In the stress of these months, United States aircraft – B-29 bombers – again moved to bases in Britain; and negotiations were begun for a wider military alliance of the Western Powers including the United States. This resulted in the signature in April 1949 of the North Atlantic Treaty, which drew in all the members of the Brussels Treaty and also the United States, Canada, Denmark, Iceland, Italy, Norway and Portugal. The new treaty was the first formal alliance made by the United States since the eighteenth century; and it also involved the most considerable European military commitment ever undertaken by Britain in peacetime.

All this encouraged the movement for some form of unity in Europe; and Churchill took the trouble to attend the foundation conference of the 'United Europe' campaign at The Hague in May 1948, and served as honorary chairman of the meeting. His support was perhaps assumed to be stronger than it really was, but at least it was not as tepid as that of the Labour government, which foresaw grave difficulties with the Commonwealth as well as with such prized concepts as nationalisation if Britain were to join.[22] Nevertheless the ex-Allied governments of Western Europe agreed early in 1949 to establish a Council of Europe, consisting of foreign ministers, and a Consultative Assembly to meet at Strasbourg. Delegates to the Assembly, although appointed by governments, were chosen to represent parties in proportion to their numbers in national parliaments; and Churchill himself went to the first meeting in Strasbourg in August 1949 in a delegation led by Herbert Morrison. This did not make for amity; and on one occasion, as Dalton, who was also a delegate, recorded in his memoirs, 'They confronted each other, in front of a crowd of astonished foreign delegates, and exchanged not only rough words but rude gestures.'[23] The disagreement was about whether a Conservative MP who was acting as a substitute for Churchill when he was away was entitled to claim any subsistence allowance from the Treasury when both he and Churchill were together in Strasbourg. But the Assembly had no power; Churchill did not stay long; and virtually nothing emerged from its deliberations.

The fact was that no prominent British political leader was prepared to accept the idea of a European Federation with Britain as a component part. Churchill remained vague in his references to British participation, and Anthony Eden was conspicuous by his absence from the discussion. The Labour leaders, being in power, were reluctant to take positive action at a time when they had other problems to deal with; their main concerns were the maintenance of Britain's position among the Great Powers, and the problems of India and the Middle East.

It was difficult to see how Indian independence could safely be achieved, in spite of the Labour Party's commitment to it as a goal. The Indian communities were so deeply divided that British withdrawal appeared likely, as Churchill feared, to precipitate a blood-bath. Nevertheless Churchill himself was committed by the Cripps Offer of 1942 to the idea of Dominion Status for India. Early in 1946 Cripps again visited India to see how the transfer could take place: this time he was accompanied by two other Cabinet ministers, Pethick-Lawrence, Churchill's old opponent at Leicester, and A. V. Alexander, his more recent colleague at the Admiralty. But the sectional strife was, if anything, worse than ever. The Muslims had a bitter and uncompromising champion in M. A. Jinnah, a lawyer who was determined to insist on partition and the creation of a new state to be called Pakistan. In February 1947 the Labour Cabinet under Attlee's leadership decided to confront the communities with the challenge of power: British rule, it was announced, would in any case end not later than June 1948.

The decision was attacked by Churchill with much of his old vigour, but once again the Conservative Party was not united, and Lord Halifax, who was of course a former Viceroy, made a speech in the Lords which gave a measure of support to the government's plans. Churchill was obliged to recognise that this was almost the end of the road for his opposition to self-rule in the sub-continent. In a gloomy speech in the Commons he proposed that the affairs of India should be determined by the United Nations, as the government had lately decided should be done in the case of Palestine. He concluded on a sombre note:

It is with deep grief that I watch the clattering down of the British Empire, with all its glories, and all the services it has rendered to mankind. I am sure that in the hour of our victory now not so long ago, we had the power to make a solution of our difficulties which would have been honourable and lasting. Many have defended Britain against her foes. Nor can defend her against herself.[24]

All the same, it was not without a certain flair that the last days of Empire were played out. Attlee had already appointed Mountbatten, the King's cousin and one of the most successful war commanders, to be the last Viceroy in succession to Wavell. Mountbatten had not only great prestige but also a true sense of urgency. In a few weeks he decided to bring forward the date of the transfer of power to August 1947, and he also acknowledged that partition was the only answer to the communal problem. Ismay had joined him as Chief of Staff, and this was a valuable link with Churchill. When he had decided on his plans, he and Ismay both returned to London to secure their acceptance, and Churchill, after consulting the Shadow Cabinet, agreed that 'it would not be right that such legislation should be deemed contentious'.[25] Thus on August 15th 1947 there emerged two self-governing dominions of the Commonwealth, India and Pakistan, out of what had been the Indian Empire.

To make things easier in the period of transition to full independence the Indian leaders – but not the Pakistanis – invited Mountbatten to continue as their Governor-General. Mountbatten had nothing to gain by accepting this task, but he agreed to do so, provided that the King and also both political parties in Britain gave him their blessing. This time Ismay was the sole intermediary with Churchill: in July he made his way to Chartwell and secured his old chief's approval.[26] Despite this, Churchill's prediction that British withdrawal would be accompanied by sectional conflict and heavy loss of life certainly came true. One other prediction, however, was falsified: he argued in the summer of 1947 that 'In handing over the government of India to the so-called political classes you are handing over to men of straw of whom in a few years, no trace will remain.'[27] A leading Commonwealth historian, Professor Nicholas Mansergh, described these words ten years later as 'one of the more memorable miscalculations of great men';[28] after twenty-five years there is no reason to modify this judgment.

It should be added, furthermore, that Churchill himself accepted the inevitable with good grace in the succeeding years. When in 1949 Nehru attended a Commonwealth Prime Ministers' Conference in London and acknowledged the position of the King as 'Head of the Commonwealth' – a new title – Churchill invited him to dinner, and the two men began a friendly relationship. At this time Churchill declared in the Commons that 'The final significance and value of the Monarchy seems to be enhanced by the way in which the King is acknowledged by the Republic of India and by the Commonwealth monarchies alike.'[29]

But if Churchill over the years had misjudged the Indian situation his attitude in this period to the Palestine problem was altogether more shrewd. He had long been personally committed to the Zionist cause, but this was by no means true of all his colleagues on the Conservative front bench. During the war, the War Cabinet had come round to the view that the best solution was the partition of Palestine, but no action to effect this was taken while the war continued.[30] The Labour government was persuaded by Ernest Bevin, its Foreign Secretary, that a separate Jewish state would not be viable; and in the early post-war years the evacuation of Egyptian territory actually led to a build-up of British forces in Palestine.

All the same, Britain's occupation derived only from a mandate of the old League of Nations, and there was also strong pressure from the United States for the resumption of Jewish immigration. In February 1947 the Cabinet agreed to refer the problem to the United Nations, and in September it announced a decision to withdraw from the mandate, a course which Churchill had suggested in August 1946.[31] In November 1947 the United Nations voted in favour of partition, and early in 1948 British troops withdrew from the country with almost unseemly speed, leaving its inhabitants to fight out their own battles. Somewhat to the surprise of British observers, the Jews succeeded in winning the civil war and establishing the new state of Israel. Churchill said late in 1948:

It seems to me very likely, although I cannot, of course, prove it, that the Foreign Secretary misjudged the relative power of the two sides, and it certainly looked on paper as if the Syrians, Egyptians and Arabs, invading from so many quarters, would win. That was not my view.[32]

He called for the early recognition of the new state, which had already been recognised by many of the other powers, including Russia and the USA.

On these questions Churchill was not always in line with the views of his colleagues, and there was likely to be occasional friction with them. But in any case, and more seriously, party leaders

572

are usually in some danger from internal revolt just after a lost election. The idea spreads that if the party has been defeated there must be something wrong with its leadership. Thus even in the supposedly deferential Conservative Party Balfour was subjected in 1911 to the successful 'Balfour Must Go' campaign, and Baldwin in 1930 was beset by the hostility of the press lords, which he withstood only with difficulty.

Churchill in 1945 had suffered a very severe defeat; and he was already over seventy years of age. These factors of themselves might have been expected to lead to an immediate attempt to replace him as leader. But no such attempt was made and, as we have seen, on his arrival in the new Parliament he was greeted with a demonstration of loyalty from his supporters. Most of the parliamentary party, at least, seemed to recognise that it was the party, and not its leader, that had failed to impress the electorate. The main disagreement was between those who thought that it was the party organisation that ought to be improved, and those who urged a new statement of policy which would prove more attractive to the electors.

There was in fact no reason why both tasks should not be undertaken simultaneously. In late 1945 Churchill appointed R. A. Butler, the former Minister of Education of the wartime years, to be chairman of the party's Research Department, with authority to develop new lines of policy. Butler enjoyed his task and in 1947 produced an Industrial Charter, for which he received Churchill's approval – typically more tacit than explicit.[33] And in the summer of 1946 Churchill persuaded Lord Woolton – a recent convert to the party, who had done well as Minister of Food during the war – to become Chairman of the party, thereby taking charge of the organisation. Woolton's first campaign for new recruits in 1946–47 was only moderately successful, however: it brought in some 226,000 new members, not a large figure compared to the big battalions of the Labour Party, which were being enlarged by the effects of the repeal of the Trade Disputes Act.[34]

Furthermore, the Conservatives failed to make any gains in by-elections, and the left-wing tendency of the country appeared to persist throughout 1946. Early in 1947 there were murmurings in the parliamentary party about Churchill's absences from the Commons and his absorption in the writing of his memoirs. James Stuart, the then Chief Whip, has recounted how he met with some seven others at Harry Crookshank's home in Pont Street,

Belgravia. The group agreed that Churchill ought to retire, and Stuart was instructed to convey the news to the leader. When Stuart gave his message, he appears to have found that Churchill had had other intimations to the same effect, for he 'reacted violently, banging the floor with his stick and implying that I too had joined those who were plotting to displace him'.[35]

But the prospects of the party began to improve a little after this. The Labour government ran into tribulations of its own, with an acute fuel shortage early in 1947, and by the summer the Conservatives had pulled ahead of Labour in the Gallup Poll.[36] Generally speaking, middle-class people were getting very tired of rationing and controls; and when Woolton launched a new recruiting campaign to secure a million new members of the Conservative Party he achieved his goal within a year.[37] All the same, the loyalty of working-class voters to the Labour Party remained obstinately firm; and it was not until November 1948, when a by-election at Edmonton, although returning a Labour candidate, showed a substantial swing to the Conservatives, that Churchill felt able to hail the result as 'another El Alamein'.[38]

Yet in spite of Churchill's personally prepared letters to each Conservative by-election candidate the Labour government continued to retain all the seats it was defending; and in February 1949, after Churchill's enthusiasm about Edmonton, the party was very disappointed not to win Hammersmith South, which would certainly have fallen on a swing comparable to that at Edmonton. The result was followed by a good deal of criticism of the Conservative leadership in the press, and a demand to Churchill from the 1922 Committee of Conservative backbenchers for a new policy statement. This was not the sort of behaviour that Churchill could accept from his parliamentary supporters; and at a meeting with them on March 3rd it was reported that he had told them firmly that he would 'not try to outbid the Labour Party by offering a programme of more extensive reform'.[39]

This attitude of Churchill's was not a novel one. Throughout the war he had resisted the idea of committing himself to detailed reforms, especially any which were likely to prove expensive, such as those of the Beveridge Report; and since then he had lectured Butler on the same subject: 'When an Opposition spells out its policy in detail ... having failed to win the sweets of office, it fails equally to enjoy the benefits of being out of office.'[40]

Consequently the 'Charters' that Butler's Research Department produced were rather vague in character. The Industrial Charter, however, accepted the nationalisation of the Bank of England and the coal industry, but demanded freedom for road haulage and for the Liverpool Cotton Exchange, which had not been re-opened. It also expressed opposition to the nationalisation of iron and steel, which was on the Labour government's programme for future legislation. Moderate and vague as they were, the proposals of the Industrial Charter aroused the wrath of the Beaverbrook Press and also of right-wing members of the Conservative Party such as Sir Waldron Smithers.[41]

But by the spring of 1949 the time had come to be prepared for a new general election. Butler drafted a more detailed statement of policy called *The Right Road for Britain*, in which Churchill took real interest, for as Butler says it was 'proof-corrected by the Churchillian pen and dignified by a Churchillian foreword'.[42] Churchill himself launched the statement upon the public in a speech at Wolverhampton in late July. By this time the Labour Cabinet was debating when would be the best time to hold the election, but Attlee announced in the early autumn that it would not take place in that calendar year.

Whether or not Churchill's defeat in 1945 was a 'blessing in disguise', as Clementine had suggested, it certainly gave him an opportunity to recover his health and energy. Towards the end of the war he had had to be lifted up out of the Annexe, where Cabinet meetings were often held, 'in a chair by the Marines'.[43] But in June 1946 he boasted to Lord Moran about his energy, and related how he had 'dined out and sat talking till two o'clock' and had then on his way home noticed a light in the Commons, indicating a session still in progress; so he had gone in, 'listened for half an hour, and then I made a very vigorous speech'. It was partly the desire to get revenge on the Labour government that encouraged him. He told Moran: 'A short time ago I was ready to retire and die gracefully. Now I'm going to stay and have them out.'[44]

Although he was now in his seventies, he was really quite fit for his age – contrary to the impression given by Moran in his memoirs, with their question-begging title *The Struggle for Survival*. In June 1947 he had to have an operation for hernia, and took two volumes of Macaulay's *Essays* to the nursing home with him.[45] Five weeks later he reappeared at the House of Commons, looking, according to the *Times* correspondent, 'extremely well'.[46] On a holiday at Marrakesh the following Christmas, however, he caught a heavy cold and, fearing complications, he asked Moran to fly out to join him. As soon as Moran had assured him that there were no complications, he recovered rapidly.[47]

Thereafter he was in fairly good health and working hard on his memoirs until August 1949, when he was staying at Beaverbrook's villa on the French Riviera. Then, while he was playing gin rummy in the small hours with another of Beaverbrook's guests, the Canadian newspaper proprietor Brigadier Michael Wardell, he suffered a loss of sensation in his right arm and leg.[48] But after a day, and after a hasty visit once more from Lord Moran, he began to feel better and observed: 'The dagger struck, but this time it was not plunged in to the hilt.'[49] At any rate he was able to go on to Strasbourg and behave there with apparently undiminished energy.

By the end of 1949 Churchill seemed to have completely recovered from this attack. His old friend Archibald Sinclair, now Viscount Thurso, visited Chartwell shortly before Christmas and found him 'recovering from a very bad cold but ... in grand form – as lively and incessant in his conversation as he was in Cabinet in old days, eating, drinking and smoking as voraciously as ever'.[50]

Meanwhile he had been engaged in writing the volumes of his *Second World War*, the advances from which – from the Houghton Mifflin Company in the United States and from Cassell in Britain – he paid into a trust fund for his children and grandchildren.[51] To obtain some immediate cash for himself, he arranged in 1945 for *Life* Magazine to reproduce a number of his paintings, for a fee of $25,000. He had been advised that to write articles in the ordinary way would hardly be worth his while, as the money thus accruing would be subject to income tax.[52] Later that year, however, he agreed to the early publication of his 'Secret Session Speeches', also in *Life* Magazine, before they appeared in book form. This led to some criticism in the British press – which was also reported in *Life*. Further, because he thought it was politically important, he wrote an article for *Life* in April 1947 expressing his approval of Truman's action over Greece and Turkey.[53]

The first volume of the *Second World War* dealt with its origins, with his own attempts to hasten British rearmament, and with his months at the Admiralty. It concluded with an account of the political crisis of May 1940. The theme of the volume was described as 'How the English-speaking Peoples, through their unwisdom, carelessness and good nature allowed the wicked to re-arm'. The final proofs were taken to America by air in February 1948, and the volume was serialised in the *New York Times* and in the London *Daily Telegraph* before being published in June, in an edition of 75,000 copies, by Houghton Mifflin of Boston. The British edition was much larger but it was held up by paper shortages and constant corrections from the author: it appeared in 221,000 copies in October.[54]

The corrections were partly due to the fact that Churchill's memory had sometimes betrayed him. He did not keep a diary, and it was easy for him to mix up dates and events. Although he was again aided by F. W. Deakin, who after distinguished war service had returned to an Oxford college, and although he had two senior professional officers – Lieutenant-General Sir Henry Pownall and Commodore G. R. G. Allen – to advise him, besides the assistance of Eddie Marsh on the proofs, mistakes still crept in. Furthermore, the whole interpretation of the pre-war period in terms of an 'unnecessary war' precipitated only by errors on the part of Chamberlain and his colleagues in confronting the 'wickedness' of Hitler, has since been criticised and considerably shaken.[55]

Thereafter, the successive volumes of the work appeared at roughly annual intervals. The first British edition of Volume II – *The Finest Hour*, covering the summer and autumn of 1940 – amounted to 276,000 copies. The same number, or even rather more, was printed of each volumes III, IV and V, but the first impression of volume VI, which was held up somewhat by Churchill's return to power and did not appear until 1954, was only 200,000. Even so, this was a formidable total.

Each volume, except volume I of the first American edition, was carefully illustrated with folding maps as well as diagrams, and great attention was paid to military operations on land or at sea. Large numbers of Churchill's personal directives were included in the appendixes as well as in the text, but the story was not quite complete as the replies to the directives – to which Churchill in any case did not hold the copyright – were not included. Early in 1949 Ismay, who was giving a hand with the work, told Harold Nicolson that he thought 'Winston is in too much of a hurry over his book'. He attributed this to a desire on Churchill's part to complete the work before the general election, which he thought would result in his return to the Premiership.[56]

It was only in these years that Churchill finally gave up the physical recreations which he had enjoyed since his youth. Late in 1948 he went out on horseback with the Old Surrey and Burstow Hunt, but this was probably his last such venture.[57] He also gradually gave up swimming in his mid-seventies, partly as a result of catching cold at Marrakesh in late 1947, partly after his stroke in the summer of 1949.[58] But he went on painting, and was delighted to have two pictures, which he had submitted anonymously, accepted for the Royal Academy in 1947; three more were accepted under his own name in 1948.[59] He was then elected an Honorary Academician Extraordinary, and, as he put it, gave Sir Alfred Munnings, the President, 'several sharp prods' to persuade him to revive the annual Royal Academy dinner. This was done for the first time in April 1949.[60] Munnings was a member of the Other Club, and this gave Churchill an opportunity for taking him to task.

A recreation which Churchill now took up for the first time was racing. His son-in-law, Christopher Soames, aroused his interest by bringing a mare to Chartwell Farm. It was July 1949, when he was getting on for seventy-five, that he registered his racing colours. The colours were as close as he could get to his father's, namely, pink, with chocolate sleeves and cap.[61] He acquired a trainer, Walter Nightingall, who came from a well-known Epsom racing family; and also a French grey colt called Colonist II, which won thirteen races for him of the value of £11,938 before going to stud at Newmarket.[62] Churchill usually went to see races in which Colonist II was entered, and he was delighted when it won – as were the great bulk of the spectators.[63]

Meanwhile, family life continued both at Chartwell and at the new home at Hyde Park Gate – where a house next door, No. 27, was purchased for the use of secretaries.[64] The children of course were now mostly away from home. Sarah was demobilised from the WAAF late in 1945, and being separated from her husband, Vic Oliver, she might have found a place in the household; but she preferred to resume her career on the stage, and went on tour in 1946 in the play *Gaslight* (by Patrick Hamilton). She made her American début in 1949, and in Georgia in October of that year she suddenly married Antony Beauchamp, an English society photographer who had served in Burma with the 14th Army.[65] Diana, of course, was married to Duncan Sandys, and bringing up a family; and only Mary, the youngest and her father's favourite, remained unmarried at the end of the war, by which time she was almost twenty-three. But in mid-February she became the bride of Captain Christopher Soames of the Coldstream Guards, who was twenty-six and whom she had met at the Paris Embassy, where he was serving as a military attaché. The wedding took place at St Margaret's, Westminster, where her parents had married.[66] Less than two weeks later Churchill's younger brother Jack died, after having been poorly for some years. He was buried, as his parents had been, in the little churchyard at Bladon, on the edge of the Blenheim Estate near Woodstock in Oxfordshire.[67] Finally, Randolph, who had been defeated in the 1945 election, and had re-entered journalism while awaiting a further opportunity to enter Parliament, had separated from his first wife, Pamela, and in late 1948 he married again. This time his bride was June Osborne, the daughter of Colonel Rex Osborne of Malmesbury, Wiltshire. The wedding took place at Caxton Hall, Westminster, and his son Winston, who was now eight, was present.[68] Late in 1949 a daughter, Arabella, was born of this marriage.[69]

Racing was one sign of Churchill's affluence in these years – although to be sure he did not lose on his investment, as the prize money was free of tax and so were his winnings on bets; but he had also become much wealthier as the result of the action of some friends, who bought Chartwell for the National Trust, it being understood that Churchill would remain there in exclusive possession until he died.[70] Churchill also bought up some of the neighbouring farms, and established Mary and his son-in-law Christopher Soames on the estate, the latter as farm manager. A herd of dairy shorthorn cattle was acquired and, almost inevitably, Churchill was elected a member of the Shorthorn Society of Great Britain and Ireland.[71]

With all his varied activities, Churchill had little interest in farming as such. He was probably more interested in the fact that farmers never seemed to have to suffer the rigours of rationing, which continued for several years after the war. But he loved animals, and had many at Chartwell more or less as pets – black swans from Western Australia, one of which, to his mortification, was killed by a fox; golden carp; and, the closest of all because it could live indoors, a small brown poodle known as Rufus or Rufie. It distressed him very much when Rufie was run over and killed by a bus at Brighton in October 1947 when his master was visiting a Conservative Party Conference there. Walter Graebner of *Life* Magazine, who had become a family friend, bought him an almost identical substitute, known as Rufie II, and he and Churchill lived on together in amity for several years.[72]

In some ways it was a royal existence that Churchill lived in these years of opposition. Although Chartwell is not a great mansion, it contained every possible convenience or gadget for the benefit of its master – who, when he went abroad, was literally treated royally. But his main object in these years was to recapture power for himself and his party in a general election, and thus to reverse the verdict of 1945. By the end of 1949 it was obvious that a new test of the opinions of the electorate could not long be postponed.

28. *On the Edge of Power, 1950-1*

CHURCHILL was on holiday with Clementine in Madeira when Attlee on January 11th announced a dissolution of Parliament for February 3rd and polling for February 23rd. He returned next day by flying-boat, to play his part in the preparations. On January 19th he wrote the preface to the Conservative manifesto, entitled *This is the Road*. It was closely based on the policy statement of six months earlier, *The Right Road for Britain*. The whole twenty-page document bore many signs of his style and phraseology. His other evident contribution to his party's cause before the dissolution was to make a formal agreement with Lord Rosebery, the son of the late Liberal Premier, and himself the President of the National Liberal Council, that Conservatives and National Liberal candidates should co-operate closely, and that in appropriate cases candidates might call themselves 'Liberal-Conservatives' or 'Liberal-Unionists'. This drew forth a personal protest to Churchill from Clement Davies, the Leader of the (independent) Liberal Party; but, as Churchill's reply indicated, Davies was not on good debating ground. In a letter for publication, Churchill pointed out:

As you were yourself for eleven years a National Liberal, and in that capacity supported the Governments of Mr Baldwin and Mr Neville Chamberlain, I should not presume to correct your knowledge of the moral, intellectual and legal aspects of adding a prefix or suffix to the honoured name of Liberal. It has certainly been done before by honourable and distinguished men.

A few days later Churchill revealed that he had offered to assign one of the twenty-minute broadcasts allotted to the Conservative Party to Clement Davies's colleague and his own old friend, Lady Violet Bonham Carter: Lady Violet was dissuaded from accepting by her party leader, but she confirmed that the offer had been made.[1]

On the whole the election was a quiet one by earlier standards. Attlee undertook a thousand-mile tour of the country – again driven by his wife, in a pre-war car; but Churchill, perhaps mindful of his previous experience, decided to make only a few forays into the provinces. All the same, it was he who made the running, so far as issues were concerned. On February 7th he spoke in support of his son Randolph, who was fighting, against Michael Foot, the difficult marginal constituency of Devonport; and here he spoke hopefully of increasing the petrol ration. The Labour response to this was rather mixed, partly because the possibility now really existed.[2] On February 14th Churchill spoke at Edinburgh, and demanded a renewed 'parley at the summit' – a proposal that produced hostile reactions in the United States as well as elsewhere abroad. Next day Ernest Bevin alluded to the topic indirectly by saying that the problem could not be solved by any 'stunt proposals', a phrase which Churchill resented.[3]

Attlee sought to carry the campaign into the enemy's camp by criticising the Leader of the Opposition himself, and on the 15th he said at Nottingham: 'Mr Churchill is a great master of words, but it is a terrible thing when a master of words becomes a slave of words, because there is nothing behind those words, they are just words of abuse.'[4] Nevertheless, people were willing to listen to Churchill in larger number than to the Prime Minister himself. According to the BBC Audience Research Service, of all the political broadcasters he secured the largest proportion of listeners – 51%, for his final broadcast on February 17th. Attlee himself had the next best proportion – 44% – and the only other speaker to gain more than 40% was Dr Charles Hill, the 'radio doctor', who after years of broadcasting on health questions had joined the Churchillian ranks.[5]

No other major issues appeared in the course of the campaign. On the Monday before polling day (February 20th) Churchill spoke at Manchester and Oldham, and reiterated his call for 'an enduring settlement with Soviet Russia'.[6] In the last few days before polling the supposedly uncommitted newspapers made up their minds how to advise people to vote – the *Daily Mirror* for the Labour Party, the *Manchester Guardian* for the Liberals, who, with 475 candidates, were attempting a comeback, and *The Times*, rather vaguely, for the Conservatives.

Churchill was freer in 1950 than in 1945 to spend time in his own constituency, and his interest in doing so was no doubt increased by the fact that this time the main parties were opposing him. He spent several days touring the constituency, and Clementine kept him company. On polling day he went to vote at St Stephen's Church Hall in South Kensington, for that was where he was now registered; but next day, although the tally of victories for each of the major parties kept in close company, indicating that he might need to respond to the call to form a government, he travelled to Woodford for the closing stages of his own count, which was taking place at St Barnabas School, Woodford Green. After his arrival at about 1.45 p.m. he still had some time to wait, and he spent it listening to the progress of the election elsewhere on the radio in the headmaster's study. When he was called out to find that he had been re-elected for Woodford by a large majority, he followed the traditional routine of proposing a vote of thanks to the returning officer, and complimenting him on the 'fairness, precision and decorum' of the occasion.[7] His opponents, of whom there were three, for a Communist had also entered the lists, formed rather a contrasting group. None could have expected to win. They were all in their thirties, and all ex-servicemen – the Labour candidate a printer who had been at Oxford and had become President of the Union; the Liberal a chartered accountant; and the Communist the full-time Secretary of the Young Communist League. The figures were:

W. S. Churchill (Conservative)	37,239	Elected
S. Hill (Labour)	18,740	
H. Davies (Liberal)	5664	
W. Brooks (Communist)	827	

The figures were not strictly comparable with any previous ones, owing to boundary changes and the fact that in 1945 neither of the major parties had opposed the then Prime Minister. The outcome of the election nationally was still, on the afternoon of the day after polling, very much in doubt, and it was only at 6.20 p.m. that it became apparent that Labour would remain the biggest single party in the new House, and only at about 8.30 p.m. that it acquired an overall majority.[8]

Nationally the total poll had been very large – it was almost 84% – and it was clear that the electors had regarded it as very largely a contest between two parties. Of those who voted, 46.1% voted Labour, 43.5% voted Conservative or National Liberal, and 9.1% voted Liberal. Although the middle class had apparently largely swung back to the Conservatives, the working class had been very loyal to the Labour Party. Evidently the enthusiasm for things Russian had quite disappeared, and the housewife did not like rationing; but there was a residual appeal about the Labour Party which the Conservatives had difficulty in overcoming. As Harold Macmillan put it in a frank and confidential letter to Churchill a few months later: 'The Socialists have got, and look like keeping, the immense advantages of full employment and high pay-packets. So far, we have only *cost of living* and the *housing muddle* against these.'[9]

Even so, a lead of 3% should have given the Labour Party a substantial working majority. But this was not so in the constituencies as they had been revised under the Labour government's own Representation of the People Act, 1948, for while old 'pocket boroughs' of the Labour Party in the centre of London and other cities had been eliminated, there were still many overwhelmingly working-class divisions – especially in the mining areas – where Labour majorities piled up excessively and were in a sense 'wasted'.[10] Of course the Liberals, as the third party in a two-party race, suffered much more severely. 315 Labour MPs were elected, 298 Conservatives and 9 Liberals. There were two Irish Nationalists, who did not take their seats, and the only other elected person technically outside the ranks of the major parties was the Speaker, Colonel Douglas Clifton Brown, who had been a Conservative. The university seats, which often elected independents, had been eliminated by the Act of 1948. The disappearance of independent members from the House was thus a feature of the election. Among the new recruits to the Conservative strength were Churchill's two sons-in-law, Duncan Sandys, elected for Streatham, and Christopher Soames, who came in for the Bedford division of Bedfordshire; but Randolph Churchill was again defeated.

The outcome of the election was thus a disappointment for all the parties. The Conservatives had recovered considerably, but not enough to take power. As for Labour, a continued government with a majority of only eight – at best – could hardly expect to pass any contentious legislation. The Labour leaders also gave the impression of being very tired. In October 1950 Sir Stafford Cripps, the Chancellor of the Exchequer, was obliged to resign owing to a spinal complaint, from which he died in April 1952. He was replaced by Hugh Gaitskell, formerly his principal lieutenant at the Treasury, and a man of great administrative ability, but relatively speaking a newcomer to Parliament, as he had first been elected in 1945. In March 1951 Ernest Bevin was obliged to leave the Foreign Office owing to heart trouble; he died in April. Attlee had great difficulty in deciding who should succeed him. Eventually he chose Herbert Morrison, who had made a good recovery from a thrombosis in 1947, but who had great difficulty in coping with a subject of which he knew virtually nothing. Worst of all, as it turned out, Attlee himself was in hospital for a time at Easter 1951 with a duodenal ulcer. Gaitskell in his Budget that year had to find extra sums for rearmament; he imposed a charge on the supply of false teeth and spectacles under the National Health Service. Factions developed within the Cabinet; and a few days later Aneurin Bevan and Harold Wilson both resigned from its ranks.

Even so, these events were probably not as important in ending Labour's term of office as was one of Macmillan's two major points – an increase in the cost of living. In June 1950 the Korean War began. President Truman felt he had no alternative but to order American troops to assist the South Koreans, who were clearly in difficulty; and he also appealed to the United Nations for aid. At a time when the Americans had lately come to the aid of the British in Europe, there could be no contention within the leaderships of the British political parties about the need to respond to the call, and so a brigade of troops was sent from Hong Kong to operate under American command. Churchill thought that if he himself had been in power at the time he would have been hotly criticised by the Labour Party. At the fortnightly lunch for the Shadow Cabinet, which he gave at the

Savoy Hotel, he remarked, 'the old man is very good to me. I could not have managed this situation had I been in Attlee's place. I should have been called a war-monger.' His colleague David Maxwell Fyfe asked him, 'What old man?' and Churchill replied, 'God, Sir Donald'.[11] Apparently Churchill always mixed up Sir David Maxwell Fyfe and Sir Donald Somervell, also a lawyer in politics though of a slightly earlier generation.

For some months it seemed that, if anything, the British economy was benefiting from the war, because of American stockpiling of raw materials from the sterling area; and at the end of 1950 the government was able to announce that Britain would henceforth be independent of Marshall Aid. But just because of the stockpiling prices rose more rapidly in Britain in 1951 than in previous years. A marked Conservative lead appeared in the Gallup Poll at this time; and whereas the by-elections in 1950 had shown a medium swing against Labour of only 1.7% in the first nine months of 1951 the corresponding figure was 5.7%.[12]

The Conservatives were so close to power after the 1950 election that it seemed almost certain that there would have been another election that year; indeed, probably only the outbreak of the Korean War prevented it. In the spring of 1950 Churchill was strongly pressed by Macmillan to make a positive response to Robert Schuman's plan for the integration of European iron and steel resources, which had been received with little favour by the Labour government;[13] and in a Commons debate late in June he said:

> It was not only our own cause but a world cause for which the Union Jack was kept flying in 1940.... The Conservative and Liberal Parties declare that national sovereignty is not inviolable, and that it may be resolutely diminished for the sake of all the men in all the lands finding their way home together.[14]

But in the end the Labour government refused to participate, and the European Coal and Steel Community – in many ways the predecessor of the Common Market – was set up without British membership in April 1951.

In August 1950 Churchill had again attended a meeting of the Consultative Assembly of Europe at Strasbourg. On this occasion, although the Schuman Plan formed one topic of discussion, the beginning of the Korean War had raised the question of defence in an urgent form, and there was discussion about a European

586

Army. A German delegation was present for the first time, and its members were entertained by Churchill at the villa which the City of Strasbourg had placed at his disposal. He made a speech at one of the formal sessions advocating 'a real defensive front in Europe', to which both Britain and the United States might contribute contingents. He listed all the other nations which might contribute, but accidentally missed out the Germans, and then had to put out a statement to correct his speech.[15] A resolution in accordance with his views was passed by 89 votes to 5, with 27 abstentions. This did not solve the problems connected with the proposal. The French were still unwilling to see any German rearmament on any large scale, and M. Pleven, the French Prime Minister, produced a proposal for a European Army in which the national contingents would be incorporated in the smallest possible units. The Americans, who were anxious to secure German rearmament, accepted this plan as the basis of European defence, without committing their own troops to it directly. It was also accepted by the Council of the North Atlantic Treaty Organisation in December 1950, and early in 1951 General Eisenhower, the successful wartime leader, was once more appointed Supreme Commander, with headquarters in Paris.

Churchill's health in this period of waiting for a new election was on the whole remarkably good, and he was given to making demonstrations of personal fitness. On October 12th 1950, for instance, he flew back to Northolt from a visit to Denmark and then immediately took another plane up to Newmarket, where he saw Colonist II win the Lowther Stakes. On the same day he flew on to Blackpool for the conclusion of the Conservative Party Conference there.[16] It was at this conference that Woolton accepted the demand from the floor of 300,000 houses a year – a considerably larger figure than the Labour government had achieved; and Churchill himself in his closing speech said that he had been 'impressed and encouraged by what I was told of the gust of passion which swept through our body yesterday about the shameful failure of the Socialists' housing policy'. Of the target of 300,000, he said, 'I accept it as our first priority in time of peace.'[17]

Lord Moran's published diary is rather bare of entries in this period, except for one which indicates that Churchill was increasingly troubled by deafness. Moran took him to see Sir Victor

Negus, an ear specialist, and Negus told him that he could no longer expect to hear 'the twittering of birds and children's piping voices'.[18] As throughout his life he had been irritated by other people whistling the disability was not without its compensations. He still took a lively interest in the annual occasion at Harrow when the boys sang their school songs: in 1950 he went there for the eleventh year in succession.[19]

At the turn of the year 1950–1 he was on holiday at his favourite resort, Marrakesh, for several weeks. Early in March his doctor, presumably Lord Moran, put out a notice to say that he was suffering from a 'localised staphylococcal infection', and was cancelling his engagements for a few days.[20] On the following day, however, *The Times* was permitted to say simply that he was 'suffering with boils'.[21] It was shortly after this that some of the Conservative backbenchers, encouraged by the swing of national opinion towards their party, discovered that by putting down Prayers against Ministerial Orders they could keep the House sitting to all hours of the night. A difficult fortnight ensued until the Labour Whips discovered in their turn that the answer to this problem was simply to move the adjournment of the House. Needless to say, Churchill enjoyed the 'parliamentary warfare', and in mid-1951 Macmillan thought he was deliberately making 'a demonstration of energy and vitality':

> He has voted in every division; made a series of brilliant little speeches; shown all his qualities of humour and sarcasm; and crowned all by a remarkable breakfast (at 7.30 p.m.) of eggs, bacon, sausages and coffee, followed by a large whisky and soda and a huge cigar.[22]

It was, however, a matter of distress to him that so many of his oldest friends were not able to endure. In September 1950 General Smuts died, and Churchill learnt of this event, as he said next day, 'with deep sorrow'.[23] Smuts was one of the few of his colleagues with whom he could still talk on terms of equality. Almost in the same category was Ernest Bevin, who as we have seen died of a heart attack in April 1951. In a brief statement about one who was after all a political opponent, Churchill said: 'I am deeply grieved at the death of my wartime comrade. A valiant spirit has passed from us. He has his place in history.'[24]

In mid-August Churchill went off to Annecy in the French Alps to join his wife, who was on holiday there after having had an operation in May. He intended to do some painting and to com-

588

plete his *Second World War* volumes, and he and Clementine spent some of their time in early September in Venice, where Churchill completed several more canvases. It would have been possible to publish volume VI of the *Second World War* – entitled *Triumph and Tragedy* – in 1952, but Churchill did not want to upset the American Presidential election of November 1952 by revealing the disagreements between himself on the one hand and Presidents Roosevelt and Truman on the other about policy in Europe in 1945. The dates of preparation of the volumes should not be judged, as they are in Lord Moran's book, from the dates of their prefaces.[25]

In late September 1951 the King was seriously ill, and had to undergo an operation for the removal of a cancer of the lung. Before this happened, however, he had already urged Attlee to hold an election in the autumn so as to ensure a reasonable degree of political stability before he (the King) undertook his proposed tour of Australia and New Zealand in January 1952.[26] In the event, the tour was never to take place; and the King was recuperating from his operation while the second election within twenty months was taking place. Parliament was dissolved on October 4th, and polling was fixed for October 25th.

The general election of 1951 differed from that of 1950 above all in the reduction of the number of Liberal, Communist and independent candidates. The Liberals numbered only 109, instead of 475; the Communists only ten instead of a hundred. There were a few seats which the Conservatives did not contest, but left to the Liberals, sometimes – as at Bolton and Huddersfield – on the understanding that the Liberals would allow the Conservatives a free run in a neighbouring contest. The Conservatives were now committed to two proposals which had not formed part of their programme in 1950 – an excess-profits tax for armament firms, and an undertaking to build 300,000 houses a year. Churchill himself wrote the Conservative manifesto, which was full of echoes of his earlier career: 'Many years ago I used the phrase, "Bring the rearguard in." ... Now we have the new Socialist doctrine ... "Keep the vanguard back." '[27]

As for the rest, the matter discussed on the party platforms was not European unity, which aroused little interest, but whether or not Churchill was a 'warmonger' because he advocated a different and stronger line in the current controversy with Persia over that country's nationalisation of the refinery and other installations of the Anglo-Iranian Oil Company at Abadan. Herbert Morrison, the new Foreign Secretary, who had himself wanted to use force but had been held back only by his Cabinet colleagues in view of the absence of American support,[28] realised the potentialities of this situation for electioneering purposes and declared in a speech on October 3rd:

> It is a great pity that Mr Churchill is still living in the kind of atmosphere that existed before the First World War.... Even in respect of Persia there is an implication of force in the mind of Mr Churchill, who thinks we have been defeated.... Would Mr Churchill say whether in his judgment the Government should have gone to war with Persia or not?[29]

Once again, therefore, the election focused around the figure of the Opposition Leader. He did not speak often outside his own constituency, but wherever he spoke his words had a marked impact. At Loughton, near Woodford, on October 6th, he replied to Morrison:

> Mr Morrison has asked me whether in my judgment we should have gone to war with Persia or not. He had no right to ask this question. The responsibility is entirely that of the Socialist Government who alone had the power and should have had the knowledge. He is only asking the question in order to gain acceptance for the falsehood he and his associates – I can hardly call them his friends – are spreading about that the Conservative Party want another world war. I am quite sure that if a strong Conservative Government had been in power the Persian crisis would never have arisen in the way it did. It is only when the British Government is known to be weak and hesitant that these outrages are inflicted upon us and upon our rights and interests. I cannot believe that there would have been any need for a war with Persia.[30]

He also replied to an innuendo in the *Daily Mirror*, which was asking 'Whose finger do you want on the trigger, Attlee's or Churchill's?'. He said:

> I am sure we do not want any fingers upon any trigger. Least of all do we want a fumbling finger. I do not believe that a Third World War is inevitable. I even think that the danger of it is less than it was before the immense rearmament of the United States. But I must now tell you that in any case it will not be a British finger that will pull the trigger of a Third World War. It may be a Russian

finger, or an American finger, or a United Nations Organisation finger, but it cannot be a British finger.[31]

A few days later, also in his constituency, he counter-attacked by pointing out that as a result of the voting at the Labour Party Conference, which had lately concluded at Scarborough, Aneurin Bevan and his supporters, although opposed to the main leadership, had emerged at the top of the poll for membership of the National Executive Committee. He suggested that this was a 'dangerous development' as it would endanger relations with the United States, and added: 'I warn you solemnly that the mass growth of the Bevan movement inside the Socialist Party ... may make the return of a Socialist Government a real blow to our hopes of escaping a Third World War.'[32] Attlee's campaign was dignified and rarely personal, but three days later, on October 12th, Churchill attacked him for remarking defensively, 'How can we clear up in six years the mess of centuries?' This drew forth all Churchill's powers of sarcasm, as he rolled off the list of British achievements in the past, all dwarfed by the 'giant and Titan' Attlee.[33]

On October 15th Churchill went north to Huddersfield to speak for Lady Violet Bonham Carter – a Liberal standing for the Colne Valley with Conservative support. Just before setting out by train he found he had a temperature, and consequently persuaded Moran to accompany him: thereupon the temperature disappeared, and all went well.[34] He said: 'In Mr Asquith's famous daughter you have one of the very best speakers, male or female, in this island at this time.... The representation of Colne Valley will certainly not lack distinction if you return Lady Violet Bonham Carter.'[35] Moran was more impressed by Lady Violet as a speaker than by Churchill himself; the latter sat on the platform during the later speeches with 'the expressionless mask of a deaf man'.[36] Next day he went on to Newcastle, to speak on behalf of Major Gwilym Lloyd George, who was, to be sure, the candidate of an official Conservative Association, but nevertheless was challenged by an Independent Conservative opponent. It must have given Churchill some satisfaction to appear on the platforms of both an Asquith and a Lloyd George; and he reckoned, no doubt correctly, that some former Liberals would be influenced in their voting by this.

The 1951 election was the first television election; but the proportion of viewers was still small, and the principal Conservative broadcast by this medium was probably seen by fewer than 10% of households.[37] Anthony Eden took part, and produced a chart to show how rapidly the cost of living had risen under Labour rule. The design of the chart was strongly and effectively criticised in a later Labour broadcast by Christopher Mayhew, who was already an experienced television performer.[38] Churchill, whose oratory was more conventional, spent the Tuesday evening before polling day (which as usual was on a Thursday) speaking at Plymouth on behalf of his son Randolph, who was again facing Michael Foot at Devonport. He made his final call for 'a strong and stable Government resting on a majority that can uphold the responsibilities and burdens of Britain in the world for three or four years at least'.[39]

Once again, in spite of all experience, he was encouraged by optimistic forecasts from Max Beaverbrook.[40] On polling day, however, the *Daily Mirror* revived its anti-Conservative campaign with a large picture of a revolver on its front page, and the question 'Whose finger? Today YOUR finger is on the trigger'. The statements that accompanied the picture led Churchill to issue a writ of libel against the paper; and after seven months the case was settled out of court by the publication of an apology, the payment of Churchill's costs, and a 'contribution to a charity to be named by him'.[41]

Whether or not the *Mirror* had anything to do with it, it appeared from the opinion polls that there was a surprising recovery in the Labour vote in the last few days of the campaign. In the end the Conservatives scraped in with a majority not very much larger than that which the Labour Party had had in 1950. There was in fact a very uniform swing of 1.1% to their side, and they secured 321 seats in the new Parliament, as against 295 for Labour and 6 for the Liberals. There were in addition three Anti-Partitionists elected for Northern Ireland. The final result had to wait until late on Friday afternoon, and Churchill could hardly have guessed it from his own result at Woodford, where no Liberal stood and yet his own majority rose by only 80 votes. His Labour opponent, William Archer, a man of 51, was a branch chairman of the Transport Salaried Staffs Association. There was also a Communist – J. R. Campbell, the editor of the *Daily Worker* and the man who had precipitated the fall of the Labour government in 1924; and Alexander Hancock, the eccentric Independent of 1945, reappeared. The result, which was announced once more in Churchill's presence, was as follows:

W. S. Churchill (Conservative)	40,938	Elected
W. A. Archer (Labour)	22,359	
J. R. Campbell (Communist)	871	
A. Hancock (Independent)	851	

As usual, Churchill made a courteous speech proposing a vote of thanks to the returning officer.[42]

This result had been completed by the early afternoon; but although elsewhere the trend of the results was clear it was not until just before 5 p.m. that it was determined that the Conservatives would have an overall majority in the new House. Attlee at once went to Buckingham Palace to resign; and within a few minutes Churchill was summoned and asked to form a government. One curiosity of the result was that the Labour Party received the largest total poll of all three parties – in fact, the largest poll that any party has received up to the present day. But because of the phenomenon of the 'wasted vote' the Conservatives had an overall majority of seventeen. Only 27 seats had changed hands, and neither Randolph Churchill nor Lady Violet Bonham Carter was elected.

Although Churchill was disappointed with the small size of the Conservative majority, he tried to buttress it by bringing the Liberals into his government as well. To begin with, he made eight senior appointments, putting Eden back at the Foreign Office and elevating Butler, rather unexpectedly, to the Exchequer. He had really wished to make Oliver Lyttelton the Chancellor of the Exchequer, but his Chief Whip warned him that Lyttelton would not be able to command the House of Commons. Churchill then invited Lyttelton to take any other post of his choice, and Lyttelton chose to be Secretary of State for the Colonies – a post not without major importance at the time of the Malayan guerrilla warfare, and one which Lyttelton's father had held early in the century.[43]

David Maxwell Fyfe really wanted to be Lord Chancellor, but Churchill asked him to serve a term first as Home Secretary;[44] and then, in line with the Prime Minister's view and pledge that the trade unions should be treated generously and should not be worried by any reversion to the 1927 Act, Sir Walter Monckton, who had not been a member of the parliamentary party for more than a few months, but who was known to the public principally as the Duke of Windsor's counsel, was made Minister of Labour.[45] The other appointments made at this early stage were in the Lords – and Churchill said that he could have made a 'very good inner Cabinet' from the Lords alone.[46] Woolton was rewarded for his work with the party organisation by becoming, as he had been during the war, Lord President of the Council. He was in fact to supervise and co-ordinate questions concerned with food and agriculture. Salisbury (formerly Cranborne) came in as Lord Privy Seal, where he was available also for co-ordinating functions.

But the oddest appointment at this stage was that of Lord Ismay – the faithful 'Pug' of wartime, when he had been Churchill's Chief of Staff on the Defence side – to be Secretary of State for Commonwealth Affairs. 'Pug' had played no part in the election, and he was fast asleep when the telephone rang in the small hours and he was invited to call upon the Prime Minister at Hyde Park Gate. He put his head under the cold tap to wake himself up thoroughly, and then hastened over, to be invited to join the new Cabinet. As he put it in his memoirs, 'I thought that the cold tap had failed to do its work and that I was still dreaming.'[47] It turned out that Churchill wanted him to examine the problems of defence pending the return of 'Alex' – Field-Marshal Lord Alexander of Tunis, who in spite of equal political inexperience was to be the Minister of Defence after he had completed his term as Governor-General of Canada. To begin with, however, it was announced that Churchill himself was once more to be Minister of Defence.

All these appointments were published on Saturday (October 27th), and they constituted more than half of the eventual Cabinet. Churchill thought it was a good idea to build up his new government in stages, but the idea did not commend itself to at least one senior Conservative who had not yet been given a post – Harold Macmillan.[48] One reason for the delay at this stage was that Clement Davies, the Liberal leader, was to be offered the post of Minister of Education. He saw Churchill in London on Saturday evening, but naturally asked for time to consult his colleagues before accepting. Churchill invited him to lunch at Chartwell on Sunday – the Attlees were having a last weekend at Chequers – but as there was no promise of advantage to the Liberal Party as a whole, such as the introduction of Proportional Representation, Clement Davies felt obliged to refuse the post.[49] The rest of the Cabinet, which in the end did not include the Minister of Education, was announced on Tuesday October 30th. Lord Cherwell re-emerged as Paymaster-General, in fact to take charge of scientific development and in particular the development of the atomic bomb; Lord Leathers was to co-ordinate transport, as he had done during the war, and also fuel and power. It was a disappointment that owing to poor health Churchill's most faithful colleague of all, Brendan Bracken, was unable to accept office.

Among the second group of appointments, Harold Macmillan was summoned to deal with a special responsibility, that of building the 300,000 houses promised in every year. Churchill told him, 'It is a gamble – [it will] make or mar your political career. But every humble home will bless your name, if you succeed.'[50] The title of his ministry was changed from 'Local Government and Planning' to 'Housing and Local Government' to emphasise the importance of housing. The total size of the Cabinet, at sixteen, was two smaller than Attlee's at the dissolution; and it was also remarkable for having a higher proportion of peers in it than any other since 1923. The Labour leaders in particular directed criticism at the idea of having ministers for 'co-ordination' – the 'Overlords', they called them – in the House of Lords.[51] But perhaps the most disappointed section of the Commons was the Conservative Party itself, for so few of its members received promotion to the higher posts of the government under the new Churchill regime.

29. *Prime Minister Again, 1951-5*

ALTHOUGH Churchill's resumption of office in late October 1951 lacked the drama of warfare as in May 1940, it was nevertheless not without its emergency aspects. Butler, the new Chancellor of the Exchequer, was promptly warned by his Civil Service advisers that the economy was on the verge of a 'collapse greater than had been foretold in 1931'.[1] He was obliged to take immediate action to cut imports, which he could still do directly owing to the existence of the controls left over from wartime, which the Labour government had found it necessary to retain. To show that he believed in other, more traditional methods of controlling the economy, he also made a token increase in the Bank Rate – from 2 to $2\frac{1}{2}\%$. In January a Commonwealth Finance Ministers' Conference was held in London to co-ordinate the policy of the whole sterling area; and hire-purchase restrictions were introduced in Britain. In March there followed a more or less stand-still Budget, in which Butler on the one hand increased the Bank Rate to 4%, introduced further restrictions upon imports, put up the duty on petrol, and cut food subsidies by £160 million, but on the other hand made concessions to pensioners, to parents of large families and to small wage-earners, two million of whom were relieved from paying tax altogether. He also wished to make the pound convertible at a floating rate of exchange, but he was voted down in the Cabinet on this.[2]

Churchill was naturally distressed that he and his colleagues could not 'set the people free', as they had promised at election time. None of the foods that were still rationed in late 1951 could be derationed in early 1952 and, so far from the promised 'red meat' being made available, the meat ration was reduced to a lower level than in 1942, when shipping had to run the gauntlet of enemy submarines. The only symbol of the government's intentions in its first few months of office was the abolition in February of the requirement for people to carry identity cards and to show them on demand – a requirement which had existed since 1939.[3] As a token of the Cabinet's own concern about the economic crisis, it was agreed that ministers normally paid £5000 a year should draw only £4000, and Churchill himself, who as Prime Minister was entitled to £10,000 a year, decided to take only £7000. These sacrifices hit some ministers more than others: Monckton, for instance, who was used to receiving substantial legal fees, was placed in serious temporary difficulty.[4] But Churchill himself, who within five weeks sold his horse Colonist II for stud at Newmarket for 7000 guineas, was evidently little worse off.[5] He also moved into 10 Downing Street, and let 28 Hyde Park Gate to the Cuban Ambassador for a substantial rent.[6]

All the same, the chastening effects of the economic crisis may have helped to account for what *The Times* called the Prime Minister's 'cross-bench mood' in addressing the Lord Mayor's Banquet at the Guildhall on November 9th.[7] He ascribed the country's difficulties partly to 'world causes', partly to 'the prolonged electioneering atmosphere in which we have dwelt for nearly two years, and especially for the past two months'.[8] Then early in December, in a Commons debate on defence, he acknowledged that it would be impossible to complete the Labour government's proposed £4700 million rearmament programme in the three years allowed, and somewhat grudgingly gave Aneurin Bevan an 'honourable mention' for 'having, it appears by accident, perhaps not from the best of motives, happened to be right'.[9]

In spite of tensions within the Labour Party, therefore, the first few months of the new Churchill government did nothing to make the Conservatives more popular in the country. The continuity between Gaitskell's and Butler's budgetary policies led the *Economist* to coin the word 'Butskellism' to describe the large measure of agreement between them.[10] It was now the Labour Party which began to obtain the benefit of popular discontent:

in the spring of 1952 it did very well at the local government elections, and Hugh Dalton in the privacy of his diary even began to consider the 'danger that we may come back too soon'.[11] *The Times* went so far as to suggest that there was 'a permanent shift of political power' to the Left.[12]

All this made the Conservative backbenchers grumble. There were only 43 members on either side who were entirely new to the Commons when it assembled after the general election,[13] and there were many of the government's supporters who felt that they should have had an opportunity to take office – an opportunity denied to them because Churchill had brought into his administration so many peers and also persons who had played little or even no part in the struggles of the preceding six years. The new government appeared to add insult to injury by failing, in the first session of the new parliament, to fulfil its two major legislative pledges – for the denationalisation of road haulage and of the iron and steel industry. On April 9th Churchill attended a meeting of Conservative MPs, who were reported to be 'restive' at the delay. Another meeting three and a half months later led to the publication of a statement saying: 'The Prime Minister made it clear that the fact that all legislation announced for the session had not been passed into law in no way represented any weakening of determination with regard to it on the part of the Government.'[14]

Naturally, Churchill did not allow either the Labour Party's local successes or the grumbles of the Parliamentary Conservative Party to precipitate him into an early general election. In fact, it was part of his 'cross-bench mood' at the Guildhall in November 1951 to plead for an end to electioneering:

> If these conditions of furious political warfare between the two halves of our party-divided Britain are to continue indefinitely, and we are all to live under the shadow of a third General Election, it will not be at all good for the main life interests of the British nation, or for her influence in world affairs.[15]

At the turn of the year he went off on a visit to President Truman in Washington, and was invited for a third time to address the two Houses of Congress in joint session. He called for American aid in making British rearmament effective, but added: 'I have come here to ask, not for gold, but for steel, not for favours but equipment.' He also implied that there would be British support of the United States in the Korean truce negotiations, which were already becoming very tortuous, and said that if a truce were reached, only to be broken, 'our response will be prompt, resolute, and effective'. By this time the Soviet Union had acquired its own atomic bombs; but Churchill congratulated the United States upon the 'vast resources of American rearmament', which, he thought, might well avert the danger of a Third World War. He also suggested to his audience an idea that met with little favour – that there might be an American 'token force' in the Suez Canal Zone, by the side of the British soldiers already there. As usual, he concluded on the note of Anglo-American partnership in world policy: 'Bismarck once said that the supreme fact of the nineteenth century was that Britain and the United States spoke the same language. Let us make sure that the supreme fact of the twentieth century is that they tread the same path.'[16]

The speech was well received, and superficial observation, as reported by the Washington correspondent of *The Times*, was that Churchill, although slower than when he had visited America during the war, was still 'alert, well informed, and as full of ideas, vivid language, and wit as ever'.[17] Dean Acheson, who was now Truman's Secretary of State, was rather more critical: he had many conversations with both Churchill and Eden, and in both he perceived 'evidences of six years in opposition and the absence of familiarity with frustrating detail and of intuition instilled by the daily pain of decision and action'.[18] But there were also rigidities on the American side. The year 1952 was an election year, and it was not likely that the administration would wish to be criticised for making political concessions to the British. The only adjustment that the Prime Minister was able to obtain of arrangements already made for NATO defence was a largely verbal one – that the Home Command of the Royal Navy should extend as far out into the Atlantic as the one-hundred fathom line.

In the course of private discussions on board the presidential yacht on the Potomac, Churchill voiced his personal dislike of the French proposals for a European Defence Community, in which, he thought, there would be too much mixing of nationalities to make an effective force. But in fact the proposals did not involve much more heterogeneity than had been characteristic of the Allied commands in Europe during the latter part of the war, and Eisenhower himself approved the plan, as did Anthony Eden.[19] Yet Churchill's view of the European Army was that it would be a 'sludgy amalgam' of nationalities;[20] and even Eden's approval was only approval from outside. In discussing the idea of Britain entering a European Federation when he spoke at Columbia University, New York, on January 11th, Eden said: 'This is something which we know in our bones we cannot do.'[21] Such an attitude, which was not shared by Maxwell Fyfe, by Macmillan, or of course by Duncan Sandys, nevertheless prevailed within the Cabinet largely by reason of Churchill's sense of Britain's need for close association with the United States, and because Anthony Eden was after all both his Foreign Secretary and his expected successor in the Premiership. But some of Churchill's old colleagues in the European Movement regarded it as a betrayal, and in particular Spaak of Belgium decided henceforward to work for the unity of 'the Six', who signed the Treaty of Rome establishing the Common Market in 1957.[22]

One reason for the failure of Britain to 'enter Europe' at this stage soon became apparent. The manufacture of a British atomic bomb had been begun in 1948, without the advantage of the exchange of secret information with the Americans, owing to the McMahon Act passed by the United States Congress, but at least with the aid of 'know-how' acquired by British scientists during their participation in the American wartime programme. The first British atomic test took place in the Monte Bello Islands, off the Australian coast, early in October 1952, and Britain thus became the third power, after the United States and Russia, to have this weapon at its disposal.

Meanwhile Churchill had felt the need for a fundamental re-examination of the strategy of defence preparations, and although from March 1952 onwards he had the assistance of Field-Marshal Lord Alexander of Tunis as his Defence Minister it was largely on his own initiative that the Chiefs of Staff were ordered to sit down together in seclusion and work out a new statement of policy for British defence. The 'Global Strategy Paper' that they produced has been described as 'a classic among military documents'.[23] It emphasised the need to rely upon deterrence – the threat of an atomic strike at the heartland of the enemy – and consequently it accepted that less importance should be attached to conventional forces. It was probably as a direct result that in

December 1952 the NATO Council agreed on major reductions in the planned levels of ground troops. In Britain, the need was now for high-quality bombers to carry atomic bombs, and the Churchill Cabinet decided to manufacture the so-called 'V-bombers' in some quantity.

The Korean War, which had been responsible for hastening the rearmament plans of the Western Powers, had by now undergone some remarkable vicissitudes. In November 1950 General MacArthur, who was then in command, had sent his troops forward far beyond the 38th Parallel which was the formal dividing line between the two Koreas. This provoked the intervention of Chinese troops in the guise of volunteers: they threw back the Allied troops, and in the course of doing so incidentally wounded Randolph Churchill, who was there as a journalist. In 1951 the line became re-established near the 38th Parallel, and truce negotiations began. They did not proceed smoothly, because many of the prisoners in Allied hands did not wish to return to Communist China or North Korea. A final armistice agreement was not signed until the end of July 1953.

As the Korean War began to sputter out, Churchill conceived the idea of a meeting of the heads of government of the major powers, as had taken place occasionally in wartime and just afterwards. Stalin died on March 5th 1953, and was succeeded as Chairman of the Council of Ministers in the USSR by M. Malenkov, a man who seemed to be more of a technician or bureaucrat than a military dictator. In May Churchill spoke of the idea of a new Locarno Pact – referring to the treaty that Austen Chamberlain made in 1925 to guarantee the Franco-German frontier.[24] This was not the best analogy to raise enthusiasm among Soviet diplomats, who had felt that the Locarno Pact was in a sense aimed against their own country. But Churchill also called for 'a conference on the highest level ... between the leading Powers'. There was a rather testy reaction in *Pravda*, but all the same the comment was added: 'The importance of Winston Churchill's offer cannot be overlooked.'[25]

It seemed worth while to try to exploit the more favourable atmosphere that had now developed, and Churchill decided, in his usual fashion, to talk first with the Americans. General Eisenhower had succeeded Truman as President after a sweeping victory at the polls in November 1952. But the new President, although warm in his friendship for Churchill, had little enthu-

siasm for a 'summit' meeting at a time when Americans were
still suffering from the shock of their losses in the Korean War
and the fact that the war had ended, not in out-and-out victory,
as Americans expected their wars to end, but in a form of deadlock. Eisenhower liked to leave foreign policy questions to his new
Secretary of State, Foster Dulles, and Dulles was also against a
high-level meeting. But finally Eisenhower agreed to meet Churchill for a preliminary conference on the British islands of
Bermuda, not far from the American coast, in July 1953.[26] Owing
to a French Cabinet crisis the date was altered to early July, but
in the end, as we shall see, there had to be further substantial
postponement.

The sense of *détente* was increased by the fact that the first week
of June 1953 saw the Coronation of Queen Elizabeth II. Her
father, King George VI, had had a major operation in the autumn
of 1951 – an event that made Churchill very anxious and distressed
– but he seemed to make a surprisingly good recovery.[27] Early
in 1952 Princess Elizabeth and her husband, the Duke of Edinburgh, began a Commonwealth tour by air, travelling first to
east Africa. The King saw the couple off at the airport, and a
few days later he went shooting, and retired apparently con-
tentedly to bed. Next morning (February 6th) it was found that
he had died in the night. The Queen – as she had now become –
and the Duke flew back at once from Kenya, and were greeted
by Churchill and other Privy Counsellors on the apron of London
airport. The Prime Minister was deeply moved by the death of
the King and by the accession of the young Queen. His memorial
broadcast was one of his best. He spoke of the King's illness:
'During these last months the King walked with death, as if
death was a companion, an acquaintance, whom he recognised
and did not fear. In the end death came as a friend.' And he also
saluted the new Queen, ascending the throne at the age of
twenty-five, and for this he called upon his own memories: 'I,
whose youth was passed in the august, unchallenged and tranquil
glories of the Victorian Era, may well feel a thrill in invoking,
once more, the prayer and the anthem "God Save the Queen".'[28]
The government's wreath at the funeral bore an inscription in
Churchill's handwriting – 'For Valour', the citation of the Victoria Cross.[29]

Arrangements for the Queen's coronation had to be made many

months in advance, and the date chosen was June 2nd 1953. It was an auspicious beginning to the reign that the preceding months saw a marked improvement in Britain's financial position, largely owing to increasingly favourable terms of trade as American stockpiling declined. This meant, among other things, that various foods could now be taken off the ration – tea in October 1952 and chocolate and sweets in February 1953. The Conservatives did well in by-elections and early in May actually won a marginal seat, Sunderland South, from the Opposition. It was apparently the first time since 1924 that a government had gained a seat in a by-election.[30] A *Times* leader-writer thereupon solemnly discerned 'a pattern which suggests that the British electors' desire for change, having been mobilised to produce great reforming majorities as those of 1906 and 1945, is then satisfied within a matter of five or six years'.[31]

All the Commonwealth prime ministers were invited to attend the Coronation, and also to take part in discussions with the British ministers. All accepted – no doubt looking forward to the pageantry and to the unique contrast of the youthful monarch and her aged Prime Minister. In April the Queen had conferred on him the Order of the Garter, and this time he had no reason to excuse himself. His work in supervising the arrangements for the Coronation was heavy enough, but to this was added the need to assume primary responsibility for foreign policy in the absence through illness of Anthony Eden, who after two operations upon the bile duct had to go off to the United States for yet a third operation by an American surgeon. Until Eden's return the Minister of State, Selwyn Lloyd, was invited to attend Cabinet meetings regularly.[32]

The Prime Minister's physician, Lord Moran, was worried by the accumulation of duties upon his patient's shoulders. Churchill had become increasingly deaf in recent months, and as he began his American trip he admitted to Moran that he was 'not so good mentally as I used to be'.[33] A few weeks later, in late February 1952, he suffered a period of aphasia, and Moran began to plot with Colville, his Principal Private Secretary, Lascelles, the Queen's Private Secretary, and Lord Salisbury, some means of persuading him to lighten his load – perhaps by going to the Lords himself.[34] But Churchill soon felt better and would hear no more of it. He attended the Coronation in the uniform of the Lord Warden of the Cinque Ports, wearing all his medals and also a Special Badge of the Order of the Garter – the so-called 'Greater George', nearly double the size of the standard badge, originally given to Marlborough by Queen Anne and later returned to the Crown and given by William IV to Wellington.[35] Amidst the pageantry of the day – marred only by cold, wet weather – Churchill was indeed, as *The Times* reported, 'a jovial and picturesque figure in his plumed hat'.[36]

In the following days Churchill presided at all the five plenary sessions of the Commonwealth Conference; and he entertained all the Commonwealth prime ministers at 10 Downing Street, inviting also the Attlees, Herbert Morrison, and Tom O'Brien, MP, retiring chairman of the TUC. He was at the coronation review of the navy at Spithead – still quite an imposing display, especially with the visiting foreign warships as well. Then on June 23rd the Italian Prime Minister, Signor de Gasperi, arrived for a two-day visit; and that evening Churchill was the host at an official dinner, also at No. 10, to the Italian guests. When the dinner was over, and Churchill himself had made an amusing speech, Christopher Soames noticed that he could not get up from his chair. Soames and Clementine managed to draw the waiters away, so that they would not see too much of the Prime Minister's plight. But several of those present noticed that his speech had become very indistinct, and assumed that he had had a little too much to drink. The Office attempted to summon Lord Moran that evening, but he was not at home, and so a message was delivered asking him to visit his patient next morning.

When Moran appeared next day he found that Churchill had suffered a minor stroke. The left side of his mouth was sagging, his gait was unsteady and his speech was slurred. Moran brought another distinguished physician, Russell Brain, into consultation, and between them they drew up a rather vague medical bulletin referring to 'a disturbance of the cerebral circulation', and advising abandonment of the Bermuda meeting and 'at least a month's rest'.[37] But even this was too explicit for Churchill's close political colleagues: taking a gamble on the chances of his recovery, Butler and Salisbury made the bulletin vaguer still: 'The Prime Minister has had no respite for a long time from his very arduous duties and is in need of a complete rest. We have therefore advised him to abandon his journey to Bermuda and lighten his duties for at least a month.'[38] They must have been encouraged by an episode which Moran does not mention and probably did not know about. As soon as the doctor left Downing Street, Churchill went downstairs and conducted the Cabinet meeting as he had originally intended. He got through it without disclosing his misfortune; and Macmillan, who was a close observer, admitted later that he noticed nothing wrong except that Churchill looked very white and spoke little.[39]

The trouble was, however, that the signs of incapacity grew worse in the succeeding days. He went down to Chartwell, where he was visited by one or two of the friends most likely to cheer him up – Max Beaverbrook at lunch on Sunday June 28th and Brendan Bracken at dinner on the same day.[40] They both found him cheerful and talkative amidst the increasing signs of paralysis on his left side. In the absence of Eden, Butler became acting Prime Minister, and he later recalled an occasion when he sat at dinner 'whilst Winston with his good arm carried to his lips a beaker of brandy'.[41] And then, after the weekend, he began to improve. He was really relaxing – reading Trollope's *Phineas Finn*, for instance, apparently for the first time. Macmillan, who visited him on July 2nd, came to the conclusion that 'these "strokes" or "seizures" are of a very mild kind'.[42]

Macmillan himself had to go into hospital for a minor operation. Meanwhile Salisbury was appointed Acting Foreign Secretary, and was given a briefing by Churchill himself for a visit to Washington, in which he was to deputise for both the Prime Minister and the Foreign Secretary.

In the summer of 1953 Churchill gradually recovered from his stroke, by resting and by waiting, as Lord Moran suggested to him, for the blood in his head to 'get round the back streets' – what doctors call collateral circulation.[43] He alternated between Chartwell and Chequers, not because he wished to, but simply to allow the servants to have a rest.[44] From Chequers on August 1st he went to Royal Lodge, Windsor, for an audience with the Queen – his first since his illness. In mid-August, on his return to Chartwell, he stopped en route at No. 10 Downing Street to see Salisbury and some of the Foreign Office officials who had accompanied him to Washington. He also underwent an examination by Moran and Russell Brain, and told them that the Queen had invited him to the St Leger at Doncaster on September 12th and then on to Balmoral for the weekend. The doctors apparently made little comment, but agreed that he was now much better and well rested.[45] On August 18th he presided at a Cabinet, which went quite well in spite of 'a long and difficult agenda'. The Prime Minister himself, according to Macmillan, was 'full of quips and epigrams'.[46]

Early in September some Cabinet changes were announced from Downing Street. Churchill had now ended the 'Overlords' experiment: Leathers was retiring, and Woolton gave up his suzerainty over food and agriculture – whose separate ministers, together with Florence Horsbrugh, the Minister of Education, now joined the Cabinet. This brought the total membership of the Cabinet up to nineteen – more than Churchill had ever had before. But the boundaries between full membership of the Cabinet and other ministerial responsibility were still not very clear, for Churchill had his 'constant attenders' in peacetime as in war.

On September 12th, a Saturday, Churchill duly went off with Clementine to see the St Leger with the Queen and the Duke of Edinburgh. It was the Churchills' forty-fifth wedding anniversary. Next day, at Balmoral, they joined the royal family at a service at Crathie parish church – which Churchill had also done forty-five years earlier.[47] Thereafter he and Clementine flew back to London in a Viking aircraft of the Queen's Flight; and on September 17th he and his daughter Mary and Christopher Soames travelled to Nice to stay at Beaverbrook's villa at Cap d'Ail. He did some painting and looked over the galleys of his book *The History of the English-speaking Peoples*, which he had drafted before the war but had then put aside. He was, however, depressed by a sense of tiredness;[48] and he was unable to gamble at Monte Carlo, as he would have liked, owing to the government's restriction of the tourist's foreign exchange allowance to £10.[49] Then as the days went by he began increasingly to worry about his closing speech for the Conservative Party Conference at Margate, due to be delivered early in October.

While Churchill had been on the Riviera, Eden had been recuperating from his operation in Greece, and both leaders returned by air at almost the same time on the last day of September. Eden must now have been wondering when Churchill would retire, but the latter's performance at Margate, assisted by one of Moran's pills, was described by *The Times* as 'a personal triumph'.[50] As for the succession, all that Churchill said was:

If I stay on for the time being bearing the burden at my age it is
not because of love for power or office. I have had an ample share
of both. If I stay, it is because I have a feeling that I may through
things that have happened have an influence on what I care about
above all else, the building of a sure and lasting peace.[51]

After the success of the speech he told Colville, his private secre-
tary, that he would stay on as Prime Minister at least until the
Queen returned from her Commonwealth tour, due to begin in
November and to conclude in mid-May.[52]

At the opening of Parliament early in November he again made
a speech which impressed his critics. 'Chips' Channon, the one-
time Chamberlainite, wrote in his diary that it was 'one of the
speeches of his lifetime'.

Brilliant, full of cunning and charm, of wit and thrusts, he poured
out his Macaulay-like phrases to a stilled and awed House. It was
an Olympian spectacle.... Then he sought refuge in the Smoking
Room, and, flushed with pride, pleasure and triumph sat there for
two hours sipping brandy and acknowledging compliments. He
beamed like a schoolboy.[53]

Later in the month he took the trouble to arrange a dinner at
No. 10 for the Jockey Club: the Duke of Gloucester was present,
and in the company were two other dukes and six earls.[54]

The Bermuda meeting of Heads of Government, which had
been postponed owing to Churchill's illness, took place at last
early in December. Churchill arrived first, in order to greet the
French Premier, Laniel, and the American President to what
was after all a British colony, albeit also an American base. The
conversations soon convinced him that it was not Eisenhower
who was in control of American foreign policy, but his Secretary
of State, Foster Dulles; and Dulles, who saw things in stark
black-and-white terms, was strongly hostile to a 'summit' meeting.
Moran reported Churchill as saying: 'This fellow preaches like
a Methodist minister, and his bloody text is always the same:
that nothing but evil can come out of meeting with Malenkov.'[55]

Dulles probably wished to be sure of getting the French to
accept the European Defence Community before making any
attempt at a *rapprochement* with Russia: indeed, not long afterwards he publicly threatened an 'agonising reappraisal' of American foreign policy, implying a withdrawal to a so-called
'peripheral' policy, if it were not passed.[56] At least it was agreed

to invite the Russians to a Foreign Ministers' Conference in Berlin early in the New Year to discuss the problems of Germany and Austria. But when Churchill came to report on the conference to the Commons he did not have much to say; and Attlee was not far wrong when he described him as 'a Father Christmas without any presents'.[57]

The question of a *rapprochement* with Russia was not the only matter which worried Churchill at this time. He was concerned about the agitation for commercial television which had developed within the Conservative Party in Parliament – not because he himself opposed the breaking of the BBC's monopoly of broadcasting, but because a substantial number of his Cabinet colleagues did. Being patricians themselves, they were horrified at the degradation of taste that might be involved in having advertising on radio and television. Churchill's own view was quite different. He recalled that the BBC had kept him off the air on controversial questions in the 1930s, and he therefore thought that it deserved to face some competition. It was in fact this view that prevailed, although to begin with it was supported in the Cabinet only by Woolton and a couple of junior ministers.[58] By a compromise, the BBC was to retain its monopoly of sound broadcasting and, although independent television with advertisement was to be permitted, the programmes were not to be directly sponsored by the advertisers as in the United States, but only indirectly through new television companies, themselves controlled by a supervising authority.

But this was not the only issue which unsettled a number of the Conservative backbenchers. A minority of more than twenty, led by Captain Charles Waterhouse, was upset by Eden's negotiations for the withdrawal of British troops from Egypt, where they were still stationed under the terms of the treaty of 1936. Churchill met the 1922 Committee on December 16th to tell them that the Cabinet was not going to be deterred from its policy by the threat of a revolt, and the party as a whole was sufficiently influenced by his eloquence to sing 'For He's a Jolly Good Fellow' as he left.[59] Churchill's support for Eden on this question was given in spite of his own instincts in the matter. His mind probably went back to the 1890s and the 'River War'; but he recognised that the overwhelming power of the hydrogen bomb now made fixed bases obsolete. It was largely by emphasising this aspect that he won the backbenchers' support for Eden's new treaty.

If there were signs of discontent within the Conservative Party, they were as nothing to the dissensions which rent the Labour Party at this time. Bevan resigned from the Labour Shadow Cabinet in April 1954, ostensibly over Far Eastern policy, but perhaps really to lead a struggle against acceptance of German rearmament. Soon, however, the issue of the hydrogen bomb, which Britain had begun to manufacture in 1952, and which had first been tested by the Americans in November of that year, came to dominate political discussion at Westminster. Public knowledge of the new weapon was delayed for over a year, as information about the first American tests was not revealed until February 1954. Churchill himself read about the devastating effect of the H-bomb not in any state paper but in a report in the *Manchester Guardian* of a statement made by Sterling Cole, the Chairman of the Joint Congressional Committee on Atomic Energy.[60] The British decision to manufacture the H-bomb, arrived at so early, was announced only in the Defence White Paper of 1955. The announcement had the effect of dividing the Labour Party still more, as Bevan and his supporters felt that the largely bipartisan attitude to defence which their front bench was still maintaining was no longer tolerable.

Meanwhile the revelations of Sterling Cole's announcement were enough to cause Churchill to request another visit to Eisenhower in Washington in order to talk over various aspects of the new situation. The two leaders met in June 1954 and, as their Foreign Ministers were also available, other urgent problems could be discussed, in particular the possibility of the French Assembly after all defeating the treaty establishing the European Defence Community. But the main upshot of the meeting was that Eisenhower agreed to sponsor more generous arrangements for the exchange of atomic information not actually forbidden by the McMahon Act, which since 1946 had been very strictly observed.

Eden had been pursuing the less spectacular but not less important task of seeking common ground for *rapprochement* with the Soviet Union in Europe and elsewhere. The Conference of Foreign Ministers in Berlin in January 1954 proved abortive so far as Germany and Austria were concerned, but it did lead to an agreement to meet in Geneva in April, to try to sort out the problems of the Far East, and in particular the war in Indo-China, where the French were engaged in a desperate and largely fruitless struggle. Although the negotiations at Geneva lasted several months, they did in the end result in a termination of this war – largely due to a certain flexibility in the Russian approach, to Eden's skill, and to the desire of the new French Prime Minister, Pierre Mendès-France, to find a solution.[61] But when it came to the debate in the French Assembly on the European Defence Community, Mendès-France felt it impracticable to exert the influence of government in its favour, and it was voted down in late August 1954.[62]

This was a critical moment for the construction of the Western defensive arrangements, and it led to a flurry of negotiation in which Eden was heavily engaged and in which Churchill had to play the host in London to a conference of prime ministers and foreign ministers. The obvious solution of the problem of German rearmament now lay in the admission of Germany to the North Atlantic Treaty itself, with certain safeguards designed to allay the suspicions of her Western neighbours. That this solution proved acceptable was partly due to carefully co-ordinated pledges from both Dulles and Eden that the troops of their respective countries would remain indefinitely on the Continent. The agreements provided not only for the admission of Germany to NATO but also for the termination of the occupation regime. Thus at last the framework of Western security in its political aspect was completed.

Churchill's visit to Eisenhower had taken place before the defeat of EDC by the French Assembly, and he found him as obstinately opposed as ever to the idea of an early summit meeting with Malenkov. But Churchill himself, feeling that his opportunity of acting as the peacemaker was running short, asked of Eisenhower whether he opposed an attempt by himself to go to Russia on what he described as a 'reconnoitring patrol'.[63] Eisenhower could hardly limit Churchill's movements, though he clearly did not like the idea; and when the Prime Minister was on the *Queen Elizabeth* on the way back to England he sent a message to Molotov, who was still the Russian Foreign Minister, proposing the meeting. The Cabinet was not informed of this message before its despatch – quite deliberately, according to Colville, the Prime Minister's Principal Private Secretary – and a first-class row blew up when Salisbury and Crookshank threatened to resign. Fortunately the Russians were also in some diplomatic disarray. As Colville later wrote: 'The crisis was resolved by the Russians themselves taking an initiative which demanded a meeting ... of thirty-two powers to discuss a European Security Plan.'[64]

In September the Western Powers agreed not to attend such a conference unless Russia would sign the Austrian Treaty, the main lines for which had been agreed in the late 1940s, and also allow free elections throughout Germany. Owing to the fall of Malenkov in the following February and the need for the new Russian regime to consolidate itself, this meant the loss of Churchill's last chance to act as the world's peacemaker.

Churchill was now given to consulting his colleagues about the date of his resignation and hand-over to Anthony Eden. The latter had married into the Churchill family in August 1952, his bride being Jack's only daughter Clarissa, then aged thirty-two. But he was now a rather ageing 'crown prince', as he was already fifty-seven by the summer of 1954, and he was still being given a succession of dates for the changeover: May of that year, on the Queen's return from her Commonwealth tour; then July; and then again September.[65] At least Eden had plenty to do with the various negotiations in which he was involved, and at least they bore fruit.

In October Churchill made a Cabinet reshuffle, which did not suggest that he was on the point of retirement. Field-Marshal Lord Alexander was allowed to leave the Ministry of Defence and retire: he had never been happy in the political world. Lord Simonds, the Lord Chancellor, also not much of a politician, was relieved of his office, which now went to Maxwell Fyfe, the former Home Secretary, who was translated to the House of Lords with the title Viscount Kilmuir. Macmillan, having by general agreement made a great success of his post of Minister of Housing, was promoted to be Minister of Defence, and Duncan Sandys, the Prime Minister's son-in-law, succeeded him at Housing. The press could not refrain from discussing the possibility of the Prime Minister's own retirement in the near future, as it seemed unlikely that he could face another election. The *Times* leader, for instance, in considering the changes that had been made, said: 'Compared with the change that has still to come they seem of little account. In many ways it is embarrassing to discuss that change.'[66]

A few weeks later there was a further reminder of the Prime Minister's great age when, on November 30th, there were celebrations of his eightieth birthday. As he enjoyed receiving presents there was no question of his not participating in the event with enthusiasm. At a special meeting of both Houses of Parliament in Westminster Hall, he received a portrait of himself presented by members of all parties, together with a commemorative book which contained the signatures of all but a handful of MPs. The portrait was by Graham Sutherland, and as Churchill said at the time it was 'a remarkable example of modern art. It certainly combines force with candour.'[67] This meant, in fact, that he did not like it. There was some reason for this, as it made him look harsh and even cruel. But Churchill enjoyed the occasion, which as he said was unique in British political history, the presentation being made by Attlee, the Leader of the Opposition, and with Churchill himself the only man alive to have held the post of Prime Minister. Two enormous birthday-cakes had been constructed, each three feet across: one was for this occasion, and one was for Churchill's private party at 10 Downing Street.[68]

Presents and greetings came in from all over the world, and the only element of embarrassment was that in accepting a portrait of Lady Churchill from the Woodford Conservatives he made a claim to have ordered Field-Marshal Montgomery in May 1945 to stack the surrendered German arms 'so that they could easily be issued again to the German soldiers whom we should have to work with if the Soviet advance continued'.[69] Whether the indiscretion arose from blurting out the truth is still not clear: it certainly caused concern among those interested in foreign affairs. But the Commons and the Labour front bench let him off lightly – Shinwell saying that he was 'sorry to engage in controversy with the right hon. Gentleman immediately after his birthday celebrations'.[70]

Of course it was obvious that his retirement could only be a matter of months. He himself had spoken of it to his closer associates for some time. In March 1954 he told Butler: 'I feel like an aeroplane at the end of its flight, in the dusk, with the petrol running out, in search of a safe landing.'[71] By early 1955 he had given up the expectation of an early summit meeting with the Russians. In February Malenkov fell from power, and it seemed likely that the Bulganin–Krushchev regime would need time to consolidate. But the 1951 Parliament had now lasted well over three years, and Churchill did not feel fit enough to fight another general election as Prime Minister. Finally he fixed on April 5th as the day of his resignation: Eden was to come back quickly from a visit he was paying to the Far East for the first meeting of the Council of the South-East Asia Treaty Organisation. On April 4th Churchill gave a dinner party at 10 Downing Street, at which both the Queen and the Duke of Edinburgh were present. Contrary to custom, he made a brief speech in proposing the toast of the Queen; and the Queen in turn proposed the toast of her Prime Minister. The Churchill family was well represented: besides Lady Churchill, the Randolph Churchills, Mr and Mrs Sandys and Captain and Mrs Soames were all present.[72]

At noon on April 5th Churchill presided over his last Cabinet. At 4.30 p.m. he visited Buckingham Palace to make his formal resignation. Next day Anthony Eden was invited to the Palace and asked to form a government. Churchill moved out of Downing Street at 5 p.m. *The Times* reported:

Before leaving he entertained all the members of the staff at a tea party, and as he walked from the house to his waiting car they stood in the hall and sang 'For He's a Jolly Good Fellow'. Smoking a cigar, and greeting the crowd gathered in Downing Street with his famous V-sign, Sir Winston Churchill drove slowly away to the accompaniment of cheers and shouts of good wishes.[73]

Churchill left office during a prolonged newspaper-strike, and this prevented the events of his resignation from being fully reported in the conventional way. This could perhaps be regarded as poetic justice, for throughout his premiership he had pursued a policy of 'appeasement' of the trade unions, and had appointed Walter Monckton as Minister of Labour virtually with the object of buying them off. It was not for another decade that the Conservative Party made up its mind that trade-union legislation was in need of revision. Meanwhile, when it was suggested that the Trade Disputes Act of 1927 ought to be re-enacted, Churchill's view was that, although the operation of the political levy was unjust, 'a wider spirit of tolerance had grown up and the question may well be left to commonsense and the British way of settling things.'[74] He knew that about a third of the trade-union membership voted Conservative – as they may have done in the days when he first fought Oldham in association with a Conservative trade-union leader – and he wished to encourage this. In the course of his premiership, many trade-union leaders were invited to join dinner parties at 10 Downing Street, and one – Tom O'Brien, MP, chairman of the TUC in 1952–3 – visited him at Cap d'Ail.[75]

To some extent it was good to have a 'wider spirit of tolerance' at work in British politics after the bitterness of earlier conflicts. But the question may be asked – it cannot yet be answered – whether the final Churchill years were not years of lost opportunity. The improving terms of trade, which kept domestic prices in check, concealed the real problems of industry and also encouraged complacency about Britain's role in the world. These were the years when the foundations were laid for the establishment of the European Economic Community by 'the Six'. Meanwhile Churchill and his Cabinet were still pursuing the will-o'-the-wisp of Great Power status for their country, and maintaining too high a proportion of expenditure upon the armed forces and rearmament to enable Britain to stay in the economic race.

Yet, for all the echoes of the past that were to be found in this later period of government, Churchill could claim to have taken the lead in many ways in adapting his country's institutions to the new post-war world. His and Eden's role as intermediaries between the United States and its rivals, Russia and China, was a vitally important contribution to a genuine form of 'appeasement'. Of the two parties, only the Conservatives, and perhaps only under Churchill, could have hastened the pace of German independence and rearmament. It was also under the later Churchill that many of the implications of nuclear warfare were worked out in the Chiefs of Staff's paper on Global Strategy – a paper which was to influence American policy as well.

It is now apparent that Churchill and his colleagues were wrong in thinking that Britain could maintain the status of a Great Power, simply by possessing the H-bomb like the Americans and Russians. The development of missiles to the point of the launching of satellites to orbit the earth and even to go to the moon implied a wealth and power which Britain did not have. Yet the process of adjusting national pretensions to a less lofty status in the world could be politically painful, as Harold Macmillan was to find in the early 1960s when his efforts to acknowledge the 'wind of change' in Africa and to join the Common Market were strongly opposed within the Conservative Party. If the later Churchill government had been relatively peaceful, it was partly because Churchill on many issues worked in step with, and not in advance of, the great body of his fellow-citizens.

30. *In Retirement,*
1955–65

VERY soon after leaving No. 10 for the last time – in fact, on April 12th – Churchill with Clementine and also Cherwell went off on holiday to Syracuse. According to Colville as reported by Moran, he played bezique for eight hours a day and painted for four.[1] But only three days after his outward flight, and after only eight days of the new premiership, Anthony Eden announced a dissolution of Parliament for May 6th and a general election for May 26th. Since the weather in Sicily was disappointing anyway, Churchill returned home after little more than a fortnight, on April 26th. Eden did not invite him to give a proper broadcast, but only to make a brief appearance on television – to be sure, a rapidly expanding medium – and this arrangement did not satisfy Churchill. Having refused to participate, he was rather at a loss for a few days.

His constituency of Woodford was, of course, safe enough. It had been reduced in size and made even safer than previously by fresh redistribution. He was formally adopted by the Conservative Association on May 9th, and a week later gave an address to his constituents in the Sir James Hawkey Hall – a memorial to his old friend and colleague. He opened with a few words of praise for the new Prime Minister, and then went on to a defence of the retiring government's record, together with an attack on the Labour Party and especially upon Aneurin Bevan, 'the politician who causes most anxiety to every friend and ally of Britain all over the world'.[2] Next day he spoke for Christopher Soames at Bedford and also for Alan Lennox-Boyd, the Colonial Secretary, nearby at Biggleswade. Two days later he spoke on behalf of John Harvey, the Chairman of the Woodford Conservative Association, who was standing at East Walthamstow; and he combined this excursion with a visit to address a meeting on behalf of John Biggs-Davidson, who was fighting Chigwell, the seat carved out of the northern part of the old Woodford constituency. All these candidates were elected for their somewhat marginal seats.

He had carefully rationed his electoral efforts this time and for the rest his only public performance was to make an eve-of-the-poll tour of Woodford itself. As usual he attended the final stages of the count late on the evening of polling-day. It resulted as follows:

W. S. Churchill (Conservative)	25,069	Elected
A. K. M. Milnes (Labour)	9261	

Churchill's opponent was an electrical engineer in his mid-forties, fighting his first campaign. There were no other candidates, and this must have accounted in part for the heavy fall in turnout – 72%, as against 82% in 1951. But some degree of fall in turnout was almost universal, and it was apparent that other people besides Sir Winston himself found the election 'boring'.[3] The change, which was obviously partly due to Churchill's withdrawal from the leading role, was all the same beneficial to the Conservative cause. The government had, after all, captured the best issue that the Labour Party had had – the need for 'summit' talks, which was in fact agreed to by the Russian Foreign Minister Molotov on May 15th. The signature of the Austrian State Treaty on the same day was also a notable step towards the pacification of Europe.

Dalton's comment on the election is revealing. The former Labour Chancellor recorded in his diary this statement:

There were no burning issues, no unemployment, & much overtime. I was reduced to arguing (1) that prices – & here I read out a list of growing prices at two dates – had risen disproportionately under the Tories who had promised to put value back into the £; (2) that Attlee rather than Eden should go to top-level talks! ![4]

In the event there was a swing to the Conservatives of 1.8%, distributed very evenly throughout the country.[5] The Conservatimes won 49.7% of the total poll, which put them well ahead of Labour, even though in aggregate the figure was less than Labour had polled in 1951. The Conservative majority in Parliament went up from 17 in 1951 to 58; it was the first time that an existing government had managed to increase its majority at a general election in peacetime since Palmerston's success in 1865.

When Parliament reassembled Churchill occupied the first seat below the gangway on the government side – the seat that he had occupied in his days as a rebel in the 1930s. But this time there were no rebellious speeches, in fact no speeches at all, and he did not attend even as regularly as he had done then, as he did not wish to attack his successor and his vote was hardly essential now that Eden's government had a comfortable majority. He preferred to spend his time preparing for publication the volumes of his *History of the English-speaking Peoples*. From mid-January to mid-April 1956 – except for two weeks – he stayed at Roquebrune Cap Martin on the Riviera as the guest of Emery Reves, his continental publisher. In late April, on Eden's invitation, Marshal Bulganin and Mr Krushchev visited Britain, and Churchill met them at an official dinner at No. 10. He had no difficulty in deciding that of the two Russian leaders Krushchev was the more important.[6] In May he was in West Germany, at Aachen – his first visit since 1945 – to receive the Charlemagne Prize for his contribution to European unity: he also met Adenauer and President Heuss at the Federal capital, Bonn. He had really become quite friendly with Adenauer, and presented him with one of his paintings.[7] In late July he returned briefly to West Germany to see his colt Le Prétendant run in a race; but the horse was the last but one in a field of twelve.[8] In September and October he spent another five weeks at Roquebrune Cap Martin.

Meanwhile in late July Colonel Nasser, the new revolutionary Egyptian leader, had announced the nationalisation of the Suez Canal, and Eden set himself the task of organising Nasser's downfall. He was, of course, especially encouraged in this course by the 'Suez Group' of Conservative MPs who had been worried about the earlier agreement to withdraw all British troops from the Canal Zone. On October 29th, a few days before the presidential election in the United States, the Israelis attacked Egyptian positions in Sinai. Eden never admitted direct 'collusion' with the Israelis, but next day Britain and France together issued ultimatums to the Egyptian and Israeli governments demanding a withdrawal to ten miles on either side of the Suez Canal. As the fighting was still taking place far to the east of the canal, the Israelis had no difficulty in accepting the ultimatum, but the Egyptians were almost obliged to refuse. At dusk on October 31st British and French bombers attacked Egyptian airfields; and Nasser thereupon closed the canal by sinking blockships, and withdrew his troops from their exposed positions in Sinai.[9]

During the next few days Eden's government came under heavy attack, partly in Parliament where the Labour Party caused such a disturbance that the Speaker was forced to suspend the proceedings for the first time since 1924; partly at the United Nations where even the United States joined in the condemnation of the Anglo-French action, and demanded a cease-fire. About fifteen Conservative MPs condemned Eden's policy, and there were resignations of junior ministers. The agony was all the worse for Eden and his immediate colleagues because the Allied forces could not arrange a simultaneous invasion to coincide with the bombing of the airfields. The landings began only on November 5th, with an airborne drop on Port Said; and troops went ashore from the fleet next morning. But the advance southwards down the canal did not last long. Heavy selling of sterling in New York confronted Harold Macmillan, who had become Chancellor of the Exchequer, with the prospect of a financial crisis; and he was transformed into the advocate of a cease-fire instead of being, as previously, the strongest proponent of those for attack.[10] The advance of the troops was therefore halted at midnight on November 6th/7th. The whole period of hostilities had lasted less than a week and the Allied casualties had been very few. Nasser remained in possession of much of the canal, but, to save the Allies' face, a United Nations force was hurriedly assembled and sent out to take their place in separating the two Middle Eastern combatants.

Churchill was upset by the whole business. It was not that he opposed Eden's policy in its entirety: on the contrary, he made a point of issuing a statement on November 4th, in the form of a letter to the chairman of his constituency organisation, saying that 'I am confident that our American friends will come to realise that, not for the first time, we have acted independently for the common good.'[11] But he was distressed by the breach that had occurred in Anglo-American relations, and he also felt that it was a mistake, having started the operation, not to see it through to its conclusion. As he told Moran, 'To go so far and not go on was madness.'[12]

The course of events had placed Eden under considerable strain, and his health for many years had not been good. He was ordered to rest, and on November 23rd he flew to Jamaica, leaving R. A. Butler in charge of the government. Soon after his return in mid-December, he and his wife dined alone with Sir Winston and Lady Churchill, and Sir Winston appeared to be trying to revive some of the Dunkirk spirit by saying, 'What a magnificent position to fight back from.'[13] But Eden's doctors decided that his health would not allow him to continue as Prime Minister. On January 9th he saw the Queen at Buckingham Palace to resign his post. On the question of his successor, as Macmillan reported, 'he had neither been asked for his advice nor had volunteered it'.[14]

It was not yet the case that the Parliamentary Conservative Party elected its leader; and the Queen in customary fashion sought advice about the succession from senior Conservatives who were not themselves possible candidates. On January 10th in the morning she first saw Lord Salisbury, who had already taken a poll of his colleagues in the Cabinet upon the question, and had found that the great majority preferred Macmillan to Butler, the other obvious contender.[15] She then consulted Churchill, who went round to the Palace in morning dress and a rather shabby old top hat, and also recommended Macmillan. As he later told Butler rather apologetically, 'I went for the older man'; but of course there were other factors.[16] Of the two, he obviously preferred the man who had not been afraid to be a rebel in the 1930s; the man who had served him abroad during the war; and the man who would, as Gladstone once said a prime minister should, 'be a good butcher'.

Churchill's confidence in Macmillan was thoroughly justified. The new government was one of reconciliation – posts being offered to and accepted by MPs from the further wings of the party, both those who had resigned from Eden's government because of the attack on Suez and those who had protested bitterly when the attack was so unexpectedly halted. Although at the outset there was a reimposition of petrol rationing, and the Gallup Poll strongly favoured the Labour Party, the standing of the Macmillan government gradually improved. The terms of trade continued to favour the British economy, and this was helpful in keeping down prices. As for Anglo-American relations, Macmillan who like Churchill had had an American mother, and who had a close friendship with President Eisenhower dating from service together in the Mediterranean campaign of 1942–3, was the ideal person to effect a restoration of good will. Churchill had sent Eisenhower a private letter urging him not to let the Suez crisis destroy the good relations between the two countries, and Eisenhower responded in a friendly way.[17] It was not very long before President and Prime Minister were meeting in the accepted fashion: in fact, their first personal contact after Suez was as early as March 1957, at Bermuda. Meanwhile Duncan Sandys, Churchill's son-in-law, who had now become Minister of Defence with increased powers over the three Services, put into effect the lessons of Suez and of the Global Strategy Paper of Churchill's government by announcing that henceforth British defence policy would be to rely primarily upon the nuclear deterrent, and progressively to cut the armed forces from some 700,000 – the existing figure – to 375,000. Only RAF Transport Command would actually be increased in size, so as to allow the rapid movement of troops from one place to another; National Service would be ended by 1960.[18]

By 1959 the Conservatives had clearly regained their lead in the opinion polls. Divisions in the Labour Party over defence policy in part accounted for this, but it must also have been due to a personal respect for Macmillan, who felt himself to be so thoroughly in control that he could undertake a Commonwealth tour and then pay a visit to Russia. The 1959 Budget was also an occasion for tax relief, with twopence being taken off the cost of beer. It was generally accepted that the election would take place some time that year. The Labour Party, led by Hugh Gaitskell since Attlee's retirement at the end of 1955, made efforts to show a common front for the expected campaign; and Aneurin Bevan, who had uttered harsh words about Gaitskell in the past, accepted his leadership from 1957 and rejected the left-wing proposal of unilateral nuclear disarmament, saying that in any high-level talks about disarmament Britain must not 'go naked into the conference chamber'.[19]

Churchill had been described by the *Times* lobby correspondent in April 1959 as 'regularly in his place just below the gangway'.[20] This was a generous remark in view of his frequent absences in the south of France; but at least he felt prepared to fight another election, and he so declared himself to the Woodford Conservative Association that month at the end of a twenty-two-minute speech. The local members greeted the statement warmly and in due course he was adopted and fought the election, which took place early in October. His only opponent was a Labour candidate, but a new one – Arthur Latham, a methods consultant aged twenty-eight, and already a Romford Borough Councillor. Churchill limited his speaking activities to Woodford alone this time, visiting the constituency for the formal adoption meeting and also for one public meeting before his tours by car two days before polling day and on polling day itself.[21]

The election results came in rapidly that evening (October 8th) and it was soon clear that there was a further swing to the Conservatives. It was just after 1 a.m. that Gaitskell in the American fashion 'conceded defeat' in a television interview.[22]

In the end the Conservatives won 365 seats as against Labour's 258, with six for the Liberals and one Independent. The national swing from Labour to Conservative was 1.1%, and this had been accompanied by a slight increase in turnout. Churchill's personal success, however, was not as great as in 1955: there was a negative swing of 1.8%, and it may be that some Conservatives had heeded the Labour candidate's special appeal for support this time 'because they are dissatisfied with the state of representation they are getting in this constituency'.[23] The figures were:

W. S. Churchill (Conservative)   24,815   Elected
A. C. Latham (Labour)   10,018

As usual, Churchill went through the process of attending the final stage of the count. He walked slowly round the hall where the counting was taking place, and 'talked and joked for several minutes' with his opponent. When the poll was declared he proposed a vote of thanks to the returning officer, as he had so often done before: then he shook hands with his opponent, gave the 'V' sign, and re-entered his car for the return journey to Hyde Park Gate.[24]

Henceforward, owing to increased infirmity, he rarely visited Westminster, although he had now succeeded to the title of 'Father of the House' vacated by David Grenfell, a Labour member continuously since 1922. He tried to make a point of attending on his birthday, so as personally to receive the congratulations of the members. He entered the Chamber on November 30th 1959, and acknowledged the good wishes of both sides of the House on his 85th birthday.[25] The following year he was ill at that time, but in 1961 he again entered the Chamber for a few minutes on his birthday. He finally announced his retirement in May 1963, to take effect at the next general election.[26] He last visited the House on July 27th 1964, four days before the end of the session;[27] and next day, in his absence, Sir Alec Douglas-Home, who was now Prime Minister, moved a motion 'putting on record its [i.e. the House's] unbounded admiration and gratitude for his services to Parliament, to the nation and to the world'.[28] The pattern of the motion followed that of one adopted to give thanks to Wellington in 1814. It was carried 'nem. con.', with support from all quarters of the House.

After his retirement from office there was still one publishing venture to keep him busy and to delay the transition to a life of complete ease. His *History of the English-speaking Peoples* had been in his mind as early as 1931, and, as we have seen, he had signed a contract with Cassell as far back as 1933.[29] When he went to the Admiralty in 1939 he had completed a draft of almost half a million words, but of course he did not have time thereafter to work on proofs. After the war he gave first priority to his war memoirs: their preparation was virtually complete when he again resumed office. The pre-war draft of the *History* was now further revised with the help of a new group of historians, of whom Alan Hodge, editor of the new journal *History Today*, was the co-ordinator.

The first volume, covering the period from Caesar's invasion to the Battle of Bosworth, was published on St George's Day, 1956 – only about a year after Churchill's retirement. As Professor Geoffrey Elton later said, it was greeted with 'a favourable but uneasy reception; historians seemed aware of the writer rather than the writing and could not disguise an almost patronising surprise at "seeing it done at all".'[30] But there were some criticisms of a specific character: the *Times* reviewer noticed that 'social and economic life' seemed to 'get short shrift'.[31] When the second volume appeared, it was even more evident that Churchill's interests were in war and politics, for although this volume covered the years from 1485 to 1688, Shakespeare was not even mentioned in the index.

The third volume carried on the story to 1815, and here Churchill could draw upon his knowledge of Marlborough's life and times. On the other hand the Industrial Revolution, which the anonymous *Listener* reviewer said rather stiffly 'is to some historians the most significant single event in eighteenth century history', was disposed of in a single paragraph.[32] Finally, the fourth volume, dealing with the remainder of the nineteenth century on both sides of the Atlantic, with a full coverage of the battles of the American Civil War – came out in March 1958. Apparently he had difficulty in writing about periods in which there were no wars, and grumbled to Moran about 1830–60 as 'thirty years when nothing happened';[33] and it was a notable American historian, Crane Brinton, who complained that there was 'disproportionate attention' given to the American Civil War, while the development of the British dominions was dealt with in 'comparative brevity'.[34] The work concluded more or less as the author himself was entering on the scene, with the South African War. Harold Nicolson wrote a generous review of it for the *New York Times*, but more frankly described it in his diary as 'really lamentable'.[35]

For the British market the initial print of the first volume was 130,000 copies, but later volumes were published in totals of 150,000. In the United States there was a separate edition published by Dodd, Mead, and there was also a Canadian edition.[36] So far as Churchill was concerned, the preparation of the volumes ended in the early months of 1957. After that, the only substantial work of his to be published was a volume of his speeches from 1953 to 1959, edited as usual by his son Randolph. The last speech in the book was delivered in late October 1959, when Field-Marshal Montgomery unveiled a more than life-size statue of him at Woodford. The title of this volume was again a reminder of his constant concern for Anglo-American association: *The Unwritten Alliance*.

Early in 1963 the two Houses of Congress decided, by large majorities, to confer honorary citizenship of the United States upon him, and in April President Kennedy signed the bill authorising this. There was a brief ceremony at the White House, at which Randolph represented his father and read his message of acceptance, including the sentence: 'I reject the view that Britain and the Commonwealth should now be relegated to a tame and minor role in the world.'[37] Dean Acheson wrily remarked that Churchill was indeed behaving like an American citizen, in that three minutes after becoming one he was attacking an ex-Secretary of State. Acheson, who had served under President Truman, had lately said that 'Great Britain has lost an Empire and has not yet found a role'.[38]

In spite of his strong ties with the United States, therefore, Churchill was as anxious as ever to keep Britain to the fore. In the late 1950s it became evident to him that it was essential to increase the number of scientists and technologists to keep up with the other great powers in what was to be 'the Space Age'. He resolved to do his bit, and in May 1958 launched an appeal for £3,500,000 to establish a 'Churchill' College at Cambridge; he himself promised £25,000 from his Eightieth Birthday Trust Fund.[39] In October 1959 he visited the site of the new college to plant an oak tree, and to announce that with a grant of a million dollars from the Ford Foundation and £50,000 from the Transport and General Workers Union – the latter in memory of Ernest Bevin – the total was now over £3,000,000.[40] The foundation stone of the college buildings was laid in October 1961 by Air-Marshal Lord Tedder, who had become the Chancellor of the University; and the first section was officially opened by the Duke of Edinburgh in 1964. The college, with an annual intake of only about 120 undergraduates a year even by the early 1970s, was not able by itself to do much to speed up the growth of British university education: but it was an earnest of what was to come – the great expansion that followed the government's acceptance of the Robbins Report in 1963.

By 1959 Churchill was eighty-five: he would have been more than human if he had been able to carry on as before. In fact he was again hampered by a succession of small strokes – in June 1955, again a year later, and also in the following October.[41] There were some events in the annual calendar that he tried very hard to avoid giving up, such as the Royal Academy banquet, the 'songs' at Harrow and, of course, the dinners of the Other Club at the Savoy. But he was now very deaf and could walk only with difficulty. He was silent in the House of Commons and made few speeches elsewhere; and a great deal of his time was spent on the French Riviera, at Roquebrune Cap Martin, or at Beaverbrook's villa at Cap d'Ail, or in a penthouse suite of the Hôtel de Paris at Monte Carlo, which was conveniently close to the casino. It was at the Hôtel de Paris in February 1961 that his pet budgerigar, Toby, escaped from its cage and – to Churchill's distress – disappeared for ever, in spite of the best efforts of his private secretary, Anthony Montague Browne (formerly of the Diplomatic Service) and of his personal bodyguard, Detective Sergeant Edmund Murray.[42]

Churchill had by now suffered the loss of many of his oldest and closest friends. In particular, Cherwell, a diabetic, died suddenly of a coronary thrombosis in July 1957; and Brendan Bracken died prematurely (he was only 57) of cancer in August 1958. Churchill had almost lost the will to live on. He told Moran on his 85th birthday: 'I feel very well. I hope I don't go on feeling very well. I don't want to waste time reading novels and playing cards.'[43] That spring he had already paid a final private visit to President Eisenhower in Washington, and had briefly seen both Dulles and General Marshall in Walter Reed Hospital – the former suffering from terminal cancer, the latter from a disabling stroke.

Yet in 1959 he made a new friend – Aristotle Onassis, the Greek millionaire shipowner, who had a luxury yacht, the *Christina*, which he based on the French Riviera. Onassis invited him and Clementine to accompany him on Mediterranean and Atlantic cruises, and on several occasions in the years 1959–63 they accepted, and visited places as far east as Istanbul and as far west as the West Indies and New York. Onassis was evidently happy to do everything he could to make things as agreeable as possible for his distinguished guest; and one advantage of this form of travel which must have been apparent to Churchill was that it took him away from the press and the crowds of photographers who otherwise would beset him everywhere.

Some of the limelight which was directed upon Churchill's own activities was shared by members of his family. They did what they could to protect their father from undue publicity; but sometimes they found that they could not avoid the harsh glare themselves. Although they were all very loyal to their father, and tended to copy his behaviour in various respects, for example by drinking heavily, they did not all have the iron constitution which was one of his greatest assets. Randolph's attempts to re-enter Parliament seem to have ended with his failure to be adopted for the safe Conservative seat of Bournemouth East and Christchurch in 1959 when the sitting member, Nigel Nicolson, was ejected owing to having opposed the Suez operation.[44] He was already in his late forties, and was proving to be a successful political journalist and biographer – his life of *Lord Derby, King of Lancashire* was published in 1959. He had an attractive country home at East Bergholt, Suffolk; but he separated from his second wife, June, in 1961.[45]

Apart from Mary, all of the Churchill children suffered the breakdown of their marriages. Diana's second marriage to Duncan Sandys seemed to be successful for many years, but they broke up in 1960, and in 1962 she decided that she 'wished to be known in future as Mrs Diana Churchill'.[46] For several months she undertook unpaid work for the Samaritans, aiding people in mental distress; but in October 1963 she suddenly took her own life with a 'single, massive dose' of sleeping tablets.[47] She was just over fifty-four years old, and her three children were now all grown up. As for Sarah, her second husband, Antony Beauchamp, had also committed suicide as long ago as 1957; but Sarah continued her stage career and at Christmas 1958 played the title role in *Peter Pan* at the Scala Theatre in London.[48] She did not find it easy to adapt to the humdrum world of provincial theatri-cals, and was in and out of court on several occasions on charges of being 'drunk and disorderly'. But in April 1962 she married again. This time her husband was Lord Audley, the holder of an ancient peerage who lived abroad a good deal, and died in Granada, Spain, in July 1963.[49]

It seemed as if only Mary had an entirely happy family life. In May 1959 she gave birth to her fifth child – Churchill's tenth and last grandchild, later christened Rupert Christopher.[50] By this time her husband, Christopher Soames, was Secretary of State for War and clearly destined for a distinguished political career, It was, however, a child of Diana's, Celia Sandys, married to Piers Dixon, son of the diplomat Sir Pierson Dixon, who late in 1962 gave Churchill his first great-grandchild, a boy who was christened Mark Pierson.[51] Churchill was used to this mixture of generations: indeed it was only late in 1964 that his own step-father – Montagu Porch, Lady Randolph's last husband – died at the age of eighty-seven.[52]

From the spring of 1958 onwards Churchill was looked after personally by a new 'man' who was not so much a valet as a nurse. This was Roy Howells, who later wrote an account of his work in this post, which lasted until Churchill's death in January 1965. As sometimes happens with very old people, his eyesight actually improved and he was able to read without glasses. He was very deaf but he had an effective hearing-aid, though he frequently preferred to have it switched off. His real weakness was that he was very shaky on his feet, and Howells got into the habit of walking closely behind him in case he stumbled.[53]

But Howells could not always be there to catch him if he fell; and in mid-November 1960 Churchill fell to the floor of his bedroom at Hyde Park Gate, and fractured a bone in his back. He had to enter St Mary's Hospital, Paddington, for a time; but after three weeks he was up, and he was able to spend Christmas with his family at Chartwell. On the whole, his recovery was quite a good one: in 1961 he was able to go out to dinner several times, taking Onassis to the Other Club on one occasion, and also attending for more than an hour the coming-out dance of his grand-daughter Celia Sandys at Quaglino's.[54]

In the summer of 1962 he had a more serious fall, which occurred shortly after his arrival at the Hôtel de Paris in Monte Carlo. Dr David Roberts, a doctor who lived on the Riviera and had a practice in the English-speaking colony there, attended him at once and arranged for him to go to the Princess Grace Clinic nearby. There a plaster was put on his leg, and next day he was taken from Nice to London in an RAF Comet which the Prime Minister had ordered to fly out for him. He then went by ambulance to the Middlesex Hospital, and shortly underwent an operation to set the bone. Within three weeks he was reported to be walking unaided, but he stayed in hospital for another five weeks, partly because of alterations to his home at Hyde Park Gate to enable him to live on the ground floor. Meanwhile, he remained tolerably cheerful, especially as films were shown in the evening in his hospital bedroom after dinner.[55]

Early in November 1962 he attended a dinner of the Other

Club at the Savoy; and he repeated the excursion a month later. But he did not go to the Commons on his birthday, and he blamed his 1962 fall for his retirement from Parliament, saying in May 1963 that 'the accident which I suffered last year has greatly decreased my mobility'.[56] His secretary, Anthony Montague Browne, was increasingly responsible for organising his life and also acted as his Press Officer. But the domestic side, although supervised by Clementine, was really managed by Clementine's secretary, Grace Hamblin. Even in this phase of his life, the staff were numerous. There were two female secretaries to deal with his personal mail; two female nurses apart from Roy Howells; and a butler and a cook.

Late in 1964 Churchill attained his ninetieth birthday, and evidently enjoyed the occasion as he always did. The day before, he appeared at the window of 28 Hyde Park Gate to greet a crowd which had gathered outside. That evening he watched with great interest a special programme on BBC television, *Ninety Years On*, which was introduced by Noël Coward and which incorporated many of his favourite music-hall songs. On his birthday itself there were, of course, many presents and messages, including a gift of flowers from the Queen. He had a champagne lunch in bed and later received in his bedroom the new Prime Minister, Harold Wilson, who conveyed to him the good wishes of the Labour Cabinet. He got up only for his dinner party, the invitations to which, apart from the Colvilles and the Montague Brownes, were limited to members of the family: all the same, nineteen people sat down to dine.[57]

But there was little now to keep Churchill's interest in life alive. His oldest friend, Max Beaverbrook, died in June 1964; Bernard Baruch, his only contemporary, was separated from him by the Atlantic; and now that he was no longer an MP the link with day-to-day politics was gone. He still enjoyed his meals, and took a postprandial cigar and glass of brandy. But on Saturday, January 9th 1965 there came a change, for that night he refused both cigar and brandy. Next day he lay in bed with no appetite or apparent interest in the world. On Monday he was examined by Moran and Russell Brain, and they found that he had had another stroke.[58] But his powers of recovery had previously been so great that no immediate announcement was made. It was not until the following Friday, January 15th, that Moran gave a first bulletin from the pavement in front of the house:

'After a cold, Sir Winston has developed a circulatory weakness and there has been a cerebral thrombosis.'[59]

It was generally realised that this stroke was likely to prove fatal. Indeed, the *Times* medical correspondent commented on the following Monday: 'Life is clearly ebbing away, but how long it will be until the crossing of the bar it is impossible to say.'[60] The Prime Minister postponed a policy statement to the Commons, and the ordinary course of politics was suspended. For several days Moran read a daily bulletin from the doorstep of the house to the newsmen and photographers who were massed in the Hyde Park Gate *cul de sac*. Meanwhile Churchill slipped into deeper unconsciousness, but still he stayed alive. According to Moran, 'for fourteen days he was not seen to move', and he must have been unaware of the birth of a baby son to Minnie Churchill, née d'Erlanger, the wife of his grandson Winston, on January 22nd. Sarah, Lady Audley, had flown home from Italy, and the other members of the family had been visiting regularly; Mary Soames sometimes took her mother out for a drive to enable her to relax a little, but the strain of the noise caused by the crowd was such that Clementine had to ask everyone to withdraw to the end of the road; it was arranged that Moran's bulletins should go direct to the news agencies.

Finally, on Sunday morning, January 24th – the seventieth anniversary of his father's death – 'his breathing became shallow and laboured', and just after 8 a.m. his life ebbed away.[61] Apart from Clementine, his three surviving children, and his grandchildren Winston Churchill Junior and Celia Sandys, four other people were present – Montague Browne, Lord Moran and the two nurses on duty, Ann Huddleston and Roy Howells.[62]

After Churchill's death, it was announced almost at once that he would have a state funeral – a privilege rarely accorded to a person not of royal blood. The decision had been made seven years earlier at the suggestion of the Queen, when Macmillan was Prime Minister.[63] The date chosen was the following Saturday, January 30th. Churchill himself had first thought of being buried at his beloved Chartwell, but several years before he died he changed his mind and decided upon a grave at Bladon, near Woodstock, in the village churchyard where his parents and his brother Jack were buried.[64] During the intervening days there were no meetings of Parliament. There was, however, a lying-in-state in Westminster Hall, and over 320,000 people filed past to pay their last respects.[65] For one short period the servicemen keeping guard at the four corners of the catafalque were replaced by the Speaker and the three leaders of the political parties. At another time the Chiefs of Staff, now four in number owing to the appointment of a Chief of Defence Staff in 1964 (the first being Earl Mountbatten of Burma) took the stand.

The day of the funeral was bitterly cold. But in the usual fashion a procession formed to take the coffin on a gun-carriage from Westminster Hall to St Paul's Cathedral for the service. The ladies of the family went in carriages, but the menfolk all walked, wearing overcoats and top hats. It was quite a long journey – all the way up Whitehall, along the Strand and Fleet Street, and up Ludgate Hill. The Queen waived her prerogative and waited in the Cathedral for the procession to arrive; with her were many other heads of state – four kings, the Queen of the Netherlands and Queen Elizabeth, the Queen Mother, and the Presidents of France – now General de Gaulle – and of Iceland, Israel, Uruguay and Zambia. Many Commonwealth prime ministers attended, as did Dr Erhart, the Federal German Chancellor, and Marshal Koniev, representing the USSR. After the service – which was enlivened by the 'Battle Hymn of the Republic' – the coffin was taken for embarkation by launch from Tower Hill to Waterloo, and as the launch left the pier there was a nineteen-gun salute and a flypast of RAF Lightning aircraft.

The final journey was accomplished by steam train from Waterloo to a station near Blenheim Palace. The locomotive was one of a post-war class called 'The Battle of Britain', and this one, appropriately, had the name 'Winston Churchill'. Leslie Rowan, one of Churchill's wartime secretaries who had been invited to join the train, later wrote:

Two single figures whom I saw from the carriage window epitomised for me what Churchill really meant to ordinary people: first, on the flat roof of a house, a man standing at attention in his old RAF uniform, saluting; and then, in a field some hundreds of yards away from the track, a simple farmer stopping work and standing, head bowed, and cap in hand.[66]

31. *Conclusion*

IN the last few years of his life Churchill was often referred to as 'the greatest living Englishman'. It is difficult to compare his career with those of previous English statesmen, because circumstances have varied so much. His long experience of high office – first joining the Cabinet in 1908 and leaving it as Prime Minister in 1955 – was surpassed only by Gladstone, who first became a Cabinet minister in 1843 and finally retired in 1894. But Gladstone was essentially a peacetime minister; and Churchill's achievement in rallying the country against its external enemies reminds one rather of the career of the elder Pitt, who had a similar self-confidence: 'I am sure that I can save this country, and that nobody else can.'[1] Churchill also had a greater versatility than either Gladstone or Pitt. If his ability as a painter was not that of a distinguished professional, it was not far short; and his work as an historian has left a remarkable corpus of work for the edification of future generations. Disraeli might compare with him in this respect, because of his novels; but he was Prime Minister for seven years, as against Churchill's eight and a half, and was in the Cabinet for only another four.

The only statesman who could compare with Churchill in his own time was Lloyd George, who was his senior by almost twelve years. Churchill readily recognised the ability of Lloyd George, first as an architect of social reform, and then as a man who could see the essential needs of war. In July 1915, when he himself was gradually being edged out of office, he wrote to Sinclair, 'L.G. is necessary to the state. He has the warmaking quality. I do not intend to allow my personal feelings to prevent my working with him.'[2] In the course of the Second World War, when Lloyd George was still thought of by some as a possible alternative leader, Churchill told Crozier of the *Manchester Guardian*: 'He may have more imagination and depth as PM than I have, but I have more experience, and know more, of war.'[3]

Churchill's active life spanned an epoch in British history. At the outset, the Empire was at its apogee, and the army was engaged in minor colonial wars in Asia and Africa in which the principal weapons were the rifle, the revolver, the sabre and the lance. When he retired, he and other heads of government were grappling with the threat of thermonuclear war; and the balance of power had altered so far that Britain could merely endeavour to exercise a moderating influence upon the two world super-powers, the United States and Russia. The strategy and tactics of war had always absorbed him, and he had played an important part in bringing to birth several of the major new weapons of twentieth-century warfare: the tank in the First World War, the craft and other equipment for opposed landings in the Second World War, and above all the atomic bomb. In both wars his own role was a vital one – but it was only after his demonstration of leadership in 1940 that he came to be recognised as pre-eminent above all other British politicians. Thereafter he had no rival.

In fact in the era of the late 1940s the challenge came not from a man but from a movement, of which the Labour Party was the political arm. Clement Attlee was not in any sense fitted to play the role of personal rival to Churchill: nor did he seek such a role. On personal grounds the two men were on good terms; Attlee had always approved of the Dardanelles operation, and in the Second World War he had served loyally in Churchill's War Cabinet. Attlee had in fact been elected Leader of the Labour Party partly because of his very modest pretensions, which seemed to contrast favourably with the arrogance of Ramsay MacDonald, the 'lost leader'. After being defeated by Churchill in 1951 Attlee and his wife went to live in a cottage just outside the grounds of Chequers, whence he was occasionally invited up for a meal by his successor, almost as if he were a retired courtier.

Attlee was asked by the *Observer* to prepare an obituary notice of his predecessor and successor as Prime Minister, and he wrote a shrewd comment in which he described Churchill as 'rather like a layer cake. One layer was certainly seventeenth century. The eighteenth century in him is obvious. There was the nineteenth century, and a large slice, of course, of the twentieth century; and another, curious, layer which may possibly have been the twenty-first'.[4] A man born in Blenheim Palace, for a time heir to the dukedom which dated from the early eighteenth century, could not but have some sense of the continuity of English life. This encouraged his interest in history, and the success of his early writings, including studies of the campaigns on the North-West Frontier of India and in the Sudan, collected journalism about the South African War, and also an impressive biography of his father, was followed between the wars by the *World Crisis*, the biography of Marlborough and the first draft of his *History of the English-speaking Peoples*. As the Second World War developed, Churchill's role became more and more like that of Marlborough – to sustain an alliance in which his own country was but one of several participants, and to develop a strategy leading to the victory of the disparate partners. But, as Attlee indicated, he had a mind keenly interested in the future as well as in the past. He enormously enjoyed the novels of H. G. Wells, the 'science fiction' of the era – he said once that he 'could pass an examination in them'.[5] They encouraged him to think of new ways of winning wars, and his friend Lindemann enlightened him about the possibilities of atomic energy long before the manufacture of 'the Bomb'.

It was in part this interest in the future that made him enjoy his visits to the United States, where so much was going on that seemed to open up new prospects for humanity. His American parentage gave him a head start in forming transatlantic friendships, and at the critical moment when Anglo-American co-operation was essential he could readily establish cordial relations with American leaders – with President Franklin Roosevelt himself, and also with the President's personal agents such as Harry Hopkins and Averell Harriman. Similar cordiality developed between him and the principal American generals, notably Generals Marshall and Eisenhower. With Russia, the other major ally against Nazism, it was not so easy. There was a legacy of distrust, partly owing to Churchill's role in the civil war after the Bolshevik Revolution. He recognised that it was essential to visit Stalin personally, so as to explain to him the strategic possibilities; and in this way he was able to overcome at least some of the previous suspicion. His belief in personal contacts of this nature came to the fore again in the early 1950s, but his object was frustrated owing to American intransigence after the Korean War, and owing to his own ill-health. All the same, the man who had been, for most people in the West, the first herald of the 'Cold War', was also the first statesman of the Western world to seek, and indeed to achieve, a degree of *détente* in the 1950s.

Churchill did not fit easily into the party system of modern British politics. He set forth in his father's footsteps as a 'Tory Democrat' critical of the leadership of the Conservative Party. But the living political leader whom he most admired – also a friend of his father's – was Rosebery, the last of the Whigs and the exponent of a new Liberal Imperialism which emphasised the cause of 'National Efficiency'. In 1903, when Joseph Chamberlain propounded the policy of Tariff Reform, and Arthur Balfour, the Prime Minister, showed no sign of completely disavowing it, Churchill had his excuse to leave the Conservative Party, which he did with a number of other Free Traders. He was after all MP for an industrial constituency in Lancashire, Oldham, which owing to its dependence upon the cotton trade was bound to suffer if Chamberlain's policy were accepted. At the general election of January 1906 he was able to secure a personal triumph in Manchester, where he fought the seat which contained the commercial centre of the city, and won it from the Conservatives. Although he was little over thirty years old, he seemed destined for Cabinet office, and secured it in 1908 when Asquith succeeded Campbell-Bannerman.

The origins of the Asquithian social reforms are still disputed by historians; but it seems that, apart from the personal ambitions of the 'Young Turks' of the Liberal Cabinet, Lloyd George and Churchill, the impulse was more a matter of keeping up with the Tariff Reformers – who promised to deal with the problem of unemployment – than to rival the nascent Labour Party, which was still regarded as an ally. For some time Churchill was content to serve as a lieutenant of Lloyd George, who was the master-mind of the strategy of social reform in the early years of the Asquith government. So, too, behind the cut and thrust of debate on Ireland and the Reform of the Lords, he agreed with Lloyd George that it might be best of all if the two major parties could form a coalition for the solution of problems which were evidently leading towards deadlock.

In 1911, with the Agadir crisis, Churchill recognised a new

imperative: the need to prepare the country, and in particular the navy – for Asquith made him the First Lord of the Admiralty in that year – for an expected clash with Germany. When the war came, he was fertile in expedients to ensure the success of British arms, but he did not have the supreme power to ensure that his plans were carried out as he wished. A section of the Conservative Party – not by any means all, for he was a warm friend of some of its leaders – was anxious for his dismissal, and this took place, by stages, in 1915. For a few months, in 1915–16, he served with the infantry on the Western Front. But then in 1917 his old ally Lloyd George, who had now become Prime Minister, summoned him to become Minister of Munitions. Henceforward, not just until the end of the war but until the fall of the Coalition in 1922, Churchill was in office with Conservative and Lloyd George Liberal colleagues – a situation which he would have liked to maintain still longer, but which the rank and file of the Conservative Party decided to terminate.

The second main turning-point of Churchill's career in party politics came between 1922 and 1924, when he was an exile from Parliament. First, when Baldwin, the new Conservative Leader, took up Tariff Reform, he rejoined the Liberal Party and fought an unsuccessful battle in a Leicester constituency; but then, when a depleted Liberal Party under Asquith decided to place the Labour Party in office, he became an Independent and was pleased to find that Baldwin had for the time being at least abandoned the idea of carrying Tariff Reform. From this moment he was prepared to rejoin the Conservative Party, and it was simply a matter of finding a constituency which would allow him to make the transition without embarrassment. When in the general election of 1924 he returned to the House as a 'Constitutionalist', he was delighted to accept from Baldwin the post of Chancellor of the Exchequer.

After the Conservative defeat in the 1929 election, Baldwin was soon under attack from Beaverbrook and Rothermere for his unwillingness to adopt a policy of Imperial Preference. Churchill also found occasion to disagree with his leader, but naturally it was not on this issue: it was rather that he objected to Baldwin's acceptance of the Irwin Declaration promising Dominion Status for India. It seems that Churchill was genuinely concerned about the dangers of Irwin's policy, but he also saw the issue as one which might bring together elements from the Conservative and Liberal Parties, and thus restore the Coalition which had broken in 1922. In this, he was evidently influenced by his friend F. E. Smith, Earl of Birkenhead, who had been Secretary for India in Baldwin's government.

But Birkenhead fell ill and died in 1930; and Churchill was left in isolation, to become even more lonely when in 1931 a National Government of all the parties was formed under Ramsay MacDonald. MacDonald's persistence in office, in spite of the fact that his National Labour group was so tiny, appears to have owed something to his desire to secure Dominion Status for India; but on this issue Churchill maintained his opposition and managed to rally a good deal of support within the Conservative Party as the Government of India Bill went through the House of Commons. He was trying to overthrow MacDonald (and Baldwin) as Baldwin had overthrown Lloyd George. The struggle continued until the eve of the 1935 general election, when Churchill acknowledged defeat and returned to the ranks of Baldwin's supporters for the succeeding contest.

He had already begun to feel alarmed about the slow pace of British rearmament, in face of the threat from Nazi Germany; but it was difficult for him to rouse the Commons, partly because he had already used his most violent language in denouncing Gandhi and the Indian Congress Party. Gradually his warnings began to be heeded by his colleagues and by members of other political parties, and by the end of 1936 he was – through no very effective organising of his own – the main speaker in a campaign to arouse the country to the danger of war. At this juncture the Abdication Crisis suddenly erupted and he felt obliged to take the part of King Edward VIII – just at the moment when MPs of all parties were acknowledging Baldwin's skilful leadership and accepting that Abdication was what their constituents really wanted. Lord Winterton later said that in almost fifty years' membership of the House this was the only occasion when he had heard a member hissed or booed.[6] When next year Neville Chamberlain took over the Premiership from Baldwin, Churchill's reputation was still not much above its nadir.

Churchill grew very impatient in the later 1930s as Chamberlain stubbornly refused to establish a proper Ministry of Defence or to accept Churchill himself back into the Cabinet. It was after all undoubtedly true that no other Conservative leader could rival his knowledge of the three Services and their supply. But, as he himself later wrote, 'Over me beat the invisible wings.'[7] He escaped all responsibility for the condition of British arms at the outbreak of war, and this served him well in the critical months of 1940, when he was still consolidating his power as Prime Minister.

Yet he had cause to appreciate the fact that in May 1940 it was the Labour Party which precipitated the crisis that led to his premiership. The Labour leaders did not insist upon a Churchill premiership: rather, they vetoed Chamberlain, and thus forced a choice between Churchill and Halifax. The decisive factor in the crisis was Halifax's recognition that Churchill had the energy and experience to assume the role of war leader, while he himself had not. For some time the Conservative backbenchers seemed lukewarm in their support of Churchill, and it was only during the Oran debate early in July that they expressed themselves warmly in his support. After his remarkable demonstration of authority in the course of the summer and early autumn, there could be no rival for the leadership of the Conservative Party when Chamberlain was obliged to give it up owing to illness.

The Liberal and Labour Parties remained loyal in their support of Churchill in spite of the fact that he had become the Conservative leader. Their discontent emerged only later in the war, on the Beveridge Report and other questions of post-war reconstruction. Their parliamentary representatives were harassed by the appearance of the Common Wealth Party, which performed remarkably well at by-elections which they were unable to contest owing to the electoral truce. But there was no parliamentary rival to Churchill after 1940, and attempts to make Lloyd George – now old and frail – into the 'queen bee' of the Opposition were stillborn.[8] Nevertheless, the reputation of the Conservative Party had sunk so low that not even Churchill's prestige could save it from overwhelming defeat in the 1945 general election.

Churchill was now over seventy, and he might well have chosen to retire from the rough and tumble of partisan politics. But he was still fit, and he therefore decided to fight another day and to win his revenge, if he could, over the Labour Party. For some years he appeared to be more partisan than at any other time since the 1920s, and he used every device that rhetoric or parliamentary tactics could suggest to bring Attlee's government to defeat. Yet it was not out of character that as soon as he was able to resume office in 1951 he virtually ignored the Parliamentary Conservative Party in forming his ministry, brought back as many as he could of the non-party men of wartime, and also did his best to recruit into his Cabinet Clement Davies, the leader of the Liberal Party. It is not surprising that Sir Derek Walker Smith, then the Chairman of the 1922 Committee of back-bench Conservatives, has described Churchill at that time as 'a formidable, isolated and elevated figure'.[9] As his eightieth birthday approached, and as it became more and more apparent that his only remaining interest was to secure a meeting of the Great Powers at the 'Summit', members of all parties looked to him as a man of Olympian stature above the ordinary level of domestic politics.

It is sometimes maintained that Churchill's career after the Second World War was something of an anticlimax. Attlee – who was certainly a partisan on the matter – described his second period of government as 'a mistake from every point of view'.[10] This ungenerous opinion does not do justice to the facts. In the spring of 1946 Churchill had startled the world with his Fulton speech, in which he warned of the Russian 'iron curtain' that had descended across Europe: this was not warmly appreciated at the time, but it was taken later to have been prophetic in character. In the late summer of that year, at Zürich, he took up the theme of European unity, and the reconciliation of France and Germany: again, he spoke ahead of his time. When he took office in 1951, the need to resist Russian pressure in Western Europe and to set on foot some form of federation between the powers had become accepted truths.

Nor was his second government a failure. A period of relaxation was desirable after the period of vigorous domestic reorganisation which had characterised the Attlee years; and Churchill was at great pains to ensure that relations between the TUC and the government, at least, should be on a friendly basis. His own interests lay largely in the field of Great Power negotiation; and if, partly for this reason, he neglected the opportunities of European unity for Britain herself, it could not be said that his personal views were more conservative than those of the bulk of his colleagues, or indeed of Attlee himself. The Global Strategy Paper, which he persuaded the Chiefs of Staff to work out as a policy for the nuclear age, was in advance of any document produced up to that date in the United States, the leading military power of the time. His second government was also successful because it was lucky: the terms of trade were steadily improving in favour of Britain in the early 1950s, and his Chancellor, R. A. Butler, could reduce taxation and remove the trammels of rationing which still afflicted the housewife. It was probably this, more than anything else, which accounted for the government's success at the polls in 1955, it being the first for ninety years to increase its grip at a peacetime election.

If a man outlives the great bulk of his contemporaries, some of his ideas are likely to seem old-fashioned to a younger generation. The idea of racial equality – of placing the Asian and the African on a par with the Anglo-Saxon – was not very appealing to Churchill. Nevertheless he had no elaborate concept of racial superiority, and he used the word 'race' in a very loose sense to mean a 'nation': he spoke, for instance, of the English and the Irish as 'two ancient races'.[11] He always sympathised with Zionism, and declared his hostility to Nazi anti-Semitism from the start of Hitler's regime. In April 1933 he declared that 'this persecution of the Jews ... distresses everyone who feels that men and women have a right to live in the world where they are born, and have a right to pursue a livelihood which has hitherto been guaranteed them under the public laws of the land of their birth'.[12]

His attitude to the British Empire itself was also that of a Victorian or an Edwardian. He tended to speak about the 'English' rather than about the 'British', and there seemed to be in his way of thinking a tacit subordinating of the Scots and the Welsh, as well as of the self-governing peoples of the Dominions, all of whom he regarded as part of the Westminster-centred 'Empire'. During the Second World War Roosevelt was inclined to take the part of the Indian Congress Party, and to assume that self-government could be achieved in India as it was in the American colonies. Yet for the sake of convenience in strategic planning he was quite prepared to abet Churchill's claim to speak for all the territories owing allegiance to the Crown – often to the grave annoyance of ministers in Canada and Australia.[13]

His lack of religious belief was perhaps more in keeping with modern views – though it was not out of line, in all probability, with the attitude of his parents and their cosmopolitan 'set'. Yet his own career was so successful that he could not forbear from regarding himself as in some way the fulfilment of a grand design worked out by an impersonal Providence. As he told the United States Congress early in 1942, 'He must indeed have a blind soul who cannot see that some great purpose and design is being worked out here below, of which we have the honour to be the faithful servants'.[14] No doubt this was language which the Congress would wish to hear anyway, but it occurs so widely in other works by Churchill that it is difficult not to believe that he accepted its truth. He was not, however, a man for personal religious observance; although he went to memorial services and the like, he was not a regular churchgoer; and frequently at Chartwell and at Chequers Clementine would attend the parish church alone or with one or other of the children. He certainly did not take with high seriousness the appointment of bishops, which was one of his duties as Prime Minister but frequently largely delegated to Brendan Bracken – the photographs of the possible candidates playing an important part in their selection.

In the last resort, the most prominent of Churchill's convictions was a sense of English patriotism, combined with an intense loyalty to the Crown, to his own family and cousinhood, and to his friends. At times this led him into acute difficulty, for instance in supporting Edward VIII when almost everyone else had deserted him, and in retaining the ageing Admiral Sir Roger Keyes, the hero of Zeebrugge, as the Chief of Combined Operations in the early part of the Second World War. His patriotism and his exceptional martial courage meant that he did not feel personally the sharp reaction of so many people in the 1930s that another war like that of 1914–18 must be avoided at all costs. Throughout his life he had been taking risks and enjoying them – first as a cavalry officer, then in the early days of flying, and then in the trenches when he wrote to Clementine that shell-fire 'did not make me jump a bit – not a pulse quickened'.[15] He was to show the same qualities in the Second World War, whether in the air raids on London or on the battle-fronts, to the alarm and concern of the officers who were accompanying him.

Naturally such a man was very well qualified to exhort others at moments of danger, as the whole world discovered in the critical months of 1940. Two other episodes in which he displayed this quality are also worth mentioning. The first occurred when he was under fire from the Boers during the derailment of the armoured train in 1899: he persuaded the already-injured engine-driver to return to his duty by assuring him that a man was never wounded twice in the same battle – and also that he would be rewarded for his gallantry.[16] The second was perhaps less effective, but nevertheless not unimpressive. Beaverbrook told Crozier, the editor of the *Manchester Guardian*, that when in 1942 they were flying together eastwards across the Atlantic – at a time when there were still many dangers in such a venture – the plane ran into bad weather: 'We saw snow beginning to fall thickly.... Churchill, who was sitting by me, said "It's all right. There's no need to worry. We can turn off to Lisbon or to the Azores, or we can turn back and return to America, so everything will be all right." And I knew that it was not true.'[17]

By the end of his career Churchill had become 'Father of the House', and it was his claim that he had always been devoted to its ways and customs. This was not entirely true, for we have seen that there were periods when his attendances were far from regular. Attlee was not unfair in saying that he was 'not a great Parliamentarian, mainly of course because he was too impatient to master the procedures'.[18] Nor was he a good debater as some of his contemporaries were, such as Lloyd George or Birken-head. He had to prepare his speeches with the utmost care, and it was of course greatly to his credit that he never spared himself in this task; but they were then, to quote Attlee again, 'magnificent rhetorical performances, but ... too stately, too pompous, too elaborate to be ideal House of Commons stuff'.[19] Aneurin Bevan put this into a rather striking metaphor: 'He had to wheel himself up to battle like an enormous gun.'[20] This was not very different from what Balfour had said of him sixty years earlier: 'It is not, on the whole, desirable to come down to this House with invective which is both prepared and violent.'[21]

On this topic, Sir Oswald Mosley, the Fascist leader, has had a word to say based upon his acquaintance with Churchill as a parliamentary colleague in the 1920s. When a Homeric quotation was unexpectedly used against himself, he asked Churchill for its provenance, and Churchill said that he had obtained it from Bartlett's *Familiar Quotations*.[22] Certainly a perusal of that work suggests one or two phrases that must later have been adapted to a Churchillian purpose, such as this one from Napier's *Peninsular War*: 'Napoleon's troops fought in bright fields, where every helmet caught some gleams of glory; but the British soldier conquered under the cool shade of aristocracy. No honours awaited his daring....'[23] When Churchill became Prime Minister, one of his first acts was to ask Eddie Marsh to recommend him a new book of quotations – perhaps feeling that Bartlett's, being American, was not quite appropriate for him in his new office.[24] It is not known what work Marsh suggested, the *Oxford Book* not being published in its first edition until 1941.

It was also true that Churchill lacked all capacity to engage in intrigue, and partly for this reason he never acquired a following until he was elected leader of the Conservative Party. Again, to quote Bevan, he was 'too much of the egotist to know about other men's minds'.[25] Archibald Sinclair said that his efforts in this direction were 'boyish and puerile', and that he was 'the most candid, ingenuous and impulsive person in the world'.[26] Such a man might not be expected to be very loyal to the House of Commons throughout his career. Nor was he: in 1955 he was offered a dukedom by the Queen, and had gone so far as to select a title – Duke of London – when he was persuaded not to accept by the man who would have inherited it from him, his son Randolph.[27]

Churchill's major historical works are sometimes criticised for being too rhetorical, and they were, as we have seen, prepared in the same way as his speeches, being dictated in the first instance directly on to a secretary's notebook or typewriter. Because he did not keep a diary, they often contain small errors of fact when he recounts from memory some episode of recent history. But he was generous both to political opponents and to subordinates, and because the books are always interlaced with documentary material they form a unique record of the times they record. It is true that much of his work between the wars was pure journalism; but he rarely allowed his work simply to be 'ghosted', and although much of it was republished in book form much more remains to be offered again to a public still interested in the career of so remarkable a man.

Journalism was, of course, an important part of his life, both at the beginning of his career and again between the wars; and his editors admired his capacity to submit his copy 'clean' and in good time. Because he knew the problems of journalism from the business side, he acquired a sense of good public relations. He read the newspapers in their first editions in the middle of the night – and not just the newspapers that he liked but all the newspapers, including the *Daily Worker*: so that when there was a spare copy of the *Worker* at the Westerham newspaper shop the local correspondent would know that he was not at home at Chartwell.[28] He soon settled upon a more or less distinctive appearance for himself to attract the photographers: there was the variety of hats, including the flat-topped so-called 'Cambridge' hat; there was the range of uniforms, from that of an Elder Brother of Trinity House to that of an RAF Commodore; and, often even when in uniform, there was the cigar, usually unlit or in the process of being lit, and, from 1941 onwards, the 'V' sign.

Yet in the last resort Churchill's most endearing quality was his evident humanity. This reflected or seemed to reflect the mood of the people in the country: there was nothing of the remote intellectual about him. The trouble that he took in making friends with birds or animals; the puckish humour that he often displayed; the manifest enjoyment with which he received honours and presents, especially on his birthday; and the ease with which he was moved to tears at the sight of human misery; all these things made the ordinary person feel that, scion of a ducal family though he was, he was instinctively on the side of the man or woman in the street. An episode of 1940 or 1941, not generally known, may serve as a final impression. It was recorded by one of his private secretaries, John Peck:

> Driving down to Chequers one Friday evening, when the bombing was at its worst, he saw a very long queue of people lined up outside a shop in a poor quarter of London, and he stopped and sent his detective to see what the shortage was that had caused it. It was a queue for birdseed. Winston wept.[29]

APPENDIX A

OFFICES OF STATE HELD BY WINSTON CHURCHILL

December 1905: Under-Secretary of State for the Colonies

April 1908: President of the Board of Trade

February 1910: Home Secretary

October 1911: First Lord of the Admiralty

May to November 1915: Chancellor of the Duchy of Lancaster

July 1917: Minister of Munitions

January 1919: Secretary of State for War and Air

February 1921: Secretary of State for the Colonies (retaining Air Ministry until April 1921)

Relinquished office on LG's resignation in October 1922

November 1924: Chancellor of the Exchequer

Relinquished office on Baldwin's resignation in June 1929

September 1939: First Lord of the Admiralty

May 1940: Prime Minister and Minister of Defence

Resigned office in July 1945

October 1951: Prime Minister and Minister of Defence

Relinquished Ministry of Defence in March 1952

Resigned as Prime Minister in April 1955

APPENDIX B

WINSTON CHURCHILL'S BOOKS (with London publishers)

The Story of the Malakand Field Force, Longmans, 1898
The River War (2 vols), Longmans, 1899
Savrola, Longmans, 1900
London to Ladysmith, Longmans, 1900
Ian Hamilton's March, Longmans, 1900
Lord Randolph Churchill (2 vols), Macmillan, 1906
My African Journey, Hodder & Stoughton, 1908
Liberalism and the Social Problem, Hodder & Stoughton, 1909
The People's Rights, Hodder & Stoughton, 1910
The World Crisis (5 vols), Thornton Butterworth, 1923–31
My Early Life, Thornton Butterworth, 1930
India, Thornton Butterworth, 1931
Thoughts and Adventures, Thornton Butterworth, 1932
Marlborough: His Life and Times (4 vols), Harrap, 1933–8
Great Contemporaries, Thornton Butterworth, 1937
Arms and the Covenant (speeches, ed. R. S. Churchill), Harrap, 1938
Step by Step, 1936–1939 (articles), Thornton Butterworth, 1939
Into Battle (speeches, ed. R. S. Churchill), Cassell, 1941
The Second World War (6 vols), Cassell, 1948–54
The Sinews of Peace (speeches, ed. R. S. Churchill), Cassell, 1948
Europe Unite (speeches, ed. R. S. Churchill), Cassell, 1950
In the Balance (speeches, ed. R. S. Churchill), Cassell, 1951
The War Speeches (3 vols, ed. C. Eade), Cassell, 1952
Stemming the Tide (speeches, ed. R. S. Churchill), Cassell, 1953
A History of the English-Speaking Peoples (4 vols), Cassell, 1956–8
The Unwritten Alliance (speeches, ed. R. S. Churchill), Cassell, 1961

APPENDIX C

SELECT LIST OF UNPUBLISHED SOURCES

The following unpublished sources have been not merely used but cited at least once in the narrative.

Official Papers
India Office Library:
   Halifax Papers (Viceroy as Lord Irwin)
   Templewood Papers (Sec. of State as Sir Samuel Hoare)
Public Record Office:
   Dardanelles Commission Evidence, Cab. 19
   Cabinet and War Cabinet Minutes, Cab. 23 and 65
   Cabinet and War Cabinet Papers, Cab. 24, 37 and 66
   Imperial Conference Minutes, Cab. 32
   War Council Minutes, Cab. 42
   Prime Minister's Papers, Prem. 1 and 4

Private Papers
Beaverbrook Library, London:
   R. D. Blumenfeld Papers
   Bonar Law Papers
   Lloyd George Papers
British Library of Political and Economic Science, London:
   Dalton Diary and Papers
British Museum:
   Balfour Papers
Cambridge University Library:
   Baldwin Papers
   Crewe Papers
   Templewood Papers

Churchill College Library, Cambridge:
  Attlee Papers
  Margesson Papers
  Thurso Papers (Sir Archibald Sinclair)
Bodleian Library, Oxford:
  Asquith Papers
  H. A. L. Fisher Papers
University College Library, Oxford:
  Attlee Papers
Princeton University Library:
  Baruch Papers
Yale University Library:
  Diary of H. L. Stimson
In private hands:
  Hickleton Papers: Diary of Lord Halifax (by courtesy of
  Dorothy, Lady Halifax)

APPENDIX D

SELECT BIBLIOGRAPHY OF BOOKS ON CHURCHILL

THE best introduction to Churchill's life is afforded by his own works, the list of which appears in Appendix B. For the serious student, there is a highly professional *Bibliography of the Works of Sir Winston Churchill* (rev. ed., 1969) by F. Woods, which also contains a list of works about him as well as by him. I must express my great indebtedness to this invaluable volume.

The official biography, based upon Sir Winston's own papers, was initiated by his son Randolph, and before he died he published two volumes in 1966 (covering 1874–1900) and in 1967 (1901–14). Since his death his former research colleague Martin Gilbert has been appointed to continue the task, and he has so far published one volume on the years 1914–16: this appeared in 1971. There are also companion volumes of documents, published in 1967, 1969 and 1972. Each companion volume is in two separately bound parts, but has consecutive pagination. Wherever possible, I have cited these volumes for reference purposes, rather than the original sources.

The principal biographers and works dealing directly with Churchill are contained in the following list. The place of publication is always London unless otherwise stated.

Ashley, M., *Churchill as Historian*, 1968.
Bardens, D., *Churchill in Parliament*, 1967.
Berlin, I., *Winston Churchill in 1940*, 1964.
Bonham Carter, V., *Winston Churchill as I Knew Him*, 1965.
Broad, L., *Winston Churchill*, 1941; last revised ed. 1956.
'Captain X' (A. D. Gibb), *With Winston Churchill at the Front* (Glasgow) 1924.
Chaplin, E. D. W. (ed.), *Winston Churchill and Harrow*, 1941.

Churchill, R. S., *Winston S. Churchill*, official biography, vols i and ii, 1966 and 1967.

Churchill, R. S., and Gernsheim, H., *Churchill: His Life in Photographs*, 1955.

Churchill, Sarah, *A Thread in the Tapestry*, 1967.

Coombs, D., *Churchill: His Paintings*, 1967.

Cowles, V., *Winston Churchill: the Era and the Man*, 1953.

Eade, C. (ed.), *Churchill by His Contemporaries*, 1953.

Fedden, R., *Churchill and Chartwell*, 1968.

—, *Churchill at Chartwell* (Oxford) 1969.

Gardner, B., *Churchill in His Time, 1939–1945*, 1968.

Gilbert, M., *Winston S. Churchill*, official biography vol. iii, 1971.

Graebner, W., *My Dear Mister Churchill*, 1965.

Howells, R., *Simply Churchill*, 1965.

Hyam, R., *Elgin and Churchill at the Colonial Office*, 1968.

Gretton, P., *Former Naval Person*, 1968.

James, R. Rhodes, *Churchill: A Study in Failure, 1900–1939*, 1970.

Marchant, J. (ed.), *Winston Spencer Churchill: Servant of Crown and Commonwealth*, 1954.

Marder, A. J., *Winston Is Back: Churchill at the Admiralty, 1939–1940*, 1972.

Marsh, E., *A Number of People*, 1939.

McGowan, N., *My Years with Churchill*, 1958.

Moir, P., *I Was Winston Churchill's Private Secretary* (New York), 1941.

Moran, Lord, *Churchill: The Struggle for Survival, 1940–1965*, 1966.

Nel, E., *Mr Churchill's Secretary*, 1958.

Observer (ed.), *Churchill by His Contemporaries: An Appreciation*, 1965.

Pawle, G., *The War and Colonel Warden*, 1963.

Reid, P. G., *Churchill: Townsman of Westerham* (Folkestone), 1969.

Stansky, P. (ed.), *Churchill: A Profile*, 1973.

Taylor, A. J. P. *et al.*, *Churchill: Four Faces and the Man*, 1969.

Thompson, W. H., *Guard from the Yard*, 1938.

—, *I Was Churchill's Shadow*, 1951.

Urquhart, F. (ed.), *WSC: A Cartoon Biography*, 1955.

Wheeler-Bennett, J. W. (ed.), *Action This Day working with Churchill*, 1968.

Young, K., *Churchill and Beaverbrook*, 1966.

APPENDIX E

GENERAL BIBLIOGRAPHY

(The place of publication is always London unless otherwise stated.)

Acheson, D., *Present at the Creation*, 1970.

Addison, C., *Politics from Within, 1911–1918*, 2 vols, 1924.

—, *Four and a Half Years*, 2 vols, 1934.

Airlie, Mabell, Countess of, *Thatched with Gold*, 1962.

Amery, L. S., *My Political Life*, 3 vols, 1953.

Anon., *Strike Nights in Printing House Square*, 1926.

Arnold, H. H., *Global Mission* (New York), 1949.

Arnot, R. Page, *The Miners: Years of Struggle*, 1953.

Ashmead-Bartlett, E., *The Uncensored Dardanelles*, 1928.

Askwith, G. R., *Industrial Problems and Disputes*, 1920.

Asquith, Cynthia, *Diaries 1915–1918*, 1968.

Asquith, Margot, *see* Oxford and Asquith, Margot, Countess of

Atholl, Duchess of, *Working Partnership*, 1958.

Atkins, J. B. (ed.), *National Physical Training*, 1904.

—, *Incidents and Reflections*, 1947.

Attlee, C. R., *As It Happened*, 1954.

Avon, Lord, *Full Circle*, 1960.

—, *Facing the Dictators*, 1962.

—, *The Reckoning*, 1965.

Barrymore, E., *Memories* (New York), 1955.

Bartlett, J., *Familiar Quotations*, 10th ed., 1914.

Baudouin, P., *Private Diaries*, 1948.

Beaverbrook, Lord, *Politicians and the War, 1914–1916*, 1928.

—, *Men and Power, 1917–1918*, 1956.

—, *Decline and Fall of Lloyd George*, 1963.

—, *The Abdication of Edward VIII*, 1966.

Bell, H., *Glimpses of a Governor's Life*, 1946.

Bernays, R., *Special Correspondent*, 1934.

Beveridge, W., *Power and Influence*, 1953.

Birkenhead, 2nd Earl of, *F.E.*, 1960.

—, *The Prof. in Two Worlds*, 1961.

—, *Halifax*, 1965.

—, *Walter Monckton*, 1969.

Blake, R. (ed.), *Private Papers of Douglas Haig, 1914–1919*, 1952.

Blake, R., *The Unknown Prime Minister*, 1955.

—, *Disraeli*, 1961.

Blum, J. M., *Morgenthau Diaries*, vol. iii, *Years of War, 1941–1945* (Boston, Mass.), 1967.

Blunt, W. S., *My Diaries*, 1932.

Boothby, R., *I Fight to Live*, 1947.

Bowle, J., *Viscount Samuel*, 1959.

Boyle, A., *Trenchard*, 1962.

Brett, M. V. (ed.), *Journals and Letters of Reginald Viscount Esher*, 4 vols, 1934–8.

Bridges, G. T. M., *Alarms and Excursions*, 1938.

Briggs, A., *Birth of Broadcasting*, 1961.

—, *The Golden Age of Wireless*, 1965.

British Institute of Public Opinion, *What Britain Thinks*, 1939.

British Officer, A, *Social Life of the British Army*, 1900.

Brockway, A. F., *Inside the Left*, 1942.

Brownrigg, D., *Indiscretions of the Naval Censor*, 1920.

Bryant, A. (ed.), *Turn of the Tide*, 1957.

—, *Triumph in the West*, 1959.

Butler, D. E., *British General Election of 1951*, 1952.

—, *British General Election of 1955*, 1955.

Butler, D. E. and Freeman, J., *British Political Facts*, 3rd ed., 1968.

Butler, D. E. and Rose, R., *British General Election of 1959*, 1960.

Butler, J. R. M., *et al.*, *Grand Strategy*, Official History of the Second World War, U.K. Military Series, 8 vols, 1956– .

Butler, R. A., *The Art of the Possible*, 1971.

Callwell, C. E., *Stray Recollections*, 2 vols, 1923.

—, *Field-Marshal Sir Henry Wilson, His Life and Diaries*, 2 vols, 1927.

Campbell-Johnson, A., *Mission with Mountbatten*, 1951.

Cantril, H., *Public Opinion, 1935–1946* (Princeton, N.J.), 1951.

Cartland, Barbara, *The Isthmus Years*, 1943.

Casey, R. G., *Personal Experience, 1939–1946*, 1962.

Chair, D. de, *The Sea Is Strong*, 1962.
Chalmers, W. S., *Life and Letters of David Earl Beatty*, 1951.
Chamberlain, A., *Politics from Inside*, 1936.
Chandos, Viscount, *Memoirs*, 1962.
Charteris, J., *At G.H.Q.*, 1931.
Chatfield, Lord, *Navy and Defence*, 1947.
Chenery, W. L., *So It Seemed* (New York), 1952.
Childs, Wyndham, *Episodes and Reflections*, 1930.
Churchill, J. S., *Crowded Canvas*, 1961.
Churchill, R. S., *Lord Derby*, 1959.
—, *Twenty-one Years*, 1965.
Cilcennin, Viscount, *Admiralty House*, 1960.
Citrine, Lord, *Men and Work*, 1964.
Clark, A., *Barbarossa*, 1965.
Clarke, T., *My Northcliffe Diaries*, 1931.
Clemens, D. S., *Yalta* (New York), 1970.
Clifford, B., *Proconsul*, 1964.
Clynes, J. R., *Trade Unions and the Law* (Oldham), 1903.
Collier, B., *Defence of the United Kingdom*, Official History of the Second World War, UK Civil Series, 1957.
Connell, J., *Auchinleck*, 1959.
Conservative and Unionist Central Office, *The Industrial Charter*, 1947.
Cooper, Diana, *The Light of Common Day*, 1959.
—, *Trumpets from the Steep*, 1960.
Cooper, Duff, *Old Men Forget*, 1953.
Coote, C. R., *Editorial*, 1965.
—, *The Other Club*, 1971.
Cornwallis-West, G., *Edwardian Heydays*, 1930.
Cornwallis-West, J., *Reminiscences of Lady Randolph Churchill*, 1908.
Cowling, M., *The Impact of Labour, 1920–1924*, 1971.
Croft, L., *My Life of Strife*, 1948.
Crozier, W. P., *Off the Record* (ed. A. J. P. Taylor), 1973.
Cruttwell, C. R. M. F., *History of the Great War* (Oxford), 1934.
Cudlipp, H., *Publish and Be Damned!*, 1953.
Dalton, H., *The Fateful Years*, 1957.
—, *High Tide and After*, 1962.
Devonport, Lord, *The Travelled Road*, 1935.
Darwin, B., *James Braid*, 1952.
Dickinson, F. A., *Lake Victoria to Khartoum*, 1910.

Dilks, D. (ed.), *Cadogan Diaries*, 1972.

Dilley, M. R., *British Policy in Kenya Colony*, 2nd ed., 1966.

Dixon, Piers, *Double Diploma*, 1968.

Dow, J. C. R., *Management of the British Economy, 1945–1960* (Cambridge), 1964.

Ehrman, J., *see* J. R. M. Butler *et al.*, *Grand Strategy*.

Einzig, P., *In the Centre of Things*, 1960.

Elibank, Viscount, *A Man's Life*, 1934.

Elletson, D. H., *Chequers and the Prime Ministers*, 1970.

Ellis, L. F., *Victory in the West*, Official History of the Second World War, UK Military Series, 2 vols, 1962–9.

Feiling, K., *Life of Neville Chamberlain*, 1946.

Fergusson, B. (ed.), *The Business of War*, 1957.

Finch, E., *Wilfred Scawen Blunt*, 1938.

Fisher, Admiral of the Fleet Lord, *Memories*, 1919.

Fitzroy, Sir A., *Memoirs*, 1925.

Forbes-Robertson, D., *Maxine*, 1964.

French of Ypres, *1914*, 1919.

Furse, R., *Aucuparius*, 1962.

Gallacher, W., *Rolling of the Thunder*, 1947.

Gardiner, A. G., *Prophets, Priests and Kings*, new ed., 1924.

—, *Certain People of Importance*, 1926.

Garnett, D. (ed.), *Letters of T. E. Lawrence*, 1938.

Gibbs, P., *Life's Adventure*, 1957.

Gilbert, B. B., *The Evolution of National Insurance in Great Britain*, 1966.

Goodhart, P., *The 1922*, 1973.

Gowing, M., *Britain and Atomic Energy, 1939–1945*, 1964.

Graubard, S. R., *British Labour and the Russian Revolution* (Cambridge, Mass.), 1956.

Greenfield, K. R. (ed.), *Command Decisions*, 1969.

Grey, Viscount of Falloden, *Twenty-five Years*, 2 vols, 1925.

Grigg, P. J., *Prejudice and Judgment*, 1948.

Guinn, P., *British Strategy and Politics, 1914–1918* (Oxford), 1965.

Gwyer, J. M. A., *see* J. R. M. Butler *et al.*, *Grand Strategy*.

Haldane, Viscount, *Autobiography*, 1929.

Halifax, Earl of, *Fulness of Days*, 1957.

Halle, K. (ed.), *Randolph Churchill: The Young Unpretender*, 1971.

Hamilton, I. B. M., *The Happy Warrior*, 1966.

Hancock, W. K., *Survey of British Commonwealth Affairs*, vol. 1, 1937.

—, *Smuts*, vol. ii: *The Fields of Force, 1919–1950*, 1968.

Hancock, W. K. and Gowing, M. M., *British War Economy*, Official History of the Second World War, UK Civil Series, 1949.

Hankey, M., *Supreme Command 1914–1918*, 1961.

—, *Supreme Control at the Paris Peace Conference of 1919*, 1963.

Harris, H. W., *J. A. Spender*, 1946.

Harrison, M., *Trade Unions and the Labour Party since 1945*, 1960.

Harrod, R. W., *The Prof.*, 1959.

Hart, Liddell, *The War in Outline*, 1936.

—, *Memoirs*, 2 vols, 1965.

Haslehurst, C., *Politicians at War*, 1971.

Hasluck, P., *The Government and the People, 1939–1941*, (Canberra), 1952.

Hassall, C., *Edward Marsh*, 1959.

—, *Ambrosia and Small Beer*, 1964.

Hervey, J. (ed.), *Diplomatic Diaries of Oliver Hervey*, 1970.

Hewins, W. A. S., *Apologia of an Imperialist*, 2 vols, 1929.

History of the Ministry of Munitions, HMSO, 11 vols, 1921.

Hoffman, J. D., *The Conservative Party in Opposition, 1945–1951*, 1964.

Holland, B., *Life of the Duke of Devonshire, 1833–1908*, 2 vols, 1916.

Hollis, C., *The Oxford Union*, 1965.

Holtby, W., *Letters to a Friend*, 1937.

Howard, M., *see* J. R. M. Butler *et al.*, *Grand Strategy*.

Huxley, E. J., *White Man's Country*, 2 vols, 1935.

India Defence League, *Prominent Supporters of the I.D.L.*, 3rd ed. (?), 1934.

Ismay, Lord, *Memoirs*, 1960.

James, R. Rhodes, *Gallipoli*, 1965.

—, *Chips: the Diaries of Sir Henry Channon*, 1967.

—, *Memoirs of a Conservative: J. C. C. Davidson's Memoirs and Papers*, 1969.

James, W., *A Great Seaman: The Life of Admiral of the Fleet Sir Henry F. Oliver*, 1956.

Jenkins, R., *Asquith*, 1964.

Jones, T., *Whitehall Diary*, 3 vols (ed. K. Middlemas), 1969–71.

Kent, W., *John Burns*, 1950.

Kerr, M., *Prince Louis of Battenberg*, 1934.

Keynes, J. M., *Economic Consequences of Mr Churchill*, 1925.

—, *Essays in Persuasion*, 1931.

—, *Essays in Biography*, 1933.

Kilmuir, Lord, *Political Adventure*, 1964.

Kimberley, Earl of (ed.), *Polo*, 1936.

King, C. H., *With Malice Toward None*, 1970.

Kirby, W. S., *War Against Japan*, 5 vols, Official History of the Second World War, UK Military Series, 1957–69.

Knightley, P. and Simpson, C., *The Secret Lives of Lawrence of Arabia*, 1969.

Kolko, G., *The Politics of War*, 1969.

Langer, W. L. and Gleason, S. E., *Challenge to Isolation, 1937–1940*, 1952.

—, *The Undeclared War, 1940–1941*, 1953.

Lavery, J., *The Life of a Painter*, 1940.

Leith-Ross, F., *Money Talks*, 1968.

Lawrence, A. W. (ed.), *T. E. Lawrence by his Friends*, 1937.

Leslie, A., *The Fabulous Leonard Jerome*, 1954.

—, *Jennie*, 1969.

Lloyd George, D., *War Memoirs*, 6 vols, 1933–6; also new ed., 2 vols, 1938.

—, *The Truth about the Peace Treaties*, 1938.

Longmore, A., *From Sea to Sky*, 1946.

Lucy, H. W., *The Balfourian Parliament, 1900–1905*, 1906.

Lyons, F. S. L., *John Dillon*, 1968.

Macaulay, T. B., *Critical and Historical Essays*, Everyman's Library, 1907.

McCallum, R. B. and Readman, A., *British General Election of 1945*, 1947.

McCormick, D., *Mr France*, 1955.

McLachlan, D., *In the Chair*, 1971.

—, *Room 39*, 1968.

Macleod, I., *Neville Chamberlain*, 1961.

Macleod, R. and Kelly, D. (eds), *Ironside Diaries*, 1962.

Macmillan, H., *Winds of Change*, 1966.

—, *The Blast of War*, 1967.

—, *Tides of Fortune*, 1969.

—, *Riding the Storm*, 1971.

Macready, N., *Annals of an Active Life*, 2 vols, 1924.

Mallet, C., *Herbert Gladstone*, 1932.

Mansergh, P. N. S., *The Transfer of Power, 1942–7*, vol. 1, 1970.

—, *Survey of British Commonwealth Affairs: Problems of Wartime Cooperation and Postwar Change, 1939–1952*, 1958.

Marder, A. J., *Fear God and Dread Nought*, 3 vols, 1952–9.

—, *From the Dreadnought to Scapa Flow*, 5 vols, 1961–70.

Marrot, H. V., *Life and Letters of John Galsworthy*, 1935.

Martin, B. K., *The British Public and the General Strike*, 1926.

Massey, V., *What's Past Is Prologue* (Toronto), 1963.

Masterman, L., *C. F. G. Masterman*, 1939.

Matloff, M. and Snell, E. M., *Strategic Planning for Coalition Warfare, 1941–2* (Washington, D.C.), 1953.

Maurice, F. (ed.), *Life of Lord Rawlinson of Trent*, 1928.

Meinertzhagen, R., *Middle East Diary, 1917–1956*, 1959.

—, *Diary of a Black Sheep*, 1964.

Menzies, R. G., *Afternoon Light*, 1967.

Middlemas, K. and Barnes, J., *Baldwin*, 1969.

Minney, R. J., *Private Papers of Hore-Belisha*, 1960.

Moggridge, D. E., *The Return to Gold, 1925* (Cambridge), 1971.

Morley, Lord, *Memorandum on Resignation*, 1928.

Morrison, Lord, *Government and Parliament*, 1954.

—, *Autobiography*, 1960.

Mortimer, R. (ed.), *Encyclopaedia of Flat Racing*, 1971.

Mosley, Sir O., *My Life*, 1968.

Murray, A. C., *Master and Brother*, 1948.

Munnings, A., *The Finish*, 1952.

Namier, J., *Lewis Namier*, 1971.

Nevinson, H. W., *Fire of Life*, 1935.

Nicholas, H. G., *British General Election of 1950*, 1951.

Nicolson, H., *Diaries and Letters*, 3 vols, 1966–8.

Nowell-Smith, S., *The House of Cassell*, 1958.

Oliver, V., *Mr Showbusiness*, 1954.

Owen, F., *Tempestuous Journey*, 1954.

Oxford and Asquith Margot, Countess of, *The Autobiography of Margot Asquith*, 2 vols, 1920–22.

Oxford and Asquith, Earl of, *Memories and Reflections*, 2 vols, 1928.

—, *H.H.A.: Letters to a Friend*, 2 vols, 1933–4.

Pankhurst, E. S., *The Suffragette Movement*, 1931.

Pelling, H., *Social Geography of British Elections, 1885–1910*, 1967.

—, *Popular Politics and Society in Late Victorian Britain*, 1968.

Percy, Lord Eustace, *Some Memories*, 1958.

Pethick-Lawrence, Lord, *Fate Has Been Kind*, 1943.

Petrie, C., *Walter Long and his Times*, 1936.

—, *Life and Letters of Sir Austen Chamberlain*, 2 vols, 1939–40.

Philips, C. H. and Wainwright, M. D. (ed.), *The Partition of India*, 1970.

Pierre, A. J., *Nuclear Politics, 1939–1970*, 1972.

Pogue, F. C., *The Supreme Command* (Washington, D.C.), 1954.

Poore, Ida, Lady, *Recollections of an Admiral's Wife*, 1916.

Pound, R., *The Strand Magazine, 1891–1950*, 1966.

Pound, R. and Harmsworth, G., *Northcliffe*, 1959.

'Raymond, E. T.' (E. R. Thompson), *Uncensored Celebrities*, 1919.

Redford, A., *Manchester Merchants and Foreign Trade*, vol. ii (Manchester), 1956.

Redmayne, R. A. S., *Men, Mines and Memories*, 1942.

Reith, J. C. W., *Into the Wind*, 1949.

Repington, C. à C., *The First World War, 1914–1918*, 1920.

Richards, D. and Saunders, H. St G., *Royal Air Force, 1939–45*, 3 vols, 1953–4.

Riddell, Lord, *Intimate Diary of the Peace Conference and After*, 1933.

—, *More Pages From My Diary, 1908–14*, 1934.

Roch, W., *Mr Lloyd George and the War*, 1920.

Roosevelt, Elliott, *As He Saw It* (New York), 1946.

Rosebery, Lord, *Lord Randolph Churchill*, 1906.

Roskill, S. W., *War at Sea*, 4 vols, Official History of the Second World War, UK Military Series, 1954–61.

—, *The Navy at War, 1939–1945*, 1960.

—, *Naval Policy between the Wars*, vol. i, 1968.

—, *Hankey*, 3 vols, 1970–73.

Salvidge, S., *Salvidge of Liverpool*, 1934.

Samuel, Lord, *Memoirs*, 1948.

Sassoon, S., *Siegfried's Journey*, 1945.

Scriven, A., *The Dartmoor Shepherd* (Oswestry), 1931.

Seely, J. E. B., *Adventure*, 1930.

Shakespeare, G., *Let Candles Be Brought In*, 1949.

Sheridan, C., *Nuda Veritas*, 1927.

Sherwood, R. E., *White House Papers*, 2 vols, 1948.

Shinwell, E., *Conflict without Malice*, 1955.

Smalley, G. W., *Anglo-American Memories*, 1911.

Snell, J. L., *The Meaning of Yalta* (Baton Rouge, La.), 1956.

Sommer, D., *Haldane of Cloan*, 1960.

Spaak, P.-H., *The Continuing Battle*, 1971.

Spears, E. L., *Assignment to Catastrophe*, 2 vols, 1954.

Spender, J. A., *Life of Sir H. Campbell-Bannerman*, 2 vols, 1923.

—, *Life, Journalism and Politics*, 2 vols, 1927.

Spender, J. A. and Asquith, C., *Life of H. H. Asquith, Lord Oxford and Asquith*, 2 vols, 1932.

Spier, E., *Focus*, 1963.

Stacey, C. P., *The Victory Campaign*, Official History of the Canadian Army, vol. iii (Ottawa), 1960.

Stalin, J. V., *Stalin's Correspondence with Churchill, et al., 1941–1945* (Moscow), 1957.

Stephens, I., *Monsoon Morning*, 1966.

Stern, A., *Tanks, 1914–1918*, 1919.

Stimson, H. L. and Bundy, McG., *On Active Service in Peace and War* (New York), 1948.

Storry, R., *History of Modern Japan*, Pelican ed., 1960.

Stuart, J., *Within the Fringe*, 1967.

Sueter, M., *Evolution of the Tank*, 1937.

Surtees, R., *Handley Cross*, new ed., 2 vols, 1901.

Sutherland, G. (ed.), *Studies in the Growth of Nineteenth-Century Government*, 1972.

Sykes, F., *From Many Angles*, 1942.

Sydenham of Combe *et al.*, *The World Crisis: A Criticism*, 1927.

Taylor, A. J. P., *Origins of the Second World War*, 1961.

—, *English History, 1914–1945* (Oxford), 1965.

— (ed.), *Lloyd George: Twelve Essays*, 1971.

—, *Beaverbrook*, 1972.

Taylor, H. A., *Jix, Viscount Brentford*, 1933.

Tedder, Lord, *With Prejudice*, 1966.

Templewood, Lord, *Nine Troubled Years*, 1954.

—, *Empire of the Air*, 1957.

Thomas, Hugh, *The Suez Affair*, rev. Pelican ed., 1970.

Thomson, D., *The Proposal for Anglo-French Union in 1940* (Oxford), 1966.

Tilden, P., *True Remembrances*, 1954.

Truman, H. S., *Memoirs*, 2 vols, 1955–6.

Ullman, R. H., *Britain and the Russian Civil War* (Princeton, N.J.), 1968.

Ullswater, Viscount, *A Speaker's Commentaries*, 2 vols, 1925.

Vansittart, Sir Robert, *The Mist Procession*, 1958.

Waley, S. D., *Edwin Montagu*, 1964.

'Watchman' (S. V. T. Adams), *Right Honourable Gentlemen*, 1939.

Webb, B., *Our Partnership*, 1948.

—, *Diaries, 1924–1932*, 1956.

Webster, C. K. and Frankland, N., *Strategic Air Offensive*, 4 vols, 1961.

Wedgwood, J. C., *Memoirs of a Fighting Life*, 1941.

Wemyss, V. M. A. Wester, *Life and Letters of Lord Wester Wemyss*, 1935.

Westminster, Duchess of, *Grace and Favour*, 1961.

Wheatley, R. R. A., *Operation Sealion* (Oxford) 1958.

Wheeler-Bennett, J. W., *King George VI*, 1958.

White, J. Baker, *True Blue*, 1970.

Williams, Francis, *A Prime Minister Remembers*, 1961.

Wilmot, Chester, *The Struggle for Europe*, 1952.

Wilson, H. H., *Pressure Group*, 1961.

Wilson, T., *Downfall of the Liberal Party*, 1966.

Wilson, T. (ed.), *Political Diaries of C. P. Scott, 1911–1918*, 1970.

Wilson, Theodore A., *The First Summit*, 1969.

Winant, J. G., *Letter from Grosvenor Square*, 1947.

Windsor, Duchess of, *The Heart Has Its Reasons*, 1956.

Windsor, Edward, Duke of, *A King's Story*, 1951.

Winterton, Earl, *Orders of the Day*, 1953.

Wolfe, H., *Portraits by Inference*, 1934.

Woodward, E. L., *British Foreign Policy in the Second World War*, Official History of the Second World War, UK Civil Series, vols i and ii, 1970 and 1971.

Woolton, Earl of, *Memoirs*, 1959.

Wrench, J. E., *Geoffrey Dawson and Our Times*, 1955.

Young, G. M., *Stanley Baldwin*, 1952.

Young, K., *Balfour*, 1963.

Zetland, Lawrence, Marquess of, *Lord Cromer*, 1932.

—, *Essayez*, 1956.

SPECIAL ABBREVIATIONS USED IN THE NOTES

C.A. for Confidential Annex.

CP for Cabinet Paper.

CV1, CV2, CV3, for the Companion Volumes of Documents to the official biography by R. S. Churchill and M. Gilbert.

F.R.U.S. for *Foreign Relations of the United States.*

Hansard references are given by volume, page and (where necessary) by date, but not by series. Unless otherwise stated they refer to the House of Commons.

LG for D. Lloyd George.

PP for Parliamentary Papers.

WP for War Cabinet Paper.

WSC for Winston S. Churchill.

WW2 for *The Second World War,* Churchill's war memoirs.

References to WSC's books are to the first London edition in all cases except that of *The Second World War,* volume 1, where the corrections of details are so numerous as to justify the use of the third London edition (February 1950).

Since details of works cited are to be found in the Bibliography, the Notes provide authors' names only, and short titles in addition only when there is more than one book by an author. Authors' initial are given only when there are two authors of the same name.

Notes

Chapter 1 (pp. 17–29)

1. *Oxford Times*, 30 May 1874.
2. *Ibid.*
3. J. Cornwallis-West, 57.
4. *Ibid.*, 58–9.
5. *Oxford Times*, 21 Nov. 1874.
6. *Ibid.*, 28 Nov. 1874.
7. *CVI*, 1–2.
8. *Ibid.*
9. Blake, *Disraeli*, 692.
10. *CVI*, 20.
11. WSC, *Lord Randolph Churchill*, i, 551.
12. Finch, 207.
13. WSC, *Lord Randolph Churchill*, i, 309–10.
14. Rosebery, 72.
15. *World*, 4 Nov. 1874.

Chapter 2 (pp. 30–41)

1. WSC, *Savrola*, 44.
2. WSC, *My Early Life*, 18.
3. Leslie, *Jennie*, 70.
4. R. S. Churchill, *Winston*, i, 45–6; A. Storr in A. J. P. Taylor *et al.*, *Churchill*, 223–4.
5. *The World*, 4 Nov. 1874.
6. *CVI*, 92–3.
7. Leslie, *Jennie*, 82.
8. *Harrovian*, 30 July, 1892.
9. *CVI*, 159.
10. Chaplin, 24.
11. Zetland, *Essayez*, 7.
12. *CVI*, 168.
13. Meinertzhagen, *Black Sheep*, 176.
14. WSC, *My Early Life*, 54.
15. *Harrovian*, 18 Feb. 1892.
16. WSC, *My Early Life*, 54.
17. *CVI*, 227.
18. Leslie, *Jennie*, 93.
19. WSC, *My Early Life*, 52.

20. *CVı*, 111.
21. Sheridan, 14.
22. *CVı*, 371.
23. *Ibid.*, 390, 394.
24. *Ibid.*, 485.
25. *Ibid.*, 423.
26. *Ibid.*, 527.
27. *Pall Mall Gazette*, 5 Nov. 1895.
28. WSC, *My Early Life*, 71.
29. *St James's Gazette*, 5 Nov. 1895.
30. *Jackson's Oxford Journal*, 2 Feb. 1895.
31. *CVı*, 553, 555.

Chapter 3 (pp. 42–67)

1. 'A British Officer', *Social Life in the British Army*, xiii.
2. Smalley, 291. According to records at Somerset House, however, the gross value of Lord Randolph's estate at his death was £75,971.
3. *CVı*, 570.
4. *Ibid.*, 977–8.
5. G. Cornwallis-West, 119.
6. *CVı*, 869.
7. *Ibid.*, 953.
8. *Ibid.*, 576.
9. *Ibid.*, 578, 597.
10. *Ibid.*, 583.
11. *Ibid.*, 584.
12. *Ibid.*, 589.
13. *Ibid.*, 600.
14. *Ibid.*, 603.
15. *Ibid.*, 676.
16. *Ibid.*, 688.
17. *Field*, 5 Dec. 1876.
18. WSC, *Malakand*, 231–2.
19. *CVı*, 697.
20. *Ibid.*, 725.
21. *Ibid.*, 724.
22. WSC, *My Early Life*, 221.
23. *CVı*, 792–3.
24. *Ibid.*, 830.
25. *Ibid.*, 797, 810.
26. *Ibid.*, 815.
27. *Ibid.*, 805.
28. *Ibid.*, 811.
29. *Ibid.*, 913.
30. 7 Apr. 1898.
31. 14 May 1898.
32. N.s. xvii (1898), 109.
33. *Ibid.*, 504–10.
34. WSC, *Savrola*, 42.
35. *Ibid.*, 27.
36. *CV2*, 811.
37. WSC, *Savrola*, 44.

38. *Ibid.*, 88.
39. *Ibid.*, vii.
40. 19 Feb. 1900.
41. 24 Feb. 1900.
42. 24 Feb. 1900.
43. 3 Mar. 1900.
44. 20 Feb. 1900.
45. 13 Apr. 1900.
46. 17 Feb. 1900.
47. 17 Feb. 1900.
48. *CV*I, 856, 942.
49. *Ibid.*, 968.
50. *Ibid.*, 970.
51. *Ibid.*, 978.
52. *Ibid.*, 979.
53. *Ibid.*, 971.
54. WSC, *The River War*, ii, 377-8.
55. N.s. xx (1899), 322.
56. 6 Nov. 1899.
57. 18 Nov. 1899.
58. 16 Nov. 1899.
59. 16 Dec. 1899.
60. 6 Nov. 1899.
61. 18 Nov. 1899.
62. Atkins, *Incidents and Reflections*, 122.
63. *CV*I, 1067.
64. WSC, *My Early Life*, 289.
65. *CV*I, 1091.
66. *St James's Gazette*, 29 Dec. 1899.
67. *Morning Post*, 29 Dec. 1899.
68. *Ibid.*, 30 Dec. 1899.
69. WSC, *My Early Life*, 317.
70. *Ibid.*, 333.
71. *Ibid.*, 341.
72. *CV*I, 989.
73. *Ibid.*, 1033.
74. *Ibid.*, 1044.
75. *Globe*, 17 May 1900; *United Services Magazine*, n.s. xxi (1900), 328.
76. 29 May 1900.
77. 15 May 1900.
78. WSC, *My Early Life*, 374.
79. *CV*I, 1222.

Chapter 4 (pp. 68–93)

1. WSC, *Thoughts and Adventures*, 52.
2. *CV*I, 698.
3. *Ibid.*, 751.
4. *Ibid.*, 938.
5. *Ibid.*, 1012.
6. *Morning Post*, 1 Nov. 1898.
7. *Oldham Standard*, 1 July 1899.

8. *CVI*, 1033.
9. *Oldham Standard*, 1 July 1899.
10. *CVI*, 1036.
11. *Oldham Standard*, 1 July 1899.
12. *Ibid.*
13. *Ibid.*
14. *Ibid.*, 8 July 1899.
15. WSC, *London to Ladysmith*, 210.
16. *CVI*, 1214.
17. *Oldham Standard*, 18 Aug. 1900.
18. *Ibid.*, 6 Oct. 1900.
19. 2 Oct. 1900.
20. WSC, *My Early Life*, 373.
21. *CV2*, 8.
22. *Ibid.*, 62, 64.
23. Lucy, 231.
24. *CV2*, 113.
25. *Ibid.*, 146.
26. *Ibid.*, 168.
27. *Ibid.*
28. *Annual Register*, 1903, 130.
29. WSC, *My Early Life*, 385.
30. WSC, *Thoughts and Adventures*, 55.
31. *Oldham Chronicle*, 25 Oct. 1902.
32. *CV2*, 184.
33. *Ibid.*, 188–9.
34. Holland, ii, 375.
35. *Monthly Review*, Nov. 1903, 28.
36. *Ibid.*, 31.
37. H. Gladstone, diary, 6 Jan. 1904, quoted H. W. McCready, 'The Revolt of the Unionist Free Traders', *Parliamentary Affairs*, xvi (1963), 189n.
38. *CV2*, 337.
39. Atkins, *Physical Training*, 70–3.
40. Clynes, 10.
41. *Hansard*, cxxxiii, 998 (22 Apr. 1904).
42. For his own account of the episode, see WSC, 'On Making a Maiden Speech in the House', *News of the World*, 25 Dec. 1938.
43. *CV2*, 355.
44. *Ibid.*, 356.
45. *Hansard*, cl, 95, 98 (24 July 1905).
46. *Ibid.*, 119.
47. *CV2*, 399.
48. *Ibid.*, 393.
49. Spender, *Campbell-Bannerman*, ii, 161.
50. See, e.g., Masterman, 97.
51. Blunt, 518.
52. *CV2*, 478.
53. 6 Jan. 1906.
54. *Manchester Guardian*, 2 Jan. 1906.
55. WSC, *Lord Randolph Churchill*, ii, 449.
56. *CV2*, 416; Bonham Carter, 126.
57. Hassall, *Marsh*, 121.
58. 11 and 12 Jan. 1906.

59. 5 Jan. 1906.
60. Leslie, *Jennie*, 273.
61. 12 Jan. 1906.
62. *Manchester Guardian*, 11 Jan. 1906; H. A. Taylor, 62.
63. *CV2*, 422.
64. *Manchester Guardian*, 4 Jan. 1906.
65. *Ibid.*; Pankhurst, 193–4.
66. Leslie, *Jennie*, 273.
67. *CV2*, 768; *Manchester Guardian*, 15 Jan. 1906.
68. *Manchester Guardian*, 8 Jan. 1906.
69. 12 Jan. 1906.
70. Pelling, *Social Geography*, 243, 415.
71. *CV2*, 427.
72. Chaplin, 16.

Chapter 5 *(pp. 94–109)*

1. *CV2*, 797.
2. Marsh, 150.
3. *CV2*, 797.
4. *Ibid.*, 497.
5. *Ibid.*, 499.
6. Hyam, 125.
7. *Hansard*, clv, 848 (5 Apr. 1906).
8. *Hansard*, clxii, 753 (31 July 1906).
9. *Hansard*, clxvii, 1138 (17 Dec. 1906).
10. *Hansard*, clii, 555 (22 Feb. 1906).
11. Marsh, 151.
12. R. S. Churchill, *Winston*, ii, 185.
13. Elibank, 118.
14. Chamberlain, 459.
15. *CV2*, 631.
16. *Ibid.*, 634.
17. *Ibid.*, 606.
18. WSC, *Liberalism*, 98 (speech 7 May 1907).
19. R. S. Churchill, *Winston*, ii, 215.
20. *CV2*, 797.
21. *Manchester Guardian*, 30 Dec. 1907.
22. WSC, *African Journey*, 21.
23. Bell, 168.
24. *Ibid.*, 170–1.
25. Marsh, 157; WSC, *African Journey*, 58–9; J. S. Churchill, 67 (on sensitive skin).
26. Hassall, *Marsh*, 138.
27. WSC, *African Journey*, 123.
28. *Ibid.*, 52.
29. 23 June 1906.
30. WSC, *Liberalism*, 81.
31. 'The Liberal Cabinet: An Intercepted Letter', *National Review*, xlvi (1906), 789–90.
32. WSC, *Liberalism*, 84.
33. *Dundee Advertiser*, 9 May 1908.
34. Masterman, 88.

35. *Daily News*, 30 Aug. 1907.
36. Gardiner, *Prophets*, 228.
37. Dickinson, 82.
38. Harris, 81.
39. W. Beveridge, 'Social Reform: How Germany Deals With It', *Morning Post*, 12, 17, 18 and 20 Sept. 1907.
40. *CV2*, 759.
41. *Manchester Guardian*, 24 Jan. 1908.
42. *CV2*, 754–5; WSC, 'My Life', *News of the World*, 24 Feb. 1935.
43. Marsh, 163.
44. *CV2*, 755.
45. Jenkins, 206n.

Chapter 6 (pp. 110-29)

1. *CV2*, 779.
2. *Manchester Guardian*, 13 Apr. 1908.
3. *Ibid.*, 20 Apr. 1908.
4. *Nation*, 2 May 1908.
5. *CV2*, 793.
6. *CV2*, 788.
7. WSC, *Thoughts and Adventures*, 210.
8. *Dundee Advertiser*, 5 May 1908.
9. *Manchester Guardian*, 5 May 1908.
10. *CV2*, 787.
11. Bonham Carter, 217.
12. *World*, 19 Aug. 1908.
13. *Nottingham Daily Express*, 7 Aug. 1908.
14. *CV2*, 798.
15. R. S. Churchill, *Winston*, ii, 268.
16. *Ibid.*, 252; Barrymore, 125.
17. Mabell, Airlie, 125.
18. *Westminster Gazette*, 12 Sept. 1908.
19. R. S. Churchill, *Winston*, ii, 273.
20. *Westminster Gazette*, 12 Sept. 1908.
21. *World*, 16 Sept. 1908.
22. *Ibid.*
23. *Jackson's Oxford Journal*, 19 Sept. 1908.
24. *Westminster Gazette*, 14 Sept. 1908; *CV2*, 934; *Riddell, Diary 1908–14*, 1; Arnold, 512.
25. Beveridge, 67.
26. Devonport, 147.
27. Masterman, 177.
28. Askwith, 127.
29. Report of the Select Committee on Home Work, *PP* 1908, viii, 18.
30. Webb, *Partnership*, 418–19.
31. *CV2*, 852.
32. See WSC's speech at Aberdeen, *The Times*, 12 Sept. 1912.
33. B. B. Gilbert, 272.
34. *CV2*, 860.
35. CP 27 June and 3 July 1908, PRO Cab. 37/94/89 and 93.
36. Brett, ii, 324.

37. *CV2*, 947.
38. Spender and Asquith, i, 254.
39. Marder, *Dreadnought to Scapa*, i, 171.
40. *CV2*, 857.
41. *The Times*, 17 Aug. 1908.
42. *CV2*, 836.
43. *The Times*, 15 Apr. 1909.
44. WSC, *Liberalism*, 199–200.
45. *Ibid.*, 279–81.
46. Masterman, 137.
47. WSC, *The People's Rights* (new ed. 1970), 6–7.
48. *Manchester Guardian*, 4 Dec. 1909.
49. *Ibid.*, 9 Dec. 1909.
50. Chaplin to Sanders, 1 Dec. 1909, Balfour Papers, B.M.Add.Ms. 49772.
51. *Manchester Guardian*, 18 Dec. 1909.
52. Bonham Carter, 186; *CV2*, 964.
53. *Dundee Advertiser*, 11 and 19 Jan. 1910.
54. Pelling, *Social Geography*, 415.
55. *Dundee Advertiser*, 19 Jan. 1910.
56. Pelling, *ibid.*
57. *CV2*, 1132–3.
58. *CV2*, 864.
59. *CV2*, 863.
60. *CV2*, 895–8.
61. Masterman, 97.
62. R. Davidson, 'Llewellyn Smith, the Labour Department and government growth, 1886–1909', in Sutherland.

Chapter 7 (*pp. 130–46*)

1. Mallet, *Herbert Gladstone*, 208.
2. *CV2*, 1141.
3. *Blunt*, 862.
4. *Ibid.*, 863.
5. *CV2*, 1152–3.
6. *Hansard*, xv, 178 (15 Mar. 1910).
7. Marrot, 283.
8. *Hansard*, xix, 1343–54 (20 July 1910).
9. *CV2*, 1198–1203.
10. *Hansard*, xix, 1354 (20 July 1910).
11. WSC, 'My Life', *News of the World*, 3 Mar. 1935.
12. *Annual Register*, 1910, 238.
13. *The Times*, 27 Jan. 1911.
14. *Annual Register*, 1911, 5. For Davies' life, see Scriven.
15. *Hansard*, xix, 1352 (20 July 1910).
16. Redmayne, 143.
17. Labour Party *Conference Report*, 1912, 27; *Hansard*, xxii, 2659 (17 Mar. 1911).
18. *Liberal Magazine*, 1914, 308.
19. *Ibid.*
20. *Hansard*, xxvi, 508 (25 May 1911).
21. *The Times*, 5 Oct. 1911.

22. For a reassessment of reasons for the 'labour unrest', see Pelling, *Popular Politics*, ch. 9.
23. *Ibid.*
24. Macready, 155.
25. *The Times*, 10 Nov. 1910.
26. *Hansard*, xxi, 55 (6 Feb. 1911).
27. Masterman, 184.
28. *CV2*, 1274, 1277.
29. *CV2*, 1278.
30. 'Employment of Military During Railway Strike', *PP* 1911, xliii, 730.
31. *Westminster Gazette*, 19 Aug. 1911.
32. *CV2*, 1287.
33. *Hansard*, xxix, 2296 (22 Aug. 1911).
34. Masterman, 205.
35. *CV2*, 1290.
36. *Manchester Guardian*, 22 and 23 Aug. 1911.
37. *CV2*, 968–70.
38. Lloyd George, *War Memoirs*, i, 36; Petrie, *Chamberlain*, i, 381–8.
39. Lloyd George, *War Memoirs*, i, 37–8.
40. *Dundee Advertiser*, 1 Dec. 1910.
41. *Ibid.*, 2 Dec. 1910.
42. *Ibid.*, 8 Dec. 1910.
43. Pelling, *Social Geography*, 389, 415.
44. *Hansard*, xxv, 1771 (15 May 1911); *CV2*, 1032.
45. *CV2*, 1113.
46. Lloyd George, *War Memoirs*, i, 44.
47. WSC, *World Crisis*, i, 51.
48. Callwell, *Henry Wilson*, i, 99, 102; WSC, *World Crisis*, i, 60–4.
49. *CV2*, 1124.
50. WSC, *World Crisis*, i, 67.
51. Haldane, 230–1.
52. Asquith to Crewe, 7 Oct. 1911, Crewe Papers C/40, Cambridge University Library.
53. WSC, *World Crisis*, i, 70.
54. Sommer, 248.

Chapter 8 (pp. 147–62)

1. *CV2*, 1316.
2. Hassall, *Marsh*, 174.
3. WSC, *World Crisis*, i, 81–2.
4. *CV2*, 1312–16.
5. Marder, *Fear God*, ii, 424.
6. *CV2*, 1486–90; *Annual Register*, 1912, 4.
7. Marder, *Dreadnought to Scapa*, i, 266.
8. de Chair, 149, 152.
9. Marder, *Dreadnought to Scapa*, i, 261; de Chair, 150–1.
10. *Fleet*, Oct. 1912.
11. *The Times*, 10 Feb. 1912.
12. Marder, *Dreadnought to Scapa*, i, 284–5.
13. *CV2*, 1638.
14. *Hansard*, i, 1757 (26 Mar. 1913).
15. Marder, *Dreadnought to Scapa*, i, 319.

16. Lyons, 343.
17. T. Wilson, *C. P. Scott*, 75.
18. Marder, *Dreadnought to Scapa*, i, 326.
19. WSC, *World Crisis*, ii, 374–5.
20. *The Times*, 15 Nov. 1909.
21. *CV2*, 1457.
22. *The Times*, 28 Nov. 1910.
23. *Ibid.*, 12 Sept. 1912.
24. *Ibid.*, 25 Apr. 1914.
25. *Hansard*, xix, 224 (12 July 1910).
26. *CV2*, 1440–7; Hassall, 162–4.
27. *CV2*, 1473.
28. A. J. Ward, 'Frewen's Anglo-American Campaign for Federalism, 1910–21', *Irish Historical Studies*, xvi (1967); J. E. Kendle, 'The Round Table Movement and Home Rule All Round', *Historical Journal*, xi (1968).
29. *CV2*, 1375–8; *The Times*, 13 Sept. 1912.
30. 14 Sept. 1912.
31. *CV2*, 1390.
32. Riddell, *Diary, 1908–14*, 37.
33. *The Times*, 9 Feb. 1912.
34. *Manchester Guardian*, 9 Feb. 1912.
35. 9 Feb. 1912.
36. *CV2*, 1392; Nevinson, 280–1.
37. *The Times*, 9 Feb. 1912.
38. WSC, *World Crisis*, i, 181–2.
39. *The Times*, 14 Nov. 1912; Viscount Ullswater, ii, 132–3.
40. Lyons, 332–3.
41. T. Wilson, *C. P. Scott*, 76.
42. WSC, *World Crisis*, i, 178.
43. *The Times*, 16 Mar. 1914.
44. *Ibid.*
45. Riddell, *Diary, 1908–14*, 204; Fitzroy, 541.
46. *Hansard*, lx, 901 (30 Mar. 1914).
47. *Hansard*, lxi, 1575 (28 Apr. 1914).
48. *CV2*, 1418.
49. WSC, *World Crisis*, i, 193.

Chapter 9 (pp. 163–79)

1. *The Times*, 4 Feb. 1909.
2. *Ibid.*, 4 Apr. 1912.
3. T. Wilson, *C. P. Scott*, 78; *CV2*, 1997–8.
4. Marder, *Fear God*, ii, 397; R. S. Churchill, *Winston*, ii, 560.
5. Masterman, 109.
6. Webb, *Partnership*, 416.
7. *CV2*, 893.
8. *The Times*, 10 Aug. 1909.
9. Masterman, 144.
10. *CV2*, 918.
11. Brett, ii, 422.
12. *Ibid.*, 423.
13. *The Times*, 27 Oct. 1911.
14. R. S. Churchill, *Twenty-one Years*, 13.

15. *CV2*, 1723.
16. Cilcennin, 42.
17. Riddell, *Diary, 1908–14*, 139.
18. WSC, *World Crisis*, i, 198.
19. *CV2*, 1417.
20. *Daily Graphic*, 5 May 1909.
21. *Dundee Advertiser*, 11 Jan. 1910.
22. Riddell, *Diary, 1908–14*, 24.
23. Darwin, 148, 179.
24. Blunt, 690.
25. *CV2*, 1781.
26. WSC, *Thoughts and Adventures*, 182–3.
27. *CV2*, 1889–95.
28. Boyle, 107.
29. *CV2*, 1922.
30. *CV2*, 893, 1087.
31. *CV2*, 893.
32. Callwell, *Stray Recollections*, ii, 246.
33. WSC, *Thoughts and Adventures*, 81.
34. *CV2*, 912.
35. *CV2*, 908.
36. *CV2*, 912.
37. *Marsh*, 167.
38. WSC, *World Crisis*, i, 119.
39. *CV2*, 1723.
40. Longmore, 30.
41. Bonham Carter, 262.
42. Chalmers, 112.
43. Leslie, *Jennie*, 299–300; *The Times*, 8 Apr. 1914.
44. Bonham Carter, 273.
45. *CV2*, 1723.
46. *The Times*, 24 May, 6 June, 4 Aug., 17 Sept. 1910; *CV2*, 1022–3.
47. Hassall, Marsh, 174.
48. Marsh, 245; Clarke, 60.
49. Masterman, 173.
50. *Manchester Guardian*, 16 Mar. 1914.
51. Blunt, 812.
52. WSC, *Great Contemporaries*, 174.
53. *Oxford Magazine*, 6 Mar. 1907.
54. *CV2*, 1032, 1089.
55. Mallet, *Anthony Hope*, 208.
56. Coote, *Other Club*, 20.
57. *CV3*, 742.
58. Masterman, 128.
59. Bowle, 74–5.
60. Masterman, 128.
61. Murray, 40.
62. Masterman, 128.
63. Brett, ii, 344.
64. WSC, *Thoughts and Adventures*, 59.
65. Grey, i, 235.
66. Riddell, *Diary, 1908–14*, 54.
67. Ibid., 106.
68. Owen, 231; *CV2*, 1747.

69. Marsh, 150–1.
70. Fitzroy, 485, 547.
71. Kent, 243.
72. WSC, *World Crisis*, i, 197.
73. Kerr, 243.
74. WSC, *World Crisis*, i, 211–12.
75. *CV2*, 1989.
76. Brett, 558; Samuel, 103.
77. WSC, *World Crisis*, i, 215.
78. *CV2*, 1990; *Unknown Prime Minister*, 220–1.
79. Oxford and Asquith, *Memories*, ii, 7.
80. Jenkins, 327.
81. *CV2*, 1996–7.
82. Blake, *Unknown Prime Minister*, 221.
83. Beaverbrook, *Politicians*, 36.
84. WSC, *Great Contemporaries*, 148.
85. WSC, *World Crisis*, i, 217.
86. Morley, 24.
87. Jenkins, 329.
88. WSC, *World Crisis*, i, 229.
89. M. Asquith, ii, 196.

Chapter 10 (pp. 180–209)

1. WSC, Dardanelles Commission Evidence, 65, PRO Cab.19/33.
2. Gretton, 166–70.
3. WSC, *World Crisis*, i, 323.
4. M. Gilbert, iii, 28.
5. WSC, *World Crisis*, i, 281 (where the visit is wrongly dated); French of Ypres, 303–4.
6. WSC, *World Crisis*, i, 345.
7. Oxford and Asquith, *Memories*, 42.
8. Seely, 189.
9. *The Times*, 27 Nov. 1914.
10. W. James, 133.
11. Maurice (ed.), 107; WSC, *World Crisis*, i, 357–8.
12. Oxford and Asquith, *Memories*, 44.
13. Bowle, 165. Cf. Cruttwell, 96; Hart, 47.
14. 13 Oct. 1914.
15. Oxford and Asquith, *Memories*, 46.
16. Marder, *Dreadnought to Scapa*, ii, 86.
17. *Morning Post*, 21 Oct. 1914.
18. Oxford and Asquith, *Memories*, 47.
19. Marder, *Fear God*, iii, 65.
20. Chalmers, 179.
21. Wester Wemyss, 186.
22. Marder, *Dreadnought to Scapa*, ii, 92–3 and 115–17.
23. WSC, *World Crisis*, i, 404–6.
24. Brownrigg, 12.
25. Marsh, 246.
26. Brownrigg, 7, 12–13.
27. Addison, *Four and a Half Years*, 50.

28. 1 Jan. 1915.
29. War Council, 25 Nov. 1914, PRO Cab. 42/1/4.
30. War Council, 1 Dec. 1914, PRO Cab. 42/1/5.
31. WSC, *World Crisis*, ii, 44.
32. *Ibid.*, ii, 98.
33. Hankey, *Supreme Command*, 265–6.
34. War Council, 13 Jan. 1915, PRO Cab. 42/1/16.
35. WSC, *World Crisis*, ii, 154–7; Hankey, *Supreme Command*, 269–70.
36. Dardanelles Commission, First Report, *PP* 1917–18, x, 446.
37. Dardanelles Commission, Evidence, *ibid.*, 203.
38. Fisher, 59.
39. Oxford and Asquith, *Memories*, 59.
40. War Council, 16 Feb. 1915, PRO Cab. 42/1/35.
41. Bonham Carter, 360, 362.
42. Marder, *Dreadnought to Scapa*, ii, 240.
43. *Ibid.*, 246–8.
44. War Council, 26 Feb. 1915, PRO Cab. 42/1/47.
45. Jenkins, 353.
46. Marder, *Dreadnought to Scapa*, ii, 248, 259–65, 275–6.
47. For a detailed but lucid account of the operations see Rhodes James, *Gallipoli*.
48. War Council, 14 May 1915, PRO Cab. 42/2/19.
49. *Morning Post*, 5 May 1915.
50. Marder, *Dreadnought to Scapa*, iii, 228.
51. See above, pp. 177–8.
52. Petrie, *Walter Long*, 185.
53. Jenkins, 339.
54. Dardanelles Commission, First Report, *PP* 1917–18, x, 426.
55. T. Wilson, *C. P. Scott*, 112.
56. Oxford and Asquith, *Memories*, 68.
57. Jenkins, 339–40.
58. S. E. Koss, 'The Destruction of Britain's last Liberal Government', *Journal of Modern History*, xl (1968), 264. On this, see also Haslehurst, 235–59.
59. Marder, *Fear God*, iii, 238; Hankey, *Supreme Command*, 316.
60. WSC, *World Crisis*, ii, 364–5; Beaverbrook, *Politicians*, 114–15.
61. Marder, *Fear God*, iii, 239.
62. Bonham Carter, 394.
63. WSC, *World Crisis*, ii, 366.
64. *Ibid.*, 369.
65. Jenkins, 360.
66. Marder, *Fear God*, iii, 241.
67. WSC, *World Crisis*, ii, 371–2; Jenkins, 360.
68. Jenkins, 360.
69. Riddell, *War Diary*, 91; WSC, *World Crisis*, ii, 366.
70. Jenkins, 361.
71. Beaverbrook, *Politicians*, 120–3.
72. Jenkins, 361.
73. Brownrigg, 35.
74. Lloyd George, *War Memoirs*, i, 233.
75. Fitzroy, 596.
76. *The Times*, 22 May 1915.
77. 22 May 1915.
78. Cynthia Asquith, 31.

79. *Ibid.*
80. K. Young, *Balfour*, 416.
81. *The Times*, 7 June 1915
82. Ashmead–Bartlett, 121–4.
83. Cynthia Asquith, 170.
84. Addison, *Four and a Half Years*, 114.
85. Leslie, *Jerome*, 321.
86. Hassall, *Marsh*, 340.
87. WSC, *Thoughts and Adventures*, 307.
88. Hassall, *Marsh*, 349; Repington, 517.
89. Marsh, 248.
90. *Ibid.*; J. S. Churchill, 31.
91. Marsh, 249.
92. Leslie, *Jennie*, 329.
93. Bonham Carter, 465.
94. Reproduced in Lavery, at end of book.
95. Beaverbrook, *Politicians*, 283.
96. WSC, *World Crisis*, ii, 391.
97. Hankey, *Supreme Command*, 376–7; Bonham Carter, 415–6.
98. Guinn, 93–4.
99. Roskill, *Hankey*, i, 212.
100. PRO Cab. 42/3/15.
101. PRO Cab. 42/4/8.
102. T. Wilson, *C. P. Scott*, 132.
103. Seely, 228.
104. M. Gilbert, iii, 563.
105. *Ibid.*, 230.
106. Hankey, *Supreme Command*, 433.
107. *The Times*, 13 Nov. 1915.
108. *Hansard*, lxxv, 1512 (15 Nov. 1915).

Chapter 11 (pp. 210–28)

1. T. Wilson, *C. P. Scott*, 141.
2. J. S. Churchill, 32.
3. Bonham Carter, 429–30.
4. Repington, 68.
5. Beaverbrook, *Politicians*, 276.
6. Seely, 233.
7. Oxford and Asquith, *Memories*, 60.
8. WSC, *Thoughts and Adventures*, 99.
9. *Ibid.*, 101.
10. Chandos, 50.
11. WSC, *Thoughts and Adventures*, 104.
12. *Ibid.*, 105.
13. K. Young, *Churchill and Beaverbrook*, 41.
14. WSC, *Thoughts and Adventures*, 108–10.
15. M. Gilbert, 537. The memorandum is printed in WSC, *World Crisis*, ii, 86–9.
16. Sueter, 53, 66.
17. Seely, 236: Blake, *Haig*, 116.
18. Beaverbrook, *Politicians*, 277; Bridges, 141.

19. Blake, *Haig*, 117.
20. 'Captain X', 21–2, 24.
21. *Ibid.*, 96; Charteris, 130.
22. 'Captain X', 49, 97.
23. Hassall, *Marsh*, 383.
24. 'Captain X', 70.
25. Beaverbrook, *Politicians*, 240–5; Macready, i, 232–4.
26. 'Captain X', 84, 89.
27. Hankey, *Supreme Command*, 490.
28. *Hansard*, lxxv, 1421 (7 Mar. 1916).
29. Repington, 191.
30. *Spectator*, 11 Mar. 1916.
31. Riddell, *War Diary*, 163.
32. Beaverbrook, *Politicians*, 280.
33. Repington, 190.
34. *Ibid.*, 191.
35. T. Wilson, *C. P. Scott*, 200.
36. 'Captain X', 110.
37. *Ibid.*, 109–10.
38. *The Times*, 10 May 1916.
39. *Ibid.*, 3 June 1916.
40. Repington, 287.
41. *Sunday Pictorial*, 16 July 1916.
42. Repington, 354.
43. Pound and Harmsworth, 491.
44. *Hansard*, lxxxxii, 500 (9 May 1916); M. Gilbert, iii, 762.
45. *Hansard*, lxxxxii, 2977 (1 June 1916).
46. Hankey, *Supreme Command*, 518.
47. Zetland, *Cromer*, 344.
48. Marder, *Fear God*, iii, 366.
49. Dardanelles Commission, Evidence, 63–4, PRO Cab. 19/33.
50. *Ibid.*, 81.
51. *Ibid.*, 85.
52. *Ibid.*, 210.
53. *Ibid.*, 195.
54. Dardanelles Commission, First Report, *PP* 1917–18, x, 462.
55. *Ibid.*, 449.
56. *Ibid.*, 463.
57. *Ibid.*
58. Riddell, *War Diary*, 241.
59. Roskill, *Hankey*, i, 359.
60. T. Wilson, *C. P. Scott*, 268.
61. *Hansard*, xci, 1785 (20 Mar. 1917).
62. *Hansard*, lxxxxii, 2011 (23 May 1916).
63. *Ibid.*, 2022.
64. Repington, i, 205.
65. *Hansard*, lxxxii, 2024 (23 May 1916).
66. E.g. Cynthia Asquith, 170.
67. WSC, *World Crisis*, iii, 190.
68. *Ibid.*, 187.
69. Churchill's standpoint is defended, at least by implication, in M. J. Williams, 'Thirty Per Cent: a Study in Casualty Statistics', *Journal of the Royal United Services Institution*, cix (1964), 51–5.
70. *Hansard*, lxxxiv, 1372 (24 July 1916).

71. *Ibid.*, 1373–4.
72. *Ibid.*, 1378–81.
73. Brownrigg, 54.
74. T. Wilson, *C. P. Scott*, 213 (5 June 1916).
75. *Hansard*, lxxxv, 2511, 2514 (22 Aug. 1916).
76. T. Wilson, *C. P. Scott*, 234 (20 Nov. 1916).
77. Beaverbrook, *Politicians*, 308.
78. *Ibid.*, 526; Lloyd George, *War Memoirs* (new ed.), ii, 1066–7.
79. Beaverbrook, *Politicians*, 492–3.
80. Riddell, *War Diary*, 232.
81. T. Wilson, *C. P. Scott*, 268.
82. *Sunday Pictorial*, 8 Apr. 1917.
83. *Ibid.*, 22 Apr. 1917.
84. *Ibid.*, 20 May 1917.
85. T. Wilson, *C. P. Scott*, 285.
86. *Hansard*, xcii, 1382–3 (4 Apr. 1917).
87. WSC, *World Crisis*, iii, 253.
88. Roch, 197.
89. Addison, *Four and a Half Years*, 347–8.
90. Beaverbrook, *Men*, 124; Riddell, *War Diary*, 251.
91. Addison, *Politics*, ii, 167.
92. Beaverbrook, *Men*, 128.
93. *Ibid.*, 130–3.
94. *Ibid.*, 136.

Chapter 12 (pp. 229–48)

1. 18 July 1917.
2. R. S. Churchill, *Lord Derby*, 280.
3. Owen. 414.
4. Hewins, ii, 152–3.
5. Lloyd George, *War Memoirs* (new ed.), ii, 1072.
6. Roskill, *Hankey*, i, 415.
7. Repington, ii, 27.
8. *Dundee Advertiser*, 23 July 1917.
9. *Ibid.*, 28 July 1917.
10. *Ibid.*, 30 July 1917.
11. *Ibid.*, 27 July 1917.
12. Repington, ii, 27.
13. *History of the Ministry of Munitions*, ii, Part 1, 77.
14. Wolfe, 126.
15. Riddell, *War Diary*, 257.
16. WSC, *World Crisis*, iv, 298–9.
17. *History of the Ministry of Munitions*, ii, Part 1, 181.
18. WSC to LG, 9 Sept. 1917, Lloyd George Papers F/8/1/11.
19. Memo. on 'Labour, Manpower and Material', 12 Feb. 1918, enclosed in J. A. Webster to H. Hamilton, 16 Feb. 1918, Bonar Law Papers 82/9/5.
20. Roskill, *Hankey*, i, 424; B. Law to E. Geddes, 31 Aug. 1917, Bonar Law Papers 84/6/113.
21. Derby to LG, 15 Aug. 1917, Lloyd George Papers F/14/4/63; Roskill, *Hankey*, i, 425.
22. WSC, *World Crisis*, iv, 311.

23. *History of the Ministry of Munitions*, ii, Part 1, 82.
24. Summary of the Reports of the Commissions of Enquiry into Industrial Unrest, *PP* 1917–18, xv, 154.
25. *The Times*, 16 Jan. 1918.
26. WSC to LG, 22 Jan. 1918, Lloyd George Papers F/8/2/6.
27. *The Times*, 8 Jan. 1918.
28. *Hansard*, xcviii, 2073 (6 Nov. 1917).
29. *The Times*, 11 July 1918.
30. *History of the Ministry of Munitions*, vi, Part 2, 75.
31. *Ibid.*, 67–8.
32. War Cab. Minutes, 26 Sept. 1918, PRO Cab. 23/7.
33. WSC to LG, 9 Sept. 1917, Lloyd George Papers F/8/1/11; Stern, 177–8.
34. WSC, *World Crisis*, iv, 339.
35. Bridges, vi.
36. Hankey, *Supreme Command*, 717.
37. Blake, *Haig*, 254–5.
38. WP, 1917, GT2553, PRO Cab. 24/13.
39. Blake, *Haig*, 271.
40. *Ibid.*, 278.
41. WSC to LG, 19 Jan. 1918, Lloyd George Papers F/8/2/3.
42. WSC, *World Crisis*, iv, 411.
43. Cruttwell, 512.
44. WSC, *World Crisis*, iv, 423.
45. *The Times*, 9 Oct. 1918.
46. WSC, *Thoughts and Adventures*, 177.
47. WSC to LG, 4 May 1918, Lloyd George Papers F/8/2/19.
48. WSC, *World Crisis*, iv, 389.
49. *Ibid.*, 481.
50. Repington, ii, 42.
51. WSC, *World Crisis*, iv, 397–8.
52. Callwell, *Henry Wilson*, ii, 68; Blake, *Haig*, 294.
53. WSC, *World Crisis*, iv, 474.
54. Hassell, *Marsh*, 450.
55. WSC, *World Crisis*, iv, 506.
56. WSC to LG, 10 Aug. 1918, Lloyd George Papers F/8/2/30.
57. Haig to WSC, 9 Aug. 1918, Lloyd George Papers F/8/2/30.
58. WSC, *Thoughts and Adventures*, 187–8.
59. WSC to LG, 9 Sept. 1918, Lloyd George Papers F/8/2/36.
60. *The Times*, 11 Oct. 1918.
61. Riddell, *War Diary*, 371; Roskill, *Hankey*, i, 612–13.
62. Roskill, *Hankey*, i, 616.
63. *The Times*, 16 Oct. 1918.
64. Hassall, *Marsh*, 451–3.
65. *The Times*, 9 Nov. 1918.
66. WSC, *World Crisis*, iv, 541.
67. *Ibid.*, iv, 543.
68. Waley, 182–3.
69. *Ibid.*, 185–6.
70. WSC to LG, 7 Nov. 1918, Lloyd George Papers F/8/2/37.
71. LG to WSC, 8 Nov. 1918, Lloyd George Papers F/8/2/38.
72. WSC to LG, undated, Lloyd George Papers F/8/2/39.
73. WSC to LG, 22 Dec. 1917, Lloyd George Papers F/8/1/21.
74. WSC to LG, 21 Nov. 1918, Lloyd George Papers F/8/2/42.
75. *Dundee Advertiser*, 4 Dec. 1918.

76. *Ibid.*, 10 and 13 Dec. 1918.
77. WSC, *World Crisis*, v, 43.
78. *Dundee Advertiser*, 27 Nov. 1918.
79. *Ibid.*, 5 Dec. 1918.
80. *The Times*, 5 Dec. 1918; WSC to B.Law, 5 July 1919, Bonar Law Papers 87/5/4.
81. *Dundee Advertiser*, 4 Dec. 1918.
82. *The Times*, 3 and 4 Dec. 1918.
83. *Dundee Advertiser*, 30 Dec. 1918.

Chapter 13 (pp. 249–78)

1. R. S. Churchill, *Twenty-one Years*, 19; *Oxford Times*, 4 Jan. 1919.
2. WSC to LG, 29 Dec. 1918, quoted Beaverbrook, *Men*, 361.
3. 16 Jan. 1919.
4. Blake, *Haig*, 350.
5. LG to WSC, 18 Jan. 1919, Lloyd George Papers F/8/3/2; Jones, i, 72.
6. WSC to LG, 20 Jan. 1919, Lloyd George Papers F/8/3/5.
7. WSC, *World Crisis*, v, 63.
8. *Hansard*, cxiii, 72 (3 Mar. 1919).
9. See, e.g., W. Long to LG, 1 Feb. 1919, Lloyd George Papers F/33/2/8.
10. *Hansard*, cxxv, 1339 (23 Feb. 1920).
11. Ullman, 14–15.
12. *Hansard*, cxxiii, 191 (15 Dec. 1919).
13. Ullman, 90.
14. *Ibid.*, 97.
15. *Ibid.*, 130–2.
16. Hankey, *Supreme Control*, 70.
17. Riddell, *Peace Conference*, 21.
18. WSC to LG, 17 Feb. 1919, Lloyd George Papers F/8/3/19.
19. Ullman, 181.
20. *Ibid.*, 199.
21. *Ibid.*, 247n.
22. Riddell, *Peace Conference*, 175.
23. Ullman, 306.
24. Jones, i, 105.
25. Cab. Minutes, 11 Nov. 1920, PRO Cab. 23/23.
26. *Daily Herald*, 3 July 1920.
27. Graubard, 100.
28. Imperial War Cab. Minutes, 31 Dec. 1918, PRO Cab. 23/42.
29. *The Times*, 12 Apr. 1919.
30. Lloyd George, *Peace Treaties*, 325.
31. WP, 13 Feb. 1919, PRO Cab. 23/15.
32. LG to WSC, 30 Aug. 1919, Lloyd George Papers F/9/1/15 (partly quoted in Owen, 518).
33. WSC to LG, Sept. 1919, Lloyd George Papers F/9/1/17.
34. Seely to LG, 4 July 1919, Lloyd George Papers F/9/1/2.
35. WSC to LG, 14 July 1919, Lloyd George Papers F/9/1/5.
36. WSC to LG, 25 Oct. 1919, Lloyd George Papers F/9/1/41; *Hansard*, clii, 390 (21 Mar. 1922).
37. *Hansard*, cxxi, 374 (12 Nov. 1919).
38. *Hansard*, cxxxviii, 1674 and 1711 (1 Mar. 1921).

39. Boyle, 342–3.
40. Callwell, *Henry Wilson*, ii, 316.
41. Boyle, 368–9; Amery, 201–2.
42. *Hansard*, cxxv, 1354 (23 Feb. 1920).
43. Sykes, 266–7.
44. Trenchard to B.Law, 9 Feb. 1921, Bonar Law Papers 100/2/12.
45. CP 1320 'Mesopotamia Expenditure', 1 May 1920, PRO Cab. 24/106.
46. WSC to LG, 4 Jan. 1921, Lloyd George Papers F/9/2/51.
47. Furse, 81–2.
48. Curzon to Samuel, 17 Jan. 1921, quoted in Bowle, 212.
49. The best work on Lawrence in this period is Knightley and Simpson, *The Secret Lives of Lawrence of Arabia*.
50. Thompson, *Guard from the Yard*, 107–8.
51. *The Times*, 12 Mar. 1921.
52. *Ibid.*, 14 Mar. 1921.
53. Thompson, *Guard from the Yard*, 115.
54. Knightley and Simpson, 140–1.
55. *The Times*, 26 Mar. 1921 and 11 Apr. 1921 (leader).
56. Lawrence, 236.
57. *The Times*, 31 Mar. 1921.
58. *Ibid.*, 2 Apr. 1921.
59. CP 3123, 115, PRO Cab. 24/126; Meinertzhagen, *Middle East Diary*, 99–100.
60. Beaverbrook to B. Law, quoted Blake, *Unknown Prime Minister*, 427.
61. Halifax, 95.
62. *The Times*, 8 June 1921.
63. Cab. Minutes, 14 Oct. 1921, PRO Cab. 23/27.
64. *The Times*, 17 June 1921.
65. *Ibid.*, 28 Jan. 1922; Dilley, 157–8.
66. Hancock, *British Commonwealth*, i, 220–1; Huxley, ii, 132.
67. Imperial Conference, 1921, Summary of Transactions, E.55, PRO Cab. 32/6.
68. Cab. Minutes, 3 Nov. 1920, PRO Cab. 23/23.
69. WSC to LG, 9 Nov. 1921, quoted Beaverbrook, *Lloyd George*, 114.
70. WSC, *World Crisis*, v, 305.
71. WSC, *Thoughts and Adventures*, 225.
72. *Hansard*, cli, 1428 (8 Mar. 1922).
73. Amery, ii, 232.
74. *Hansard*, clv, 1712 (26 June 1922).
75. *Ibid.*, 1749.
76. Macready, ii, 653.
77. WSC, *World Crisis*, v, 307.
78. *Dundee Advertiser*, 28 July 1917.
79. *The Times*, 25 July 1919.
80. *Ibid.*, 5 Jan. 1920.
81. *Ibid.*, 16 Feb. 1920.
82. *Ibid.*, 17 Mar. 1920.
83. Sir W. Sutherland to LG, n.d. (? May 1920), Lloyd George Papers F/22/1/33.
84. *The Times*, 1 May 1920.
85. LG to A.Chamberlain, 22 Mar. 1922, Lloyd George Papers F/7/5/21.
86. A.Chamberlain to LG, 23 Mar. 1922, Lloyd George Papers F/7/5/22; also quoted Owen, 613.
87. McCurdy to LG, 17 Mar. 1922, Lloyd George Papers F/35/1/38.

88. WSC to LG, 26 July 1920, Lloyd George Papers F/10/3/22.
89. WSC to LG, 24 Mar. 1920, Lloyd George Papers F/9/2/20.
90. *Ibid.*; cf. WSC's letters to LG and Curzon in June 1921, quoted Beaverbrook, *Lloyd George*, 245 and 259.
91. Cab. Minutes, 4 June 1920, PRO Cab. 23/21.
92. WSC to LG, 23 Sept. 1921, Lloyd George Papers F/9/3/87.
93. WSC, 'The Unemployment Situation', CP 3345, 28 Sept. 1921, Cab. 24/128.
94. LG to WSC, 1 Oct. 1920; WSC to LG, 8 Oct. 1920. Both quoted in Beaverbrook, *Men*, 400–7.
95. War Cab. Minutes, 5 and 15 Aug. 1919, PRO Cab. 23/15.
96. Beatty to Countess Beatty, 23 Feb. 1922, quoted Chalmers, 371; Roskill, *Naval Policy*, i, 337.
97. For more details, see Rhodes James, *Memoirs*, 129.

Chapter 14 (pp. 279–97)

1. *The Times*, 17 Oct. 1922.
2. *Ibid.*, 23 Oct. 1922.
3. W. M. Walker, 'Dundee's Disenchantment with Churchill', *Scottish Historical Review*, xlix (1970), 102.
4. *Ibid.*, 98–9.
5. *Dundee Advertiser*, 16 Nov. 1922.
6. *Ibid.*, 10 Nov. 1922.
7. *Ibid.*, 7 Nov. 1922.
8. *Ibid.*, 13 Nov. 1922.
9. *Ibid.*, 14 Nov. 1922; *Manchester Guardian*, 14 Nov. 1922.
10. Gallacher, 45.
11. *Dundee Advertiser*, 17 Nov. 1922.
12. Oxford and Asquith, *H.H.A.*, ii, 37.
13. WSC to Fisher, 18 Nov. 1922, H.A.L. Fisher Papers, Box 1 (Bodleian Library).
14. WSC, *Thoughts and Adventures*, 213.
15. *Hansard*, clx, 316 (15 Feb. 1923).
16. WSC to B.Law, 3 Mar. 1923, Bonar Law Papers 112/12/2.
17. Hankey to B.Law, 8 Mar. 1923, Bonar Law Papers 112/13/3.
18. *The Times*, 26 Oct. 1923.
19. McCurdy to LG, 12 Oct. 1923, Lloyd George Papers G/13/1/10.
20. *The Times*, 12 Nov. 1923.
21. *Ibid.*, 17 Nov. 1923. Actually Pigg said 'Hellish dark, and smells of cheese'. Surtees, ii, 125.
22. WSC, 'My Life', *News of the World*, 31 Mar. 1935.
23. *The Times*, 20 Nov. 1923.
24. *Ibid.*, 22 Nov. 1923.
25. *Ibid.*, 1 Dec. 1923.
26. Pethick-Lawrence, 127.
27. *Ibid.*, 128.
28. C. Cook in A.J.P. Taylor, *Lloyd George*, 307.
29. Jenkins, 500.
30. WSC to Lady Bonham Carter, 8 Jan. 1924, quoted in Cowling, 395.
31. *The Times*, 18 Jan. 1924.
32. T. Wilson, *Downfall*, 267.
33. *The Times*, 25 Feb. 1924.

34. *Daily Mail*, 11 Mar. 1924.
35. *The Times*, 21 Mar. 1924.
36. WSC to Baldwin, 7 Mar. 1924, quoted Rhodes James, *Memoirs*, 194.
37. Rhodes James, *Memoirs*, 194–5.
38. Brockway, 153.
39. WSC, *Thoughts and Adventures*, 213.
40. *The Times*, 12 Mar. 1924.
41. *Ibid.*, 8 Mar. 1924.
42. Brockway, 154.
43. *Daily Mail*, 12 Mar. 1924.
44. Brockway, 155.
45. Pethick-Lawrence, 130.
46. WSC to Salvidge, 23 Mar. 1924, quoted in Salvidge, 271.
47. Salvidge, 273.
48. *Ibid.*, 275.
49. *The Times*, 26 Sept. 1924.
50. *Woodford Times*, 26 Sept. 1924.
51. *The Times*, 9 Oct. 1924.
52. *Ibid.*, 13 Oct. 1924 (election address).
53. *Ibid.*, 10 Oct. 1924.
54. *Ibid.*, 24 Oct. 1924.
55. *Ibid.*, 3 Nov. 1924.
56. K. Young, *Churchill and Beaverbrook*, 71.
57. Jones, i, 302.
58. I. Macleod, 110–11.
59. G. M. Young, 88.
60. Duff Cooper, 137.
61. Jones, i, 303.
62. K. Young, *Churchill and Beaverbrook*, 73.
63. Salvidge, 278.

Chapter 15 (pp. 298–325)

1. WSC, 'The Minister Who Has to Say No', *News of the World*, 30 Apr. 1939.
2. Grigg, 55.
3. Leith-Ross, 89.
4. Grigg, 178.
5. Boothby, 45.
6. Moggridge, 16.
7. *Ibid.*, 34.
8. WSC to Baldwin, 12 Dec. 1924, quoted Moggridge, 40.
9. 28 Jan. 1925.
10. WSC, 'Liberalism', *English Life*, Jan. 1924.
11. Moggridge, 46.
12. *Ibid.*, 46–7.
13. Leith-Ross, 92.
14. 21 Feb. 1925, reprinted in Keynes, *Essays in Persuasion*, 235–6.
15. WSC to Niemeyer, 22 Feb. 1925, quoted Moggridge, 54.
16. Grigg, 182–4.
17. WSC, 'Montagu Norman', *Sunday Pictorial*, 20 Sept. 1931.
18. WSC to Baldwin, 15 Dec. 1924, Baldwin Papers 2.26.
19. Quoted in Roskill, *Naval Policy*, i, 447.

20. Chalmers, 405.
21. N. Chamberlain diary, quoted Feiling, 131.
22. *Hansard*, clxxxiii, 72 (28 Apr. 1925).
23. N. Chamberlain diary, quoted Feiling, 131.
24. *Hansard*, clxxxiii, 90 (28 Apr. 1925).
25. *Ibid.*, 179 (29 Apr. 1925).
26. *The Times*, 13 July 1925.
27. Keynes, *Economic Consequences*, 8.
28. A. K. Cairncross in *Economic History Review*, xxiv (1971), 305.
29. WSC to Baldwin, 15 Dec. 1924, Baldwin Papers 2.26.
30. *The Times*, 9 Oct. 1924.
31. Roskill, *Naval Policy*, i, 450.
32. Rhodes James, *Memoirs*, 213.
33. Templewood, *Empire of the Air*, 275.
34. Cab. Minutes, 30 July, 1925, PRO Cab. 23/50.
35. A. Mason, 'The Government and the General Strike', *International Review of Social History*, xiv (1969), 5–8.
36. *Hansard*, cxciv, 1515 (22 Apr. 1926).
37. Roskill, *Naval Policy*, i, 478–82.
38. *Hansard*, cxciv, 1687 (26 Apr. 1926).
39. *Ibid.*, 1717.
40. *Ibid.*, 1723.
41. *Ibid.*, 1890 (27 Apr. 1926).
42. Strike memoir (undated), Templewood Papers, V.8, Cambridge University Library.
43. Percy, 132.
44. Rhodes James, *Memoirs*, 243.
45. *Ibid.*, 237.
46. Anon, *Strike Nights in Printing House Square*, 34.
47. *British Gazette*, 13 May 1926; *Hansard*, cxcvii, 2218 (7 July 1926).
48. Rhodes James, *Memoirs*, 244–5.
49. Jones, ii, 44.
50. Rhodes James, *Memoirs*, 247; Reith, 108–12.
51. Rhodes James, *Memoirs*, 242.
52. Jones, ii, 44.
53. Cab. Minutes, 7 May 1926, PRO Cab. 23/52.
54. Ismay, 57–8.
55. Rhodes James, *Memoirs*, 245.
56. *Hansard*, cxcvii, 2216, 2218 (7 July 1926).
57. Martin, 90, 94.
58. *Morning Post*, 14 May 1926.
59. Jones, ii, 36.
60. WSC to Baldwin, 9 June 1926, Baldwin Papers 18.37.
61. Rhodes James, *Memoirs*, 258.
62. Jones, ii, 76.
63. *Ibid.*, 73.
64. Rhodes James, *Memoirs*, 258.
65. Jones, ii, 78.
66. WSC to Baldwin, 10 Sept. 1926, Baldwin Papers 18.52.
67. Jones, ii, 85.
68. Page Arnot, 487.
69. WSC, 'The Coal Situation', CP 368 (1926), PRO Cab. 24/181.
70. *Hansard*, ccv, 61–2 (11 Apr. 1927).
71. *Ibid.*, 101.

72. *Ibid.*, 238 (12 Apr. 1927).

73. Macmillan, *Winds of Change,* 238.

74. WSC to Baldwin, June 1927, Baldwin Papers 5.125.

75. Feiling, 144–5.

76. *Ibid.*; Macmillan, *Winds of Change,* 240.

77. *Hansard,* ccxvi, 845 (24 Apr. 1928).

78. *Ibid.*, 872.

79. 21 Apr. 1929.

80. *Hansard,* ccxxvii, 69 (15 Apr. 1929).

81. *Ibid.*, ccxvi, 939 (25 Apr. 1928).

82. *Ibid.*, ccxxvii, 30–1 (15 Apr. 1929).

83. K. Young, *Churchill and Beaverbrook,* 104–5.

84. Memo. by LG, Lloyd George Papers, G/4/4/23.

85. 'Resignation of the Second Baldwin Government', Templewood Papers, V.4, Cambridge University Library.

86. *Woodford Times,* 31 May 1929.

87. *The Times,* 27 May 1929.

88. Jones, ii, 191.

89. Cab. Minutes, 3 June 1929, PRO Cab. 23/60.

90. 15 June 1929; see also memo. cited in note 85.

91. Grigg, 193.

92. WSC to Baldwin, 22 Feb. 1925, quoted in Jones, i, 311. See also 'Trade Union Legislation', CP 365 (1926), PRO Cab. 24/181.

93. *Hansard,* ccv, 238 (12 Apr. 1927).

94. Leith-Ross, 88, 95.

95. Grigg, 208.

96. For a discussion of the proposed 1887 Budget see WSC, *Lord Randolph Churchill,* ii, 190–210.

97. Cab. Minutes, 6 June 1928, PRO Cab. 23/31.

98. Rhodes James, *Churchill,* 166.

99. Roskill, *Naval Policy,* 556–7.

100. WSC to Baldwin, 15 Dec. 1924, Baldwin Papers 2.26.

101. Cab. Minutes, 18 July 1928, PRO Cab. 23/58.

102. *Economist,* 13 Apr. 1929.

103. Leith-Ross, 118.

104. Grigg, 174.

Chapter 16 (pp. 326–44)

1. WSC to LG, 29 June 1921, Lloyd George Papers F/9/3/63.

2. Leslie, *Jennie,* 354.

3. Oxford and Asquith, *Memories,* ii, 197.

4. Principal Probate Registry, s.v. 1921: Porch, Jennie.

5. R. S. Churchill, *Twenty-one Years,* 17.

6. Labour Party, *Report of 18th Annual Conference* 1918, 12.

7. Hamilton, 437.

8. Riddell, *Peace Conference,* 261.

6. Labour Party, *Report of 18th Annual Conference* 1918, 12.

10. Tilden, 117.

11. Jones, ii, 77.

12. Fedden, *Churchill at Chartwell,* 7–8.

13. *Westerham Herald,* 18 Aug. 1923 and 15 Mar. 1924.

14. *The Times,* 13 Nov. 1924 and 22 Jan. 1925.

15. WSC, *Thoughts and Adventures*, 193–5.
16. *Ibid.*, 196–8; Riddell, *Peace Conference*, 105.
17. Marsh, 397.
18. R. S. Churchill, *Twenty-one Years*, 20 and 24.
19. *The Times*, 21 Apr. 1922.
20. Birkenhead, *F.E.*, 441.
21. P. Sassoon to LG, 28 Apr. 1922, Lloyd George Papers F/45/1/13.
22. R. S. Churchill, *Twenty-one Years*, 49.
23. *The Times*, 6 Apr. 1920.
24. Duchess of Westminster, 227.
25. C. Lowther to R. Blumenfeld, 10 Aug. 1916, Blumenfeld Papers Lowt.2.1.
26. Sheridan, 133.
27. Gibbs, 51.
28. See Coombs.
29. *The Times*, 24 July 1921. This picture, entitled 'The Hills of Moab', does not appear in the above catalogue.
30. WSC, *Thoughts and Adventures*, 314.
31. Woods, 51–4.
32. WSC, *World Crisis*, i, 24; *Blackwood's Magazine*, xxiii, 708.
33. *Nation*, 14 Apr. 1923.
34. 10 Apr. 1923.
35. WSC, *World Crisis*, ii, 489.
36. Sydenham of Combe *et al.*
37. See above, Chapter 11, note 69.
38. *Nation*, 9 Mar. 1929, reprinted in Keynes, *Essays in Biography*.
39. J. S. Churchill, 21.
40. *Ibid.*, 26; Diana Cooper, *Light*, 93; Cartland, 77.
41. R. S. Churchill, *Twenty-one Years*, 48.
42. *Ibid.*, 26; Thompson, *Guard from the Yard*, 140.
43. Jones, ii, 67.
44. R. S. Churchill, *Twenty-one Years*, 27–8.
45. *Ibid.*, 48–50; *The Times*, 21 Jan. 1927.
46. WSC to Baldwin, 6 Nov. 1924, Baldwin Papers 27.2.
47. Sarah Churchill, 25.
48. WSC to Baldwin, 17 Apr. 1925, Baldwin Papers 6.328.
49. WSC to Baldwin, 2 Sept. 1928, Baldwin Papers, 36.76.
50. *The Times*, 2 Nov. 1928.
51. *Ibid.*, 11 Oct., 18 Oct. and 2nd Nov. 1928.
52. Boothby, 45.
53. K. Young, *Churchill and Beaverbrook*, 92.
54. Wedgwood, 117; but for a slightly different view, see Coote, *The Other Club*, 16.
55. Grigg, 177.
56. WSC in Lawrence, 201.
57. Garnett, 521.
58. Birkenhead, *The Prof.*, 128–9.
59. Jones, ii, 67.
60. *Ibid.*, 68.
61. R. S. Churchill, *Twenty-one Years*, 63.
62. Hassall, *Marsh*, 287, 405 and 466; Sassoon, 77.
63. Hassall, *Marsh*, 498.
64. K. Young, *Churchill and Beaverbrook*, 89.
65. 'Raymond', 103.

66. Curzon to WSC, 13 June 1921, quoted in Beaverbrook, *Lloyd George*, 255; Waley, 248 and 269.
67. Hewins, ii, 302.
68. Amery, ii, 497.
69. Bridgeman, 'Political Notes', quoted Roskill, *Naval Policy*, i, 37.
70. *Hansard*, cxxv, 1362 (23 Feb. 1920).
71. Amery, ii, 204. Cf. Wyndham Childs, 158; Coote, *Editorial*, 96.
72. WSC, *Thoughts and Adventures*, 213.
73. Macmillan, *Winds of Change*, 176.
74. Holtby, 245–6.
75. CP 80 (1927), PRO Cab. 24/185.
76. Briggs. *Birth of Broadcasting*, 271.
77. *The Times*, 11 Feb. 1928.
78. Cab. Minutes, 29 Feb. 1928, PRO Cab. 23/57.
79. Briggs, *Golden Age*, 130; Webb, *Diaries*, 166.
80. *Sunday Express*, 5 Dec. 1920.
81. *Ibid.*, 12 Dec. 1920.
82. LG to Balfour, 21 June 1923, Lloyd George Papers G/1/17/1.
83. 7 Nov. 1924.
84. *The Times*, 9 Dec. 1924.
85. *Ibid.*, 26 Sept. 1924.
86. Spender, *Life*, i, 164.
87. Cowling, 428.
88. 'A Gentleman with a Duster' (i.e. H. Begbie), *The Mirrors of Downing Street* (1920), 108.
89. 10 Aug. 1924.

Chapter 17 (pp. 345–65)

1. K. Young, *Churchill and Beaverbrook*, 110.
2. WSC, 'The Dole', *Saturday Evening Post* (Philadelphia), 29 Mar. 1930.
3. *The Times*, 13 Aug. 1929.
4. WSC to Baldwin, 29 June 1929, Baldwin Papers 164.36.
5. *Hansard*, ccxxix, 125 (3 July 1929).
6. Amery, iii, 18.
7. Jones, ii, 229.
8. Nicolson, i, 41–2.
9. WSC to Baldwin, 16 Oct. 1930, Baldwin Papers 31.172.
10. Baldwin to WSC, 21 Oct. 1930, Baldwin Papers 31.171.
11. Middlemas and Barnes, 557.
12. *Ibid.*, 578.
13. Winterton, 161.
14. WSC, *India*, 35.
15. WSC, 'Egyptian Independence Proposals', CP 1803 (24 Aug. 1920), PRO Cab. 24/111.
16. WSC's notes on Montagu to LG, 8 Dec. 1920, Lloyd George Papers F/40/3/38.
17. Irwin to Salisbury, 3 Dec. 1929, Halifax Papers, India Office Library, Mss.Eur. C152.18.369.
18. Irwin to WSC, 26 Dec. 1929, *ibid.*, 385.
19. WSC to Irwin, ? Jan. 1930, *ibid.*, 19.1.
20. K. Young, *Churchill and Beaverbrook*, 115–16.
21. WSC to Baldwin, 24 Sept. 1930, Baldwin Papers 104.51.

22. Rhodes James, *Memoirs*, 355.
23. WSC, *India*, 40 and 46-7.
24. *The Times*, 13 Dec. 1930.
25. WSC, *India*, 68.
26. *Hansard*, ccxlvii, 744 (26 Jan. 1931).
27. I. Macleod, 140.
28. WSC, *India*, 94.
29. *The Times*, 17 Mar. 1931.
30. *Ibid.*, 18 Mar. 1931.
31. Nicolson, i, 81-2.
32. *Woodford Times*, 18 Sept. 1931.
33. *The Times*, 9 Sept. 1931.
34. WSC, 'The Way Out of the Crisis', *Daily Mail*, 2 Oct. 1931.
35. *Woodford Times*, 23 Oct. 1931.
36. *The Times*, 12 Sept. 1931.
37. *Hansard*, ccxlvii, 1021 (28 Jan. 1931).
38. *Ibid.*, cclix, 121 and 132 (11 Nov. 1931).
39. *Ibid.*, cclxvi, 684 (26 May 1932).
40. Hoare to Willingdon, 31 Mar. 1933, Templewood Papers, India Office Library, Eur. Mss. E240.2.654; *Hansard*, cclxxvi, 1047-8 (29 Mar. 1933).
41. R. A. Butler, 51.
42. *Indian Empire Review*, Oct. 1935, 380.
43. S. C. Ghosh, in his otherwise valuable article, 'A Case Study of the Indian Problem, 1929-1934', *Political Studies*, xiii (1965), 198-212, fails to make clear the distinction between the IES and the IDL.
44. *The Times*, 8 and 12 May, 1933.
45. *Ibid.*, 29 June 1933.
46. *Indian Empire Review*, July 1933, 2.
47. *The Times*, 7 Oct. 1933.
48. Redford, ii, 289.
49. *Hansard*, cclxxxviii, 714-15 (16 Apr. 1934).
50. Hoare to Willingdon, 10 May 1934, Templewood Papers, Eur.Mss. E240.4.1058.
51. *Hansard*, ccxc, 1738 (13 June 1934).
52. *The Times*, 27 June 1934.
53. *Sunday Dispatch*, 1 and 22 July 1934; Redford, 287.
54. *The Times*, 29 Mar. 1934, 5 Oct. 1934.
55. *Ibid.*, 5 Dec. 1934.
56. *Westerham Herald*, 26 Jan. 1935.
57. *The Times*, 6 Feb. 1935; Rhodes James, *Churchill*, 211-12.
58. *The Times*, 8 Feb. 1935.
59. *Ibid.*, 31 Jan. and 5 Feb. 1935.
60. *Ibid.*, 13 Dec. 1934.
61. *Hansard*, ccxcvii, 1641 (11 Feb. 1935).
62. *Hansard*, cccii, 1915-16 (5 June 1935).
63. *Ibid.*, 1925.
64. Hoare to Willingdon, 20 Apr. 1934, Templewood Papers, Eur.Mss. E240.41045.
65. Wrench, 266ff.
66. *Hansard*, cccii, 1911 (5 June 1935).
67. Briggs, *Golden Age*, 135-7 and 144.
68. India Defence League.
69. Bernays, 109.

70. *Ibid.*, 183.
71. 'Watchman', 117.
72. *Ibid.*
73. Joint Committee on Indian Constitutional Reform, *PP* 1932–3, viii, 1777.
74. *The Times*, 30 Oct. 1933.
75. Halifax, 125; Templewood, *Nine Troubled Years*, 103.
76. R. A. Butler, 58–9; R. J. Moore, 'The Making of India's Paper Federation, 1927–1935', in Philips and Wainwright, 54–78.
77. *Hansard* (Lords), lxxv, 402 (5 Nov. 1929).

Chapter 18 (pp. 366–98)

1. WSC, 'United States of Europe', *Saturday Evening Post*, 15 Feb. 1930.
2. *New York Times*, 12 Dec. 1931.
3. WSC, *Arms and the Covenant*, 38 (23 Nov. 1932).
4. *Ibid.*, 45.
5. *Ibid.*, 65 (23 Mar. 1933).
6. *Ibid.*
7. WSC, *WW2*, i, 69.
8. Hollis, 190–1.
9. *The Times*, 25 Feb. 1933.
10. *Ibid.*, 28 Feb. 1933.
11. *Ibid.*, 15 Nov. 1933.
12. WSC, *Arms and the Covenant*, 111 (7 Feb. 1934).
13. *Ibid.*, 123 (8 Mar. 1934).
14. *Ibid.*, 125.
15. *Hansard*, cclxxxvi, 2073 (8 Mar. 1934).
16. WSC, *Arms and the Covenant*, 180 (28 Nov. 1934).
17. *Hansard*, ccxcv, 882 (28 Nov. 1934).
18. U.S. Strategic Bombing Survey, *Overall Report* (1945), 11.
19. *Hansard*, cccii, 367 (22 May 1935).
20. *Ibid.*, cclxx, 632 (10 Nov. 1932).
21. Rhodes James, *Memoirs*, 401.
22. Birkenhead, *The Prof*, 178.
23. WSC, *WW2*, i, 135.
24. Birkenhead, *The Prof*, 182–3.
25. *The Times*, 23 Feb. 1935.
26. Wrench, 322.
27. WSC to A.Chamberlain, 1 Oct. 1935; WSC, *WW2*, i, 156.
28. *The Times*, 4 Oct. 1935.
29. WSC to Baldwin, 7 Oct. 1935, Baldwin Papers 47.113.
30. *The Times*, 29 Oct. 1935.
31. 'Mr Churchill on his Fight', *Daily Mail*, 8 Nov. 1935.
32. *Woodford Times*, 15 Nov. 1935.
33. *The Times*, 12 Nov. 1935.
34. Nicolson, i, 228; WSC, *WW2*, i, 162.
35. *The Times*, 9 May 1936.
36. Petrie, *Chamberlain*, ii, 408.
37. I. Macleod, 193; Rhodes James, *Memoirs*, 410; *The Times*, 16 Mar. 1936.
38. Rhodes James, *loc. cit.*
39. Avon, *Facing the Dictators*, 347.

40. Nicolson, 251.
41. WSC, *Arms and the Covenant*, 313–14 (6 Apr. 1936).
42. WSC, *Step by Step*, 41 (26 June 1936).
43. *Ibid.*, 53 (10 Aug. 1936).
44. WSC, *WW2*, i, 191 and 611–12.
45. WSC, *Arms and the Covenant*, 331–2 (21 May 1936).
46. WSC, *WW2*, 143 and 608–11.
47. Winterton, 216–17; Croft, 285; *News Chronicle*, 25 May 1936.
48. Winterton, *loc. cit.*
49. 'Parliamentary Deputation, July 1936', PRO Prem. 1/193.
50. *Ibid.*
51. *Ibid.*
52. *Hansard*, cccxvii, 1144 (12 Nov. 1936).
53. *The Times*, 26 Nov. 1936.
54. C. T. Stannage, 'The East Fulham By-Election', *Historical Journal*, xiv (1971), 165–200; R. Heller, 'East Fulham Revisited', *Journal of Contemporary History*, vi (1971), no. 3, 72–96.
55. Inskip in *Hansard*, cccxvii, 742 (10 Nov. 1936), but it is fair to add that he applied the words to the whole preceding decade.
56. *The Times*, 8 June 1936.
57. V. Bonham Carter in *Daily Telegraph*, 9 Mar. 1965; Spier, 22.
58. Duke of Windsor, 135.
59. Birkenhead, *Walter Monckton*, 129–30.
60. Beaverbrook, *Abdication*, 65.
61. Duke of Windsor, 365.
62. Citrine, 357; V. Bonham Carter in *Daily Telegraph*, 11 Mar. 1965; Spier, 64.
63. WSC to Baldwin, 4 Dec. 1936, quoted Middlemas and Barnes, 1009.
64. Duke of Windsor, 382–3.
65. Beaverbrook, *Abdication*, 80.
66. Middlemas and Barnes, *loc. cit.*
67. *Sunday Times*, 6 Dec. 1936.
68. Nicolson, i, 284.
69. WSC, *WW2*, i, 197.
70. Rhodes James, *Memoirs*, 415.
71. Duke of Windsor, 409.
72. *The Times*, 1 June 1937.
73. *Ibid.*, 5 July 1937.
74. WSC, *WW2*, i, 219.
75. *Ibid.*, 220–3; Avon, *Facing the Dictators*, 463.
76. *The Times*, 8 Oct. 1937.
77. *Evening Standard*, 7 Jan. 1938, reprinted WSC, *Step by Step*, 204.
78. Minney, 130.
79. WSC, *WW2*, i, 231.
80. COS Report, 'Comparison of Strength', CP 296(37), PRO Cab. 24/273.
81. Cab. Minutes, 8 Dec. 1937, PRO Cab. 23/90A.
82. Avon, *Facing the Dictators*, 499.
83. 'Watchman', 133.
84. Macmillan, *Winds of Change*, 548.
85. 19 Mar. 1938.
86. WSC, *Into Battle*, 42 and 53 (5 Oct. 1938).
87. *Ibid.*, 263–5.
88. *Ibid.*, 272–3.
89. Duff Cooper, 232.

90. Diana Cooper, *Light*, 242.
91. Birkenhead, *Halifax*, 400; WSC, *WW2*, i, 277.
92. Nicolson, i, 370.
93. Macmillan, *Winds of Change*, 559.
94. Nicolson, i, 371; McLachlan, *In the Chair*, 141.
95. V. Bonham Carter in Spier, 11–12.
96. WSC, *Into Battle*, 42 and 53 (5 Oct. 1938).
97. Nicolson, i, 375–6.
98. WSC, *WW2*, i, 296; *The Times*, 5 Nov. 1938.
99. *The Times*, 7 and 11 Nov. 1938.
100. British Institute of Public Opinion, 20.
101. Atholl, 229.
102. The point is not elucidated in A. J. P. Taylor, *Beaverbrook*.
103. *Woodford Times*, 27 Jan., 17 Feb. and 17 Mar. 1939.
104. *The Times*, 11 Mar. 1939.
105. WSC, *Into Battle*, 78 (14 Mar. 1939).
106. *Hansard*, cccxlvii, 1846 (19 May 1939).
107. WSC, *WW2*, i, 317.
108. *Ibid.*, 327–8.
109. Feiling, 406.
110. *The Times*, 18 Aug. 1939.
111. WSC, 'The Terrible Twins', *Collier's*, 30 Sept. 1939.
112. WSC, 'The Age of Government by Great Dictators', *News of the World*, 10 Oct. 1937.
113. WSC, 'What Price Freedom?', *Answers*, 24 Oct. 1936.
114. WSC, *Step by Step*, 313 (30 Dec. 1938).
115. Gardiner, *Certain People*, 60.
116. *The Times*, 13 Nov. 1936.
117. 11 Dec. 1936.
118. Cantril, 195.
119. WSC, *WW2*, i, 162.

Chapter 19 (pp. 399–418)

1. The journey may be documented from R. S. Churchill, *Twenty-one Years*, from J. S. Churchill, *Crowded Canvas*, from WSC's articles in the *Daily Telegraph* and the *Daily Mail*, and from the Baruch Papers in Princeton University Library.
2. R. S. Churchill, *Twenty-one Years*, 73.
3. WSC, *Strand Magazine*, Aug. 1931, 147.
4. WSC, *Daily Telegraph*, 9 Dec. 1929.
5. WSC, *Strand Magazine*, Aug. 1931, 150.
6. WSC to Baruch, 1 Nov. 1930, Baruch Papers.
7. WSC, *Daily Mail*, 5 Jan. 1932.
8. *Ibid.*, 4 Jan. 1932.
9. Moir, 31.
10. *New York Times*, 31 Dec. 1931.
11. WSC to Baruch, 18 Jan. 1932, Baruch Papers; Clifford, 188–9.
12. WSC, *Daily Mail*, 23 Mar. 1932.
13. WSC, *Collier's*, 5 Aug. 1933.
14. Moir, 82–3.
15. *New York Times*, 24 Jan. 1932; *The Times*, 19 Mar. 1932.

16. The total can be calculated from Woods.
17. 20 Oct. 1930.
18. *Daily Telegraph*, 9 Mar. 1965.
19. Hassall, *Marsh*, 567; WSC to Baldwin, 24 Sept. 1930, Baldwin Papers 104.51.
20. 2 Nov. 1931.
21. Woods, 228.
22. Hassall, *Marsh*, 575.
23. WSC, *Marlborough*, i, 7; Ashley, 139.
24. Ashley, 1.
25. WSC to Feiling, 19 Sept. 1932, quoted in Ashley, 235–6.
26. Ashley, 138; Woods, 69.
27. Hassall, *Marsh*, 576–7.
28. *English Historical Review*, xlix (1934), 716 and 718–9.
29. *English Review*, lix (1934), 708.
30. Namier, 230.
31. *Sunday Times*, 11 Sept. 1938.
32. J. H. Plumb in A. J. P. Taylor *et al.*, *Churchill*, 136.
33. Ashley, 210.
34. *New York Times*, 22 Feb. 1933; *Westerham Herald*, 25 Feb. 1933.
35. Moir, 100.
36. Hassall, *Marsh*, 614; Ashley, 33 and 36.
37. Pound, 1.
38. *Ibid.*, 3–4.
39. K. Young, *Churchill and Beaverbrook*, 124.
40. Pound, 153.
41. Moir, 170; Chenery, 210.
42. Moir, 166.
43. Baldwin to Davidson, 2 Sept. 1934, quoted Rhodes James, *Memoirs*, 401.
44. Pound, 5.
45. Hassall, *Ambrosia*, 24 and 28.
46. Halifax Diary, 12 May 1943, Hickleton Papers A7.8.12.
47. WSC, *WW2*, i, 73 and 178.
48. Vansittart, 497 and 499.
49. WSC, *WW2*, i, 72–3.
50. Baker White, 161.
51. Spier, 22.
52. Moir, 53.
53. *Ibid.*, 71–2.
54. Westminster, 230.
55. *News Chronicle*, 29 Aug. 1930.
56. *The Times*, 10 and 13 Dec. 1932.
57. Sarah Churchill, 51–2.
58. Oliver, 104 and 118.
59. See Forbes-Robertson.
60. Baldwin to Davidson, 2 Sept. 1934, quoted in Rhodes James, *Memoirs*, 401.
61. WSC, *News of the World*, 13 Jan. 1935.
62. WSC, *Daily Mail*, 6 Feb. 1936.
63. Forbes-Robertson, 249.
64. *New York Times*, 8 Jan. 1938.
65. *The Times*, 9 and 30 Jan. 1939; Citrine, 330–6.
66. Diana Cooper, *Light*, 155.

67. J. S. Churchill, 59.
68. *The Times*, 10 Dec. 1931 and 4 Aug. 1936.
69. E.g. Ashley, J. S. Churchill, Moir, Oliver.
70. Ashley, 24.
71. Birkenhead, *F.E.*, 551.
72. B. Liddell Hart in A. J. P. Taylor, *Churchill*, 200.
73. Duchess of Windsor, 212.
74. WSC to Baruch, 30 July 1931, Baruch Papers.
75. Baruch to WSC, 25 Sept. 1930 (telegram), *ibid.*
76. Sarah Churchill, 38.
77. See, e.g., Col. G. R. Lane-Fox to Halifax, 4 Mar. 1931, Halifax Personal Corr., India Office Library, Mss. Eur. C152.1y, p. 358.
78. *The Times*, 31 Oct. 1936.
79. Birkenhead, *The Prof*, 155.
80. *Hansard*, cccxxxviii, 2034 (19 July 1938).
81. *New York Times*, 3 Dec. 1937.
82. WSC, *News of the World*, 13 Jan. 1935.
83. *The Times*, 27 June 1929.
84. WSC, *News of the World*, 13 Jan. 1935.
85. *The Times*, 25 Oct. 1937.
86. *Westerham Herald*, 16 Sept. 1933.
87. Sarah Churchill, 48; Fedden, *Churchill and Chartwell*, 47.
88. *Daily Sketch*, 15 Mar. 1934.
89. *Hansard*, ccliii, 104 (2 June 1931).
90. WSC, 'The Truth about Myself', *Strand Magazine*, Jan. 1936, 281.
91. *Hansard*, cclxxiv, 1860 (22 Feb. 1933).
92. Briggs, *Golden Age*, 135.
93. *The Times*, 12 Aug. 1931.
94. WSC, *Strand Magazine*, Jan. 1936, 286.
95. Liddell Hart, *Memoirs*, i, 220.
96. WSC, *Answers*, 4 Aug. 1934.
97. *The Times*, 2 Apr. 1938.
98. *New York Times*, 19 Apr. 1938.

Chapter 20 (pp. 419–39)

1. WSC, *WW*2, i, 361.
2. *Ibid.*, 362–3.
3. *Ibid.*, 364.
4. *Ibid.*, 365.
5. Oliver, 126.
6. Pawle, 20. This book, *The War and Colonel Warden*, is based on Commander Thompson's recollections.
7. *Ibid.*, 31.
8. Fraser in Marchant, 80–1.
9. Wheeler-Bennett, *King George VI*, 391 and 416.
10. Pawle, 30.
11. Harrod, 180–7.
12. Fraser in Marchant, 78–9.
13. Pawle, 30–1.
14. WSC, *WW*2, i, 386.
15. *Ibid.*, 391.
16. *Hansard*, cccli, 1244 (26 Sept. 1939).

17. *Ibid.*, 1246 and 1250.
18. *Ibid.*, ccclii, 686 (17 Oct. 1939).
19. Hoare, War Diary, Templewood Papers, XI.II, Cambridge University Library.
20. *Hansard*, ccliii, 254 (8 Nov. 1939).
21. *Ibid.*, 266.
22. Templewood, *Nine Troubled Years*, 409–10.
23. Hoare, War Diary, Oct.–Nov. 1939, Templewood Papers, Cambridge.
24. Roskill, *War at Sea*, 100.
25. WSC, *WW2*, i, 507.
26. *Ibid.*, 410.
27. *Ibid.*, 411.
28. *Ibid.*, 495.
29. *Ibid.*, 644–5 and 647–8; Pawle, 41–5.
30. WSC, *WW2*, i, 498.
31. *Ibid.*, 504.
32. *F.R.U.S.: Diplomatic Papers, 1940*, i (General) (Washington, D.C., 1959), 83–4.
33. McLachlan, *Room 39*, 126–7.
34. Shakespeare, 229.
35. Woodward, i, 79.
36. WSC, *War Speeches*, i, 169 (11 Apr. 1940).
37. Roskill, *War at Sea*, i, 174–5.
38. Nicolson, ii, 70.
39. Roskill, *War at Sea*, 177–8.
40. Macleod and Kelly, 257.
41. *Ibid.*, 260.
42. Chatfield, ii, 179; Ismay, 110.
43. WSC, *WW2*, i, 530.
44. *Ibid.*, 537.
45. *Ibid.*, 565.
46. Ian Jacob in Wheeler-Bennett, *Action This Day*, 163.
47. Avon, *Reckoning*, 84; Templewood Papers, XII.3, Cambridge.
48. Avon, *Reckoning*, 73.
49. Hervey, 324.
50. WSC, *War Speeches*, i, 109 (1 Oct. 1939).
51. *News Chronicle*, 1 Jan. 1940.
52. *Ibid.*, 8 Apr. 1940.
53. Amery, iii, 339.
54. Boothby, 195.
55. Amery, iii, 355.
56. Nicolson, ii, 75 (4 May 1940).
57. Amery, iii, 358.
58. Morrison, 172–4.
59. *Hansard*, ccclx, 1283 (8 May 1940).
60. *Ibid.*, 1362.
61. *Ibid.*, 1150 (7 May 1940).
62. Dalton, *Fateful Years*, 306.
63. Margesson to Baldwin, 4 Mar. 1941, Margesson Papers.
64. Avon, *Reckoning*, 96–7.
65. WSC, *WW2*, i, 597 (but WSC has the date wrong).
66. R. A. Butler, 84.
67. WSC, *WW2*, i, 598.
68. Avon, *Reckoning*, 97; Templewood, *Nine Troubled Years*, 432.

69. Rhodes James, *Chips*, 249–50.
70. War Cab. Minutes, 10 May 1940, PRO Cab. 65/7.
71. Dalton, *Fateful Years*, 311.
72. War Cab. Minutes, *loc. cit*.
73. WSC, *WW2*, i, 599.
74. Wheeler-Bennett, *King George VI*, 444.
75. Dalton, *Fateful Years*, 312; WSC, *WW2*, i, 600. The timing is based on the Diary of WSC's engagements sent to him in Sept. 1946 by T. L. Rowan, then Attlee's Principal Private Secretary; copy in Attlee Papers, Univ. College, Oxford.
76. Dalton, *Fateful Years*, 312.
77. Dalton, *Fateful Years*, 313n.
78. WSC., *WW2*, i, 601.
79. *Ibid*.
80. A. J. P. Taylor, *English History, 1914–1945*, 475.
81. See, e.g., Feiling, 422; Dalton, *Fateful Years*, 307; Wheeler-Bennett, *King George VI*, 444.
82. Halifax Diary, 9 May 1940, quoted in Birkenhead, *Halifax*, 454.
83. Hervey, 326.
84. Nicolson, ii, 59.
85. *News Chronicle*, 1 Jan. 1940.
86. Wheeler-Bennett, *Action This Day*, 48–9.
87. Lady Oxford to Dawson, quoted Wrench, 410.

Chapter 21 (*pp. 440–60*)

1. WSC, *WW2*, ii, 11–12.
2. *Ibid.*, 10.
3. Colville in Wheeler-Bennett, *Action This Day*, 49.
4. Meetings of Ministers, 111A and B (11 May 1940), PRO Cab. 65/7.
5. *Ibid.*, 111C (12 May 1940).
6. K. Young, *Churchill and Beaverbrook*, 140–1.
7. Dalton, *Fateful Years*, 317–18.
8. Shinwell, 146.
9. Dalton diary, 18 May 1940.
10. Nicolson, ii, 85.
11. Labour Party *Conference Report*, 1940, 123–5.
12. WSC, *War Speeches*, i, 181.
13. *The Times*, 14 May 1940.
14. *Hansard*, ccclx, 1503 (13 May 1940).
15. *Ibid.*, 1510.
16. *Ibid.*, 1522.
17. Halifax diary, quoted Birkenhead, *Halifax*, 456.
18. Colville in Wheeler-Bennett, *Action This Day*, 49–51.
19. *The Times*, 6 June 1940; Halifax diary, 5 June 1940, Hickleton Papers A7.8.4.
20. *The Times*, 18 May 1940.
21. Nel, 22.
22. Dilks, 312.
23. War Cab. Minutes 120, 13 May 1940, PRO Cab. 65/13 (C.A.).
24. War Cab. Minutes 122, 14 May 1940, PRO Cab. 65/7.
25. *Ibid*.

26. WSC, *WW2*, ii, 38.
27. *Ibid.*, 42–3.
28. *Ibid.*, 46.
29. Ismay, 130.
30. *Ibid.*, 131.
31. Spears, i, 292–316.
32. WSC, *War Speeches*, i, 191–6.
33. Avon, *Reckoning*, 117.
34. Ismay, 144.
35. WSC, *WW2*, ii, 161; Woodward, 258.
36. See Thomson, *The Proposal for Anglo–French Union in 1940*.
37. WSC, *War Speeches*, i, 206–7.
38. Roskill, *War at Sea*, i, 242–5.
39. WSC, *WW2*, ii, 211.
40. *Ibid.*
41. Nicolson, ii, 94.
42. Owen, 749.
43. *Ibid.*
44. War Cab. Minutes 140, 26 May 1940, PRO Cab. 65/13 (C.A.); Baudouin, 57–8.
45. *Ibid.*
46. War Cab. Minutes 141, 27 May 1940, PRO Cab. 65/13 (C.A.).
47. WSC, *War Speeches*, i, 199.
48. *The Times*, 29 June 1940.
49. Einzig, 208–21.
50. *News Chronicle*, 8 July 1940.
51. Wheatley, 37.
52. Halifax to Hoare, 8 July 1940, Templewood Papers, XIII.20, Cambridge.
53. Boyle, 718–20. Cf. Ismay, 188, on the problems of the high command.
54. Richards, i, 156.
55. Bryant, *Turn of the Tide*, 197–8.
56. WSC, *WW2*, ii, 233.
57. *Ibid.*, 238–45.
58. *The Times*, 1 Aug. 1940.
59. Pawle, 75.
60. WSC, *WW2*, ii, 276.
61. WSC, *War Speeches*, i, 255.
62. Pawle, 77.
63. Ismay, 180.
64. WSC, *WW2*, ii, 297.
65. *Ibid.*, 323–5.
66. Pawle, 57.
67. *Ibid.*, 81–2.
68. *Ibid.*, 82.
69. WSC, *War Speeches*, i, 267.
70. Ismay, 183–4.
71. WSC, *War Speeches*, i, 259 (17 Sept. 1940).
72. WSC, *WW2*, ii, 306.
73. Kennedy to Hull, 10 June 1940, *F.R.U.S.: Diplomatic Papers, 1940*, iii, 35.
74. WSC, *WW2*, ii, 355.
75. Langer and Gleason, *Challenge to Isolation*, 516.
76. *Ibid.*, 573.

77. Woodward, i, 337.
78. *Ibid.*, 364.
79. Langer and Gleason, *Challenge to Isolation*, 750.
80. WSC, *War Speeches*, i, 244.
81. Woodward, i, 383.
82. 5 Oct. 1940.
83. *BBC Handbook, 1941*, 80.
84. Nicolson, ii, 93.
85. *News Chronicle*, 8 Aug. 1940.
86. WSC, *War Speeches*, i, 278–80.
87. *The Times*, 10 Oct. 1940.
88. *Ibid.*, 12 Sept. 1940.
89. WSC, *WW2*, ii, 646.
90. Kennedy to Hull, 27 Sept. 1940, *F.R.U.S.: Diplomatic Papers, 1940*, iii, 48.
91. *Sunday Times*, 13 Oct. 1940 (comment by 'Atticus').

Chapter 22 (pp. 461–80)

1. Wheatley, 89 and 95.
2. War Cab. Minutes 239, 2 Sept. 1940, Cab. 65/15 (C.A.).
3. Collier, 496.
4. War Cab. Minutes 244, 5 Sept. 1940, Cab. 65/15 (C.A.).
5. War Cab. Minutes 232, 22 Aug. 1940, Cab. 65/14 (C.A.).
6. *Ibid.*
7. *Ibid.*
8. For an account of the pact, see Langer and Gleason, *Undeclared War*, ch. 1.
9. WSC, *WW2*, ii, 500–1.
10. Langer and Gleason, *Undeclared War*, 239.
11. *Ibid.*, 249.
12. Owen, 752.
13. Birkenhead, *Halifax*, 467–70.
14. Sherwood, i, 239.
15. *Ibid.*, 246.
16. *Ibid.*, 244.
17. *Ibid.*, 255.
18. *Ibid.*, 257.
19. Birkenhead, *Halifax*, 473–4.
20. Winant, 47; Menzies, 47.
21. Avon, *Reckoning*, 133.
22. *Ibid.*, 180.
23. WSC, *WW2*, iii, 63 and 90.
24. Woodward, i, 528.
25. WSC, *WW2*, iii, 148–9. The phrase was thought of by Alec Cadogan. See Dilks, 366.
26. Colville in Wheeler-Bennett, *Action This Day*, 62; WSC, *WW2*, iii, 308.
27. WSC, *WW2*, iii, 228.
28. *Ibid.*, 308.
29. *Ibid.*, 303.
30. Dill to Auchinleck, 26 June 1941, quoted J. Connell, 247.

31. Chandos, 223–4; WSC, *WW2*, iii, 311–12.
32. J. R. M. Butler, ii, 543.
33. WSC, *WW2*, iii, 355.
34. Halder, quoted in A. Clark, 96n.
35. War Cab. Minutes 61, 19 June 1941, PRO Cab. 65/18.
36. Colville in Wheeler-Bennett, *Action This Day*, 89.
37. Bryant, *Turn of the Tide*, 258–63.
38. Dill to Auchinleck, 25 Oct. 1941, quoted Connell, 326.
39. WSC, *WW2*, iii, 493.
40. Roskill, *War at Sea*, i, 348.
41. Roskill, *War at Sea*, i, 395–418; WSC, *War Speeches*, i, 421–2 (27 May 1941); Rhodes James, *Chips*, 307.
42. See FDR's notes, *F.R.U.S.: Diplomatic Papers, 1941*, i, 341.
43. For the meeting, see also Theodore A. Wilson, *The First Summit*; Dilks, 395–402; WSC, *WW2*, iii, chs. 23 and 24.
44. WSC, *WW2*, iii, 384.
45. *F.R.U.S.: Diplomatic Papers, 1941*, i, 369.
46. Dilks, 398.
47. WSC, *WW2*, iii, 382.
48. Dilks, 396.
49. *Ibid.*, 402.
50. Gwyer, iii, Part I, 125.
51. *Hansard*, ccclxxi, 880 (7 May 1941).
52. *News Chronicle*, 9 May 1941.
53. War Cab. Minutes 86, 25 Aug. 1941, PRO Cab 65/19.
54. Beaverbrook to WSC, quoted K. Young, *Churchill and Beaverbrook*, 308.
55. WSC to Hopkins, 28 Aug. 1941, quoted War Cab. Minutes 88, 1 Sept. 1941, PRO Cab. 65/19.
56. WSC's Report on Atlantic meeting, War Cab. Minutes 84, 19 Aug. 1941, PRO Cab. 65/19.
57. Langer and Gleason, *Undeclared War*, 892.
58. Kirby, 17.
59. WSC, *WW2*, iii, 379.
60. Matloff and Snell, 36.
61. Dill to WSC, 15 May 1941, quoted J. R. M. Butler, ii, 581.
62. Kirby, i, 166–7.
63. Gwyer, iii, Part I, 280.
64. WSC, *WW2*, iv, 43.
65. Kirby, i, 161.
66. Duff Cooper, 292–3.
67. Kirby, i, 85.
68. WSC, *WW2*, iii, 538.
69. *Ibid.*, 540.
70. War Cab. Minutes 111, 11 Nov. 1941, PRO Cab. 65/20.
71. Bryant, 301.
72. Rhodes James, *Chips*, 307.
73. Dilks, 402.
74. McLachlan, *In the Chair*, 189.
75. R. A. Butler, 89.
76. Avon, *Reckoning*, 276–7.
77. Diana Cooper, *Trumpets*, 73.
78. For the relations between WSC and Bracken see Stuart, 106–7.
79. Elleston, 106; *The Times*, 27 Sept. 1941.

80. Sarah Churchill, 56–7.
81. Cudlipp, 160 and 166.
82. King, 101.
83. *Ibid.*, 107–12.
84. *News Chronicle*, 3 Nov. 1941.
85. *Ibid.*, 23 Oct. 1941.
86. War Cab. Minutes 98, 29 Sept. 1941, PRO Cab. 65/19.
87. War Cab. Minutes 106, 27 Oct. 1941, PRO Cab. 65/19.
88. *Hansard*, ccclxxiv, 2035–6 (11 Nov. 1941).
89. Rhodes James, *Chips*, 312–13.

Chapter 23 (pp. 481–97)

1. WSC, *War Speeches*, ii, 132 (8 Dec. 1941).
2. WSC, *WW2*, iii, 573.
3. Stuart, 105.
4. Roskill, *War at Sea*, i, 566–7.
5. WSC, *WW2*, iii, 573.
6. *Ibid.*, 574.
7. *Ibid.*, 583.
8. *Ibid.*, 584.
9. *Ibid.*, 589.
10. War Cab. Minutes 116, 20 Nov. 1941, PRO Cab. 65/24 (C.A.).
11. He had addressed the Bahama Legislature in January 1931. See above, p. 402.
12. WSC, *War Speeches*, ii, 143 and 151.
13. Moran, 16.
14. *Ibid.*, 17.
15. Matloff and Snell, 381.
16. WSC, *WW2*, iii, 603.
17. Pawle, 155–9.
18. WSC, *War Speeches*, ii, 170.
19. Nicolson, ii, 207–8.
20. *Hansard*, ccclxxvii, 622–3 (27 Jan. 1942).
21. WSC, *War Speeches*, ii, 189 (29 Jan. 1942).
22. WSC, *WW2*, iv, 81.
23. Roskill, *War at Sea*, ii, 149–61.
24. WSC, *WW2*, iv, 74.
25. Dilks, 437.
26. Casey, 168.
27. R. A. Butler to Hoare, 6 Mar. 1942, Templewood Papers, XIII.19.
28. *The Times*, 25 Feb. 1942.
29. WSC, *WW2*, iv, 178.
30. *Ibid.*, 180.
31. Mansergh, *Transfer of Power*, i, 445.
32. *Ibid.*, 110–12.
33. Stephens, 31.
34. Mansergh, *Transfer of Power*, i, 721–2.
35. *Ibid.*, 764.
36. *Ibid.*, ii, 198.
37. WSC, *WW2*, iv, 314.
38. Gowing, 145 and 159.
39. WSC, *WW2*, iv, 343–4 and Bryant, *Turn of the Tide*, 407–8, contain

slightly different variations of the story. The offer of an armoured division in the first instance is confirmed by CIGS's report to War Cab., Minutes, 27 June 1942 PRO Cab. 65/30 (C.A.); and by entries in the diary of Henry Stimson, 22–5 June 1942, Yale University Library.

40. Nicolson, ii, 231.
41. *Hansard*, ccclxxxi, 528 and 538 (2 July 1942).
42. Avon, *Reckoning*, 332–3; Bryant, *Turn of the Tide*, 419.
43. L. J. Meyer, 'The Decision to Invade North Africa', in Greenfield, 129–53.
44. Hancock, *Smuts*, ii, 377–8.
45. Tedder, 321.
46. Bryant, *Turn of the Tide*, 448–9.
47. WSC, *WW2*, iv, 430.
48. For Harriman's report see Sherwood, ii, 616–17.
49. WSC, *WW2*, iv, 435.
50. *Ibid.*, 444.
51. Howard, iv, 33–4; Moran, 63.
52. WSC, *WW2*, iv, 464.
53. Pawle, 199–200.
54. Howard, iv, 128–36.
55. WSC, *WW2*, iv, 539.
56. WSC, *War Speeches*, ii, 342.
57. *Ibid.*, 343.
58. Howard, iv, 62.
59. WSC, *War Speeches*, ii, 344.

Chapter 24 (pp. 498–521)

1. WSC, *WW2*, iv, 541.
2. Stalin to WSC, 6 Dec. 1942, *Stalin's Correspondence*, i, 82.
3. Macmillan, *Blast of War*, 243.
4. Howard, iv, 245.
5. Bryant, *Turn of the Tide*, 535.
6. WSC, *WW2*, iv, 611.
7. WSC, *War Speeches*, ii, 376–89 (10 Dec. 1942).
8. War Cab. Minutes 12, 20 Jan. 1943, PRO Cab. 65/37 (C.A.).
9. Sherwood, ii, 691; Coombs, 13 and 63.
10. WSC, *War Speeches*, ii, 404 (3 Feb. 1943).
11. Moran, 88.
12. WSC, *War Speeches*, ii, 425 (21 Mar. 1943).
13. *Social Insurance and Allied Services* (HMSO Cmd. 6404, 1942), 6.
14. *Ibid.*, 164.
15. War Cab. Minutes 153, 16 Nov. 1942, PRO Cab. 65/28.
16. Memo of 25 Nov. 1942, PRO Prem. 4/89/2/687.
17. War Cab. Minutes 8, 14 Jan. 1943, PRO Cab. 65/28.
18. WSC, *WW2*, iv, 861.
19. *News Chronicle*, 26 June 1943.
20. *Ibid.*, 1 July 1943.
21. Howard, iv, 354.
22. *Ibid.*, 362.
23. WSC, *WW2*, iv, 678–81; Woodward, ii, 625ff.
24. Pawle, 235; Dilks, 527.
25. Moran, 94.

26. WSC, *WW2*, iv, 707.
27. *Ibid.*, 722–3.
28. Avon, *Reckoning*, 388–9.
29. Wilmot, 12–13 and 129; Bryant, *Turn of the Tide*, 33. For a more balanced view see R. M. Leighton, 'Overlord Revisited', *American Historical Review*, lxviii (1963).
30. Howard, iv, 419.
31. *Ibid.*, 419.
32. *Ibid.*, 466.
33. *Ibid.*, 502.
34. *Ibid.*, 506.
35. WSC, *WW2*, v, 73.
36. Howard, iv, 561.
37. *Ibid.*, 564–5.
38. War Cab. Minutes 81, 5 June 1943, PRO Cab. 65/34.
39. Fergusson, 290.
40. Howard, iv, 592 and 693–4; WSC, *WW2*, v, 110–11 and 128–9.
41. WSC, *War Speeches*, ii, 513.
42. *Stalin's Correspondence*, i, 142.
43. Avon, *Reckoning*, 410.
44. WSC, *WW2*, v, 287.
45. *Ibid.*, 289.
46. *Ibid.*, 296–300.
47. *Ibid.*, 301; Roosevelt, 159.
48. WSC, *WW2*, v, 303.
49. For accounts of this episode see *ibid.*, 329–30; Roosevelt, 188–91.
50. WSC, *WW2*, v, 343.
51. *Ibid.*, 354.
52. Moran, 151.
53. WSC, *WW2*, v, 376.
54. *Ibid.*, 377.
55. *Ibid.*, 538.
56. *Ibid.*, 394.
57. *Ibid.*, 401.
58. For a detailed account, with references to Lucas's diary, see M. Blumenson, 'General Lucas at Anzio', in Greenfield, *Command Decisions*.
59. WSC, *WW2*, v, 432.
60. WSC, *War Speeches*, iii, 82 (22 Feb. 1944).
61. WSC, *WW2*, v, 450.
62. Ehrman, v, 2–3.
63. Roskill, *Navy at War*, 311–13.
64. Webster and Frankland, i, 323 and 332.
65. Casey, 166, gives an instance of this revulsion.
66. Ehrman, v, 308 and 310–11.
67. Avon, *Reckoning*, 448–9 and 450–2.
68. WSC, *WW2*, v, 468.
69. *Ibid.*, 518.
70. *Ibid.*, 521.
71. *Ibid.*, 338.
72. Ehrman, v, 324–5.
73. Avon, *Reckoning*, 442–3.
74. WSC, *WW2*, v, 546–51; Wheeler-Bennett, *King George VI*, 601–6.
75. Avon, *Reckoning*, 452.
76. *Ibid.*, 453.

77. *Ibid.*, 424.
78. WSC, *WW2*, v, 340.
79. *Ibid.*, ch. xii; Ehrman, v, 93–102.
80. *The Times*, 24 Dec. 1943.
81. War Cab. Minutes 74, 21 May 1943, PRO Cab. 65/38 (C.A.).
82. Halifax diary, 6 May 1943, Hickleton Papers.
83. On this see Rowan in Wheeler-Bennett, *Action This Day*, 263–4.

Chapter 25 *(pp. 522–47)*

1. The official histories may be consulted on this: the British account by L. F. Ellis, *Victory in the West*, i; the Canadian by C. P. Stacey, *The Victory Campaign*; and, of the various US volumes, see esp. F. C. Pogue, *The Supreme Command*.
2. Stacey, 51–2 and 66.
3. Nicolson, ii, 375.
4. WSC, *War Speeches*, iii, 155–7.
5. WSC, *WW2*, vi, 11; Bryant, *Triumph*, 213–15; Pawle, 303–4.
6. Stacey, 151.
7. Nel, 142.
8. WSC, *WW2*, vi, 35–6.
9. Bryant, *Triumph*, 234–5.
10. WSC, *WW2*, vi, 22–4.
11. *Ibid.*, 27–8.
12. Collier, 406–7.
13. Smuts to WSC, 23 June 1944, quoted WSC, *WW2*, vi, 54.
14. WSC, *WW2*, vi, 90.
15. *Ibid.*, 58.
16. *Ibid.*, 61-2.
17. *Ibid.*, 79–85.
18. Pogue, 265.
19. WSC, *WW2*, vi, 94.
20. Dixon, 114.
21. WSC, *WW2*, vi, 107.
22. Stalin to WSC and FDR, quoted in WSC, *WW2*, vi, 120. Stalin's attitude to the Poles has not found many supporters in the West, but among them is Kolko, 115–20.
23. Moran, 173.
24. WP (44)483, 30 Aug. 1944, PRO Cab. 66/54.
25. Moran, 179; Blum, iii, 369–73.
26. Blum, 377–8.
27. Ehrman, v, 520–2.
28. WSC, *WW2*, vi, 142.
29. Pogue, 281–2.
30. WSC, *WW2*, vi, 197.
31. *Ibid.*, 198.
32. War Cab. Minutes 89, 10 July 1944, PRO Cab. 65/43.
33. WSC, *WW2*, vi, 205; Avon, *Reckoning*, 486.
34. WSC, *ibid.*; Nel, 151.
35. For details, see Pawle, plate opposite p. 404.
36. *Ibid.*, 320–1.
37. 'Conditions in France and Belgium', WP (44) 551, 3 Oct. 1944, PRO Cab. 66/56.

38. Avon, *Reckoning*, 494; Duff Cooper, 340.
39. Duff Cooper, 341.
40. WSC, *WW2*, vi, 218.
41. Roskill, *War at Sea*, iii, Part 2, 168–9.
42. Kolko, 183.
43. WSC, *War Speeches*, iii, 295 (8 Dec. 1944).
44. WSC, *WW2*, vi, 259.
45. *Ibid.*, 252.
46. McLachlan, *In the Chair*, 257.
47. WSC, *WW2*, vi, 258n.
48. FDR to WSC, quoted WSC, *WW2*, vi, 262.
49. Avon, *Reckoning*, 501.
50. Nel, 158.
51. Pawle, 339–40.
52. Macmillan, *Blast of War*, 627–9; Pawle, 341–2.
53. War Cab. Minutes 176, 30 Dec. 1944, PRO Cab. 65/48 (C.A.); Avon, *Reckoning*, 502–3.
54. Pawle, 330.
55. *The Times*, 1 Dec. 1944.
56. *Ibid.*, 2 Dec. 1944.
57. *Ibid.*, 5 and 13 Dec. 1944.
58. WSC, *WW2*, vi, 233.
59. Pogue, 310.
60. For an account of the offensive, see C. V. P. von Luttichau in Greenfield, *Command Decisions*.
61. WSC, *WW2*, vi, 243.
62. *Ibid.*, 245; Pogue, 400–1.
63. WSC, *War Speeches*, iii, 354–5.
64. Avon, *Reckoning*, 506.
65. Attlee to WSC, 19 Jan. 1945, Attlee Papers, Churchill College.
66. WSC to Attlee, 22 Jan. 1945, *loc. cit.*
67. Webster and Frankland, iv, 483.
68. *Ibid.*, 494.
69. *Ibid.*, 383.
70. *Ibid.*, iii, 112 and 117.
71. WSC, *WW2*, vi, 300.
72. Moran, 220–1; Nicolson, ii, 435.
73. WSC, *WW2*, vi, 314.
74. *Ibid.*, 314.
75. *Ibid.*, 315.
76. Dilks, 707.
77. For a recent account, see Clemens, esp. 274–9.
78. Snell, 72.
79. WSC, *War Speeches*, iii, 389 (27 Feb. 1945).
80. Avon, *Reckoning*, 513.
81. WSC, *WW2*, vi, 346.
82. WSC, *War Speeches*, iii, 394.
83. *Hansard*, ccccviii, 1515–16 (28 Feb. 1945).
84. WSC, *WW2*, vi, 363–5; Bryant, *Triumph*, 432–9.
85. WSC, *WW2*, vi, 388.
86. *Ibid.*, 391.
87. *Ibid.*, 409; Pogue, 443–4.
88. WSC, *WW2*, vi, 412.
89. Avon, *Reckoning*, 529.

90. WSC, *WW2*, vi, 434.
91. WSC, *War Speeches*, iii, 435.
92. Hancock and Gowing, 517.
93. WSC, *War Speeches*, vi, 446.
94. Quoted in Wheeler-Bennett, *Action This Day*, 96n.
95. Dalton diary, 28 Nov. 1944.
96. Nicolson, ii, 437.
97. WSC, *WW2*, vi, 498. The phrase 'iron curtain' had been used a few days earlier by the new German Foreign Minister, Count Schwerin von Krosigk. See *The Times*, 3 May 1945.
98. WSC, *WW2*, vi, 483–4.
99. *Ibid.*, v, 340–1.

Chapter 26 (*pp. 548–62*)

1. WSC, *War Speeches*, iii, 254 (31 Oct. 1944).
2. WSC, *WW2*, vi, 511.
3. *Ibid.*, 514.
4. *Ibid.*, 514–15.
5. *Ibid.*, 515–16.
6. Dalton, *Fateful Years*, 458–9, and Dalton diary for 19 May 1945.
7. Labour Party *Conference Report* 1945, 87.
8. For the text, see Attlee, 135–8.
9. WSC, *War Speeches*, iii, 474 (22 May 1945).
10. Dalton, *Fateful Years*, 462.
11. *Ibid.*, 463.
12. WSC, *War Speeches*, iii, 479.
13. 5 June 1945.
14. McCallum and Readman, 143.
15. WSC, *War Speeches*, iii, 490 (15 June 1945).
16. McCallum and Readman, 148–9.
17. *Ibid.*, 154.
18. *The Times*, 25 June and 5 July 1945; Pawle, 385; *Woodford Times*, 6 July 1945.
19. *News Chronicle*, 11 June 1945.
20. WSC, *War Speeches*, iii, 499 (30 June 1945).
21. *Woodford Times*, 6 July 1945.
22. *Ibid.*, 13 July 1945.
23. Pawle, 387.
24. Pawle, 388–90; Moran, 255–66.
25. Moran, 279.
26. WSC, *WW2*, vi, 553.
27. *Ibid.*, 556–7.
28. Pawle, 390–1; WSC, *WW2*, vi, 582–3.
29. Dilks, 759; McCallum and Readman, 240.
30. WSC, *WW2*, vi, 583.
31. Pawle, 399 and 401.
32. WSC, *WW2*, vi, 583.
33. On this see B. B. Gilbert, 'Third Parties and Voters' Decisions: the Liberals and the General Election of 1945', *Journal of British Studies, xi* (1972).
34. Wheeler-Bennett, *King George VI*, 636.
35. WSC, *War Speeches*, iii, 503.

36. Pawle, 403–4.
37. *Manchester Guardian*, 27 July 1945.
38. WSC, *WW2*, vi, 508–9.
39. The lists are in PRO Prem. 4/64.
40. *Daily Mail*, 25 Sept. 1945, quoted in Hoffman, 27.
41. R. A. Butler, 128–9.
42. See, e.g., poll published in *News Chronicle*, 23 Aug. 1943.
43. McCallum and Readman, 43.
44. Moran, 277.
45. Cantril, 275.
46. *News Chronicle*, 12 Mar. 1945.
47. 'Programme for July 1945', CP 58, 3 July 1945, PRO Cab. 66/67.
48. WSC, *WW2*, vi, 583.

Chapter 27 (pp. 563–80)

1. See above, p. 205.
2. Avon, *Reckoning*, 551.
3. Chandos, 329.
4. R. A. Butler, 131.
5. See Stimson and Bundy, ch. xxii.
6. Storry, 230.
7. *The Times*, 16 Aug. 1945.
8. Sarah Churchill, 91.
9. *Ibid.*, 94; Moran, 300–1.
10. WSC, *Sinews of Peace*, 49 (28 Nov. 1945); *The Times*, 29 Nov. 1945.
11. WSC, *Sinews of Peace*, 95–103.
12. *The Times*, 14 Mar. 1946.
13. Williams, 163.
14. *Ibid.*, 109.
15. Attlee to WSC, 13 Mar. 1946, quoted in Williams, 164–5.
16. WSC, *Sinews of Peace*, 44 (16 Nov. 1945).
17. Macmillan, *Tides of Fortune*, 155.
18. WSC, *Sinews of Peace*, 199 and 201.
19. WSC, *Europe Unite*, 79–80 (14 May 1947).
20. Truman, ii, 111.
21. WSC, *Europe Unite*, 295 (21 Apr. 1948).
22. See, e.g. Dalton, *High Tide*, 317.
23. *Ibid.*, 321; Morrison, 278–9.
24. WSC, *Europe Unite*, 25 (6 Mar. 1947).
25. Ismay, 422; WSC, *Europe Unite*, 103 (3 June 1947).
26. Ismay, 430; Campbell-Johnson, 132.
27. WSC, *Europe Unite*, 145 (27 Sept. 1947).
28. Mansergh, *British Commonwealth Affairs*, 226.
29. WSC, *In the Balance*, 55 (28 Apr. 1949).
30. Bryant, *Triumph*, 321.
31. WSC, *Sinews of Peace*, 194 (1 Aug. 1946).
32. WSC, *Europe Unite*, 499 (10 Dec. 1948).
33. R. A. Butler, 145.
34. Hoffman, 85; Harrison, 28 and 62.
35. Stuart, 147.
36. Butler and Freeman, 159.
37. Hoffman, 90.

38. *The Times*, 15 Nov. 1948.
39. *News Chronicle*, 4 Mar. 1949, quoted in Hoffman, 187; Goodhart, 146–8.
40. R. A. Butler, 135.
41. Conservative and Unionist Central Office, *The Industrial Charter*, 24–6; Hoffman, 154–5 and 165.
42. R. A. Butler, 152.
43. WSC, *WW2*, vi, 512–13.
44. Moran, 313.
45. *Ibid.*, 320.
46. *The Times*, 17 July 1947.
47. Moran, 322.
48. K. Young, *Churchill and Beaverbrook*, 284–5.
49. *Ibid.*; cf. Moran, 333–5.
50. Thurso to Beaverbrook, 19 Dec. 1949, quoted in K. Young, *Churchill and Beaverbrook*, 287.
51. K. Young, *Churchill and Beaverbrook*, 289.
52. Graebner, 12–13; *Life*, 7 Jan. 1946.
53. Graebner, 14–15; *Life*, 28 Jan., 4 Feb. and 25 Feb. 1946; 14 Apr. 1947.
54. For its publishing history, see Woods, 111–26 and 351–6; also Nowell-Smith, 229–31.
55. Serious reinterpretation began with A. J. P. Taylor, *Origins*, and continues.
56. Nicolson, iii, 163–4.
57. *The Times*, 29 Nov. 1948.
58. Graebner, 34; *The Times*, 26 Aug. 1949.
59. *The Times*, 29 Apr. 1947 and 24 Apr. 1948.
60. *The Times*, 29 Apr. 1948, 29 Apr. 1949, and 28 Apr. 1950; Munnings, 140–1.
61. *The Times*, 22 July 1949; G. Gilbey in Eade, 472.
62. Mortimer, 62 and 224.
63. See, e.g., *The Times*, 23 Sept. 1949.
64. Graebner, 88.
65. *The Times*, 18 Oct. 1949.
66. *Ibid.*, 12 Feb. 1947.
67. *Ibid.*, 28 Feb. 1947.
68. *Ibid.*, 3 Nov. 1948.
69. *Ibid.*, 9 Dec. 1949.
70. *Ibid.*, 9 Aug. 1946.
71. *Ibid.*, 1 May 1947; Graebner, 93–4.
72. Graebner, 97–102.

Chapter 28 (pp. 581–95)

1. Nicholas, 84–7.
2. *Ibid.*, 96.
3. *Ibid.*, 103–4.
4. *The Times*, 16 Feb. 1950.
5. Nicholas, 127.
6. *Ibid.*, 112.
7. *Woodford Times*, 3 Mar. 1950.
8. Nicholas, 287.
9. Macmillan, *Tides of Fortune*, 195.

10. See Appx. by D. E. Butler in Nicholas, 306–33.
11. Nicolson, iii, 191.
12. D. E. Butler, *General Election of 1951*, 19–20.
13. Macmillan, *Tides of Fortune*, 193–5.
14. WSC, *In the Balance*, 302–3 (27 June 1950).
15. *Ibid.*, 351 (11 Aug. 1950); *The Times*, 12 Aug. 1950.
16. *The Times*, 13 Oct. 1950.
17. WSC, *In the Balance*, 400–1 (14 Oct. 1950).
18. Moran, 338.
19. *The Times*, 24 Nov. 1950.
20. *Ibid.*, 2 Mar. 1951.
21. *Ibid.*, 3 Mar. 1951.
22. Macmillan, *Tides of Fortune*, 322.
23. *The Times*, 12 Sept. 1950.
24. *Ibid.*, 16 Apr. 1951.
25. Moran, 786; Macmillan, *Tides of Fortune*, 354.
26. Wheeler-Bennett, *King George VI*, 792–3.
27. Conservative and Unionist Party, *Manifesto, General Election 1951*, 3.
28. Dalton diary, 2 July 1951.
29. *The Times*, 4 Oct. 1951.
30. WSC, *Stemming the Tide*, 128.
31. *Ibid.*, 130.
32. *Ibid.*, 139 (9 Oct. 1951).
33. *Ibid.*, 142.
34. Moran, 346.
35. WSC, *Stemming the Tide*, 147.
36. Moran, 347.
37. D. E. Butler, *Election of 1951*, 75.
38. *Ibid.*, 77–8.
39. WSC, *Stemming the Tide*, 175 (23 Oct. 1951).
40. K. Young, *Churchill and Beaverbrook*, 290; Moran, 343.
41. *The Times*, 24 May 1952.
42. *Woodford Times*, 2 Nov. 1951.
43. Chandos, 343–4.
44. Kilmuir, *Political Adventure*, 190.
45. Birkenhead, *Walter Monckton*, 274.
46. Woolton, 365.
47. Ismay, 453.
48. Macmillan, *Tides of Fortune*, 362.
49. *The Times*, 30 Oct. 1951.
50. Macmillan, *Tides of Fortune*, 364.
51. Morrison, 45–52.

Chapter 29 (*pp. 596–615*)

1. R. A. Butler, 157.
2. *Ibid.*, 159–60.
3. *Annual Register, 1952*, 14.
4. Birkenhead, *Monckton*, 274–5.
5. *The Times*, 6 Dec. 1951.
6. Moran, 373.
7. *The Times*, 10 Nov. 1951.
8. WSC, *Stemming the Tide*, 189.

9. *Ibid.*, 204 (6 Dec. 1951).
10. *Economist*, 13 Feb. 1954, quoted in Dow, 77n.
11. Dalton diary, 9 Apr. 1952.
12. 5 Apr. 1952.
13. *Annual Register, 1951*, 60.
14. *The Times*, 10 Apr. and 25 July 1952.
15. WSC, *Stemming the Tide*, 189 (9 Nov. 1951).
16. *Ibid.*, 220–7 (17 Jan. 1952).
17. *The Times*, 14 Jan. 1952.
18. Acheson, 600.
19. *Ibid.*, 598–9.
20. Normanbrook in Wheeler-Bennett, *Action This Day*, 41.
21. Avon, *Full Circle*, 36.
22. Spaak, 219–25.
23. Pierre, 87.
24. WSC, *The Unwritten Alliance*, 53 (11 May 1953).
25. *The Times*, 25 May 1953.
26. *Ibid.*, 23 May 1953.
27. Wheeler-Bennett, *King George VI*, 788–90; Moran, 339–42.
28. WSC, *Stemming the Tide*, 237–40 (7 Feb. 1952).
29. Moran, 373.
30. D. E. Butler, *Election of 1955*, 12.
31. *The Times*, 15 May 1953.
32. *Ibid.*, 8 Apr. 1953.
33. Moran, 353.
34. *Ibid.*, 373ff.
35. *The Times*, 29 May 1953.
36. *Ibid.*, 3 June 1953.
37. Moran, 408–11.
38. *Ibid.*, 411.
39. Macmillan, *Tides of Fortune*, 516.
40. Moran, 412–13.
41. R. A. Butler, 170.
42. Macmillan, *Tides of Fortune*, 518.
43. Moran, 412.
44. *Ibid.*, 442.
45. *Ibid.*, 450–1.
46. Macmillan, *Tides of Fortune*, 522.
47. Moran, 472; *The Times*, 14 Sept. 1953.
48. R. A. Butler, 171.
49. K. Young, *Churchill and Beaverbrook*, 302.
50. Moran, 477; *The Times*, 12 Oct. 1953.
51. WSC, *Unwritten Alliance*, 67 (10 Oct. 1953).
52. Colville in Wheeler-Bennett, *Action This Day*, 125.
53. Rhodes James, *Chips*, 479 (3 Nov. 1953); Macmillan, *Tides of Fortune*, 526–7.
54. *The Times*, 18 Nov. 1953.
55. Moran, 508.
56. Avon, *Full Circle*, 57.
57. *Hansard*, dxxii, 586 (17 Dec. 1953).
58. H. H. Wilson, 79.
59. *The Times*, 17 Dec. 1953; Moran, 513.
60. *Manchester Guardian*, 18 Feb. 1954; Colville in Wheeler-Bennett, *Action This Day*, 121.

61. Avon, *Full Circle*, Bk 1, chs. 5 and 6.
62. Spaak, 175; McCormick, 179–82.
63. Macmillan, *Tides of Fortune*, 535.
64. Colville in Wheeler-Bennett, *Action This Day*, 135–6.
65. Macmillan, *Tides of Fortune*, 540.
66. *The Times*, 18 Oct. 1954.
67. WSC, *Unwritten Alliance*, 202.
68. *The Times*, 30 Nov. 1954.
69. WSC, *Unwritten Alliance*, 196 (23 Nov. 1954).
70. *Ibid.*, 205 (1 Dec. 1954).
71. R. A. Butler, 173.
72. *The Times*, 21 Apr. 1955: News Summary for 5 Apr.
73. *Ibid.*, N.S. for 7 Apr.
74. WSC, *Stemming the Tide*, 139 (9 Oct. 1951).
75. Moran, 394–5; *The Times*, 28 Sept. 1953.

Chapter 30 (pp. 616–31)

1. Moran, 653.
2. *Woodford Times*, 13 May, 1955; WSC, *Unwritten Alliance*, 254.
3. Moran, 656.
4. Dalton diary, 1955, Ms. headed 'Election'.
5. D. E. Butler, *Election of 1955*, 199.
6. Moran, 694.
7. *The Times*, 15 May 1956.
8. *Ibid.*, 30 July 1956.
9. Thomas, 142–3.
10. *Ibid.*, 162–3.
11. *The Times*, 5 Nov. 1956.
12. Moran, 709.
13. Avon, *Full Circle*, 575.
14. Macmillan, *Riding the Storm*, 184.
15. Kilmuir, *Memoirs*, 285.
16. R. A. Butler, 195.
17. For WSC's letter, see Macmillan, *Riding the Storm*, 175–6.
18. L. W. Martin, 'The Market for Strategic Ideas in Britain: the Sandys Era', *American Political Science Review*, lvi (1962).
19. Labour Party *Conference Report*, 1957, 181.
20. *The Times*, 20 Apr. 1959.
21. *Woodford Times*, 11 Sept. and 2 Oct. 1959.
22. Butler and Rose, 189.
23. *Woodford Times*, 25 Sept. 1959.
24. *Ibid.*, 16 Oct. 1959.
25. *Hansard*, dclxiv, 871.
26. *Woodford Times*, 10 May 1963.
27. *The Times*, 28 July 1964.
28. *Hansard*, dcxcix, 1237 (28 July 1964).
29. Ashley, 210; Nowell-Smith, 237.
30. *Listener*, 12 Dec. 1956.
31. *The Times*, 23 Apr. 1956.
32. *Listener*, 17 Oct. 1957.
33. Moran, 704.

34. *New York Herald Tribune Book Review*, 16 Mar. 1958, quoted in *Book Review Digest*, 1958.
35. *New York Times*, 16 Mar. 1958; Nicolson, iii, 346.
36. Woods, 136–40.
37. *The Times*, 10 Apr. 1963.
38. *Ibid.*, 6 Dec. 1962; A. Schlesinger in K. Halle, 282.
39. *The Times*, 15 May 1958.
40. WSC, *Unwritten Alliance*, 328 (17 Oct. 1959).
41. Moran, 693 and 708.
42. *The Times*, 15 Feb. 1961; Howells, 81.
43. Moran, 762.
44. *The Times*, 4 Mar. 1959.
45. *Ibid.*, 29 July 1961.
46. *Ibid.*, 7 Mar. 1962.
47. *Ibid.*, 25 Oct. 1963.
48. *Ibid.*, 19 Aug. 1957 and 31 Dec. 1958.
49. *Ibid.*, 27 Apr. 1962 and 9 July 1963.
50. *Ibid.*, 19 May 1959.
51. *Ibid.*, 19 Nov. 1962.
52. *Ibid.*, 10 Nov. 1964.
53. Howells, 24.
54. *Ibid.*, 74.
55. *Ibid.*, 86–99.
56. *The Times*, 2 May 1963.
57. Howells, 164–76.
58. *Ibid.*, 179.
59. *The Times*, 16 Jan. 1965.
60. *Ibid.*, 18 Jan. 1965.
61. Moran, 790.
62. Howells, 178 and 184–5.
63. Moran, 739 (27 Apr. 1958).
64. *Ibid.*, 764 (16 Dec. 1959).
65. Ministry of Public Building and Works, *The Lying-in-State and Funeral of Sir Winston Churchill, 1965* (n.d.), 8.
66. Rowan in Wheeler-Bennett, *Action This Day*, 265.

Chapter 31 (pp. 632–44)

1. Macaulay, 397.
2. WSC to Sinclair, 30 July 1915, Thurso Papers, Churchill College.
3. W. P. Crozier, in A. J. P. Taylor (ed.), *Off the Record*, 334 (29 May 1942).
4. Attlee in *Observer* (ed.), *Churchill by his Contemporaries*, 24.
5. *Sunday Pictorial*, 23 Aug. 1931.
6. Winterton in *Observer* (ed.), *Churchill by his Contemporaries*, 49.
7. WSC, *WW2*, i, 162.
8. The phrase occurs in R. Stokes to LG, Lloyd George Papers G/19/3/37.
9. Quoted in Goodhart, 160.
10. *Observer* (ed.), *Churchill by his Contemporaries*, 34.
11. WSC, *World Crisis*, iv, 352.
12. WSC, *Arms and the Covenant*, 82 (13 Apr. 1933).
13. For Canada, see e.g., Massey, 350–4; for Australia, Hasluck, 347.
14. WSC, *War Speeches*, ii, 151 (26 Dec. 1941).

15. *CV3*, 1467 (28 Mar. 1916).
16. WSC, *My Early Life*, 260.
17. Crozier, *Off the Record*, 287 (19 Feb. 1942).
18. *Observer* (ed.), *Churchill by his Contemporaries*, 21.
19. *Ibid.*, 22.
20. *Ibid.*, 58.
21. *Hansard*, cl, 119 (24 July 1905).
22. Mosley, 105.
23. Bartlett, 537.
24. Hassall, *Ambrosia*, 87.
25. *Observer* (ed.), *Churchill by his Contemporaries*, 58.
26. Crozier, *Off the Record*, 340 (25 Mar. 1943).
27. Lady Juliet Duff in *Sunday Times*, 31 Jan. 1965.
28. Reid, 66–7.
29. *Atlantic Monthly*, ccxv (1965), 70.

Index

Gold Standard, 300–3, 305–6, 309, 355

Gorst, J. E. (*later* Sir John), 24, 77

Greece, Battle of (1940–1), 466–7, 473, 478; troubles on German evacuation (1944–5), 528, 534–6, 541–2

Greenwood, Arthur, 437, 440, 450–1, 488, 502, 545

Grey, Sir Edward, 78, 122–3, 140, 164–6, 174–5, 177–8, 184, 192, 197, 205, 238, 477

Griffith, Arthur, 268–9, 271

Grigg, P. J. (*later* Sir James), 298–300, 302, 312, 324–5, 330, 489, 551

Guest, Ivor (*later* Lord Wimborne) (WSC's cousin), 125, 172, 205, 227, 330

Guest, F. E. ('Freddie') (WSC's cousin), 114, 172, 244, 266, 274, 288, 330, 348

Haig, Gen. Sir Douglas, 213, 233, 237–41, 250–1

Haile Selassie, Emperor, 374, 542

Haldane, R. B., 78, 121, 146, 150, 174, 199

Halifax, Lord (*earlier* Edward Wood and Lord Irwin), 266–7, 344, 570; Viceroy of India, 348, 350–1, 353, 363, 365; Foreign Sec. (1938–40), 386, 389, 397, 432, 437, 440–2, 447, 451, 459; seen as potential premier (1940), 433, 435–6, 638; Ambassador to USA (1940–6), 464–5, 520

Hamilton, Gen. Sir Ian, 65, 193–5, 203, 205–8, 327

Hancock, Alexander, 534–5, 557, 592–3

Hankey, Maurice, 191, 207–9, 218, 220, 230, 233, 255, 283

Harriman, Averell, 465–6, 472, 476, 495, 634

Harris, Air Marshal Sir Arthur, 516, 538

Hart, B. Liddell, 406–7, 417

Heligoland Bight, Battle of (1914), 181

Henderson, Arthur, 225, 234, 248

Herbert, A. P., 286, 415

Hitler, Adolf, 366–8, 370, 374–6, 395, 462, 577; and Czechoslovakia

(1938–9), 388–92, 408; in war, 422, 430, 454, 469–71, 482, 487, 507, 515, 525, 529, 538; death (1945), 544, 556

Hoare, Sir Samuel, 308, 311–12, 320, 324, 344; Sec. for India (1931–5), 357, 360, 362, 365; Foreign Sec. (1935), 371–2, 374–5; later career, 375, 423–4, 427, 432

Hopkins, Harry, 464–5, 472, 474, 476, 494, 500, 520, 634

Hore-Belisha, Leslie, 384, 432

Horne, Sir Robert, 251, 265–6, 284, 369, 377

Hozier, Lady (Blanche) (WSC's mother-inlaw), 114–15, 173

Hussars, 4th, 41, 48, 51, 501, 564

Hydrogen Bomb (H-bomb), 608–9, 614

Imperial Conference (1921), 266-8; (1930), 347; (1944), 518

India, 48–55, 66, 68–9, 221, 259, 267; constitutional reform in, 348–53, 355, 357–65, 371, 417, 438, 486, 489–90, 520, 570–2, 636–7, 640

India Defence League, 358–9, 361, 363

Indian Empire Society, 351, 358

Inskip, Sir Thomas, 375–7

Iraq, 259, 261–5, 468

Irish Free State Act (1922), 270, 340

Irish Home Rule, 69, 78, 91, 111, 140, 349; Bills, 1st (1886), 26; 3rd (1912), 158

Ironside, Gen. (Sir) Edmund, 253, 256, 431, 447, 452

Irwin, Lord, *see* Halifax, Lord

Ismay, Maj. Hastings (*later* Gen. Lord), 314, 432, 438–9, 444, 446–7, 455–6, 491, 578; a Minister, 594

Israel, 572, 619, *and see* Palestine

Jellicoe, Adm. Sir John, 148, 181–2, 193, 223, 283

Jones, Tom, 257, 296, 313–4, 316–7, 338, 346

Joynson-Hicks, (Sir) William, 91, 93, 110–1, 291, 312, 314

Jutland, Battle of (1916), 223, 334

N